NOTHING LESS THAN VICTORY

NOTHING LESS THAN VICTORY

An Oral History of
D-Day

RUSSELL MILLER

MICHAEL JOSEPH
LONDON

MICHAEL JOSEPH LTD

Published by the Penguin Group
27 Wrights Lane, London w8 5tz
Viking Penguin Inc., 375 Hudson Street, New York, New York 10014, USA
Penguin Books Australia Ltd, Ringwood, Victoria, Australia
Penguin Books Canada Ltd, 10 Alcorn Avenue, Toronto, Ontario, Canada m4v 3b2
Penguin Books (NZ) Ltd, 182–190 Wairau Road, Auckland 10, New Zealand

Penguin Books Ltd, Registered Offices: Harmondsworth, Middlesex, England

First published in Great Britain 1993
Copyright © Russell Miller 1993

Typeset by Datix International Limited, Bungay, Suffolk
Typeset in 11½/13 pt Garamond
Printed in England by Clays Ltd, St Ives plc

A CIP catalogue record for this book is available from the British Library
ISBN 0 7181 3328 5

The moral right of the author has been asserted

The author and publishers would like to thank the following for permission to include copyright material:

Anthony Sheil Associates Ltd for *Six Armies in Normandy* by John Keegan; Pen & Sword Books Ltd for *Ten Commando* by Ian Dear and *Typhoon Pilot* by Desmond Scott; Robson Books Ltd for *Six of the Best* by Jimmy Edwards; and Weidenfeld & Nicolson Ltd for *By Sea and Land: The Story of the Royal Marine Commandos* by Robin Neillands.

To the veterans of Normandy

'We will accept nothing less than full Victory!'

DWIGHT D. EISENHOWER
6 June 1944

CONTENTS

Illustrations		xi
Foreword		xiii
1.	NIGHT RAIDING	1
2.	THE INVASION OF THE YANKS	11
3.	DRY RUNS AND WET RUNS	34
4.	SPIES AND LIES	58
5.	BEHIND THE ATLANTIC WALL	79
6.	SEALED!	100
7.	ON THE MOVE AT LAST	121
8.	SUNDAY 4 JUNE 1944	143
9.	MONDAY 5 JUNE 1944	159
10.	CHOCKS AWAY	177
11.	THEY'RE COMING!	221
12.	OMAHA	246
13.	SWORD	301
14.	JUNO	320
15.	GOLD	335
16.	UTAH	361
17.	THEY'RE HERE!	373
18.	IS IT THE LANDING?	387
19.	AFTERNOON	411
20.	HOME FRONT	439
21.	THE END OF THE DAY	447
	Notes	475
	Bibliography	485
	Index	487

ILLUSTRATIONS

MAPS (*by Raymond Turvey*)

Front endpaper: The disposition of forces.
Back endpaper: The landings.

PLATES (*copyright holders are indicated in italics*)

1. General Eisenhower. (*Popperfoto*)
2. General Montgomery. (*Topham*)
3. The heads of the Allied Expeditionary force for Europe. (*Hulton-Deutsch*)
4. Field Marshal Rommel. (*Hulton-Deutsch*)
5. Royal Marines recruits training. (*Hulton-Deutsch*)
6. British troops practising an assault. (*Topham*)
7. The exercise at Slapton Sands, Devon. (*Topham*)
8. A typical German machine-gun nest. (*Barnabys*)
9. German soldiers setting up a fence. (*Barnabys*)
10. US servicemen checking a Mustang P51B. (*Barnabys*)
11. A Hawker Typhoon. (*Camera Press*)
12. A Messerschmitt 109. (*Barnabys*)
13. Rows of guns for D-Day. (*Imperial War Museum*)
14. A German gun emplacement. (*Camera Press*)
15. A company of German infantry. (*Hulton-Deutsch*)
16. A typical scene on the south coast. (*Imperial War Museum*)
17. A Royal Artillery convoy in Kent. (*Barnabys*)
18. A German guard keeping watch for saboteurs. (*Barnabys*)
19. A Bren Gun Carrier passing a pub. (*Barnabys*)
20. American troops en route to an embarkation port. (*Imperial War Museum*)
21. Pilots of No. 453 Australian Spitfire Squadron. (*Popperfoto*)
22. A US army unit being briefed. (*Imperial War Museum*)
23. General Eisenhower briefing paratroopers. (*Topham*)
24. A British convoy assembling. (*Barnabys*)
25. Gliders and tugs preparing for take-off. (*Topham*)
26. US troops ready to embark in landing craft. (*Topham*)

27. An LCVP landing craft with its complement of GIs. (*Hulton-Deutsch*)
28. US troops board an LCI (L). (*Imperial War Museum*)
29. Grim-faced GIs aboard a landing ship. (*Imperial War Museum*)
30. An American driver shaving. (*Popperfoto*)
31. Colonel Nathaniel R. Hoskot.
32. Major Peter Martin.
33. Sergeant John R. Slaughter.
34. Oberleutnant Helmut Liebeskind.
35. Obergefreite Heinrich Severloh.
36. Two Consolidated Liberators of the USAF. (*Imperial War Museum*)
37. Part of the Allied Armada. (*Topham*)
38. Landing craft forming up. (*Topham*)
39. HMS *Warspite*. (*Imperial War Museum*)
40. HMS *Rodney*. (*Imperial War Museum*)
41. British sailors man an anti-aircraft gun. (*Imperial War Museum*)
42 & 43. Two of the famous Robert Capa photographs of the first landings. (*Magnum Photos*)
44. Scottish troops landing in France. (*Topham*)
45. US troops under fire. (*Topham*)
46. Men of the Regiment de la Chaudière coming ashore. (*Topham*)
47. Lieutenant George Honour on an X Craft.
48. Royal Marine Commandos. (*Camera Press*)
49. Survivors of a capsized craft wade ashore. (*Imperial War Museum*)
50. Survivors of a capsized US landing craft give artificial respiration to a colleague. (*Imperial War Museum*)
51. British troops taking cover. (*Imperial War Museum*)
52. British troops moving forward on Sword beach. (*Imperial War Museum*)
53. A GI is tended to by a US medic. (*Topham*)
54. The Sixth Airborne Division's landing zone near Ranville. (*Imperial War Museum*)
55. A British tank and glider near Ranville. (*Topham*)
56. British airborne troops digging in, with their glider in the background.
57. The scene on Omaha beach. (*Popperfoto*)
58. Canadian wounded wait for transfer. (*Topham*)
59. The first news of the invasion comes out in England. (*Popperfoto*)

FOREWORD

This is the authentic story of D-Day as it has never been told before –
entirely by those who took part, on both sides. It is compiled from
many sources – from letters home, diaries, memoranda, official
reports and from innumerable interviews with veterans in the United
States, Canada, Britain, France and Germany.

D-Day was the greatest amphibious operation the world has ever
seen, a truly staggering feat of logistics which involved putting
ashore in Normandy a total of 176,475 men, 3,000 guns, 1,500 tanks
and 15,000 other assorted vehicles. Some 11,000 ships were committed
to the invasion force; 10,500 air sorties were flown.

Allied commanders secretly predicted that as many as 10,000 men
might die in the initial assault. They were, thankfully, overly pessimistic – less than 2,500 Allied soldiers were killed on D-Day and
total casualties were fewer than 12,000, of whom 6,600 were
American, 2,500 British and 1,000 Canadian.

But none of these figures meant anything to the men who were there.
Soldiers neither know, nor care, about grand strategy, the big picture;
what they care about is trying to stay alive and trying to make sense of
what is happening immediately around them. For the soldiers huddled
in the assault craft approaching the beaches, for parachutists waiting to
jump into the unknown night, for men packed into wooden gliders
swooping down onto the Normandy countryside and braced for
impact, for German troops in bunkers and trenches along the Atlantic
Wall, D-Day was nothing but fear, confusion, noise, muddle, chaos . . .
hysteria and horror interspersed with flashes of heroism and humour.

Their voices predominate here, but there are many other voices
worthy of contributing to the story, as the invasion force was
assembled and trained in the months leading up to 6 June 1944.

Women and children in wartime Britain say what they think about
the Yanks . . . the Yanks say what they think about Britain.

German troops occupying France say what they think about the French . . . the French say what they think about the occupiers.

Commandos describe their reconnaissance missions at night to the coast of France . . . resistance fighters talk about sabotage.

Tetchy memoranda document the disagreements between the Allied generals, admirals and air marshals planning the operation . . . boffins talk about floating harbours and swimming tanks.

The men who dreamed up elaborate deception plans explain how they were put into operation . . . German officers tell how much they knew about the upcoming invasion.

As the inexorable build-up continues, the men who are to take part in this moment of history describe their feelings, the anti-climax of the twenty-four-hour postponement, the tortuous crossing of the Channel, the eventual storming of the beaches and the bloody struggle to gain a foothold on French soil.

The story ends at midnight on 6 June 1944, with the last, poignant, voices: the British officer who takes a midnight stroll on Sword beach and finds he is not walking on seaweed, as he thought, but on a carpet of dead bodies; the exhausted American paratrooper on guard duty who can only keep himself awake by pulling the pin from a grenade and holding it tightly in his hand; the German soldier sitting in a bunker, with the enemy on the roof, helplessly radioing for orders . . .

These are the true voices of D-Day.

It is extraordinary, given the passing of the years, how well the events of that day are remembered by the men who were there. Some can recall, almost minute by minute, what happened, even to the extent of relating, word-for-word, exchanges under fire with their mates. Of course, for many of them it was their first taste of the horrors of war, and as such it was obviously an unforgettable experience. But even for hard-bitten veterans of earlier battles, taking part in the Normandy landings would forever remain seared in their memories.

Old soldiers are always happy to talk about their past campaigns, but getting them to talk about their *feelings* is not so easy. Soldiers are not trained to have emotions. I wanted, in this book, to try and get an understanding of what it *felt* like to be at Normandy, to know what men were thinking as they approached the beaches, to try and appreciate what it meant to be there.

That it was terrifying there is no doubt. Robert Capa, the war photographer, whose personal courage was beyond question, was so frightened on Omaha beach that he could not hold his cameras still enough to load more film. Yet soldiers, British soldiers in particular (American veterans are much more willing to articulate their emotions), will often not admit to fear. They take refuge in platitudes about being well trained and having a job to do and just getting on with it.

But with time it was possible to break through the barriers of natural modesty and reserve and gently tap the reservoir of rarely aired inner reminiscences, to try and understand what it was like to be in Britain in those early months of 1944 and what it was like to be nineteen years old and to be part of the greatest invasion force ever assembled. All the extracts are in the vernacular, as they were written or spoken.

So this book does not purport to be a military history – enough books have been written about D-Day to fill a substantial library.

It is a book about being alive in 1944, being young, and being at war.

It could not have been put together without the patient help of all of the veterans who gave freely of their time to talk to me, who sent tapes or wrote wonderfully detailed accounts if it was impossible for us to meet. I took all their accounts on trust; if memories are faulty or time has embroidered reality, so be it. They were indisputably there, and that was enough for me.

Doctor Stephen Ambrose, director of the Eisenhower Center at the University of New Orleans, generously made all his files available to me, an invaluable contribution to the story. Elsewhere in the United States, I would like to thank archivists at the National Archives, Washington DC; the US Army Military History Institute, Carlisle, Pennsylvania; the George C. Marshall Foundation, Lexington, Virginia; the Dwight D. Eisenhower Library, Abilene, Kansas; the Vernon R. Alden Library, Ohio University, Athens, Ohio; and at the Hoover Institution, Stanford, California. In Canada, the archivists at the University of Victoria, British Columbia, were unfailingly helpful.

In Britain my thanks go to archivists and librarians at the Public Records Office, London; the BBC Sound Archives; the Imperial War Museum; the National Army Museum; the Normandy Veterans Association; the Royal Marines Museum, Eastney; the Airborne Forces Museum, Aldershot; the D-Day Museum, Portsmouth; the Liddell

Hart Centre for Military Archives, King's College, London; the RAF Museum, Hendon; the Glider Pilot Regimental Association; the Royal Engineers Corps Library; and the Commando Association. The editors of many regimental magazines and secretaries of regimental associations also provided valuable assistance.

Finally, I want to pay loving tribute to my wife, Renate, whose contribution was such that she really ought to be listed as co-author of this book. Not only did she conduct all the interviews in France and Germany, but she transcribed more hours of tape than either of us would ever want to count. I could not have completed this book without her.

CHAPTER ONE

NIGHT RAIDING

By the beginning of 1944, planning for Operation Overlord, the code name for the invasion of Europe, was well advanced. Hitler himself recognized that an Anglo-American landing on the western coast of Europe would be the decisive battle of the war and ordered defences in the west to be strengthened, even at the cost of depleting his already beleaguered army in Russia. The problem for the German High Command was to know where the Allies would strike. Most senior generals, including Rommel, believed that the attack would come in the Pas de Calais area, where the English Channel was at its narrowest. The Allies encouraged this belief by concentrating night raids on the Pas de Calais coast. Meanwhile, the real reconnaissance was continuing, quietly, further along the coast, in Normandy . . .

Major Logan Scott-Bowden, aged 24, Royal Engineers:

My job was beach reconnaissance, to swim ashore at night from a midget submarine or some other vessel and to carry out a reconnaissance of the beaches where we would be landing on D-Day. Some people reckoned it would be extremely difficult to do an accurate reconnaissance on an enemy-held beach and get away with it, so we arranged a demonstration at Brancaster beach in Norfolk, which was geologically very similar to the beaches in Normandy. We sailed out in an LCT and swam ashore in the dark period. Sentries had been posted all over the place but we managed to crawl past them, get our samples and take them back. Afterwards they checked all the information we had obtained and found it to be correct and I think that played a considerable part in getting permission for the reconnaissances to take place, because it had been ruled by Churchill that no reconnaissances should take place without his specific authorization.

There was great concern about the bearing capacity of the beaches on the Normandy coast. We needed to know what vehicles would be able to cross the different beaches and where trackways would need to be laid. All kinds of research had been carried out on the subject. Professor Bernard, chief scientific officer to Combined Operations, read up the geological history of the Normandy beaches in five languages. He had the books all over his desk, I remember, when I went to see him. Another expert who was called in was Sir Malcolm Campbell, who had done a lot of work on bearing capacity of sand for his record-breaking attempts in Bluebird. It was worked out, by and large, that if there were about fourteen inches of sand above clay or peat the going would be all right.

Although it wasn't yet the dark period, it was suddenly decided that New Year's Eve wouldn't be a bad time to do a quick reconnaissance. It was during the briefing for this operation that I realized, for the first time, that D-Day would take place in Normandy. It was something about which the entire world was speculating and in a strange way knowing this information was really an appalling burden as people were speculating all the time about where and when it would happen. It's frightfully difficult for people nowadays to realize how wonderfully security-minded the whole nation was at that time, which helped one to keep one's mouth very firmly shut.

We went over on an MTB. It was not a very pleasant night, the wind was rising, blowing up the Channel. As we went in, to our absolute astonishment the lighthouse which stands back from the beach up on a bit of high ground behind Luc-sur-Mer was operating. It started drizzling and raining a bit, so that was perhaps advantageous, but being exposed every so often by the beam of light was not a good prospect; you feel extraordinarily naked in such situations, even when it's pretty dark.

From the MTB we transferred to a small, shallow-bottomed reconnaissance craft, the kind that was used for hydrographical surveys. We were quite a way offshore, because the MTB had to carry on as if it was on a normal patrol. We went in on this craft some two miles, I suppose, and then, well outside the breakers, my sergeant, Bruce Ogden-Smith, and I went into the water to swim ashore. We were wearing a primitive sort of wetsuit based on the old-fashioned diver's suit and were equipped with wrist compasses, watches, torches and all the essential things one needs to do a reconnaissance and get back to the recovery vessel. We each carried a dozen long tubes, numbered in phosphorous on the top, in a bandolier on our backs, and the idea was to take a sample from various parts of the beach, noting on the underwater writing tablets which were strapped to our arms approximately where each sample had been taken.

We were aiming for a point about a kilometre to the west of Luc-sur-Mer, but the current was very strong and we were actually carried east towards the village. We could see the houses silhouetted by the lighthouse beam and we realized we would be screened to some extent from the beam, so we made our way straight in. We could hear some carousing going on in the village; the Germans were obviously celebrating the New Year and so we didn't think they would be all that alert. We crawled back along the beach, making sure we kept below the high-water mark so that our tracks would be obscured by the rising tide. After a while we began to walk but soon we were no longer screened from this damned lighthouse beam and we had to flatten ourselves every time it swept by.

When we got to the area where we were due to carry out a detailed survey we started taking samples from the beach, filling up our tubes. We came across a large outcrop of peat, which had been suspected from aerial photographs, but by and large we thought the area would turn out all right from the point of view of bearing capacity. When we had each filled about eight tubes I reckoned we had got enough and so I said 'Let's go.'

That's when the trouble really started, because the breakers were quite heavy and we were positively bogged down with our bandoliers and all our other kit. We had a go at getting out and were flung back. We waited and watched for a bit, then had another go and were flung back a second time. The prospects didn't look too good. We went out into the water as far as we could and watched the rhythm of the breakers, hoping that we would time the moment to get out. Bogged down as we were and out of our depth, it was quite a feat to get through a breaker but on the third attempt, having timed it right, we managed it and swam like hell to make sure we weren't pitched back in again. I swam a little further out than Ogden-Smith and for a moment I thought we had got separated, but then I heard him yelling. I thought maybe he'd got cramp, or something, so I swam over to him, and this is quite true, when I got close enough I found out that all he was yelling was 'Happy New Year!' I forget what I said to him; I think I swore at him, then wished him a happy New Year. He was a good chap, a marvellous fellow.

We swam out to the point we thought would be our rendezvous and started flashing our torches. We had to be careful, in the rough sea, that we didn't swing around and start flashing in the wrong direction, but after what seemed to be a rather long time, we at last saw the prow of a craft coming to pick us up.[1]

Lieutenant Commander Nigel Clogstoun-Willmott RN, aged 33, on board the recovery vessel:

Scott-Bowden and Ogden-Smith were both pretty puffed and very seasick when we pulled them in and I don't think they could tell me very much other than 'OK, we got most of what we wanted to get. Let's go, for God's sake!' They actually brought back samples of what was supposed to be peat, and samples of sand, mud and shingle. They also had a bit of a look at where there might have been minefields and got some idea of possible exits from the beach. Scottie reckoned that there weren't any mines at that time.

The trip home was rather traumatic because the weather blew up. The boats didn't have very good throttle controls and no lights, of course. It was raining hard and blowing up more and more and we had to get back to the rendezvous twenty miles out at sea and I was a bit doubtful that we would be able to do it. We were crashing into high seas, there was water everywhere and the other boat couldn't keep station on us very well. We lost touch with each other two or three times and in fact at one point I had to go right round and try to find them again. Eventually we lost them altogether and it was very worrying because if they had been caught it would have compromised everything.

However, we both, in the end, made it to the rendezvous just before dawn was breaking, after four very unpleasant hours. We climbed on board the MTB, very damp and very cold.

I think I was probably told about the Second Front back in August 1943. I must have been one of the first people who knew, not the exact date, but the moon and tidal conditions and where it was in Normandy. I had to know because, as the commanding officer of a

Combined Operations Pilotage Party, I had to say whether we could reconnoitre the area and what would be needed.

The task of the COPP teams was to reconnoitre the beach areas, the rocks below high-water marks, the minefields and beach exits. There were about three or four specific things we had to cover. They said 'We want to know what goes on on the beaches and, if you can get any more, we'd be glad to have it.' We operated mainly with midget submarines, sometimes with native craft, and occasionally fast launches – whichever happened to be appropriate – and worked out of them by canoe and swimming.

Some six months before the invasion, the thing they were most worried about were dark areas on some of the beaches, which were said to be peat. They had gone right back into pre-Norman and even Roman history, I suppose, and apparently the Romans had dug up peat from these very places and if these dark areas were peat it would be too bad and they would have to think up some means of getting vehicles and tanks over it. That really was the number one priority that we had to discover on our first operation, on New Year's Eve, 1943.

For our next operation, about a month later, we used a midget submarine, which was towed by a trawler. We were released about half-way across the Channel and made our own way under our own steam, as it were, from there on.

I was on the bridge, more or less literally strapped to a post. Where one sat was not a conning tower, just the sort of top of the control room. You had a telephone down to the control room, which didn't work very well, and you clung to this schnorkel thing.

Eventually I sighted the coast and we took bearings on it so we knew where we were. It was getting on for dawn at this stage. We were heading for a point to the west of Port-en-Bessin and Vierville to recce all that stretch of beach and cliffs. The first place you could see very clearly was Port-en-Bessin. It was pretty near daylight by then and again one wondered would anyone see us, but we were such a tiny speck and were about two miles out, I think, and not going very fast. I wanted to go in on the surface because once we were submerged our maximum speed was only about three knots. Surface speed, we could do about seven or eight and it made a big difference. And if we had to go too far under the surface, the batteries soon ran out, so I risked staying on the surface for longer than I should have done. What you do is always a choice of one evil against another.

Anyway, it was rather interesting seeing Port-en-Bessin and the cliffs each side of it quite clearly in daylight. We dived a couple of miles after that and started creeping in and looking at the defences through this tiny periscope, which was about as thick as a man's thumb. We went in quite close, I should think as close as 100 yards from the edge of the water, and we could see people on shore bulldozing and improving the defences, making ditches.

We did a lot of that during that day and I think we had a little sleep during the afternoon. There were five of us on board the submarine and it was very crowded, of course. We had a little electric cooking ring and that was about all. We ate when we could, but we had some sort of a routine, first thing in the morning and last thing at night. In a sub you work the other way round, you have breakfast at suppertime and suppertime at breakfast, usually. We cooked bully beef or something like that. You could lie down on the floor plates, but there were no beds or anything like that, you just found a corner where you could prop yourself up. There were always two people on watch out of five.

There was a disgusting device which was a lavatory, but it was in the wet and dry chamber, a little compartment about two foot wide which you flooded to get somebody out while you were under water. So you can imagine it was always wet and disgusting. It had to be pumped out and that could only be done when you were at a certain depth, otherwise the detritus could be seen on the surface.

That night we surfaced to charge the batteries. That meant going out quite a long way, so that the noise of diesel wouldn't be heard. Charging the batteries took two to three hours, then we came in and crept carefully to the beach. In fact we actually grounded, on purpose, because I was determined to touch the soil of France.

We had a long sounding pole and I remember making soundings as we went in on the surface. I was on the casing, conning the boat in. It was fairly calm that night, much calmer than the first operation. The only other person on the casing was Scottie, all dressed up in his swimming gear, who was going to go in again.

We waited off about a couple of hundred yards and took samples of the current, tidal stream and soundings, all of which were noted. We all had sortie schedules, which you had to memorize, so I knew roughly when and where he ought to come back, abreast some bluff or the other, and then, sure enough, we saw the little blue light shining.[2]

Scott-Bowden:

The main anxiety always was that the recovery would fail. Our lives were dependent on an ordinary torch which, in our amateur way, we waterproofed and fitted with a directional cone so that we could shine it out to sea without being observed from the land. We trained so much and under so many varying conditions that one's confidence about being recovered was good, but nevertheless the anxiety was always there. If the recovery failed, our orders were to cut through the wire defences with the wire clippers we always carried and make our way as far inland as possible and the Resistance would be alerted to look out for us. We carried little photographs of ourselves so that they could provide us with the necessary papers.

I insisted that we wore badges of rank on the sweaters we wore under our swimming suits because we were well aware that Hitler had issued orders that all commandos were to be shot. I thought that if I was wearing a major's crown and Bruce Ogden-Smith was wearing sergeant's stripes, no one could pretend we were anything other than soldiers, until such time as we had disposed of our suits and the Resistance had given us some clothes.

We didn't carry any poison pills or anything like that, although we had been led to expect that if we were captured we would be taken straight to Paris for interrogation by the Gestapo. I made it absolutely clear at SHAEF [Supreme Headquarters Allied Expeditionary Force] that I couldn't guarantee that I might have something squeezed out of me about what I knew about D-Day. I have the utmost admiration for those fantastic people who have been tortured and failed to say anything, but I said I couldn't guarantee that I would be able to keep my mouth shut.

Our next operation was about three weeks later, in a full dark period. This time we went over in a midget submarine to do a reconnaissance of one of the American beaches. It was Omaha, although we did not know it by that code name at the time. There were five of us in the submarine: the skipper and engineer, the commander of the operation, Nigel Clogstoun-Willmott, and the two men who were to swim ashore – myself and Bruce Ogden-Smith. With everything we had to stow on board, it was very, very cramped. We were towed half-way across the Channel by a converted trawler, then we slipped the tow and submerged to complete the crossing. We had to surface for a while to re-charge the batteries and went in the following morning. We had to be careful because there were minefields laid across the Cherbourg peninsula, but the Navy was secretly keeping some channels swept for hydrographical operations and so we were restricted in our approach.

To our considerable surprise, we found a fleet of small trawlers fishing more or less opposite the cliffs leading out of Pointe du Hoc. Nigel spotted a soldier in the bow of one of them and gave the periscope to me to see if I could identify his unit. I was able to see this fellow quite distinctly, with his collar up and his rifle slung over his shoulder. I could even see the shape of the curved pipe he was smoking, one of the German cherrywood pipes; very complacent. To avoid the nets, we passed right underneath this trawler.

We developed a technique of bottoming at periscope height and taking bearings on everything we could see through the periscope. Often we could see things which weren't visible from aerial photographs – even aircraft flying at fifty feet couldn't see underneath camouflage, for example. We were looking for a worm's eye view and were able to see an awful lot. The extent of the fortifications and concrete work was simply enormous and I could see soldiers using a horse and cart to excavate stuff away up an incline and deposit it somewhere over the top of a ridge. We were able to confirm what type of emplacements were there and what kind of guns they were likely to have. When we had finished in one section, we would ease out and bottom at another point and take fresh bearings. In this way we were able to prepare an extensive panorama of the foreshore defences on Omaha beach and confirm many of the air photographic interpretations.

It was quite a tricky operation because it was easy to upset the trim of a midget submarine bottomed on a wavy beach. If someone moved inadvertently it could put the bottom off or put the stern up, so one had to be very careful the whole time. Whoever was on the periscope would take an overall look around every so often to make sure there weren't any other craft about.

As soon as it got dark, the first thing we had to do was surface to charge the batteries. During this time we changed into our swimsuits in the area above the battery compartment. It was only about two feet ten inches high and you had to be quite a contortionist to get in there. I wouldn't care to try it today. We swam ashore from about three or four hundred yards. This time we had to test the firmness of the beach with augers, seeing how far we could push them into the sand. The plan was to survey the left-hand sector on the first night and the right-hand sector on the following night. The first night the operation went according to plan and was quite straightforward.

The following night it was more difficult, because the sea had gone unexpectedly calm and that was the one condition we didn't like, because you felt extremely naked in a calm sea. We were very careful about how we went in, easing our way in with the tide, but we were spotted by an alert sentry, who shone his high-powered torch directly at us. We just stayed very still in the water. We were more or less opposite the village of Vierville, on the right-hand side of Omaha beach. We gradually eased our way out and swam to the east, to a place that seemed quieter, at least there were few buildings. We got up to the back of the beach and had a look around, put some samples of the pebbles in a little bag and then left. The recovery went perfectly smoothly.

Clogstoun-Willmott:

We picked him up without any real difficulty and he had had a moderately adventurous time. Again, he was nearly trodden on by a sentry and was in quite good form. Then there was this awful business of getting him out of his suit which was unlined and very difficult to get off. He was exhausted and so was his sergeant and it was an awful business in that tiny space, rather like doing everything under a dining-room table. It was very, very wet in those subs and the condensation was terrible.

We did the same thing next day, looking around further along the beach. These all turned out to be American beaches, although of course we didn't know that at the time. While we were wandering around the bay, trying to take observations and bearings, I saw a fishing boat buzzing past within about eight feet of us. We suddenly found we were surrounded by them and every other one had a German soldier on board to make sure the French fishermen did not decamp over the Channel and that sort of thing. We quickly pulled down the periscope and dived immediately; it was really rather alarming.

We hadn't seen them before. We should have done but we were so intent on what we were doing that they must just have come round the point without us noticing. Of course we couldn't see anything low, like a fishing boat, very well because the periscope didn't go very much above the water and was always being covered by waves.

Anyway, that gave us a start and the next thing we heard was a sort of 'whang, ping', a sound like an instrument string being twanged, and after a bit we noticed little spurts of spray and reckoned we were being fired at. This was during the second or third day. We thought, well, they must have discovered us and were sending MTBs and trawlers and anti-sub vessels and God knows what and aircraft that would be able to see us through the water, which was very shallow.

After a second lot of firing, which went on for about half an hour, we reckoned they probably hadn't taken alarm but thought we were a good thing to practise their musketry on. We reckoned the soldiers were just having a go at a good aiming mark and didn't realize it was a sub. You see we were moving so slowly, there was no feather of water and just a little stick sticking up like that and, if we moved at all, it was about half a knot, so it probably didn't look like a periscope. Luckily they didn't hit us because we would have been blind if they had.

We were going to do another night's recce but there wasn't really very much point in it. We thought it was time to go, after all there was a great deal to be lost if we were caught, and torture, probably. We had a rather phoney cover story. I had a picture of myself on a French identification card and, though I did speak very bad French fairly fluently, none of the others did. Our plan if we were caught was to skedaddle into the interior and pretend we were what our identity cards said we were, mostly Apaches, sort of illegal characters trying to work the black market, of which there were quite a lot in Normandy. That was my cover and the others had something similar, but it was all a bit shaky and would not have survived torture.

CHAPTER TWO

THE INVASION OF
THE YANKS

The American troops pouring into Britain in preparation for the opening of the Second Front found everything, from the customs of the people to the warm beer served in pubs, strange. But, eminently adaptable like soldiers everywhere, they soon settled in. And while the British continued to gripe about the Yanks being 'over-paid, over-sexed and over here', few could resist their charm, generosity and lack of guile . . .

John Keegan, prep-school boy, aged 10:

Towards the end of 1943 our backwater [in the West country], which British soldiers had garrisoned so sparsely for four years, overflowed almost overnight with GIs. How different they looked from our own jumble-sale champions, beautifully clothed in smooth khaki, as fine in cut and quality as a British officer's – an American private, we confided to each other at school, was paid as much as a British captain, major, colonel – and armed with glistening, modern, automatic weapons, Thompson sub-machine-guns, Winchester carbines, Garand self-loading rifles. More striking still were the number, size and elegance of the vehicles in which they paraded about the countryside in stately convoy. The British Army's transport was a sad collection of underpowered makeshifts, whose dun paint flaked from their tinpot bodywork. The Americans travelled in magnificent, gleaming, olive-green, pressed-steel, four-wheel-drive juggernauts, decked with what car salesmen would call optional extras of a sort never seen on their domestic equivalents – deep-treaded spare tyres, winches, towing cables, fire-extinguishers. There were towering GMC six-by-sixes, compact and powerful Dodge four-by-fours and, pilot fishing the rest or buzzing nimbly about the lanes on independent errands like the beach buggies of an era still thirty years ahead, tiny and entrancing jeeps, caparisoned with whiplash aerials and sketchy canvas hoods which drummed with the rhythm of a cowboy's saddlebags rising and falling to the canter of his horse across the prairie. Standing one day at the roadside, dismounted from my bicycle to let one such convoy by, I was assaulted from the back of each truck as it passed by with a volley of small missiles, which fell into the ditch beside me. When I burrowed in the leaves I unearthed a little treasure of Hershey bars, Chelsea candy and Jack Frost's sugar cubes, a week's, perhaps a month's ration, of sweet things casually disbursed in a few seconds. There was, I reflected as I crammed the spoil into my pockets, something going on in the west of England about which Hitler should be very worried indeed.

For a time it was only as the distributors of haphazard largesse that the Americans impinged, though the town soon began to be surrounded by encampments of neat, weathertight wooden huts, again altogether superior in quality to the straggling settlements of corrugated iron which housed British units. But gradually personal contacts were made, first by our pretty, black-ringleted, Welsh nursemaid, Annie, who had appeared soon after the evening when a drunken British parachutist had made an assault on the bedroom window of her dottily pious predecessor. Annie came to us from a convent, where she had emphatically not been preparing to enter the sisterhood. The look assumed by my mother, as Annie swayed towards GI territory in the centre of town on her afternoons off, her pink, plump and rather wobbly legs covered for the outing in a bottled brown preparation called liquid stockings which did wartime duty for the real thing, implied a nagging anxiety that she was flirting with another sisterhood, from which the convent had presumably been enlisted to rescue her. But though silk stockings materialized to replace liquid ones, as did supplies of Hershey bars and Spearmint on a scale which rapidly devalued mine, Annie was apparently asked to give nothing in return or, if asked, not pressed. My mother's alarm subsided.

The American presence had swollen that spring to almost all-pervading proportions, so that there seemed more Americans than natives in the district (as there may well have been). American transport monopolized the roads, American uniform became as commonplace as that other uniform of the penultimate war years, the high-shouldered overcoat, wedge-heeled shoes and turbaned head so often seen on its arm. American accents, much enjoyed, much, if badly, imitated, passed as an alternative to local dialect and some of the ease, nonchalance and generosity of American manners had permeated and softened local formality. The feudal west would never be quite the same again, and a good thing too thought many, particularly the young. We relentlessly patriotic little prep-school boys, imprinted with our idea of the paramountcy of the British Empire, to which we knew the United States represented a principle in some way antithetical, held out longest against American charm. I particularly resisted admitting that the US Navy had demoted the Royal Navy to second place among the world's fleets, even after the facts told me differently. But in time it got to us too. There was something in particular about the jeeps, and the way they were driven with one high-booted leg thrust casually outside the cab, which softened even the most chauvinistic ten-year-old heart.[1]

Pfc Vernon W. Tart, aged 26, 618th Ordnance, 174th Ordnance Battalion, 6th Engineer Special Brigade:

We pulled into Liverpool in daylight and pulled up alongside the pier, but we weren't allowed off the ship, or even on the decks. We had to stay below deck, so we all took turns at the portholes, sticking our heads out to see what was what, hollering to people on shore of course, and all that.

When night time came we were allowed topside and formed up and marched off the ship. There was a delegation who gave a short welcome speech and a small band playing, and after that was over we marched through the streets of Liverpool to the railroad station. This was my first view of any war damage or anything and I was fascinated, looking to the left and right at the ruins of buildings and the rubble in the streets, block after block. This was as a result of the Blitz, of course.

We finally ended up at the railroad station. The platforms were dimly lit with very low-wattage bulbs and we were given 'at ease' and put our baggage down. Being a train buff I was amazed at the size of the locomotive and the cars. I could reach my hand out and put it on top of the boiler of the engine.

So we boarded the train. Talk about sardines in a tin. We had all our luggage, rifles, packs, duffel bags, everything with us, all crowded together in the coach. We were warned strictly: DO NOT RAISE THE BLINDS. Everything was under blackout, so that is how we travelled across Britain. We couldn't see anything of England or anything else, but we managed to get some rest.

Finally, in the early dawn, we pulled into a town which we found out was Exeter, on the English Channel. We disembarked from the train and formed up and started marching up what we later found out was the High Street to a big stone and brick barracks, which I understand was the home of the Devonshire Regiment. We were billeted in there, which was fairly good, and I had my first leave in an English town. It was only for like a six-hour pass, but it was something.

Of course it was evening, and under blackout. I went into the nearest pub, though I'm not a pub man, I don't drink at all, but none the less you can't go to England without going into a pub. I went in just about the time for them to close up and the barkeep was pounding on the bar with a big stein saying 'All right, ladies and gentlemen, time please. Mind my license.' I thought that was great.

I walked around a little bit and there was a crowd of people at a bus stop, so I sauntered up and got talking with a girl. She was just a working girl, I'm sure, not a prostitute. She was just there with a crowd and she was just interested in me as a GI, because we were among the first in that area, and of course I was fascinated with her as an English girl. All of a sudden a light was sprung in my face and voice said 'All right! All right! Break up the blinking party. Move on.' I was outraged, but I was not about to create an incident, so I said nothing and just walked away. That stuck with me as my introduction to an English town, although I found out later that not all the English were like that.

After about a week in Exeter we boarded a train again and headed down the coast, a very scenic ride on the Great Western Railway, and ended up in a small town called Torquay, which was an English summering place and watering hole and very nice. We marched into the center of town and there was a sort of small park down there where two quonset huts were set up. One was a kitchen and one was a mess hall and outside was a huge pile of hay. As we entered the area, they handed us mattress covers which we were told to fill with straw. With a mattress full of straw, a duffel bag, rifle, pack, helmet and all, we were loaded down like mules, but we formed up and started marching.

There was a couple of British NCOs with clipboards at the head of the column and as we marched up what we later found out was Forest Hill Road, we were told off, so many men into various houses on each side of the road. The English were required by law to accept troops if they had any room, which they had to register with the authorities ahead of time. Of course, they were paid for it.

I and three others ended up in the home of the Bond family in about the middle of Forest Hill Road, in a typical row house, all steps and stairs, with a little garden and a gate in front. We four were assigned two rooms, which was good, and we met the Bond family. They were rather strange. Mr Bond was probably the nicest one, poor old fellow. He worked down in the coal yards unloading coal, so we did get a little extra ration of coal which helped out on heating, since coal was in short supply like everything else. Mrs Bond was a cripple in a wheelchair, but strangely enough she was very sexy and she immediately started making advances to one of our guys, much to our amazement.

We lived there for quite some time and that was a good deal. Being that we were billeted in private homes, we had no passes and so we could go anywhere we wanted after duty hours. They had buses running into town and in town they had libraries and bookstores and a theater in which they had not only movies but plays, now and then, which I enjoyed. Of course, being GIs we were richer than Croesus, so we had the best seats in the house, naturally.

There were a few restaurants down there but we were advised not to use them, to go to our quonset hut for meals, because food was in short supply in England. But being lazy GIs, we'd always go to a restaurant if we were downtown. Their favourites were sausages and chips. Chips are French fried potatoes and the sausages looked and smelled beautiful, although inside them was nothing but mashed potatoes. But they were edible, and it was nice sitting there in a restaurant on the waterfront.

We used to take a bus to and from Forest Hill Road. It was a double decker running with blackout lights instead of headlights, but that driver knew his business. We would swoop down one road and make a sharp left turn at the bottom and every time I swore the bus was going to tip over, although it never did. It used to get so dark up there sometimes that when we got off the bus we couldn't find the house at all. We had to feel along the stone walls until we approximated where we were and then we'd go in and look close.

Just up the top of the hill was a fish and chip shop which was very popular. For two and six, that's about equal to a quarter in our money at that time, we could get a good helping of fresh fish and chips, but you had to bring a newspaper or something to carry it in. There were no bags available. The only time we couldn't get them was when they ran out of oil, which was fairly frequent. Whenever they had oil the word would go round to everybody, civilians and soldiers alike, that the fish and chip shop was open.

We used to be routed out in the early morning and marched down to the quonset hut for breakfast, then we'd form up for the day's activities, whatever they were. In most cases it was field exercises and marches. We had some pretty long marches. I remember one that ended up at an RAF airfield called Honiton where we looked over the Spitfires. That was rather interesting, but it was a long hike, something like twenty miles, and we were pooped when we got back. But the cooks were always on the ball and would have coffee and doughnuts ready whenever we got back and that made up for it.

Another detail I had was driving a jeep and going round all the houses at four in the morning and rousing the cooks. Then I had to rouse out the squad leaders who in turn were entrusted with getting their squads up and moving. We'd go in through the back doors of the houses to root out the people we needed. Doors had to be left unlocked, it was part of the requirement. It was strange, thinking of my own home, to be doing this, but it was part of war. Nobody resented it particularly. Later on as more troops kept coming in they had to set up pyramidal tents outside the town and so they weren't as lucky as we were, living right there in the town.

One of my goals was to see London while I was in England and when I got a four-day pass we took the Great Western Railway up to London and stayed in the Red Cross building near Marble Arch. We saw all the usual fun places, the Tower of London and St James and Downing Street and the British Museum. We found an Englishman who showed us round on a foot tour.

On the last day when we were getting ready to come back we heard the air raid sirens go off. People were swarming down into the underground. I had a friend named Magg, Lester Magg, and he took one look and said 'I'm not staying up here, I'm going.' I vacillated. I wanted to see the raid very much, so I stayed out and he went down.

I went into a side street and there were a number of Englishmen there, also waiting for the raid. We had been told before we went to London to carry our gas masks and if we got into a situation like that to lay in the gutter as some protection from the blast. So I had my mask and all and we were looking up at the sky and you could hear the drone of the German engines up there. All of a sudden, a great big chandelier flare lighted up, almost overhead, which lit up the area as bright as day. One of the English fellows said 'Blimey, here it comes' and dived for the gutter. I was right there too. About that time I was sorry I hadn't gone down into the underground, because bombs really started coming down. There was a tremendous display of rockets and anti-aircraft fire and searchlights and bomb blasts and fires. As it turned out, it was the biggest fire raid since the Blitz. When the all-clear sounded and the trains started moving and we began our journey south-west out of London, you could see the fires, huge fires, burning for miles and miles. That was certainly an experience.[2]

Letters home from Pfc Robert W. McCormick, Medical Detachment, 696th Armored Field Artillery Battalion, stationed at Kington, Herefordshire:

Dear Folks,
Well as you could guess we have arrived at our destination. I can't tell you where it is but I think I'll be able to tell you before too long. Maybe not though. You said dad wondered about the ship. Well I don't think I can say much but it was a new ship and on its maiden voyage. It was and so was I. I don't think the ship got sick however. We came in convoy and all in all it was a good trip. We had a short service by the chaplains on arrival.

The American Red Cross served coffee and doughnuts just before we got on the ship. We were all given a package containing soap, a book, mints, shoe strings, razor blades and other things in a handy little bag. We have been served coffee and doughnuts several times since. Believe me the American Red Cross does a lot at home and abroad. I can't describe our ship but I bet it was a lot better than either one pappy was on.

We are encamped in barracks here. Not billeted as dad was.

Perhaps you should meet the censor. Mom & Dad, this is Mr Suesz, the unit censor, Mr Suesz, my parents. That makes everything legal now.

The one thing I miss most is the movies and radio we had in the States. Outside of that we aren't missing out on much I don't think.

You wanted to know what to send me. One thing I could use is a knife. Not a fancy one but just any ordinary pocket knife would be o.k. Of course I'm always interested in eating material. I don't know if you can send that or not. Some ice cream would be o.k. too. We had ice cream on board ship however.

I managed to bring along my gloves and sweater that you sent home for Christmas. My peaked hat from Camp Grant I had to get rid of.

Well that's all for now. I'll write more later.

     Love,
       Bob.

Dear Folks,

Well it is Sunday here and since it's 3.30 p.m. here I suppose your about to go to church or at church at this time while I am now looking forward to supper.

I had a pass to go to town Fri night. I had a real nice time and the English people seem to be quite friendly considering having a lot of Americans thrust upon them. Over here the Negro has equal station with the white. They have no racial predjudice [sic] whatsoever. We were out walking over the countryside last night. We must have walked several miles. We passed one farm and saw a sick lamb laying in the pasture. George Bayer and I looked him over but I don't have much hope for him. We talked to the farmer and he asked how we liked England. He mentioned that we probably didn't have very many hedge fences back home. We told him no they were mostly wire.

We get our laundry done free over here but we can send only 9 pieces a week. We should be getting paid before long so I may send home some money.

Paper is very scarce over here so if you get a chance to send some light weight air mail stationery, plain. We can get the envelopes o.k. so far. If I had to do it over I'd bring a lot more stuff than I did. Plenty of fellows brought more than five pounds.

I may go to town tonight. You can buy things to eat at the YMCA canteen. They have a drink called 'Orange Squash'. It's like orangeade.

Well I'll write again tomorrow I think.

     Love,
       Bob.

Dear Folks,

Well I didn't receive any mail from you yesterday or today but I imagine that is to be expected . . .

We were in to a near by town yesterday. We had lunch at the YMCA and looked over the town. These British towns are very neat little places. When they have a park it is very neatly kept and in the summer time I imagine it will be very beautiful. We went to see a show later in the afternoon. It wasn't too bad and not too good. We have to stand in a que, which is a line, to get our tickets. There was an RAF band playing there also. The RAF are the boys who have the nicest uniforms in the British service. The army uniforms are like coveralls, only of wool. The RAF is a very pretty blue and is cut just about like ours with shirt and pants and blouse.

We rode on a bus and there are all kinds of uniforms here in England. I mean in the British service. Practically everyone wears one kind of uniform or another. Both women and men. They have the WLA the Women's Land Army which are like Farmerettes. There are WAAFS for the air force and Women Auxiliaries for the army and navy. You see quite a few automobiles on the road. Not a lot but some. These double decker buses are really something. They look as though they would tip over.

I got my rations from the PX tonight. Only one candy bar per week but that's better than none I guess. If you have any old candy lying around I'd be glad to eat it. In fact any food is greatfully accepted. We get good enough food understand but we just can always eat a little more. We get pancakes quite a lot which is alright by me. We have quite a bit of fruit, fresh and canned, also a little juice now and then.

Well I guess that's all for tonight. We are making a spot of tea before retiring. We filched it out of the officers mess by way of a friendly cook. We also got hold of some sugar. One of our fellows has a cook friend. Write when you can.

     Love,
      Bob.

Dear Folks,

Well it's Sunday again over here in England. We slept till about eight o'clock this morning and some of the fellows are still sleeping.

I went to town last night on pass. We had some fish and chips which is fish and french fried potatoes. I went to the Cinema also.

There was a double feature playing. 'Topper Takes a Trip' with Connie Bennett and Roland Young and 'Bombers Moon' with George Montgomery and Annabelle. They are both a year or so old but I had never seen either one. They had a really beautiful little Theater there. It looked like a very new theater. It was modern in every respect. It cost 2–9 to sit in the balcony which is supposed to be the best seats. They are allowed to smoke in the balcony. This creates quite a lot of haze but it was still a pretty nice theater.

I got a letter from you yesterday. I think you should be starting to get some of my letters before long.

You ask if I am still doing the same work as before. Yes I'm still punching a typewriter most of the time. We have classes besides but I'm still clerking for the detachment . . .

I think I may go out this afternoon for a while. The sun is shining brightly and it is really a beautiful day here. We have a lot of daylight too it seems to me. It doesn't get dark till about 8 o'clock here.

Well there isn't any thing particularly thrilling to report here as everything is pretty routine. We were told yesterday that we are now eligible to wear the ETO campaign ribbon. (ETO is European Theatre of Operations) it is that little green black brown and white ribbon. I guess we'll be issued some soon. In about $2\frac{1}{2}$ months I'll be eligible for a good conduct ribbon too. That's red and white stripes. You have to be in a year before you get it and then sometimes they don't. My year is officially up the 7th June.

Well I'll write again tomorrow if we don't have any night problem.

> Love,
> Bob.[3]

Private George 'Mac' McIntyre, aged 33, B Company, 4th Engineers:

We unloaded at the small hamlet of Berry Pomeroy, near Totnes in Devon, the vacation centre of southern England. There weren't more than a dozen structures in sight, the most important an ancient town house, or mansion, built by Henry the Eighth. Bernie Myers, George Holodnak and myself were fortunate enough to draw a small room in the mansion itself, while the rest of the company were billeted in Nissen huts spread around the grounds. In the townhouse, or mansion, or whatever it was, we had the advantage of gas heating, while the boys in the huts depended on small coal stoves. The English mornings were cool, and it was quite an advantage.

Our English money came through a few days later and timidly we began to make the mile and a half trip into Totnes. We weren't timid very long for we found the average English citizen a very friendly person. Naturally, the first place many of us headed for were the English pubs. We found the barkeeps friendly and honest, an important factor when you consider we didn't know the true value of English pennies, shillings and pounds. We found the English shilling went just a little further than an American quarter. Pubs are nothing less than the working men's club, where people gather to discuss weather, politics or crops over a glass of the best. When I say glass, I mean pint, and it was usually something called 'bitters' – a weak beer.

We soon became acquainted with English national pastimes, cribbage and darts, but I really began to 'live' in England when I met a few of the finer families – the Princes, the Bawls and the Maddocks – at the White Horse, a pub at the top end of Totnes. I finally adopted the Princes, or should I say they adopted me? I spent practically all of my off-time at their home and usually had my Sunday dinner with them. At first I felt quite embarrassed when I ate their food, knowing they were strictly rationed, but when I found I could repay them with surplus sugar, butter, flour and fruit from our own company kitchen, I didn't feel so badly about it.

Under the Army system of food logistics, there could be no leftovers, and, if there were, the officers of the company didn't object to the boys taking them to friends in town. Then, too, I could trade or buy tobacco and cigarettes from the few non-smokers in the company. Mr Prince and his sons really appreciated whatever I could get for them. English tobacco then sold for about two dollars a quarter pound, and cigarettes for forty-five cents a pack, both in scant supply.

I wrote to my wife, Betty, and explained the situation and she began sending packages containing food and other odds and ends not available in Britain. Now raisins were a delicacy at the time and the English ration was a quarter of a pound per month per family. When you could get a bun or muffin in England, your luck was measured by the number of raisins it contained: two, average; three, good;

four, excellent. I'll never forget the time I managed to get ten pounds of them from kitchen surplus. Mum Prince all but cried when I presented them to her. When I managed to secure a few fresh oranges and lemons from the kitchen, the people in the entire block came to look at them, including a couple of youngsters who had never seen the fruit before.

Irene, the Princes' nineteen-year-old daughter, was a conductress on the local bus line – they gave her a choice between that and the Land Army – and I made many a bus trip free of charge. There was no chicanery involved whatever, for the drivers often refused to take a fare from an American soldier, especially if he was a friend of someone working for the line. The average English citizen knew that, without American aid, their country would go down to defeat and they showed it in their hospitality to the American soldier. They went without, themselves, in order to show the 'Yanks', as they called us, that we were welcome.[4]

Naina Beavan, aged 16, clerk, Portsmouth:

The Americans arrived while I was still at school and they more or less took over our beautiful school. They used to put on fantastic concerts, I think Glen Miller was even there one night, but the fact was they were taking over our classrooms and we were shoved in at one end and had to have the old classrooms.

I left school at fourteen and went to work in the office of Chapman's Laundry, which did dry cleaning. All the Americans had beautiful uniforms and they could afford to have them dry cleaned. It was four shillings and sixpence to have a uniform cleaned and the Americans would bring in three at a time whereas our sailors would only ever bring in one.

One girl I worked with was stunningly attractive, a peroxide blonde. I thought she was fantastic. Her main ambition was to get as much money as she could out of any service person, so we always had a shop full of Americans giggling and laughing.

There was one called Baxter who I thought was marvellous. I only knew him as Baxter and he used to come in and bring all these Hershey bars, and of course chocolate was rationed at that time. He used to say he would look out for me at the concerts at the school and the girl I worked with, the one I was telling you about, used to tell me that I ought to go and have a good time, that I would never get the chance again. But I never did go. I was absolutely terrified. My mother was always telling me to be careful, that awful things could happen to me.[5]

Staff Sergeant R.A. Wilkins, aged 27, C Company, 149th Engineer Combat Battalion, 6th Engineer Special Brigade:

We arrived in Liverpool on January 8, 1944. We boarded a train which took us to a little village in southern England called South Brent. We were billeted in little quonset huts. It was rainy, cold and miserable. It seemed like it rained every day we were out marching and hiking on the moors. We certainly had our share of blisters.

On January 22 they took us to the town of Paignton in trucks. They took the truck down the street and they'd stop and say 'All right, three of you out here.' They'd march you into this house and say 'These are your American troops that are going to be staying with you.'

I can remember the place that I went to. Their name was Glover. He was a retired piano dealer from New Zealand or Australia. Our boots were muddy and everything about us, I suspect, was offensive, certainly to Mrs Glover. She made us remove our boots outside before she would even let us come in the house. We immediately thought this was going to be a very difficult situation and weren't happy with it at all.

But after we had become acquainted with the Glovers, they treated us like we were their own sons. Everything was blacked out and we didn't do much going out at nights unless we were on training missions. Mr Glover, who told us he was known as the Piano King of Australia, would give us piano concerts in the evening and it was a truly amusing experience. I had no doubt he was quite a wealthy person because he had a lovely home and we used to play pool with him in his pool room and he would take us to his club and buy us drinks. Of course their car was in the garage, jacked up. They rode around on bicycles.

The people in that part of the country made a lot of sacrifices for the war effort. Many of them were not able to use their farms and some had to sell off their herds of cattle. But they accepted the Americans quite well and were really good to us.

Each time we would leave to go on mock invasions we didn't really know whether it was the real thing or not. But then it came time for the real invasion and the public seemed to know pretty much what was going on. When we left the Glovers to get on the train for the sealed camp, they cried.[6]

Lieutenant Colonel Nathaniel R. Hoskot, aged 32, 507th Parachute Infantry, 101st Airborne Division:

We were quartered in the cricket pavilion on the sports field belonging to the Players tobacco factory in Nottingham. We used to play them at baseball on Saturdays and cricket on Sundays; we weren't very good at cricket and they weren't very good at baseball so it sort of evened itself out. It was a lot of fun. Some of our guys were farm boys and they had never even *heard* of cricket. It was a very pleasant time for me, we had a lot to do and the people were delightful to us. The relations between the Americans and the British couldn't have been nicer and the people in the factory were very tolerant because our trucks were always tearing up their playing fields; they used to give us a bushel basket of cigarettes every Saturday, those thin short ones that everyone smoked then.

Local ladies' groups would organize teas and invite soldiers and officers along. Our army rations were very good for bartering. We got two bottles of whisky a week and a case of beer per man, something like that, and it was much more than the local people had had for a long time, so if you were invited out you could always take along something, like a piece of ham, that would be welcome. We had all the material things you could want, in fact it was almost embarrassing at times because we had so much more than the local people had had for a long time.

British beer took a bit of getting used to and you'd go to a restaurant and get something like bangers and bubble and squeak, but once you had caught on to the language it was fine. I think the soldiers enjoyed it there, I really think they did.[7]

Sergeant Owen L. Brown, aged 22, HQ Company, 2nd Ranger Battalion:

When we arrived at Warsash [Hampshire], Mrs Downs, the wife of a British Army general serving in India, said she had room for eight Yanks. We were greeted at the door by the maid. As the last Yank walked in, the maid reached down, picked up her bag, and left. She refused to work for any damn Yankees. The lady of the house did all the cooking and cleaning while we were there.

The house we were in had 1594 chiselled in the fireplace mantel, and it is still a very solid structure to this day. It was constructed by putting up a framework of hand-hewn timbers and my bed was in the roof area, between crossbeams holding the sides together. When I tried to get up in a hurry, I would hit my head on a beam. This was a particular danger after spending a few hours at the local pub, when beer made me run for the bathroom in a hurry. The bathroom was on the second floor landing, so I had further to go than the rest of them.

Mrs Downs had purchased the home right after their home in London had been bombed. The only people she knew in Warsash was the butcher. With the strict rationing the English had, it was hard to get meat. Mrs Downs came home with many parcels labelled 'rabbit' or 'chicken' that contained mutton. We actually sat around the table in the dining room as a family. Her favourite dish was mutton roasted with quarter potatoes cooked in the meat around it and served with brussel sprouts.

We did learn to enjoy this, as it made a change from our GI mess hall.[8]

Article in Army Talks, 15 March 1944, by American scientist Margaret Mead, aimed at explaining Britons to the Americans:

To an American a British town is puzzling. He doesn't know what to do there. He doesn't know how to nurse a pint of beer in a pub all evening. At home he didn't go into bars except to drink. If he didn't drink he went somewhere else, to the pool room, or the bowling alley, or the corner drug store – or he stood on the corner, if the town was small, and watched the passers-by.

Houses had front porches; he could call on a girl and sit on the porch and talk, or go out in a car. He didn't have to get right inside other people's houses at first. The first time he called on a girl he didn't get into the family circle. Because American houses are heated all over, other members of the family can be shooed out of the living room when a girl has callers.

But in a wartime British town he finds pavements so crowded that people who stand on street corners are a nuisance. There are relatively few places to go, unless he is so fortunate as to be stationed in or near a town with an American Red Cross Club. If he goes to a pub, he thinks the only thing he can do there is to drink. If he makes friends with anyone his own age, girl or boy, and they take him home he finds himself embarrassingly right in the middle of the family – when he gets in the door.

Then he can't tell what sort of manners people are likely to have by the houses they live in or by the clothes they wear or by the way they talk. When American soldiers get invitations from British homes they very often don't accept them. They are afraid that there will be only middle-aged people there – and very often they are right, with all the young people called up.

And when they do go they sometimes find out they didn't do the right thing, and that their very casual 'Thanks a lot', with the 'lot' half swallowed as they dive out of the room, isn't the way their hostess, who stood in line an hour to get sultanas for the cake, expected them to behave. But they know hardly anything of rationing.

On my recent journey about Britain I was asked, in one form or another, over and over again, why Americans talked so big, why they boasted so, why they threw their weight around. As one A.T.S. said to me: 'The trouble with Americans is that when they are good at something, *they say so.*' If I had instead been journeying in the American middle west, I should have been asked: Why are the British so superior? Why do they act as if they were more perfect than anyone else? Why do they look down their noses?

Unless it is possible to get behind the irritating American 'boasting' and the irritating British patronizing and recognize that both people disapprove of the strong bullying the weak and it's just a question of WHO is strong, the speaker or the listener, a great deal of misunderstanding results. Americans, used to the person who is talking treating them as if they had to be impressed, get annoyed when the British quietly assume that they will be automatically impressed.

If Americans and British people are to form a picture of each other which will make it possible for them to cooperate when there is no war to make that cooperation urgent, it is important that Americans should come to respect British accomplishment. This should be easy, British people will say, proud of their tremendous record in the war, proud of their production of planes, proud of the RAF, proud of their long constitutional history, proud of their political genius. But although they are very proud of these things, they haven't any very good method of showing them to other people.

The British code doesn't permit a lot of boasting about production figures or plane hits. It isn't very easy to demonstrate to a machine-minded young American, who thinks in numbers and quantities, how well the spirit of compromise has worked.

The truth of the matter is that the things which Americans are proud of are easy to show other people. They can be seen and ridden in and counted. Many of the things of which the British can be most proud of are very difficult to see, some of them are almost impossible to describe.

When boys and girls do go to the same school in Britain, they act as if they were still going to separate schools. To an American eye, the absence of flirting and back chat among secondary school boys and girls is astonishing.

Of course, this is very confusing to British girls who haven't had any practise in wisecracking. Some of them are insulted by the speed and assurance of the American's approach and turn chilly and unapproachable, and make him feel that Britain is a cold – and then he will add – little country. Some of them take his words which sound like wooing, for wooing, and give a kiss with real warmth, which surprises him very much. Some of them thought the Americans were proposing when they weren't and proceeded to take them home to father.

Yet because American boys and men think that the pleasantest way to spend an evening is going out with a girl, the casual social relations between American boys and British girls are very important. Americans have to learn to adjust to the different pace of personal relations in Britain, not go so fast at first, and British girls, and British men who get to know Americans, need to learn that while the Americans seem to move very fast at first, are quick to use first names, tell the story of their lives, state how much money they used to make, and show pictures of their kid sisters, afterwards they go more slowly than the British, enjoying each step in getting acquainted, and then they feel cheated if a relationship moves too fast.

If the British people learn that the initial intimate use of first names and terms of endearment are only greetings and don't mean anything, are really neither intimate nor rude, the Americans' first impetuous approach will seem less breathtaking.

Unless Americans can have an opportunity to work informally with British people, listen to discussions, sit in on small committees, get a feel of the way things are done, they may come away from

Britain with very little understanding of those aspects of British life which have a first claim on their respect. This is one of the reasons why more informal participation of Americans in British life is desirable.

If, for instance, no one has bothered to tell the British people that Americans don't set the same store that they do on standing upright, and see no harm in taking the weight off one's feet by leaning against the nearest wall, they will judge the Americans who do it as undisciplined, spineless people, because those are the judgements which they pass on the members of their own society who lean against walls.

Leaning against a wall doesn't mean the same thing to the average young American as it does to the corresponding young man in Britain. Neither does chucking a girl under the chin, telling a joke, riding in a car, or taking a drink. They all mean something quite different. Every detail of behaviour, because it is part of a different character, a character developed in a new country in the machine age without any shadings from a pre-industrial period of society, contrasts with the British character.

Once they recognize this, British people can learn to know Americans as members of another society, a society which is based on the same traditions but has developed them very differently.[9]

Article by Major Thor M. Smith, press officer to General Eisenhower:

I 'live' here now. I have been here so many months, that I have long since ceased to feel like a visitor. In fact, that's my answer whenever I'm asked the invariable English opening greeting of 'How do you like it here?' But in those early days my reply was an enthusiastic 'Fine' and that type of response always seemed to be unexpected – but pleasing to them none the less. Most of us are adjusted to everything new . . . the wartime restrictions, the different accent, the unusual (to us) customs, the people, and the country itself. But it's still fun to recapture some of those original impressions, and to remember some of the more outstanding differences that attracted our attention during the first exciting weeks.

Definitely No.1, and at the top of the list for all time, is the reception we were accorded, every last one of us. The hospitality, the genuine friendliness, the desire to co-operate, really overwhelmed us.

Let's be frank about it, most of us came over here with a chip on our various and respective shoulders. Dr Goebbels had done a good job in the States, too good a job. He had thrown a wedge of distrust between us. We actually expected that we would be unwelcome, that Yanks and Tommies would be fighting in the pubs and in the streets, that we would be rebuffed and discriminated against. Looking back on it now, it seems silly. But the problem was gravely serious, even to the brass hats.

Small booklets were published and distributed to each American soldier, telling him how to 'get along' with the British. The way this so-called problem has turned out sums up like this: it's impossible for the English and Americans to live together, work together, play together and *fight* together without getting to know each other mighty well, have a wholesome respect for each other and finally really *liking* each other. Dr Goebbels found that out. After a few more feeble efforts in that direction, he gave up. There were too many goodwill ambassadors working against him.

Every soldier's letter home was a glowing testimonial to the way we had been welcomed. Fact is, of course, that there was a fertile ground for the original distrust. The unofficial pre-war emissaries for each country had been bad. The so-called 'bridge of understanding' created by the movies had led the English to think everyone in America was a Chicago gangster, a Texas cowboy, a 52nd Street playboy or a Dead End kid. The English were amazed to find out that we were just regular people. For our part, we expected the English to be walrus-mustached, monocle-wearing Colonel Blimps. Since I have been here, I have seen the grand total of seven people wearing monocles.

Pubs are a tremendous factor in Anglo-American relations. In my own experience and among my own close personal friends, I know of countless cases of Englishmen establishing extremely cordial relations with our boys by using the opening gambit 'Won't you have a drink with me?' The so-called British reserve breaks down completely inside of a pub. A lot of friendships and a lot of real understanding is developed over a glass of beer. Minor differences fade into insignificance when you discover so many points of common interest and agreement.

One evening a group of us went into the famous Cheshire Cheese, just off Fleet Street. I stepped up to the bar ahead of the others and was immediately hailed by a group of Royal Navy boys who insisted that I join them. They thought that I was alone, but when the others came up, they demanded that they be allowed to buy all of us drinks. It developed that they had just returned on a convoy from New York, and they had been feted so splendidly there that they were out on a personal crusade to do the same for every American they met in England. On another occasion a quiet little man stepped up and asked to buy me a drink with the explanation 'I have a son that's training with the RAF in your country. In Arizona. Do you know where that is?'

A popular toast, when raising the glasses high hereabouts, is 'Bung ho!' First time we heard it, we fell into hysterical laughter. But now we 'Bung ho!' ourselves with equanimity. In fact, it's our favourite greeting.

Of course, by the same token, pubs are wonderful places for a fight. What few fisticuffs have developed between our soldiers and the British have occurred in or just outside a pub. That is to be expected. Because after a man gets a few drinks under his belt, he forgets all the little lessons in Anglo-American relations he learned in the booklet.[10]

Pfc David Kenyon Webster, Company F, 506th Parachute Infantry, 101st Airborne Division:

We were stationed in Aldbourne, which became our home. If the boys wanted to raise hell, they went to Swindon or London; around Aldbourne they acted with restraint, sipping their beer quietly in The Bell or The Cross Keys or the other pubs. Naturally, everybody got a little raucous, especially on the nights the beer and liquor rations came in, but on the whole there were very few fights and not many breakages. We got settled enough in town to become steady customers of the three bakers, who slipped us a lardy cake now and then, and to know most of the local inhabitants by sight, if not by name. Gradually the people thawed out and began to speak to us. A few men in the battalion even married Aldbourne girls. Since our mess hall was on the other side of town from our barracks, we had to march through the village on our way to and from meals. The reassuring sight of civilian houses and civilian people made life seem more normal and homelike than it had been in a vast, barren army camp like Fort Bragg.

Our own physical set-up wasn't too bad. F and Headquarters

Companies lived in Nissen huts, while D and E Companies savoured the comparative luxury of one-storey wooden barracks. The Nissen huts were dark and gloomy and very dusty, but we improved them as much as possible by painting the interiors with gaudy blue, white and red enamel and installing radios, which we purchased at outrageous prices in Swindon. (Our first-squad noise box, a triumphant cabinet affair for which we paid £33, or $132, received only the BBC and the German propaganda station.) The floors of those Nissen huts were made of a tar-like compound so soft our double-deck bunks sank into it and formed cavities all over the surface. We fixed that by putting boards under the bunks but, clean as we would, we could never get rid of the dust which collected in the holes left behind. Small Victorian coal stoves provided a semblance of heat during the winter.

Sanitary facilities left much to be desired, however. Our toilet, an unimposing wooden shanty, housed a pair of stone troughs and two rows of wooden seats on honey buckets. The toilet paper, when it was present for duty, was coarse brown, very wartime English stuff. That latrine was no place to linger on a cold night.

The shower room and wash room were adequate, if somewhat primitive. Despite coal rationing, we managed to have enough hot water, provided, of course, the latrine orderly didn't goldbrick and let the fire go out. Once in a while a clogged drain would flood the place. There were five showers for our two companies of about 250 men, but this was enough, because nobody was very shower-conscious in the cold climate. We washed our hands and faces and shaved in helmets filled with ice water in a building across the street. We looked back on our life in camps in the States as a period of great luxury.

Living conditions weren't the only things which had changed since we left Fort Bragg. Our diet, hitherto so rich in such accepted staples as fresh milk, fried eggs, and oranges and apples, suddenly dried up on us, and powdered milk, powdered eggs, dehydrated apricots and dehydrated potatoes became the order of the day. Once or twice a month we got fresh eggs, but we were never given fresh milk while we were overseas. Although it seemed to me that we got more steak in England than we had in the States, the rest of our food, poured from cans, suffered a serious decline in quality. We were not subjected to a constant diet of Spam, however. As a matter of fact, I could never see the point of all those jokes about Spam, because as far as the 506th, which missed the pre-Africa, or Spam, period in England, was concerned, we ate the dish only as a variety item, never as a regular. I personally found the powdered eggs hardest to take; even though the cooks converted them into omelette pancakes, they could never disguise their definably dry, dull flavour to taste like real eggs.

Since our PX goods were now rationed, chow hounds accustomed to completing an inadequate meal at Toccoa by stuffing themselves with candy, crackers, Coke, and beer at the PX found themselves cut off without relief in Aldbourne, where our weekly ration consisted of seven packs of cigarettes, three candy bars, one pack of gum, one cake of soap, one box of matches, one package of razor blades, and sporadically, washrags, towels, combs, crackers, coathangers, etcetera.[11]

Celia Andrews, housewife, Signett Hill, Burford, Oxfordshire:

One lovely summer morning I was shaking a duster out of the window when much to my surprise a jeep went past with American soldiers in it. One of them saw me and said to the driver: 'I'm coming back!' Not long afterwards, lorries, tanks and troops in their hundreds arrived. After being so quiet at Signett Hill it seemed so strange to see so many people about.

There was a piggery just up the road that had been built by the local farmer but never used. It was improved and made into living quarters for the men. Naturally, as they marched past I was often in the garden with my children and they used to call out to me. At first I was aloof, but then realized how stupid that was and I started to talk to some of the fellows.

One I called Virginia, as he came from that part of the country, another one was called Richard and his mother had a chain of beauty salons. A sergeant was called Tommy and had a friend, an Italian American, Mike, who was engaged to a girl called Mary, who he adored. He bought a record called 'Wait for me Mary' and used to come and play it on our gramophone.

One day I was just about to go to Burford, a walk of one and a half miles, to the shops, when a lorry went by and seeing me the driver said 'Would you like some sugar?' I thanked him and didn't like to say no, so I ran in to fetch a basin. The driver said 'That's no good, it's too small.' So back I went for a larger basin and he proceeded to fill both basins with sugar. I thanked the driver very much and he said he'd put some tea over the wall.

When I came back from Burford my Grandma, who was staying with me, said a lorry had stopped and someone had put a large box over the wall. When I looked inside the box I found there was thirty-six pounds of tea and several large boxes of corn flakes! When I next saw the driver I thanked him, yet he never attempted to take advantage of this and I only occasionally saw him passing in his lorry.

All the Americans were very kind to my children, yet only Mike and Tommy ever came to the house (and then only when my husband was there). We met them in Burford one evening when they recognized our very old Austin Seven Tourer. They hailed us and asked for a lift and were quite excited at having a lift in such a car (which had cost us £5!).

I remember, too, the planes and gliders practising, dropping large baskets, several of which fell almost in our garden. The Americans from up the road used to practise marching and hiding at the same time; I used to see them crouching and I wondered then what their future would be.

Several of the fellows bought bikes but so many of them fell off while learning to ride that they were forbidden to keep them in the camp. One day several chaps came to our door and asked if they could keep their bicycles in our shed. We agreed, of course. When it was rumoured that they would be leaving I asked them what they wanted to do with their bikes and they said I could sell them and keep the money, as they were grateful for being allowed to use the shed.

When they all eventually left and all the lorries were rumbling past I had such sad feelings, wondering where they were all going. I heard later, from a girl who was engaged to one of them, that practically all those boys were wiped out.[12]

CHAPTER THREE

DRY RUNS AND WET RUNS

Outside of the senior planning staff, no one knew when or where the invasion was to take place, but as the pace of training increased most soldiers knew that the big day was not far off . . .

Corporal Bill Bowdidge, aged 22, 2nd Battalion, Royal Warwickshire Regiment:

We were stationed at a camp in Sussex and we knew we were going to be among the assault troops on the invasion, but we didn't know where or when that would be. We knew that one of our roles would involve rapid movement because a few weeks before D-Day the whole company, from the commanding officer downwards, was issued with folding bicycles! I didn't think much about it at the time; when you're a junior soldier you just take whatever comes. I don't think anyone thought what are we doing this for?

I mean you're not paid to think, you just do it, accept it. I can't remember anyone saying 'What on earth are we going to use these for?'

There was time for us to take our bikes out on the Sussex roads to practise what we called 'cycle marches' – riding out in platoons like a pre-war cycle club, all bunched together, three abreast – and new drill movements were devised. The company would fall in in the usual way with the front wheels of our bicycles pointing to the right at an angle of fifteen degrees, the officers in front of their platoons holding their bicycles in the same way and the company commander, with his bicycle, facing the company. He would give the command to come to attention and turn to the right in column of route. To achieve this, we in the ranks would do a smart right turn and at the same time shuffle our bikes backwards and forwards so that they were facing in the right direction. While this was going on the officers would wheel their bikes to take up position at the head of their platoons and the sergeants went to the rear. The OC would then shout over his shoulder, 'D Company, quick march!' and off we would go. After a few paces the order would be, 'D Company, prepare to mount,' and then, 'D Company, mount!' At this we would all swing our legs over and ride on, still trying to keep our dressing to the left. It was great fun.

Of course we had to carry normal marching order, weighing about fifty pounds, on our backs and consequently we all suffered from saddle sores.[1]

Felix Branham, aged 22, T Company, 116th Infantry, 29th Division, US Army:

We were in a British barracks at Crown Hill outside Plymouth. It was some six or eight miles from the edge of the moors, which is a miserable, horrible place to be at any time, much less training. We were hungry all the time, on half rations. We would go to the mess hall, and you could smell the food, and you would wind up getting half of what you expected. You'd get half an orange, half a slice of bread. You would get maybe a small ladle of powdered eggs – horrible. If someone has never tasted powdered eggs, you can't imagine how they tasted or what they looked like.

We had powdered onions and powdered potatoes. In this day and time we would call them instant onions, instant potatoes, instant eggs, but we called it powdered. It came out of cans, big five, six, seven gallon cans full of powder in granulated form like washing powder, or cornmeal. That's the way it looked, only it was colored.

They would take these sugar beads and add water to make syrup. Cooks would. Officers would visit us from supplies and say 'Do you know how many sailors are dying to bring you this food?' and 'Don't do this' and 'Don't do that' and 'Watch what you eat' and 'Don't waste this' and 'Don't waste that'. So many times I went to the mess hall and came away just as hungry, or hungrier, than I was when I got there.

Our training was rough, we never had nothing easy. We would get up and run four miles in twenty minutes and this was before breakfast. We would have to run two or three mile obstacle courses with some of the damnedest obstacles that anybody could think of. Sometimes we thought the Devil had thought up some of those obstacle courses. Golly no one, but no one, realized how horrible our training was. We would take two or three thirty-mile hikes a week. We would leave Crown Hill, march six or seven miles to a poor little town, Tavistock, which was our division headquarters, then go onto the moors. The fog would be so low and thick that if you stood up, straight up, you could see probably no more than four or five feet. But if you got down to below three feet you could see a long distance. I can't describe it.

I was born in Charlottesville, Virginia, and I was never in the northern part of the country or in Canada, where the tundra is and where the cold is. The higher you went on the moors the deeper the swamp got. It would be covered with blocks of ice at times and it was miserably cold.

A lot of the guys broke out with hives from the impregnated clothes which we'd have to wear out on these exercises. If you laid your hand on your chest the hives would be that thick, almost. It made them awful deathly sick.

We trained with different units. We would get with a group of commandos, rappelling down cliffs, climbing up again, climbing down cargo nets. When we trained with the British or the Free French or other allies, we always tried to outdo them. We would work with Combined Operations and go out on different landing craft in the English Channel. We would make landings all along the coast, up and down the beaches of the British Isles from Liverpool to Bristol and from Penzance to Plymouth. We went out on LCTs, on LCVPs, on LCIs, on British ships and American ships in every form.

In the meantime we were having assault training schools. We swam through tanks of water with full equipment on. We threw various hand grenades. We were shown various types of enemy grenades and enemy weapons and how we could use them if we landed and misplaced our weapons. They would show us how to attack pillboxes, what to do if we became separated on a hostile shore. We learned Morse code, we could flip it with a light. If we were abandoned and they had to come and save us, then we would be able to give a signal from a hidden place on shore.

We learned how to make various charges. Various people would volunteer and become demolition men. I myself was busted from squad leader a couple of times so I joined a demolition team. I carried a 50-pound pole charge and a 50-pound satchel charge made of burlap and TNT. I figured 'OK if I make the Second Front and I get hit with all the explosives I would be carrying, then it would all be over real quick.' If it had to be, that's the way I wanted it to be.

We never thought of going back home, although when we had a chance to sit around barracks, to write letters, or clean up equipment, or rest up before the next day's gruelling grind, we'd always gab about home. It was the main topic, always home and the ones we'd left behind.

We were always conscious that some day we were going to have to make a landing, go in and destroy the enemy and get the job over with. We didn't talk of dying, unless it was a joke. We used to kid a guy who had this beautiful ring and used to carry a big wad of money, seven or eight hundred dollars. His name was Gino Ferrari. I used to say to him 'Ferrari, when you hit that beach and you fall, man, I'm going to get your wallet out.' And another guy would say 'Yep, and I'm going to have that ring.' And we sat around and thought about that, but never thinking that that would really happen. What else did we have to talk about?[2]

Pfc John Barnes, aged 19, A Company, 1st Battalion, 116th Infantry:

By February '44 I had joined the 1st Battalion barracked on the edge of Dartmoor in the little village of Ivybridge in England. The boys of A Company came over two years earlier, after being federalized from the National Guard. They were all in the Guard together from one town in Virginia, a town named Bedford. I felt a bit out of things as a New Yorker. They all knew each other as old friends from home and I felt lonelier than I had ever felt before in my life. My feelings didn't improve as the southern boys were bragging that their outfit was slated to be the assault unit in the landings to start a second front in France. They had been training a long time and they were ready. I wasn't.

Within a few weeks, the four platoons of A Company were reorganized into six boat teams. I felt gloomier than ever, but the boys were right. We were going to be the assault force as combat opened on the northern shores of France. Our training became very serious. We learned to attack pillboxes as a team. I was in Boat Team Number Two under Lieutenant John Clements. Out on the moors we would practice landings from an imaginary boat. Men would line up in three columns, ten men each. The first three out of the boat were riflemen. They would fan out when the ramp went down and take up protective fire positions. Next came two men who carried bangalore torpedoes, long lengths of pipe containing dynamite. These were shoved under barbed wire to blow a pathway. The next men were designated as wire cutters to help clear the gap. Then came machine gunners to cover us, next 30mm mortar gunners and ammo carriers. Lastly, a flame-thrower team and a dynamite team to get close to the pillbox and blow it up.

The pillbox, we were told, was the way the Germans built up their defensive set-up. Huge concrete structures, two or three feet thick, round like an old-fashioned pillbox, with a small hole from which they could fire their guns. It was to this small hole which we were to direct our attack. The last members of the assault team scrambled up to the target, running the last steps, setting the charge, then hurling it inside the hole and running back shouting 'Fire in the hole!' A few seconds later the dynamite would go off, and our team would charge forward firing and shouting success. We practiced this routine every day, over and over. Each man knew his job. We worked together. It was different from the basic training in the United States. We took it very seriously and the officers made it more serious when they began to set up groups of sharp-shooters to fire freely at us in our dry run.

One time, one of the boys set off a charge that had a short fuse. It blew up in his face. I was glad I didn't see him, thank God. They said he still had his helmet strap down below his chin and after that we never wore our helmet straps buckled, except for parades or guard duty.[3]

Verse composed by Captain Maurice Clift, company commander
115th Infantry, to metre of 'Sea Fever' by John Masefield:

> I want to go out to the moors again,
> To the fog and the rocks and rain,
> To the gorse and the marsh and muddy pools,
> Wherein the boys have lain.

I want to go out to the moors again,
To retrace each painful stride,
To look again at the hills wherein,
The sheep and rabbits hide.

I want to go again to the moors,
To follow their winding trails,
To stand again on their lonely slopes,
In the cold and the rain and the gales.

Oh, I'll go out to the moors again,
But mind you and mark me well:
I'll carry enough explosives,
To blow the place to hell.[4]

Sergeant John R. Slaughter, aged 19, D Company, 1st Battalion, 116th Infantry:

D Company were quartered in Nissen huts in Ivybridge on the edge of the moors in Devon, about twelve miles from Plymouth. It was the end of the winter and the windswept moors were a foreboding place to train. There were no trees and the mushy, spongelike soil was constantly under clouds, fog and cold, misty rain. The battalion spent much of the time training and sleeping out on those God-forsaken hillsides.

We were in the initial stages of amphibious training. Endurance and strength tests called 'burp-up' exercises were given to monitor physical fitness. Those who passed earned the Expert Infantryman's Badge and an extra $5 in the monthly paycheck. Failing to qualify meant transfer to a non-combat outfit.

Some of the criteria for the Expert Infantryman's Badge was running 100 yards in twelve seconds with army shoes and clothing, doing thirty-five push-ups and ten chin-ups, running an obstacle course within the prescribed time and qualifying on the pistol, rifle and machine-gun ranges. It really was not that difficult, and the officers allowed some cheating so some of the men could pass. Despite this, a few could not pass and were transferred.

Amphibious training began in earnest when the regiment moved to tented camps in Hampshire. The training area was selected because it resembled the terrain and beaches of Normandy. Slapton Sands near Dartmouth was a sloping expanse of sand and shingle guarded by an arm-pit deep salt marsh which had to be crossed before assaulting simulated fortified bunkers. The company hiked all day dripping wet on the cold and windy moors and slept that night in the same damp clothes. It was one of the most miserable experiences I can remember as a soldier.

One of the men in my squad, Pfc Joseph Alvalio, from Brooklyn, was only recently drafted and hadn't fully embraced the system. When he crossed the lake he lost a $6 machine-gun water can in the murky water. On learning of this mishap, Captain Schilling, the company commander, screamed at me: 'Slaughter, what in the hell's the matter with your squad! Bust him to private! He pays for the water can and he's going to learn to take care of the equipment.'

Each day for a week I had to oversee Alvolio's punishment, which was a two-mile run up a mountainous path to a swimming pool, where he had to wade through the cold water, fully clothed with all his equipment. The pool had a skim of ice over it and on the first day Alvolio slid into the water and went straight to the bottom. He was a poor swimmer and I had to pull him out of the water. From then on I only required him to wade in the shallow end and get wet, then we both ran quickly down the hill to camp for inspection by Sergeant Obenshain, who grinned and said sarcastically, 'Must be nice to have a private swimming pool, eh, Private?'

Dry runs preceded the actual drills. Mock-up landing craft and cargo nets set the stage for the actual landings from LCAs and LCVPs. Nets were hung from high makeshift walls and the troops practiced climbing them with full field equipment.

Loading and unloading dummy landing craft, exiting in columns of threes, peeling off left, center and right, then quickly moving into a perimeter of defense. Crawling under barbed wire with live machine-gun grazing fire just inches overhead and live explosions, strategically placed, detonating all around, lent realism to these exercises.

The battalion was schooled in the use of explosives. Satchel charges and bangalore torpedoes were excellent weapons for blowing holes in barbed wire and neutralizing fortified bunkers. Bayonets were used to probe for hidden mines. Poison-gas drills, first aid, airplane and tank identification, use and detection of booby traps, foxhole digging, unarmed combat and weapons training gave us the confidence that we were ready.

The build up of troops and supplies multiplied daily. While we were away on an exercise, black troops moved into Ivybridge. Everyone knew that Ivybridge belonged to the 1st Battalion, 116th. The village simply could not support any more troops. Acrimony led to fighting between the newcomers and the battalion. One of the men found his girlfriend had been with one of the new arrivals and it soon became apparent that the troops had to be separated.

Every other night was off-limits for one race or the other and, to make matters worse, when the blacks were in town the Military Policemen were whites, and vice-versa. The trouble got worse and there were several stabbings. One of our mortar platoon sergeants was caught leaving camp with a sub-machine gun, heading for town and intending to 'clean the place out'.

I was selected for MP duty one night and paired with a soldier from one of the rifle companies. After the pubs closed that night a mob of black soldiers, fortified by beer, came up the street shouting obscenities and acting belligerent. It was beginning to look ugly and my partner and I backed into a doorway. One of the men, a rather large sergeant, was carrying a pistol. I called for him to drop his weapon. He hesitated and I fired my carbine into the ground at his feet. He dropped the pistol and the crowd dispersed. This temporarily ended that crisis but the problem persisted until we finally moved from Ivybridge to the assembly area in Dorset.[5]

William C. Smith, aged 20, F Company, 115th Infantry Regiment:

Ranger training at the Commando training base in Scotland was unique and tough. Needless to say, it was during this period I was introduced to landing craft. Probably during the five or six months' Ranger training we made half a dozen or more practice landings from LSTs and from a craft designated LCVP. I think that stood for Landing Craft Vehicles and Personnel. LST I guess meant Landing Ship Tank. I don't know, they came up with some of the craziest designations for those things.

The training on landing craft was as realistic as they could make it. They used live ammunition, which was fired over your head. Occasionally they fired a live artillery shell over your head so you could get used to the sound of artillery, and as you crossed the beach they would detonate dynamite that had been buried in the sand beforehand.

I recall one landing we made real early in the morning when it was pitch black. I mean, you couldn't see your hand in front of your face. The sailor pulled up to the beach, let the ramp down and off we went. Next thing I know, there was water up to my mouth. How I ever got ashore and didn't lose my rifle I'll never know. As I recall, I think half of the people that came off that landing craft that morning lost rifles, packs, web belts, the whole bit. That was one miserable day.

After training in Scotland we were sent to a little town on the southwest coast of England called Bude. It was a summer resort town and the government had taken over rows of houses where we were living.

Our training there consisted of field training, marches, lectures, pretty much that sort of thing. Most of the marches were forced marches, double-time marches. We'd run for five minutes, walk for five minutes, or walk for five minutes, run for ten minutes. It was always run and walk, we never did just walk.

What I always remembered about those marches was just a short time into them your boots would get to feeling like they weighed a ton. The canteen beating on one hip would have you really tee'd off. A commando knife on the other hip, bouncing up and down, had you tee'd off. The hand grenade bouncing on your belly didn't help any. The rifle sling digging into your shoulder and the helmet on your head bouncing up and down, beating your brains out, sure didn't help any. The only thing I can say is that it's amazing what a guy will go through for his country.[6]

Lance Corporal John 'Bill' Bailey, aged 22, 52nd Oxfordshire and Buckinghamshire Light Infantry:

We were doing some exercises blowing up bridges down near Exeter and I remember one day, a Sunday it was, we had stopped for lunch. The officers had gone off to have a meal in a pub and we had forty minutes or so to hang around with our cheese and corned beef sandwiches. We were used to this, it didn't worry us, it was the system, the way it was done.

Anyway, it was a pretty miserable sort of day and a little group of us was walking along the road and we passed what seemed to be a social club in a kind of hall and there were dustbins on one side and some American soldiers, coloured men, were emptying their mess tins and they were throwing chicken away.

Well, most of us hadn't seen any chicken for years and we stopped and stared and as we did so a chap came out – it turned out later he was the QM – and asked us if we had eaten. We said, well, we've had our sandwiches, but he took us in anyway and fed us with all the chicken that they were going to ditch. It was all good stuff, too. Afterwards they gave us ice cream and apologized that all they had left in the barrel was vanilla.

They *apologized*! I don't suppose any of us had seen ice cream since before the war started. I'm a great lad for ice cream. It didn't matter to us whether it was pink, white brown or whatever, it was ice cream.[7]

Sergeant Major Jack Vilander Brown, aged 29, 147th Essex Yeomanry:

We knew that we were training for the second front because when we went up to Scotland the colonel there, who was a regular, held a conference and said 'I've got some news, we're going to form part of the second front.' Then he added 'It's most disappointing. We're in the second wave, not the first wave.' He was quite upset about it. Well, he soon had his wish, because Monty increased the number of bridgeheads and beaches and he then held a second conference and told us we should all be 'pleased to learn' that we were going in on the first wave after all.

Then we went up to Scotland to practise with the Navy at Rothesay. We were practising these running shoots – you've got a flat-bottomed thing with four self-propelled guns, two in front and two at the back, and they fire as they go in. Once the initial range is given they just keep firing continuously. I think we fired between 150 and 200 rounds each gun continuously on the way in.

We came down south in March, to Brandon, and we were issued with all our equipment. We then went off to Bournemouth and took over the largest hotel, the Carlton, on the seafront. There was nothing in there, of course; they'd stripped everything, carpets, furniture, the lot. Practically every day we went out on these exercises on these LCTs. We used to start more or less from the Needles and go towards Studland Bay. We used to land on Studland Bay, fire live ammunition, all sorts of things, then trundle with our tanks back through Bournemouth, waking people. We were supporting the Sherwood Rangers' Yeomanry, who were equipped with DD tanks, which were all very hush hush. They were using the swimming tanks on exercises but they were always kept very close, in the inlets round Sandbanks and Poole, and whenever they moved they always tried to keep them hidden. Still, we could never understand why spies and people didn't see us, why the Germans never picked us up.[8]

Trooper M.E. Mawson, wireless operator, 13th/18th Hussars:

We got wind that there was something going on, something secret, high and mighty, when we went to Yarmouth to do our training in what turned out to be a tank that could swim. At the same time we were given training in the Davis Submarine Escape Apparatus. That nowadays is completely archaic, because breathing oxygen has been discovered to be dangerous, but nevertheless it worked at the time. We sat in an old tank turret at the bottom of a deep pit and thousands of gallons of water was poured on to us, giving us just a few seconds to don the apparatus. One of my companions tapped me in the darkness and knocked off my nose-clip as he went up. My remarks when I surfaced did not originate from a 'good home'.

I couldn't swim but I didn't mind the Davis apparatus because you could breathe. See, if I get my head under water I panic, probably the reason why I could never learn to swim satisfactorily, although enough people tried to teach me.

Up at Suffolk they had a lot of flamethrowers and flail tanks and Shermans with whips on them – 'Hobart's toys' they were called, after General Sir Percy Hobart. They were all supposed to be top secret, but people told me that they'd actually seen them driving down the street. I don't know if it's true.

There was a lot of experimenting with tank stability vis-à-vis the necessity of loading as much ammunition as possible along with a variety of supplies never conceived by us before and all aimed at our well-being and contributing to a 'we can't lose' atmosphere. We put in so many extra fittings – racks around the turrets for shells and so on – that we had to have a full-scale exercise to see if the wretched things would still float. I even had an extra shelf welded in my turret for a row of Penguin paperback books. My mother said that they might come in handy to read some time. Of course, with tanks, you always did your best, if you had ability, to make yourself comfortable, unlike the PBI. It was what we called home modification. If you didn't like something some place you moved it, and if someone from the Army Vehicle Inspectorate came round to inspect your tank it was just too bad. I saw one tank unit rumbling up a road with an upright piano strapped on the back.[9]

Corporal William Merifield, aged 31,745 Tipper Company, RASC:

We were living in a tented camp somewhere in Essex, alongside the London-to-Southend road. The first we knew that something was in the offing was when we were told that all our vehicles would have to be waterproofed.

We were issued with large tins of plastic, similar to plasticine, and yards of adhesive tape, and told to get on with it. There were no handbooks about how to proceed as nothing like this had been tried before. Each driver was responsible for his own vehicle and had to work out his own method.

Basically what it involved was applying plastic around all the electrical parts likely to come into contact with water and to fix a 'snorkel' onto the air intake of the carburettor. All oil breathing holes had to be left to the last possible moment before immersion.

As it was all trial and error, every vehicle had to be tested by driving it through a specially constructed trough, built of concrete. A ramp of about 25 degrees led down into the water, which was about four feet deep and 20 feet wide, and there was another ramp on the opposite side to climb out onto dry land.

There were lots of problems with vehicles stalling in the water. When this happened, they were hauled out by a breakdown vehicle, but the driver involved had to get into the water to attach a tow chain to the axle of his failed vehicle. After several vehicles had passed through the trough the water was very oily and muddy, as well as freezing cold. No one wanted their vehicle to fail and it wasn't long before we got everything right.[10]

Sergeant Jack Harries, A Company, 9th Battalion, The Parachute Regiment:

On Sunday church parades at Bulford Garrison Church we were required to attend in full battle order with weapons and leave them outside on the lawn and at the end of the service Brigadier Hill would arrive and suggest we all went on a 'nice stroll' before lunch. No one could refuse, of course, but the stroll usually consisted of anything up to eight or ten miles which usually developed into more of a run than a march, such was the pace of Brigadier Hill at the front. Maybe that was why he had the nickname 'Speedy'.

Long marches and training by night and sleeping by day was also included. Saturday-morning cross-country runs, with no exceptions, were also included. The importance of having good feet was essential and I recall the whole battalion was required to parade each morning and sit down around the football pitch where an interesting period was spent soaking our feet in methylated spirits in our mess tins, coupled with soaping our socks and using dubbin on our boots. It must have looked a bit strange, but it paid dividends.

The Bulford Special was the train that always started from Bulford sidings when we were granted a weekend pass. It left at 11.58 a.m. for Waterloo and we then caught the last train back from Waterloo to Salisbury, arriving in the early hours of Monday, when trucks would pick us up for Bulford. Failure to catch the correct train from Waterloo meant one had to get a later train which only stopped at Porton, which meant an eight-mile stroll across Salisbury Plain, arriving at barracks just about in time for breakfast. That route was followed by many.

Trips on the Bulford Special were often amusing and I recall one occasion when, as usual, all the chaps going on leave were doing their best to acquire extra rations to take home to their families, which by coincidence was the same time that rations always seemed to be short in the cookhouse. One day on arrival at Waterloo, instead of the usual stampede through the ticket barrier, a squad of Military Police was waiting on the platform to march all the chaps on the train to the underground railway passage below, where we were all lined up and a systematic search started of all clothing, small-packs and attaché cases, etcetera. The result was not without humour as the piles of provisions in front of each squad would have provided a banquet, including eggs, bacon, sugar, dried milk, rice, prunes, semolina, tinned fruit, etcetera, etcetera – the list seemed endless. The funniest moment was when a certain sergeant of A company was asked to open his case, which he did and in addition to food a frying pan clattered onto the stone floor. Rumour had it that the railway porters had a field day as chaps who had suspected that something was up quickly jettisoned packages onto the railway lines before leaving the train.[11]

Sergeant Len Drake, aged 24, 22nd Independent Parachute Company:

I joined 22 IPC at Larkhill early in January '44. Our role was to be pathfinders for the main body of parachute troops.

Approximately every two weeks we were supplied with one truck per platoon in which we tried to travel as far from Salisbury Plain as possible. One favourite place was Bournemouth, which was swarming with Yanks and the arrival of thirty British paratroopers, although usually split into groups of pals, usually created a noticeable furore, especially when the Yanks' monopoly of the local girls was contested. Inevitably a few punch-ups took place, but we always returned to camp feeling much better for our break from training.

The 'borrowing' of vehicles was rife among the paras, but none more so than in 22 IPC. We had possibly the champion in this field – an angelic-looking ex boy soldier who on one occasion actually borrowed a double decker bus and, with one of his pals as conductor, brought a busload of troops back to Larkhill, leaving the vehicle to be picked up by its owners the following morning. His downfall came when he was caught driving a US Army vehicle out of their camp. The 22 IPC corporal detailed to escort him back to the company described how he found the culprit handcuffed to a chair and covered by two US military policemen with loaded weapons.

It would have been a mammoth task for the police to investigate all the stolen vehicles, a large proportion of which were service vehicles in any case. It was a common sight, especially on the Monday after some unit had had a free weekend, to see abandoned vehicles dotted about Larkhill.

Larkhill and Salisbury Plain as a whole were teeming with troops of all descriptions. Our company had no Naafi and, much to the owner's delight, we used to frequent the Jubilee Café across the road from our quarters. We were also made honorary members of the Civilian Club in Larkhill – a great privilege and much envied by other units. We also had access to the ATS Naafi, known as Smokey Joe's, arranged through the girlfriends of one of our sergeants.[12]

*Captain John Tillett, aged 25, 52nd Air Landing Battalion,
Oxfordshire & Buckinghamshire Light Infantry:*

We had quite a few people killed while we were training in gliders; I
was nearly killed myself. Coming back from a flight out over the sea
during our main pre-D-Day exercise, I think we got caught in the
slipstream of aircraft ahead of us and the glider started to whirl about
and suddenly the tow-rope broke while we were still about three or
four miles out to sea. There was no hope of getting back to land and
so we had to prepare for ditching in the sea.

On board with me was the regimental sergeant major, the padre,
about six signallers, a jeep and a fully-loaded trailer – everything, in
fact, that we would carry for the landing itself. Our main worry was
that the lashings that held the jeep and trailer would break under the
impact and if they did so we would all almost certainly be killed.

It took about four or five minutes to get down and I think I can
remember saying to the padre, as we were going down, that perhaps
he ought to say something, but he didn't. We also had on board an
RAF wing commander who had come along for the ride. He was
bracing himself against the same bulkhead as me and looked absolutely terrified. He'd probably ditched in the sea before and knew
what it was like. To us it was a novel experience.

Actually, it is amazing how hard water is, it's like running into a
brick wall at eighty miles an hour. Although the sea was very calm,
we hit it with a hell of a crash and the pilot and myself and all the
people in the front of the glider just shot out the front of the thing,
straight through the fuselage. Next thing I can remember is actually
waking up under water and when I got to the surface I was in the sea
about thirty yards in front of the glider.

I couldn't move my legs much because I had smashed my back and
neck a bit. The glider floated for a while and we all got back on it
until we were picked up by a Walrus flying boat.[13]

*Flying Officer Jimmy Edwards, aged 24, Dakota Pilot, 271
Squadron, RAF:*

It was decided that as one of our jobs was going to be glider-
tugging, it would be an improving experience for all pilots actually
to go up in one of these fearsome contraptions, so that we could
appreciate for ourselves the difficulties involved at the other end of

the tow-rope. Accordingly, a few of us were despatched to RAF Brize Norton, where the training of Army personnel to fly the Horsa glider was in progress.

We were only there for two or three days and I was only airborne four times, but it put years on me. They were using the Whitley bomber as a tug and this ancient dilapidated machine was scarcely up to the task. I did two trips sitting beside the pilot in one of these and each time it seemed as if we would never get off the ground. But this knuckle-whitening experience was nothing compared to the two trips I was forced to make in a glider.

The Horsa was constructed on rudimentary lines of three-ply wood and piano wire, and was designed to be crash-landed on enemy territory, and was therefore regarded as entirely expendable. The pilots of the Glider Pilot Regiment were all volunteers, some sergeants and some officers, and they had been given a very swift and sketchy course of basic training on Tiger Moths. The fellow whom I sat beside did the whole thing as if he were loading up a machine-gun and finally, when he was ready for take-off, he was sitting ramrod-backed with the stick shoved forward by rigid arms as far as it would go. To double the terror, the very first trip was at night. I can just recall a pitch-darkness, relieved only by the stabbing flames of the Whitley's exhausts in front of us.

We were airborne first and stayed above his tail until we had climbed in a gradual turn to 2,000 feet. And then our pilot pulled a lever and we were alone, and I knew that the only way to go was down. The Horsa had immense manually-operated flaps, so we had some sort of control over our rate of descent, and we managed to juggle our way to the threshold at a reasonable height. Then, with a last wrist-cracking application of flap, we sank down and hit the deck with an almighty crunch. After that, silence . . . except for the sound of my heart beating.

I never sat in a Horsa again, but on the many subsequent occasions I towed them I had a lively understanding of what those Army boys were coping with.

There were two tricky moments in a take-off with a Horsa behind you. Firstly you had to take up the slack on the rope by gently letting the aircraft roll forward until the glider pilot, who could talk to you through a wire in the rope, told you when the rope was taut. If you opened the throttles too suddenly you could either break the rope, or you could yank it out of its two attachments to the glider's wings.

Then, when you had at last applied full power and had got the Dak's
tail up and were accelerating, albeit painfully slowly, down the
runway, the glider would get into the air before you and manoeuvre
up to about 20 feet in order to get out of your slipstream. So, for a
few moments, he was up and you weren't! And if he was ham-fisted
enough to get too high he would lift your tail so that your nose
dropped and you had a hell of a job to get up at all.

It's not difficult to imagine the language that went flashing along
the rope at times like that. Once you had climbed to a reasonably safe
altitude, you could all relax, but there was no question of putting on
'George', the automatic pilot, while the Horsa was wallowing behind
you.

If you ran into bad weather and there was a danger that your
glider pilot would lose sight of you in cloud, he could opt to go into
the 'low-tow' position. This involved his pushing his nose down and
bucketing through your slipstream until he was a few feet beneath
you and he then relied on some crazy string device that ran from the
hawser to an instrument in his windscreen. This was meant to help
him fly 'blind' behind you and was known colloquially as the 'angle
of dangle'. I never knew a glider pilot who had any faith in one of
these contraptions.

When you reached your destination and your Army mate behind
you reckoned he was in the right position to make a landing on the
airfield, he only had to pull a lever and the tow-rope fell away from
his wings. We then made a slow run over the prepared field and
dropped the hawser into it so that it could be used again. In an
emergency, or in bad weather, it was a matter of some delicacy as to
who disengaged himself from the rope. If the glider unhitched, the
Dak pilot would take the rope home with him; if the tug unhooked
the glider, its pilot would hang on to the hawser until he was down.
In each case, the theory was that if a court martial resulted, whoever
was in possession of the hawser was exonerated.[14]

3 April 1944

OVERLORD   TOP SECRET
GLIDER PILOT ADMINISTRATION INSTRUCTIONS

1. The attached Administration instructions deal with all administration prior to and after a successful landing on the Continent.
2. All the attached instructions are general, and a guide to Wing

Commanders. Situations may arise, where they will differ with the situation, and therefore may have to be altered at the last moment. An administration order will be issued prior to each operation.

3. The Corps Commander wishes the vital importance of strict administrative discipline to be emphasized to all ranks. Scrounging, Hoarding, Waste, and failure to comply with orders, completely upsets all administrative forecasts and planning. Any attempt to secure 'Private Nest Eggs' or unnecessary stores by making demands in excess of strict requirements, can only result in other troops receiving less than their essential needs and their being placed in jeopardy . . .

DRESS

The following dress will be worn by all operational pilots.

Battle Dress V.
Smocks Airborne.
Full Equipment (Pouches will be included).
Water Bottle.

1st Pilots to carry:-

Compass.
Watch.
Binoculars (if considered necessary by Wing Cmdrs).
Pith helmets to be worn during flight, Steel helmets carried and worn after landing.
Personal Anti-Gas Equipment will be carried.
Formation Signs will be worn.
Regimental Titles will Not be removed.
Berets will be taken.

The following is the suggested content of a haversack, but may be amended at Wing Cmdrs discretion.

Hold-all containing – knife – fork – spoon – shaving kit – comb – tooth brush – toothpaste – soap (for 14 days – 2 tablets).
Toilet paper.
Length of 4 × 2.
Mess Tin – 2 × 24 hour rations inside if possible.
British Emergency Ration.
Box of Matches – Safety Type.

Sterilizing Outfit.
1 pair of Boot laces.
2 pairs of Socks.
Cigarettes as required.
Beret.
Cooker (Hexanine Type).
Razor Blades.

RATIONS
Landing Rations. Each man will carry the following:-

(a) Emergency Ration.
(b) 24 hr Ration including 20 Cigarettes.
(c) Tommy Cooker (Hexanine Type).
(d) Water Sterilizing Outfit.
(e) Chewing Gum & Box of Matches.

The above (excluding Emergency Ration) are for use during the first 48 hrs AFTER landing. It is essential that troops should not break into these rations before take-off, or during transit.

Arrangements will be made for a meal prior to take-off, and chewing Gum, and boiled sweets will be issued as necessary.

The Emergency Ration will not be opened without the express order of an Officer. This should be made clear to all concerned.

Limited quantities of Rum will be available in the initial stage from normal sources, issued (on Medical advice) on authority of an Officer not below the rank of Colonel. Issues will only be made to men who have finished their work, and can be allowed a rest . . .[15]

Private John Chalk, aged 23, 1st Battalion, The Hampshire Regiment:

There was no need for us to be told officially that the 'Big Do' was coming off, we all knew that. What we didn't know was where or when. We presumed we would be an assault brigade, owing to our experience of assault landings in Sicily and Italy, and the type of training we were doing. I don't think I ever heard it referred to as Operation Overlord, but I guess we all knew it would be France, somewhere. Those sort of things didn't seem to bother us old campaigners much (I had joined as a boy soldier in 1935). We knew it was our job and we would do it to the best of our ability.

Meanwhile we were back in our own county, in a tented camp near Fawley in the New Forest, and soldiers, being what they were, we attempted to make the most of what we had. This certainly wasn't a lot, being under canvas in a gloomy, damp forest, with nothing much to do in our spare time and recurring malaria cropping up.

The acute shortage of beer was one of the main bugbears. The influx of thousands of servicemen into the south of England was draining the pubs dry and the breweries couldn't cope with the extra demand. Local pubs would only have enough beer for two or three nights a week and then they would be sold out in one-and-a-half to two hours, consequently they didn't open up until eight or half past eight in the evening. Word soon got around which pub would have beer and long before opening hordes of soldiers would be outside ready.

My cousin's wife was managing a pub in Blackfield, about two miles from the camp, and myself and four of my friends became 'privileged' customers there when beer was available. We would already have a table full of beer when the doors were thrown open to admit the waiting troops. Within an hour supplies would be sold out. We had to pay for our privilege, of course, by collecting and washing glasses.

One could go into Southampton when off duty. A three-mile walk would bring you to Hythe, where the ferry ran across to Southampton. It was not a very large ferry, nowhere near big enough to accommodate all the troops who wished to use it. The last ferry back from Southampton was at 9.30 at night, and this was always overcrowded. To miss the last ferry meant a long trek back around the head of Southampton Water. Sometimes the ferry was missed because there were just too many people for it to take, and often on a Sunday night it moved off with men still trying to jump on, some actually missing and getting a good soaking, but always plenty of hands to pull them out.

Whilst at Fawley training tended to get 'bigger', by that I mean not just training as a company or battalion, but as a brigade, with other arms of the services involved. There was one rehearsal at Studland Bay and another at Hayling Island, involving Navy, Air Force and artillery firing over our heads. It was around this time that we were becoming aquainted with all the unusual armoured vehicles we would no doubt be working with – flail tanks for clearing mines, flame-throwing tanks, swimming tanks and tanks for all sorts of jobs.[16]

Lieutenant Colonel Donald V. Bennett, 62nd Armored Artillery:

As we were going to be required to participate in the pre H-Hour bombardment of the beach by firing our M7s from LCTs we asked if we could send A Battery down to Slapton Sands to try this out on an LCT borrowed from the British.

We mounted four M7s in the hull of the tank hold of the LCT, two up and two back. These LCTs were made in two halves and welded together. They had a centre line that went from the bow ramp all the way back through the bridge to the stern. We tied an aiming stake on the bow ramp as an extension of the centre line, then we laid all the pieces parallel to the centre line of the LCT, so we were able to fire the Howitzers in the direction the LCT was pointing.

Now, we put the battery Exec up on the bridge, which is a narrow catwalk about six inches wide, and he straddled the centre line. Previously, we had picked aiming points on shore from aerial photos. Every time the aiming stake started coming across the aiming point, the battery Exec said 'Fire!' and the gun with a round in the tube at that time fired. Then we had another man on each piece and all he did was keep the levelling bubble level. When the bow would go up he would turn this way, and when the bow would go down he would crank the other way, just keeping the bubble level. We had another man on the range drum of each Howitzer. We figured out that we were doing about five knots, which is about 200 yards a minute. So we had a man up on the bridge next to the battery Exec with one of these big dishpans that the Army has in the kitchen kit, and a wooden potato masher. Every thirty seconds another man with a stop watch would say 'Time' and then, wham, the man would hit the dishpan and each piece decreased range by 100 yards.

Once in a while you could see where your shot was landing, since all we were doing was firing at the beach. If it 'walked' into the water, you would just add 200 yards to it; if it started 'walking' too far up the beach, you would drop 200. We did this, firing about 100 rounds per piece, on that exercise.

But the interesting part was that we didn't know what the LCT would stand. We started out with charge number one and it barely got over the bow. Finally, we settled on charge number five. We had seven charges on the 105mm Howitzer at that time. When we fired all four pieces with charge five that gave an awful jolt to the LCT. We could open up about 9,500 yards offshore with charge five, thus we were going to be able to put an awful lot of fire on the beach.

I said, 'We're going to do it this way. Let's go in, we've done enough', and I went into the crew compartment of the LCT, which is just behind the tank hull compartment; just a steel plate separates it from where the M7s were. I was seated right up against the compartment at a table about 14 inches wide, drinking a cup of coffee because I was frozen, it was so darn cold.

All of a sudden – Karoom! Everything came down on us and I went roaring out of there. It turned out that my battery commander couldn't stand that I hadn't tried out charge number seven and so after I had gone into the compartment, he loaded up those four pieces with charge seven and fired them. The LCT literally backed up in the water and we sprang about ten leaks. We started back towards the harbour since we were in the English Channel about 8,000 yards out at this time and we were sinking.

We had some of our gun crews manning the mechanical pumps, pumping as best we could. We went into the Dartmouth river. We had gotten on the boat up near the Naval Academy but coming back we were about 400 yards from there and it was obvious we were going to sink before we got there, so we just put it into the shore. As we left, the British lieutenant came out and said: 'What about my boat?'[17]

Sergeant Ewell B. Lunsford, aged 24, 4th Medical Battalion, 12th Division:

We pulled maneuvers there in England and went out in the Channel one week in a convoy of seven ships that got torpedoed by German E-Boats. We lost five of the nine ships.

The whole end was knocked off the one that I was on. I was down in the hold with the vehicles, gasoline and ammunition just packed in there. I heard one torpedo come sliding down the side of the hull, but it didn't explode. Then the next one caught the stern end and tore off about thirty feet all the way across to the end. It was like there was a big door back there, but we didn't sink.

I managed to get up on top. The tracer bullets were thick as hair on a dog's back. I saw one of those little old E-Boats in the moonlight. The guys were firing on it and I saw it hit and it just broke in two and went down in three minutes. Everything in it went down with it.

It happened about one or two o'clock in the morning and we just sat there the rest of the night, trying to keep all the GIs under control. Me and another sergeant had one section of the ship and it took a lot of pleading and begging to get them to stay in place and not go up on deck. But we got them quieted down finally and didn't let anybody get out, but just kept them in there.

Next morning, a British tugboat came out and pushed us into Plymouth. I've forgotten now whether it was three or four out of the nine ships they didn't sink that night. There was never anything in the paper about it. Nothing was ever said about it, but when they took us ashore they marches us way back out in those woods, away from everything. Wouldn't let us talk to anybody. They wouldn't let anybody see us or talk to us or anything for a week or two, then they sent us back to our company. Security didn't want it known that they lost all those ships.[18]

Joe Palladino, aged 19, 462nd Amphibious Truck Company, 1st Engineer Special Brigade:

I drove an amphibious truck, a DUKW, which we called 'ducks'. It was a very versatile vehicle. It not only hauled cargo but it was just the right width, with notches on the side, to fit five or six stretchers across, so it could haul wounded. It had a gun mount for a 50-calibre machine gun and it had a central air system that deflated or inflated the tyres as needed, when you were in soft sand on the beach. It was really something.

In early May we formed a convoy and went to Plymouth, where there was a whole line-up of LSTs and we proceeded to load onto these landing craft. We all figured this must be it, that we were going into the invasion of France. But it was just a rehearsal, a practice session for what was to come.

As we were loading onto the LSTs, I was just about to load when they stopped me and told me that it was full and to go to the next one. So I was the first DUKW on the next LST.

We went out into the Channel and there were about 50 or 60 ships sitting out there, and that night our convoy was attacked by Nazi E-Boats, similar to our torpedo boats. They did quite a lot of damage and the other LST that had half our outfit on was sunk. Only three of our men survived.

The LST that I was on had a torpedo miraculously right under it, scraping the bottom. I consider myself pretty lucky that I got out of there all right.[19]

Private Sam Jacks, aged 19, 83rd Field Artillery:

About three weeks before we hit the beach we was out on an exercise called Exercise Tiger. I always stayed on the topsides on one of them LSTs. I thought well if a shell comes in at the bottom and explodes you just had it. So I stayed on the topsides so I could be like a damn frog and jump in the water if I had to. So I was laying up on the topside of that thing, wrapped up in an old bed robe full day there one morning.

We was practicing these landings on a little old place called Slapton Sands and somehow or another they all got messed around. This here German wolf-pack, I'd guess you'd call it, torpedo boats or whatever the hell they was, they came down on us. The first time it cut loose he shot a torpedo off one of them things. Well, it went in on the bottom of that damn LST that I was on and it hit. Well, he realized then that there wasn't no big ships about so he lightened up his reins and the next time he knocked the hell out of us in the back end. Although we didn't sink, he did sink a couple more of them and we lost 740 men right there.

Them Germans slipped in there and sunk the hell out of them couple of LSTs and we'd lost them 740 men. And after that tragedy there that night, we were impounded and they swore they'd cut our damn heads off if we divulged it. I never did quite understand why, but later they said it would be a breakdown of morale to the other soldiers and this that and the other.

My brother was a captain, and I guess he would have gotten busted if Eisenhower had ever known it, but he come to see me about a week before we left out and told me 'I thought I better come see you 'cause the next time you go out doing this amphibious training you ain't coming back. You gonna hit the beach.' He was with Eisenhower headquarters but he wasn't supposed to tell me that, but he swore me to secrecy. I never did tell nobody, ever.[20]

CHAPTER FOUR

SPIES AND LIES

Operation Fortitude, the code name for the Allies' cover and deception plans was one of the remarkable successes of the war. False trails were laid, false armies created, every possible trick played to confuse the enemy; meanwhile, vital intelligence gathering continued . . .

Brigadier Richard Barker, signalmaster for Home Forces, appointing Colonel Rory MacLeod to command a phantom '4th Army':

Rory, old boy, you have been selected to run a deception operation for SHAEF from Scottish Command. You will travel to Edinburgh and there you will represent an army which does not, in fact, exist. By means of fake signals traffic you will, however, fool the Germans into believing that it does exist and, what is more, that it is about to land in Norway and clear the Germans out of there. The whole thing is an important part of the coming invasion of France. You are to keep the Germans fully occupied in Norway so that they don't reinforce the units in France from there . . . It is terrifically important that it should be a success.[1]

Letter from General Eisenhower to the Prime Minister, dated 25 March 1944:

Dear Prime Minister,
I do not know whether the suggestion I am going to make is practicable or whether it will be repugnant to you personally.

The large-scale exercise which it is necessary to carry out about 3rd–5th May will seriously detract from the degree of surprise that Plan 'Fortitude' is designed to achieve, if the enemy should interpret it in the true sense, as our final rehearsal. Accordingly everything possible must be done to convince the enemy that this exercise is the first, and that Operation Overlord is the second, of a series of exercises which must be carried out before D-Day.

I, therefore, submit for your considered opinion the proposal that when you next address the Nation you include a statement somewhat in the following terms: 'It will be necessary to hold a series of exercises during the next few months which, being unprecedented in scale, will call for many restrictions on the public. These must be borne with patience and it is the duty of every citizen to refrain from speculation.' I consider that such an address, framed in your own words, would greatly assist in concealing from the enemy the date of Overlord . . .[2]

Winston Churchill, reviewing the state of the war in an address to the nation, 26 March 1944:

We shall require from our own people here, from Parliament, from the press, from all classes, the same cool strong nerves, the same toughness of fibre which stood us in good stead in those days when we were all alone under the German blitz.

And here I must warn you, that in order to deceive and baffle the enemy as well as to exercise our forces, there will be many false alarms, many feints and many dress rehearsals . . .

Colonel Francis P. Miller, OSS, head of Sussex Operation:

I was assigned staff responsibility for planning, organizing and mounting an operation called 'Sussex'. The purpose of this operation was to gather strategic military intelligence through agents placed behind the enemy's lines prior to D-Day and during subsequent operations. Strategic intelligence meant information regarding enemy reserves (the location and deployment of particular units), indication of targets for bombing such as munition dumps, bridges and railway yards and any other data which might be of value to our offensive operations. Organization of such an operation was a complex undertaking. It involved recruiting agents, training them for months in field techniques and skills, endowing them with new personalities, furnishing them with appropriate clothes and gadgets, dropping them at designated spots, and above all insuring that they would be met by competent reception committees who would take them to three different 'safe houses' on successive nights so that the Gestapo would lose the trail.

An operation of this kind required an impressive variety of equipment. The British were far ahead of us in the invention of tools for espionage, and among other things had perfected a ground-to-plane phone which they allowed us to use. The Germans had become expert at locating ordinary radio transmitters, but the radio waves from this phone went skyward in a cone and the Germans could not pinpoint the source with their regular direction-finders. Mosquito planes based in England, with receiving sets installed, flew out over the channel to listen to the reports of agents who used these phones.

Sussex was one of the few operations with which I have had anything to do that was carried through to a wholly successful conclusion. I glow with a bit of pride now when I think about it. Fifty-six agents dropped behind the enemy lines with not a single miscarriage in reception arrangements: a thousand messages received back from those agents and only three of them were caught in the line of duty and executed by the Germans.

Of those three none, as far as we could tell, revealed any information about other agents during torture prior to execution. One of the three had been dropped at Chartres. He was equipped with a ground-to-plane phone and before D-Day reported that the Panzer Lehr Division was being held in reserve in that area. When reporting his voice indicated stress of emotion and we feared for him. A few days later he was caught.

The Panzer Lehr Division was the best equipped division in the German army and its presence in France had not been known to either American or British headquarters. Montgomery's chief of intelligence remarked later that spotting that Division alone was worth the entire Sussex operation.[3]

Average Standard List of Equipment Supplied to Sussex Operation Agents

CLOTHING

Two complete sets of clothing of French or European make. (Large quantities of assorted European clothing obtained from refugees, etcetera, have been received from Washington.)

COMMUNICATIONS EQUIPMENT

For W/T Operator:

1 TR-1 (U.S.) or Mark 7 (British) Radio set.
1 Mark 21 (British) emergency set.
2 Batteries.
2 Battery acid, bottles.
1 Generator and stand (operated on bicycle wheel).
W/T communications plan and codes.

For Observer:

1 Klaxon set (Ground to plane voice wireless communication. Given to certain teams only, as there are not enough available to supply all.)
2 Batteries.
1 Power Pack.
2 Battery acid, bottles.
1 Generator and stand.
Communication plans and codes.

Trading or Personal use equipment
(French trade-marks, but fabricated in England.)
Laundry soap.
Toilet soap.
Chocolate bars.
Cigarettes.
Matches.
Saccharine.
Coffee and/or tea.
Tobacco.
Fuel kits.
Meta tablets.
French flashlights (batteries, bulbs).
Bicycle repair kits.

Bicycle inner tubes.
First aid kit (French).
Medical Kit (British).
Magnifying glass.
Rations.
Flasks of whisky or brandy.
Toilet articles (some with concealing devices).
Sewing Kits.
Any odd item on special request, e.g. pepper, which one agent requested to drive off dogs.

Weapons and Special Equipment
·45 automatic and 3 clips.
Bakelite grenades.
M1 Carbine (in some cases only, in addition to other weapons).
Compass.
Field glasses.
Set of maps of region.
Rulers.
Q.B. pads (quick burning).
Signalling flashlight, with green and red strips (for eventual receptions).
Spare batteries and bulbs.
L tablets (lethal suicide tablets).
K tablets (knock-out tablets).
Escapist knife.
Escapist hack-saw set in rubber.
Wrist watch.
Rings (with concealed compass, or secret space for L tablet or message).[4]

Staff Sergeant Leonard Levenson, aged 27, Divisional HQ, 82nd Airborne Division:

I knew about D-Day very early on because of my job. When you were approved to go into what we called the war room, you were called 'bigoted'. By May there were voluminous plans, volumes of stuff; the war room, which was a hut, had a couple of annexes to it and one war cupboard was full of maps. I knew that the British were going to be there somehow, but we didn't have plans for the British end of it. We had complete plans for the First Army part of it – we were at the western end – and we were working on that for weeks, solid weeks.

The interesting thing is, we were permitted out at night, there was no restriction on this – I'm talking about myself, all the other men and all the officers, a group of 30 to 40 people, all of them having either complete or partial knowledge of what was going to happen. I know I travelled to London a couple of times, other guys did, people were travelling all over. I've read that there were a couple of breaches of security, by officers, not by men, but fortunately, they didn't hurt us.

When you got to be part of this deal, the way I was and the group I was with, we felt we could do anything, we weren't afraid of anything. It sounds a little stupid, but it was so. You get caught up in it after a while. Everybody was apprehensive, I think, I certainly was apprehensive about it, scared even if you want to use that word, but not terrorized, not cowardly or craven.

We all wished it would happen sooner rather than later because I think we felt the later it got, the worse it would be. I think that most of us felt it had to be done. Well maybe it was better if *they* had to do it rather than we had to do it, but we're gonna have to do it, and there was not too much else we could do about it.[5]

Brigadier A.E.M. Walter, Commander British Mulberry B Port Construction Force:

The research, designing, building, towing across the Channel and planting of the artificial harbours, code-named Mulberries, on the beaches of Normandy was probably the greatest wartime engineering feat of all time. My memories of those three months leading up to D-Day are of eternal conferences, eternal planning and everlasting sailing schedules, because each piece of the jigsaw had to sail from England at an exact time to reach the other side and be fitted in according to a tight programme always hoping that the sea and the Germans would not interfere; chasing around the country trying to meet units; plans changing and an ever growing sense of bewilderment at the sheer size of the enterprise.

One particular memory was terrifying and I can still go cold at the thought of it. After a long and tedious morning of meetings, Petrie (my naval opposite number) took me to lunch at the In and Out Club in Piccadilly. As was the custom, we took our black bags, carefully locked, into lunch and for security's sake put them down on the floor beside our feet and never let them go – or so I thought. After lunch, we returned to Norfolk House and I found that I had left my bag under the table at the club. My papers contained plans of the Mulberry and it would not have taken German intelligence much effort to locate the beach.

I have never forgotten the horror of that moment of discovery. Execution at the Tower would have been a comforting and welcome release, but would not have lessened the damage. I rang the club immediately and again I have never forgotten the calm voice of the Hall Porter saying: 'Yes sir, a bag was found beside one of the tables and I have it here quite safe in the office.' I broke the record time between Norfolk House and the club to retrieve that bag. As far as I could see, the papers were intact.

I reported the incident immediately to Intelligence, expecting that I would now sever my brief connection with 21 Army Group and go to the Tower, especially as we had recently heard on the grapevine of a senior American officer who had spoken out unwisely and had been returned promptly to the States for punishment. However, after much checking and interviewing, it was decided that no harm had been done and I was returned to store in a battered condition.

Early in May I had to be told the planned date of D-Day and this was a great burden, especially after my lapse of security – I was even scared of babbling in my sleep. For the last week my headquarters moved to some rather nice empty houses down by the shore at Selsey and we took with us from Norfolk the large model of the harbour at Arromanches. We were very worried about having it down there on the shore, in case we were attacked, and so in addition to the permanent guards, the bravest of the clerks were assigned to die destroying the model at all costs, if attacked.[6]

Hanson W. Baldwin, military editor of the New York Times:

The *New York Times* office then was in the Savoy Hotel, where I had a room; the former office in Fleet Street had been bombed out. I remember surrendering my ration tickets for horrible breakfasts of spam and dried eggs (almost inedible) or dried mushrooms on toast. There was no other choice.

Ray Daniell was the head of the *New York Times* London bureau and a whole crew of *Times* men had been assembled to cover the invasion. At nights we would gather in the *Times* office suite, hiding the increasing tension as the slow days passed by, playing The Game, a variation of charades and a fad that was sweeping Britain.

Then, at last, I got the word: report outside the north-west entrance of the Admiralty, near the Mall, about eight the next morning, 22 May, with all equipment ready to go.

The accredited naval correspondents – in uniform and complete with typewriters, cameras, helmets, gas masks, baggage – assembled conspicuously in the heart of London. There must have been several score correspondents – British and American and a few French, representatives of press services, individual newspapers, radio chains and stations, a few magazines and numerous photographers.

With escort and conducting and public relations officers, there were probably close to 100 people milling about in the open near the Admiralty in the midst of London's rush to work. It was a *very* conspicuous assemblage and it was meant to be.

Somehow, some of us had gotten the word. The 'brass' confessed after they had herded us inside the Admiralty. This was a 'dry run'. We were journalistic guinea pigs serving a three-fold purpose: to test the administrative machinery of assembling, transporting and escorting war correspondents assigned to the Navy; to provide an opportunity for correspondents to inspect one of the crowded invasion ports; and, most importantly, to try a deception ploy, a minor part of a vast cover pattern that screened D-Day, intended to fool any German spies still at large in Britain.

We played it for real. The group boarded a train bound for somewhere on the South Coast, where at every port from Dover to Land's End and around into the Bristol Channel and the Irish Sea 3,000 ships and vessels of the invasion fleet, crammed with thousands of men and the hopes of two continents, were waiting.

We were, we found, bound for the picturesque port of Fowey in Cornwall, a peacetime fishing port and a mecca for vacationers during the August Bank Holiday, crammed now, gunwhale to gunwhale, with US LCIs.

In Fowey, we walked around the little town, inspected the congested harbour and I looked up an LCI skipper to whom I bore a message of love and a photograph from his fiancée in the States. Then, in compensation for the long and futile train trip, we were bussed to Menabilly House, a manor on the outskirts of Fowey. It was the home of Daphne du Maurier, the English novelist, master of the Gothic romantic-suspense genre, then internationally famous for her best-seller, *Rebecca*.

Miss du Maurier was the wife of Lt.Gen. F.A.M. Browning, commanding British airborne troops. He was, of course, on the verge of D-Day, conspicuous by his absence. But his wife, her mother and the young Browning children took on the task of offering tea and whisky to a clamouring crowd of correspondents.

Miss du Maurier was the epitome of graciousness and English understatement, the setting unforgettable. The Brownings lived in a half-ruined, ancient Cornish manor house and had restored to a liveable condition only a part of it – as I remember, about half – before the war stopped additional restoration.

The half-ruined portion, windows blank or boarded, was very evident; the whole house was ivy-covered, the long-neglected garden here and there showed signs of cultivation and conversion from flowers to vegetables. There was a small lawn and then the tall grass, rippling in the wind off the Channel sloped down to the high cliffs that loomed over the sea.

It was a fitting setting completely in keeping not only with Miss du Maurier's novels, but with the sense of hidden dread, prayerful hope and controlled suspense that permeated the air of England before D-Day.[7]

BIGOT TOP SECRET – 26 April 1944

To: London Headquarters, SOE/SO

From: Supreme Headquarters Allied Expeditionary Force

Subject: Deliveries by air to Resistance groups

1. Study of the deliveries by air during the April moon has shown that there was an undue emphasis in the 'OVERLORD' lodgement area. There is a danger, therefore, that the GERMANS may have been able to make deductions which compromise the security of the operation.
2. In order to counteract any such deductions, deliveries during coming moon periods will be made in such a manner as to throw the emphasis on to the cover area. This emphasis should be at a ratio of at least 3 to 1 until such time as a daily check of successful

operations indicates a revision of the ratio is desirable. No restriction is placed on the area south of the line, the LOIRE-ORLEANS-LUXEMBURG, which may be used as an alternative area in the event unfavourable weather conditions preclude operations in the cover area, but the urgency of deliveries to the cover area is emphasized.

3. You will submit a plan for deliveries during the May moon to this Headquarters as early as possible for approval and will report the result of operations daily to this Headquarters.

4. For the purposes of security and cover the attached statement may be presented to operational personnel concerned:

In the past, restrictions imposed primarily by weather have caused deliveries in BELGIUM and N.E. FRANCE to fall considerably below requirements. During the coming moon periods, therefore, there is a special demand for stocks of arms and equipment in these areas to be brought up to the scale essential for future operations. In making this operational demand, it is fully realized that the risk of increased losses to aircraft and crews will be entailed.[8]

André Heintz, aged 24, student, member of the Resistance in Caen:

We had to keep the Allies informed on the progress of 'Rommel's Asparagus' – those stakes that were planted in open fields around Caen – and about minefields. Quite often, for their own safety, the Germans marked them with little yellow flags with cross bones drawn on them. The problem, which was rarely solved, was how to differentiate the real minefields from the fake ones. Farmers not able to use their fields always reported to the local authorities, so instead of going on long rounds it was much more efficient to get the information from the local Mayor's office or, even better, from the tax collector's office, because he could provide us with a very precise survey map.

Beside the information that we gathered from our own authority, we would often get questionnaires through our Resistance groups, either inspired by the leaders in Paris or from queries received by radio in England.

I remember how I used to meet with my Resistance leader, from the Cahors-Asturie network, in a church in Caen. That church had entrances on two different streets so that each of us entering on a different side were never seen together outside. In the church we would kneel side by side at the 6.30 mass in the morning; we thought that the Germans would not be so active at such an early hour. We talked together as little as possible, but exchanged missives – his was the new questionnaire and mine were the answers I had been able to find out from the previous one.

I must confess that there were two types of questions that always puzzled me. When a bunker had been found we could describe what type it was as the number of models was limited, but I am afraid we could not always be very accurate about the calibre of the guns. When the guns were brought in, the area was evacuated. If by any chance a local farmer had seen the guns, it was rare luck.

The other thing that often caused a blank in my answers was the last question – how many men would be necessary to invest a certain defence post or headquarters? It was very difficult for inexperienced people like us to assess the answer to such a question. The only thing it did, in fact, was to make us think it was not fair to ask such questions unless D-Day was getting near. Other questions were perfectly useless, like finding out passwords which were changed every day.

In order to find out about troop movements, which was one of the most common requests, the best way to confirm some hearsay was to go to the bus terminal and join the long line of people waiting for the bus. By broaching a conversation about the weather, you were sure to be told the news from different villages and it was always such a relief when occupying troops left that people were bound to mention it. Then you had to pretend you had to check some luggage or that you had forgotten to buy your ticket. It usually saved you having to make a trip yourself.

It was more difficult to identify a new unit when it arrived. The best way was to find out where the soldiers gave in their laundry and if you had a friend there he could read the numbers of the units for you on the shirt collars. It was also reported on the soldiers' graves, but you had to wait until one died!

Little details had their importance. When we were all expecting the opening of the Second Front, my mother heard a storekeeper ask a German soldier who was on the coast what he would do if there was a landing the next day. His answer was 'I shall behave like the mussels', in other words stay in his shell and avoid the fight. The other type of information required was about industrial plants, boats and docks, but Caen was never a very busy port or a very industrial city. More important from a military point of view were the ack-ack guns and any changes in their location had to be immediately reported by radio.

But radio operators ran great risks as they were so easily detected; after nine minutes of transmitting they could be found out. Ours – we called him the 'pianist' – loved the summer because he felt safer transmitting from the middle of a wheat field where he said his aerial could hardly be seen.

I remember once when a farmer was indignant to see one of his fields taken over to build bunkers to set up a battery. It was on the top of cliffs at Longues-sur-Mer some six miles from Bayeux. Unfortunately the farmer did not know anyone in the Resistance to report it to until he discovered that his nephew, Arthur Poitevin, who was blind, was in touch with the Resistance in Bayeux. He made contact with him and the boy managed to get a pass to visit his uncle in the 'forbidden zone' by the coast. Of course the Germans could not suspect a blind boy of spying.

When he was with his uncle, Arthur paced up and down the field next to the bunkers and back in Bayeux he was able to give the figures to Jean Guerin, who was an expert at reading maps and coding messages. Jean pinpointed the four bunkers on the map, made up his message, coded it and signed it with his assumed name, 'Alain Chartier'. (Chartier was a fifteenth-century poet who wrote 'La Belle Dame sans Merci', which Keats translated and turned into a beautiful poem of his own.)

Our radio operator was not a specialist trained and parachuted from England with a code. He transmitted 'blind' and, to let us know the message had been received, we had to wait for a transmission from the BBC that included the last word of our message.

At the time it was not only forbidden to listen to the BBC but all wireless sets had been confiscated. I had built a crystal set hidden in an empty tincan with beans on top, so Jean Guerin, who was a friend of mind, told me, 'If you hear anything about Alain Chartier, let me know.' Two days later I heard on the BBC 'Alain Chartier, poète bas-normand, est né à Bayeux' (Alain Chartier, a poet from Lower Normandy, was born in Bayeux). It was two days before I saw Jean again but when I finally met him and told him the message had gone through, he said, 'Don't mention it. We sort of guessed it because the

Germans are already circling round with their direction-finding truck.' Fortunately we had been given the registration numbers of six of those trucks and one in our group in Bayeux had spotted one. The Germans were always furious at never understanding the BBC messages, but they had heard the word 'Bayeux' and had decided to investigate there. Of course, for safety, all radio transmitting had to be stopped in the area for nearly three weeks.[9]

TOP SECRET   7 May 1944

EIGHTH MONTHLY PROGRESS REPORT TO SHAEF FROM SFHQ LONDON
APRIL 1944

GENERAL
The outstanding features of the month can be outlined as follows:-

(a) The MAQUIS areas continue to become stronger and better equipped. GERMAN counter-measures have increased and attacks on the organized MAQUIS now amount to small scale military operations.

(b) Resistance Groups are still suffering from arrests by the GESTAPO, but these losses in the field are partially compensated for by the record number of agents which were despatched during April.

(c) An agreement was reached between SHAEF and the AFHQ whereby operational control and coordination of Resistance Groups in SOUTHERN FRANCE has been transferred to SHAEF for the purpose of giving maximum assistance to OVERLORD.

(d) General KOENIG has been appointed by General DE GAULLE as the French commander of the patriot forces in those parts of France which fall within the zone of OVERLORD operations.

GENERAL SABOTAGE
The weight of current sabotage is steadily increasing in spite of several important GESTAPO penetrations of SF organizations in the field. Examples of recent attacks are:

(i) All machines and precision tools at the TOULOUSE powder factory were sabotaged; stocks of raw materials set on fire; 30 100-HP motors and the water supply lines destroyed.

(ii)   The copper factory at MONT BARTIER was successfully attacked, thus depriving the NAZIS of 90 tons of copper per month.

(iii)   A power plant and a GERMAN supply depot north of ALDERIEU were sabotaged by explosives and fire.

(iv)   Successful attacks on 80 high tension electric pylons in AVEYRON and EGUZON held up industry in PARIS and TOULON for nearly two days.

(v)   The TINKEN ball-bearing factory in PARIS was put out of action by the destruction of its transformers, presses and Blanchard machines.

(vi)   In an attack on the factories of CIE FRANCAISE DE RAFFINAGE and REGIE AUTONOME DES PETROLES in the BOUSSENS district, six transformers and 10,000 gallons of oil were destroyed. These factories produced 200 tons of oil per month for GERMANY.

(vii) The HOTCHKISS plant at PARIS, manufacturers of anti-tank guns and spare parts for marine engines, was sabotaged.

(viii) The cement works at BEAUCAIRE were blown up resulting in a three weeks' delay in production.

(ix)   Railway sabotage continues to flourish. In April, 153 locomotives were reported sabotaged. During 1944, more than 850 locomotives have been attacked by agents or groups operated by SF HQ. Thirty trains were derailed by members of Resistance Groups in April. These included four troop trains and resulted in considerable ENEMY casualties.

(x)   The small steel railway bridge over the HAUTE SOANE canal at LAVILLIERS was destroyed by explosives.

PREPARATIONS FOR D-DAY

Plans for Interference with Communications

(i)   The total number of railway targets in all stages of preparation is now 998, but because of previous arrests, 199 of these must be considered as doubtful. The targets ready for demolition upon receipt of these orders from the SF HQ now total 159 for the SOE/SO Controlled Groups in FRANCE, and 258 for the ALLIED FRENCH Resistance Groups.

(ii)   The total number of road cuts which are confirmed as ready for demolition in FRANCE is 23. Those targets which have been

reconnoitred but which are not yet prepared and ready because
of a lack of supplies total 78.

(iii)   The total number of telecommunication targets which are
ready for demolition upon receipt of orders from SF HQ is 24.
The total number reconnoitred, but at present lacking stores
and final preparation, is 34.

(iv)   In addition to the planned demolitions shown above, instructions issued to all Resistance Groups under the heading
'GENERAL DE GAULLE TASKS' call for maximum
interference with road, rail and telecommunications upon
receipt of the D-Day 'action' orders from SF HQ.

(v)   SF organizers in NORTHERN FRANCE have been
instructed to prepare cuts on a number of specified sections of
trunk cables. These are planned with a view to isolating the
principal communication centres in the OVERLORD area.

(vi)   Arrangements have been made for the PTT trunk communication specialists (more than 700 in number), after receiving their
action orders from SF HQ, to effect technical sabotage of their
local installations and then go into hiding. Thus it is hoped
these experts will be available to assist in repairing the trunk
network in FRANCE as the invasion progresses.[10]

Lieutenant George Lane MC, aged 29, X Troop, 10 Commando:

We were doing small-scale raiding across the Channel from
Newhaven, crossing on moon-less nights in an MTB then going
ashore in a small boat called a dory. We had many different jobs to
do – take samples from the beaches, photograph the obstacles, check
on the disposition and strength of the coastal defences, things like
that. Sometimes we had to try and snatch a prisoner to bring him
back for interrogation.

Almost everyone in X Troop was a foreigner. I am a Hungarian;
my real name is Lanyi Gyorgy. I was studying English literature at
London University when war broke out. I wanted to fight against
the evils of Nazism and was accepted into the Grenadier Guards but
the Home Office intervened and said that as a foreigner I could only
join the Alien Pioneer Corps. I didn't relish the idea of fighting with
a pick and shovel, so I managed to get a job with SOE and from
there I transferred to the Commandos.

One day my company commander, a wonderful Welshman called

Bryan Hilton-Jones, sent for me and told me that Mountbatten had come up with an idea to make better use of foreigners serving in the British army. He thought that with their specialist knowledge and languages they could form a secret troop to undertake hazardous operations. Hilton-Jones asked me if I would like to be a part of it and I said 'You bet I would.' We asked for foreign-born volunteers interested in doing something more useful than they were already doing and interviewed an enormous number at the Great Western Hotel in Marylebone Road. About 100 were eventually selected for training in North Wales and it was from that nucleus that X Troop was formed. We were all given false names and army numbers to conceal our real identities and we began small-scale raiding at the end of 1943.

In mid-May I was briefed for a special mission. This is the story I was told. An RAF plane was strafing a strong-point on the beach near Calais and his aerial torpedo fell into the sea short of the target. As it exploded, it set off a series of simultaneous explosions in a very definite pattern over a large-ish area. When the scientific chaps saw the pictures, they were worried that it was some kind of new mine we knew nothing about. They didn't know whether it was electric or pressure or release or magnetic; they didn't know anything about it. It was decided that someone should be sent over to bring one back. The operation was given the code name Tarbrush.

Our first raid was on the night of 15 May, but all we could find were ordinary Tellermines fixed to the top of stakes driven into the sand. I recognized what they were and took one off and brought it back. They nearly died of fright when I presented it to the chaps at Newhaven. As it had been underwater they said the corrosion had played havoc with the mechanism and it could have gone off at any minute. I was ticked off.

We went over again on the following night to have another look, but had to turn back because of bad weather. On the night of 17 May we tried again. They were pretty certain that the linked explosions were probably caused by corrosion, but they wanted to be sure there was nothing we had missed. This time I took with me a Sapper officer by the name of Roy Woodbridge. He was a mine expert who had won the Military Cross lifting mines at El Alamein. I also took an infra-red camera to photograph obstacles on the beach. Two NCOs – Sergeant Bluff and Corporal King – accompanied us.

We landed near Onival some time after midnight. After a quick look round I sent the two NCOs back to the dory while Roy and I went further along the beach. I told them to wait for us until three o'clock. As we moved off into the night there was a tremendous amount of noise: two enemy patrols suddenly opened fire. I don't know whether they had spotted us or whether they had spotted each other, but we were certainly in between them and we flattened ourselves on the sand, making ourselves pretty scarce, as you can imagine. The two patrols fought a tremendous battle over our heads. I suppose we might have laughed if we had felt a bit safer, but we didn't laugh much. Eventually they must have hit each other because we heard a few screams and they withdrew.

We made our way back to where the dory should have been waiting for us but it wasn't there. All we could find was our rubber dinghy. By that time it was raining like hell. We thought that if we were going to be caught, it would be better to be caught at sea, so we got into the dinghy and began paddling, trying to get as far away from the coast as we could before dawn. Shivering in our wet clothes, we tried to keep our spirits up by talking about the possibility of a Catalina flying boat being sent out to find us and take us home. It was then that Roy told me he should have been on his honeymoon. He had only got married a couple of days before he was sent on this job. There he was, the poor bugger, instead of being on honeymoon he was with me in a rubber dinghy almost certain to be captured.

By the time it was light we were quite a way out but still clearly visible from the shore. We saw a motor boat heading out towards us from the direction of Cayeux-sur-Mer and we decided to get rid of all our equipment and throw it overboard. We had a fanciful notion that if we pretended to be destitute there might be a chance of shooting our way out, overpowering the crew and pinching their boat. But they were, of course, highly trained Germans and when they came close and began circling our dinghy we found four or five Schmeisser machine guns pointed at us very menacingly. We realized there was no chance of them making any silly mistakes and so, with a somewhat theatrical gesture, we threw our pistols into the water and put our hands up.

They very slowly came alongside, searched us, tied the rubber dinghy to their boat and took us into Cayeux-sur-Mer. I was soaked to the skin, very unhappy and very uncomfortable. I asked them if we could dry ourselves, pretending to be a Welshman because I knew my accent would give me away very quickly. As we were entering the harbour I noticed that the boat reduced speed and the crew were being very, very careful. It was obvious the harbour was very heavily mined and I thought back to how just a few days before we went happily straight through it in the middle of the night without a second thought. It was an incredible bit of luck that we weren't blown to bits.

We were separated when we got ashore and I was put in some underground place which was very damp and cold. I felt very unhappy and uncomfortable. Then the interrogation started. A good-looking chap came in, I think he was a captain, and he began by saying, 'Of course, you know we'll have to shoot you because you are obviously a saboteur and we have very strict orders to shoot all saboteurs and commandos.' I said I didn't think it was a good idea and so he said, 'All right, what were you doing?'

Roy and I had decided to pretend that we had been shipwrecked and we knew it was vital that we stuck to our story. I told them I didn't really know what had happened except that we had had some bad luck and our ship had been hit and we had been told to get into the dinghy and that is what we had done.

On raids I used to wear a polo neck fisherman's jersey over my battledress, thinking that if anything happened I could quickly take it off and put it under my battledress. That is what I did that night. We had removed our commando and parachute badges, but they were quite cute – they examined my battledress top very carefully and could see where the badges had been. They knew we were commandos.

The interrogation was very unpleasant. They kept threatening me and I kept saying I'm sorry, I can't tell you anything important because I don't know anything important. It went on for a long time. They wouldn't give me anything to eat or drink and I felt bloody peckish, as you can imagine. Then suddenly a medical chap came in and I thought, 'My God, what's going to happen now?' But all he did was blindfold me and tie my hands behind my back. Then I was told to stand up and, as I did so, my trousers fell down because they had taken my belt away. Somebody pulled them up and I was taken outside and pushed into the front seat of a car.

We started driving and I tried to ask where we were going, but no one answered. Then, as I lay back in the seat, I realized they had tied the blindfold so tightly that I could see underneath it, through the gaps on either side of the bridge of my nose. I leaned right back as if I was trying to get some sleep and tried to see where we were going. The French never took their signposts down and I noticed that the last signpost was to a place called La Petite Roche-Guyon. When we arrived I was pulled out of the car and they took my blindfold off and untied my hands so I could hold up my trousers.

I looked up and caught a quick glimpse of an old castle nestling against a cliff with some curious trees growing out of the rock to the same height as the chimneys. Then I was quickly shuffled inside and taken to a room where, much to my joy, I was given a cup of tea. I had been left alone in the room and I realized that the door was not locked. I opened it slowly and the biggest Alsatian I have ever seen jumped up and barked at me, so I quickly closed it again and sat down.

After a little while a very elegant officer came in and, to my amazement, we shook hands. He spoke beautiful English. 'How are things in England?' he said. 'It's always very beautiful at this time of the year, isn't it?' I asked him how he knew England so well and he said his wife was English. As he seemed so friendly I told him I hadn't had anything to eat for days and I was very hungry. He immediately apologized and sent for some food – very nice chicken sandwiches, which tasted superb.

As I was eating, he said, 'Do you realize you are going to meet someone very important?' I said, 'No. Who? Hitler?' He did not take any notice and continued, 'Before you are taken in, you have to give me your word as an officer and a gentleman that you are going to behave like one.' I told him I always behaved like a gentleman. 'Very well,' he said, 'you are going to meet his Excellency Field Marshal Rommel.' I said I would enjoy that very much, as Rommel was rather admired by the British army. He asked me if I would like to clean up a bit when I had finished my sandwiches. I was pretty grubby by then, of course, and I remember he lent me a nail file to clean my fingernails.

I was taken up some stairs and shown into a beautiful room, a library, and there was Rommel, at the far end, sitting at a small writing-table. I remembered stories of people being unnerved by being made to walk the whole length of a room, but it did not happen like that at all. Rommel immediately got up, walked towards me, motioned to a round table on one side of the room and said, 'Setzen Sie sich.' I pretended I could not understand and looked at the other officer, who told me to take a seat at the table.

Several other people came in, I think one of them was an admiral, and we then had this most extraordinary conversation. Rommel looked at me and said, 'So you are one of these gangster commandos, are you?' When it had been interpreted I pretended to be very annoyed and said to the interpreter, 'Please tell his Excellency that I do not understand what he means by gangster commandos. Gangsters are gangsters but the commandos are the best soldiers in the world.'

Rommel frowned and said something about having had some very unfortunate experiences with commandos pretending to be dead and then shooting the German medics who had gone to help them. 'You know you are in a very serious situation,' he added, 'because we think you are a saboteur.' I replied that I didn't think he would have invited me to see him if he seriously believed I was a saboteur.

Rommel laughed suddenly. 'Oh,' he said, 'so you regard this as an invitation, do you?' Certainly, I replied, and a great honour. He laughed again and everyone else laughed and the atmosphere became very relaxed and congenial. Then he asked, 'How's my friend Montgomery?' I told him I didn't know anything about Montgomery other than what I read in *The Times*, which was an excellent newspaper. 'Yes, I know,' he said. 'I get a copy every day via Lisbon.'

The conversation then turned to the invasion. Rommel asked me if I thought it was really going to happen and I again said that I didn't know any more than what I read in *The Times*, but I certainly believed it would take place. He said something about how it would be the first time the British army would have to do some fighting for themselves and went on at length about how they were always getting others to do their fighting for them. Being a Hungarian, it was difficult for me to keep a straight face.

Then he asked me where I thought the invasion would be coming. I said that as a junior officer I certainly didn't know, but if it was up to me I would probably go for the shortest crossing because that way you would get the least casualties. He nodded slowly then said, 'You know it is a great pity that Germany and Britain are not fighting together against the Russians. They are the real enemy in Europe, they are the ones who are going to create real trouble, not us.' I said I thought there were too many differences between us for us ever to be on the same side, giving as an example the Jewish question, but he dismissed it as the responsibility of the politicians, not the military.

I had the feeling that our conversation was coming to an end. It was such an extraordinary situation that I could not resist trying to prolong it. All my life I have been a pretty gregarious chap and I was enjoying myself tremendously, so I asked the interpreter if, as the Field Marshal had asked me so many questions, I would be permitted to ask a few of my own. Rommel laughed again when my question had been translated and nodded. I said what I would most like to ask was whether it was a feasible proposition for a victorious army to both conquer and govern a hostile country.

Rommel then produced the most wonderful dissertation explaining how the army was uniquely qualified to take over the efficient running of a country. The French people, he claimed, had never been so happy and so well organized. I said I would like to have seen them for myself, but I had been blindfolded. With that he turned to his ADC and asked if it was really necessary to blindfold me and the ADC blustered about how dangerous all commandos were and how it was essential to take all precautions.

That was really the end of our conversation. I was taken out of the castle, bundled into a car and driven straight to the Gestapo headquarters in Paris. It frightened the life out of me when I realized where I was, but I was only interrogated in the most half-hearted manner. I am sure that Rommel must have interceded on our behalf and that he prevented both Roy and I from being executed.[11]

CHAPTER FIVE

BEHIND THE ATLANTIC WALL

Most of the German soldiers manning coastal defences in France no longer believed the war could be won and so waiting for the invasion was both tedious and nerve-racking. There was only one certainty – that it would *come . . .*

Feldmarschall Gerd von Rundstedt, commander in chief West:

The strength of the defences was absurdly overrated. The 'Atlantic Wall' was an illusion, conjured up by propaganda – to deceive the German people as well as the Allies. It used to make me angry to read the stories about its impregnable defences. It was nonsense to describe it as a 'wall'. Hitler himself never came to visit it, and see what it really was. For that matter, the only time he came to the Channel coast in the whole war was back in 1940, when he paid a visit on one occasion to Cap Gris Nez.[1]

Gefreite Werner Beibst, aged 18, Infantry Division, 15th Army:

I was sent to the Channel coast, between Hardelot-Plage and Le Touquet, in December 1943. We were never actually in a village, as such, all that was banned by the military, and there were no French people there either, presumably evacuated. In this place, there were already bunkers – partly bunkers dug into the ground and partly concrete – right on the coastline and from there one could look over practically the whole beach area.

Some of these bunkers had guns in them already, because the

invasion was expected in this area. But we had no idea at all when this invasion would be. The very best information, which to all intents and purposes was illegal, came from the English broadcasts, which we could pick up very clearly since we could see the English coast from where we were, on a fine day. You could receive the medium wave on our radio sets without too much difficulty, though of course it was strictly forbidden, as it was in all Germany. At home, stickers were distributed and attached to radio sets with the instruction 'Do not listen to enemy broadcasts'.

Anyway, on the coast we listened to broadcasts in German which presumably came from the BBC. Although they may have been propaganda to some extent, they were actually quite informative. Through them we found out about how the rest of the war was progressing and we discovered many things that were completely unknown to us. At that time, I had the impression that many people thought the war was not going well for Germany, although we certainly never discussed it; one simply didn't.

We discussed the individual actions of the war among ourselves, certainly, but mostly we were expected to be informed by the bulletins issued by the regimental staff and we were expected to believe what we read – which we largely did, unless of course we had heard the English broadcasts. It made us question what we were reading and a certain doubt began to creep in.

From time to time, there were small commando raids on the coast. The English came at night in their rubber dinghies or small speed boats, landed and overpowered the occupants of some of the bunkers, whom they duly took back to England. This was naturally a tremendous shock for those people – the commandos arrived silently, all dressed in black, no one saw them at all. They overpowered the guards and carried them off in their boats. It was only discovered next day, when the bunker was found to be empty.

They instituted a special training course in how to react, should one be threatened in this way. One of my comrades, on being asked what he would do in such a situation, as a joke, replied, 'Well, go with them, of course!' It was not the expected answer, naturally. We were supposed to respond by fighting and defending the bunker. This was somehow typical of the situation at the time, that people were making remarks like that. The atmosphere was already becoming somewhat defeatist.

On the whole, morale was not good. It had a lot to do with the fact that the infantry was simply not well looked after. The food was very, very bad. In Germany, at home, provisions were also pretty poor. Then there were differences between the navy, the air force and the infantry, which had the lowest possible status. We always seemed to get very bad sausage and 'Army Bread', very black, horrible bread which had been stored for so long the middle of it was quite mildewed. Whenever anyone in our group went home on leave, we usually begged him to bring bread back when he returned.

It was impossible to buy stuff from the neighbourhood because there were practically no French people left in the area. I can recall only one occasion when I bought something from a French person. It was a fish, and I had only been able to do the transaction because I had learned a little French at school and was able to speak to him.

At that time I don't think we cherished many patriotic feelings any longer. I think I probably was homesick, but certainly it was the first time I was away from home. My parents were very concerned about me and I was an only child. But on the other hand, they were grateful that I was sent to France and not Russia. While still at school, we discussed the war, particularly during history lessons, and mostly from a rather positive point of view. I simply never dreamed that I would end up fighting in a war. We were sure it would end quickly.

We never thought about the future at all. We were getting reports from home about the raids and how nothing was really working there any more. The post was very unreliable and so contact with home faltered a bit. We were never able to communicate properly with our families. We could write letters but never really say anything and we were not able to phone them. This was pretty troubling because we knew the Russian army was penetrating westwards and we were all concerned about our families.

One of our main duties was to keep guard in two-and-a-half-hour shifts, throughout the day and night, just looking at the sea. There were occasionally bombing raids. Then there was Rommel's idea – I heard later that it had come from him – to fell trees, pines or some other kind of trees that grew abundantly in that area. These were to become 'Rommel's Asparagus'. Anyway, it was our job to fell these trees, knock off the branches and then horses were used to drag the trunks out of the woods, back to the coast. Then we had to wait for the tide to go out to plant the trees really far out on the sand. All this we did more or less without any kind of mechanical help. It was terribly difficult work and required huge numbers of people. Once the trees had been erected, mines were planted on the seaward side of the trees. This was all intended to catch the landing craft that we expected to land in that area. We spent April doing this work.

We were really strained by the work. During the day, we worked felling and dragging the tree trunks and then at night we had constant watch, such that we could never really sleep properly. We were all quite young at the time, seventeen or eighteen years old, and we really needed our sleep and decent food, but got neither. The bunkers were frightfully primitive, sometimes they were only earth bunkers and we had to live in them; the bombing raids made it impossible to live any other way. There weren't any houses in the area anyway, though there must have been beach huts at one time on the beaches.

In our bunker there were eight men sharing; sometimes it was twelve and very restrictive and unpleasant. No one could move and the sleeping-bunk, well, it was not unlike being in a submarine. Washing arrangements were very primitive and we could never take our clothes off to sleep because we had to keep our uniforms and our boots on at night.

I was really only properly scared during the bombing raids which were often quite close to where we were. Sometimes they happened during the day, when we were out on the beach, fully exposed, erecting these Rommel Asparagus in the sand. When the raids came, all we could do was throw ourselves down in the sand. A number of people in my group were actually killed on these occasions.

Our only contract was to shoot on enemy landing craft to prevent them landing and that was our single objective. I don't think we ever thought about actually meeting the enemy face-to-face. At that age, I don't think we had the mature consideration to weigh up the possibilities, I had not even finished my schooling. We lived from one day to the next.

There was a rather dramatic incident one night in this forested area in which we lived when we heard the sound of a shot. Immediately, we all took up our 'alarm' positions and found one of our comrades lying in a bunker with a wound in his leg. First he said he had been shot by a sniper. There were known to be French partisans in the region but it was highly improbable anyone had penetrated our area as it was surrounded by minefields. Pretty soon it emerged that he had shot himself.

Normally, the penalty for this was death. He was taken away and put in hospital. (By pure coincidence, I met him later in a P.O.W. camp and he told me he had been taken to Brussels, where there was a huge military prison, and he had actually been sentenced to death. It was only thanks to the Americans, who were advancing very swiftly on Brussels with their tanks, that he was able to get away.) He must have been absolutely desperate to do a thing like that.[2]

Obertleutnant Fritz Ziegelmann, chief of staff, 352 Infantry Division:

It became gradually clearer that an invasion might occur that summer. We were supported therein by information in the German press about Russia's demands for an active, decisive participation on the Western powers in the war. This view was supported by the strict censorship ordered in England, the curbing of diplomatic privileges, and of resistance to enemy landing craft on the south coast of England and by the cancellation of all furloughs for all commanding and general staff officers from March onwards.

Careful attention to the tides also indicated that the highest command reckoned with an invasion soon. From a conversation my Division commander had in May with Field Marshal Rommel – whom he knew very well – he seemed to expect the beginning of the invasion in August.

The distribution of our own forces was definitely determined by the possibility of the enemy – by isolating the Cotentin peninsula – coming into possession of the spacious Cherbourg harbour and, with additional forces from the captured bridgehead, of undertaking the push for Paris. In the 352 Infantry Division's sector the main thing was to reinforce the left wing at the mouth of the Vire and strengthen with reserves the danger points of the landing sectors by St Landeul and Arromanches.

The grouping of the reserves was a hobby of Field Marshal Rommel. It was his opinion that he could *destroy* the enemy with an attack in front of the MLR, consequently in the water. On the occasion of his visit in May, I was reproached because I did not bring the reserves (a rifle company without heavy weapons) close enough to the coast. He wished every soldier to be able to concentrate his fire on the water. My query that the length of our sector (fifty-three kilometres) and the weakness of our rearward constructions made it possible for the enemy to infiltrate less heavily occupied sections and that to counter this assault reserves were necessary behind the lines, remained unanswered.

In May Hitler gave orders to hold each foxhole to the last man and the last cartridge. An abandonment of the battle area during engagement was thus impossible.

Assuming that enemy landings would only take place at high tide, obstacles of all kinds were erected on the interior beach, so that their upper parts projected. *Tschechen* hedgehog defences, pile-driven stakes of metal and concrete, as well as wooden trestles, were set up here and partly charged with deep water or surface mines and H.E. It turned out that in the course of time these obstacles filled up with tidal sand and had to be dug again. During the storms in April, the mass of these obstacles were torn out and the mines exploded. It was necessary to begin again. Considering that the wood had to be cut in the Foret de Cerisy, that it had to be carried at least thirty kms in horse-drawn vehicles (lack of fuel), had to be logged by circular saws (limited supply) and rammed by hand, which took a long time and was particularly difficult on account of the rocky foreground, results were still surprisingly good.

In the second half of May the possibility of a landing at lower water was discussed. The construction of obstacles to the seaward of the former coastal obstacles was begun. But it was impossible to build these obstacles in proper depth. In the sectors of steep coast by Longues and St Pierre-du-Mont we reckoned with the employment of enemy commandos who could climb up the steep cliffs with special equipment. On both steep gradients, old 24cm shells were embedded by the engineer battalion which, after touching a trip wire, came rolling down and, with an effective splinter range of 600 metres, exploded over the water.

To cope with local unrest and to arrest bailed-out air crews, hunting patrols on bicycles or motor cycles were organized in each regimental sector. Through their employment, a small number of air crews were handed over to the interrogation service of the air force in Caen.[3]

Obergefreite Werner Kortenhaus, aged 19, 4th Company, 22nd Panzer Regiment:

As D-Day drew closer and closer, so the condition of alertness was stepped up. The troop had been put on alert several times in the preceding month on orders from above that 'it is possible that they might come.' By the end of May we were at a high level of alertness. We pulled a lot of sentry duty and this was very exhausting. If you started at 20.00 hours you had to walk without halting for two hours, backwards and forwards, over the same area. At 22.00 two men came to relieve you, always two men. You weren't allowed to speak to each other and you had to keep a distance of two metres apart. This was strongly policed. They wanted to achieve a state of total concentration on the part of the guards on the terrain they were supposed to be watching. Soldiers who were caught chatting were punished for their pains. From 22.00 you could go and lie down for two hours, certainly not on a bed but somewhere in a French household, probably on the floor.

Two hours on and two hours off. At 04.00 I was able to lie down again and at 06.00 I did my third watch, and by then I was absolutely finished. During the day, the watch was at four-hourly intervals. It was better during the day, but at night, walking non-stop for two hours, two hours were very long, and usually without being able to talk, so it was very boring. Sometimes we were able to hide and have a chat, always keeping an eye out for the officers.

The worst kind of guard duty was to have to stand in the turret of one of the five tanks and look up at the sky for two hours. Everyone who did that fell asleep, and if the unfortunate guard was found to be asleep he was locked up.

What sources of information did we have? They were lousy. We had no 'free press', but one that was totally censored by the Nazis. In the newspapers we only read what they wanted us to read and, as far as radio was concerned, most German families only had quite small radio sets, if they had one at all. It was called the 'people's receiver' and only broadcast on one wavelength – achieved with some difficulty – news considered to be suitable for public consumption.

Richer people had larger sets and could receive a much wider range of wavelengths, even English ones. During wartime, however, there was a law which stated 'anyone who listens to the enemy network will be sentenced to death.' I don't know if any of these sentences were pronounced or carried out, but I do know that we lived under a pressure called, 'For God's sake, don't get caught.' Many people did listen to the enemy network but they were very scared and it was important not to be noticed. But if one really listened – and I did – and heard that, for example, the Germans had shot two Norwegians in Norway (the BBC reported this actual incident) my immediate reaction was, this cannot be true, it is propaganda. No German would readily shoot a Norwegian. That was what we believed at that time.

When we lived in the homes of French families we lived very closely with them. A French family was obliged to offer a room to the German army. Straw was put on the floor and sometimes as many as five of us, that is one tank crew, slept in a room. Straw wasn't so bad.

I recall a very nice elderly couple who had had to give us a room. They were very friendly to us at the beginning, took us upstairs and showed us the room. After a while, they simply stopped speaking to us. Today I understand. Those people suffered because we were just young boys at the time and terribly noisy, and in that room upstairs we fried eggs and of course that wouldn't have pleased this old couple at all – the noise, smell of cooking and everything.

Usually we and the French were very friendly with one another. We were strictly disciplined to behave decently towards the French and anyone who behaved otherwise was severely punished. There was an incident of theft, in which a French lorry was broken into, and the thief was imprisoned for several months. Then there was an incident in which a German soldier, under the influence of drink, urinated in the corner of a cinema. He got four or five months' detention and the whole company had to pay a penalty by doing extra exercises. Although we were forbidden to do anything that damaged relations with the French, there was no great contact with them because of the language difficulties. We mostly consorted with each other.

We often discussed the Allied landing, and where it might be, among ourselves. We thought, let them get here, we'll throw them out again. We genuinely believed – and we were always being told – that we were so strong we would throw them out in no time. But then we also thought there were several thousand German aircraft ready to come and give us air support. We firmly believed that.

We were young men and, in a way, we burned for a little action. We had rehearsed and practised things for so long that we wanted to see some real action at last. Also, we were simply too naïve to grasp what war actually meant, we had no idea. We had lived in France for a year. Others, of course, had experienced the Eastern front and knew what it was all about, but we didn't. Very few of our officers or other ranks had had any experience of the front lines. Our daily life had so little to do with war. All we ever did was dig in, exercise and do guard duty, and a few other little technical things – practise radio calls, clean our weapons.[4]

Oberleutnant Helmut Liebeskind, aged 22, adjutant 125 Panzer Grenadier Regiment, 21 Panzer Division:

In May we moved closer to the coast, in the countryside around Caen. Already in May, even in April, we were expecting an invasion. It was the subject of daily conversation. It was known that the British troops were being trained for a large invasion. We read in the papers, the German papers and Swiss papers, that Stalin was urgently in need of another front.

We knew that in the upper echelons of command there were two schools of thought. The first was that the Allies would come over by the shortest route, that is from Dover to Calais. The second claimed that the enemy would probably come from that quarter where he would not necessarily be expected, and that meant Normandy. In the somewhat pig-headed fashion of German land-war thinking it was deduced that the British would first have to find themselves a harbour and win it in order to have sufficient supplies to continue to support the invasion. It was therefore all the more surprising, and even shocking, when it transpired that the Allies had built their own harbours and brought them along with them.

I calculated that it would be in Normandy for the simple reason that we had been posted there. We sat there and thought, well, this is where it will be. We were waiting for it almost daily. We were pained and deeply disappointed that our aerial reconnaissance results were so meagre. Their sorties were largely unsuccessful and were very swiftly repelled by anti-aircraft fire. What little they did get was very thin.

At the time, we had no idea that the British knew so much about us and our deployment. Apparently, they even had maps of the area with our names and locations printed on. We had been told about the precision of enemy intelligence and were warned to be careful, there were even posters distributed with the slogan, 'Caution, the enemy is listening.' We were always conscious of this danger and therefore always spoke in veiled tones, never in clear text.

At one point there was a rumour that the Allied invasion would come at that very moment when the Allies in southern Italy occupied Rome. It was conjectured that the occupation of Rome and the invasion of the north would occur simultaneously.

It did get on our nerves a bit, the constant orders to stand-to and then stand-down, but at least it meant there was some movement. It would have been a lot worse, if we had been in a state of tension the whole time. We were not on alert all the time, don't let anybody tell you we were. We didn't sit in our foxholes the whole time waiting for the invasion. The days passed in a fairly normal fashion. We did training exercises and were warned to have our ammunition at the ready.

It was common gossip among the troops that Rommel and Geyr von Schweppenburg, leader of Panzer Group West, had had a dispute, a difference of opinion, about how the Panzer corps could best be deployed; whether they should be positioned immediately by the water's edge or held back until the opposition appeared and could be annihilated in open battle, which we felt capable of doing. Rommel believed the latter possibility was not viable. Guderian [Inspector General of Armoured Forces] kept out of this dispute. He preferred a kind of compromise because he wanted to take advantage of whatever flexibility was left, and this meant positioning the tanks partially to the front and partially to the rear without tearing them apart.

Like all the others, he was convinced that within three days we would have to drive the Allies back into the sea. I remember he said, 'If we are not in a position to throw the English and the Americans back into the sea within seventy-two hours, then not only is this campaign lost, but also the war itself.' He said this with great confidence and conviction.

Guderian was right, though we did not want to believe him at the time. He had wanted to motivate us with these words, but unfortunately it had the opposite effect. Those of us who were more reflective thought about this afterwards for some time and asked ourselves, 'Just how smart is this prognosis? If we do not succeed within seventy-two hours, what will happen, then, in the 100th hour, for example? Do we tell our soldiers, look, Guderian said we've got to get this finished in seventy-two hours, and we haven't, so the war is lost.'

Actually the possibility of achieving this feat within seventy-two hours was not very likely. We had reckoned already that American back-up supplies would be so great that we would barely be able to do a thing. The single thing of which we could dream were the wonder-weapons, the V1 and V2 rockets.[5]

General Walter Warlimont, deputy chief, Armed Forces
Operations Staff:

Hitler was the first one to decide for himself that Normandy was the most probable spot for the invasion and on 2 May he ordered anti-aircraft and anti-tank weapons to be reinforced all through Normandy and Brittany. His view was based partly on intuition and partly on intelligence received about troop movements in the British Isles. Two main troop concentrations had been noticed there: one in the south-east, with mainly British troops and one in the south-west, consisting mainly of US troops.

We generals thought along the lines of our regular military education and were all prepared for a landing in the Channel zone between the Seine and the Somme. We thought this was the most likely area because it was the shortest crossing from the British Isles, it provided the shortest route to Germany and the industrial Ruhr, it had at least one big harbour, Le Havre, which was better situated than Cherbourg and had better communication with the interior and finally the enemy air force had better possibilities to support the attack because it was closer to its bases.

Hitler based his theory on the idea that the enemy would aim to build up a stable front, including a big harbour, and that there was no better place on the whole coast than the Cotentin peninsula. We were not convinced that he was right, but he kept harping on about it, demanding more and more reinforcements in that sector.

However, as time went on, we recognized that a landing in other parts of Europe further to the north was becoming more and more improbable as the British troops were grouped more and more in the south. The position of the US troops especially led Hitler to anticipate an attack launched against the west coast of Normandy.

We attached great importance to the Resistance movements in the interior and tried to determine the place of landing by noting where most parachute baskets were dropped. But the drops became so widespread that it no longer helped us.

We also managed to get into some of the Allied radio nets. Radio transmitters were dropped from planes to be used by enemy agents in France to inform about our movements. We intercepted some of these and used them to communicate with enemy stations. We had the impression that this action was not noticed by the enemy. We also found out that there were special catchwords with which the enemy prepared for operations and by which means the French underground were going to be warned of the day and hour of the attack.

I am not sure whether Rommel and Rundstedt were convinced Hitler was right. More and more in recent months, since Hitler had assumed the role of military expert, he would talk at great length and in broad terms at the twice-daily operational meetings. These meetings, attended by up to twenty officers, would be held at 13.00 and close to midnight. Hitler would speak honestly, but seldom directly to any individual or individuals. He would speak 'out of the window'.

His line was that the impending invasion of France would be the decisive event of the coming year. He said: 'It will decide the issue not only of the year, but of the whole war. If we succeed in throwing back the invasion, then such an attempt cannot and will not be repeated within a short time. It will then mean that our reserves will be set free for use in Italy and the East. Then we can stabilize the front in the East and perhaps return to the offensive in that sector. If we don't throw the invaders back, we can't win a static war in the long run because the material our enemies can bring in will exceed what we can send to that front. With no strategic reserves of any importance, it will be impossible to build up sufficient strength along such a line. Therefore, the invader must be thrown back at his first attempt.'[6]

Feldwebel Rainer Hartmetz, aged 19, No.2 Company, Schell Battalion, 77 Division:

My company was stationed at Frénouville, a small village off the Caen-Lisieux road – a castle, two bistros, a church and 200 inhabitants. Three of our platoons were placed in the castle, my platoon in a school building.

Each morning at five o'clock the company assembled and disappeared into the fields or forests for combat training – assault, defence, counter-assault. Training in squads, in platoons, in companies. In the afternoon we did weapons drill, changing the barrel or the lock of the machine gun (we succeeded in changing the lock in five seconds and the barrel in three). We learned to fire in bursts of four or five rounds – the Spandau had a theoretical firing rate of 1,700 rounds a minute. We made job rotation – machine gunners changing over to 81 mm mortars, riflemen to machine gunners, mortarmen to weaponless training, a kind of karate. In the park behind the castle we had a shooting range for machine guns, trenches for hand-grenade fighting. The training became a kind of sport.

The presence of the soldiers changed the village completely and I felt a little sorry about it, for I loved that lousy village. Before we appeared it must have been very peaceful. They hadn't seen Germans since 1940; now there were more than enough. You couldn't miss them in the few streets, couldn't not hear the fire bursts of their weapons from the shooting range behind the castle.

It was worst in the evenings, in the two cafés, which were very small, just four small tables and sixteen chairs. Around the tables would be French farmers drinking their calvados and playing dominoes. German soldiers would fill the narrow room, standing along the walls, at the bar, glasses in their hands and passing other glasses to the boys sitting on the steps outside. All in all there was no serious trouble between the French and the Germans. A team from our company, which changed from day to day, had the job of getting the boys out of the bars at 9.30 and back to the castle.

Sometimes at nights we did fifty-kilometre marches, each man carrying weapons and ammunition. There were moments when we thought we were dying. We didn't feel no more our feet, our arms.

We didn't know much of the shape of German troops in France. Our battalion came from Russia, and that was another world. When we came to France we knew we would have another adversary – the British. We didn't give a damn for the Americans, they didn't exist for us on the battlefield, only in Western stories and films, and they seemed very far away to us. We had the feeling that fighting the British would be more of a human fight, with more human rules. We knew the British were tough fighters, but there would be human rules and we didn't want the fight to escalate to the mercilessness like against the Russians.

We never got the idea to surrender to the British, but there was a certain temptation to give up sooner than was necessary. Surrender seemed the last chance of surviving in a hopeless situation. We countered the temptation with feelings of honour and responsibility, honour as a soldier, responsibility for Germany. But what was Germany? A country filled with people – my parents, my teachers, my girlfriend, my young friends in the Hitler Youth, the neighbours?

Or the Nazi leader of the block, or the town, or the region? Those fat guys in brown uniforms with big patriotic words in their mouths? No, not those guys!

If we fight for our country, we also had to fight for the Nazis, who we didn't like. We thought that if we ever won the war, there would have to be another war, a civil one, to get rid of the Nazis. It was a very simple and primitive way of thinking, but it came out of our emotions, experiences, education and propaganda.

On Sunday mornings we had classes. We sat on the grass behind the castle and Second Lieutenant Hans Peill, my platoon leader, informed us of things which the army thought were important – politics and news of the war – because we didn't often get a chance to see a newspaper. He tried to avoid Nazi propaganda and he succeeded mostly.

Most interesting of all for us were things connected with our future adversary. What was the difference between fighting the Russians and the British? What about their armies? What about their weapons? Their tactics? I tried to fool around a little and asked Lt Peill about their food. There was a lot of laughing as he said, 'Boys, if you get to be P.O.W.s, you'll get a lot better food over there than you ever get in the German army.'[7]

Hauptmann Curt Fromm, aged 25, commanding 6 Company, 100 Panzer Brigade, 22 Panzer Division:

We were based at Yvetot and the company's tanks were scattered around Deauville, Trouville etc. as part of the Atlantic Wall fortifications. We always had a very good relationship with the French people. I said that I thought we ought to make the very best of the situation in those difficult times. I asked them to refrain from harming my soldiers and for my part I offered to mediate or resolve any problems they might have as a result of the occupation – you know, like someone stepping out of line or behaving badly because he was drunk; that they should come straight to me and I would see that the offender was punished. And I kept my word. As a result, my relationship with the French was always the very best. I even had a French girlfriend.

We were billeted in a school where we had a couple of gardeners and planted vegetables in the school garden, which we grew and harvested. It was a really peaceful time. We bought butter and meat from the farmers and I had French friends in Paris to whom I always took some produce when I visited them. They used to call me the 'little king of Yvetot'.

I was pretty certain that there were members of the Resistance among my friends (I didn't know this for sure, rather I suspected it) but, in order to steer clear of any danger, I simply agreed with them never to discuss politics or religion. It was not a dangerous situation, it truly was not. I used to play tennis at a tennis club where there were several members of the Resistance and, on one occasion, there was a tennis match against another club and I was asked not to come to the club in my army uniform that day. I told them I didn't have any civilian clothing at all, so my friends scratched around and dressed me in civilian clothes and presented me as a British, or possibly Dutch, pilot who had been shot down and who had been dragooned into playing tennis for the club.

We realized that an invasion was expected but none of us knew much and my own rank was too low for me to know much more than anyone else. But through my French friends we heard stories and there was a joke going around, 'Where have all the Germans in Paris disappeared to? To the Bois de Boulogne. Why? To stick the leaves onto the trees. Why? Because Churchill said that there would be an invasion before the leaves fell from the trees.'

We took the possibility of an invasion seriously, of course, but more or less relied on the safety and impenetrability of the Atlantic Wall. In the upper echelons of the German army it was assumed that the invasion would come around the Pas de Calais.

We had these so-called 'Rommel's Asparagus' in the area and used the local French peasants to fix them in the ground for us. There were no forests in the neighbourhood at all and the tree trunks had to be brought in from some distance away. I gave a speech to the French peasants and told them that we needed their help to set these things up, in order to prevent parachutists or gliders landing. I told them that after the war they could then have the wood and use it for heating. I also made the point that if they helped us now, planting these stakes, then we would help them with the next harvest. I enlisted the help of the local priest to persuade them, had a glass of wine with him, and the farmers helped us. My unit was the first to finish its section and even received a commendation from Rommel himself.

Our daily life consisted of mainly exercises and, for the officers, discussions about the terrain, drives to the sea to examine the routes to the coastline, reviewing plans in the event of an alarm. But in our hearts we didn't believe it would come in our area.

Of course we wanted to go home, but we had a job to do and had been brought up in such a way that we did our duty before leaving. But I no longer believed we would win the war. I not only no longer believed it was possible but had not believed we could win the war even before that time.

Before the invasion, I had to give lectures to my troops. Among the officers there were Nazis who charged me with accusations of defeatism when I said that we were living off glorious retreats on the Eastern front. Nothing came of the charges because my commanding officer knew me and I was known for needling the hierarchy. It had not been intended as defeatism, more as a tease.[8]

Gefreite Heinz Herbst, aged 23, H Company, 613 Long-Range Reconnaissance Unit:

We were based at Lambersart, near Lille, away from the coast because we had very valuable listening equipment which we wanted to protect from air raids. To all intents and purposes, we were the eyes of the army – espionage in England was no longer very viable at that stage.

In the army, every unit has a particular call sign, from the divisions right down to the individual companies. We monitored Allied frequencies so painstakingly that we were able to detect the signs for each unit and establish where each one was by the way each call sign was directed. In that way we were able to discover not only that individual units had been transferred but where they had gone.

The English were rather slacker and less disciplined than we were. At Christmas, for example, they would break all the rules and transmit in clear text, which was utterly forbidden for us. They did not bother to transmit in code or in ciphers as they did for the rest of the time and so we heard them transmitting 'Goodbye' and 'Happy Christmas'. We even heard them wishing each other happy birthday. In the methodology of transmission, the operator's ear was so well schooled that he could recognize the style of his counterpart even when it was coming from some other location. There were even recognizable characteristics in Morse code that we could detect. One operator might linger on a 'dash' or falter with a 'dot' and those of us who listened on the frequency would be able to recognize the individual operator and we referred to them by nicknames we had given them.

We thought the invasion would be around Calais, but the English deceived us. Again and again, we heard on the airwaves that they seemed to be giving orders to start extensive troop movements towards the environs of Dover. We heard both the English and the American orders to move. I have to admit it was very skilled, because it caused us to think that that was where the invasion would come from. This was very obvious as far as the military forces were concerned, because it meant only a two-hour crossing or so, instead of a journey lasting three times that, as it finally turned out.

We were therefore aware of what seemed to be a great massing of troops in the Dover area. We heard, for example, reinforcements being called in and ammunition transport ordered up and where it was sent to, and tank movements. Again and again, new units appeared. We had more and more call signs to deal with and we were bewildered by the numbers of troops that were being massed.

It was all coded in letters and numbers and these messages were sent to the de-coders, who got to work on it. We did round-the-clock duty – six hours on and then twelve hours' liberty and then six hours' duty again. Occasionally, you got twenty-four hours free. We started in the morning and went on until midday, then the next shift came on and worked until evening and a third shift came on and worked all night through. This cycle was kept up the whole time and was operated in all the aspects of the work – listening, locating, decoding, translating and teletyping, round the clock until you lost all sense of time. It was very tense, exhausting for those who were on listening duties, because there were times when for hours you heard absolutely nothing.

This was particularly the case just before the invasion, when we went for days without hearing a thing. It was so dead that at times we thought the war was over. Of course, this turned out to be deliberate radio silence on the part of the Allies and there were those among us who said that such a deep silence undoubtedly presaged enormous events.

We were never able to talk about our work and what we heard, naturally, but in fact there was not much opportunity as we were shielded from the other units; we had no contact with other units; we were an independent group and kept pretty much to ourselves.

I certainly was scared for my life, anyone who said he wasn't scared was lying. Everybody was scared. We discussed such things often among ourselves but never with officers present. It is unimaginable now, when you think of the times, but we had a comrade in our team who came from Munich and who had a great liking for the poet, Heinrich Heine. At night, when there wasn't much happening, he would read out Heine's poems to us. Such an act was unthinkable as Heine was completely banned and it was dangerous to read his work. And we had another chap in our team from Cologne who dragged a huge case around with him, everywhere he went. The RSM kept telling him that the case had to stay behind, nevertheless the case continued to go everywhere with him. And in that case there was a gramophone and an entire collection of jazz records of Louis Armstrong, which were also prohibited as being decadent. This sort of thing was going on. And how we listened to English music! And what is more, we listened to it in the presence of officers, even though it was strictly forbidden, but you see, we had to monitor the BBC broadcasts and they played music. We assumed that they might interrupt the music to make significant announcements, so we had to listen to the music. In that respect, I think we were a rather informal unit.

I really did enjoy the work, though. In a way it was fun and something quite out of the ordinary. To me, it did not seem to have all that much to do with the military. It was in some ways a bit like a thriller.

The people in our unit could think for themselves, and through their activities listening to the enemy they were in possession of information which they would not under normal circumstances have ever heard and the effect of that was to sharpen their senses even further. Knowing what we knew, it made us realize what madness it all was. But we did not oppose it because we would have ended up in Russia. So we thought, well, better here than frost bite in Russia. The most we could do was discuss it endlessly among ourselves, but there was never any question of a palace revolution – we were, after all, the tiniest cogs in the mechanism. None of us in the unit were either great fighters or great idealists: we did our duty and that was that.[9]

Gefreite Aloysius Damski, aged 21, 352 Regiment:

I am a Pole. I was impressed into the German army in February 1943. I was working in the office of a munitions factory in Blomberg when the manager called me in and said I could either go into the German forces or be declared 'politically undesirable', which almost certainly meant a concentration camp. I was only twenty years old and I loved life, so I chose the army.

After training I was sent to Normandy, to a mixed unit of Poles, Czechs and Russians under the command of German NCOs and officers. Most of the older men had no faith in Hitler and believed that Germany could never win the war.

My job was fire control, co-ordinating the fire of three batteries positioned between Arromanches and Asnelles. The batteries were equipped with old-fashioned horse-drawn artillery – ordinary field guns on hard rubber tyres, not emplaced in concrete but in open field positions. Each had about 400 shells. There was no real shortage of ammunition, but considerable shortages of minefield equipment. We used to plant scraps of metal in a field to decoy mine detectors, wire it off and put up '*Achtung Minen*' signs. Most of the minefields in our area were false.

I was billeted with an old French lady who was very sympathetic and kind because I was a Pole. She used to give me extra food and things. There was very little recreation, apart from occasionally being allowed to go into Bayeux. I sometimes went out with French girls, but most of my spare time was spent drinking. Wine was very cheap, only twelve francs a pint, and my wages were equivalent to 350 francs every ten days.

I used to listen to the BBC on the radio. The lieutenant in charge of our section listened too, but he would always vigorously deny the claims made by the British, saying they were 'rubbish', but it didn't stop him listening. One day he called me into his office and said, 'I am speaking to you not as an officer, but as a man. How German do you feel now?' I replied, 'Well, since we are talking like this, I will tell you the truth. I was born in Poland, I was educated in Poland, both my parents are Polish and still live in Poland. How can I feel anything but Polish?' The lieutenant said nothing, but was always a little 'reserved' with me after that.

Before any German radio programmes there was always a little signature tune, *Heute wollen wir ein Lliedlein singen, Denn wir fahren gegen England* (Today we are going to sing a little song because we are marching on England). It caused a great laugh among the men, to such an extent that they had a joke about 'walking on the water with wooden clogs'.[10]

Leutnant Heinrich Fuerst, aged 30, medical officer, 706/8 Festungsdivision:

We were living under tension, expecting the invasion, and there were the constant air raid attacks. We knew it would come. The morale wasn't bad, although there was a lot of doubt that we could win the war. That was pretty clear. After the debacle in the East, particularly after Stalingrad, it was pretty clear that the war couldn't be won. Half-way sensible people knew it.

We discussed it a lot and the people who were there, you could trust them. The army still – that was one of the reasons I was glad to be in the army – even during the war, was unpolitical. You could say a lot more things in the army than you could say as a civilian, particularly in the last few years of the war. If you said the wrong things as a civilian and sombody reported you, you'd had it; in the army you could risk a bit more.

My fellow officers and I knew that things were looking bad for Germany. They were very sensitive people. They knew it and, of course, there was the other side – the awareness of what was going on at home, that the home front was as much a 'front' as the front was. It was very worrying for us, that people were getting killed in the cities. That was all part of the pressure.

Of course we felt patriotic. We were fighting for Germany; the Nazis could go to hell! You separated your country from who was running it and we knew that it was a bunch of criminals but there was nothing we could do about it.

We knew that the invasion had to come some time soon and that when they came they would come in force. The situation was like you were sitting on a tropical beach, well protected, but expecting a huge hurricane to hit in the next forty-eight hours. We couldn't run and hide, we had to stay, what else was there to do? It was not a very pleasant prospect, knowing you had a good chance to get killed.[11]

Generalstabsoffizier Hubert Meyer, aged 30, senior general staff officer, 12 SS Panzer Division (Hitlerjugend):

We went to Evreux to visit the air force squadron that performed reconnaissance flights over England and asked them how much they knew and could they judge how far advanced the Allied plans were. The air commodore there told me that he had been unable to penetrate airborne defences in England for weeks because of the fighters and flak and that he simply could not say how far advanced the invasion plans were. That was all the information we needed to know that it was going to be soon.[12]

Von Rundstedt to Hitler, 30 May 1944:

It is true that the hour of invasion draws nearer, but the scale of enemy air attacks does not indicate that it is immediately imminent.[13]

CHAPTER SIX

SEALED!

In the latter half of May 1944, the invasion troops began to be moved into special transit camps, where they were isolated behind barbed wire prior to embarkation on the fleet of ships waiting along the south coast to take part in the largest amphibious operation the world has ever seen . . .

Letter from Gunner Ernest Brewer, G Battery, 5 RHA, 28 May 1944:

Dear Ma,

Well it looks as though I've well and truly had it now. We are all confined to this dump we have moved into; the camp is sealed – so they say. It seems a rotten trick not to tell us beforehand so that we could let you know that it might be our last time at home. I said it seems a rotten trick – rather it *is*. We are, so far as I can understand, kept here for security reasons, though I myself can't see what we could give away. We don't know anything.

Wish Con many happy returns for today for me. Did she walk home from the hospital or did you have to carry her? I suppose she is walking now.

I suppose the next time I see Danny he will be in uniform – a real soldier. Tell him I am sorry I won't be home Wednesday for a final booze-up before he joins H.M. forces and the best of luck, he needs it. He'll find the Army ain't so bad, but they will muck you abaht. I am now witnessing *the* classic example.

Well I'll be seeing you. Don't forget to give Tich my blue suit for
his birthday.
> Yours
> Ern

PS What's the betting on where we're going and when?[1]

Private Dennis Bowen, aged 18, 5th Battalion, East Yorkshire Regiment:

We weren't told we were going to a sealed camp in Canning Town.
We were just told you're being drafted tomorrow, parade with your
kit at so-and-so hours. So we went down to a railway station, got
onto the train and some time later arrived at Canning Town. We
were marched from the station to this camp, which was a canvas
camp built on a bomb site. The camp was only three-quarters built;
in fact, we had to put up the barbed-wire fence ourselves, that was
part of our duties. We still didn't really know anything. We assumed
we were going to be drafted abroad, but not on an invasion.

It was quite curious. Surrounding the bombed area were civilian
houses and the local Londoners were saying, 'You'll be going abroad
soon,' but they weren't saying, 'You'll be doing the invasion.' Then
we were paraded at evening time and it was said, 'You are now all
confined to camp, no one will be allowed out.' That was the first
warning. In fact, sentries were posted all round, patrolling the
perimeter to keep us in. It didn't particularly bother me, because I
found a way I could get out so I could go to the cinema and get back
in. It didn't make a lot of difference because I had no secret
information or anything. If anybody spoke to me, all I could have
said was that we were going abroad.

I just got out through a hole in the wire. Lots of other people did,
too, but of course we weren't stupid enough to go off and do
anything silly. We'd go to the cinema and then crawl back in. In fact,
the sentries would see us but they turned a blind eye. They were
soldiers like ourselves. There were probably five, six hundred people
in that camp, but no more than 100 went out. I did it three or four
times. I don't know what the penalties for going out were because I
never got caught and I never heard of anyone else getting caught and
being punished, so whether officially a blind eye was turned, I don't
know.

When the camp was sealed there was no further contact with the civilians. They weren't even allowed to come up to the barbed wire. That was really the thing that upset us more than being told we were confined to camp. A lot of the men used to go to people's houses for a cup of tea or something. That was suddenly stopped. The sentries were instructed to keep the civilian population away from the wire and the civilians were just told the camp was out of bounds and they weren't to come anywhere near. There wasn't any real bother. The troops who were there were well behaved rather than well disciplined. They weren't particularly smart, boot-polished, foot-stamping soldiers, but they were all well behaved.

There was a camp cinema and a concert party came down from London and gave us an open-air concert, which was very well received. It was a professional performing party which, we were told, was playing in the West End. It was variety, you know, comedians, a girl in short clothes riding a trick cycle, that kind of thing. It was given in the open air because the weather was quite good. There weren't any air raids at that time.

We had to remain within the barbed wire the whole time and I found that period absolutely boring, which was really the reason I was determined to go under the wire and get out, to relieve the boredom. All this time, we still did not know when it was going to happen. Then one day there was a pay parade, and we marched up to the table and saluted and they counted out these peculiar blue and white square notes, which were called 'invasion money'. Then, of course, we knew we were going to France but we still thought that we were reinforcements and that we would be going AFTER the invasion to be sent as reinforcements to the units who had suffered casualties.

[The 5th Battalion was part of the 50th Northumbrian Division, which had been fighting in the desert and had done the invasion of Sicily and when they were brought back to England they felt they had done their bit. It was accepted, or at least expected, that if there was going to be an invasion of Europe it would be done by troops in divisions that had been in the UK since Dunkirk.]

Suddenly it came right out of the blue that the 50th Northumbrian Division were going to do the invasion, to be the initial landing troops. I was ready for it. I had enlisted as a boy and, although I had only spent twelve months in the band, we were constantly doing repetitive training and so I personally felt that I was well-prepared. It might sound big-headed, but I was keen to go, I was quite happy to go, I wasn't the slightest bit bothered that I was going to be sent into action. I was good on weapons and on drill – for what use that is – and I'd been a junior NCO instructor in the depot. I was quite happy. I knew I was a good shot, I knew that my field craft was pretty good; in fact I thought that I was better trained than the men who had actually been in action! They were more battle-wise, more battle-crafty, but as far as training was concerned, I, as an individual, considered myself a pretty slick, well-trained soldier.

As soon as we got the French money, we were told to put it in a secure place and keep it. But of course everybody immediately started playing cards for it. We didn't understand what the value of French francs was, they were meaningless bits of paper to us. I played cards for it, win some, lose some; I know when I got on the boat I didn't have the same amount that I had started with.

The cry in the camp was 'Let me out!' If there were three or four of you walking down to the Naafi and you saw a sentry walking on the other side of the wire, someone would always shout, soldier to soldier, 'Let me out, let me out!' It was funny because on the day when we were leaving the camp to march to the boats, somebody in the line called back at the camp 'Let me in!'

We were taken from that camp in a mixed draft, men from quite a number of units, mostly infantry but some engineers. We were marched down to either the West India or East India Dock, where we got onto an old troopship. It must have been the back end of May, about the 28th or 29th, when we sailed off down the Thames and out to sea and put out sea anchors and just laid there. Then small drafts began to be taken off the boat and taken away to, well, we didn't know where. Powered craft would come alongside and men would scramble down the side and get into them and off they'd go.

One man actually took off, jumped over the side of the boat and swam off to the breakwater, amid great cheers! I never knew or heard of anybody else doing that, or anyone making a deliberate attempt to get away by pretending to be sick or self-inflicting wounds. I did later in Normandy, but not on the boat.

Then came the time when myself and three or four other lads were taken down and put onto the boat and found ourselves being transferred into a landing craft, with landing craft assault slung on the side. Then I knew I was going to be part of the invasion, with the 5th Battalion. I found myself posted into a platoon with a company of men who knew they were going on the invasion but they still didn't know when or where. The company commander greeted us and said, 'I'm glad that you lads are here, you're reinforcements.' I presumed that men had either fallen sick or hurt themselves on the boat and we were there to replace them. He said, 'I'm sending you to Sergeant Mayhew's platoon,' and Sergeant Mayhew came along and said, 'Right, you lads are now with my platoon and this is Corporal Stevenson and he is going to be your corporal.' All these soldiers had secretly been my heroes. Corporal Stevenson was a man who'd been in the desert, done the invasion in Sicily. It was nothing to him, the fact that he was doing another invasion, although he wasn't right keen on it. They were still feeling a bit jaundiced at the prospect of having to do the invasion. It was just general moaning, you know, 'Why the hell did it have to be us. There's bloody blokes been here in England all the bloody time and they have to send us . . .' It was resentment, rather than objection. Their main interest was to get the war over and get back home.

I was very pleased to be going into action with men who were skilled fighting men. They weren't particularly slick on things like daily rifle cleaning, they weren't bothered about that, but they were seasoned troops who knew what it was all about. They knew enough to make a pot of tea under the most difficult circumstances. They were very, very good. Their usual phrase was, 'Stick by me and I'll see you're all right.' There was no question of anybody attempting to be heroes, no question of anybody saying, 'I'm going to get a medal.' All they were interested in was keeping their heads down.[2]

Rifleman Patrick Devlin, aged 20, 18 Platoon, C Company, 1st Battalion, The Royal Ulster Rifles:

In the transit camp, behind the barbed wire, where we were kept locked in after being briefed on the D-Day operation, we had a special pay parade. The table was covered by an army blanket, sitting behind it was the company commander, the CQMS and the orderly-room corporal.

When my name was called, I marched to the table, saluted and was asked to sign for a military 200 French francs (i.e. £2 sterling). I was also asked to take three condoms. We had never been given these before. I was RC and refused them. I said to the major, 'I thought we were going to France to fight, sir.' I could see he was embarrassed and did not say anything. The colour sergeant saved the day by telling me it was orders from high up. He said, 'Take them, Wee Joe, and give them away.' He always called me Wee Joe after the Northern Ireland MP, Wee Joe Devlin. To prevent further embarrassment I took them and gave them away. I often wondered if we would we have been issued with condoms if we had been invading any other country than France.[3]

Sergeant W.E. Wills, 2nd Battalion, The Devonshire Regiment:

We were living in tents in the New Forest, near Beaulieu in Hampshire, in a camp run by the Americans. The tents, when we first saw them, were delightful and snug. Each had four camp beds and a small solid-fuel stove. Unfortunately we were told to remove the camp beds and the stoves and keep ourselves warm by having another six men in each tent. Our American hosts were flabbergasted.

The camp was hidden in thick woods, tents were camouflaged and no washing lines or clothing was allowed outside. Very quickly the walkways became quagmires. Our American hosts did their best to make us feel at home, but American-style messing takes a bit of getting used to. Many were the requests for good old Irish stew, or 'Irish spew', as our hosts were wont to call it.

All ranks were confined to camp for security reasons but many were able to use their West Country knowledge of field craft to find ways of getting through the perimeter barbed wire to slink off for a drink in various pubs. The locals knew we were there, of course, and they could guess why, but not where, we were going, or when. In these circumstances security was maintained – for we didn't know where or when, either.

Cinema performances, in huge marquee tents, were nightly and before each cinema show there was a record-request programme lasting about forty-five minutes. A 'disc jockey' had an easily accessible stack of records and would endeavour to satisfy requests shouted from the waiting audience. One night he was on top form and was heard to call, 'Request from Butch from Idaho, Deanne Durban and The Kiss.' Next was, 'Request from a Limey – "The White Cliffs of Dover".' When this ended, 'Special request from Elmer from Michigan – shut the fucking thing off.'[4]

Archibald Doon Campbell, Reuters war correspondent:

One morning we were all summoned to a large conference room where a colonel, a very distinguished looking colonel, told us our assignments. He called out, 'Campbell, Doon, Reuters, Marine Commandos.'

So, there I was in this commando camp, feeling terribly ill-at-ease because these men were limbering up and were in superb shape, doing Tarzan acts from the trees. I was in a bell tent and found common ground with the chap immediately to my right, who was the padre, a nice fellow. The others were very agreeable, didn't make me feel uncomfortable, but I felt utterly ill-equipped and unprepared to join them, they were so absolutely honed to prefection for this assault, this job they were going to be doing on D-Day, and there I was, with no particular training or preparation for it.

On the Sunday before embarking, there was a church service. I described it as a Galilean scene, these great big brawny men lying around and the pulpit a mound of earth. This padre got up and preached the most appalling sermon in which he said something like, 'We're shortly going into the big fight and it will be a very messy affair. You're going to see your mates without their arms, no legs, but it is God's cause and if it wasn't God's cause, I wouldn't touch it with a bargepole.' That was the expression he used, I wouldn't touch it with a bargepole.

The effect was tremendously dampening, it somehow affected our morale terribly, to an extent that Lovat [Commander No.1 Special Service Brigade] saw the situation and went up into the pulpit unrehearsed, and in French and English did a sort of Agincourt speech: 'Gentlemen, you've been given a proud task. On you so much depends in this next phase of the war. I am sure you will acquit yourselves in a way that your children and your children's children will say they were men, they were giants in those days.' He completely restored the situation and got everybody buoyant again. Lovat had sent for the padre after the service and told him he would not be going in on the first wave because of the damage his sermon had done to the men's morale.

I went off to the mess for lunch, feeling very uncomfortable. As I was walking back to the tent I was a few paces away when I heard a rifle crack. I saw the canvas move, went in, and there was the padre. He'd shot himself.[5]

Mary Verrier, Hants 12th Detachment, VAD, Portsmouth:

Our preparation and training for D-Day mainly consisted of getting our mobile ambulance ready and getting our standard of nursing and care up to 100 per cent and being mentally prepared. We didn't really know to what extent we would be of value; it was a bit of an unknown.

D-Day of course was a secret, an absolute secret, but we began to smell a bit of rat when we started to prepare a lot of pack-dressing drums by the score, stacking them away with dates on. We were trained so we could do it blindfold. I remember saying then that something was going on. Then we had some camouflage nets delivered at the end of our first aid post and we had to thread pieces of yellow and green camouflage through the nets.

One night there was a hilarious incident. There was a small air raid going on, nothing of any note. If a full moon was up those days you knew something was going to come over so we all prayed for dark days and wet, windy nights. But this night I was in the first aid post and we were a bit busy with a few civilians – people falling down potholes, things like that. There was still a blackout and those were the hazards of living in that environment.

Anyway, I was in the first aid post and this army chap came in, obviously a despatch rider, with tattoos all over his arms. He said he'd lost his way and wanted to know the way to Fort Widley. I thought it was a bit funny because he said he'd come from the Marine barracks and there was only one road out of Portsmouth. When he said he didn't know where he was I thought, 'Not half you don't. You're Fifth Column, that's what you are.'

So I took him down to the end of the post where we had two long cupboards under the concrete. He went in and I shut the door behind him and locked it. I went back and was immediately called to help in the theatre and forgot all about this chap.

It wasn't until the early hours of the morning someone happened to hear him bashing on the door and let him out. It turned out he was genuine and had some despatches for General Eisenhower. He got stripped of his sergeant's stripes for being an idiot and I got a severe reprimand from Matron.[6]

Alan Winstanley, aged 19, leading telegraphist, Royal Navy:

It was going to be our job to provide communications as to the state of affairs back to the UK as well as to the ships in the bombardment fleet. It was no use, for instance, some warship two or three miles out at sea knocking hell out of its own people because of lack of communications. If the troops moved forward quicker than anticipated, someone needed to tell them that they had done so. Otherwise there'd have been a lot of problems for the blokes on the ground.

We lived under canvas on Southampton Common, where we spent most of our time keeping the sparkers [wireless telegraphists] refreshed in Morse. I'd sit on the steps of one of the WT wagons with a small oscillator and give Morse lessons. All the sparkers would sit round on the grass with their pencils and pads and I would just transmit whatever we had, some paragraphs out of a book, maybe make up some supposed coded signals. It was purely to keep everybody fully up to date with Morse, so they didn't get rusty.

From Southampton we went across to Ipswich and the moment we got there the order went out for all camps in the UK to be sealed. This was obviously because D-Day was getting near. If I remember rightly, there were a number of civilians in the camp who just got caught in it because they were either delivering supplies or doing something else. That was their hard luck; they were sealed in like the rest of us. It was the same with the Naafi personnel: most of them were locals, but they were not allowed to go back home. Once the camp was sealed, that was it for them as well. The only people allowed out of the camp were despatch riders. No one else was allowed out.

I think the idea of the camp being sealed was because obviously certain people did know more than we did and, if you had some subversive element around, any information was likely to leak out. I'm not saying that anybody else knew much more than us, although obviously the higher-up officers must have had a much better clue. But there was no risk going to be taken of anything being given away.

For the next three weeks life was just sort of living in tents in a field. There was really nothing to do except keep the sparkers in what you might term top gear as regards reading Morse. In addition, some of the Marines taught us tips about survival, things like if you have six pieces of wood, a hammer and a few nails you can build yourself a latrine, which is always a useful thing. Another thing was how to make yourself a little fire to boil some water by scooping a channel in the ground in the direction of the wind, filling it with some small sticks or whatever's burnable, lighting it and in no time you've got a sort of miniature furnace going. The wind blows through the channel, acts like a wind tunnel and you stick your dixie can on the top of it and you can soon have yourself a cup of tea. It all sort of passed the time away.

To break the monotony some of the army boys took us on a tour of the sewage works which had been built, because there must have been thousands of military personnel – army, navy, RAF – in this camp. I couldn't say how many thousands, but it was big enough to require a miniature sewage works of its own. I remember them taking us round and at the end giving us a glass of water to try and persuade us to drink it to prove that when they'd purified the water it was absolutely perfect for drinking. I think we drank it with a little bit of an intrepid feeling. But as none of us kicked the bucket afterwards, obviously we believed that they must have been right.

We had been in the sealed camp near Ipswich for about three weeks when we were suddenly told that the Naafi was throwing a party. I must say they did go to town. There was nothing spared that night; everything was absolutely free. It was a sort of free party-cum-dance and I must say it was the only time I ever had anything free from the Naafi in the five years I was in the services. It didn't make us feel like condemned men being granted our last wish; we just enjoyed it. This was the Friday night before D-Day.[7]

Sapper A.J. Lane, aged 23, Field Squadron, Royal Engineers:

In preparation for the great day, we were for a few weeks placed into special security areas which we called 'concentration camps' because of our confinement and lack of communication with the outside world. Because of the tight security required for such a major operation, where surprise was all-important, the spearhead troops with their dangerous knowledge had to be constrained within well-defined limits, orders and regulations.

Inside the camp we REs had little time for worrying about what lay ahead. Much work had to be done in preparing ourselves, our equipment and weapons for the big test, which was sure to prove fatal to any weakness, failure or unreadiness on our part.

It was expected that for the real task our first efforts would have to be directed towards blasting obstacles above and below sea water. A good deal of our time in the camp was therefore spent in making up neat packages and parcels of explosives into ready-made waterproof charges. These were designed so as to be rapidly placed on the various obstacles for equally rapid demolition. Many boxes of good old-fashioned Durex rubber goods were used – or misused – for the purpose of waterproofing igniter switches, the safety pins of which could be extracted within the stretched outer skin of the Durex covering. They were also used for the protection of wrist watches and other personal items. There was also no doubt that many were hopefully secreted away in reserve for purposes more to do with love than war.[8]

Sapper Benny Jordan, aged 22, 3rd Parachute Squadron, Royal Engineers:

By the time May rolled around our unit was ready for anything. I felt on top of the world, I was finally happy with army life, I didn't have a care in the world and all my mates were in the same frame of mind. None of the other fellows ever discussed the approaching big day ahead; they were just enjoying themselves from day to day and week to week.

When we travelled on liberty trucks to the various small towns around the Salisbury area at weekends we could see the great comradeship of the other units of the 6th Airborne Division. If there were any problems at any of the dances or in the pubs all of the Red Berets stuck together. Even if we didn't know a group of people passing by, if they were wearing red berets, we nodded to one another.

About this time we had a visit from Field Marshal Montgomery. The 3rd Parachute Brigade were formed up in a large 'U' shape outside Bulford. Monty walked by our ranks wearing a red beret at a distinct angle, followed by about a dozen officers of various ranks, when Wee Johnny MacMillan, one of the many characters in 3 Para, called out from the back, 'Ask him if he has done his night jump?' The night jump was the last qualifying jump for para wings. All the officers following Monty were startled by the outburst but Monty kept going. Monty told us to gather around him and he told us we would be playing an important part in the invasion. Even at this point it didn't sink in to me that this day would play such a great part in history. I know all the other fellows felt the same way. None of us had ever seen action before, and all of us were excited about the big day that was approaching. I didn't see any sign of nerves among the men; all I saw was great enthusiasm.

About the third week in May we left Bulford for an unknown

destination. After several hours' driving we finally came to a makeshift camp in the country with a fence around it. We were joined by the 1st Battalion, The Royal Ulster Rifles, of the 6th Airlanding Brigade. We found out later we were somewhere near Swindon.

After a day or so, we started our briefing on what our objective would be for the invasion of Europe. The 3rd Parachute Squadron's task was to destroy every bridge over the River Dives from the sea to Troarn, on the extreme left flank of the invasion front. We all had to gather around a table in a Nissen hut and view a great variety of pictures of a three-tier road bridge outside the small town of Troarn. We were informed this was our main objective and it was to be destroyed at all costs to prevent enemy tanks from crossing it. I remember at one briefing standing at the back of the assembly as our captain, Freddy Fox, told everyone that, 'No matter how many men it will cost, the bridge has to be destroyed.' There was a lot of mumbling from the men. When all the fellows got together over a cup of tea in the canteen we were confident our job wouldn't be too hard. I can honestly say I didn't see any fear in any of my mates, especially during our drinking sessions in the makeshift canteen and singing popular Irish songs with the Ulster Rifles.

Our troop of forty men went out every day to a small village nearby that had a similar bridge to the one at Troarn. Two of our sections would practise placing charges on the bridge, while the other two sections were in the pub, which was about fifty yards away. The locals asked many questions about what we were up to and we told them it was just the usual army bull, something to keep us busy.[9]

Sergeant Major Jack Vilander Brown, aged 29, 147th Essex Yeomanry:

At that time we had no idea of where the invasion was going to be. When we went back to these camps, near Beaulieu – ours was B6 – we weren't sealed in to begin with. They were marvellously well run, the arrangements, everything, were absolutely fantastic. Everything was in the right place at the right time, everything was there.

We were in there for quite some while and we thought things might be getting near when we were told to send any surplus kit home. We were issued with French money, with Dutch money, with Belgian money and Italian money. I remember thinking at the time, God, we can't be going to Italy.

When we were sealed in, the joke was that you could only get out if you were dying. I had a sergeant, a jolly nice bloke and a regimental soccer player, too, who was ill and I sent him to the MO and he did die, too, poor chap, but even the hospitals were probably guarded in case a bloke started to talk under the anaesthetic!

Then we went to these briefing tents. That would have been probably about the middle of May, about a week before we boarded the boats. The briefing tent was a big tent and in front of us was the beach on which we were going to land, everything – a model, pictures, everything. I always remember this because we were to look out for a sunken ship to try to make certain we knew where we were. The thing that amused me was that on the charts and things, the names of the places were all American, like Pittsburgh, that sort of thing. Well, you know, with all due respect, anybody who had had a decent education and had paid a little attention to geography, would have looked at it and known where they were going to land.

This was all explained and after a bit one young chap said, 'I see that there is an order of battle for about a month after D-Day. What shall we be doing after that month?' And the briefing officer said, 'Well, I'm sorry you asked me that, because the majority of the units that take part in the initial assault will no longer be coherent units after a month.' That's what he said! And I thought, 'Dear oh dear', but I never told a soul, never told anyone in the troop. It was an extraordinary thing to say, but he did.

I don't think we went over there with the idea that we were going to lose, but I don't think, either, that we went over there with the idea that it was going to be easy, a quick job. We didn't. But we thought, look, he might be a bit wrong, we might be lucky.

We had bivi tents at Beaulieu. I was in a tent with about five other sergeants. The waggon lines, as we called them, where all the tanks were, were some way away. I had one of these airborne forces kind of collapsible motor cycles, with a puff-puff engine, to visit them and I remember after going about 100 yards you had to stop and take the plug out and wipe it on the seat of your trousers.

We practised twice at night. There were an awful lot of troops going down to the hards and the strange thing is that, although we knew when we were going for good, the people on the hards didn't. There was a chap in charge of this hard and I always remember, the second time he said, 'Well, you're off today!' I didn't say anything and he said, 'Yes, this is it,' and gave us some extra rations, which I took. Anyway, we all loaded up and then, of course, we all came back.

They weren't supposed to know when we were actually going but, of course, we did. It was rather strange how we did. They suddenly announced that evening, for those who wanted to go, there was going to be a communion service. Then we had what we called 'the last supper' – a magnificent meal, American stuff with egg and tinned fruit and things we hadn't seen. Absolutely marvellous. But then we knew. That would have been towards end of May, 28th or 29th, because we went down that night and loaded on and we went out into the Solent and tied up to these buoys.[10]

Journal of Lance Bombardier C. Morris, 3 Troop, 6 Commando, 28 May 1944:

Once again we made our departure from Brighton, this time assembling at Hove station in the early hours of the morning around 04.00 hours, despite which quite a crowd had gathered to see us off, for somehow everyone sensed that this time we would not be returning. Troop officers and SiMs called the roll and everyone turned up, which was in itself a very good show, even though some of them had to be nearly carried. Wasting as little time as possible we entrained and drew out of the station midst the waves and tears of our many friends.

At Southampton we were taken by troop transports to what turned out to be our final grouping centre. This was a mass of tents on either side of the main road around which was a heavy barbed-wire fence. On entering we were shown to our troop areas and explained the whereabouts of the Naafi and cinema, etc. The whole affair was organized and run by Yanks and seemed very good, the food being excellent. All the lads were amazed at the amount of white bread and other luxury foods that were available.

On the day of our arrival everyone was allowed out of camp, much to the dismay of the local inhabitants, for all the lads were walking around armed to the teeth with guns, knives, hatchets and everything imaginable. The general direction appeared to be the beer houses, which soon ran dry for they had not been prepared for anything like this. After all interest in the town was finished, everyone made tracks for camp again, where we found quite a change. During our absence it had been sealed and surrounded by security police, who now informed us of the camp orders which had been put into force, the most important of which was that we were not allowed to converse with any passing civilians and if any of the latter were caught they would be thrown into jail. Also we were not allowed to talk to any of the camp staff re any of our training and the camp was filled with security personnel in many guises whose job was to catch you out if possible. All this could only mean one thing – this was It.

The weather was sweltering and in a nearby park equipped with a swimming pool the local beauties were tripping around in swimsuits in full view and looked very tempting indeed. Three of the camp staff soon tired of this confinement and jumped it. They were missed on the evening roll call. A net was immediately thrown over the locality and a search made. The missing men were found in a beer house, which was immediately closed and customers, proprietors and deserters were thrown into jail, likewise a woman talking through the wire to her husband.

No chances whatever were being taken. On several occasions the Yankee guards, who were armed with .22 rifles, opened fire on civvies loitering near the wire.

All time off in between briefings was spent playing sport and keeping fit, the camp being well equipped with football pitches and many other facilities. Our lads seemed to prefer all-in handball, which was about the roughest game we could find. We made a couple of short trips in organized parties through the town, much to the embarrassment of the local girls, for every time we passed one the lads let out a wolf howl, which always caused laughter. Most of the girls took it in good part for the lads meant well enough and there was no fear of us getting off the lead.

We also made a test run out of camp, consisting of a five-mile run with full-scale ammo and equipment, approximately ninety pounds. Orders were issued that on no account were we to talk to anyone. Our course was mostly over fields and rough country, but on our way back we had to pass through the park and the crowded swimming pool was a sight for sore eyes, for we were all sweating and could have done with cooling off. Many people threw questions at us, but learned nothing.[11]

*Pfc Carl Cartledge, aged 21, Intelligence & Reconnaissance
Section, 501st Parachute Infantry Regiment:*

Early in May my team of six men were left behind at Hampstead
Marshall to guard the sand tables. At the time we thought the
invasion was on and that we were going to miss it, but it was only an
exercise. There were two sand tables, each in a small wooden
building surrounded by two rolled barbed-wire fences. On one sand
table was the 501st's area in Normandy and on the other were all the
beaches, with every road, house and hedgerow in place. They looked
like one would see the landscape from about 5,000 feet.

There were two of us outside the barbed wire twenty-four hours a
day, one at the front gate, one at the back, each armed with a sub-
machine gun. Our orders were to stop anyone approaching and ask
them to produce their Bigot card. They were to place it in their right
hand, next to their cheek, then advance. Their picture was on it. Any
deviation from this, we were to capture, or kill, them.

The front gate to Hampstead Marshall was locked and no one
came night or day until about the fourth night, when a command car
drove up with black half-lights on and stopped about fifty yards
away. I was at the gate and flashed my light on them.

There were six people in the car. The driver stayed seated. General
Eisenhower and his aide got out, along with Air Marshal Tedder and
two aides. I halted them, asked for their Bigot cards, and then
advanced them forward. General Ike came up first, put his Bigot card
by his cheek and gave his famous smile. And so did his aide. Of
course, no salutes were exchanged. Neither Air Marshal Tedder nor
his aides could produce their cards. It was a breach of orders, but I
recognized him and opened the gate.

General Ike was the last to go in and as he passed me he clapped
his hand on my shoulder and said, 'How's it going, soldier?' 'Just
fine, sir,' I answered. He knew the Air Marshal had breached orders
and that I hadn't made a big deal out of it. We all knew how miffed
some of the English brass was that Ike, an American, had been
chosen to lead the invasion.

On some of those nights we listened to the radio in our tent.
Johnny Mercer and his Music Shop had some good records, but so
did Axis Sally and Lord Haw Haw. One night Axis Sally said, 'And
tonight I want to dedicate the next record to you boys with the 501st
Parachute Infantry at Hampstead Marshall. We'll be waiting for you.

And now, "Shoo-Shoo Baby" to all of you. And by the way, boys, you might tell the clock keeper in Newbury that the clock is two minutes off.'

In the middle of May the 501st returned to Hampstead Marshall. They had been on Exercise Eagle, another rehearsal for D-Day. A few days later, we sent our jump suits and boots to be impregnated against gas attack. They came back thickened by a whitish substance that even air couldn't get into. They always felt sticky after that.

About this time, Air Marshal Tedder predicted an 80 per cent casualty rate for the airborne troops on D-Day. Our training and orders were changed. We would be making the landing at 12.30 at night, seaborne troops would come onto the beaches at 06.00 hours and during that time difference of five-and-a-half hours, all gunfire would be considered enemy. We would seek and destroy with knives and grenades only and would fire only as a last resort.

We were issued new combat knives with leather ties to strap onto our boots and practised with them every day in hand-to-hand combat with each other, leaving the sheaths on. We learned to throw them, but not too well. Some of us bought commando knives in London. I sewed a straight razor into the lining of my canteen cover. We were instructed how to kill through the jugular and voice box, for a silent death.

There was a lot of game at Hampstead Marshall. Some of our team went hunting deer with knives only. I never got a deer, but I threw at a rabbit once. It stuck in the ground just under his belly. One of my team, Frederick Becker, dived on a buck deer from a tree. He hit it with a knife half a dozen times, was thrown to the ground, hung on and finally killed it. We were learning that it wasn't going to be that easy.

Around this time about fifty intelligence people from parachute regiments were given a special assignment to check security. We were to drop singly on different installations, determine which unit was there and get off the base without getting caught.

I became an air force staff sergeant with coveralls and baseball cap and mess kit. I jumped on an airfield, went to breakfast, got the information and walked off the base through the runways and never had a question asked. I heard one of us was dressed as a German major in air force uniform, all except for the swastika. He parachuted into London, took the underground to Trafalgar Square in the morning, walked the Mall to the British Admiralty building, went up the steps and got a drink of water. An English officer bumped into him at the fountain and said, 'Excuse me.' So much for security.[12]

Sergeant John R. Slaughter, aged 19, D Company, 1st Battalion, 116th Infantry:

Some time in late May we were sent to Blandford and put behind barbed wire. We were fed the best food we'd ever had in the army – steak and pork chops with all the trimmings, topped off with lemon meringue pie, were items on a typical menu. The officers became friendlier and it seemed that the men were a bit kinder to each other. We were treated royally: we could sleep late, we had recreation, played football and baseball and boxed and had tremendous movies every night – *Mrs Miniver*, with Greer Garson and Walter Pidgeon was one of the favourites. It was really fattening us up for the kill.

We were also issued with brand new equipment and the new weapons had to be test fired and zeroed in on the firing range. Unlimited amounts of ammo were given to each of us for practice firing. We sharpened our bayonets, honed them finely and got ready for one of the biggest adventures of our life. We couldn't wait.

Just prior to D-Day a German plane flew over and dropped some bombs and the 29th Division had casualties there in the marshalling area.

One thing about the British Isles at that time, on every vacant lot, every road, there were tanks, trucks, ammunition, weapons of all kinds you couldn't believe. Everybody could see that this was definitely going to be invasion and that it was going to be a tremendous force.

After we got into the marshalling area we were shown what our objective would be on D-Day. We were told we would land on Dog Green sector of Omaha beach, in front of the Vierville draw. We were shown a sand-table mock-up of what the landing area would look like: they even had the steeple of the Vierville church that we were to be guided on and electric lights simulated shell bursts to enhance the realism. They told us we would have twenty-one pillboxes in our area but that only one or two would actually be manned. The troops guarding the area were old or were Russian or Polish nationals conscripted into the German army and that they would not fight very forcefully and that we shouldn't have any trouble just going in and marching across the beach, so we weren't worried too much about the beach.[13]

Pfc William E. Jones, aged 25, 1 Company, 8th Infantry Regiment, 4th Division:

We were in England just before the invasion, a couple of weeks, probably. We had a formation and Colonel Van Fleet came out and said, 'Now boys, we're going on an expedition that the whole world will be watching. There's never been anything like it in history, as to the size of the armada that will cross that English Channel. But we want 110 per cent performance out of every man here and if there's anyone here who thinks he can't perform the way he should and the way we want him to, all he has to do is step out of the formation. He'll be transferred to a non-combat unit. There will never be anything against your records. All we want are people that will perform.'

He waited about five minutes. Nobody moved an inch. We were very confident in ourselves. We were one of the crack divisions in the whole army.

When we left our barracks there in Honiton we went to a marshalling area outside of Plymouth. It was behind barbed wire. Once we went in there, nobody was allowed to go through that gate again until we left.

While we were in that marshalling area there was one character who really sticks out in my mind – Private Huffstickler, from North Carolina. At one time he had been a professional boxer and he was one of the roughest characters I've ever met, and one of the nicest. Every day he would come by and ask us if we needed anything. Anything we wanted – canned peaches, pineappple, anything you can imagine, he would come back with it before the night was over. He'd raid the supply house every night. He had a skylight he went through and would come back with canned goods, mostly. When we left there we had the floor set full under our bunks with the stuff that we were unable to eat. We'd been starved from that kind of thing for a long time and he supplied all our needs while we were there.

We'd taken training with the English commandos and they used a garrotte to slip up behind enemy sentries, pull that thing round their necks and choke the fool out of them. One night Huffstickler asked if anybody wanted one of those things and of course everybody did. He came in about two o'clock in the morning and said, 'Here's your garrottes.' He'd got eighty-eight of them. That sucker took all the string out of the piano down at the recreation hall. He made a big joke out of it. It was real funny to him.

I didn't see him after we had hit the beach until we got to Cherbourg. He was in a little old Renault tank with a buddy of his, just room enough for two of them to sit in, with a box full of French money and a case of cognac.[14]

Private Joe Minogue, 7th Armoured Division:

We spent six weeks at Beaulieu, Lord Montagu's estate. It was really like a concentration camp, because we had to be checked in and out all the time. I think this is where the soldiers began this business of bleating like sheep. Whenever an officer had to account for his men, they all began bleating like sheep. It was a bit of light relief, I suppose, because of the peculiar situation we were in we were all edgy and getting a bit nervous about the invasion. One day when we were waterproofing the tanks the divisional commander, Percy Hobart, popped his head under a tank and said, 'We're expecting 70 per cent casualties, you know, but if any of you chaps get there I'll see you after D-Day.'

While we were down there the only thing we had to do was waterproof the tanks, get all the guns and ammunition ready and make absolutely sure that anything mechanical was going to work when we wanted it to work. It was really rather a boring period in some respects, because unless you were on guard you were stuck in this pine forest with absolutely nothing to do. We couldn't go anywhere at night of course and at one stage, just for a bit of diversion, people set fire to the Naafi tents. That was really the only excitement available.

Of course during this period we were all thinking about the invasion. We didn't know where or when we were going and fear feeds on delay, of course, so we used to have these long discussions with each other about the kind of things that might happen, you know, whether we'd ever get off the beach alive and all the rest of it. I wouldn't say we were cowards, as such; I mean, I think everybody who was involved in the invasion was afraid. Later one learned that basically this is what war is about: it's really two groups of very frightened men facing each other. But we didn't talk to each other very much about our particular fears.

As tank men I think we had two main worries. One was the danger of being trapped inside a tank that was on fire and the other, because we were soldiers and used to being on land all the time, was a fear of water. I really think we were more terrified of being drowned in that damned tank than anything else. One thing we did do was get a hacksaw and cut about thirty pounds worth of very valuable metal from inside the turret of our Sherman tank so that if there was any danger of drowning, the two of us in the turret could grab the driver and co-driver and pull them to safety. We really were scared of going down the ramp of the landing craft into deep water so that the whole tank would be submerged and we would just be drowned.[15]

CHAPTER SEVEN

ON THE MOVE AT LAST

During the first days of June the assault troops began embarking on the ships that would take them to Normandy. Most of them were relieved that the long months of training and waiting were finally over . . .

BBC correspondent Frank Gillard describing last-minute preparations:

England has become one vast ordnance dump and field park. I've driven through it today for the best part of one hundred miles, the roads crammed with military traffic and lined, often enough on both sides, with vehicles of all kinds, just pulled off and parked on the verges. There is plenty of cover to be had this time of the year and for all its concentration this stuff is well hidden from observation from above. In every wood and copse, in leafy, dead-end lanes and side roads, often in private gardens, under quarries and embankments, there it all was – trucks, ambulances, tanks, armoured cars, carriers, jeeps, bulldozers, DUKWs, vehicles of all kinds, vast, really vast numbers of them. And great mountains of stores, weapons and ammunition, rations, bridging equipment, tyres, timber – millions of tons, often with special railway tracks laid from dump to dump around great areas of dispersal.

And everywhere today we have met the columns of men in battledress. Men marching, men running, men deploying on exercises, men being transported here and there by the thousand in trucks and lorries. Men testing their equipment, tuning up their engines, waterproofing their vehicles, raising great sweeping clouds of yellow dust as their tanks bump and crash along the test tracks.

We saw the temporary homes of these men – acre upon acre of camouflaged tenting, tents spread out everywhere. Hundreds of them just simply pitched by the roadside on the grass verges. The people who actually live in these parts must feel as if some mammoth circus has suddenly sprung up round them.

Certainly, in the whole history of the world, there never has been such a vast concentration of all the paraphernalia of war in so small a space. Right in the midst of it all, just as I turned for home, I passed a field where twenty-two men in khaki shirts and battledress trousers and heavy hobnailed boots were having a quiet knock-up game of cricket. They made me think of Francis Drake and Plymouth Ho.[1]

Mrs Marjorie Box, housewife, Holbury, Hants:

We had soldiers living just across the road from us. They were warned not to talk to civilians, but the officers in charge turned a blind eye and we were invited to join them for a drink on the night before they were due to leave.

The officers had given them a barrel of beer and they asked me if I would bake for them and gave me all the ingredients, much more than I needed.

That evening we had a lovely time, the men were singing and drinking and, unbeknown to me, adding rum to my husband's mug of beer. He got very merry and what a time I had getting him upstairs to bed. When my husband does have one too many, which is not very often, he starts to laugh and that night everything to him was hilarious. There I was trying to get him to bed and the soldiers were outside, shouting do you need any help and suchlike.

We, and about three other couples, were up at dawn to see them go. We waved till they were out of sight, me with tears streaming down my face. They left before I could make them the cake and I knew they had found this way of just giving us some very rare rations.

I often wonder how many of them came back.[2]

Private George 'Mac' McIntyre, aged 33, B Company, 4th Engineers:

After repeated show-down inspections, each one supposed to be final, we loaded on trucks and headed for a then unknown port of embarkation. We had written our final notes to the folks at home, at least until we hit the coast of France. Of course, we knew that the letters would not be mailed until the invasion was well under way, but we wanted our folks to know that we were well on 2 June 1944. Our convoy was long and there were many stops. Along with the regular equipment of the combat soldier, we were given an extra carton of cigarettes, several Hershey bars, and a French–English phrase book. To pass away the time, we practiced our French on each other. We laughed and joked outwardly, but an undercurrent of fear could be felt.

At last we reached the crest of a long hill and looking off into the distance we could see the English Channel. Down our convoy crept, and from chance civilians we met we learned that the town we were entering was Dartmouth. When the trucks could go no further, Captain Smith gave the order to unload. We had been on the trucks so long that we obeyed with alacrity. The footing beneath was steep and bumpy and several of the boys were dragged to their knees by their loads as they disembarked from the trucks.

We could see that we still had about a quarter of a mile to go to the edge of town, so we shifted our loads as best we could and stumbled down the steep incline. As we approached, an informal reception committee of children and dogs met us. There were the usual cries of 'Any gum, chum?' and those of us who could reach a stick or two passed it out. As we reached the first street of the city, some of the older people joined the parade. Others watched from doorways and windows, or gathered in groups to offer encouragement as we marched along.

Our route was still on the downgrade, but the footing was better now for we were walking on smooth-worn cobblestone streets. Judging by the sounds, we were getting very close to the harbour, although the camouflage was so deceiving we could see nothing yet. Abruptly, we made a sudden turn through a cleverly disguised gap in a barbed-wire barricade, and we entered the harbour itself. Here we found field kitchens already set up and immediately formed a show line, each man helping the fellow ahead get his mess equipment from his knapsack. The meal was excellent, one of my favourites – macaroni cheese, peas, carrots, mashed potatoes, bread, butter and coffee. For dessert we had fruit salad.

One of the fellows near me griped because there was no ice cream, but I think he was just sounding off. Jack Moyer, always a comic, yelled, 'Eat hearty, me mates, for tomorrow it's K Rations.' We were all sweating it out and didn't know what the morning would bring. In fact, none of us was absolutely sure that the present preparation was the real thing, or just another dry run. A fraction of our mind hoped it was another dry run, but we also knew that D-Day had to come.[3]

Diary of Lieutenant General Lewis H. Brereton, 1 June 1944:

All plans for the Big Show have been completed. The invasion is only a matter of days and hours away. It is almost beyond comprehension how much work went into the planning for the invasion. Ninth Air Force's plan for Operation Neptune alone – that part of Overlord that has to do with the landing on the Continent – consisted of 847,500 words covering 1,376 pages of legal-size paper using both sides. It was $4\frac{1}{2}$ inches thick and weighed ten pounds, three ounces.[4]

Captain Robert M. Miller, aged 30, commander Company F, 171st Infantry, 29th Division:

The operational plan for our regiment was thicker than the biggest telephone book you've ever seen. It must have been three inches thick. I remember our regimental commander, Colonel Paul R. Good, nickname Pop Good, after everything was over and the briefing was completed, he stood up, picked it up and I saw he was attempting to tear it in half, but it was so thick that even that strong man couldn't do it. So he simply threw it over his shoulder and said something like, 'Forget this god-damned thing. You get your ass on the beach. I'll be there waiting for you and I'll tell you what to do then. This is so much paper. There ain't anything in this plan that's going to go right according to plan, so get on the beach and do what common sense tells you to do. I'll be there and we'll decide then where we go from there.'[5]

Diary of Captain Douglas Aitken, medical officer, 24th Lancers:

The weather is falling off a bit today. I spend the morning arranging the vehicles in their correct order along the road. Have now got things in the common-sense order – the leading vehicle is first on and last off, with tanks in the rear of the column. We leave in a rather hungry state at midday in two deep columns; Ian and I go with the leading vehicles of the first column. Only seven miles to the docks, but the trip is a slow one.

American military police in a jeep lead us all the way. We pass over well-known roads and I must say I take a deeper than normal interest in these last glimpses of England. The local people are wondering if this is the real thing. We have a number of organized stops and innumerable cups of tea laid on at several places. In the towns, where we have more halts and more tea, the people take a little more interest, but security police keep everyone segregated and there is no mixing. The girls look much more attractive when we know we won't see any for a long time to come. Three attractive ones pass on bicycles on their way to tennis; they look very cool and very English. I occasionally find myself thinking foolish thoughts about not coming back or being away for a hell of a long time.[6]

Pfc Bruce Bradley, aged 24, radio operator, B Battery, 29th Field Artillery Battalion:

The assembly area near Torquay was alive with nervous excitement. Troops like highlanders in kilts, paratroopers, a visit from Ike, people having mohawk haircuts – a shaved head where the hair was just down the middle. I guess some of it was bravado. I saw the movie _Jane Eyre_ in a tent theatre, something to do while waiting. Funny, after all these years, I can recall the name of a movie, but some of the events escape my memory.

Finally the word came and we marched down through the town just before daylight. People were out in force giving the V for Victory sign. I carried a radio, four grenades, a carbine and a .45 pistol, extra ammo for the carbine, a Mae West jacket. It was like a big inner tube, when you inflated it with a C2 cartridge, you could float with it. I also had a first aid kit, some binoculars and a combat knife that had brass knuckles on it, an item I hoped I would not have to use. The first aid kit had morphine in it as well as sulfa.[7]

***Diary of Major George L. Wood, 6th Battalion, Durham Light
Infantry:***

The men are in good spirits. They know now that the real 'party' is
on. They are fit and well, have had little work to do in the past three
days. To keep ourselves amused we have had Ensa concerts, cinema
shows and, best of all, we ran our own unit sports which we
thoroughly enjoyed and which did more to foster good comradeship
than anything which I had seen for some time past.

We have had a visit from Anthony Eden. A most pleasant and
cheerful man and a great personality. Shook hands with him. He was
most interested in our past history, especially as he has a family
connection with this Battalion. He walked round our camp. Very
interesting to note how easily he conversed with the men. They all
seemed to enjoy his conversation and are all smiles.

Our Brigade Commander talked to the men this morning. As he
spoke, confident in manner, direct gaze, a little touch of humour and
lastly 'Good luck and God speed to every one of you', one could
read in the faces of the men their admiration for him. Their complete
trust in his leadership. Their growing confidence in this so-called
Second Front. They know it will be successful. Monty said so. Their
only doubt: 'I wonder how I shall come through all this?'

... We marched out of our camp this morning [3 June] and
embussed beside the gates. There is a small boy standing just outside
the gate. He attracts the attention of all eyes. On his jersey he is
wearing our Regimental and Divisional signs. On his chest is pinned
the ribbon of the Africa Star with Eighth Army clasp. I find myself
thinking whether any of our men feel as proud of their Africa Stars
as this little boy so obviously does. If so, they certainly don't show it.
But then they always hide their true feelings. It is not always easy to
know what the men are thinking. However, they are all cheerful this
morning. Smiling and whistling, waving and calling to the girls as
pass them en route for the docks. People gaze from their windows,
stand on the pavement and wave. Somehow one has the feeling that
they know 'this is it'. Some are very cheerful and shout 'Good luck,
get it over quickly'. Others look sad, some silently weeping. Perhaps
they have a husband, son or sweetheart whom they know will be on
this move also.

My thoughts are very mixed. What a grand set of men. Hope we
don't lose too many of the old faces this time. Already they've seen

so much and done so much. They know what it's all about, what to expect, they've done it before. No false illusions. War is not a pleasant pastime, besides we cannot possibly hope for such an easy landing as we had in Sicily. The English countryside is at its best. So lovely. How long will it be before we see it again? I believe this thought is in everyone's mind. I wonder what my wife is doing at this moment? It's such a nice day, I expect she is taking the baby for a walk. Lord, how heavy and irksome this equipment feels. Christmas-tree order the troops call it. However we can't do without any of it, it's all essential. I suppose we will sail tonight. I have never been sea-sick before. Hope we have a smooth crossing.[8]

Sergeant Hyman Haas, A Battery, 467th Anti-Aircraft Artillery Battalion:

I remember going through last-minute briefings. One man, Lieutenant Colonel Mumford, spoke to us. He left no doubt in our minds that we were going to fight. His last words stuck in my mind: 'Take care of yourselves, because if you don't we'll replace you.' We knew what he meant.

There were religious services. I can remember being at a mass for the Jewish boys with a Catholic priest holding mass on one side and a Protestant minister holding a service for the Protestant boys on the other. It was really strange – everyone praying in different religions and denominations, each watching the other. If you know anything about Jewish religious services, you know that when a Jew is praying he wraps himself in a prayer shawl and wears phylacteries, especially in the morning. We had a rabbi who was fully equipped, wearing a prayer shawl which completely covered him. I felt very strange, as though somebody was saying a prayer for the dead. This sticks out in my mind.

Of course we did other kinds of training. For the first time we saw something which later became Cinerama. They showed us this tremendous motion picture screening of enemy aircraft coming at you. It looked so natural. We had to try and aim at it; it was a very good exercise.

Right next to us in the marshalling area was a Ranger battalion. We would see them. For some strange reason they were kept in a separate area. What I mean by separate is that I think there was a fence between us, a wire fence. I think they sort of meant to keep us apart. But still, you know, you get to talking. They said they had a suicide mission coming up. We heard that they would have to scale a cliff, which seemed like suicide to me.

The thing that sticks out in my mind is the type of men they were. They looked like big, mature men. You know it's very hard to know how others see you, it's possible I was viewed in that same manner by somebody not knowing I was the sergeant of a section, but these men looked to me very capable, mature and tough. But they were very solicitous. As I recall, a young boy – he looked to me to be about seventeen or eighteen – was with them and these men, these tough-looking guys, took care of him like a father would his son. I often wondered what happened to that young fellow. I know many of them were killed.

I don't remember anybody speaking about what it might possibly be like in combat, yet, of course, it was on our minds, always wondering 'How will I do?' It really scared me. As I recall, what really frightened me was that I wouldn't measure up. I might be too frightened to move. That frightened me more than anything else. I never thought about being killed or hurt or anything, never gave it a thought.[9]

Constable Sidney Booth, Portsmouth:

My job was to keep people away from Southsea Common, on the seafront, because it was a prohibited area. No one was allowed there unless they had a lawful excuse and if any stray person started to walk across there we used to check them and escort them back to the road.

When the troops started moving off our job with the Military Police was to follow the convoys of vehicles and make sure they didn't throw out any letters or make any form of communication as they went along. Some of them were slinging out letters for people to post, things like that, which was taboo.[10]

Ursula Norton, aged 10, schoolgirl:

The whole of Southsea front was closed off to the public and most of the houses had been requisitioned by the Services. I lived within the restricted area with my grandmother, who ran a hotel which was used by all the top dogs.

To get to school I had to have a special pass. Woe betide me if I did not have it with me; twice I was taken to the police station because I had forgotten it. My satchel was searched every time I passed through the barrier. I often wondered what they were looking for in a ten-year-old's satchel.

Troops lived in all the large houses in Alhambra Road, where I lived, and my three-year-old cousin, Malcolm, was made the soldiers' mascot. I can see him now in his little soldier's hat, jacket and stripes, lined up to march with the men around to a large house on the corner of Mansion Road and Granada Road, which was used as a canteen. They all thought the world of him. He was three.

Being a child I did not appreciate the seriousness of the situation. It was all so exciting watching the exercises – every day landing craft would make attacks along the beach.

One day the area of beach in front of Canoe Lake, which was the Boom Defence Headquarters, was suddenly fenced off with barbed wire. Being an inquisitive child, I went to investigate. I remember climbing through the wire and tearing my dress in the process when suddenly men appeared from nowhere with loud hailers, shouting at me not to move, but to stay right where I was. I was so scared I could not have moved if I had wanted to. I was standing in the middle of a minefield and all I could think of was what my grandmother would say when she found out I was somewhere I should not have been.

This exciting period came to an abrupt end on the night my Grandmother's hotel had a direct hit. Many people said the bomb was meant for South Parade Pier as it was full of ammunition for D-Day. My whole family and the guest staying at the hotel were all buried under the rubble and the troops stopped all their exercises and worked day and night to dig us all out.

When we were finally rescued we went to live with my aunt in her flat opposite, as we were told we still could not leave the restricted area. This was because the D-Day operation was about to commence. It was all to be so hush-hush that I was not allowed to go to school.

My cousin, my Aunt Audrey and I went down to the beach to wave goodbye to all our friends. Many men were sitting on the beach waiting their turn to enter the boats. An American major who appeared to be giving the troops encouragement took Malcolm and I out in his boat and I was told afterwards that taking us right out among the troops did a lot for their morale.

While we were on the beach a lot of men came up and spoke to us and asked our names. Others took our photos. One man with a beard hugged us both and burst out crying. I remember him telling me he had a little girl just like me that he had left behind. Some soldiers asked us to post letters and we were made to hide them. I think they had been ordered not to write home at that late date.

The thing that stands out in my mind more than anything was the way they were all throwing their money at us. 'It will be no use to us when we are in Germany,' they said. My cousin and I ran home and got two buckets to put the money in. I can't remember how much we had but I can remember when we got home, my Gran gave us a good hiding for taking money from the men.[11]

Violet Bingley, St John's nurse, aged 18, Bow, East London:

My twin sister and myself were industrial nurses working in a factory at the Royal Victoria Docks at Silvertown and for several days we watched the invasion craft arriving just outside the docks. During those few days when troops were stationed near the docks I spoke to many of them and understood the fear of those who were young like myself.

On Sunday 4 June we were on our way home from church when we saw the start of the movement of troops to the docks. Hundreds of vehicles containing vast numbers of soldiers, most singing, most guessing where they were going and putting a brave face on things. Some, like my husband, were very young indeed and frankly worried.

As each vehicle turned from Barking Road into the docks, volunteers were stopping everyone with collecting boxes to provide every soldier with five Woodbines and a bar of chocolate.

As one truck passed the soldiers inside sang 'Two little girls in blue' to my sister and me. We were both in our uniforms. Even today, I still get a lump in my throat when I hear that song.[12]

Colin Wills, BBC reporter:

Some of them shout farewells, some of them sing. Some are silent. Some of them laugh, some smile, some look thoughtful, some look grim. One thing is common to all of them – an unmistakable air of purpose and resolve. You will now hear some of them calling out:

'Hello, Betty darling – how're you getting on? Back soon when it's all over – don't get worried. George.' 'Cheerio, mother – keep smiling. Up John Smith.' 'Hello, some public house. Save us a pint!' 'We're off on a little trip. Love to you all. Frank.' 'Hello, Mum and Dad. This is Derek speaking. All the best. We're going to give Jerry all he gave us at Dunkirk, and, boy, we're going to give it to him strong.'[13]

Noel Monks, war correspondent, **Daily Mail***:*

I have never been prouder of being a newspaperman than at the assignment of duties handed out to the few Commonwealth correspondents who were to land with the British forces in Normandy. We had been taken, in great secrecy, to Monty's HQ in the south of England and there, in a magnificent old house, we were given our tasks. Not one of us knew to which unit we had been allotted, nor when we would be landing; nor, until this meeting, *where* we would be landing. Around me sat old colleagues who had come with me all the way from the dark days in France, and even beyond that, like Ronald Monson and Matt Halton from Spanish Civil War days.

As my colleagues' names were called out, they were given their assignments and asked 'Is that all right?' Of course, they all said yes. There was Chester Wilmot and Leonard Mosley – 'With the airborne forces.' 'Yes sir!' they said. Then came Doon Campbell of Reuters: 'Commandos. H-Hour minus five minutes.' The very first men to land on the beaches. 'Yes sir!' said Doon, patting his artificial left hand. Colin Wills of the BBC, lanky, laconic Australian: 'First wave, infantry assault.' Col just grinned his 'Yes, sir' and looked as though someone had left him a fortune . . .

My assignment was with the 3rd Division with an outfit that, following close on the heels of the Commandos, had the task of clearing our beach of mines and other obstacles for the following infantry.

It was a moving experience to hear the correspondents accept their duties so happily, so wholeheartedly, without question, though each knew from hard experience the dangers ahead.

When we had all been given our assignments, we wandered out into the waning afternoon sunlight and sprawled on the lawn. We began assessing each other's chances of survival. None of us were over-optimistic of coming out of this all in one piece, as we had so far emerged from other beach landings, but we were certain of one thing – we wouldn't swap this assignment with anyone for anything.

Nothing could stop us now. We were in purdah as far as our editors were concerned.

We had tea on the lawn, chatted a little more, then, as the sun was setting, our jeeps called to take us to our various units.[14]

Lieutenant George Elsey, aged 26, on board the USS Ancon:

We were lying at Plymouth when, two or three days before the operation, our war correspondents came on board and were secured with us. They couldn't leave, just like the rest of us. The correspondent who was the object of the greatest curiosity was Ernest Hemingway. He came on board with a bandage round his head through which some blood had already soaked through. He looked very heroic and warlike, but the gossip was that he'd gotten drunk the night before and fallen down.

I didn't talk to him at all. All the officers who knew what was going on were told to stay the hell away from the correspondents.[15]

Telegraphist Clifford Palliser, aged 19, on board HMS Largs:

As we had no proper duties until D-Day we did odd jobs on the ship and one of us collected messages from the signal office in Naval HQ ashore. He did this twice daily, with an armed Royal Marine as an escort, even though they only had a couple of hundred yards to walk and did not leave the dockyard. One of the Wrens who worked in the signal office was his cousin and he would have a short conversation with her on each visit.

On 2 June this chum came back and said the next time we left harbour it would be the real thing. We asked him how he knew and he said that whenever he called at the signal office his cousin always said she would see him later, or tomorrow, or in a couple of days. That time she had said she would see him some time and best wishes.

Those trips for my chum stopped from then.[16]

Private Dennis Bowen, aged 18, 5th Battalion, East Yorkshire Regiment:

We passed the time playing cards, sing-songs, that kind of thing. Each night, as dusk fell, it was surprising how the ship went quiet. There were a couple of lads who had mouth organs and they would play and sing and the song would eventually be all round the ship.

Everybody tried to get up onto the deck and join the singing. In the morning, at reveille, we sang 'Beautiful Dreamer'.

I realized that I was going to be part of something that was going to be big. I didn't realize how big, although when you stood on the deck and looked round, you couldn't see anything else but ships, north, south, east and west. Some had barrage balloons on. I don't really know what I sort of expected. I know that what I eventually found was not what I expected. I felt quite safe because I was among these experienced soldiers who had spent three years almost continually in action and I was absolutely certain that they would carry me through.

We didn't talk about our chances, only individuals said things like, 'If I get shot I hope I get shot in the head.' People didn't want to get shot in their stomachs, or their private parts, or lose a limb, nobody wanted that. There was no real fear.

It wasn't boring on the ship. We had a proper routine of getting up in the morning – pickets on all night, of course – went for breakfast, a cafeteria system, you went through with a metal tray with indentations on. Food was good. Then you would have a muster parade, the usual sort of ship's stations. We had to wear white life jackets all the time. If you went to the toilet you had to take your life jacket. You get used to that army thing, you know, 'Hurry up and wait'. I think we were basically a little bit on the idle side. If they said there is going to be a weapons parade – which there was – you'd go, 'Oh, bloody hell, I don't really go for this, I'll be glad when all this bull is over.'

It was on the Sunday when they suddenly appeared with blackboards and photographs and things and said this is where you are landing and this is our objective. It was a mass briefing, all the men were paraded on the mess deck, company level. He told us it was going to be a difficult job, but that the beaches would be well softened up by naval gunfire and most of the beaches would be cleared of mines and obstacles. There will be some German snipers still firing at you but we don't expect any German armour and we don't expect any heavy German artillery. This was rather pooh-poohed by the men who had been in action before, but I suppose I believed it.

He didn't try to make any false picture and he said there will be casualties and men wounded. 'What I don't want is people picking up wounded men and taking them back in order to get back on the ship. If they are wounded there are already people who will look after them. If your pals are wounded, leave them, the object is to get as far inland as we can. We must not hang about on the beach; the most dangerous place will be the beach. Take my advice and get as far forward as you can away from the beach. If there is going to be any enemy fire, it will be on the beach. The sooner you get off the beach, the happier I shall be and the safer you shall be.'

We still didn't know when it would be, so we then went back to our normal routine of playing cards, playing crown and anchor and telling each other how many girls we'd been with etcetera. There was any amount of crown-and-anchor boards and gambling schools that went on hour after hour after hour. We went to bed, got up next day, thought we were going that day, didn't. The rumour went round that it had all been cancelled, we were all going back to the UK, someone else is going to do the job, thank God! But of course, when we went to bed that night we were told tomorrow morning there would be an early reveille because we were going ashore. That was it.

I did get to sleep that night. I didn't know, of course, what it was all about, how horrific it was going to be. The men who had done it before, they already knew what it was going to be like, so it was nothing to them.[17]

Diary of Technical Sergeant Richard T. Wright, combat correspondent, US Marines:

I met a new personality on the ship this morning. He is Royal Marine J.T. Wenn, general manager of 'Bookies Incorporated' and at times has a very grim sense of humour.

He passed on a 'Second Front Handicap' form offering odds on this ship's future, after or before we finish our job of blasting German coastal defences. Here's the way he figures the future:

> 5 to 2 that this ship will be sunk by shore batteries.
> 4 to 1 that we will be sunk by dive bombers.
> 6 to 1 that we will be sunk by low-level bombers.
> 8 to 1 that we will hit a mine.
> 10 to 1 that we will be sunk by a glider bomb.
> 13 to 1 that we will be shot up by fighters.
> Last, but not least, 2 to 1 that we don't get back at all.

It is generally agreed that Marine Wenn is the ship's comedian – at least he gets his share of laughs.

Sergeant Kilpatrick [US Marine photographer] and I played a little handball on the deck this afternoon, much to the amazement of the Royal Marines, who can't figure out why we need such a big glove, that is until they tried catching the ball themselves.

Kilpatrick accompanied me on a jaunt ashore this p.m., where we found plenty of servicemen, no beer, no women, not much to eat and besides which we were broke, so we came home.[18]

Diary of Leading Signalman I.J. Gillen, on board the corvette HMS Camrose:

We are at anchor in Weymouth Bay, off Portland; arrived here May 28th and have had no contact with the shore at all. This is generally thought to be because we are about to take part in some large-scale operation; none of the officers seem to know what is in the wind and we can think of no reason for keeping the ship so long in one place, after having been so busy the past four weeks. The harbour is quite a bustling place, crowded with American and British ships of many types, including the ubiquitous merchantmen. Landing ships and landing craft come and go hourly, and in fact everyone seems to be on the move except one group, which remains quiet at anchor. It consists of *Camrose*, two other corvettes – *Lunenberg* and *Baddeck* – the old French battleship, *Courbet*, and two tugs, *Samsonia* and *Growler*. *Courbet* is no longer a proud fighting ship; built in 1909, of 22,000 tons, she was scuttled in a port in Africa during France's dark days. She had been completely submerged and the mark of the water-line was still visible on her towering foremast when we first saw her. No effort has been made to clean her up and most of her big guns have been cut off at the turrets. Some new AA guns have been mounted on her, but this gives us no idea as to why she has been raised and brought here. We made several trips to her in our whaler, the first time on a legitimate search for fresh bread and vegetables – we have no yeast for baking and get no supplies from the shore. The first party to board her found her crew most hospitable, and possessed of a plentiful supply of rum and wine. They were an odd lot, in a way; there were about a hundred Free French matelots and a smaller number of British Army AA gunners. Both made us welcome, being as glad as we were for a change of any sort. A few of the huge mess decks had been cleaned up enough to provide temporary quarters and the refreshments came up in all sorts of odd dishes and jugs from one of the huge dark caverns in this dead ship. None of the men aboard her knows where she is going, but they are all 'travelling light' with a minimum of kit and equipment.

Today, Sunday, was a special occasion on our ship – we had 'divisions' for the first time since leaving our own country. Divisions is a sort of ceremony designed to make a sailor truly grateful for the Sundays it is omitted. It means all hands turn to and clean up the ship, while every man hackles and harasses his junior. Then, when so ordered, you change into your number one uniform and clean up the mess you have just made doing so. Then, while giving your uniform a final brush over, you try to think of a place to hide or a legitimate excuse for dodging divisions. The effort is usually in vain, so when the quartermaster pipes 'Hands fall in', away you go with the rest and fall in with your own division (seamen, stokers, etc.). A corvette has no clear deck space large enough for this purpose, but we assembled in some sort of order on the forecastle head. After being inspected, we were addressed by the 'Old Man', who told us we will soon see some action . . .

In the afternoon, a privileged few, myself among them, were told enough to make it quite clear why we were waiting here. We have aboard secret orders for 'Operation Neptune', the invasion of the continent. Our part in the opening phase is relatively small, but of many such small parts a mighty machine has been built. We are to escort *Courbet* across the Channel to a place in the Seine bay, the site of one of two proposed artificial harbours – the 'prefabricated ports' which are the foundation of the plan. Our destination is known by the code name 'Mulberry B' and *Courbet* is to be sunk to form part of a breakwater there. We now await the signal which will tell us to carry out our orders.[19]

Private George 'Mac' McIntyre, 4th Engineers, on board LST 47:

At ten o'clock by my watch we were summoned to the crew's quarters for a briefing. I never saw so many men packed into such a small space. I'll never forget Captain Smith's opening words as long as I live: 'Well men, this is it! Tomorrow morning at six o'clock, by order of General Eisenhower, the invasion of France begins. We are to hit the beaches of Normandy . . . I want every man to check his equipment and keep it nearby. Remember, your rifle is your army wife, so take it to bed with you. Sleep in your clothes and be ready to move out.'

We realized that there wouldn't be much sleep that night, but we went back to our quarters to round up our equipment. There were important decisions to make regarding the personal belongings each of us would take, for these had to be cut down to a minimum. Extra cigarettes, writing paper, shaving articles, and other odds and ends picked up in several years of army life were separated and stuffed into our duffel bags.

I had previously decided what I would take with me: just my prayer book, my rosary, a few choice snapshots of the folks at home, writing paper, a pencil and a small penknife. These items, along with the $4 in French money the army had allowed us, were placed in a waterproof bag. I was about five minutes deciding which pocket I would carry the bag in. I finally decided on the top pocket of my fatigue jacket, probably influenced by the fact that the prayer book might deflect a bullet.

With our preparations made, we settled back for some subdued conversation, or quiet reflection. Naturally we all thought of the morrow. Where would we be if we were still alive? One boy said he would dig in on the beach and stay there indefinitely. At the other end of the conjecture was a boy who would be making love to a French girl in Paris by sundown. Most of us were sensible and sober enough to realize that if the invasion went according to schedule, we would be from three to four miles inland by nightfall the following day.

Personally, I prayed: didn't use a prayer from a book, or even one I made up myself. I just remembered something Joe Louis, the heavyweight champion, had uttered when questioned about the outcome of the war. If I remember correctly, he said, 'We're on God's side and we can't lose.' The words lulled me into a restless slumber. I knew that the folks at home would be praying too and would take over when I might not be able to find the time myself.[20]

Lieutenant John Mason Brown, USNR, on board USS Augusta, flagship of the Western Task Force:

Men begin going to church as battles draw near. The toughest sailors; the guys whose speech is as a rule proudly, patently uninfluenced by the liturgy, they all begin going to church, even if they haven't bent an elbow to lift a hymnal in months. The church services were held in the hot confines of the Forward Mess Hall.

Captains, messboys, petty officers, yeomen, gunners, marines, cooks, junior officers and soldiers – we had all come unordered to this service which we suspected of being the last one, well, the last one before the invasion. We had all come, or almost all, including the fellows who seem incapable of avoiding in every sentence a certain blunt, four-letter word which serves as a whole dictionary, since they are given to using it as noun, adjective or verb, and using it abusively as if it had no association with pleasure.

They were all there, facing on the improvised altar a red triptych in which two angels, serene in spite of having been drafted, went calmly about their war jobs, the one employing his, her or its Botticelli fingers to support a bomber, the other a destroyer. The hymns were properly amphibious – 'For Those in Peril on the Sea', 'Onward Christian Soldiers' and 'O God, Our Help in Ages Past'. They were those sturdy standbys in which, comfortably familiar as they are, men keep rediscovering new meanings when danger rewrites them.

On the front page of the typed leaflet handed to each man, the young Chaplain, Lieutenant R.G. Gordon, had printed from the eighth verse of the 121st Psalm words radiant with reassurance: 'The Lord shall preserve thy going out and thy coming in from this time forth, and even for evermore.'

On the same leaflet, under the heading of 'Our Purpose', he had also quoted from the Atlantic Charter the article which reads 'To destroy Nazi tyranny and establish a peace which will afford to all nations the means of dwelling in safety within their own boundaries, and which will afford insurance that all the men in all the lands may live out their lives in freedom from fear and want.'

All of us, I think, gathered in that hot messroom and further warmed by the emotion stirred there, had been grateful for the happy appropriateness of being reminded just then of these words. Each confused man on every crowded ship needed to be prodded into remembrance of the reason for the ordeal about to come.[21]

Letter from Major R.M.S. Maude, 246 Field Company, Royal Engineers:

My dear Mum,
You certainly won't get this letter until after the event, as it were, but

I hope it won't be delayed too long. I thought you might be interested to know what we are doing, and how we are all feeling now.

I am writing this on board the ship in which we go across. At the moment, of course, we are at anchor off the coast of England, surrounded by a great many other ships and craft.

We embarked yesterday afternoon. We had lunch in camp and then got into buses and drove – very slowly – down to the harbour. We were all crowded anyhow onto the buses. The men were all very cheerful, cracking jokes and cheering every girl we passed on the way. You would never have dreamed, except for the amount of equipment we were carrying, that we were not going on another exercise. I must say I didn't feel any different myself.

I have known for over a year that we would eventually go off on this, or something similar, and I used to dread the last preparations and the final parting from friends and England, but in actual fact (fortunately) I haven't minded at all, now that it is really happening. We all feel very confident and optimistic about the result of the landings, and we all think it is going to be a walk-over – at first, anyway. Also it simply doesn't occur to anyone as a possibility that anything unpleasant can possibly happen – to other people, yes, but not to oneself – so naturally nobody worries about it.

And also we are all intensely interested to see how this thing which we have been planning so long and training for so long does work out in practice. I want to see the effect the terrific preliminary bombardment has, and what France is like after four years of occupation, and what the Germans are like, and all sorts of things like that. So it is something I am really looking forward to, and the unpleasant things that are bound to happen don't seem to me as possibilities at the moment and don't disturb me at all.

The atmosphere on board is so far quite normal. I have a lot of friends and we have an amusing time pulling each other's legs, and we feed like Kings – terrific food, like peacetime. There are six of us in my cabin – a gunner called Llewellyn, who is very nice and good looking, and David Smith, another Sapper major who I like very much, and three other gunners, only one of whom I know at all well.

Others in the ship are Charles Boycott, who was at Bradfield with me, and Dick Goodwin and Geoffrey Riley and lots of other pleasant officers, mostly from the Battalion in our Brigade. We don't know yet when D-Day is, but we think it is likely to be Tuesday, or possibly Wednesday – providing of course the weather is OK. At the moment it is much too windy and rough. Curiously enough, the first unsuitable day for about a month. It always does that. On practically every exercise it has been the same – perfect weather until we embark, and then a gale or storm gets up.

About ten days ago an RE major – J.A. Crawford – turned up from COHQ and announced that he was coming with us as a spectator! So I took him under my wing and we became great friends. He is an amusing chap – a bit of a rogue, and lazy as hell, but amusing, and we talked the same language to each other and made each other laugh a lot, so it was great fun having him and a wonderful change to have somebody to talk to, especially at this time. It has made me quite human!

. . . Mail is being delivered to us over there almost as soon as we arrive so I hope there will be something from you as I haven't heard anything from you for some days. I hope you have been getting some of my letters, but I am afraid they haven't been very good ones recently for obvious reasons – and there probably won't be any more for some time as I shall be rather busy for a few days! Anyway, please don't worry, I am sure to be all right and no news is good news.

I have been washing all my clothes in Puritan soap. Rather fun! I must stop now and get my maps sorted. I hope you get this, but you can never tell these days. So annoying the way these ships get sunk!

All my love to you, and don't worry.
   Your loving
    Rodney.[22]

Radio operator Vernon L. Paul, on board LST 983, US Navy:

I was on watch from eight to twelve on the night of the 4th. We had these frequencies we were supposed to guard. One of the voice frequencies was supposed to be strictly monitored and we were not to transmit on that frequency under any circumstances.

So I was in the shack all by myself, tired and looking forward to being relieved so I could hit the sack. There was nothing on the radio except the usual signal noise. The secured frequency was cooking away, nothing on it, then I heard what sounded like a transmitter coming on the line.

I said to myself 'It can't be. No one would dare transmit or break radio silence on that guard channel.' Then I heard, very softly, a voice say 'Who dat?' And then I heard another transmitter coming up to power and a voice, a bit louder: 'Who dat saying who dat?' And then another saying, 'Who dat saying who dat when I say who dat?'

And finally the whole channel opened up with everyone, it seemed, saying, 'Who dat?' and, 'Who dat saying who dat?' and the whole thing went crazy. It sure broke the tension for a lot of radio operators on watch.[23]

TOP SECRET. *Memorandum from Colonel Charles 'Stoneface' Canhan CO 116th Infantry, to be read by commanders to all personnel:*

1. The long-awaited day is near and I want to wish each one of you the best of luck in your forthcoming venture. There is one certain way to get the enemy out of action and that is to kill him. War is not child's play and requires hatred for the enemy. At this time we don't have it. I hope you get it when you see your friends wounded and killed.

2. Learn to take care of yourself from the start. Remember the Hun is a crafty, intelligent fighter and will not have any mercy on you. Don't have it on him. He will try to outwit you. Be on the alert.

3. Fighting a war is the same as any athletic event, only war is for keeps. It is you or the enemy. Teamwork is the essence of success. You have the tools, the best in the world, and it is up to you to see that they are used properly.

4. Remember when you run into the enemy, contain him with the minimum to stop him, then move around and strike him in the flank or rear. In all your contacts with him be ruthless, always drive hard. The Hun doesn't like Yankee drive and guts. If you close on him, use your bayonet, show him that you can take it and dish it out. Don't be caught napping. Don't let your Yankee curiosity get you blown up by a booby trap or mine.

5. Take care of your arms and equipment. Conserve your ammunition, make every shot count. Keep your weapons cleaned and oiled. Their proper functioning at the right time may mean your life.

6. Do not eat 'K' and 'D' rations prior to D + 1. You won't get anymore until D + 2.

7. The Navy and Air will give us plenty of support. General

Montgomery was very optimistic in his talk to the officers yesterday. At this time no one knows how much resistance we will get on D-Day. We may be able to walk in without trouble, we may have to fight for every inch of ground, to the last man. Be prepared to fight for your life to meet the worst and make up your mind now that you are going forward regardless and that no Hun on God's Green Earth can stop you. We are going forward and it is a one-way street. We are not giving ground at any time and not leaving until the job is done.

8. I have the utmost confidence in your ability to take it and dish it out. There is one final word of warning. The Hun will try and lower your morale by firing artillery or mortars in your area during the time our artillery is firing in an effort to make you believe our artillery is firing on us.

9. To each one of you Happy Landing and come off those craft fighting like hell.[24]

CHAPTER EIGHT

SUNDAY 4 JUNE 1944

While the vast invasion fleet waited for orders to sail, the storm clouds were literally gathering and Eisenhower faced the toughest decision of his life . . .

General Walter Bedell-Smith, Chief of Staff to Supreme Commander:

From the beginning it had been clear that the choice of D-Day depended on the weather. We proposed to cross the treacherous waters of the English Channel with more than 5,000 ships and hundreds of smaller ship-to-shore craft to assault a coast bristling with determined troops and all manner of fixed defences. The hazardous operation would hang on four factors of weather.

First, we wanted low tide so that the underwater and half-hidden beach obstacles could be seen and destroyed by our demolition crews. The low tide must be late enough in the morning for an hour's good daylight to permit the saturation bombing of defences which would precede the landings themselves. But it must come early enough in the morning so that a second low tide would occur before darkness set in. Without the second low tide we could not land the follow-up divisions.

For the airborne landings behind Utah Beach and at road centres around Caen, timed for 02.00 hours on D-Day, we needed a late-rising full moon so the pilots could approach their objectives in darkness but have moonlight to pick out the drop zones. For the naval craft and transports, we must have a reasonable sea and good visibility to reduce the perils of navigation in crowded waters and to keep troops from arriving at the point of assault so seasick they could not leave their ships. Finally, we hoped for a fair wind blowing inshore to drive the smoke and dust of battle towards the enemy.

Two of these requirements were within the ready prediction of the meteorologists. They could tell us when we should have the low tide and the full moon. During the four days in early June, they said, the exact conditions – barring storms – would be forthcoming: on the 4th, 5th, 6th and 7th. The ideal day was June 5.[1]

Group Captain James Stagg, RAF, Chief Meteorological Officer, SHAEF:

After the fine weeks of April and early May the weather changed and by the end of May there seemed to be nothing on our weather charts but a series of great depressions of almost winter-like intensity. General Eisenhower and his commanders met twice a day and I was required to attend to advise them on the weather prospects for D-Day. At the evening meeting on Wednesday 31 May, I warned them that conditions for the oncoming weekend – especially over Sunday night and Monday morning, the crucial times for Overlord – were going to be stormy.

I kept a diary and made notes before and after each of the conferences, but the long-room in which they were held remains vivid in my memory. It had the appearance of having been the library of Southwick House [SHAEF's Portsmouth headquarters]; the walls were lined with empty bookcases. In the half of the room closest to the door, easy chairs and couches were arranged informally in two or three roughly parallel arcs facing towards three more chairs usually occupied by the Supreme Commander, his Deputy, Air Chief Marshal Tedder, and his Chief of Staff, General Bedell-Smith. Behind them was the war room, where the disposition and current movements of Overlord forces were displayed on vast wall maps. The Commanders in Chief and their deputies usually sat in the front row of the seats facing the Supreme Commander and other officers would usually be sitting on the arms of chairs in the rows behind. The setting and atmosphere was completely informal and reminded me of nothing so much as an after-lunch meeting of the mess committee in a senior officers' mess in the Royal Air Force.

According to my notes, assembled in the room on the evening of

1. General Eisenhower talking to an American soldier during pre-invasion manoeuvres in England (February 1944).

2. General Montgomery addressing the British First Airborne Division.

3. The heads of the Allied Expeditionary force for Europe. *Back, l. to r.*: General Omar Bradley, Admiral Sir Bertram Ramsey, Air Chief Marshal Sir Trafford Leigh-Mallory, Lieutenant General Walter Bedell-Smith. *Front*: Generals Eisenhower and Montgomery.

4. Field Marshal Rommel at Caen.

5. Royal Marines recruits training with bayonets.
6. British troops practising an assault from landing craft.

7. A scene from the infamous exercise at Slapton Sands, Devon, in which 749 GIs were killed after a German E-Boat attack.

8. A typical German machine-gun nest.

9. German soldiers setting up a fence round a minefield.

10. US servicemen checking the fuel level on a Mustang P51B. Note the cigar!

11. A Hawker Typhoon of the type used on D-Day for strafing and rocket attacks.

12. A Messerschmitt 109.

13. Rows of guns forming part of the huge accumulation of new equipment prior to D-Day.

14. A German gun emplacement on the French coast.

15. A company of German infantry somewhere on the Western front.

16. A typical scene on the south coast of Britain on 5 June 1944.
17. A Royal Artillery convoy passing through a Kent village.

18. A German guard keeping watch for saboteurs.

19. A Bren Gun Carrier passing a pub in the south of England.

20. American troops en route to an embarkation port.

21. Pilots of No. 453 Australian Spitfire Squadron being briefed at Ford airfield in May 1944.

22. A US Army unit being briefed. *Front, l. to r.:* Privates Albert V. Ottolino, Howard D. Krant and J.H. James.

23. General Eisenhower briefing paratroopers before they take off for France.

24. A British convoy assembling.

25. Gliders and tugs preparing for take-off.

26. US troops ready to embark in landing craft that will take them to larger craft lying off the coast.

27. LCVP landing craft with their complement of GIs.

28. Climbing out of an LCVP, US troops board an LCI (L).

29. Grim-faced GIs aboard a landing ship.

Friday 2 June, were General Eisenhower, Air Chief Marshal Tedder, General Bedell-Smith, the three Commanders in Chief (Admiral Ramsay, General Montgomery and Air Chief Marshal Leigh Mallory, with his deputy, General Vandenberg), the Deputy Chiefs of Staff (General Gale and Air Vice Marshal Robb), the Chiefs of Staff to the Commanders in Chief (Admiral Creasey, General de Guingand and Air Vice Marshal Wrigglesworth) and the SHAEF Chiefs of Divisions (Generals Bull and Nivens).

When I had expanded this statement there were questions, but not many. General Eisenhower pressed me hard for my opinion about the weather on Tuesday and Wednesday, June 6 and 7, but I could only reply that it was unlikely to be worse than that on Sunday and Monday – not, in retrospect, a helpful remark.

Without any preliminaries, General Eisenhower started the meeting by saying, 'Well, Stagg, what have you got for us this time?' 'Broadly,' I replied, 'I can only confirm the picture I hope I left you with last evening. The whole situation from the British Isles to Newfoundland has been transformed in recent days and is now potentially full of menace. In the last twenty-four hours there has been no clear indication how it will go, better or worse, but, at the best, weather in the Channel for the next two or three days at least will be very different from what we hoped for. Until at least Tuesday or Wednesday there will be much cloud; at times skies will be completely overcast, especially in the west of the area and winds will be from a westerly point, often force four and up to force five at times.'

When I had expanded this statement there were questions, but not many. General Eisenhower pressed me hard for my opinion about the weather on Tuesday and Wednesday, June 6 and 7, but I could only reply that it was unlikely to be worse than that on Sunday and Monday – not, in retrospect, a helpful remark.

Of all the senior officers I met in those days, General Eisenhower himself, Admiral Creasey and General Morgan were, I think, the most sympathetic to our work and the most understanding of our difficulties. Admiral Creasey and General Morgan also had a beguiling knack of relieving tension at difficult times. Before the evening meeting on the following day, Admiral Creasey said to me: 'Well, I hope you have some reassuring news for us tonight. You know, when you went out from yesterday's meeting I remarked to the company, "There goes six feet two of Stagg and six feet one of gloom." Is that how you really felt?' I smiled and said, 'I'm sorry, sir, I didn't intend that my face should be used as a barometer. But you were right and I'm afraid I don't feel much happier now.'

That night I told the conference: 'Gentlemen, the fears my colleagues and I had yesterday about the weather for the next three or four days have been confirmed. The whole weather set-up over the British Isles and, even more so, to the west over the north-east Atlantic, is very disturbed and complex. We cannot have much confidence in what will happen and how it will happen from day to day. Even for tomorrow the details are not clear. But we do know now that the extension of the Azores anticyclone towards our south-west shores, which some of us thought might protect the Channel from the worst effects of the Atlantic depressions, is now rapidly giving way. It can no longer be expected to act as a bumper to push the depressions northwards. A series of three depressions are strung out across the Atlantic from north Scotland towards Newfoundland, and, as things are at the moment, we think they will all pass through the north of the country. They are all vigorous and one or more of them may have further intensified by the time they reach the British Isles. That is the broad picture as we see it and the sequence of events in the Channel resulting from it is likely to be this: from tomorrow winds will be from between the south-west and west, force 4 to 5, maybe 6 at times, on the English side of the Channel and 3 to 4 along the French coasts. They will continue fresh, even strong at times, till Wednesday when we think the main front of one of the depressions will come through the area. It will then be squally for a time with heavy showers. There will be much cloud, often ten-tenths, with its base down to 500 to 1,000 feet, especially in the morning. Breaks in the cloud cover will occur during the day, especially inland, with amounts decreasing to nil to five-tenths, and with variable amounts in the Channel itself and along both coasts. Visibility will be 3–4 miles but 5–6 miles inland and in the afternoon. There is a risk of fog in all sea and coastal areas until Monday.

Throughout this recital General Eisenhower sat motionless, with his head slightly to one side resting on his hand, staring steadily towards me. All in the room seemed to be temporarily stunned: the gloom attributed to me last night had now fallen on everyone. Admiral Ramsay broke the grave silence: 'Are the force 5 winds along the Channel to continue on Monday and Tuesday?'

'Yes, sir.'

'And the cloud on those days?'

'As the situation is at this moment I could not attempt to differentiate one day from another in regard to cloudiness through the whole period.'

Air Chief Marshal Tedder asked: 'What will the conditions be like after Wednesday?'

'Not by any measure settled. But the cold front then expected should clear the warm air from the Channel and there will be less persistent cloud. There should be alternating deteriorations and clear ridge weather for a period.'

Air Chief Marshal Leigh Mallory asked: 'What will the conditions be like for heavy bombers taking off from bases early on Monday morning?'

'Ten-tenths stratus cloud, 3,000 feet thick and with its base down to 500 to 1,000 feet; there will also be considerable amounts of cloud at 8,000 to 12,000 feet.'

'And what will the enemy have then, for their aircraft?'

'Inland over France weather will be better than over England, but along the French coasts skies will be overcast, with cloud down to 500 feet at times, as on our side.'

General Eisenhower listened with close attention to the questions and answers, and he seemed to me to be watching particularly the effect the answers had on the questioners and the rest of the company. He turned to me for a final question: 'Now let me put this one to you. Last night you left us, or you left me, with a gleam of hope. Isn't there just a chance that you might be a bit more optimistic again tomorrow?'

'No, sir. As I had hoped you would realize yesterday, I was most unhappy for the prospects for Monday and Tuesday. Even then the whole weather situation was extremely finely balanced and slow to show which way it would develop. Last night, it is true, we thought there might be the slightest tip towards the favourable side; but tonight the balance has gone too far to the other side for it to swing back again overnight.'

The Supreme Commander said: 'You certainly gave me the impression that you didn't like anything about the business,' and for that remark I was thankful – he had not been unprepared for the evening's forecast.

The procedure was for myself and my colleagues to remain in the hall in case we were required again; we usually had to wait only a few minutes. But that evening we waited an hour or more from 10.15 p.m. Then General Bull came out and told us: 'The Supreme Commander has made a provisional decision to hold up the operation on a day-to-day basis. Some of the forces will still sail tonight but

General Eisenhower and his commanders will meet again at 4.15 a.m. tomorrow to hear what you have to say. They will then decide definitely whether the first assaults will be postponed from Monday to Tuesday.'

As I came out of Southwick House about midnight, Air Chief Marshal Tedder passed, lighting his pipe. He turned to me, smiled, and said, 'Pleasant dreams, Stagg.'

As far as I could take in at a glance the same company as had attended the meeting five hours earlier were again there at 4.15 a.m. that Sunday morning. The tension in the room was palpable. On a nod from the Supreme Commander, serious and unsmiling, I immediately confirmed that in the interval since the last meeting no development had occurred which allowed any substantial change in the forecast I had then presented.

I understood Admiral Ramsay to say that he was prepared to go ahead though he did not like the prospect, and General Montgomery was against delay. But Air Chief Marshal Leigh Mallory said he could not carry out his bombing programme if cloud formations were going to be as bad as I had forecast them and Air Chief Marshal Tedder upheld this view. General Eisenhower said: 'In that case, gentlemen, it looks to me as if we must confirm the provisional decision we took at the last meeting. Compared with the enemy's forces ours are not overwhelmingly strong. We need every help our air superiority can give us. If the air cannot operate we must postpone. Are there any dissentient voices?' There were none.[2]

Major E.H. Lassen RAMC, commanding officer 21 Field Dressing Station:

The day dawned dull and cold with grey clouds scudding across the sky as we climbed on to the three-tonners that were to take us to the hards of the embarkation point. Steel helmet on head, festooned with equipment, surgical haversack, large pack, two 24-hour concentrated food packs, water bottle and revolver dangling precariously at my waist, I gloomily reflected that I would sink like a stone if there were any nonsense over the landing.

The three-tonners stopped alongside the hards and troops at the head of the convoy began to clamber out of their vehicles and into the waiting landing craft, which were already bobbing about ominously in the choppy waves. I turned away from that depressing scene and saw on the other side of the road the only other living soul out and about on this grey morning – a lone policeman, just one stolid, but somehow comforting, British bobby who stared without apparent interest at the reluctant activity before him.

The contrast between him and us was just too much. What in the name of fortune was he doing there anyway – to see that we didn't run away and arrest us if we did? Lucky sod, he'd be off duty in a couple of hours and home in time for tea. But we, we were going down to the sea in ships, landlubbers to a man.

How precisely it came about I am not sure, but it appeared that some of the movement of the troops in front had stopped. Some who had already got on to their craft were actually getting out again. Then, in another few minutes, there was a general scramble back into the lorries as the news filtered through: 'Disembark. D-Day postponed. Everyone back to camp.'

The lorries reversed and we climbed back into them, numbed and empty of all feeling: a non-event. Even the policeman had gone. Soon we were back at the camp which we had left just a few hours before and which we had never expected to see again in our lives. Anticlimax. Total anticlimax.[3]

Edward C. Boccafogli, aged 24, B Company, 3rd Platoon, 508th Parachute Infantry:

On the night of June 4 we were all ready to go. At 9.30 we loaded into C47 airplanes at Falkingham aerodrome. Everyone was very nervous, very tense. We took off, being we were in the first lead group. We flew around for about an hour, and then word came that the invasion was called off for twenty-four hours due to the bad weather. They said that there was one of the worst storms in many years in the Channel.

When we landed back at the airfield it was really a letdown. It just seemed to take everything right out of your stomach. That night there were very heavy rains. A couple of tents collapsed; one was hit by lightning. Next morning, the fellows were trapped underneath the canvas because of the weight of the water.

One thing I remember very well was one young kid, I don't think he was more than seventeen years old, his name was Johnny Daum, a blond, tow-headed kid. In the morning he was standing there, staring

into space. I went over to him and said, 'What's the matter, Johnny?'
I get emotional just thinking about it. He said, 'I don't think I'll
make it.'

I said, 'Nah, you'll be all right.' I sort of shook him, because he
was like in a daze. As it turned out, he was one of the first men killed
in Normandy.[4]

Major E.H. Steele-Baume, second in command, 7th (Light Infantry) Parachute Battalion:

Our transit camp was some fifty miles from our airfield at Fairford.
This meant that we had to go to fit our parachutes the day before we
took off. On June 3 we went to the airfield for the fitting of
parachutes. It was an odd feeling, quite different from that
experienced before an exercise. Most people had, naturally or
artificially, acquired an air of indifference as to how well the parachute
had been packed. This time it was a little different. Everyone seemed
to be inspecting their 'chute minutely; every tie, every buckle, was
tested and re-tested. Our fitted 'chutes were then packed in a warmed
store to prevent them getting damp.

We returned to our camp and organized a concert for that night.
Despite the general tension and the fact that everyone was looking
constantly at the sky, trying to assess the weather, the concert was a
great success. The wind was rising, and it became apparent that we
should get some pretty rough falls if we jumped in it. It was not long
before the anticipated postponement arrived.

I think the next twenty-four hours were the most unnerving of the
whole operation. There was nothing to do. It was no use trying to
go through the briefing again. Everyone had been keyed to the
highest pitch and it was irritating in the extreme to have a postponement. It was interesting to walk around the camp and watch the
reaction of individuals. At one point I came across a man surrepti-
tiously practicing his leap into space off three steps; at another I
came across a very bloodthirsty creature who was grinding his
fighting knife on a step and declaiming his intention vis-à-vis the
Boche in a particularly gruesome and telling manner. (One officer
bet his batman that he would not kill a Boche with his knife – the
batman won.)

Most people were writing one more letter to be posted after we
had gone.[5]

Flying Officer Jimmy Edwards, Dakota pilot, 271 Squadron,
RAF:

We had all felt that D-Day was looming and our suspicions were
confirmed when the station intelligence officer issued an edict that all
aircrew moustaches were to be shaved off. His reasoning was
somewhat convoluted. We were all to carry passport-size photographs
of ourselves which, if we were unlucky enough to be shot down,
could be pasted into false identity cards supplied by the French
underground movement. He thought that RAF-type handlebar
moustaches looked far too British so, before the photos were taken,
off they had to come. We appointed one of the senior WAAF
officers as Official Shearer and with great merriment, and not a little
beer, she performed the solemn ceremony.

I was one of a group of Daks which were to go over the night
before and drop gliders on various special targets like bridges and
gun-emplacements, so that these could be captured before the main
onslaught took place. We did our best to memorize the lie of the land
from maps and reconnaissance photographs and the day before the
'off' all the Dakotas and Horsas were duly marshalled on the
runway.

There were going to be so many machines in the air over the
beachhead that to simplify identification all Allied aircraft were to be
painted with wide black and white stripes on the wings and fuselage.
This was such a well-kept secret that we didn't know about it
ourselves until the day before D-Day and it had to be done so
speedily that our ground crew couldn't possibly cope with the task in
the short time available. Accordingly, all the aircrew had to rally
round and out we went to the dispersal points armed with large
whitewash brushes and lent a hand sloshing the stuff on to the wings.
I was wearing my second-best peaked cap which was already splitting
open at the front of the peak, and the addition of liberal amounts of
white paint added to the rakish appearance. The CO eyed my get-up
with a disapproving look, but said nothing. This was hardly the time
for bullshit.

The postponement placed a great strain on all of us; conversation
was not very brisk and in the Mess drinking was sporadic and
merriment short-lived. Every spare bit of grass on the aerodrome
was occupied by the tents of the troops going with us, and their
nerves were pretty taut as well. Some of the remarks tossed to us

'boys in blue' as we went to the comparative luxury of our Nissen huts were definitely bordering on the unfriendly. We were all strictly confined to company and I sat on my bed, in an uncharacteristically sombre mood, and wrote a letter to my mother.[6]

Lieutenant Stephen L. Freeland, USNR, commander LCC No. 70:

When our convoy finally formed on the afternoon of June 3, LCTs strung out in two columns about ten miles long and behind them 90 LCMs bucked and banged in four columns, with our LCCs acting as outriders. From my station at the tail of the starboard columns, the line of ships stretched forward out of sight even then, and the convoy was not yet complete.

We headed east with more than a full day's run ahead of us before we turned south for the final leg of our journey to the shores of Normandy. Tides run strong through the Channel, upwards of six knots in some places, and since our convoy was scheduled to proceed at five knots that meant some straining for the LCTs. Breakdowns that first night appeared to be frequent. At least, we stopped often, a tricky business for the LCMs, who'd be barreling along at top speed with a following sea and suddenly find themselves climbing the fantails of the LCTs ahead. All night long we could hear them banging around like tin-framed bass drums.

Soon after sundown, which came about 10 p.m., the sky became overcast, the breeze freshened, and the sea grew rougher. Occasionally the overcast would break and the moon would light up the ghost-white hull of a British LCT. Morning of the 4th was gray and gusty. We were getting thoroughly wet and well slammed about by the steep chop building up on our starboard quarter. We'd done what we could to stow all personal gear securely, but an LCC in a sea has a snappy roll with a kind of walloping wriggle tied onto it that can jar the fillings out of your teeth and soon our small free space below decks looked like the steerage of an old Black Ball liner – a confused litter of sleeping men and miscellaneous gear. One green-faced gunner's mate hoisted himself wearily topside explaining 'Sleeping down there is damn rugged duty.'

Matters were uncomfortable enough while we were underway; when we were forced to lie to, which was often, we slopped and sloshed around even more unhappily. Trying as that was physically, there was an indecisiveness, an apparent lackadaisical quality to our progress, that tired us as much as the beating we were taking from the sea.

Along about nine o'clock we were taking heavy spray over the bow. The interval between the waves was just right to have us burrowing into each one. Then we got a signal in the clear 'Post Mike One – Postpone D-Day one day.'

Our convoy, however, went bucketing along just as though nothing had happened. About 15 minutes later the signal was repeated and 15 minutes after that. I was a little worried, since we were still moving along our invasion course. I signaled Jim White in the LCC 90, who was bringing up the rear of the port column, and he replied that he hadn't heard any message. That had me really bothered until we got another signal from the 90 saying that their radio hadn't been working in the first place.

From time to time ships off the screen would come within range of our blinker and of course we'd pass along the message to them. They always acknowledged, but maybe they didn't get what we said. After all, rolling and pitching and squirming as we were, our signalmen had to be a combination of chimpanzee and acrobat to flash messages anywhere near the ship he was sending to. A little more than two hours after we got the first radio signal, we got orders to accompany the LCMs back to Weymouth to take aboard fresh water and fuel. It was a long wet haul against wind and tide, with rain squalls to complicate matters, but eventually at six in the afternoon we entered the delightful calm waters of Weymouth harbour.[7]

Lieutenant George Honour RNVR, aged 25, 12th Submarine Flotilla, Commander of midget submarine X 23:

Our job was to act as a navigational marker for the invasion armada. We arrived off the French coast, near the mouth of the River Orne, about four o'clock on Sunday morning, just as dawn was breaking. I had a quick look through the periscope and saw a cow on the beach and a fixed light on the pier. I didn't expect them to leave any lights on. You could see the flare path of Caen airport and planes landing. Our brief was to make our marker position, that was the first thing. We could see the Orne and we knew we were too far to the left, so we moved along the coast and got a fix from a couple of churches. Once we had fixed our position bang on, there was nothing to do but wait.

We had a galley on board with a nice little cooker, a thing called a 'gluepot', and took it in turns to do the cooking. We ate sort of standard rations, bully beef, baked beans, things like that. Really with the five of us on board, there'd be two sleeping, three fiddling around or navigating and then a change round. There were two bunks, one over the batteries and one in the control room. The loo was inside the escape hatch, which opened up to the front and back compartments. One of the major problems was the condensation, everything dripped, everything was damp.

We had a quick look round during the day on Sunday. The X craft had a very thin periscope which would have been hard to spot. We could see staff cars moving about and later on there were lorry loads of Germans coming down to the beach, playing beach ball and swimming. That amused us because they obviously hadn't any idea we were there or what was soon to happen. They were having their Sunday make and mend, *spielen* or whatever they did in Germany, and there they were, lorry-loads of Germans coming down having a lovely time. You could see them actually in the water. I should think there were one or two Olympic swimmers, they seemed to be going at a hell of a pace. I don't think they had any swimsuits on, although I couldn't be sure as we were lying about a mile off the beach.

We didn't dare surface until between midnight and two o'clock on Monday morning. Then we got these coded messages which said, 'Not coming on Monday.' We had been told that, if it was postponed, we were to go down and wait twenty-four hours and have another go the following night, which is what we did. We went down for another twenty-four hours and waited all day. We didn't bother to keep an eye on the shore any more, we thought by then that we had seen everything we ought to see and really there was no point in looking round.

So we just sat there. There were always jobs to do and a certain amount of maintenance. But we were getting a bit soppy, too. We'd had about forty-eight hours of oxygen and it's almost as good as a strong Bass, so you start to get a bit gaga. It's a bit like being half canned, half-tight, being shut in like that on oxygen. We played poker dice, we all lost a fortune but that was about all you could do.[8]

Group Captain James Stagg:

That day was a day of dreadful tension. Here was the whole business completely suspended. I knew, we all knew, that there could be only one day's deferment. If there had to be another day because of continuing depressions then all the landing craft would need to return to base so that the soldiers and forces on them could stretch their legs and get fresh food on board and re-fuel. Then the operation would have to be deferred for a whole fortnight until the next tides were right and at that time our charts were so black in the Atlantic, there were so many depressions bringing such storms and such amounts of cloud, that there didn't seem to be any prospect of getting the operation going at all.

Then, mercifully, miraculously, the almost unbelievable happened at about midday. We spotted two reports from the Atlantic indicating that there just might be an interlude between two depressions moving towards Ireland and therefore, ultimately, into the south-west approaches. If the interlude was long enough, and if it arrived in the Channel at the proper time, it might just allow the operation to get started again.

As on preceding occasions in the last four days – to me it seemed like four months – the senior officers were assembling in the library at Southwick House, settling informally into their couches and easy chairs, when we arrived at 9.30 p.m. I stood just inside the door to deliver the news.

'Gentlemen, since I presented the forecast last evening some rapid and unexpected developments have occurred over the north Atlantic. In particular a vigorous cold front from one of the depressions has been pushed more quickly and much further south than could have been foreseen. This front is approaching Portsmouth now and will pass through all Channel areas tonight or early tomorrow. After the strong winds and low cloud associated with that front have moved through there will be a brief period of improved weather from Monday afternoon. For most of the time the sky will then be not more than half covered with cloud and its base should not often be below 2,000 to 3,000 feet. Winds will decrease substantially from what they are now. Those conditions will last over Monday night and into Tuesday. Behind that fair interlude cloud will probably increase again later on Tuesday with amounts up to eight-tenths to ten-tenths at times overnight Tuesday/Wednesday. From early

Wednesday until at least Friday weather will continue unsettled – variable skies with cloud ten-tenths and base height down to 1,000 feet for periods of not more than four to six hours at a time but interspersed with considerable fair intervals. Wind will be westerly throughout; force four to five along English coasts, force three to four on French coasts and probably less, force two to three, along sheltered stretches on that side of the Channel.'

Admiral Creasey put the first question after a rather prolonged silence. 'Is there a chance that conditions over Wednesday to Friday could be better than you have pictured them to us?'

I hesitated before replying. 'Yes, sir. There is a fair possibility that the depression which we expect to bring temporary deterioration later on Tuesday may move in a more north-easterly direction than is assumed in the forecast. If that happens both cloud and wind conditions will be more favourable than those I have given.'

General Eisenhower asked, 'Can you say anything about the weather beyond Friday?'

'No, sir. From the way we think things are now going in the Atlantic and from the fact that we are now in June, not January, despite what has happened – both those aspects suggest that if the weather turns out as we expect until Friday, then there should be a fair chance of improvement again after that. But after the shake-up in the whole weather situation which we are going through it cannot be expected to re-settle itself very quickly: conditions must continue to be regarded as very disturbed.'

Air Chief Marshal Tedder then asked, 'What confidence have you in the forecast you have given us?'

'I am quite confident that a fair interval will follow tonight's front. Beyond that I can only repeat that the rates of development and speeds of movements of depressions in the Atlantic have been exceptional for the time of year. I cannot therefore have much confidence in this state of affairs quietening down immediately after Tuesday.'

Both Air Chief Marshal Leigh Mallory and General de Guingand questioned me further about the details of cloudiness expected overnight Monday/Tuesday. 'What exactly did you intend to convey when you said "less than five-tenths?" Did you mean that about half the sky would be persistently covered?'

'No, sir. After the low cloud has cleared with the passage of the front on Monday and particularly through Monday night, the amount of cloud at any time will probably be nil to two-tenths for much of the time. When the amount increases to five-tenths it will not be in one continuous sheet but well enough broken for the moon to shine through the gaps.'

Leigh Mallory asked, 'Have you consulted with the meteorological people at my headquarters about these matters?'

'Yes, sir, and they have agreed with the operational implications of the forecast as I hope I have presented it: very good visual bombing conditions from Monday evening into the forenoon of Tuesday, followed by good, intermixed with poor, periods till Friday.'

Admiral Ramsay spoke about the need for his aircraft to spot and report on the bombardment of shore installations by heavy naval guns, and asked about the height of the cloud expected overnight Monday/Tuesday. 'Its base should be no lower than 2,000 to 3,000 feet.'

In case there should be further questions about the weather, we waited while General Eisenhower began to discuss the position with his chiefs. The atmosphere was tense and grave.

Admiral Ramsay said, 'Let's be clear about one thing to start with. If Overlord is to proceed on Tuesday I must issue provisional warnings to my forces within the next half-hour. But if they do re-start and have to be recalled again, there can be no question of continuing on Wednesday.'

Air Chief Marshal Leigh Mallory was still anxious about the effectiveness of his heavy bombers. 'With the cloud conditions Stagg has given us, there's certain to be difficulty getting markers down accurately and the bombing will therefore suffer.' Some of his colleagues seemed to think this was an unnecessarily pessimistic view, but Air Chief Marshal Tedder supported Leigh Mallory: 'Yes, the operations of the heavy and medium bombers will probably be a bit chancy.'

General Eisenhower put the question directly to General Montgomery: 'Do you see any reason why we should not go on Tuesday?' Montgomery's reply was immediate and emphatic: 'No, I would say – go!'

After some further discussion of the possible difficulties for the Allied bombers and the countervailing advantages to the night forces of the enemy if conditions turned out poor for our interceptor aircraft, the Supreme Commander started his summing up: 'After hearing all your views, I'm quite certain we must give the order for Tuesday morning. Are there any dissentient voices . . .?'

At this stage, General Bull conveyed to me by a nod that we were not likely to be further required, so we withdrew. In the hall just outside the conference room, groups of senior staff officers of all three services were standing about in little knots, waiting to hear what had been decided. From a side door a naval officer came forward carrying a sheaf of papers and asked, 'What do you think the decision is going to be?' He explained that he had sets of signals ready to suit different contingencies. He did not have long to wait. General Eisenhower came out almost immediately. As he made for the main door, he came over and said: 'Well, Stagg, we're putting it on again. For heaven's sake hold the weather to what you told us and don't bring any more bad news.'[9]

CHAPTER NINE

MONDAY 5 JUNE
1944

Eisenhower's message to the troops:

Soldiers, Sailors and Airmen of the Allied Expeditionary Forces!: You are about to embark upon the Great Crusade, towards which we have striven these many months. The eyes of the world are upon you. The hopes and prayers of liberty-loving people everywhere march with you. In company with our brave Allies and brothers-in-arms on other Fronts you will bring about the destruction of the German war machine, the elimination of Nazi tyranny over oppressed peoples of Europe, and security for ourselves in a free world.

Your task will not be any easy one. Your enemy is well trained, well equipped and battle-hardened. He will fight savagely.

But this is the year 1944! Much has happened since the Nazi triumphs of 1940–41. The United Nations have inflicted upon the Germans great defeats, in open battle, man-to-man. Our air offensive has seriously reduced their strength in the air and their capacity to wage war on the ground. Our Home Fronts have given us an overwhelming superiority in weapons and munitions of war, and placed at our disposal great reserves of trained fighting men. The tide has turned! The free men of the world are marching together to Victory!

I have full confidence in your courage, devotion to duty and skill in battle. We will accept nothing less than full victory!

Good Luck! And let us all beseech the blessing of Almighty God upon this great and noble undertaking.[1]

Note written by Eisenhower and put into his wallet:

Our landings in the Cherbourg-Havre area have failed to gain a satisfactory foothold and I have withdrawn the troops. My decision to attack at this time and place was based upon the best information available. The troops, the air and the navy did all that bravery and devotion could do. If any blame or fault attaches to the attempt it is mine alone.[2]

CBS News, New York, 11.00, 5 June:

Up in Western Europe we've been plastering the German defences near the Channel coast for days . . . still no hint as to when the great invasion will begin.[3]

Brigadier E.E.E. Cass, commander 8th Infantry Brigade:

At about noon I set off to join my HQ ship, HMS *Goathland*, a Hunt class destroyer, in Portsmouth dockyard, but on the way the car broke down and we were stranded in the streets of Portsmouth. Time was pressing, and as always happens on these occasions, nobody was about to help us, but just in the nick of time an RN lorry hove in sight driven by a Wren. It was found to be full of dirty washing, but there was no time to be lost and we squeezed in and drove off. A good deal of amusement was given to the dockyard police when we arrived at the main gate and they looked in the back and saw what the cargo was, but we pressed on and drew alongside the gangway of our ship and jumped out of the back accompanied by various bits of washing. Perhaps the bosun's pipes trilled a little as we went up the gangway, but they kept straight faces under what must have been great provocation.

We soon sailed and saluted HMS *Victory* as we left the harbour and joined the stream of ships making for the open sea and the point south-east of the Isle of Wight known as Piccadilly Circus, from where the swept channels, all marked by dan buoys, led to the various beaches. The weather was cold, with a strong wind and heavy seas that made the ships pitch and roll heavily while the landing craft, with their flat bottoms, skated from side to side in a quite alarming manner. The afternoon passed slowly and the weather showed no sign of getting any better, but in spite of the spray that swept over the deck we managed to hold a service, a simple ceremony attended by sailors and soldiers alike, on the eve of battle.[4]

Diary of Captain A.D.C. Smith, No.4 Commando:

We embarked in a grotesque gala atmosphere more like a regatta than a page of history, with gay music from the ship's loudhailers and more than the usual quota of jocular farewells bandied between friends. It was a perfect summer evening, the Isle of Wight lay green and friendly, and tantalizingly peaceful, behind the tapestry of warships. At 21.00 we set out to war with Lord Lovat's piper playing in the bows. It was exhilarating, glorious and heartbreaking when the crew and troops began to cheer and the cheers came faintly across the water, gradually taken up by ship after ship ... I never loved England so truly as at that moment.[5]

Wireless Operator A. Baker, 4th/7th Dragoon Guards:

We eventually sailed off down the Solent at midday. Major Baker called all the 4th/7th chaps into the Captain's cabin, which was about the size of a double bed, and told us where we were headed. It turned out to be a little place between Caen and Arromanches called La Rivière. Our particular stretch of the beach was known as King Red beach and our rendezvous was at the village of Ver-sur-Mer.

Major B read out messages from Eisenhower and Montgomery, and told us that he personally thought we should all be very honoured to be in on this affair. I think most of us felt that we could have stood the disgrace of being left out of it.[6]

Sergeant Frank Murray, aged 22, HQ Company, 18th Infantry:

On the night of 5 June we left Weymouth Harbour and as we passed each ship that was anchored the men on board would salute as we passed.

That night, I was laying on my bunk next to my best buddy. We had received a mail call from home prior to leaving. While in England he had taken a furlough to Scotland and met a girl who he fell in love with. When his furlough was up and he returned to Weymouth, his girlfriend followed him and got a room in nearby Dorchester and they managed to see each other.

Well, anyway, he had written to his former girlfriend in the United States and she had written back and that was the letter he read to me that night. She had written that 'instead of being a war bride, I hope your girlfriend's a war widow.'

Well, she got her wish. He was killed in Normandy.[7]

Ross Munro, correspondent *The Canadian Press, on board HMS* **Hilary,** *3rd Division HQ Ship:*

What a spectacle that armada made sailing steadily south to France! On our right were lines of LCTs, carrying our self-propelled artillery regiments, infantry and tanks. The lines extended for two or three miles, with the craft low in the water and all flying the white ensign of the Royal Navy. On the other side of us were more LCTs and beyond them were scores and scores of landing ships of every type and size. Some had been at Dieppe and were going back to France, taking Canadians into battle again. Others had been on the North African landings, at Sicily, Reggio, Salerno and Anzio. They were the veterans of combined operations. Other ships were new. They came right from the yards in the United States, Britain and Canada.

Troopers, cargo boats, supply boats and hundreds of small craft were there. Through this shipping, fanned out over the Channel, were the protecting escort ships of the navy. Behind us was the Canadian destroyer *Algonquin*, in light blue camouflage, which curiously was the same colour as the battle patches of the 3rd Division. A flotilla of small landing craft, carrying commandos, lurched through the sea beside the *Algonquin*, taking each wave with a graceful lob of her bow while the little craft nearly foundered.

Other destroyers weaved through the fleet; corvettes and frigates kept a vigil for submarine attacks. Overhead were patrols of Spitfires, winging out from England in relays until dark.

On board you would never have known at first glance that this was one of the greatest nights in history. The officers gathered in the wardroom as usual for a drink before dinner. They sat down to a good meal. There was some talk of the operation, but not a great deal. A naval officer at our table recalled his yachting days around Cowes away back in peacetime.

This seeming indifference is common before big actions, and it always covers an undercurrent of electric emotion, but this time I had thought that possibly the sheer magnitude and drama of these hours would stir the participants to a point where they should display some excitement. It was just the same as before. It might have been another manoeuvre. Looking around the wardroom as the officers smoked their pipes and cigarettes after dinner, I thought how similar it was to those training days when we had made landings on the English coast.[8]

Diary of Captain Douglas Aitken, medical officer, 24th Lancers:

We are on our way. Still a bit heady from the correspondent's booze last night; barged into the chief engineer's cabin to find Ian and the CBC war correspondent with one or two of the ship's officers drinking an odd drink made from pure alcohol which has something to do with torpedoes, to which they add lemons and oranges. Very tasty and very potent. I only had two. The captain shows me round the bridge, including the radar – all beautifully fitted and very interesting. Try to write home but it seems a hopeless task and no certain knowledge of when any letters will reach home. The crew say they will take them back and post them in England.[9]

Pfc Joseph S. Blaylock Sr, aged 24, B Battery, 20th Field Artillery, 4th Motorized Division:

That afternoon we began to pull out of the harbour. We could see we were joining a lot of other warships after we got out. There were big battleships and cruisers and destroyers that were escorting us and that was a sight to see. Just as far as you could see there were ships.

After we set sail we went back down below and at about 10.30 we had a church service. Colonel Bryant from division headquarters gave the sermon. I remember that. He was once our minister on the base where I went to church, so I enjoyed that very much and he came back by after the sermon and said a little prayer for me and I appreciated that very much.[10]

Sergeant John R. Slaughter, aged 19, D Company, 1st Battalion, 116th Infantry:

I remember Captain Schilling's last pep talk on board our LSI, HMS *Empire Javelin*. The company was assembled below deck and the skipper was standing about half-way up a steel stairway. He had us at ease as he leaned against the railing.

He had assembled us for a last meeting before loading onto

landing crafts. We listened intently over the roar of the ship's engines to every word he said. We were sitting on the floor and some in the back of the room were standing. The mood was solemn and Schilling was also rather subdued as he said, 'This is the real McCoy . . . the dry runs are over, the amphibious assault training is concluded.' We knew what he meant and it was a relief to know that finally we were doing something that would shorten the war.

The endless training on the moors of southern England, day after bloody day, had caused one of the men to say, and he spoke for all of us, 'I'll be damned glad to get in there and get it over with, just to get a rest.' The training was so severe that the thought of a shooting war didn't scare any of us. We didn't know what it would be like to see one's buddy blown to hell.

Captain Schilling said he was 'proud to lead this company into battle . . . the enemy would be well trained and would fight like hell to protect its homeland.' The sector we were to occupy, Dog Green, on Omaha Beach, would have fortified bunkers protecting the Vierville draw, but only one or two of them would be occupied. The report was that the quality of the troops defending our sector would not be first-rate soldiers. Polish and Russian volunteers and over-age German Home Guard would be the under-dog opponent and he didn't expect them to be fanatical defenders.

He stressed 'Cross the beach fast, gain the high ground and get into a perimeter of defence. The enemy has a large reserve force that can counter-attack in twenty-four hours and ten minutes. By then the tanks and heavy artillery will be in place and you should be able to repel their best efforts.'

He said that each of the company's landing craft should guide in on the Vierville church steeple, which was a prominent landmark that could be seen from the sea. The last thing he said was, 'When I call the roll in Isigny [the Division's objective, nine miles inland] tonight, I want everyone to say "Here!" Good luck!'

Schilling's words sent a chill up my spine and the hair stood on my neck. I don't remember any cheering or loud hoots from the men, but they were, as I was, 'fired up and ready.'[11]

Pfc William E. Jones, aged 25, 1 Company, 8th Infantry Regiment, 4th Division:

While we were headed across the Channel nearly all of us painted something on our field jackets, usually the name of our state or something. Of course, I had Tennessee on mine. There were very few people from Tennessee on that thing, but someone walked up to me as I was standing at the rail and said, 'What part of Tennessee are you from?'

I looked around and it was a friend of mine who lived a few miles down the road from me. Well I was really glad to see that old boy, his name was Thurman Charlton. He was in the Coast Guard, a coxswain on one of the landing craft.

While we were talking Charlton asked me, 'If you don't make it, is there anything that you want me to tell the people at home?' Of course, I felt like a big dog anyhow, so I said, 'Just tell them that we went down swinging.'[12]

Brigadier the Lord Lovat DSO MC, commander 1st Commando Brigade:

There was a knifing wind in the Channel. Rupert Curtis described the sea as 'lumpy' when I joined him on the bridge.

The weather had changed since we left the shelter of the Isle of Wight; so flat was it in Stokes Bay that a New Zealand boat officer's gramophone playing 'Hearts of Oak' carried over and beyond our ships as the brigade supped off biscuits, American plum duff and self-heating soup.

Waiting for the darkness, Derek [Mills-Roberts] clambered over from his motor launch to mine. Immediate worries were over, with time to unwind before touch-down. Now the parcel was in the post and out of my hands. The navy found a half-bottle of gin. Later, amid unseemly merriment, Peter Young, another bachelor, was summoned to attend the party – not, as expected, for a fond farewell, but to study some remarkable information in a paperback discovered below decks. The guidance in Dr Marie Stopes' *Marital Advice for Young Couples* was full of surprises. Soft beds and hard battles had something in common after all! The officers returned to their commands, shaken by the revelations – hopping across lengthening shadows on gently heaving decks. An amplified band played 'Life on

the Ocean Wave'; I took my boots off for a last kip on Rupert's bunk
and slept well. I can snore through any form of disturbance, provided
I go to bed with a quiet mind.[13]

Hanson W. Baldwin, military editor, the New York Times, assigned to the USS Augusta:

On Monday, June 5, *Augusta*, with hundreds of ships and craft ahead
and astern of her, got under way from Plymouth Harbour, headed
south into the Channel towards the 'great adventure'. The sea was
choppy; mists hung low over the waters as we steamed independently
at about 15 knots through a swept and buoyed channel towards the
Bay of the Seine. It was an eerie passage, almost sepulchral in the light
fog. Visibility was adequate but limited.

On the way, the loudspeaker told us of the fall of Rome the day
before – brief cheers. Then, out of the mist, we passed the battleship
Texas; then *Black Prince* and *Glasgow*, wearing the White Ensign, the
Frenchmen *Georges Leygues* and *Montcalm*, a swarm of destroyers. In
mid-afternoon, I was startled briefly when we tested our 20-mm and
40-mm AA guns.

Towards nightfall we speeded up and then sat down in the
wardroom to steak, mashed potatoes, frozen green beans and cream
peas, with the usual jokes about 'the last supper' and feeding the
condemned men. Minute after minute, hour after hour, we passed
great convoys of slow-moving landing craft, some of them making a
rough crossing, all of them crammed with the youth of Britain and
America.

Some men waved, or raised a hand; there was an occasional cheer
or yell, but for the most part the foreknowledge of what was to
come, the storming of the beaches, and the querulous pangs of
seasickness, dampened overt greetings.

Few in *Augusta* slept much that night; the adrenaline was flowing.
It was after midnight before a smudged line, low on the horizon,
revealed the coast of France. Then, as we closed, we heard the faint
hum, distinct above the *Augusta*'s blowers and the creaks and groans
of a ship in a seaway, of aircraft engines – bombers and troop carriers
bound for France.[14]

Flying Officer Colin Woodward, 161 Squadron, RAF:

I was the pilot of a Stirling on a mission to drop agents behind enemy lines and that night we had a special briefing during which it was emphasized that we should maintain absolute radio silence, no matter what we saw.

We were on our way out from Tempsford in Bedfordshire at about 3,000 feet when we were suddenly confronted by the most awesome sight. The whole night sky, high above and filling the entire area in front of us, was filled with myriads of red, blue and white lights rotating very slowly like one vast coloured whirlpool.

It seemed impossible not to be engulfed, and we were without lights. Although we knew that something was going on, we were not aware that the French landings were imminent and so there was no explanation for the phenomenon. It was only later we discovered that the lights were the gliders and their tugs marshalling in the area of Benson.

All the members of my crew, except the rear gunner, crowded into the cockpit in amazed disbelief. Because of the dead quiet of the radio silence, the sight was unbelievably uncanny. Suddenly the spell was split wide open when a Canadian pilot must have accidentally pressed his transmitting button in his excitement. 'What the fucking hell,' he said, 'are those bleeding lights?'[15]

Lieutenant H. 'Nick' Knilans, USAF, attached to 617 Squadron RAF:

At the beginning of May we were told that the Squadron would be doing no more operations for a month as we would be training for a special operation. An English scientist, Dr Cockburn, wanted us to simulate a large convoy of ships, fourteen miles wide and heading across the Channel at seven knots.

Eight crews would fly for four hours. Eight more would take their place for another four hours. They would all be dropping 'window', the aluminium strips we had dropped around Hamburg. The pilots would have to do some precision flying: each plane would fly thirty-five seconds on course, make a controlled turn and fly a reverse course for thirty-two seconds, then a slow turn back on the first course while throwing out more window. I would be starting the original course slightly ahead of where the previous lot dropped in the water. Thus, there would be no interruption blips on the German radar. I had to fly at 200 m.p.h. in a series of circles that carried me forward at only 8 m.p.h. I would have to do this for two hours before a second pilot would take over.

On 5 June Wingco Cheshire briefed us for the operation. He said the invasion would begin that evening. My wave of eight planes would take off at 23.00, we would fly our circular flight pattern over the water for two hours before being relieved by eight more planes at 03.00.

There were twelve air crew aboard R-Roger, my Lancaster. Another crew had come along to share the flying and windowing duties. Harry, my navigator, guided us into position. I began my hour of very intense flying duty – on course, turning, levelling out, on course, turning, minute after minute. All the time Harry's voice was droning in my earphones.

'Tighten the turn, you're two seconds slow . . . You're three feet too low . . . On course, on course . . . Begin turn now! . . . Ease up, you're three seconds fast . . .'

This went on for an hour. I had to keep within four seconds elapsed time and within five feet of altitude at all times. It was a relief to have the other crew take over. Pilot Officer 'Caz' Castognola slipped into my seat, his navigator took over from Harry, and three of his crew relieved those of mine who had been dropping window bundles at four-second intervals for an hour.

When the second wave took over from us we had to return to base at an altitude below 1,000 feet. It was only later that we learned the ruse worked to perfection.[16]

Corporal Maurice Chauvet, French Troop, No.4 Commando:

10.30 p.m. We now know where we are going. We shall land tomorrow at H Hour + 20 – 7.30 a.m., west of Ouistreham. Up till now, this part of France has been for us nothing more than maps and snaps. For twelve days we have been learning by heart the minutest details about the roads in the area we are going to invade, but all this had been too abstract. It had not sunk in that we were actually landing in France. I needed to see those proper names on the map, then the operation meant something: liberation. I think that we all felt the same way. With the maps we had been given Montgomery's message: very English but very friendly.

All we can do is wait. I feel very tranquil, have no special desires at all. The sea is rather rough, and the LCI is rocking rather more than when we were training, but I'm not bothered. I am thinking of the cigarettes I have in the pocket of my battledress, and I hope that they will not be soaked when I disembark. I am in the bows of the LCI in a small cabin five or six metres square. It has two ladders leading to the deck. When the hatch is closed, the only light is an electric one. On either side are wooden benches, rather like the ones you see in a railway station. The fact that 25 men with all their equipment can squeeze into such a small space is amazing. The radio sets take up a lot of space. The light is dim and though the walls are painted white it is hard to distinguish the faces of my comrades sitting opposite. Their faces are familiar, of course, but I do not know their real identities. In the Free French Forces you seldom know who you have in front of you, most have changed their names, especially in the Commandos. Often during the last years we felt we were just mercenaries, but since we have joined No.4 Commando we have felt at home. The Colonel speaks to us in French and the last months have been pleasant.

There is what sounds like thunder in the sky above us and I go on deck. It is hundreds of planes flying above us, most of them towing gliders. This is the 6th Airborne Division which will be dropped inland from where we're going to land in about an hour. If we do not succeed in joining them in the morning, they won't survive. It is cold outside and I go back below. The room is dim but warm. In a corner I can see a young boy who found out a few days ago that his English girl friend is pregnant. He applied to get married, but was told it was impossible. So he went to the Colonel and explained that he knew he was going to die on the first day and that he wanted to give his son his name. Somehow the Colonel arranged it and he got married just before he went to Titchfield camp. He is certainly going to die, and he knows it. I am wondering whether soldiers in earlier wars had the same premonition that they were going to die but carried on just the same.

The cabin is full again, no one can sleep, no one is hungry. Silently we wait with our equipment around us. In our group there are graduates, workers, all mixed together, brought together because they were disgusted with France in 1940, or just because of personal matters. They have chosen to live among commandos and to die if necessary and be buried with the words 'Unknown Allied Soldier' on their graves.[17]

Pfc Robert Koch, C Company, 116th Regiment:

We knew we were going to be in the first wave because our colonel had won the toss and chosen to be first. Maybe if it had been me I might have chose third, but he took first, so we were first.

When we boarded the ship the weather looked so bad we wondered if it would ever clear up and whether the whole thing would be called off. We weren't aware of what was going on except through rumours. There were rumours that we might go to Africa and come up that way and then we heard the whole thing had been changed and we were going to Norway. They were all truthful rumours because the fella that told you said he got it right from the general himself.

We played cards, relaxed as much as possible, thought about our families and prayed. I myself was not a church-going individual but I enjoyed reading the scriptures in the Bible at that time because I knew what was ahead of me and realized that if there was any time in life I needed God on my side it was then.

We would try to play different games, to entertain ourselves and get our minds off the real objective, but we would drift back into quietness, more or less thinking about our homes and things like that.

Quite a few boys wrote letters and gave them to friends to send home or see that their parents got them. They were farewell letters. Some boys said that they knew they'd never make it. We used to tell them we thought they were talking like crazy, because we weren't going to get hurt. Basically I was speaking for myself. Frankly I never thought I'd get hurt, I never thought I'd be shot at, I felt confident that I'd make it.

However, I did more praying during that period of time than I think I've ever done in my life and I don't regret it. I think it was with the help of God, and the sincerity of my prayers, that helped get me through. I wasn't yellow, but I was scared, no question about it. I was scared to death.[18]

Captain James Milnor Roberts, ADC to General Gerow,
commander V Corps, US Army:

We weighed anchor and left Portland naval base around, I'd say, two
o'clock in the afternoon. The boatswain's mate blew everybody to
attention on the ship and shortly thereafter they put on a record of
Winston Churchill. Churchill gave a very inspirational message to the
troops, telling them that they were the flower of their country, they
were going to liberate the European Continent from the dark forces
of Hitler, which might otherwise prevail for a thousand years, and all
this good stuff. Shortly after that there was another record, this time
by Franklin Roosevelt and along the same lines, that 'All of you
finest people of our American youth are in the prayers of your
countrymen here in the United States, and we know you'll succeed
and you have our fondest wishes, etcetera.'

So, we all thought, isn't that nice? If you had a couple of violins
you could put it to music. Well then, about half an hour later, the
aide men passed out two rubbers to everybody on the ship! I couldn't
believe it. This kid came up to me and said, 'Captain, I have this for
you,' and he gives me two rubbers. He said, 'I also have two rubbers
for the General.' I said, 'I heard we were going to war. What do you
think we ought to do with these?' He said, 'I don't know, but I have
the orders.'

We thought this was absolutely hilarious. I don't know whose
idea it was to pass out rubbers to everybody in the invasion force,
but they did. As a matter of fact, some of them were put to good use,
mine in particular. I had a very nice watch. It was a Universal
Geneva, twenty-one-jewel watch, which had been given to me the
year before by my father and I thought it was just simply great that I
had this nice watch.

On D-Day it was obvious that I might get soaking wet and I felt
that if my watch got soaked with sea water it would be the end of it.
So I thought hmm, I'll put it in a rubber. So I got the rubber out and
I put the watch in it, tied it up very securely and put it in my pocket.
I tried to get my wallet in the other rubber, but it wouldn't stretch.
So, as a matter of fact, during the actual landing I got soaked
completely up to my neck and if it had not been for the rubber my
watch would not have survived.[19]

Captain Robert Neave, aged 26, second in command, B Squadron, 13th/18th Royal Hussars:

While on the ship, waiting to go, I remember writing a letter, sitting in the hot sun and having this feeling that you could walk across to the Isle of Wight; the impression I had was that you could literally walk from Portsmouth Harbour to the Isle of Wight, just by stepping from LCT to LCT on the ships moored there. The letter was either to my parents or my girlfriend. You weren't allowed to write anything very much and I remember having to read all the poor old troops' letters. It was a fairly harmless exercise, but one used to skim through them because one was expected to, to make sure that they didn't say anything silly.

I remember a sort of feeling of release that we were at least away from the shore and on our way, a certain sort of feeling of, 'Well, thank God, we've got this far.' Not that we had survived so far, but thank God we had got no more commitments to training and that it was going to happen.

I don't think one talked about it very much, but in the back of one's mind one rather looked forward to it. Don't forget, we were a very, very good regiment. We were a regiment that was a family concern in many cases, people had had fathers who commanded. It was a family concern and we had some very good chaps. I had the highest possible opinion of the morale. I don't remember any feelings of impending disaster or anything of that sort.

On the crossing I remember going up on deck with the captain and looking in front of us and there was nothing! Absolutely nothing, just sea. Then I can remember looking behind me and seeing the place absolutely solid with pinpoint lights; it was the most extraordinary feeling. It looked as if one was at the centre of the most enormous armada and the sensation was really very dramatic. This was in the middle of the night, before it started to get unpleasant. I remember seeing stars in the sky as well and it was a very remarkable feeling to know that the whole of the British army was launching itself upon the French coast.

To say one had feelings of destiny wouldn't be quite right, but to say one hadn't wouldn't be quite right either. I heard later that one chap was clever enough to read to the troops the St Crispin's day speech from Shakespeare's *Henry V*; I thought it was remarkable that he could do it. Someone else read the Lord's Prayer, which I thought was very intelligent. My feelings afterwards were that this is the sort of thing one ought to have done and didn't.

I was not sick at all; I was surprised that I wasn't, but I wasn't. I got a little sleep. I interfered with the chaps as little as possible. I went back down to find out if they were all right, had had their grub, that the tanks were secure. I asked them if they wanted any help from me over anything at all, but some of them were very sick and they wanted to be left alone. They had their own thoughts as well, which I did. I went down again in the middle of the night, found half of them were asleep and the other half, very dozy, so I left them alone.

I remember getting up and saying to myself, well, this is it. One was very young, very keen, very well trained and one had an absolute 100 per cent feeling that one was going to survive, no question of it.[20]

Journal of Lance Bombardier C. Morris, 3 Troop, 6 Commando:

We had a good stock of food on board, including tinned soup, cocoa and packets of biscuits, so we all had a good feed. Also swallowed sea-sickness pills that were distributed.

The sea seemed to be getting rougher and our craft began to toss and roll so much that it was all we could do to keep on our feet. The lads seemed to have quietened down somewhat. Many of them, including the sergeant major and the skipper were old campaigners and probably knew what we were going to run into. Some played cards and others just sat thinking and talking. Ginger Caldwell, one of my bren-gun mates, and myself got down on the floor to have a sleep, covering ourselves with our blankets, but our sleep was very broken because the storm grew worse and we were thrown all over the place. I think the boat did everything bar capsize and to make matters worse we now began to have terrible headaches owing to the pills we had taken preventing us from relieving our stomachs of the food it obviously did not want. We felt that bad we began to wish we were dead and I do not think any of us really worried about the coming events.[21]

Dr J.H. Patterson, RAMC, medical officer No.4 Commando:

It was tea-time when I noticed the minesweepers beginning to creep out and I realized the show was on. At lunch-time I had been

offering heavy odds that it would be cancelled again. I felt appalled
when I looked at the sea. It was blowing half a gale from the south-
west and banking up black and beastly for what promised to be a
dirty night. The 'Operation On' signal came through; we were issued
with real maps and real place names. Our job was to land at zero plus
thirty on Red Beach (Sword) – that is to say, on the extreme left
flank of the whole invasion.

Now all the shipping was quietly sailing out through the booms. It
was wonderful to watch the steady stream of craft slipping out past
the Portsmouth forts, silent and orderly, with no sirens or fuss, their
balloons marking those already hidden by intervening ships.

The wind howled and it rained in vicious scuds. The skipper said
in his speech: 'The High Command must be counting heavily on
surprise, for the Germans must surely think that not even Englishmen
could be fools enough to start an invasion on a night like this.'

Feeling small, I set about my final packing. I spliced my identity
discs on a new string and gloomily hung them round my neck. I
dished out sea-sick tablets and morphine and talked to all the troops
on final medical plans. I had a heated tussle with the brigade major
on the subject of the rum issue, finally settling that the troops could
have it thirty minutes before landing and not prior to getting into
the LCAs. With cold and sea-sickness ahead, this would have been
folly.

I had a bath ('washing off the B. coli in case you stop one', as the
naval doctor said), ate a huge dinner of I don't know what, soaped
my socks, dressed for battle, and, after midnight, rolled utterly
wearily into my bunk.[22]

Percy Wallace, coastguard stationed in hut on the top of St Alban's Head:

During that day those of us at St Alban's Head witnessed something
no man had seen before. Close under the headland I looked down on
the landing craft; I could see the troops in battledress on board.
Beyond them, line after line of tank landing craft side by side,
escorted by motor launches. Then came the armed trawlers, the
ocean-going tugs and behind them, echelons of mine-sweepers. Out
to sea, destroyers and frigates took up their stations. On the horizon,
coming up from the west beyond Portland, the battleships and heavy
cruisers waited. Throughout the day, the ships weighed anchor and

by dusk the sea was empty once again. Then the sound of aircraft in the sky. I said to my wife, 'This is it.' Later, when we were going to bed, we looked at one another for a moment. I said quietly, 'A lot of men are going to die tonight. We should pray for them.'[23]

BBC French Service, 21.15 hours:

Today the Supreme Commander directs us to say this: 'In due course instructions of great importance will be given to you through this channel. But it will not always be possible to give these instructions at a previously announced time. Therefore you must get into the habit of listening at all hours.'[24]

Diary of Guillaume Mercader, member of Alliance Resistance network, Bayeux:

I was, one last time, to meet Delente in Paris and was to be informed of an imminent landing and this by means of the announcement of two messages to be broadcast by the BBC the day before the one which was going to be the D-Day. For our region we had to listen at 6.30 p.m. for the words, 'It is hot in Suez' and, 'The dice are on the carpet.'

At the end of the afternoon, upon return from a mission in Lamberville, I already noticed a very important and unusual activity of the Allied air force. In Bayeux, as early as 6 p.m. the radio was turned on in my cellar. At 6.30 p.m. the first message said: 'It is hot in Suez. It is hot in Suez.' Then, the second came: 'The dice are on the carpet. The dice are on the carpet.' Twice again, as well as some other messages that did not concern us. Stunned by listening to these messages, an instant emotion invaded me, but quickly enough I came to myself and, after having turned off the radio and climbing the steps from the cellar four at a time, I informed in the first place my wife of what I had heard. I then took my bicycle and went to contact my principal responsible people of an imminent landing.[25]

General Blumentritt, Chief of Staff C-in-C West, on being told of BBC broadcast:

What kind of general, my children, would announce a forthcoming invasion over the radio? You can forget it.[26]

General Richter, commander 716th Infantry Division at Caen,
addressing weekly staff conference:

I have received a warning that the invasion will be launched between
the 3rd and the 10th. I should perhaps add, gentlemen, that we have
received similar warnings every full-moon period and every no-moon
period since April.[27]

General Walter Warlimont, deputy chief, Armed Forces
Operations Staff:

The weather was right for an invasion and we had been alerted to the
possibility for some weeks. Our chief intelligence source was the radio
and our intercepts revealed that the invasion would take place on the
morning of 6 June 1944. This information was relayed to headquarters
on the afternoon of 5 June. Hitler knew it and General Jodl knew it,
but the information was not made available to the troops in Normandy.

In Hitler's eyes, General Jodl, unlike other men, did not make
military mistakes. General Jodl knew the state of alert under which
the troops in northern France were operating and did not consider it
necessary to give out another order. Furthermore, there had been a
number of other false alarms prior to this one.[28]

Rommel's weekly situation report to von Rundstedt:

Estimate of overall situation. Systematic continuation and intensifica-
tion of enemy air-raids and more intensive mine-laying in own
harbours . . . indicates an advance in the enemy's preparations for
invasion. Concentration of air attacks on coastal defences between
Dunkirk and Dieppe and on Seine-Oise bridges confirms presumption
as to *Schwerpunkt* [area] of large-scale landing . . . Since 1.6.44 increased
transmissions on enemy radio of warning messages to French Resistance organizations, [but] judging from experience to date, [this is] not
explicable as an indication of invasion being imminent . . .[29]

CHAPTER TEN

CHOCKS AWAY

As the great armada ploughed relentlessly across the stormy waters of the Channel, the airborne forces who were to secure vital bridges and ground behind the beaches prepared for their drop into the Normandy night, by parachute and glider . . .

Sergeant William T. Dunfee, aged 21, 1 Company, 3rd Battalion, 505th Parachute Infantry:

There is no greater bore than waiting around to go into combat. You know damned well there is nothing you can do to change anything. Everyone sweats it out in his own way. We all put on a happy face for appearance's sake. I observed one young replacement who was really down. I got the company 'barber kit' out and told him he needed a haircut, that I wanted him to look good when we entered Paris. I was able to talk him out of his funk and trim his hair in the process. I assured him that every man in that hangar was as scared as he was, including myself. I feel I relieved him of some of his anxiety. I hope so anyway; he was one of the first killed.[1]

General Matthew B. Ridgway, commander 82nd Airborne Division:

Knowing that it might be death that awaited me, in the last moment before I left my quarters for the take-off fields I had sat down to say my last good-byes, to try to express something of the deep pride I felt in the men with whom I was now to go into battle. On the bottom of my own photograph, knowing that somebody would find it if I did not come back, I wrote these lines: 'To the members of the 82nd Airborne Division, with everlasting affection and appreciation of life shared with them in the service of our country. May their incomparable courage, fidelity, soldierly conduct and fighting spirit ever keep for this Division a place second to none in our Army.'

It was no masterpiece of literary composition, I know. But it expressed my feelings. And as I took my place in the plane in the hard bucket seat, and buckled my seat belt tight around me, I felt a great serenity. All that I knew to do had been done, and I was ready to accept whatever was to come. From then on, there was no backward glancing to happy days gone by, no inner tremors brought on by fearful imaginings of what might lie ahead. My soul was at peace, my heart was light, my spirits almost gay.

The mood of the men around me seemed equally tranquil as we lifted up, engines roaring, to join the great sky train that was on its way to France. I looked at my watch. It was 10 p.m., June 5, 1944.[2]

Lieutenant General Richard 'Windy' Gale, 6th Airborne Division:

Before we took off, Sir Trafford Leigh Mallory came round all the stations to bid us farewell and success in our venture. Among others who came down to see us was Wing Commander Dennis Wheatley [the novelist], who was at that time employed in the War Cabinet offices. He brought with him a bottle of the most delicious hock I ever remember tasting, and he drank to our health and success. I am by nature superstitious. I was, therefore, very touched when as a token or talisman of good fortune he gave me a small crusader sword; this I believe he had had for years. On my last exercise in England I had the good fortune to pick up a four-leafed clover. Superstition is a very funny thing and I am never quite sure how deep it runs. All I do know is that there is so much in life that is without apparent reason, so much that is so completely unforeseeable, so much that just baffles reason, that I do not laugh at little superstitious fads.

During the few days I had been on the station I had got to know the station commander and his staff very well. I remember I had once said that I liked treacle very much indeed. It was a thoughtful, friendly, and very charming gesture, therefore, when Group Captain Surplice handed me a tin of treacle to take to France just as I was emplaning.[3]

Sergeant Thomas B. Buff, Division HQ Company, 101st Airborne:

We had gotten to our aerodrome around three or four o'clock on the afternoon of June 5. Briefing was over; everyone having been briefed and briefed again. Now, everyone was on hand. All officers were there with the men of their particular section, casually going over plans and alternate plans, checking maps, technical equipment, etcetera. Last-minute preparations for an early morning 'vertical invasion' of Fortress Europe went forward in exactly the same manner as had been done for our many problems or field exercises. There was no visible sign of nervousness, tenseness, brooding, doubt, and certainly not fear. Time and again we had gone through this very same procedure in our training to equip ourselves for the moment so near at hand; at least we hoped it was near at hand and that this would not develop into the well-known dry run.

While we were blackening our faces and hands, Butler, Bill Smith and Phil Romano, who had already completed their make-up, combined forces to put on an ad-lib minstrel act for us. We laughed until our sides hurt at their mad antics, their exaggerated Southern drawl.

General Taylor had already spoken to the officers and men. Unfortunately for us, this occurred before we reached the airdrome. It was he who, as a tribute to his predecessor, Major General William C. Lee, asked each of us to yell 'Bill Lee!' as we left the door of our plane over France. All of my friends, and all of the line company boys with who I later talked, bellowed 'Bill Lee!' when making their exit.[4]

Sergeant Jack Harries, A Company, 9th Battalion, The Parachute Regiment:

To say that one moved off to the aircraft in a smart soldier-like manner would be untrue. We all looked like pregnant ducks carrying everything but the kitchen sink. I don't think any of us felt we would jump from the aircraft – we would fall out perhaps with some help from the RAF despatcher with a boot in our backs.

Now for a mental check. What was I carrying? A sten gun, which would eventually be stuffed inside the parachute harness against my chest. Webbing equipment and small pack which contained so much that I intended to jump with this in my arms with it attached by a length of strong string to the D on my parachute harness so that I could let it down after I was free of the aircraft so that it would hang below me and I would hopefully find it on landing at the end of the string. Four sten magazines filled with 9mm ammunition, a spare small box of 9mm, two 36 Mills grenades, one phosphorous grenade, two sticks of plastic explosive for the anti-tank grenade, mess tin, knife, fork, spoon, twenty-four-hour ration pack, map, message pad, entrenching tool, parachute helmet, maroon beret, mirror, bootlaces, spare socks, singlet and briefs, small towel and washing and shaving kit, pay book, handkerchiefs, writing paper, envelopes, pen, pencil, binoculars, torch, French money, field dressing, one packet (three) contraceptives, toilet paper, boiled sweets, camouflage smock, boot polish/dubbin, blanco and brush, comb, plus of course any personal items.

In addition to this there were the escape gadgets hidden around the clothing – two brass buttons sewn onto the flies of my trousers which, one balanced on the other, formed a compass, a small metal saw about four inches long bedded in rubber and sewn into my trousers, a small compass sewn into the lining of my jumping smock together with two silk maps of the area. A bonus tucked into my smock was half a bottle of brandy which had been issued to officers and senior NCOs for medicinal purposes.

Memories still come back to me as we staggered towards the aircraft. It was strange, the chaps seemed reticent to talk to one another and even the usual jokes were quiet. I wondered about my wife and little five-year-old daughter, who had no idea where I was at that moment. I wondered if they were having an air raid, which was usual being only some twenty-five miles from central London. If that was the case then they would no doubt be in the Morrison shelter, which doubled as a table, in the living room. I knew it was no picnic, having spent so much time in an air raid shelter, particularly as our second baby was expected in about six or seven weeks. When would I see the new baby? I told my wife I was volunteering for parachuting and asked her if she minded. Her reply must have been typical of many wives: 'If that's what you really want to do and it helps finish the war quicker, then I don't mind.'5

Lieutenant Parker A. Alford, 3rd Battalion, 501st Parachute Infantry:

After blackening our faces, sharpening our knives and checking our equipment for the 100th time, we got into formation and walked to the airfield. This was about 10 p.m. On the way to the airfield we were swinging along, some of us singing, and a little old Cockney lady ran up and said 'Give 'em hell, Yanks.' A lump came into my throat, both of fear and pride.

We waited at the airfield for about thirty minutes and at about 10.30 p.m. Colonel Johnson, our regimental commander, came to see us. He had a pearl-handled .45 on each hip, knives in his belt and many hand grenades on his person. He came roaring into the hangar in his jeep and gave a short pep talk.

As he grabbed a dagger from his boot, his concluding remarks were, as I recall: 'Before I see the dawn of another day I want to stick this knife into the meanest, dirtiest, filthiest Nazi in all of Europe.'

He returned the knife to his boot and a great roar went up from all portions of the hangar. As these young men applauded their commanding officer, you knew this thing had to succeed.[6]

Staff Sergeant Leonard Levenson, aged 27, Divisional HQ, 82nd Airborne Division:

When the time came to go, someone neglected to tell the company commander that me and another guy were over with the 101st HQ, so he said, well, if he's not here, we'll put someone else in his place. So they took this kid and assigned him to where I was supposed to be, in a glider with a trailer full of maps. So when I finally showed up I was put in with a group that was full of scraps, you know, a guy from here and a guy from there.

Finally, we drew our grenades and we got the ammunition and we got all the stuff and we had the flags sewn on and we had the funny money and we had the maps and we got this little printed message from Eisenhower. They lined us up. It was still daylight but it must have been ten, ten-thirty, when the company commander read the message from Eisenhower and gave the men an opportunity to say a prayer and that was it. There was no leading of a prayer, just the opportunity to say a prayer. I didn't, I was the only guy that didn't. I didn't believe in it, that was my belief, not to say a prayer.

Then we went off to the field, I guess trucks took us over there. By that time it was dark, but not completely dark, kind of twilight. And we loaded and we took off and as soon as we took off, it was like a big relief. You know, hell, here we go. There was a whole lot of tension before that, the whole day was very tense, everybody wanted to be left alone, there was very little kidding around that day, it was dead serious. But once the glider took off, I remember I was kind of relaxed. I smoked, we all did, kidded around a little bit.

Chances of survival? That's the kind of thing you kept to yourself, you didn't talk to people about that. Nobody ever told us that only 50 per cent of us were going to make it. I wasn't a rifleman. If I was a rifleman, I would have thought of it, perhaps. If I was in the First Division coming in over the beach, I would have thought of it. Those poor bastards, that was carnage. Everybody thinks of parachutists as something tough, but what we did was nothing compared with what they had. I wasn't gung ho, even if it sounds gung ho, but I knew I had to go because I had a job to do.

The glider I should have been in landed behind German lines – of course we were all behind German lines, but this was way behind. The kid who took my place was wounded and was taken to a German field hospital. It was bombed by the RAF and he was killed, this kid who took my place. He's buried in Normandy in the cemetery right above the beach. He came from Cincinnati and his name was Raymond Jungclas.[7]

Pfc George Alex, aged 19, 82nd Airborne Division:

First thing we did, flying over, was pitch our gas masks out the door. We didn't want to be carrying any gas masks with us. We figured the Germans wouldn't use gas and we didn't want to jump with the darn thing. It wraps round you and it's an uncomfortable thing to carry. The English Channel must be full of gas masks, thousands of them.

As the time was getting closer I was getting nervous, getting butterflies in my stomach. I was hoping I wouldn't run into the same problem we had when we were making our drop into Sicily and our own navy shot us down by mistake. It only takes one man to pull the trigger and then everybody else follows suit. I thought, well, this might happen again and I hope it doesn't. During our briefing we were told that the entire coast of France was mined, heavily mined, fields were flooded, poles were stuck in the ground to keep our gliders from coming in. So we didn't know what to expect and of course we expected the worst.

All this is going through your mind. You're wondering: What am I doing here? Why did I volunteer? Am I crazy? You know it is getting close to daylight and it is getting close to the time to go. Then one man gets air sick and pulls his steel helmet off to heave into it. And then everybody else down the line follows suit. Everyone is heaving, dry heaves, waiting, waiting to get out of that aeroplane. We are all sick and the plane stinks and we are ready to get out any time. Let's get the green light on and get out of this place.

When the time came to go, out the door we went. We didn't hesitate for one moment. We were happy to get out of that thing, so off we went. Yes, I was afraid. I was nineteen years old and I was afraid.[8]

Flight Lieutenant P.M. Bristow, Dakota pilot, C Flight, 575 Squadron:

The first to get airborne in the last of the daylight were all towing gliders. Never shall I forget the first one of all for he had just about used up all the runway and was still on the ground. Around the periphery of the airfield stretched a low dry-stone Cotswold wall and a load of shingle had been tipped against the wall at either end of the runways. It may have been imagination, and remember the light was failing, it may have been a despairing heave back on the control column or it may have been a bit of both, but it seemed to all of us who were watching that the Dakota ran its wheels up the shingle bank and was literally catapulted into the air.

Aircraft carrying paratroopers started their take-off about an hour later and not until it was quite dark. There should have been a full moon that night but there was 10/10ths cloud cover so the night was dark. We had normal runway lighting for take-off but no navigation lights were used and we had to observe strict radio silence. Our signal to go was a green light from the control caravan at the end of the runway and we went off at pretty long intervals of say one minute, or thirty seconds. There was certainly no sign of the aircraft ahead of you by the time it was your turn to go. The whole flight was scheduled: so long after take-off and turn onto such and such a course, after another interval turn to a different heading, with time to leave our coast at Littlehampton, time to make landfall in Normandy and a time to drop. Streams of aircraft were going off from several other airfields, many destined for the same DZ, so they all had to be interlocked. So far as I could judge, the staff work was good.

We were supposed to be flying in vees of three and I was third in my vee so I kept my throttles well open to catch up with the others in front. Formation flying is not a normal part of a transport pilot's expertise, but we had done a little in the preceding months, but not at night, yet here we were on a particularly dark night. I eventually caught up with the fellows in front and found there were four of them! I decided I would be much more relaxed if I dropped back and flew on my own.

Bill Dyson, my navigator, was giving me regular fixes from his Gee Box [a navigational device developed for night bombing] and confirmed we were on course and running to time. We had taken off at 23.30 and were due to drop at 01.00. Our stick went down within thirty seconds of the exact scheduled time.

We were carrying twenty paratroopers and an Alsatian dog that had been trained to jump from the back of a lorry. On a temporary rack fitted below the belly of the aircraft we carried a number of small anti-personnel bombs. We had been briefed to drop these as we crossed the Normandy beaches so that if there were any defenders they would be encouraged to keep their heads down. There were also a couple of folding motor cycles in cylindrical canisters.

Shortly before we made landfall something exploded on the land right ahead. A vast sheet of yellow flame lit up the sky for a second or two and in that time I saw a line of aeroplanes all going the same way, all at the same height and I realized I was part of a mad game of follow-my-leader. I made myself think I was all alone on a night exercise on Salisbury Plain, but kept very keyed up to take smart evasive action if I got close enough to anyone else to see them. I felt the slipstream from other aeroplanes in front from time to time, but once that rather shattering fire had died down I never actually saw another.

Bill Dyson and the Gee Box brought us in for a perfect landfall and Robbie Burns and I found we could see enough to make our way visually to the DZ. Robbie was an RAF navigator, just out of Ulster University. He was a bright boy. There were not always enough pilots for every crew to have a second pilot so I was given Robbie as a map reader.

We had been told that we should be crossing heavy-gun emplacements and that our bombers would be dealing with them before we arrived to prevent them bombarding the navy. Whatever had happened to them had burned them up to such effect that we passed over a number of glowing plates of ferro-concrete. The heat must have been generated inside but here was the topside of a concrete roof glowing like a red-hot plate of steel. I have always wanted to know more about those glowing gun-pits.

Rebecca-Eureka was working by now to lead us in. This was a short-range homing device actuated from a portable ground station. Now the illuminated direction tee could also be seen and we were almost there. The paratroopers had all been standing lined up with the red light on – well back from the door opening – and at this point they got the amber and would go on the green.

Doug Struke, my Canadian wireless operator, was acting jumpmaster and was able to speak to me down the intercom and he told me all was ready and well. I had started the drop at the right height, the right speed and all was as right as we could make it until I lost contact with Doug. I should wait for him to tell me it was OK to open up, but he was silent and we were steadily losing height and advancing on the Germans who were clearly belligerent as witness the flames in the sky not long before. I was sure that it was one of our lot that had bought it, though I was later told it was a Stirling. A moment later Doug came through again to say everything had gone and I opened throttles, made a climbing turn to port and disappeared into cloud where we all felt nice and snug.

When he re-joined us in the cockpit Doug told us that the dog, who with his handler was last to go, had followed the others all the way to the door and as it came to his turn to follow his handler out he decided this was not the same thing at all as jumping from the back of a lorry, had backed away from the door and retired to the front of the fuselage. Doug had had to unplug himself from the intercom, catch the dog and literally throw him out.[9]

Sergeant Louis E. Traux, 1st Battalion, 506th Parachute Infantry:

The front men were jumping. The first twelve men got out pretty close together. I was running down the aisle. Suddenly the plane was hit in the left wing by flak. The wing went straight up. My left shoulder crashed into a window. With ammo, a 1903 Springfield rifle, twelve grenade-launcher rounds, two cans of blood plasma, two cans of distilled water, gas mask, helmet, K rations . . . I must have weighed 225–250 pounds. Stripped, I weighed 130. I was surprised the window didn't break. The pilot was fighting to right the plane. When he succeeded, I was appalled at the view which greeted me – I was the only one standing.

Four men lay in a tangled heap on the floor. I realized it was almost impossible for them to stand up with their equipment loads. Also that an absolute sequence had to be maintained or we'd have a glob of human hamburger dangling outside the door at 150 miles an hour. One man dived out of the door head first. I stepped over the top of two men. The closest man to the door crawled out head first. I grabbed the ammo belt in the centre of the man I thought next and gave him a heave out nose first. The next man made it crawling on his own power. I reached up and pulled the salvo switch which released the machine gun and mortars attached to the bomb racks under the plane, then I dived out.[10]

Corporal J. Frank Brumbaugh, aged 23, 1 Company, 508th Parachute Infantry Regiment:

Just before we got on the aircraft the Red Cross, for the first and only time in my life, gave us something that we didn't have to pay for – two cartons of Pall Mall cigarettes which I stuffed inside my pants on the inside of each leg.

We took off either from North Witham or South Witham, I can't remember which, just before midnight and picked up flak as we were crossing the Channel Islands. I swear it was solid enough to walk on. The plane was all over the sky. It wasn't hit, to my knowledge, but there were shells bursting all over the place. We carried this solid flak all the way over to where we jumped.

We were supposed to jump at an altitude of 450 feet, which would give us only ten or fifteen seconds in the air before we hit the ground. Unfortunately the pilots did not get down to that level. From the time I spent in the air I would guess we jumped at 2,000 feet, or slightly more. In retrospect it was a beautiful drop because there were so many fireworks. Everything on the ground was firing up at the plane and there were shell bursts, red tracers, white tracers, green tracers.

I couldn't see much of the ground – it was more or less of a blur – but I watched all these tracers and shell bursts and everything in the air around me. A stream of tracer, obviously from a machine gun, looked like it was coming directly at me. Intellectually I knew I could not be seen from the ground under my camouflage chute, but the stream of tracer still came directly at me. In an obviously futile, but normal, gesture, I guess, I spread my legs widely and grabbed with both hands at my groin as if to protect myself. Those machine-gun bullets traced up the inside of my leg, missed my groin but split my pants, dropping both free cartons of Pall Mall cigarettes onto the soil of France. That is something I will never forget.[11]

Sergeant Len Drake, aged 24, 22nd Independent Parachute Company:

Our role was to be pathfinders for the main body of parachute troops. We were to drop at 00.20 hours, followed by the main body at 00.50 hours. Our task was to mark the dropping zone at Ranville, then to clear the landing area for the gliders which were due in at 02.30. I was assigned to be the bodyguard to the company commander, Major Lennox-Boyd.

As second in command of the stick, one of my duties was to allocate jumping positions and distribute loads. Accordingly, I placed myself at number two, behind Major Lennox-Boyd. A couple of days before take-off I agreed to allow Corporal Corbett to move up the stick to the number two position as he was worried about jumping with the Eureka radar set in a basket on his back. I took his place at number three, a decision I came to regret.

Our operational aircraft was the Albemarle, a medium bomber converted for parachuting with an exit hole in the floor roughly in the shape of a bath with two doors which clipped back inwards when jumping took place. One of the Albemarle's little quirks was the need for everyone to crowd forward in order to get the tail off the ground during take-off.

We emplaned and crowded forward ready for take-off and after a few heads had popped in and wished us good luck the doors were closed and we commenced to taxi to the runway. At this time my feelings were of pride to be in the vanguard of the invasion and some apprehension regarding the take-off, not helped by a remark from the pilot as we emplaned that we were carrying a 'hell of a load!' As the engines revved up and we sped down the runway, squeezing ourselves as far forward as possible, it seemed like hours before, to my great relief, we lifted off. Our take-off time was 23.20 hours.

In the plane it was difficult to talk because of the noise and I cannot recall any conversation at this time. When twenty minutes before the drop, the order was passed down to open the doors, everyone got to their feet and shuffled back to clear the way. I cannot recall if there was any light in the plane, but I could see the major struggling to open the doors. He managed to secure one door back against the bulkhead, but then he fell backwards through the half-open door, with his elbows resting on each side and his feet facing forward at the edge of the hole. With the door partially open the noise was now deafening. I yelled at the corporal in front of me to pull the major in and he indicated that he couldn't do it. It was then I realized my extreme folly in agreeing to change jump positions.

With great difficulty I pushed past the corporal and attempted to pull the major in, but with the Eureka in a kitbag strapped to my leg I found it impossible. I released the kitbag and tried again, but the major's own kitbag was caught in the plane's slipstream and this, plus his body weight and the arms and ammunition he was carrying, made an extremely heavy load.

While I was battling to pull the major in I noted we had crossed the coast and I knew if he dropped he would be over land, so I mouthed and indicated to him that he must drop. I released my hold on his webbing and away he went. I saw the static line pull the bag off his chute and the chute start to develop.

I was now straddling the aperture and in front of the number two in the stick. He could not possibly jump in that position as our static lines would become tangled, so I shuffled back behind the number two and instructed him to open the remaining half of the door, only to be told he could not manage it. I again had to struggle by him and secure the door in the open position. While I was doing this, the order 'Running in!' was received. As I was going back to my position the red light came on, followed almost immediately by the green. I passed a request back to the pilot for another circuit, which he proceeded to execute.

We were flying at the operational height of 450 feet and had been attracting flak since crossing the coast. As we turned for our second run we were flying through a curtain of flak. Having retrieved my kitbag there was no way I could strap it back on my leg before the drop and grasping the kitbag with all my strength I jumped and as I exited the slipstream I flung the kitbag horizontally with all my strength. I felt as though my arms were being pulled from their sockets and it also had the effect of spinning me like a top. I was still whirling like a dervish when I hit the ground and, although I was a bit dizzy, I was unhurt. I had a feeling of great thankfulness that I had made it to the DZ.[12]

Flight Lieutenant Denys S.C. Brierly, 570 Squadron, RAF:

I was the pilot of an Albemarle due to take part in paratroop-dropping operations in the Cabourg area. We had been carefully briefed for many days beforehand on the expected weather conditions, the configuration of the ground and pinpoints on the way in. Our vital pinpoint was a small farmhouse on the cliffs from which we were to turn on course for the dropping zone. To allow for changes in weather conditions, we were shown film of the coastal area and the run-in in every possible condition of light, from bright moonlight to almost total darkness, though the final weather briefing just before take-off indicated light cloud over the French coast at 2,000 feet, with the probability of some moonlight over the actual dropping zone.

The key to the success of the operation lay in identifying the farmhouse on the coast, then turning on course and flying for about forty seconds, following which we should recognize the dropping zone, which lay between two large woods.

As we took off after midnight there was a fair breeze with frequent cloud at 5,000 to 6,000 feet, interspersed with clear areas and bright moonlight. Crossing the Channel we descended to a height of 500 feet, the bomb aimer lying in the nose of the aircraft to pinpoint the vital farmhouse on the coast.

The weather deteriorated, the cloud was much lower and thicker than we had expected, and in consequence we missed the pinpoint in the darkness, although we did pick up the coastline as we crossed it. We turned on our course, set the red light for the paratroopers to prepare to drop and flew for the required 40 seconds at 500 feet with flaps down at 120 m.p.h., but failed to pinpoint the dropping zone.

We turned back, found the coast again – though not the vital pinpoint – and again set course without success in locating the DZ. We tried a third time, again without success. The flack was becoming embarrassing and we were having to take evasive action. By now we were well out of our time phase – the bombing of the coastal ports by Bomber Command had begun and at 500 feet we felt every explosion like a toy balloon in a gale. Each time an explosion took place we bounced a couple of hundred feet or so and it was on one of these occasions that the leader of our paratroop stick – still waiting for the order to jump – was jerked through the hole, head downwards, and completely blocked it!

I could hear through the intercom the verbal and physical efforts of my wireless operator and gunner to pull him out, but he was solidly stuck and there was no future staying over France in the constipated condition in which we found ourselves. There was nothing for it but to get the hell out, so we set course for home, climbed into thick cloud at 7,000 feet and reached home some three hours after take-off with the unfortunate paratrooper still blocking the hole.[13]

Charles Bortzfield, aged 19, flight engineer, 100 Squadron, 441st Troop Carrier Group:

About 23.00 hours, 5 June, our engines were started. Over one hundred planes were lined up half-way down the runway and around the perimeter of the field on the taxiways. Hundreds of propellers spun furiously as they awaited the go signal.

The signal came and two abreast the C-47s roared down the runway. Finally it was our turn. I was in my position between the pilot and co-pilot. Lieutenant World pushed the throttles full forward. We were rolling, tail up, then airborne. The air was a little rough at this point from all the prop wash of the planes ahead of us. We dipped a wing once in a while, mushed a little bit, but finally levelled out into a smooth flight.

We were in a formation of nine planes, three v-groups across. Later we would form up with other groups. I guess our formation was a hundred miles long, maybe a thousand airplanes or more.

I went back into the passenger compartment to talk to the lieutenant in charge of the paratroopers. He wanted to know how far we had to go and where he was. It wasn't easy to converse back there because the jump door was off and the roar of the engines and the wing noise was very loud. I went back and forth a number of times as we were crossing the Channel to keep the lieutenant informed of our location.

As we approached the French coast, I had to take up my position right across from the jump door and next to the paratrooper lieutenant. At this time I had to take off my helmet and put on my headset for the intercom radio, to be in communication with the co-pilot. If the signal light system was shot out, I would have to yell to the paratrooper lieutenant when to jump.

I could see tracers floating up towards us and searchlights probing the sky to give the German gunners targets to shoot at. At about 01.00 we reached our drop zone and all of a sudden I went down on one knee. The green light came on and the paratroopers jumped out into the dark night. One yelled as he passed me by 'Are you hit?' I said, 'I think so.' 'Me too,' he replied, and out the door he went.

After they were gone it was my job to pull in the static lines, but I felt to weak to do so. I got out of my flak suit and hobbled forward to the navigator's compartment. I sat down across from Sergeant Small, our radio operator. He looked at me and said I was hit. I told him I couldn't pull in the static lines and he would have to go back and do it. He went back, but didn't have enough strength to pull them in by himself, so I yelled to Lieutenant Stewart, our co-pilot to help.

Sergeant Small came back, cut away my jacket on my left arm, cut off my right pant leg and applied sulfa powder to my wounds. We were back over the Channel now, headed back for England. Lieutenant World came to look me over and wanted to give me a shot of morphine. I declined, because I was afraid we might still have to abandon our aircraft. I could smell 100-octane gasoline inside the cabin and this is not a normal condition and if I had to use a parachute I didn't want to be doped up. I found out later my parachute was hit also and was full of holes.

The left engine on the plane was very rough, not running right at all, so I guess it also took some flak. We finally got back to England and Sergeant Small got us clearance to land at the first air base we could find because we were afraid we wouldn't make it back to our home base.

We started our approach and the pilot lowered the landing gear and yelled back to me that he had no hydraulic pressure left. I asked him if they had a green light and he said 'Yes' so I said 'Land it', hoping to myself that we had tyres left and a long enough runway to roll to a stop without using the brakes, which would not work without hydraulic pressure.

I don't remember if they had sufficient pressure left to put the flaps down, but anyway we were lucky and landed safely.

An ambulance took me to a first aid station and from there I was sent to hospital. I was taken to an operating room where they patched up a broken right leg and four holes in the left arm and hand. I was a real celebrity at this hospital, because at that moment I was their only patient. All the patients had been evacuated to make way for D-Day casualties. The doctors really interrogated me, because they now knew the invasion was on.

I was probably back in the ward by 6.00 a.m., when the boys were hitting the beaches.[14]

Sergeant John Wilson, aged 23, A Squadron, Glider Pilot Regiment:

On my glider I had a jeep, trailer, two motor bikes, ammunition, rations and water and, to the best of my knowledge, seven men.

Yes, I was frightened, or possibly tense more than anything, and the co-pilot was much the same. We talked very little on the way over. We'd been warned to watch out for Messerschmitt 210s, which were the latest German fighters, and half-way over the Channel we saw one of them coming towards us. I felt the hair on the back of my head stick up and sweat run down the back of my neck. The Messerschmitt 210 was armed with 60mm cannon which were used for knocking submarines out and I expected this thing to open up and blast us out of the air. I always remember hearing over the intercom the panic that was going on in Albemarle tug aircraft, with the pilot saying to his gunner, 'Watch the bastard! Watch the bastard!' We could see the guns go round and I thought, 'Hell fire, something's going to happen.' And at the last minute this aircraft rocked its wings in recognition, dropped its flare and it was a Mosquito with engine trouble going back to base. Anyhow, that was quite an excitement . . . a terrifying bloody experience.

When we were coming over the coast we could see the anti-aircraft fire coming up. There was twenty-one of us going in line astern and I was number three and we could see this ack-ack coming up and we felt, well, all right, this is what we've got to go through and this is what it was all about. But you still felt yourself tense up and your tongue stuck to the roof of your mouth and you were very jittery. As we went over – we knew where we were going, we could see the flares – there was two shells burst above us and two below and we knew that the next one would probably knock us out.

The tug aircraft dived to get below the next shell and then we were low enough for the ground people with 20mm cannon to open up on us. We flipped off and went straight for the landing zone because we hadn't got sufficient time to do the normal approach. We did as best we could but we were lower than we should have been. We could see very little other than a cluster of red flares and a cluster of green that had been put out by the pathfinders. We should have landed from green to red but we just went straight for it because we were losing height badly.

When we landed, we did what we called a 'kangaroo'. We bounced, because we were not at the right altitude, and then hit a house. I never saw the house until we were about twenty-five yards from it. There was one hell of a bloody noise and I got this terrible pain from the waist down, virtually paralysed. My co-pilot was killed outright. Somebody came to try and drag us out. He stood me up on my legs but both legs were smashed and the pain was intense. I never felt a pain like it. I lost consciousness then. I just remember saying, 'Leave me, leave me. I'll be all right when it's daylight.'

When I came round two-and-a-half days later I was still in the glider. They'd come round to bury the dead and found that I was still alive. But I lost one leg.[15]

Sergeant Dan Furlong, aged 21, 508 Parachute Infantry Regiment:

We were right over the Channel Islands when the firing first started and then we got small fire all the way in. We got hit when we crossed the coast. You could see the shells come up, they looked like roman candles, balls of fire, and when they hit it sounded like somebody threw a cake of nails against the side of the plane. We got hit three times by an 88 and I don't know how many times by 20mm. The first 88 hit the wing and took about three feet off the tip, the second took the light panel off and the third went through the floor, blew a hole about two feet across and exploded inside the plane, killing three men and wounding four others.

There was so much confusion and smoke in the plane you didn't know what was going on, there were static lines and parachutes all over the place. I was scared, probably as scared as I ever was in my life. I thought the plane was going to crash and I was screaming for the guys to get out and they finally got the message and went. I was the last out. I fell in the hole in the floor with one leg before I got to the door, then I just dove out, head first. I was probably no more than 200 feet from the ground because when my chute popped open, my feet hit the trees, that's how low I was.

A big branch broke off as I went through a tree and I landed flat on my back in a cement cow trough. It was full of water, you bet it was.

Basically we hit pretty close to where we were supposed to be, but we were very scattered. I was completely alone. There was a farmhouse back up about 150 yards from where I dropped, so I snuck up to it and inside I could hear Germans talking. I was going to sneak away and was going round the side when one of them came out. Maybe he heard me or something and came out to check what was going on. He came round the corner. I was standing flat against the wall and I killed my first German right there. I hit him on the side of the head with my rifle butt, then gave him the bayonet treatment. Then I took off, ran like hell.[16]

Harold Canyon, aged 20, HQ Company, 2nd Battalion, 508 Parachute Infantry Regiment:

I was number six man in the stick. We were told that we may receive some fire from the Germans as we passed a couple of islands off the coast of France. I remember how helpless I felt at the time while sitting in the airplane. There was absolutely nothing you could do to improve your situation in the event you were fired on. Absolutely nothing you could do. You were completely helpless.

Next I remember the plane was being hit in the front section with machine-gun fire and then they ordered us to stand up and hook up. I remember how hard it was to stand up with all the weight that was strapped on me. It took considerable effort. I hooked up and then we started out the door and just as I approached the door the top of the airplane opened up. It had been hit by some type of explosive shell.

As I turned into the doorway the plane started a right-wing dip going into its death spiral. It took everything I had to get over the threshold. It seemed to me the threshold was just a little bit more than chest high as I rolled over and got out. I was the last man out of the plane.

When I felt the opening shock of the chute, more by habit than anything I looked up to check the chute and I remember seeing clusters of tracer going through it. I hit the ground with one leg up, trying to get my trench knife out, but fortunately didn't break anything. I lay there momentarily, fully expecting a German to run up and stick me with a bayonet, but nothing happened, which quite surprised me.

I had landed in front of a German bunker, about thirty yards away, but someone who had hit the ground before me had dropped a gammon grenade in it and put it out of order. I cut all the straps that were binding me, grabbed my carbine in one hand and ran for the hedgerow.

I lay against the bank for a short while, then saw two Germans approaching on the other side of the hedgerow. We had orders not to load our weapons until we were organized, so my carbine was not loaded. As the Germans approached, I fully intended to let them go by, but just in case I unscrewed the cap on my gammon grenade.

When they got just opposite me they noticed me and ducked. I sat there and waited as one of them started slowly rising. I saw the top of his head and when I saw his shoulders I threw the gammon grenade. At the same time he fired and a bullet passed through the crotch of my outside pair of pants. The muzzle blast knocked me out and when I came to my face was in the bank, in the dirt, my mouth was open and blood and spit were trickling out. I could hear but I couldn't move. I thought I was dead and that this was the way people died. I heard moaning on the other side of the hedgerow, so I knew my grenade had had some effect.

After a while it got quiet on the other side of the hedgerow. I don't know how long I was out to begin with or how long it took before I could move. I heard and saw someone approaching on my side of the hedgerow and it turned out to be a couple of paratroopers. They shouted the challenge 'Thunder' and I replied with the password 'Flash', but apparently they didn't hear me. Next thing I saw was a ball of fire and a bullet hit my helmet and glanced off. I rolled to my left and started swearing and a second bullet went through a couple of layers of paper maps folded in my left hip pocket. They quit firing when they heard my swearing. Swearing turned out to be one of the best passwords. No one can swear in American like an American, or in English like an Englishman.

I'm not too sure what happened then. We talked, I think, for a minute and laid down and waited. The next time I looked up I was all alone again. I decided it was kind of useless to move around in the dark as it was too difficult to identify anyone. I noticed a kind of brush-filled gully some short distance away, so I ran for that and dove into it.

I was lying on my back in the dry brush, my trench knife under me and my carbine off to my left when I heard two Germans approaching. You could tell Germans by the amount of leather they wore; you could hear it creak as they walked. They stood over me and looked down at me. There wasn't anything I could do, just play dead. I waited. I had to go to the bathroom very badly and I went. It's quite possible the Germans mistook what they saw for blood.

After a while I opened my eyes and saw they had gone, so I crawled deeper down to the bottom of the gully and lay there and went to sleep. Just before falling asleep I heard a glider come crashing through the trees.[17]

Corporal J. Frank Brumbaugh, aged 23, 1 company, 508th Parachute Infantry Regiment:

I landed extremely hard, with all the weight, in the middle of a small field. I was unable to unbuckle my chute, so I cut my way out with my trench knife, put my rifle together, stripped the radar transmitter of its cover, put the antenna together, plugged it in and turned it on. This was a few minutes after midnight.

Then I went looking for my partner, who had obviously landed some distance from me. Once we were together, we went back to the radar set. On the back of it there was a thing to unscrew, about the size and shape of an army canteen lid. It was attached to twenty-five feet of black nylon fishing line and inside the set was a shaped charge and detonator. Our orders were to pull this cord and blow the thing sky-high at 6.30 in the morning to prevent the Germans knowing what frequencies we were using. If we were about to be captured or got into a firefight or anything, we had to blow the set up immediately. It was highly secret.

I went around the periphery of this small field and heard German voices on the other side of a hedgerow. I sneaked up through the brush and saw two German officers talking to each other, apparently totally unaware that we were in the field right next to them. Well, I couldn't shoot; we were ordered not to shoot unless it was totally in self-defense, but just to be as quiet and as secret as possible. Of course, the main thing was to keep the beacon in operation as long as possible.

But when I saw those two German officers, in my mind's eye I saw two beautiful Lugers, which was a souvenir I wanted very badly. Since I couldn't make any noise, I tossed a white phosphorous grenade down at their feet. This makes a small pop when it goes off, very little noise, but it devastates anything in the area and can't be put out. It burned the two officers to death.

I got back out of the way and waited until the thing had finished burning. When I went to collect my Lugers the Germans were hardly recognizable as humans. Unfortunately for the Lugers, the ammunition had exploded in the clips and blown the Lugers apart so they were totally worthless. So that was not the best idea I'd ever had, but at least it got rid of two Germans, my first two Germans.[18]

Corporal John Mescki, aged 21, 13th Battalion, The Parachute Regiment:

Our officer, Tiger Lee, was the first out. Number two was his batman, Dougie Sharp from Cheadle, number three was a fellow called Nutter who had a water diviner strapped to his leg and this got stuck in the door and the dispatcher kicked him out. I said, 'Don't kick me out, don't push me,' because I didn't want to spiral. So I just jumped out and when I jumped out it was very quiet, beautiful and quiet, just the noise of the aircraft and my chute popping open.

When I hit the deck I heard these footsteps. We used to have cartoons stuck up on the wall of the camp showing Germans running at you with bayonets and the caption was, 'Jump to it! Don't just sit there.' So I got up out of my chute and ran off into the hedge and when I turned round I saw it was cows.

I carried on about another fifty yards and I thought, 'Well, I'm lost here,' because I realized there was electric and telephone wires going across the field and I knew from the photographs of the DZ that there was no such thing, so I was pretty lost. I came to another hedge and intended to jump through it, but I got stuck half-way. Then I heard some footsteps and I thought, 'Oh, hell, I've had it,' but it turned out to be two friends, one who had broken his arm and the other who had burned his fingers on his chute.

We went straight down this road together and heard a noise like a tank, so I said, 'Let's get behind the hedge and throw some grenades.' So we pulled the pin from our grenades, ready to throw them over the hedge, and who should come riding past was a man and a woman on bikes with milk churns on the sides. They rattled just like a tank. Luckily, we kept the pins and rings and pushed them back on, peeked out and they disappeared round the next crossroad.

We got back on the road, realizing we should go in a northerly direction, when a Typhoon came over. I thought it was going to strafe us, so we dived in the hedgerow and found a little path leading into a wood. I said, 'If we stay off the road, we'll make it.' After a while I saw this farmhouse, and I got my binoculars out and looked at it. There was smoke coming out of the chimney, but it was well protected from the road. I thought we could get round the back without anyone noticing and I went round and saw the door was open. It was now getting on for about six o'clock in the morning. I knocked on the door and this French lady came. She didn't look surprised, she just looked at me and said, '*M'sieur?*' I asked her if there were any Germans in the house and she said no and so I said, 'I've got two wounded comrades, can you look after us?' She said yes, enter if you wish. I said can you give us any idea where we are and she showed us on a little tiny railway map where we were. I said the British will be here in three days, will you hide us? She said yes, and took us out to a barn. We were there for three months.[19]

Lieutenant Colonel Nathaniel R. Hoskot, aged 32, 507th Parachute Infantry, 101st Airborne Division:

As we crossed the coast it started to get kind of foggy and we could see the flak getting closer and closer. We would have dropped about two-and-a-half minutes after crossing the coast, but the pilot made a turn to the right, to the south, and kept going for about five minutes right across the damned peninsula. I was sitting by the door, so I unhooked and got up, intending to ask the pilot where we were going. When I was about half-way to the cockpit, there was a rattle and the plane dipped. We'd been hit in the right wing, but we straightened out. I went back and hooked up, ready to get out of there as soon as possible. The crew chief, a sergeant, came back and said the pilot thought he could make it back to where we wanted to go. But I could see we were still going south and then we got hit again, on the other wing, and this time it caught fire. The sergeant came running back and said, 'He wants you to get out.' By this time we were standing up and ready to go. We wanted to be any place but that place, so out we went. We were at about 700 feet, not very high, but high enough. Just as my chute opened, I looked to the right and saw the plane was going down in flames. It crashed before I landed, maybe a mile or two miles away. I looked around, but couldn't see any other parachutes in the sky.

I landed in a field with a big pond in the middle of it. A couple of guys landed after me in the pond, but it wasn't very deep and we had no trouble getting them out. We had these damn cricket things and you could hear crickets all over the place, but I couldn't tell which were the real crickets and which were these tin things. We finally found seven guys of the thirteen who were on the plane. I don't know what happened to the rest, whether they didn't get out or whether they went in the opposite direction, or what. I don't know. So that's what we ended up with, eight out of thirteen.

It was about 1.15 in the morning, a very clear moonlit night. How did I feel? Well, I'd like to have sat down and cried. I had absolutely no idea where we were and I was supposed to lead these guys, and they had no idea where we were either. They kept asking what are we going to do now, colonel? We went down to one end of the field and there was a gate and we could see a little bit further. We got oriented and I knew we had to go north, or at least I thought we did, so we started north, a couple of guys out front, a couple at the rear. We went along for about an hour at a pretty good clip; I could see all these airplanes in the distance but couldn't hear anything. It got a little eerie. All of a sudden it was daylight. I thought we can't walk down this road in broad daylight without knowing where we are. I thought, well, I don't know where the hell we are, but a little ravine opened up off the side of the road so I thought, well, let's go in there, sit down and try to figure out what to do.

We had some radio equipment and code machines with us which we figured we ought to get rid of. We didn't want to get caught with it, so we dug a hole and buried the stuff. There was a bunch of telephone wires running into this ravine so we cut out a couple of hundred feet and then we went on. We came to a crossroads with a bunch of signs on it, but none of the places were on my map so we turned to the east as I figured we were probably somewhere opposite the British zone.

About 6.30 or 7.00 we went into this orchard at the side of the road. A couple of guys wanted to take the apples, but I didn't think it was such a good idea as they were green, or something. So we sat back under a hedge and ate part of our C rations, and then one of the sergeants and I crawled forward to this farmhouse. About a hundred feet behind the house there was an outdoor toilet and out comes this old farmer, pulling his suspenders over his shoulders as he goes into this place. It was funny, really, just like a movie. The sergeant looked at me and I looked at him and I said, 'Well, we might as well.' So we went up to the outhouse, waited for the guy to come out and stuck a gun in his back as the door opened. You've never seen a more surprised Frenchman, or any other nationality, in your life! We pointed at the American flag sewn on our sleeves but it didn't seem to make much impression on him. He didn't speak any English but I said the one French word I knew for friend, *ami*, and finally it dawned on him and he beckoned us into the house.

We walked in and there was an old lady and a younger woman who must have been his wife and two girls, maybe ten and thirteen, getting ready for breakfast. They gesticulated and we gesticulated and nobody was getting any place until they finally brought out a calender advertising some farm equipment and I wrote down that I wanted to get to Ste Mère-Eglise and pointed to the date and the clock. Well, they'd never heard of Ste Mère-Eglise. We weren't getting any place except they knew we were Americans. But we might just have well come from Mars because they didn't have a telephone, didn't know anything about the invasion. They offered us a cup of coffee and we took it.

Then the farmer took the sergeant to the door and pointed down the road, holding up fingers and after a little time we finally got the message that there were two people coming down the road. There was a little bit more pantomime and we finally got the message that a German patrol stopped by the house every morning for coffee. Sure enough, in about fifteen minutes, down the road came two Germans on bicycles. They pushed us into a back bedroom and I insisted the two young girls came with us in case the farmer told the Germans we were there.

The Germans came in, stayed for about fifteen minutes and pretty soon got on their bicycles and went down the road. We heard the farmer speaking to them in German and my sergeant knew a few words in German so we got along a lot better after that. We never thought about trying out German. Well, the upshot was that he didn't know where Ste Mère-Eglise was and had no idea where Carentan was, but I think that was because we weren't pronouncing it properly. We finally decided we weren't getting any place, so we

told them to be quiet and got the other guys together and decided we
had better get out of there and lay up for the day.[20]

Sergeant William T. Dunfee, aged 21, I Company, 3rd Battalion, 505th Parachute Infantry:

At about 02.00 hours the green jump light finally came on and it
didn't take long to empty the aircraft. When my chute opened I
figured I had it made. We were still drawing AA fire, but I was out
of that 'flying coffin'. Looking around I spotted Jim Beavers next to
me and our equipment bundle off to one side. Then, looking down, I
saw C-47s flying below us. That scared the hell out of me and I
started cussing them. I didn't want to be turned into a hamburger by
our own air force. They had jumped us at over 2,000 feet and dove
down on the deck. Those rotten bastards were going to kill us.

While descending I regained my composure, since it appeared we
were going to make it down in one piece. I told Jim I would meet
him at the equipment bundle. He landed on one side of a hedgerow
and the bundle and I landed on the other. By the time Jim joined me,
I had the bundle unrolled and the bazooka and ammo out. We loaded
up and headed for Ste Mère-Eglise. It was easy to locate – that's
where most of the firing was coming from.

While crossing several fields I noticed a couple of gliders coming
down. One landed in an orchard, the other seemed to be trying to
land on the porch roof of a farmhouse. I couldn't help but question
the pilot's 'smarts', my recent experience having prejudiced me
against all pilots.

We heard what sounded like a box-car flying through the air and
hit the deck. I think it was a 16-inch naval shell that hit in a field
nearby. It rained chunks of earth and rock for what seemed like
several minutes.

Jim and I joined a group on the outskirts of Ste Mère-Eglise. Our
battalion commander, Lt Col 'Cannonball' Krause, ordered all
bazookas forward. We went to the designated area and were ordered
to stand by until needed.

Establishing a perimeter defensive position, we dug in to await the
counter-attack that came all too swiftly. The enemy really socked it to
us with 88s and 'screaming meemies'. The 88s were using either timed
or proximity fuses, because we were receiving air-bursts. The 'Nebelwerf-
ers' were so erratic you couldn't tell where their rockets would land.

We learned in a hurry the safest place to relieve one's bladder was in the bottom of a foxhole. If Mother Nature required further relief you were in very serious trouble. We learned in a hurry to cut laterally into the side of your foxhole for a place to hide the family jewels.

We suffered a number of casualties during this bombardment. The most gruesome was when a rocket landed among three men in a mortar squad. They were all killed and the explosion must have detonated a 'gammon grenade' in one of the men's pockets, for the secondary explosion literally blew him to bits. His head, chest and right arm were all that remained. One of our men remarked, 'That's what you call going to hell in a hurry.' He didn't mean it to be callous or unfeeling, it just seemed appropriate at the time.[21]

Lieutenant Charles E. Sammon, commanding light machine-gun platoon, 2nd Battalion, 505th Parachute Infantry Regiment:

I landed flat on my back in a small orchard, completely exhausted and so bound up in equipment I could hardly move. About that time a figure appeared in the darkness and I couldn't decide if it was a friend or foe. I got my pistol out and waited until he was about three feet from me. I had decided that I wasn't going to wait very long before I pulled the trigger, but that I would give him a split second to say the code word. I said 'George' and he said 'Washington' and we both sighed with relief. We picked up several more men as we walked toward the assembly point, where I was finally able to get almost all of my men and their equipment together. Colonel Vandervoort instructed me to set up my platoon in a defensive position about one mile north and east of the town of Ste Mère-Eglise. There was no enemy activity in our area at this time, although I could hear some firing in the distance.

We found the area assigned to us by the battalion commander and I established three machine-gun positions which I felt would give us good protection. I then set up a platoon command post and together with my runner took turns wrapping up in a parachute in order to get a little sleep. Dawn was just breaking as I started out with my runner to check the three positions to make sure everything was in order, but as I approached the first position I called out to the corporal who was in charge and received an answer back in the form of a long burst from what was unmistakably a German machine gun.

The bullets hit the dirt at our feet and the two of us hit the ditch beside the road. What had happened became very clear to me at this point: the Germans must have infiltrated our positions during the night and either killed or captured my men. As I lay there in the ditch with bullets whizzing over my head I was not only scared, I was thoroughly disgusted with myself and I felt helpless to do anything about the situation.

I decided we should turn around in the ditch and attempt to crawl back to our own position. We had gone about half-way, with the bullets clipping the tall grass over our head, when my runner suddenly panicked and got up to run. I tackled him just as a long burst of fire hit all around us and from then on I kept my hand on his foot as we continued to crawl up the ditch. We were making fairly good progress when an American machine gun began firing at us from our own position. Since we were approaching from the direction of the enemy and were unable to stand up to identify ourselves, I could see no way out of our predicament. This time, however, the Germans came to our rescue. A barrage of artillery fire forced the American machine-gunner to abandon his position just long enough for us to jump up and make a run for it.

All was confusion back in our own position. The Germans had infiltrated so well and struck so suddenly that no one knew what was going on. I managed to round up the remnants of my platoon and set up a machine gun to keep firing at the German position so they wouldn't attempt to advance further. I also got a man armed with a carbine and rifle grenades to start firing grenades into their position. The best discovery, however, was a mortar man from one of the rifle companies with a complete mortar and a supply of ammunition. In parachute drops this is a rare find, as often some vital part will be missing as a result of the drop. With grenades and mortar shells falling into their position, the Germans had no choice but to move. They couldn't go back as we had set up a machine gun to cover their retreat. One by one they attempted to go over the top of their protective embankment into the ditch I had used an hour earlier. There were about twenty men in the position and about half of them made it into the ditch; the rest were either killed or wounded as they came out.

From my position on the flank I ran across about fifty yards of open ground to a position right over the ditch in which the Germans were working their way into our main defenses. I threw a gammon grenade, headed back to the protection of my ditch and disappeared over the side just as a German fired at me with a machine pistol. I waited for a loud explosion that never came; the grenade misfired. Since they knew where I was I was hesitant about going back, but about this moment a lieutenant from the airborne engineers, I believe, came running over and said he had three or four men with him and would like to help. We crawled up the embankment so I could show him what I was trying to do. As we cautiously poked our heads over the top a machine gun cut loose and we both slid back down the embankment. When the firing stopped I got up, but he didn't, so I rolled him over. He was shot right through the head.

I decided to give it another try, as the Germans were getting closer all the time. I pulled the pins on two fragmentation grenades and started across the open area again. This time they went off just as I got back to my position and the firing stopped. I looked carefully over the top of the embankment and, believe it or not, a white flag was waving back and forth on the end of a branch. Soon a German soldier climbed over the top carrying the flag and started in our direction. Two or three of the dead lieutenant's men were with me and were all for shooting him. I pointed out that he was unarmed and that we had to honour any attempt to surrender. He turned out to be a German doctor, aged about thirty-five, who spoke fluent English. He explained that many of his men were dead or wounded and that they wanted to give up. I told him we would not stop firing unless he returned and got all the Germans to throw down their arms and come out with their hands over their heads. He agreed to do this and returned to his position. We sat there waiting for something to happen, but we didn't have to wait long. Shortly after he disappeared we were the recipients of the heaviest barrage of mortar and artillery fire I had ever experienced. It was obvious his 'surrender' was all part of a plot and we were forced to abandon the position and return to the area where the rest of my men were entrenched.

The German firing was very light now and with ten or fifteen men we started a counter attack. As we were setting up our machine guns we heard the drone of aircraft and looked up to see the sky full of C-47 cargo planes towing American gliders. As I recall the time was about 8 a.m., however I am not too sure about this. The planes made one circle and started to cut loose the gliders. We watched helplessly while one glider after another attempted to land in the fields around us and crashed. When they hit something all the equipment inside tore loose and hurtled through the nose of the glider, killing or injuring the men in front of it. I doubt if 10 per cent of the gliders landing on that field did so without crashing and very few of the men who landed were in any shape to fight.

We started to haul the wounded glidermen and pilots into our position, out of the German artillery fire, and did what little we could in the way of first aid. We did not have a medic with us at the time. I gave one badly injured pilot a shot of morphine from my first aid kit and while I was trying to help another soldier one of my men gave the same pilot another shot of the same sedative. About this time we received heavy bursts of machine-gun fire and from the sound of it the Germans had regrouped and were starting another attack. It was apparent to me that we couldn't hold our position but I hesitated to leave as I knew we could never make it out with the wounded. In the end I decided to leave the wounded behind and hope that the Germans would treat them all right. As we scrambled out of one end of the position, the Germans scrambled in the other. We couldn't use our mortar or rifle grenades now as there were too many of our own wounded in the position, but for some reason, unknown to me, they decided to try and get out. We killed or wounded several and when we knew there were only a few left we rushed the position and captured the rest. I figured later they had probably lost communication with their artillery and mortars. Our glider people were still there, although one had died in the meantime. One of my men started to give a badly injured glider pilot a shot of morphine but he weakly raised his hand to say that he had had two shots from us previously and couldn't feel a thing.

Shortly after that I received orders to return the platoon to headquarters in Ste Mère-Eglise.[22]

Sapper Benny Jordan, aged 22, 3rd Parachute Squadron, Royal Engineers:

When it was my turn to jump the plane hit an air pocket and I sank to my knees. I was struggling to regain my feet, but the plane kept dropping. I was instantly pushed out of the door, head first, by the RAF dispatcher.

When my chute billowed out I found it hadn't opened properly. My wrists were tangled with the shroud lines and the butt of my rifle was pulling my chin upwards, so I was looking towards the sky. I struggled to look for our colour signal on the ground and in the event had a comparatively good landing, in what appeared to be a very large ploughed field.

The night was dark and there was a great deal of noise. Many planes were flying overhead and men were still jumping out of aircraft. One plane was in flames and it looked like the pilot was trying to keep it airborne. I had the impression we dropped at the edge of the DZ as there were no troops in my vicinity. When I landed I immediately discarded my parachute and took out my knife and slashed off a piece of my chute and stuffed it into my pocket for a souvenir. Just then I heard Corporal MacDuff call out, 'Is that you, Benny?' I made my way to him in the darkness.

MacDuff and I started running towards our containers. By now the noise had greatly increased – I don't know if it was shellfire or mortars – and the entire DZ was being raked with machine-gun fire intermingled with tracer bullets around waist high. This being the first time any of us had been in action we ignored what was happening around us. We knew by reaching our containers we would be joined by more of No. 1 Troop. While we were dashing to the containers we heard a tremendous swishing noise. It was becoming louder and louder every second. All of a sudden, a giant glider landed and skidded along the ground in the same direction as we were heading and about fifteen yards to our left. The thought struck me at the time that we could easily have been run over by it.

When we reached our containers many of our men were still missing. We managed to pull out our trolleys and all our explosives and other equipment. We heard the sound of hunting horns. We knew this was for the benefit of other units to assemble at their RVs. At this particular stage men were hurrying in every direction.

We stayed at our RV until more men joined us and then our company commander gave orders to move out. Our trolleys were laden with explosive charges and equipment. One man guided each trolley at the rear while two men were in front, pulling it with toggle ropes. I was on one of the ropes, pulling as hard as I could. It was tough going, across ploughed fields. I wasn't thinking about Germans so much as who would relieve me when we got to the road.[23]

*Major 'Rosie' Rosevere, aged 30, officer commanding 3rd
Parachute Squadron, Royal Engineers:*

I was delighted when I was told what our job would be, delighted. It was
the best job, blowing up bridges. My unit was to be split in two. One
troop went with the Canadians to blow the bridge at Varaville and my
headquarters and the rest of my squadron, which was two troops, were
with the 8th Parachute Battalion. We had to blow the bridge at Troarn,
on the main Caen road, and two lattice-girder bridges nearby at Bures.

We took off at about, oh, ten or eleven o'clock at night, something
like that, and the flight was uneventful apart from a bit of flak. I was
standing at the door ready to jump but I thought we were over the
wrong DZ and I was bloody right. The red light came on much too
quickly after we crossed the coast – the DZ was much further inland
– and we were too soon out of the plane. But there was absolutely
nothing we could do about it.

Night landings are not as terrifying as you might expect, because
in a way when you can't see the ground you make a better landing;
when you see the ground you sort of try and put your feet on it, try
to adopt a great position, whereas at night you don't have that
opportunity. I landed in the middle of a field fifty yards from the
beacon put out by the pathfinders. It would have been perfect except
that I was on the wrong DZ. We collected our containers with the
explosive as quickly as we could and found the folding canvas
trolleys that we were going to use for transport, loaded them up and
formed up, ready for a long march. About this time, a jeep and trailer
belonging to a field ambulance unit appeared out of the murk. It was
packed to the gunwales with bottles of blood, instruments, bandages
and splints and field-dressing equipment. I thought it might be good
to have some transport, so I told the driver to follow me.

We set off through Hérouvillette and cut the telephone wires as it
seemed a reasonable thing to do. I think the Germans had pulled the
bed clothes a bit too high that night, because we had no opposition
at all, through Escoville and the *forêt du* Bures. We came to a point
where it was necessary to make a plan, so I told the driver of the jeep
that I would need his vehicle and we unloaded all the medical
supplies and re-loaded the trailer with special charges and detonating
equipment that we needed for Troarn bridge. I sent number 2 troop
through the woods to deal with the Bures bridges and set off, with
seven other chaps, in the jeep through the murky gloom for Troarn.

When we were getting near, beggar me if we didn't run smack into a barbed-wire barricade across the road. By the time I saw it it was too late. We couldn't ram it, because barbed wire is hopeless stuff and gets wrapped round everything, but by the grace of God one of our chaps had some wire-cutters with him and he cut us out. We stopped short of a crossroads at the edge of town and I sent a couple of chaps forward to look round the corner and here a really farcical situation developed. While they were looking in one direction, a German soldier appeared on a bicycle from the other direction. Well, I suppose in hindsight we should have stuck a knife in the chap, but what happened was that someone shot at him and that really set things going.

All we could do was jump aboard the jeep and make the best pace we could. I suppose we had about half a ton of explosives in the trailer and there were seven of us on the jeep, with me driving, so we couldn't make very high speed. As we came into the centre of the town, the firing started from various windows and from the ground as well; there seemed to be a Boche in every doorway firing like mad. Our chaps were firing back. One German rushed out with an MG34 and put it down in the road, but we were too quick for him and he had to whip it out of the way or we would have run him over. But he was terribly quick getting it out again and a stream of tracer went over our heads. The only thing that saved us was that there was a steep downward hill leading out of Troarn and he couldn't depress his gun far enough.

We raced down the hill, picking up speed all the time, and I nearly lost control of the darn thing. There was an appalling swerve and I think that's where we lost one of our men, our bren gunner, when he fell off the trailer.

When we got to the bridge it took us less than five minutes to set all the charges across the centre of the biggest arch and down she went.

Obviously we couldn't go back through the town, we were definitely *persona non grata* there, so we took to the fields and finally arrived back at brigade headquarters. On the way we passed a farmer milking a cow and I told him in French that liberation was at hand. He was most unimpressed.[24]

*Lance Sergeant Bill Irving, aged 22, 3rd Parachute Squadron,
Royal Engineers:*

I lost my kitbag on the way down and so I must have been one of the
few parachutists to arrive on the ground without a weapon. After I
had landed my immediate reaction was to get a weapon. I knew that
the weapons containers would have landed upstream, as it were, and
it was a fairly clear night and I could see the aircraft coming in from
a distance and that if I went in that direction I would find the
containers. They had a sort of telescopic arm fitted to them and when
they hit the ground one arm went up and had a light on it, I think
blue meant explosive, red meant weapons. So I headed back up the
flight path to find the containers and at that stage I realized that there
was something amiss because gliders were coming in, so either we
were in the wrong place or the gliders were in the wrong place.

I had just found the weapons containers and was trying to get one
open when I heard a movement – there was a lot of shooting going
on, a lot of tracer fire, you know it was getting very hot – on the
grass and I pounced on this figure with my fighting knife and found
it was Sapper O'Leary, who nearly bottomed me for it. He was
crawling up to do his job and unload the weapons containers and was
pretty surprised when I pounced on him.

By then I realized we weren't where we should be and out of the
blue I heard one of the boys shouting, 'Are you sappers?' and I said,
'Yes,' and – this is one of the things I can never work out – I turned
round and someone gave me a length of rope with a horse attached
to it and said, 'If you're sappers, you've got a lot to carry, you can
use this.' It was a horse which he'd caught running around like a mad
thing. I think he just wanted to get rid of it, which he did, promptly.
It wasn't any good to us but, you know, I felt, what a crazy world. I
took the horse, gave it a whack on the flank and off it went into the
darkness.

By that stage I realized we were not on a dropping zone where we
were meant to be and I started to worry how the devil we were going
to get together to do our job. Truthfully, I hadn't an earthly where I
was, except that I was in France. But somehow or the other life
sorted itself out and I found myself with a group of about a dozen
other sappers and then Major Rosevere turned up, don't ask me how,
and people started to assemble.

It was probably an hour or so before we got a party together and we set off under Major Rosevere. At this time he had acquired a jeep and trailer and we set off for Troarn. I was sitting on the front with the sergeant of 1 Troop, Joe Henderson, sort of front gunners. We were still confident, don't ask me why, that it was all going to be well.

At a certain stage we were on one of the roads leading to Ranville and decided that the telephone wires should be cut and I was dispatched to go up this pole and cut them. Now I had climbed telephone poles many times in mock exercises, but could I get up this pole? No way. I was carrying such a load of stuff that I got about half-way up and that was it. So the wires remained uncut.

As we went further down the road we got more apprehensive about the Germans. We came to a house where there was a little light on about twelve feet from the ground and someone – I don't know whose idea it was – decided we should have a look. So again I was appointed to take a look and one of my mates lifted me up so I could look inside. I expected to see a German sitting there but instead, when I looked in, there was a woman tucking up her child in bed. It was so unexpected. I had expected to see a German sitting there and thought he might shoot, instead of that I looked in on this ordinary family scene. I think I remember this more clearly than anything else.

On we went, towards Troarn. Just short of the main crossroads in the town we went crash-bang through a barbed-wire entanglement stretched across the road and got stuck. We had to cut the jeep loose and I found myself with wire cutters under the jeep with everyone getting impatient about the time it was taking to get disentangled. Rosevere was very helpful, shining a torch on me, and I felt very conspicuous. But there wasn't a sound, wasn't a shot, although we were all expecting a hail of gunfire.

When we cleared that we went on into Troarn and when we got to the crossroads I was dispatched to go ahead and see if all was clear. At that stage it was just about daylight and I had just signalled for the jeep to come forward, that all was clear, when I turned round and a German came whistling past me on a bicycle, obviously returning from a night out. He quite clearly hadn't seen us, but was polished off before he knew what had happened. I grabbed him and the lieutenant shot him. Rosevere said, 'That's done it,' and as we started to go through the town the Germans started firing at us.

The farther we went the more fire there was and the faster Rosevere drove the jeep. I was sitting on the front, blazing away with my sten gun at anything that moved. One German with a machine gun rushed out into the road to really have a go at us and changed his mind because he got the hell out of it. Rosevere was driving like mad, zig-zagging from side to side. We lost Sam Peachey, the rear gunner, who was thrown off the back of the trailer but it was really crazy that we could get through the town and only lose one chap. When we got to the end of the town, I don't know how I got there but I was lying flat on the bonnet.

I don't think we were on the bridge more than a minute to a minute-and-a-half, laying the charges and wiring it all up and then Rosevere beckoned everyone back onto the jeep. I asked him if he wanted to light the fuse and he said, 'No, you do it,' which I did and the bridge went up with a great bang.

The Germans could obviously see us from Troarn and so we ditched the jeep and set off across the fields into a wood and went deeper into the wood for maybe half an hour and then called a halt for a rest. After all the excitement we were desperately tired and we literally dropped down and I'm sure we all went to sleep, I'm sure we did.[25]

Lieutenant Colonel T.B.H. Otway, 9th Parachute Battalion:

A key German coastal-defence battery at Merville near the mouth of the Orne commanded the beaches on which the left flank of the British Third Division was to land. Our job was to silence that battery. The brigadier described the job to me as 'a stinker'. He was certainly right. I landed in the last place I wanted to be, pretty well on top of the German headquarters. Wilson, my batman, actually went slap through the glass roof of a greenhouse in the garden. We decided to make a hurried exit. When, eventually, I got to the rendezvous, almost the first man I recognized was my 2IC. 'Thank God you've arrived,' he said. 'The drop's a bloody chaos; there's hardly anyone here.' He wasn't exaggerating. By this time it was nearly two o'clock. Suddenly Wilson appeared and offered me a small flask as if it were a decanter on a silver salver. 'Shall we take our brandy now, sir?' he said.

Time went by and more men arrived, but only a few at a time. By 02.30, 150 officers and men had turned up. Five hundred were missing. We had one machine gun. Everything else – mortars, anti-tank guns, mine detectors, wireless sets – was missing. An attack didn't seem to stand much chance of success but that coastal battery had to be knocked out by 5.30 a.m. I decided to advance, come what may. The fight was short and terrible and very bloody. Like many men, I suppose, I had no great fear of being killed but the horror of being mutilated swept over me when the moment came to go through the wire into the enemy fire. Quite irrelevantly, I wandered what Wilson would think of me. I shouted, 'Come on!' and ran for it. In the circumstances, it was the only thing to do. My adjutant was hit by a burst of machine-gun fire beside me. In half an hour, the battle was over and the Merville battery had fallen. The Very light success signal was fired but for us there was no feeling of elation. In just thirty minutes of furious hand-to-hand fighting, I had lost exactly half the remnants of my force. Inside the German battery, seventy-five British paratroopers, officers and other ranks, were lying dead or wounded.[26]

Captain Hal Hudson, 9th Battalion, The Parachute Regiment:

There was a cloudy sky, but the moon was bright behind the clouds and there, below me, I saw the DZ, the RV and the surrounding country more clearly than I had ever done on an exercise or a practice drop. It was perfect, except that I landed in a tree.

Convinced that a fat German was sitting at the bottom of the tree with his rifle aimed at my backside, I disentangled myself from my harness in double quick time and dropped safely to the ground. As I was in the last aircraft bar two, I knew that by the time I arrived at the RV the battalion would be deployed and battalion HQ set up. I set off across the field, following the ditch I knew so well from the aerial photographs and the model, and arrived at the battalion HQ RV. Nobody was there.

I recall vividly the feeling of horror and the rapid draining away of self-confidence. Could I have completely misread the topography? There seemed to be no other possible explanation. After a minute or two I retraced my steps along the ditch, when suddenly a figure appeared out of the shadows. I threw myself to the ground and said, in the best barracks style: 'Halt, who goes there?' The figure replied, 'It's me, sir.'

The tension of the last few minutes caused me to lose my cool. 'Don't be so bloody silly,' I said. 'You're supposed to say "Friend" and then I ask you to give the password.' 'Sorry sir,' he said. 'V.' 'For victory,' I said, and felt better.

After making a few casts in the battalion HQ area we found elements of several platoons. I then went back to the area where I had landed and was relieved to see one or two containers with their lights showing and troops taking them up. At this point seven civilians, two women and five men, suddenly appeared, apparently returning from the village. By this time several 9 Para soldiers were with me, on their way to their respective RVs. I therefore accosted the civilians and, in my usual execrable French, demanded to see their papers. These they produced, and I examined them in the light of my pencil torch. They meant nothing to me, but I think it impressed the wretched civilians.

When I got back to battalion HQ several people had arrived, including the CO, who said, 'Where the hell have you been?' After a bit of explanation, I told him about the civilians and asked him what to do about them. 'Shoot them,' he said.

I do not normally dispute orders from my superiors, nevertheless I demurred. 'If they were not people the Germans trusted,' said the CO, 'they would not be allowed in this area. Shoot them.' He was under some tension at the time.

Back I went to the civilians. It was a worrying moment. By chance there was a sort of barn nearby. I herded the civilians into this barn, told them that a sentry was posted outside and that if they showed themselves in the next four hours they would be shot at once . . .[27]

Major Allen J.M. Parry, commander A Company, 9th Battalion, The Parachute Regiment:

I was to command the battalion RV party, which would land on DZ Victor thirty minutes before the battalion, locate the RV and there set up light aids to assist the main body to find it as quickly as possible after landing. After a most uncomfortable flight of seventy minutes' duration, the doors were opened and we awaited the signal to leap. As those in front of me left the aircraft I shuffled along on my backside, the prescribed method, to the edge of the large aperture. Arrived at this point, it was quite impossible to avoid falling through the hole.

I hoped I had been dropped in the right place but had, at first, no means of knowing. After divesting myself of my harness, I extracted a map and an air photograph or two and began to study them with my torch. I was, however, none the wiser regarding my whereabouts.

It was reasonable to expect that at least one or two of my party would have made their presence apparent to me. But no, there was no movement or sign of them.

I decided I must move off in a westerly direction, dragging my heavy kit bag and hoping I would eventually encounter the all-important RV. I had not gone far, however, when I became aware of the drone of heavy aircraft overhead. Until now I had given no thought to the 100 Lancasters that were to attack the Merville battery at midnight-thirty. In a matter of seconds I became, as I thought, the target of this mighty force dropping 4,000 pound bombs. As these missiles rained down upon me I bit the dust and resigned myself to eternity. I could see huge columns of earth going skywards as the bombs struck and I had no doubt that I could not survive such a punishment.

I heard the crash of falling masonry as bombs hit the village of Gonneville-sur-Merville, less than one kilometre away to the north-west. After what seemed an age, although it was only the ten minutes scheduled for the attack, I found I was still alone and, indeed, had all my limbs intact. I offered profound thanks and continued on my way.

As I was approaching a narrow gravel track I heard human voices. At first I could not be certain what language they were speaking, but after a brief interval I realized they were talking Canadian English. A company of the 1st Canadian Para Battalion was, I know, to drop in the same DZ at the same time and then launch an assault on a known German HQ in a château at Varaville, a short distance to the east. These voices, then, must emanate from them.

Two soldiers, unaware of my presence, then appeared and froze as I challenged them. I demanded of them the password. They didn't know it – so I told them and remonstrated with them for making so much noise. I saw that between them they carried no weapons and they explained they had lost them on the DZ. Seeing that I was carrying a sten gun one of them asked if they could have it. At first I said no, but after negotiations decided to hand it over as I had a pistol and I felt they could make more use of the sten than I could. After giving them the magazine they bade me good night, or good morning, and disappeared into the gloom.

With this incident over I crossed the track and found myself in an orchard. At this point I became conscious of movement about thirty metres away. I watched for a few moments and was able to discern the outline of what I clearly hoped was a British soldier. As I approached stealthily, I realized it was none other than my batman, who had arrived first, and alone, at the RV. After congratulating him on his skill and bidding him good evening, he said, 'Well, what happened to you?'

The time was close to that of the landing, at midnight-fifty, of the battalion. I started to unpack my haversack and removed the Aldis lamp in its box and connected up the dry batteries. Having located the bushy-topped tree which was the RV, I invited Private Adsett to climb it with the lamp and be prepared to flash it in due course. He declined the invitation and observed that, as I was the person in charge of the RV party, it was my task to climb the tree. This I did, without further discussion.

Very shortly afterwards I heard the aircraft approaching the DZ and began to flash the Aldis lamp, which evidently had the desired effect as soldiers began to come into the RV. At about this time, two Horsa gliders containing a miscellany of stores and two others containing a six-pounder and an anti-tank gun, should have landed. Of these there was no sign.

In due course the CO arrived at the RV and I informed him of the numbers and equipment present. Both were disappointingly small. The battalion was due to leave the RV to begin the approach march at 02.35 hours, but at this time the battalion strength was no more than about 120. The CO decided to wait a further fifteen minutes, during which time another thirty or so reported. Clearly some reorganization would be necessary. The battalion had no mortars, only one machine gun, no anti-tank guns, a very few bangalore torpedoes, no tape, no mine detectors or aids for negotiating the anti-tank obstacles. More important, the entire half-troop of sappers with their prepared charges were missing, as were many complete sub-units of the battalion.

At 02.50 hours the CO ordered the approach march to begin. The route to the FUP [forming-up point] covered a distance of about 2,200 yards and took one-and-a-half hours. En route we met a representative of the battery recce party, who reported that the bombing attack had missed the battery, which was still 'alive'. The ground assault would, therefore, proceed, but not as originally planned, due to the missing 75 per cent of the battalion and much of the equipment required.

Upon arrival at the FUP the CO placed me in command of an ad hoc party that would execute the assault. I was given three officers and about fifty other ranks and I quickly divided them into four parties, one for each casemate. I allotted myself No. 1 gun.

On my signal to deploy, the four parties made their way as best they could through the outer fence and were then confronted by the principal wire obstacle, which was ten feet deep. This had to be negotiated in battle-school style, with soldiers assisting each other through, and over, it. However, before this was reached it was necessary to cross the minefield, which was known to vary in depth from fifty-five to seventy-five feet. As it had not been possible to make the planned gaps, it was a case of every soldier for himself. Inevitably, some were killed and wounded.

As we crossed the minefield, enemy fire was opened and increased rapidly. I was conscious of something striking my left thigh, my leg collapsed under me and I fell into a huge bomb crater. The rest of my party, unaware that I had been struck, continued towards No. 1 casemate, firing from the hip.

In the bottom of my rather personal bomb crater, I assessed my position. My left leg was numb and my trouser leg was soaked in blood. Having a minuscule knowledge of first aid I removed my whistle lanyard and tied it to my leg as a tourniquet. My knowledge was evidently too limited, as I applied it in the wrong place. Realizing, after a brief interval, my error, I removed it, thus restoring some form of life to my leg; sufficient, at any rate, to enable me to clamber out of my hole and continue with my appointed mission.

I eventually arrived at the entrance to No. 1 casemate to find a mêlée of my own soldiers and those of the opposition, a number of whom were standing, very frightened, with their arms raised. All around lay dead or dying soldiers. As I entered the enormous casemate it was possible to discern only two or three of my party. I was somewhat weakened by the loss of blood and passed through the casemate to the firing aperture at the far end where, to my intense dismay, I saw not a 150mm gun, as was to be expected, but a tiny, old-fashioned piece mounted on a carriage with wooden wheels. I estimated it to be a 75mm and it was clearly a temporary expedient, pending the arrival of the permanent armament. This was an awful anti-climax, and made me wonder if our journey had really been necessary.

The problem now was to deal with the gun. We all carried sticks of plastic explosive, detonators and fuse wire and I instructed a sergeant to make up a suitable charge which was placed in the breech of the gun and detonated. We re-entered the casemate, now full of acrid smoke, and upon inspecting the gun I was reasonably satisfied that sufficient damage had been inflicted upon it to prevent it playing a part in the seaborne assault, which was due in about two-and-a-half hours' time.

I left the casemate with the object of visiting the others to ascertain the situation, but as I hobbled towards No. 2 casemate I met Lieutenant Dennis Slade, the assistant adjutant, who informed me that the remaining guns had been adequately immobilized. The signal officer carried into battle a clapped-out old pigeon in his battledress blouse. He released the hapless bird which was optimistically intended to home on some place in the United Kingdom with a 'success' message attached to it, but it was seen to fly off in an easterly direction – towards Berlin.

It was after 05.00 hours and getting light, and as the *Arethusa* was to pour fire onto the battery at 05.50, withdrawal became all-important. There were quite a few soldiers still in there and, as best I could, I shouted to them to make their way out. I felt weary and was not as mobile as I would have wished. Slowly, and with some difficulty, I made my way to the point of exit, where I saw what can only be described as an urchin's soap box on wheels. This seemed to me a godsend and I decided to mount it and begin my withdrawal. By lying on my back on the trolley, and propelling myself with the heel of my right foot, I was able to make very slow progress. It was, however, exhausting, and I considered my chances of reaching the rallying point remote. As I was reflecting upon my chances a sergeant of my company came into view, took off his toggle rope, attached it to my chariot and proceeded to drag me along the dusty track to the rallying point. During this journey, while shells were still landing nearby, I drank several mouthfuls of whisky from the flask which, attached to my belt, I regarded as an important part of my battle accoutrements.[28]

Lieutenant Alan Jefferson, 9 Para:

I was about half-way down the track to the Calvary [rallying point] when an extraordinary sight met my eyes. It was Allen Parry riding in what looked like a child's home-made cart and propelling himself along with a rifle butt. One leg was sticking up in the air and he used the other to prod at the ground. He was waving and shouting in a manner far removed from his normal, quiet behaviour and I thought he must have gone barmy. 'Sorry I can't give you a lift!' he called.[29]

Captain Hal Hudson:

I was just short of the gap in the wire when something hit my right buttock. I assumed it was a piece of earth, or a stone, thrown up by mortar or shell fire. I was extremely surprised to find myself thrown on my back and assumed that some sort of blast must be responsible. However, on attempting to get back on my feet, I found that I was unable to do so. I put my hand on my right buttock and was very surprised indeed to find it smothered in blood. I felt no pain, but a curious weakness. Lying on my back, looking towards the battery, through the gap in the wire made by the bangalore torpedoes, I saw a stream of machine-gun tracer which appeared to be uninterrupted. Through this gap were pouring the assault troops. I do not know how it happened, but they seemed to be going through.

I could see the German troops outside the gun emplacements; presumably others were in the casements. With infinite pains I took up my revolver, aimed carefully at the nearest German, and pulled the trigger. The bullet went straight through my left foot.

This self-inflicted wound caused me the most exquisite pain. Dawn was coming up. The troops had destroyed the guns, the survivors were returning through the minefield to reassemble for the attack on the next objective. A soldier, I don't know who, stopped beside me and said, 'Are you all right, sir?' I said I thought I was, but something had hit me on my right side. He bent down and looked. I can still hear his involuntary intake of breath.

At that point Terence Otway came running down the pathway through the mines. He stopped beside me and said, 'Are you all right?' 'I think so,' I said. 'He's been hit in the stomach,' said the soldier. 'Oh bad luck,' said the CO. 'We've got the battery, Hal.'

I take it as eternal credit that I did not say what he could do with the battery.[30]

Captain John Madden, C Company, 1st Canadian Parachute Battalion:

C Company had been chosen to land half an hour before the rest of the 6th Airborne Division in order to clear the dropping zone of enemy resistance.

I landed in soft pastureland, crouched low against a hedge and signalled with my tiny coloured light for the others. Within a few minutes I was joined by two of the men; there had been ten men in my stick but of the remainder there was no sign.

We pushed on alone. The few seconds I had delayed in jumping would have brought us about a thousand yards too far inland, so I led the way back towards the coast. We crouched, hidden in the long grain of a field we were about to cross, when a small group of soldiers came towards us. When they came nearer we were relieved to see that they were three of our own. They slid down beside us and as they lay there panting we could hear German soldiers shouting and tramping in the next field. I had orders to avoid all trouble. Never in the history of warfare were orders so implicitly obeyed.

We by-passed the enemy and made for our objective, the château at Varaville, but after half an hour's wandering we realized we were lost. The most feasible thing to do was to contact a farmer and find out where we were. A few minutes more and I sighted a rambling group of buildings that looked like a dairy. It didn't seem too friendly: flashlights cut into the night, doors slammed and foreign tongues babbled. The fact that the babble didn't sound German offered no consolation. Many of the troops opposing us were Czechs and Poles.

We made our way to the road leading into the farm. I gathered my men around me on the roadside and gave them the plan of approach. Right in the middle of my orders, a German soldier rode past on a bicycle. He looked down at us and we up at him. He displayed only the slightest curiosity; not wanting to alarm him, we carried on as best we could to deceive him into thinking that we were also German soldiers. We must have succeeded, for he pedalled on at his normal rate.

I decided to cross the road and strike clean away, but as our boots sparked on the stony surface of the road there was a cry of '*Halt!*' We dashed onto the grass verge and into the doubtful protection of the shadows. I could see the cyclist turn round. What had made him start back? I didn't know or care. I checked my gun, waited while he cycled nearer. I could see his figure outlined in silver against the moon. He was wearing a soft hat and had a rifle slung over his shoulder. I motioned the men further into the darkness of the hedge, stood up and when he was exactly opposite me squeezed the trigger. The bicycle wobbled and with a clatter he fell off and lay still on the road.

In the awful silence that followed we heard the rattle of equipment and the scuffle of feet running towards us. It wasn't safe to stay in that vicinity, so we made off across the fields and along the numerous hedgerows. At last we found the damp and odious protection of a swamp. It took a long time to cross it and we were exhausted by the time we reached the other side. That, and the fact that it was now too light to move around, decided me to hole up until we could capture a German vehicle or contact a French peasant. With that in mind, I chose a small copse that lay by a narrow lane.

The sergeant took the first watch and I fell into an exhausted sleep.[31]

Captain B.C.E. Priday, 52nd Light Infantry:

I shall always remember the odd feeling I had as we went into a steep left-hand turn, losing height rapidly and finding myself looking straight out and down through the doorway into the darkness and the clouds below. I shouted as loudly as the others, for I did not want to be temporarily deaf when I reached the ground owing to the increase in atmospheric pressure as we lost height. We soon straightened out, still losing height, and rather more quickly than I expected we hit the ground. We hit it very hard, for it was extremely dark and the pilots could hardly see, and bounced up into the air again. We seemed to poise for a minute with our nose in the air and then we came crashing to earth once more, tearing along the ground at terrific speed. The wheels must have come off or the floor of the glider broke up and the seats came adrift. We came to a standstill, the people on my side almost lying on their backs.

With difficulty we got out of the wreckage. We were all out by 00.22 hours. Instead of recognizing my surroundings, they were completely strange to me. It is true that we landed by a waterway and a bridge, but they were not the ones I had learned to recognize so well over the weeks beforehand from photographs and models.

We were in the wrong place.[32]

CHAPTER ELEVEN

THEY'RE COMING!

The French people woke up on the morning of 6 June 1944 to find that the day for which they had been waiting so long had at last arrived; for the German occupiers, it was the day they had dreaded for so long . . .

Georges Gondrée, proprietor of the Café Gondrée, Pegasus Bridge:

A few minutes after one o'clock I was woken by my wife. At that time we slept in separate rooms; not because we wanted to but because that was the best way of preventing German troops from being billeted upon us. She said to me, 'Get up. Don't you hear what's happening? Open the window.' I was sleepy and it took me some time to grasp what she meant. She repeated, 'Get up. Listen. It sounds like wood breaking.' I opened the window and looked out.

It was moonlight, but I could see nothing, although I did hear snapping and crunching sounds. My wife, who speaks good German, suggested she should ask the sentry standing at the bridge what was happening. She leaned out of the window and did so and I could see the sentry's face clearly in the moonlight. His features were working and his eyes were wide with fear. For a moment he did not speak and I then saw he was literally struck dumb by terror. At last he stammered out one word, 'Parachutists.'

'What a pity,' my wife said to me, 'those English lads will be captured.' We both thought that what the sentry had seen was the crew of a bomber bailing out, but then firing broke out almost immediately and we took refuge in the cellar with our two children.

We could hear the sound of the battle outside and at one point there was a knock on the door and a German voice called out ordering us to leave the café and walk in front of the German troops. We stayed where we were until my wife persuaded me to go upstairs and see what was happening.

I am not a brave man and I did not want to be shot, so I went upstairs on all fours and crawled to the first-floor window. There I heard talk outside, but could not distinguish the words, so I pushed open the window and peeped out cautiously. I saw in front of the café two soldiers sitting near my petrol pump with a corpse between them. I called to them in French, but I could not understand their reply. I think one said, '*Armée de l'air*' and the other said something like 'English *Flieger*.' I still thought that they belonged to the crew of a crashed bomber, but I was worried by the clothes they had on and also by the fact that they seemed to be wearing black masks.

I went to another window overlooking the canal and saw two more soldiers who lifted their weapons and pointed them at me. By then there were a number of flares burning in the sky, so that I could see quite plainly. One of the soldiers said to me '*Vous civile?*' I replied, '*Oui, oui,*' and added something else which I don't remember. The soldier again said, '*Vous civile?*' and after a moment I realized that these were the only words of French he knew. I was for twelve years a bank clerk in Lloyds Bank in Paris and I therefore speak good English, but I did not wish to let that fact be known at that moment, for I was still not sure who they were. One of them then put his finger to his lips and gestured with his hands to indicate that I should close the shutter. This I did and went back to the cellar.

Nothing more happened for some time and then we heard the sounds of digging in our vegetable garden outside. We looked through a hole in the cellar and there was a wonderful air of dawn coming up over the land. We could see vague figures moving about, but I could hear no guttural orders, which I always associated with a German working party. I turned to my wife and said: '*Ils ne gueulent pas comme d'habitude.*' The light grew stronger and I began to have serious doubts whether the people I could see were in fact the crew of a bomber; their behaviour seemed to me to be very strange. I told my wife to go to the hole in the cellar, listen and tell me if they were speaking German. She did so and presently said that she could not understand what they were saying. Then I, in my turn, listened and my heart began to beat quicker, for I thought I heard the words 'all right'.

Presently there was a knock at the door. I opened it and was confronted by two men with blackened faces. I realized then that it was paint, not masks, which they were wearing. They asked in French if there were any Germans in the house. I said no and invited them, with gestures and smiles, into the bar. They were reluctant at first, but I persuaded them to come down into the cellar, where I pointed to my wife and children. For a moment there was silence, then one soldier turned to the other and said, 'It's all right, chum.' At last I knew they were English and burst into tears.[1]

André Heintz, aged 24, student, member of the Resistance in Caen:

Towards the end of April the wife of my new leader made me learn by heart several messages, six I think, that I was to listen out for on my crystal set. These were the famous messages in connection with the preparations for D-Day. There was a special message for each area. For region M (Normandy), the warning message was *L'heure du combat viendra* and it was heard on 1 June. The the messages for action were *Les dés sont sur le tapis* and *Il fait chaud à Suez*, which meant to try and hinder all German lines of communication for the next twelve hours. If I remember right there was also *Les enfants s'ennuient au jardin*, which fortunately was never heard because it meant cancellation.

After the first message I had to send a postcard of the Bayeux Tapestry with just *Bons baisers* written on it to those of our network who were in hiding or away with the maquis, so that they would join us and complete our headquarters.

After the second message I passed the word and spent the night watching the German 716th Infantry Division headquarters, near where I lived in Caen. We had heard many planes going overhead from 11.20 p.m. onwards and after 3.30 in the morning the rumbling of an intense shelling in the distance towards the sea made us think that the navy was destroying defences along the coast, the position and shape of which I had sent information back to England during the previous months.

After the D-Day messages I had had to keep all the information so secret that I did not even tell my mother. At two o'clock on the morning of 6 June she was woken by all the noise outside and she said to me, 'It must be the landing, André, don't you think so?' I just answered, 'I don't know.'

Towards the end of the night, when with all the rumbling in the distance it became obvious that something important was happening, she again asked me if it was D-Day and I just told her that we had better fill some bottles with drinking water because I was not sure how long water would be available. She hurried down into the cellar and buried her jewels and most treasured possessions and she also cooked some potatoes because she guessed the gas would soon be cut off, and it was.[2]

Raymond Paris, aged 20, assistant to the notary, Ste Mère-Eglise:

I lived in the notary's house and the leader of our Resistance group, whose name was M. Maurice, lived in the house opposite. One day he asked me if I could get him some information. You must understand the notary's house was frequently visited or occupied by Germans and at one point it was the Command HQ of TODT, those Germans who were involved in the construction of the Atlantic Wall, so you can imagine why it was of interest to M. Maurice. I supplied him with the information he wanted and that is how I got into the Resistance; eventually I became a specialist in preparing false documents. You understand, all young people were called up for *Service de Travail Obligatoire* – forced labour – in Germany. Most people tried not to go, but for that it was necessary to have false papers. I made many, many false identity cards for my comrades, as well as ration cards.

I had an uncle who lived in the Calvados, who also took part in the Resistance and who was wanted by the Germans. He had been arrested with false papers and identity documents that I had made for him and, since those false papers carried the stamp of Ste Mère-Eglise, I was afraid the Germans would start looking in Ste Mère and would discover I was his nephew. So I went into hiding, in a farm about sixteen kilometres from here. I stayed in touch with my family and knew that I was not being looked for, so I returned to Ste Mère from time to time to visit my parents, or to see my *Chef de Résistance*, or my friends.

It was thus by chance that I was in Ste Mère on Monday, June 5th. I was at home, visiting my family, when I heard on the radio a message which concerned our particular Resistance network. Oh, yes, I certainly remember it, everybody who had been told to expect a message knows it to this day. Ours was *Les dés sont sur le tapis* – the dice are on the carpet. That was the sign for us that the invasion was imminent. That was all, we had no orders at all. Normally, I suppose we would have cut the telephone wires. But, for a start, we did not have the right to own a radio set – the Germans had confiscated all radio sets and if they had found one in our house we would have been arrested, at the very least.

Now, I heard the message at about 8.30 p.m., I think, something like that. The curfew was at 9 p.m., after which we had no right to go outside. There were patrols in the streets and you would have been arrested if you had been found outside without a permit. Someone like a doctor or a vet would have had a *laissez-passer*, but not ordinary people like us.

I don't need to tell you that I was very excited indeed that the invasion was finally going to happen. I was exalted, I had never dreamed that the invasion would start at Ste Mère. I was lying on my bed, fully clothed, on the second floor. The window was wide open and at ten o'clock, it was not yet quite dark, I heard two friends of mine calling to me that there was a fire over at Julia's, an old lady who lived in a house on the other side of the town square. From my window I could already see the light from the fire, I called my father, who was a fireman, and we went down as fast as we could to see if we could find a pump. We also went and woke up another fireman whose house was directly opposite the hangar where the pumps were kept and got him to ring the warning bell.

We took one of the two pumps, with buckets, hoses and nozzles, and went up the road towards the house. It was hard work for us because the hoses were very heavy and we were soon out of breath. We stopped suddenly because we saw an enormous wave of aeroplanes coming from the west to the east. Immediately, we thought there was going to be a bombing raid, but what really surprised us was that they were so low. We realized straightaway that they were American planes, one could see that, but we also noticed that there were black and white stripes painted around the wings and the fuselage, something we had never seen before. The wave of planes passed on over us and we continued on our way with the hoses, which we set up by the house that was on fire.

When the alarm bell started to ring out, about sixty or seventy people appeared, including many Germans. We set up a chain of buckets from the pump and, while we were passing the buckets up the chain, a second wave of aeroplanes arrived, equally low and similarly large in numbers and coming from the same direction.

Everybody passing buckets gazed up at the planes, all of us afraid that bombs would fall. The Germans who were with us on the square turned their machine guns on the planes, which seemed to be completely unaffected. They passed on, about five or six minutes after the first wave.

About two minutes later, at the very most, a third wave arrived, equally low and equally numerous. It was still not quite dark and there was a full moon that night and we were able to see that the side doors of the aeroplanes were open. We suddenly saw men jumping out of all the aeroplanes and their parachutes opening. I was standing on the edge of the square shouting, 'That's it, it's the invasion!'

Some of the parachutists landed as close as four or five metres from where I stood. I could see them pulling on the strings of their parachutes to cushion their landing. All the Germans who were there on the spot with us, it goes without saying, began to fire at the boys who were coming down. There was a parachutist who fell directly into the lime trees just by the pump and some of us helped him down and out of his harness.

At that moment I found myself in the street, ten or fifteen metres from the pump, when a nearby German soldier suddenly lifted his machine gun to fire on a parachutist. I tapped him on the shoulder, saying, 'Don't shoot, civilian,' to distract him. The parachutist was very lucky as the German soldier did not fire. However, a few seconds later, the very opposite occurred. I saw a parachutist fall into the trees, where he remained hanging helplessly, and before he could make the slightest movement, he was shot by some German soldiers. Almost immediately afterwards, another parachutist became tangled up in the trees and, once again, the Germans shot him.

It was getting too dangerous for us, because the Germans were firing all around our ears, they were panic-stricken. Those who experienced the *parachutage* will never forget it because there was the sound of the bell, which was still tolling and sounded very lugubrious, the noise of the airplanes, the bursts of automatic gunfire, the shouts and cries of the German soldiers, the cries of the French and the screams of the women, who obviously were terrified. It was Dante-esque.[3]

Alexandre Renaud, pharmacist, mayor of Ste Mère-Eglise:

Gathered in one of the bedrooms, windows closed, at about 2 a.m., we heard a noise of motors on the main highway. The moon had set, so we couldn't see anything. But judging by the shouts we could hear in German, it sounded as though the anti-aircraft unit was leaving. Motor cycles went by at full speed. A few automobiles, their lights out, set off for Carentan. Then all was quiet, except for the sound of machine guns in the belfry letting off long rounds of fire.

I opened a window slightly: the planes were still flying overhead, but very high up. Once in a while, we would hear a faint, short rattling noise that sounded like a partridge calling its chicks. Around three o'clock, on the square under the trees, the flash of lighted matches appeared, followed by the red glow of lighted cigarettes. It looked as though men were lying at the base of the trees. We whispered about it for a long time – were they Germans or British?

Little by little the night began to dissolve and as the contours became more precise we were astonished to see that the town was occupied neither by the Germans nor the British, but by the Americans. The first thing we recognized were the big round helmets we had seen illustrated in German magazines. Some of the soldiers were sleeping or smoking under the trees; others, lined up behind the wall and the town weighing building, stood with their weapons in their hands, watching the church, which was still held by the enemy.

Their wild, neglected look reminded us of Hollywood movie gangsters. Their helmets were covered with a khaki-coloured net, their faces were, for the most part, covered with grime. Since we were used to the stiffness and impeccable appearance of the Germans, the Americans' uniforms really seemed neglected to us. Machine-gun belts were slung over their shoulders, then draped around their waists. In addition to their machine guns, each man had a huge revolver strapped to his thigh. They cut a really inelegant figure in their loose fatigues.

A parachutist who looked like all the others came and knocked at my door, introduced himself as a Captain Chouvaloff and asked if I could tell him where he could find the local German commander.

I offered to accompany him.

'Ok,' he said. He offered me some chewing gum and we set off together. He didn't speak. A young man from the town joined us, but the captain didn't trust him. He walked with me in front of him, then, taking out his gun, ordered the youth to kick open the door. The commander, together with his entire anti-aircraft unit, had taken off.[4]

Unteroffizier Rudi Escher, aged 23, 1058 Infantry Regiment, 91st Airlanding Division:

We didn't know when the invasion would come, we only knew, that is, it was said, that it would come. We talked about it a lot among ourselves. The morale of the troops was fairly good because we had, despite everything, a fairly decent life in Normandy with no action. The French people were quite friendly. We all had our doubts about whether Germany could win the war, but we knew we had to do whatever was directed from above. We were not particularly well-informed or well-equipped. We had plenty of ammunition, but it was the wrong sort. In truth, we hardly had the means to sharpen our bayonets.

On the night of 5 June, about eleven o'clock, it was still fairly light. There were two sentries in the church tower at Ste Mère-Eglise and the rest of us had had the evening free. To kill time we cycled around the church square on our bikes until it was time to turn in. We slept in the church tower and as we were turning in an aeroplane went over very low and the sentry on duty saw eight or ten parachutes starting to descend. We thought it was the crew ejecting from a crippled plane. Our orders were to track down and capture any enemy parachutists, so we grabbed our weapons and went off in the direction where we thought they had landed, leaving two sentries in the church tower. It was dark by then and they must have hidden, for we found nothing.

When we got back to the village about an hour later, it was obvious the invasion had begun. More planes were coming over and parachutists were dropping everywhere – one was hanging from the church spire, even though there were two guards still up there. There was nothing they could do about him because their weapons were in their sleeping quarters below. Some parachutes were caught up in the trees, but the men attached to them had already disappeared. Also I should mention there was a corner house on fire and the local people were trying to put out the blaze.

Naturally, with Americans landing everywhere we were afraid for our lives, so we assembled on the church square and discussed what we should do. Several of my men had gathered up a few bits of equipment that had either been lost or discarded by the Americans. We got some cigarettes and chocolate and thought we were doing pretty well out of it.

We still had a telephone link with our unit, which was dug in two kilometres from the village. A sentry made contact to ask what we should do and we were told, initially, to stay put. There was by now quite a bit of shooting and while we were standing by the church wondering what to do one of our men fell down dead, shot through the heart. After this, we decided to return to our unit. There were only about six of us and there was very little we could do.

Leaving our dead comrade behind, we retrieved our bicycles, which were stored in a barn, and cycled back to our unit, one behind the other, each of us frightened of being shot by the Americans.[5]

German War Diary, 7th Army High Command:

01.30. Chief of Staff, 84th Army Corps, reports parachutists have been dropped since 01.05 hours in the area east and northwest of Caen, St Marcove and Montebourg, both sides of the Vire and on the east coast of Cotentin.

02.00. Chief of Staff of the 84th Army Corps reports to the Chief of Staff of the 7th Army High Command: Further airborne landings in 716 Inf. Div. sector. Area at the east coast Cotentin seems to be expanding from Ste Marie-du-Mont to Montebourg. There is fighting by Le Ham. Very large forces are approaching in the area east of Cherbourg and further west in the area of Jersey.

02.05. G-3 of the 15th Army High Command informs the G-3 about further airborne landings at Pont-l'Evêque.

02.15. Chief of Staff informs Chiefs of Staff of Army Group B: Larger landings mainly airborne and mostly in the vicinity of the 716th Inf. Div., southern part of the east coast Cotentin and diagonally through Cotentin at the narrows of Carentan. Small parts already annihilated. Motor noises can be heard from the sea on the east coast of Cotentin. Admiral of the channel coast reports ships spotted in the sea around Cherbourg. Chief of Staff suggests attaching the 91st Airborne Division. Chief of Staff of Army Group B judges that at present it is still a local affair. Chief of Staff is of the opinion that it is a major action.

02.30. Strong airborne landings to the depth of the vicinity of Pont-l'Abbé.

02.40. G-3 of Army Group B reports: According to Commanding General of Group 'West', it is not a major action . . .[6]

02.15. Pemsel, Chief of Staff, 7th Army, report to Speidel at Rommel's HQ:

Engine noises audible from sea on east coast of Cotentin. Admiral, Channel Coast, reports ships located by radar off Cherbourg.

02.40. Message to Pemsel:

C in C, West, does not consider this to be a major operation.[7]

Gefreite Walter Hermes, aged 19, motor-cycle messenger, 1st Battalion, 192nd Regiment, 21st Panzer Division:

I was stationed at Carpiquet airfield just outside Caen. I had an upper bunk by a window from which I could look across the airfield. In the middle of the night I was woken by the sound of heavy machine-gun fire and I leaned out of the window and saw 'Christmas tree' flares hanging in the sky. I woke the others and said, 'Look at this, we're going to be bombed for certain tonight.' Then we heard the sergeant major yelling at everyone to get dressed because 'The English have landed.'

I reported to the sergeant major's office and he said to me, 'Do you want to see our first prisoner? He's standing right there behind the door.' I quickly turned round and saw not a man but a life-size dummy made of some kind of rubber and hung all over with firecrackers. There were some more firecrackers in boxes on the sergeant major's desk. I said, 'By God, if the Allies expect to win the invasion with this sort of thing, they're crazy. They're just trying to scare us.'[8]

Commanding Officer 711th Infantry Division, 16th Army, stationed to the east of Sword beach:

The night of 5/6 June passed off quite peacefully until shortly after midnight. We had been in the officers' mess until about half an hour after midnight and were just on the point of going to bed when we heard the sound of aircraft flying very low over the billets.

When we went outside, we could see several low-flying planes circling over divisional headquarters. There was a full moon that night, but it was rather stormy, with low, black, slow-moving cloud formations, between which the planes could be clearly perceived. Just as I went back into the mess to arm myself, someone outside shouted, 'Paratroops!' Rushing out into the open again, I saw several parachutes still falling around the headquarters.

Meanwhile flak installed in the strong-point had opened fire. Immediately on the alarm being sounded the strong-point was manned, according to plan, with clerks, dispatch riders, drivers and batmen. While the adjutant was organizing the defence of the strong-point, I ordered the alarm to be sounded for the entire Divisional sector and reported to the headquarters of 81st Army in Rouen.

In the meantime, the first prisoners – two had landed in the strong-point itself – were brought in, but they could not, or would not, give any details about the operation. Although air activity and our anti-aircraft fire had ceased temporarily and everything seemed peaceful again, it was quite clear to me that this was the beginning of the long-expected invasion, although I was unsure whether it would take place here or if this was only a feint.

As far as I could make out, the paratroopers intended to capture the divisional headquarters; I therefore ordered immediate reinforcement of the strong-point by a pioneer company from St Arnold, which arrived at about 03.00. In the meantime reports came in from various regiments and I was able to get a picture of the situation. There were numerous paratroopers and supply gliders reported between Touques and Orne and local reserve troops were brought at once into action against the enemy.

The paratroopers did not succeed in concentrating themselves into fighting units on account of the counter measures taken by us. Most of the paratroopers were hiding themselves and, when discovered, surrendered without resistance. The prisoners belonged to a British and Canadian battalion of the Second British Airborne Division. One could get very little out of them, but they seemed to be sections which had lost their way. Instead of jumping between the Dives and the Orne, they had mistaken the Dives for the Orne because the Dives had been dammed up. One of them stated that it had originally been intended to land in the territory around Cabourg, but the plan was abandoned on account of obstacles of a new kind being discovered there.[9]

Obergefreite Anton Wuensch, aged 23, 2nd Company, 2nd Battalion, 6th Parachute Regiment:

I was in charge of a seven-man heavy mortar unit located on a ridge between the villages of St Hilaire and Le Mesnil, to the south of Carentan. From the beginning of May we had been more or less on alert all the time and my orders in the event of an invasion were to hold the ridge, so we were dug in with foxholes covered by wood or tarpaulin and camouflaged.

Every evening about eight or ten men, from my unit and from the other two mortar units dug in on either side, would come across to my foxhole to talk things over, smoke a few cigarettes and drink a lot of calvados. I always had a good supply.

On the night of 5 June no one came over; we had had a bit of a party the night before and everyone was feeling a bit under the weather. It had been very warm that day, so I went to sleep on the straw in the bottom of my foxhole just in my underclothes.

Some time between midnight and one o'clock I woke up. I was only half awake but I thought I felt the earth shaking. As I lay there, becoming fully conscious, the shaking stopped for a moment, but then I could hear the sounds of many planes and explosions and the shaking started again. I noticed the sand and earth on the edge of the foxhole was beginning to crumble and I stood up, saying to myself, 'Good God, what's this?'

I crawled out of the foxhole and looked up at the sky. It was clear and the stars were shining. To the north, the noise was getting stronger and stronger. Still in my underwear, I walked up to the top of the ridge and looked north towards Carentan. I was stunned by what I saw. Hanging in the sky, slowly drifting towards the ground, were bunches of red, green and white flares which we called 'Christmas trees'. I could also see tracers and anti-aircraft fire weaving up into the sky. All I could think of was that there was a fantastic thing happening, but there was no alarm.

I ran back to the foxhole and tried to wake Sergeant Klopp, but he was a man who would sleep even if you fired a mortar in his ear, and all he did was roll over and groan. I went across to the other foxholes and began waking the other men; I pulled one man, Friedolin, out of his foxhole by his ankles and he wasn't too happy about it. Then I went back and finally got Klopp awake by shaking him and yelling at him, 'Come on, come on, wake up!'

We got dressed quickly, put on our equipment and went up to our prepared positions on the ridge, about twenty yards in front of the foxholes. It was about 1.15 by the time we got there and someone said, 'Now the shit starts.' A runner came from the company commander to say that the highest alert had been ordered and we were to stay in our positions. Friedolin was moaning all the time, saying he was hungry and trying to bum cigarettes. Around three o'clock he announced he was going to eat his iron rations, so I said to him, 'Don't ask me for food two or three days from now.' He replied, 'To hell with you. The carnival has started. Tomorrow you may all be dead, with cold arses.'[10]

Oberst Werner von Kistowski, aged 45, commander Flak Assault Regiment No. 1:

My unit was dug in at a place called La Cambe, at the mouth of the Vire near Grandscamp. On the evening of 5 June I drove to St Lô, to the headquarters of the 84th Corps, to get approval to draw more gasoline. I was driving back to La Cambe with my engineering officer when I saw Christmas-tree flares in the sky and I said to my companion, 'I think the mess is starting.'

When we got back to our headquarters, I went to the farmhouse where I had a room and wrote a letter to my wife, Ruth, breaking it off when I heard waves of bombers coming over. I went down to my headquarters and found there were reports of paratroopers dropping. I called in the communications officer and told him to send a coded message 'LL', which meant the invasion had started, to 84th Corps.

The bombing which then began was absolutely hideous, just murder. We all cowered in foxholes as the bombers laid pattern after pattern across our position. It did not seem we could possibly survive the pounding. When we climbed out of our holes we were all shivering, but every time we thought it was over another wave of planes came in.

While I was in my foxhole I could follow the path of gliders being towed over the river and passing over Grandscamp and all the time I kept wishing that my foxhole was smaller. It seemed much too wide amd I felt that every shell, every bomb, was aimed directly at me. Instinctively I tried to make myself as small as possible, tried to duck and crawl inside my helmet. Every time the bombing let up I lifted up my head and shouted to my communications officer, 'Schmidt, are you still there? Then I called to my adjutant, 'Gelaubrecht, are you still alive?'

The bombs dropped from the planes detonated just above the ground and I thought how much worse it was than the forty consecutive nights of bombing I had endured in Berlin in 1943. At one point Schmidt called out from his foxhole, 'Now I know what my wife is going through in the Ruhr.'

When it finally stopped the air was filled with the acrid smell of cordite, both from our own guns and the explosives. I stood up and saw, one by one, heads appearing. Very slowly the men came out of their foxholes and looked around. Everyone was black and covered with dust and everyone was trembling. I was absolutely amazed to discover we had lost only one man killed and three wounded.[11]

Gefreite Klaus Herrig, aged 21, wireless operator, German Navy Signals Corps, Le Havre:

Some fools believed in the first months of 1944 that Germany could still win the war, but I wasn't among them. I couldn't believe it by then. I think about half my colleagues felt as I did. Everyone could see that we were not invincible, as we had always been told. The outcome of the war was a dangerous thing to discuss – you could only do it with friends, or people you felt you could trust – because in every unit there was a spy or two from the political side who would be watching and listening all the time.

I worked in the telephone exchange at Le Havre every third night. Many of us listened to Radio Calais, a radio station based near Canterbury which broadcast news and all sorts of propaganda. German emigrants, speaking perfect German, gave us the latest news from the front. It was strictly forbidden to listen to it and if you had a comrade on duty with you who you were not sure of you couldn't do it. But I listened whenever I had the chance.

Our existence was really quite peaceful. Our relationship with the French was more correct than friendly. We used to go to the local café for a beer, but there were no strong personal connections. Our discipline was good and the German troops, in general, behaved themselves.

News from home made us very concerned for the well-being of our families because of all the air raids. Allied aeroplanes were coming more frequently and in greater numbers all the time. I managed to get a telephone connection to my parents in Trier from time to time, so I knew they were safe and sound. It was strictly forbidden to have private talks on the military net but you could sometimes do it and get news from home.

We expected the invasion to come that summer and waited for it with mixed feelings. It was a strange situation. If the invasion came, we thought it might be the end of the war and that was what we wanted, to get the thing over with and finished and to go home. On the other hand we feared for our lives, as every soldier does, because we knew it wouldn't be fun. So I had mixed feelings: I knew I had to do my duty as a soldier but in my innermost heart I just hoped for it to be over.

We had no idea precisely when or where the invasion would come. Personally I thought it would be in the Pas de Calais, at the narrowest part of the Channel. I thought the Allies would take the easiest route.

We had to alternate guard duties – one night in the telephone exchange, one night in the telecommunications centre and one night on guard outside our bunker. I was on bunker duty on the night of 5 June and between two and three in the morning there was a telephone call to say that English and American troops had landed in Normandy.

I was told to take the news to the officers in the canteen next door. They were having some kind of celebration, a reunion or something, and were having a good drink. At first they wouldn't believe it. They thought it was a joke.

Then we heard that airborne troops were landing near Le Havre. Our infantry went out to investigate and found they were only dummies, dropped as a distraction. I think most people still believed that the invasion was a feint and that the real invasion was still to come.

As far as I was concerned, I didn't know whether I believed it or not. It was the old feeling of fear and hope – fear for your well-being and secret hope that it would all be over as soon as possible.[12]

Oberleutnant Helmut Liebeskind, aged 22, adjutant 125 Panzer Grenadier Regiment, 21 Panzer Division:

We received word that the invasion would not be on that day [6 June] because the weather was so poor. Three days earlier, it had been a possibility. From 5th to 6th, it was practically written off. And we believed that. I must reflect now that we Germans are not seafaring folk. As land rats, there are none better and we decided that there would be no invasion. Readiness was scaled down a little and that told us that the high command had assessed the situation accordingly.

On the evening of 5 June I returned from reconnoitring the roads around Troarn with my scouts and went straight to the regimental orderly room, in an old school in Villemont, where the duty officer reported to me that there had been several phone calls reporting some bombing activity. I then went to my quarters, which were just round the corner, and changed into a clean tunic because I wanted to go and eat. I went to the officers' club which was in a small château in the next village and had dinner. It was then that we heard the first disturbing reports about heavier bombing raids and denser overhead flying, so I went back to the regimental orderly room.

By then it was about midnight. We could hear the sound of engines in the air and there was a low but thin cloud base. I was standing on the road in front of the school, looking up, wondering what on earth was going on up there, when suddenly we saw, through breaks in the cloud, the shadowy forms of multi-engined bombers with freighter gliders attached.

We rushed indoors and phoned through the report at once. We knew now it was coming, that it was the build-up to an airborne landing. When we received the first notification of parachutists and gliders here and there, we told ourselves that we should first establish whether or not this was the actual 'D-Day' or if it was a diversion to attract us away from the real landing, which might actually be happening in Pas de Calais. Reports then began to come in thick and fast and we learned about the landings at Ste Mère-Eglise, but still no word of a sea landing.

Our 2nd Battalion was already on stand-by but we alerted the 1st Battalion and the ancillary regimental units. They all moved out until they reached the Route Nationale, but there the column stopped because there were no orders forthcoming to attack or anything.

We sat upstairs in the orderly room and attempted to clarify the situation, telephoning the 716th and 711th Divisions to ask if anything was happening in their areas.

Then a British military surgeon who had been taken prisoner was brought in. He stood there and we asked him his name and where he had come from. He answered with name, rank and number. We rang the division and they sent him to divisional HQ as soon as possible. The poor pig, we thought at the time.[13]

Hauptmann Curt Fromm, aged 25, commanding 6 Company, 100 Panzer Brigade, 22 Panzer Division:

On the night of the invasion, at about 11 p.m., I received a phone call from a Frenchwoman whom I did not know and she said to me, 'Captain Fromm, all of us wish you the best of luck in the next few hours.' I was somewhat perplexed by this.

I had a small radio for which I had made a leather case so I could carry the radio around with me. Yes, of course, I listened to the 'enemy' broadcasts, who didn't? The music alone was worth the risk! But as it happened, one of my fellow officers was due to go on leave that very night and he was returning to Wiesbaden, which is close to where I lived, so I gave him my radio and a few valuables that I wanted to save for sentimental reasons, to take home for me. I was concerned that they would be destroyed in an air raid.

I regarded the telephone call as a sign that something was about to happen and, sure enough, shortly afterwards came the alarm. It came from regimental HQ in two stages, first make ready and then stand by. Acting according to previously agreed plans, we packed our possessions, loaded the tanks and prepared our ammunition so we were ready to move off. There were seventeen tanks in four groups and I rode in the commander's tank at the head of the column.

We could already see that Falaise and Caen were burning and realized that we would not be able to take that route. We began to feel a little uneasy by this time. Our objective was Riva Bella, at the mouth of the Orne, about sixty kilometres away. According to our plans, we should have taken two-and-a-half to three hours to get there, but we had not reckoned on not being able to go through Falaise and Caen.

Somewhere to the west of Caen we received information that the English airborne landing was happening nearby, that paratroopers were being landed and freighter-gliders were also landing and that local defence forces, which consisted mostly of old or sick soldiers and which were ill-equipped, were not in a position to repel them. It was thought that the British had even dropped small tanks.

Part of the regiment was dispatched to sort this out and my section, hidden to the best of its ability, just waited for them for the next three or four hours. This sortie, which began during the early hours, when the light was still poor, was successful and the invaders were annihilated but it meant that our plans had now irrevocably broken down as we were not able to make up the lost time. We never made it to Riva Bella.[14]

Generalstabsoffizier Hubert Meyer, aged 30, senior general staff officer, 12 SS Panzer Division (Hitlerjugend):

I was living in the same house in Normandy as the division commander, at Tillières-sur-Avre, about forty kilometres from the coast. On the night of 5 June my wife was staying with me, on a visit. It was totally illegal, but I hadn't had any leave for ages. That night the brigade leader, Major General Witt, came upstairs and knocked on my door and said, 'On your feet, Meyer, the invasion has begun!'

I got up, dressed quickly, and went downstairs and telephoned 711 Infantry Division headquarters. They said, 'No, it's not the invasion. They aren't paratroopers, they're just straw dummies.' So I thought, well, I'll go back to bed.

Half an hour later, the Major General came upstairs again, knocked on the door and said, 'Wake up! The invasion has begun and this time it's the real thing!' I told my wife to go on sleeping, went downstairs and once more telephoned the 711th. This time they said yes, paratroopers really have dropped, but they didn't know how many there were.

We immediately put the division on standby so that we could advance at a moment's notice, but no orders came through from the army command centre or from the commander of Panzergruppe West. No alert, nothing.[15]

Irmgard Meyer, aged 24, wife of Hubert Meyer:

At the time, I was living in Stuttgart at my parents' house. I had two children and was expecting the third. Suddenly, with no warning, at the end of May there came a car, an open car driven by my husband's driver and a lieutenant who told me that all leave had been suspended and that my husband wanted to see me once more and I was to go immediately to Normandy before 'things began to happen'.

I knew what was happening. People were always talking about the possibility of an invasion, it was an open secret that the English and the Americans were both expected somewhere up there. At that point, I simply wasn't thinking about my children and my family, I just wanted to see my husband one more time, because neither of us knew whether we would see each other again. I was always afraid for his safety, always. Naturally.

I had a cousin who lived in the area and she said she would take care of the children, so off I drove to Normandy in an open car. We set off in the morning and arrived that same evening. My husband had a house at Le Rousset d'Acon, a pretty house with a garden. It was a beautiful spring, warm, and I can still remember the scent of the jasmine when I arrived. The house belonged to a painter or a sculptor, I remember, as there was a studio in the large garden. There was a young French girl who cooked asparagus for us.

For a while it was just like peacetime. I lived there with my husband and he drove off each morning as if he were going to work. Then, my husband's commander, the major general, said his wife was also there and that we should move with them into the château in Tillières. It was not so nice, there were too many people and we were never alone, we had constantly to make conversation with other people in the evenings. I was not so happy there. But there was a large lake and we could swim.

In the afternoons all the commanding officers would drop in. I remember Max Wuensche in his splendid black tank uniform and Kurt Meyer – another Meyer – from a Panzer grenadier regiment whose wife was also pregnant with her fifth child. He used to say to me, 'Little Meyer, I'm going to have my son before you do!' And it turned out to be true. He had four daughters and his wife gave birth to a son. We had two daughters and had a third.

On the night of 5 June we all stayed up a long time round the fire and chatted and went to bed late. I remember my husband and the division commander went into another room for some private discussion, but everything was peaceful.

Then, later in the night, we were woken up by a knock on the door and a voice saying, 'Wake up, the invasion's started.' My husband got up and said to me, you stay here and sleep and wait and see what happens. I was so tired that I genuinely did go back to sleep. At 5 a.m., my husband came back and told me, 'They have landed, but I don't know where and you have got to get out of here as quickly as possible. Get up immediately and pack. You can't take anything with you because you are going in a car with two other women (Frau Wuensche and Frau Witt), who are going to Munich and you go on to Stuttgart.' I just took my bag and wanted to take my husband's camera home with me, but he said, 'No, I need that, I want to take pictures of the invasion.' I couldn't persuade him. Everything had to stay behind, even our dog. I looked out of the window and for the first time really comprehended just how serious things were. It was a dull day and outside I saw General Major Witt, quite alone, sitting on a garden seat at a table, his head in his hands, as if he already knew what vast event was hanging over him and the huge responsibility, leading young people into battle, that went with it. And then all the other commanding officers arrived, ready to march, with steel helmets at the ready, pistols and grenades and they all took their leave. It really dawned on me how serious this day was, the way those men were taking leave.

So I went downstairs and Frau Witt and Frau Wuensche were already there, and another young woman whose husband was a *Sturmfuehrer*. She was crying, crying bitterly, since she, too, was saying goodbye to her husband, although she wasn't actually coming with us in the car. Frau Witt, Frau Wuensche and I – I don't think any of us cried; we had, after all, already experienced some four or five years of war and had said our goodbyes so often before; we were somehow used to saying goodbye. But I will never forget how bitterly this young woman wept – ten days later, her husband was dead, along with General Major Witt. She must somehow have sensed it.[16]

Hauptmann Ernst During, aged 28, commander heavy machine-gun company, 914 Regiment, 352nd Infantry Division:

My unit was stationed at Brevands, at the mouth of the Vire river between Isigny and Carentan. In front of us was a unit made up of half-invalid soldiers who manned the pillboxes of the so-called Atlantic Wall. My position was about 500 yards from the sea.

We had only been in Normandy a few weeks and we had spent all our time reinforcing the defences, putting up wooden poles with wire nets in between, digging trenches and building an observation platform on a big tree from which we could overlook the entire coastline. We believed the invasion would come any day, but none of us, me included, thought it would come in our sector.

Early in June the whole regiment was put on 'first-alarm' alert. This meant that everyone had to sleep in the pillboxes or trenches. But I had been in Russia for several years and everything in Normandy seemed child's play compared to what we had put up with in the East, so I didn't take much notice. I had a nice soft bed in the schoolhouse where I was quartered, about a couple of hundred yards from my command post, so I carried on sleeping there. I had made friends with the schoolteacher, a Monsieur Le Chevalier, and his family.

On the evening of 5 June I had dinner with the Chevaliers, as usual, and went to my roon at about 10 p.m. I noticed that there was a lot of air activity, but this was not particularly unusual and I had got used to it in the last few weeks.

I had been asleep for a couple of hours when I was woken by the sound of heavy explosions. I looked at my watch. It was 00.15. There was the noise of many planes coming from the direction of St Mère-Eglise. I thought to myself, 'This is it!' I got dressed as quickly as I could – actually I put my boots on the wrong feet and didn't notice it until the following day – picked up my tommy gun and ran downstairs. As I opened the schoolhouse door I saw two black men standing motionless on the other side of the street. I shouted, 'Who goes there?' There was no answer, so I lifted my tommy gun and fired. I don't know whether I hit them or not; I didn't stop to look.

When I got to my command post I telephoned battalion headquarters, two miles to the rear, and said, 'Paratroopers have landed here.' The answer came back, 'Here, too,' then the line went dead.

There was heavy bombing and artillery fire from the sea and then I saw the sky was filled with huge shadows – they were gliders coming in our direction. I ordered my men to attack with their heavy machine guns and we succeeded in shooting one down.

Then I heard strange sounds – a kind of 'click, click, click' at regular intervals. It sounded like the castanets of Spanish dancers. I couldn't explain it. As our wireless contact had been broken off, I felt very uneasy and isolated, but my experience told me to stay put in our position and wait until morning.

Dawn came at around 4.30 and I climbed up to the observation platform on the tree. It was then that I saw the enormous, fantastic concentration of ships out to sea, hundreds of them stretched out for a breadth of three or four miles. They were lying out there like a huge flock of sheep and I couldn't understand why the *Luftwaffe* didn't strike. In the direction of Ste Mère-Eglise I could see naval artillery covering the shuttle operation of fast landing craft. I was left in no doubt that this really was the invasion.

Back at my command post I sent a messenger to battalion headquarters, but he could not get through. Allied paratroopers camouflaged in the hedges shot at him from every direction. At about 6.00, however, about 150 men from battalion headquarters broke through to our position, bringing with them about twenty-five to thirty Allied prisoners, with blackened faces, that they had taken on the way.

I could speak English reasonably well and I got talking with an American captain of about my own age. He seemed very scared. He kept saying, 'Take everything you want, but don't shoot me.' It seemed they had been convinced by their propaganda that all Germans were killers. To get him over this idea I offered him one of my cigarettes and he gave me a Chesterfield. We sat and smoked silently and gradually he seemed to realize that I was just a soldier like him, nothing else.[17]

06.00. Telephone conversation between General Walter Warlimont, deputy chief of operations OKW, and Jodl:

W: Colonel General, sir, this is Warlimont.

J: Yes, yes.

W: Blumentritt has just called and told me that in the judgement of OB West the real invasion has begun. He backs his opinion because of the several parachute landings and sea landings which have taken place in Normandy. Furthermore, OB West wants the OKW reserves immediately. He asks that they should be released at once so that they can be brought up to the immediate invasion areas to repel landing.

J: Are you so sure of this? I am not sure that this is the invasion. According to all the reports I have received this could be part of the Allies' deception plan. In my opinion it is necessary to wait for more information.[18]

Gefreite Werner Beibst, aged 18, Infantry Division, 15th Army:

Around the beginning of June, the bombing raids seemed to be stepping up and the hinterland around Pas de Calais was absolutely flattened. This seemed to us confirmation that this was where the invasion would come. We believed this to be true and so, surely, did the supreme commanders of our army. Of course, this was deliberate tactics by the Allies.

In our section, something really unlikely happened. There was only ever one sentry on watch and he had to wake his relief after two-and-a-half hours. But because of the constant pressure and stress, one of the sentries fell asleep and almost exactly at the beginning of the day of June 6th, every last one of us was asleep.

Suddenly, from outside, we heard the most awful noise and it was some NCO screaming at us to wake up, the invasion had begun. We were totally surprised by it. It was barely dawn. We leapt to our feet and staggered outside. It was a very stormy sort of day, very bad weather, but we could see these vast numbers of ships, unbelievable numbers, sailing right past us.

We still didn't know where the landing was actually going to be but clearly, by that time, it had already happened. The sight of the ships was almost inconceivable, they just covered the water.

We stood there, doing nothing. There was not much we could do, the action was too far away to start marching towards it and anyway we were expecting this second wave. So we stayed in a more or less permanent state of emergency. It was dreadful; we just kept on looking at the water.[19]

Major Werner Pluskat, aged 32, 352 Artillery Regiment, 352nd Division:

My unit comprised three batteries, each with five guns, covering an area from Port-en-Bessin to the Les Moulins draw [Omaha] and my headquarters was at a château at Etreham about four miles from the coast.

I was woken up at about twelve by the sound of anti-aircraft fire. I telephoned the regimental headquarters and asked what was happening but they said they didn't know. Then I telephoned the intelligence officer at divisional headquarters and he said, 'It's not clear yet, but we think US paratroopers are landing to the left of us.' I didn't know whether to get up or not; there had been so many false alarms and no one seemed to be taking the thing too seriously, although there was still a lot of bombing and anti-aircraft fire in the distance.

About twenty minutes later I got a call from the regiment and this time I was told, 'It seems the invasion is beginning. You better get all your men to their battle stations right away.'

I got dressed immediately, woke my two ordnance officers and the three of us drove in a staff car to our advanced forward headquarters, which was a bunker overlooking the coast near the village of Honorine. It was about one o'clock by the time we got there.

I remember feeling very excited. We'd been waiting for this thing so long that we were glad it was coming, so we could get it over with.

The night was very dark and a little misty. I looked out at the sea through my artillery binoculars but there was absolutely nothing to be seen. Everything was terribly quiet. The sea was calm and there was a moon, but there were no lights, nothing to be seen out there at all, partly because of the mist on the sea and partly because of clouds passing across the moon. Finally I turned round to one of the ordnance officers and said, 'Just another false alarm.'

But even then I can remember having doubts. Even though I couldn't see anything, it seemed unnaturally quiet. A little while later we heard some explosions in the distance and some gunfire, but there was no word from regiment or division about what was happening. Then we heard bombers coming over and hitting targets inland.

Hardly a word was spoken between us in the bunker, but the tension was increasing all the time. As the first grey light of dawn began to creep across the sky I thought I could see something along the horizon. I picked up my artillery binoculars and stepped back with amazement when I saw that the horizon was literally filling with ships of all kinds. I could hardly believe it. It seemed impossible to me that this vast fleet could have gathered without anyone being the wiser. I passed the binoculars to the man alongside me and said, 'Take a look.' He said, 'My God, it's the invasion.'

I took one more look, then reached for the telephone and called Major Block, the intelligence officer at divisional headquarters. 'There must be ten thousand ships out there,' I told him. 'It's unbelievable, fantastic . . .' Block said, 'Look, Pluskat, are you really sure? The Americans and British together don't have that many ships.' I just said, 'For Christ's sake, come and look for yourself,' and then, because of the disbelief in his voice, I said, 'To hell with you,' and threw down the receiver.

We watched, absolutely petrified, as the armada steadily and relentlessly approached. It was an unforgettable sight; I don't think I had ever seen anything so well organized and disciplined. At about four o'clock in the morning the fleet began manoeuvring in front of us and I realized that the battleships were getting ready to fire. I telephoned Block again and asked for permission to fire. He replied,

'No, no. We're too short on ammunition. No gun must fire until the troops are nearing the beaches.'

To my horror and amazement, I could clearly see the guns of the fleet being elevated as they swung slowly round to point in our direction. A lilac-coloured Very light was fired from one of the ships. It went about 150 feet into the air and I remember thinking that it must be a much better type than we had, ours rarely went higher than about fifty feet.

Suddenly we saw planes approaching from the sea and begin bombing the beaches. The bombing continued for a solid forty minutes. There were thunderous explosions all around us, but we were relatively safe behind the thick walls of the bunker.

But then the bombardment from the sea began. The shells screamed like a thousand express trains and all seemed to be converging on our position. One of the first shells hit the base of our bunker and literally shook it. I was thrown to the ground and my binoculars were smashed. There was dust, powder, dirt and splinters of concrete all over the place and, although many of the men were shouting, no one seemed to be hurt. The firing continued, shell after shell pounding the bunker.

It was unbelievable to me. I was completely dazed and unable to speak and all the time the bunker was shaking. I remember looking at my watch. It was six o'clock. All my communications had been cut except for an underground cable which ran back to the château where the divisional headquarters was. This telephone kept ringing with demands for a report on the situation. The bunker was swaying to and fro, filled with dust and dirt, and everyone inside was lying on the floor.

I picked up the phone and someone said, 'Please give an exact location of where the bombs are falling.' I shouted back 'For God's sake, they're falling all over. What do you expect me to do, go out and measure the holes with a ruler?'[20]

CHAPTER TWELVE

OMAHA

Omaha beach was an unforgettable nightmare for the men of the US 1st Infantry Division, many of whom were pinned down under murderous fire for most of the day. Unknown to the assault troops, a crack German infantry division had moved into the sector to stiffen the defences ...

05.30. Lieutenant Arthur Newmyer, USNR, speaking over the public address system of Rear Admiral Hall's flagship, the Ancon, off Omaha beach:

In a few minutes, coinciding with the first break of dawn on this historic day, the most tremendous naval bombardment ever to blast out against the European continent will start.

During the night our warships – battleships and cruisers – protected from enemy submarines and E-boats by their screen of destroyers, went ahead of us as we neared the Baie de la Seine. They took their position, ready to pour fire at the enemy gun emplacements, as we lined up in the transport area.

The *Ancon*, leading the transport group in Rear Admiral Hall's force, arrived at the transport area at 02.30. We dropped anchor at 02.51. We are now on the port side of the transport line in Force O. We are approximately 200,000 yards – ten miles – off the beach.

The APAs [Auxiliary, Personnel, Assault, combat-loaded transports] already have lowered their LCVPs, which are milling about their mother ships, waiting for the bombardment to open up, waiting for their time to go in.

Our big ships are in very close to bombard in this assault. The *Texas* is going to fire at 12,000 yards. The *Arkansas* is going to fire at a range of only 6,000 yards. At those ranges those 14-inch guns mean business.

Battleships, cruisers, destroyers and monitors are going to blast at Hitler's Normandy defenses with rapid fire, concentrated fire, pinpoint fire, for forty minutes before the first troops hit the beach. We know where Hitler's guns are. They are banked in concrete and they will be hard to knock out. But we are going to give them an awful wallop.

In addition to the warship firepower I spoke about before, we have some more items to dish out. Our LCTs carry medium tanks, and these tanks will be cutting loose on the way in. They are scheduled to hit the beach at exactly H Hour, 06.30. Just before the tanks hit the beach, our rocket ships, carrying many banks of rockets apiece, will open up.

The infantry, in our LCVPs, will hit one minute after our tanks hit, at H plus one minute.

We have air bombardment helping us blast out those Nazi gun emplacements. They have been blasting for the past twenty-four hours. During the night, paratroopers landed behind the enemy lines to help cut off enemy reinforcements.

The Armies that are going to land are part of the British Second and the US First Armies. Together they are known as the 21st Army Group. The First Army is commanded by Lieutenant General Omar Bradley, who was aboard the *Ancon* during the Sicilian invasion. He is aboard the *Augusta* right now. Until General Bradley establishes his headquarters on the far shore, General Montgomery will command the Allied armies, the 21st Army Group. General Montgomery is the man who chased Rommel across the North African desert until tens of thousands of Italians and Germans surrendered in Tunisia. Reports from Germany indicate that Rommel is Hitler's first choice to face General Montgomery again.

If so, he hasn't long to wait. The naval bombardment is about to begin. H Hour is fast approaching. The liberation of Europe is on the way![1]

Corporal Gilbert G. Murdoch, A Company, 116th Infantry:

The hour came round and we all went up in a single file to the upper deck and so out through the double blackout curtains to the main deck. It was very dark out and there was still no sound from the shore.

Promptly at four o'clock the transport stopped engines and we all clambered over the iron rails into the landing craft which hung from the side of the ship. Each man was helped in and his equipment handed over to him. I maneuvered myself into the bow of the craft, where I had station. Voices could be heard all over, calling to friends in other boats.

I can distinctly remember looking at George Reach, who was the assistant flamethrower in my boat team and how he smiled back there in the dark. He was my special pal and a young fellow of eighteen and not too heavily built. I wondered at the time how he would make out carrying the sixty-pound can of fuel. Little did I know that just a few hours later on the beach he would swim out to a knocked-out tank and save my life, for I had by that time been nicked in the ankle and couldn't have made it in by myself. Just as the davits were lowering us into the water I called goodbye to the third of our little triumvirate, Robert Bruce, who was in another boat.

We hit the Channel with a thud and away we went. The men started taking their seasick pills; in fact one guy took half a bottle of the darn things and was practically walking in his sleep when he went off the craft. As we went in toward the beach we could see the colored flares that the amphibious engineers had placed. As we passed the last flare, after being in the water for almost two hours, the battleship *Texas* fired. We could see the flash, hear the roar of the shell overhead, then hear the report as it left the muzzle. Soon we saw the flash on the shore, then heard the bursting shell explode. It all seemed weird.

Rocket barges gave us our first real fright. They started to fire their huge banks of rockets and seemed to fire on the upward roll, so their huge load of rockets dropped a few hundreds yards in front of us, still a good two miles offshore. One guy yelled, 'Well there goes our holes on the beach!' By this time some of the guys were seasick and some were arguing over little things that didn't count. Some guys, like myself, were just standing there in the boat, thinking and shivering.[2]

Captain Charles Cawthon, CO Headquarters Company, 2nd Battalion, 116th Infantry:

Blowing spume had soaked us before we hit the Channel. It seemed we would surely swamp, and life belts were inflated, not only on our persons but on reels of telephone wire, radios and demolition packs, in the hope that if they were lost in the surf they would float ashore. The expansion of perhaps a hundred belts added to the bulk already crowding the craft, and so we rode, packed in an open can, feet awash in water and altogether cold, wet and miserable. It seemed that we were slamming into waves with enough impact to start any rivet ever set.

After about an hour of circling, the control launch passed a signal and the craft carrying us – the second wave of 116th RCT – peeled off into line and began battering through heavy seas toward Normandy. Thirty minutes ahead was the first wave; twenty minutes behind would come the third.

For the next two hours the line pitched and rolled toward Normandy and a gradually lighter horizon as we closed with the dawn of June 6. There was no attempt to talk above the roar of the engines, wind, slamming of the waves, and the laboring of the bilge pump that managed to keep up with the water washing in. We stood packed together, encased in equipment, dumb with the noise and with the enormity toward which we were laboring. I recall offering no prayers and having no particular worries, other than whether we were coming in on Dog Red sector.

A haze of smoke, barely darker than the gray morning, was the first sign of the shore, and then the line of bluffs emerged. Our craft shuddered to a halt on a sandbar, two hundred yards off shore. We were in among the beach obstacles: big, ugly structures partially covered by the rising tide. The coxswain failed on a couple of attempts to buck over the bar and then dropped the ramp. This may well have been fortunate for us as well as prudent for the coxswain – a landing closer in probably would have drawn artillery, mortar and machine-gun fire that was knocking the first wave apart. As it was, the German gunners had too many targets close by to bother with one more distant.

Where Channel and shore met was a wavering, undulating line of dark objects. Some of the larger ones, recognizable as tanks and landing crafts, were erupting in black smoke. Higher up the beach was another line of smaller forms, straight as though drawn with a ruler, for they were aligned along a bank of shingle stone and seawall. Scattered black forms were detaching themselves from the surf and laboring toward the line. Looming up between beach and bluff through the smoke and mist was a three-storey house. Such a structure was a landmark of the Dog Red sector, but I could not see the beach exit road. I believe we had come in on target, but I ceased worrying greatly over whether we had come in or not.[3]

Sergeant John R. Slaughter, aged 19, D Company, 1st Battalion, 116th Infantry:

As we approached topside a steady drone of the bombers going to their targets could be heard overhead and we saw bomb explosions which were causing fires that illuminated the clouds in the dark sky. We were twelve miles off shore as we climbed into our seat assignments on the LCAs and lowered by davits to the extremely heavy sea. The Navy hadn't begun its firing because it was still dark. We couldn't see the armada because of the darkness, but we knew it was there.

Prior to loading, friends said their goodbyes and good luck. I remember finding Jack Ingram, an old friend from Roanoke, who had his equipment together and was waiting for the order to load. I asked him how he felt and he said, 'I'm OK. Good luck, see you on the beach.'

On deck just prior to landing, Sergeant Robert Bixler ran his hands through his blond hair and said 'I'm going to land with a comb in one hand and a pass to Paris in the other.' The feeling among most of the men was that the landing would be a 'walk-in' affair, but that later we could expect stiff counter-attacks. This didn't worry us too much because by then tanks, heavy artillery and air support would bolster our defense until the beachhead grew strong enough for a breakout.

We loaded into our assigned stations on the landing craft and were lowered into the sea by davits. The Channel was extremely rough and it wasn't long before we had to help the craft's pumps by bailing water with our helmets. The cold spray blew in and soon we were soaked. I used a gas cape as shelter from the spray. Lack of oxygen under the sack caused seasickness.

A few thousand yards from shore, we rescued three or four survivors from a craft that had swamped and sunk. We left the rest in the water as we did not have space. I could see the battleship *Texas* firing its fourteen-inch guns broadside into the coastline. In minutes, the giant swell from the recoil of those guns nearly swamped us, and added to the sickness and misery.

About 200 or 300 yards from shore we encountered artillery fire. Near misses sent water skyward and then it rained back on us. The British coxswain said he had to lower the ramp and for us to quickly disembark. I was stationed near the front of the boat and heard Sergeant Norfleet counter: 'These men have heavy equipment and you *will* take them all the way in.' The coxswain begged, 'But we'll all be killed!' Norfleet unholstered his .45 Colt pistol, put it to the sailor's head and ordered, 'ALL THE WAY IN!' The craft proceeded, plowing through the choppy water, as far as it could go.

My thinking, as we approached the beach, was that if the boat didn't hurry up and get us in I would die from seasickness. This was my first encounter with this malady. Wooiness became stomach sickness and then vomiting. Thinking I was immune to seasickness, earlier I had given my 'puke bag' to a buddy who had already filled his. Minus the paper bag, I used the first thing at hand, my helmet. At this point, death is not so dreadful. I didn't care what the Germans had to offer, I had to set foot on dry land.

About 150 yards from shore I raised my head despite the warning from someone to 'keep your heads down.' I could see the craft to our right were taking a terrific licking from small arms fire. Tracer bullets were bouncing and skipping off the ramp and sides as they zeroed in on the boat, which touched down a few minutes before we did. Had we not delayed a few minutes to pick up the survivors from the sunken craft, we might have taken the concentration of fire that boat took. Great plumes of water from enemy artillery and mortars kept sprouting close by.

We knew then that this was not going to be a walk-in. No one thought that the enemy was going to give us this kind of opposition on the water's edge. We expected Λ and B companies to have the beach secured by the time we landed. The reality was, in the sector where we touched down, no one had set foot. This turned boys into men. Some would be very brave men, others would soon be dead men, but all of those who survived would be frightened men. Some wet their britches, others cried unashamedly, and many just had to find it within themselves to get the job done. This is where the discipline and training took over.

As we approached the beach the ramp was lowered. Mortar and artillery shells exploded on land and in the water. Unseen snipers concealed in the cliffs were shooting down at individuals, causing screams from those being hit. The water was turning red from the blood. The noise from artillery fire, the rapid-fire rattle from nearby MG42s, and naval gunfire was deafening. The smell of cordite was something that would forever become fixed in our minds, always associated with death and destruction.

I was stationed on the left side of the craft and about fifth from the front. Norfleet was leading on the right side. The Englishman had escaped to the rear. The ramp was in the surf and the front of the steel craft was bucking violently up and down.

As my turn came to exit, I sat on the edge of the bucking ramp trying to time my leap on the down cycle. I sat there too long, causing a bottleneck and endangering myself as well as the men that followed. The one-inch steel ramp was going up and down in the surf, rising as much as six or seven feet; I was afraid it would slam me in the head. One of the men was hit and died instantly. There were dead men in the water and there were live men as well. The Germans couldn't tell which was which. All were coming in with the tide. It was extremely hard to shed the heavy equipment and if one were a weak swimmer, he could drown before inflating his life preserver. I had to inflate mine to get in, even though I was a good swimmer. I remember helping Private Ernest McCanless, who was not a very strong swimmer, to get closer in, so he wouldn't drown under all the weight.

There were dead men floating in the water and there were live men acting dead, letting the tide take them in. I was crouched down to chin-deep in the water when I saw mortar shells zeroing in at the water's edge. Sand began to kick up from small arms fire from the bluffs. It became apparent that it was past time to get the hell across that beach. I don't know how long we were in the water before the move was made, but I would guess close to an hour. Initially I tried to take cover behind one of the heavy timbers and then noticed a mine tied to the top, so I made the wise decision not to go for it. Getting across the beach became an obsession. The decision not to try never entered my mind.

While lying on the sand behind one of the log poles, I watched a GI get shot trying to cross the beach, running from my right to left. He was probably from the craft that touched down about fifty yards to our right. An enemy gunner shot him and he screamed for a medic. One of the aid men moved quickly to help him and he was shot too. I'll never forget seeing that medic lying next to that wounded GI and both of them screaming. They both died within minutes.

The tide was rushing in and later waves of men were due, so we had to get across. I gathered my courage and started running as fast as my long legs would carry me. I ran as low as I could to lessen the target but since I am 6ft 5ins I still presented a good one. I had a long way to run, I'd say a good 100 yards or more. We were loaded down with gear and all of our clothes were soaking wet. As I ran through a tidal pool with about six or eight inches of water I began to stumble. I accidentally fired my rifle close to my right foot but finally caught my balance and continued to the sea wall.

Reaching the slanted sea wall, I looked back for the first time and got a glimpse of the armada out in the Channel. It was a sight to behold. I also saw that Williams, Pvt Sal Augeri and Pvt Ernest McCanless were right behind. I didn't see Norfleet until later. Augeri had lost the machine-gun receiver in the water and I had gotten sand in my rifle. We still had one box of MG ammo but I don't believe we had a weapon that would fire. The first thing I did was take off my assault jacket and spread my raincoat so I could clean my rifle. It was then I saw bullet holes in my raincoat. I didn't realize I'd been shot at. I lit my first cigarette. I had to rest and compose myself because I became weak in the knees.[4]

Lieutenant Ed R. McNabb, H Company, 116th Infantry:

My wave, the H plus thirty one, got away from the rendezvous area in good shape, and one almost blundered out of the mineswept channel, but swung back just in time. When we were several miles offshore we could make out flashes and smoke ashore and thought we could see tanks on the beach. Coming in closer I took the look-out position on the port side of the bow, while my company commander hustled the men into their gear.

I was concentrating on the beach, trying to recognize our landing beach. I could see pretty clearly that there was a hell of a lot of fire in the area in front of us. There were two big splashes of fire that I thought were our flame throwers. They turned out to be German flame shells.

We had a young naval officer in our boat who was in command of our boat division. He was doing well and when we got close inshore he suddenly passed word up asking if I recognized the beach. I wasn't too sure to begin with and when he asked that I wasn't sure of anything. We went on in anyway.

The bluffs were covered with smoke and the lower part of a draw mouth was visible. This could be any one of three places. I was worried because none of us knew which it was. My company commander looked it over for a while and then told the naval officer to 'Take us on in, there's a fight there anyway.'

By the time we were around 300 to 400 yards offshore the smoke had cleared and we recognized Les Moulins draw. Our beach was right in front of it! We weren't drawing any fire yet, but there was plenty on the beach. Small arms with tracer in plenty, and HE bursts were all over it.

It was a sickening feeling to come into that beach when we saw it. I don't know whether anyone was actually afraid; we'd built up a feeling of spirit that drowned that. My company commander, the naval crew and I could see what was about and what it meant. We kept the men's heads down so that they wouldn't see it and lose heart. The tanks were still at the water's edge, some firing, some on fire. Men from the assault companies were taking shelter around these tanks and in the water. The majority of these were wounded and many dead were floating in with the tide. The enemy artillery was laying a curtain of fire at the water's edge and MG and mortar fire covered the area from the artillery to high-water mark.

We ran our boat in alongside a burning LCT on Dog Red beach at about H plus thirty-five and floundered through around seventy-five yards of water which was about chest deep at first. Company and platoon HQ had come through the artillery in pretty good shape and had stopped temporarily in the supposed cover of the beach obstacles and waited to see how the men with the heavy weapons came out of the water. The mortar squad from my boat was unable to carry the waterlogged equipment in the water so they dragged it to the water's edge and were attempting to pick it up when a shell hit and knocked out all but three of them. We looked for the craters that the Air Corps and the Navy had promised us in the beach. There were none.

We moved out across the beach. There were about 400 yards of sand between water and cover on Dog Red. I ran into a burst of MG at about the center of the beach and was hit in a couple of places in the left shoulder. Lieutenant Tomasi, our battalion surgeon, was close by and ran over and cut off my equipment under fire and sent me back to the water's edge if I could make it. I didn't make it, but the tide came up and I washed ashore in front of the three-storey house on Easy Green. Doc Tomasi and two of his medics, one was a man called White, were collecting wounded and dragging them up there and working on them.[5]

Pfc John Barnes, aged 19, A Company, 1st Battalion, 116th Infantry:

About 3.00 a.m. we were called out to get ready. Instead of our regular packs, we had been issued assault jackets, a sort of vest-like garment with many pockets and pull-strap fasteners to yank off in a hurry. In the various pockets we stored K-rations, a quarter pound of dynamite with fuses, hand grenades, smoke grenades, medical kit (a syringe and morphine). Besides our regular M1 clips, we had two slings of ammo belts slung across our shoulders. On our backs, we carried an entrenching tool, a bayonet and a poncho, and whatever else we could stuff in. As an assistant to the flame-thrower, I carried his rifle and pack. Our rifles were wrapped in a protective cellophane wrapper with an inflated tube to keep them afloat. Altogether, our equipment weighed about seventy pounds. It was an awkward assortment, around which we buckled a rubber lifebelt, inflated by CO_2. The buckle in my belt was defective, but I didn't bother with it since it was a last-minute addition and I had no thought of using it.

Up on deck, we were lined up in boat teams. Everyone checked each other's equipment. I don't remember any famous last words, but we shouted to friends in other boats. Since we were going to be first to land, we were first to get off the ship. After climbing aboard the assault craft, we were lowered to the sea. Immediately, the boats began bobbing up and down in the high waves. It was still dark as we moved away and began circling in a holding pattern.

One by one, the men began to get sick, heaving their late-night meal over the side, or into their helmets, or anywhere. Gradually, we saw shapes of other boats, many small ones and many larger hulks and planes were droning overhead by the hundreds, flying towards the coast. Now we could see anti-aircraft fire lighting up the sky and tracers arcing the night. The seasickness seemed to end as more men watched the sight: large flashes inland marked the horizon as the planes dropped their bombs. Then a flash, and a mighty roar, came from one of the black hulks. It was the guns of the big battleship we were just under.

Dawn lightened, and we could see more and more ships and more planes in the sky. We were entranced by the scene. Someone shouted, 'Take a look! This is something you will tell your grandchildren.' No one asked the question, 'What if we don't live?' At this point we were excited, not frightened.

As the day grew brighter, our boat stopped circling and we headed in. Large craft unleashed massive rockets towards the beach. Smoke clouded the lower coastline and we could just see the bluffs and, above that, the single spire of the church. It was Vierville. We knew it. We were right on target. The LCA roared ahead, buffeting the waves.

Suddenly a swirl of water wrapped around my ankles and the front of the craft dipped down. The water quickly reached our waists and we shouted to the other boats on our sides. They waved in return. The boat fell away below me and I squeezed the CO tubes in my lifebelt. Just as I did, the buckle broke and it popped away. I turned to grab the man behind me. I was going under. I climbed on his back and pulled myself up in a panic. Our heads bobbed up above the water. We could still see some other boats moving off to the shore. I grabbed a rifle wrapped in a flotation belt, then a flamethrower that was floating around with two belts wrapped round it. I hugged it tight, but still seemed to be going down. I was unable keep my head above the surface with all the equipment I was carrying. I tried to pull the release straps on my assault jacket, but I couldn't move. Others shouted at me. Then Lieutenant Gearing grabbed my jacket and, using his bayonet, cut the straps. Some of the others helped release me from the weight. I was all right now. I could swim. We counted heads. One was missing: Padley, our radio operator, who had a big SCR 300 radio on his back. No one saw him come up.

Across the water, we heard rapid-fire shots. Our company in the other five boats had landed. I felt a strange sense of relief. Sergeant Laird wanted to swim towards the shore. We were roughly one thousand yards out. 'It's too far,' said Lieutenant Gearing. 'We'll wait and get picked up by some passing boat.' But no one stopped. They were all loaded down in the water going towards the shore on their own missions and their own schedules.

Suddenly we heard a friendly shout of some Limey voice from one of the assault craft. It was a coxswain from the *Empire Javelin*, the same troopship we had left at four o'clock that morning. We had been in the water more than three hours.[6]

Staff Sergeant William H. Lewis, aged 22, Anti-Tank Platoon, 1st Battalion, 116th Infantry Regiment:

We left the LCT before daylight so we could rendezvous. We just lowered the ramp and drove the DUKW down it into the ocean. We had to circle round and round waiting for the time to go. We lost half the DUKWs in the rough seas while awaiting the signal. The DUKWs, not very seaworthy, would ride up a swell and instead of coming back down it would go into it, and go under. They just shipped water, turned over sideways and sunk.

As dawn began to break, we received the signal and headed in to shore. I remember the battleship *Texas* firing broadsides into shore while we were close by. It was God awful, terrible explosions – muzzle blast in our ears – when they fired. The smoke ring passed by us and it looked like a funnel of a tornado, growing larger and larger and finally dissipating. Then they fired another one. I don't believe we should have been that close because we actually felt the muzzle blast. All kinds of ships were firing. A French cruiser, painted in camouflage, did a good job of getting close to shore, inviting the Germans to do battle. She shelled the hell out of the beach. All the ships did a great job except the LCT rocket ships which didn't get close enough to hit their targets. Destroyers came within a thousand yards of the shore and let go their five and six inch guns. It must have been terrible on the other end of that artillery. The flash of the big guns was blinding and the explosions from the muzzles were deafening.

The DUKW was piled high with equipment like an overloaded barge. The coxswain had to use great skill, guiding us through the water and maneuvering in the waves so we didn't turn over and sink. If we headed into a trough he knew we were going to turn over, so he kept the bow into the waves.

When we got to the metal obstacles, we saw a man hanging onto one of them. He yelled to us for help. We kept going on past him because we were out of control. Platoon leader Lieutenant Leo Van de Voort yelled, 'We are out here to kill people, not to save them. If you want on this damn thing you'd better jump on!' The soldier grabbed hold and climbed aboard.

We sheared a pin in the motor and lost power. We were between the obstacles and their Teller mines and drifting helplessly sideways into the mines which could be seen sticking out of the water. We brushed one of them more than once but it failed to explode. I suppose salt water had deteriorated the firing mechanism.

We were 110 minutes or so after the first wave. They began to machine gun the DUKW so we jumped out of the thing into deep water. I jumped into the water and by standing on my toes my head was barely above water except when a wave crashed over me. The natural assumption was the closer one goes into shore the more solid the footing is going to get. That wasn't true because sand had built up around the obstacles and I stepped off into a hole. I was a good swimmer and wasn't afraid of water, but the equipment was pulling me under. We carried about 60 pounds of equipment. Every time a wave crashed over, I felt for the bottom and kept paddling until I felt the bottom again. I wasn't about to go back the other way, I'll guarantee you that. We kept going in and I don't know how we did it. The water was dancing to the tune of that damn machine gun which was firing all around us.[7]

Sergeant William B. Otlowski, Cannon Company, 16th Infantry:

We left England with DUKWs. They are amphibious trucks which carried the 105 cannons, ninety pounds of ammunition and ten men with full battle equipment. These DUKWs didn't prove very good in rough water, because I think we lost every one before we got to the beach.

When I got my men on the DUKW and tried to get off the ramp the rough water put us on the up side as we were almost off the ramp and it hit our rudder and bent it. So, while all the other DUKWs are lined up heading for the beach, we are in the water going round in little circles and can't straighten out, can't go anywhere, just drifting further and further away from the ships into deeper water.

The coxswain running the thing, the navy boy, decided to shut off the motor, which was a mistake because when you shut off the engine you shut off the pumps and it started to fill with water and what happened was we sank.

As we sank and all the men went floating free, I yelled at them to keep together and hold hands and keep in a circle. It wasn't easy – everybody was in shock. The only thing that really floated was our bedrolls. We made them up army style. If you make up a bedroll right, water doesn't get into it and it becomes a float. I swam around grabbing bedrolls and giving them to the men. Our rifles went down, our helmets were knocked off and any weight that we had was dropped so we could float.

We hung on until we were picked up by a Higgins boat that was going off to the beach way off to the right. We landed on that beach, the ramp dropped down and the platoon that was on board ran out into the water, but none of them got up on shore. There was nothing we could do. We had no ammunition, no rifles, no helmets, so I yelled at the coxswain to get the hell off that beach.

We pulled back out to deep water and I asked him if he could find a boat that was heading for my beach, Omaha Red. He inquired of a floating barge that came through. It was a great big thing loaded with trucks, jeeps and an airplane with the wings folded back. It was some kind of service company, with a second lieutenant in command. I don't know who they were, but evidently they were heading for the right beach.

So we transferred to the barge and headed back towards the beach again, only this time we were going to the right beach, so we felt a lot better, even though we were soaking wet and freezing.

The barge hit the beach about thirty feet away from the sand. I don't know if we hit an underwater obstacle, or what, but we stopped that far out. The lieutenant decided to test the water and told the jeep to drive off. It promptly sank in about ten or twelve feet of water. As the driver came floating up and got back on the barge, a German 88 fired a shot at us. It hit to the right and I knew from my experience with 88s in Africa and Sicily that they were taking aim. I knew what hell that damn gun can do.

The second shot went to the left of us and I said to the lieutenant, 'Lieutenant, that's an 88 and the third one's going to hit right in the middle. Get the men off this fucking boat.' He said, 'Sergeant, stay where you are!' And I said, 'To hell with you, Lieutenant. If you want to die, go ahead. OK men, let's go.' I called my men and we jumped off into the water and swam to the beach. We picked up rifles, ammunition belts and helmets as we scooted across the beach to where some men were up against the cliff.

As I turned round to look, the third round from the 88 hit right smack in the middle of that damn barge with that lieutenant and all the men on it.[8]

Staff Sergeant Victor 'Baseplate' Miller, aged 23, E Company, 5th Ranger Battalion:

So we headed for the coast and as we approached it didn't look like we should. It was obscured by smoke. The grass was apparently burning there from the many shells that had landed on it and as we got closer we could see tracers going down the beach. It didn't look very promising.

Anyway, as we got closer and closer, we could see more and more detail. There were the obstacles, these triangular pieces of steel sticking up there with mines dangling from them, and they looked formidable. And, of course, the bullets were still flying. You could see the tracers and shells coming in as we proceeded inward.

We ultimately got to a point where the British coxswain on our boat said, 'I'm aground, I'm aground!' He dropped the ramp and Lieutenant Anderson said, 'All out,' jumped in the water and disappeared beneath the waves. Someone in front of the boat reached down and dragged him back in.

Sergeant Charles Van der Voort, I think it was, simply put his tommy gun in the ribs of the coxswain and said, 'I think you had better get us ashore.' I might say that our boat, under those circumstances, probably got closer to the beach than any other, because we were able to get out without getting into water deeper than our knees.[9]

Major Thomas S. Dallas, Executive Officer, 1st Battalion, 116th Infantry:

As we were being lowered in the Command Group boat from the davits of HMS *Empire Windrush* it became stuck for thirty minutes directly under the ship's 'head'. It could go neither up nor down. During this half hour, the bowels of the ship's company made the most of an opportunity which Englishmen have sought since 1776. Yells from our boat were unavailing. Streams, coloured everything from canary yellow to sienna brown and olive green, continued to flush into the command group, decorating every man on the boat. We cursed, we cried and we laughed, but it kept coming. When we started for the shore, we were all covered with shit.[10]

Sergeant Debs H. Peters, 121st Combat Engineers:

An LCI with a flat bottom was a terrible thing to ride in. The interior of the vessel was full of vomit and smoke, so I stayed on deck to get some fresh air, in spite of the rough seas. We started in on time and when we got about 400 yards offshore the skipper told us to unlash the ladders. The boatswain and I went forward and we were taking the rope from the ladders to make them operational when we came under heavy machine-gun fire. The boatswain, and some of the other men around me, were killed.

About that time, we were hit in the stern by something. I don't know if it was a mine or an 88, but we lost headway, turned sideways to the waves and were parallel to the beach for a few seconds. Then we were hit directly midships and blew up. Those of us on deck were set on fire with flaming fuel oil and we all just rolled overboard.

I fell into the water and went down like a rock before I discovered that I hadn't pulled the string on my life preserver to release the CO_2 cartridges. A few seconds after it inflated I came up to the top. The Germans were raking the sea with machine-gun fire, fast-firing weapons and mortars. The Germans had fixed telephone poles in the sea bed with mines attached to them to stop landing craft and these offered some protection. I held onto one of these poles until I could get my breath, then I moved on to another one. I finally got within about fifty yards of the shore.

On my way in I met a Captain Bainbridge that I knew, not from my unit, but from another unit. We started in together and I said, 'When we get into shallow water where we can stand up, let's come out real fast, because otherwise we'll never make it across that stretch of sand.' He agreed. We came out as fast as we could but we were so heavy with water and sand that I could only just about stagger.[11]

Second Lieutenant Kent T. Lundgren, A Company, 1st Medical Battalion:

Immediately on touching the shore, the enemy opened fire on the LCI with machine guns, 47mm and heavier artillery. Several direct hits were made, going through the front holds, the control room and the forward deck, killing several men and severely wounding several more.

Immediately Captain Hahn with an aid man went into No.2 hold to give medical aid and administer plasma to a critically injured patient. Captain Apanasewics was on the starboard side also giving aid and treatment to critically wounded.

The beach at this place was not satisfactory for a landing so the LCI was withdrawn from land a few hundred yards and then came in again to make another landing to the right. On this second landing we succeeded in reaching the shore and the port side ramp was lowered and men started getting off. About twenty men from A company had got into the water when the enemy again opened fire, hitting the ramp and blowing it off the side of the boat into the water, at the same time badly wounding some of the men as they came off the ship. During this time other direct hits went into the holds, setting two of them on fire. By this time the holds and deck were littered with dead and wounded and when the third hold caught on fire there were still several men in it, and since the opening to this hold was on the inside they were becoming quite panicky. We succeeded in getting them through the door to the outside deck.

However, there was a critically injured patient in the officers' cabin immediately above and in front of the opening to No.3 hold. Another man and myself went into the cabin in the face of terrific heat and blinding smoke and carried the helpless patient to the deck.

The control tower by this time was full of smoke. The ship was listing badly to starboard and was rapidly sinking. It was also getting out of control, swinging around with the tide so that the port side was exposed to the shore. The enemy was still firing and some hits were scored on the port side. The crew finally got the badly listing ship out into the water further from the shore, the fire was extinguished and we started with the dead and the wounded back to the *Chase* to be evacuated.[12]

Sergeant Bob Sales, aged 19, B Company, 116th Infantry:

About 100 yards from the shore the English coxswain said he couldn't get us in any closer. As the ramp lowered, enemy machine guns opened up, firing directly into our boat. Captain Zappacosta was first off and first hit. Staff Sergeant Dick Wright, communications sergeant from Lynchburg, was second and he was also hit as he left the boat, falling into the water. A medic was third and I didn't see what happened to him. Being fourth, I caught my heel in the ramp and fell sideways, out of the path of that MG42 and this undoubtedly saved my life.

All the men that followed were either killed by the Germans or drowned. As far as I know, no one from my craft was ever found alive.

The captain screamed, 'I'm hit!' I tried to get to him but he was lost in the surf. It became obvious that we were in mortal danger. Men were all around me in the water bleeding from wounds and screaming for help. Knowing that the landing craft was the target, I got away from it as fast as I could.

The first thing I did was shed my SCR300 radio and my assault jacket. That radio was heavy and I suppose it's still at the bottom of the Channel. Mortar and artillery shells were landing all around and one hit so close that it knocked me groggy. Luckily a log floated by with a Teller mine attached. I grabbed it until my head cleared. I stayed behind the log, pushing it in front of me, using it as a shield, until I reached the beach.

The first person I saw on the beach that I recognized was Sergeant Wright. He hollered over to me that he was badly hit. Trying to raise up on his arms he was spotted by a sniper and was shot through the head. I didn't try to go to him because I knew that he was dead.

While pinned down on the beach, I watched incoming landing craft being shot at. One of them carried battalion surgeon Captain Robert Ware, a man I knew from my home town, Madison Heights, Virginia. The doctor had flaming red hair. I watched him as he disembarked and that machine gun opened up, cutting him down. I'll never forget his helmet flying off and seeing all that red hair. I'll swear that scene haunts me to this day.

I crawled on my belly, using the dead and wounded as a shield. Some time later I saw Mack Smith from Shepherdtown, West Virginia, and some other B Company men taking shelter behind a sea wall. Some of them were badly wounded. I bandaged Smith's eye, which was laying out on his face. I kept crawling back to the water's edge, dragging men out if they were still living. I didn't bother if they were dead. I pulled out quite a few. A medic helped me give them first aid and comfort.

The first enemy soldier I saw was a prisoner. They had him on his knees and his hands were over his head. He didn't look so tough, but those guys up in those cliffs were plenty tough. You can't imagine how helpless it was to be lying on that beach and those snipers shooting everything that moved.

At this point we were not sure the invasion would succeed. Our company was shot up so badly that there was no organization and we didn't know what the other sectors were doing. We felt helpless and alone.[13]

Pfc John R. Slaughter:

We had trouble going in, we were taking a little bit of water and we were bailing out and we also had to stop a couple of times to pick up some people, some survivors from a capsized boat. That delayed us and we were pretty well loaded down when we finally got in close and the shells were hitting the water, and we could hear the machine guns and a few mines exploding.

We were about twenty-five yards off the beach when they dropped the ramp. We were in the surf and it was real rough. The front of the boat was going up and down and they were shooting at us. Some of us were going over the side because some were getting shot as soon as they got off the front. One man went off the ramp when it was way up in the air and it came right down and hit him on the head and killed him.

I jumped off the side and was bobbing around in the water. It was still way over my head and I made my way to one of the landing obstacles. They were shooting into the water with 88s and mortars and so we just floated out there for a while until things quietened down. I just bobbed around trying to act like I was dead because I had a friend near me in the water who was hollering and waving his arms and carrying on and he was shot by a sniper on the cliff. So I didn't act like I was swimming, I just let the tide take me in.

There was a landing craft beached in front of us with a GI going around in the propeller and there were people on the beach with no heads and no arms. It made me so sick that I couldn't eat or drink for three days.

There was a pal of mine from Chicago with me as we got to the edge of the water and I said to him, 'Let's go,' and we took off across the beach and ran.

I really didn't think I would make it, I didn't think there was any way you could get across that beach and survive. I really thought that was my last day, but you don't want your friends to know that you're afraid, so you bluff, you know, act big and tough, but really you're scared to death.

It was a long, long beach and a long run and I could feel the tracers going by. Bullets hit my heel and my canteen and went through my pack, but didn't touch me. One buddy ran ahead of us and fell on the beach. We were so loaded down with equipment that he stumbled and fell and they shot him and he fell into a puddle of water which turned red.

When I got to the sand dunes I looked back and saw one fella try to run and they shot him and then a medic went over to him and he got shot too.

It was all very disorganized because we lost nearly all our officers, and people just laid around, not knowing what to do. If the Germans had counter attacked we could not have held. We'd thrown our hand grenades away or lost them because when you're floating around in the water you start unloading some of your weight and so we didn't really have any weapons at all.[14]

Sergeant Joe Pilck, aged 26, G Company, 16th Regiment, 1st Infantry Division:

The first wave was to hit at 6.30 a.m. That was E and F companies. My company, G, was to hit at 7.00. We were supposed to help E or F company, whichever one needed help most. But everyone needed help. We had to help ourselves.

The Channel was so rough the waves would splash over the boat. We were scared at first. After a while we got seasick, cold and wet. Then we couldn't wait to get inland.

As we were riding around out in the Channel the Germans spotted some of our boats and started shooting artillery at us. With the rough water and the Germans shooting at us, a couple of our soldiers were real nervous types. We were passing the bucket down to anyone who had to vomit. One of the soldiers said, 'Hurry up. Pass the bucket, I have to shit.' Another man replied, 'Just do as I did. Shit in your pants.'

When we first hit the beach it was low tide. After a couple of hours the tide started to come in and it washed many of our wounded buddies and some that were dead back into the Channel. We also took cover in the water from the machine-gun and artillery fire.

After being on the beach awhile, one of our tanks came ashore. I ran towards it to take cover and two of my buddies had the same idea. After a short time the Germans started to shoot at the tank, so I said to myself, 'Get the hell away from this tank or you'll get killed.' So I ran back to the same spot where I was before. I reached in my gas mask for some cigarettes and saw it was full of bullet holes. As I looked back at the tank I saw it backing up to take cover in the water. As it did so, it ran over my two buddies and killed them right there.

At this time I heard one of the officers saying, 'There are two kinds of soldiers on this beach. Those who are dead and those who are about to die. So let's get the hell off this damned beach!' I can't say if I was scared or not. Mostly I was thinking of getting captured because it looked like the invasion was a failure.

It was one hell of a mess. There were supposed to be thirty-six tanks come on shore to help us. We were told six made it to the beach. The rest sank. We could see some of the tank crews floating around on rafts or in lifejackets. We were told the air force was going to drop about 500 tons of bombs on the beach to make shell craters we could hide in and to knock out some of the barbed wire and obstacles. Not one bomb hit the beach.

Nothing went right for us. It was one big mess. Everybody lost a lot of men. I found myself saying the rosary and other prayers whenever I could find a moment to do so. This was pretty often. I used my fingers to count the ten Hail Marys.[15]

Pfc Harry Parley, aged 24, E Company, 116th Infantry:

As our boat touched sand and the ramp went down I became a visitor to hell. Some boats on either side of us had been hit by artillery; I was aware that some were burning and some were sinking. I can't recall if there were cries from the wounded. The air was thick with smoke and the roar of exploding shells. I shut everything and concentrated on following the man in front of me down the ramp and into the water. I stepped off the ramp into a deep pocket in the sand and went under the water completely. With no footing whatsoever and with an eighty-pound flamethrower on my back I was unable to come up. I knew I was drowning and made a futile effort to unbuckle the flamethrower harness. Inadvertently, I had raised the firing arm, which is about three feet long, above my head. One of my team saw it, grabbed hold, and pulled me up out of the hole onto solid sand. Then slowly, half-drowned, coughing water and dragging my feet, I began walking towards the beach. I was unable to run.

Ahead of me in the distance, as I came across the sand, I could see high bluffs rising above the beach. I knew, of course, that enemy fire was being directed down onto the beach from those bluffs and I could see the survivors of the landing already using the base of the bluffs as shelter. Machine-gun fire was hitting the beach and as it hit the sand it made a 'sip-sip' sound like someone sucking on their teeth.

What I found when I finally reached the sea wall at the foot of the bluffs is difficult to describe. I can only call it disorganized chaos. Men were trying to dig or scrape trenches or foxholes for protection against incoming fire. Others were carrying or helping the wounded to shelter. We had to crouch or crawl on all fours when moving about. To communicate, we had to shout above the din of the shelling from both sides, as well as the explosions on the beach. Most of us were in no condition to carry on. All we could do was try to stay alive for the moment.

Along the beach I could see burning wreckage and equipment, damaged landing craft and, of course, men trying to get off the beach. The enormity of our situation came as I realized that we had landed in the wrong beach sector and that many of the people around me were from other units and were strangers to me. What's more, the terrain before us was not what I had been trained to encounter. All disorganized, all trying to stay alive, I remember removing my flamethrower and trying to dig a trench while lying on my stomach.

Scared, worried, and often praying, I tried to help some of the wounded. One or two times I was able to control my fear long enough to race across the sand to drag a helpless GI out of the water and save him from drowning in the incoming tide. That was the extent of my bravery that morning.

When clear thinking began replacing some of our fear, many of us accepted the fact that we had to get off the beach or die where we were. Word was passed that a small draw providing access up the bluff had been found and that attempts were being made to blow the barbed wire with bangalore torpedoes and find a way up through the mines. As I worked my way up the draw I could hear the bangalores blow, followed by other explosions. By the time I reached the opening in the wire, a few men had already gone through. I could see them picking their way up the slope. As I started up, I saw the white tape marking a safe path through the mines and I also saw the cost paid to mark that path for us – one or two GIs had been blown to death and another, with both legs gone, was being attended to by medics.

Anyhow, before I could reach the top of the bluff, word was shouted that we were to come back down, because the navy was about to shell the area above us. For some unexplainable reason, we didn't come all the way back down; maybe it was the fear of triggering some undetected mine. I remember foolishly standing about forty feet below the top of the bluff and watching in amazement the power and accuracy of the navy fire landing just above me. I could even look back across the water and see the ship firing its guns. I think it was the USS *Augusta*.

The shelling ceased in about fifteen or twenty minutes and we continued our climb to the top. During the delay, I traded my BAR automatic rifle for an M1 with another GI. He wanted more firepower and I wanted less weight to carry.

Finally reaching the top, I found an area entirely devoid of vegetation, marked by shell craters and covered by a maze of trenches, dug-outs and firing positions. I also saw the enemy for the first time. Two German prisoners, hands on head, were being passed back down the slope. They had Asian features and they were smiling.[16]

Pfc Warner 'Buster' Hamlett, aged 27, F Company, 116th Infantry:

It was critical that we hit the beach at low tide, because thousands of obstacles with mines attached lined the beach. At high tide, many of these were concealed. Many assault craft stopped far short of the beach, in fear of hitting mines. As the men jumped into the water, it was often over their heads. Heavy equipment caused them to be pulled down into the rough water. The two coxswains, two young sailors on our boat, saw what was happening to other boats and they drove our craft into the sand as far as possible. We were in only four feet of water as we cleared the ramp. Constant 88 artillery shells, machine-gun fire and rifle fire criss-crossed the beach, mowing down helpless soldiers who couldn't find cover or fire their sand-clogged rifles.

I was to take my squad to the left of the boat. However, machine-gun fire was ripping the water and hit several of our men, so I turned to the right with my squad. After we were in the water it was every man for himself. I waded parallel to the beach with my squad because the heavy fire was directed towards the boats. As I was going towards the beach I saw Lieutenant Hillshure go down on his knees as a shell exploded. He fell into the hole caused by the explosion and died there on the beach.

When I finally reached the edge of the water, I started to run towards the sea wall under a deafening row of explosions and bullets. I saw a hole about seventy-five feet away, so I ran and jumped in, landing on top of O.T. Grimes. As soon as I caught my breath, I dashed forward again, but had to stop between the obstacles in order to rest. The weight of wet clothes, sand and equipment made it difficult to run.

One of the South Boston soldiers, Mervin L. Matze, had run straight to the sea wall and was motioning for us to come on. At the same time he was yelling, 'Get off the beach!' Our only chance was to get off the beach as quick as possible because we were sitting ducks. While resting behind the obstacles, Private Gillingham, a young soldier, fell in beside me, white with fear. He seemed to be begging for help with his eyes. His look was that of a child asking what to do. I said, 'Gillingham, let's stay separated as much as we can 'cause the Germans will fire at two quicker than one.' He remained silent as I jumped up and ran forward again.

I heard a shell coming and dove into the sand, face down. Shrapnel rose over my head and hit all around me, blowing me three or four feet. My rifle was ripped from my hand and my helmet went twenty-five or thirty feet in front of me. When I started to jump up and run, a sharp pain hit my spine from my neck to my lower back. I pulled myself by my elbows to my rifle, then retrieved my helmet and dragged myself into the hole the shell had made. As soon as I felt stronger, I got out of the hole and ran forward as machine-gun bullets kicked up sand to the right of me. As the bullets came closer I dropped to the sand and waited to be hit. I looked up to see the bullets hitting on my left side. Again, I jumped up and ran, falling down each time machine-gun fire came close. I continued doing this until I reached the sea wall.

The shell that injured me took Gillingham's chin off, including the bone, except for a small piece of flesh. He tried to hold his chin in place as he ran towards the sea wall. He made it to the sea wall where Bill Hawkes and I gave him his morphine shot. We stayed with him for approximately thirty minutes until he died. The entire time, he remained conscious and aware that he was dying. He groaned in pain but was unable to speak.

We were forced to wait at the sea wall until wire cutters could cut the tremendous web of wire that the Germans had placed on top of it. During this time, Lieutenant Ernest Wise of F Company was directing his team behind the sea wall when a bullet hit him in the forehead. He continued to instruct his men until he sat down and held his head with the palm of his hand before falling over dead.

Germans began firing mortars, trying to knock out those few of us who had made it across the beach and were waiting behind the sea wall. They also shot out a type of fire bomb that contained a yellowish powdery substance that would ignite everything it touched. One of these bombs exploded so close to me that the yellow powder got on my clothes, but fortunately there was not enough to ignite. The Germans took advantage of the men that jumped up to avoid the powder and heavy mortar fire caused shrapnel to rivet the air, injuring one of my squad, Pfc Tway from Wisconsin. He was hit in the back and leg. I looked around to see who had survived and most were injured in some way.

We waited at the sea wall until the time to cross over the path cleared by the wire cutters. As I crossed the wall, I thought I saw my brother, Lee, lying face down dead. His clothes had been blown from his body. The back of his head looked just like Lee, but I chose not to know for sure. (It was weeks before I learned that Lee, who was in the 16th Regiment, had also survived the first wave.)

As we crossed the sea wall, Germans in pillboxes fired on each man as he dashed forward. After crossing the sea wall, the ground provided more protection, with small bushes and gullies. As I examined my injuries, I realized a large hole was torn from the jacket and shirt on my shoulder. My skin was not touched.

We took time to reorganize and planned to knock out the pillboxes. First we tried direct attack using TNT on the end of long poles, but this was impossible because the Germans could shoot the men down as soon as they saw them coming through the barbed wire strung in front of the pillboxes. It was then decided to run between the pillboxes and enter the trenches that connected the boxes. These trenches gave the Germans mobility and a means of escape. We entered the trenches, slipped behind the pillboxes and threw grenades into them. After the explosion we ran into the boxes and killed any that survived the grenade. Rows of pillboxes stood between us and the top of the cliff. Slowly, one by one, we advanced. The bravery of the soldiers was beyond belief. They were determined to do their job, whatever the cost. During this time, other boat waves of soldiers were joining us to push the Germans beyond the cliffs.

When we got near the top of the cliff, I talked to Sergeant England, who had also been injured. He told me I was pale and I showed him my leg, which was now swelling and turning different colours. My spine was sending jabbing pains through my body.

Sergeant England told me to go back to the beach and get a medic to tag me so that I could be transported back to a ship. The two of us returned to the beach. As I painfully walked back to the beach, thousands of bodies were lying there. You could walk on the bodies, as far as you could see along the beach, without touching the ground. Parts of bodies – heads, legs and arms – floated in the sea. Medics were walking up and down, tagging the wounded. As I stepped gently between my American comrades, I realized what being in the first wave was all about.[17]

Pfc George Roach, aged 19, A Company, 116th Infantry:

I was the assistant flamethrower. I had an M1 rifle and a five-gallon drum of flamethrower fluid, plus assorted wrenches and a cylinder of nitrogen. It was heavy, that's for sure. My job was to follow the flamethrower – Sergeant Greenstreet I believe his name was – wherever he went and in the event that his tank became empty we could make a switch. I don't know how that was going to be accomplished because I don't think we ever really practiced it to that extent during the practice invasions.

As our assault craft came closer to the shore I could hear and see rockets from the ships being fired at the coast. The sea was very rough. We were given little sick-bags and most all of us used them one time or another. As we got closer to the shore the British guys in our boat kinda said to us, 'You know we're going to drop this ramp and as soon as we do we're gonna back out, so you guys better be ready to get off. Our instructions are to get you in and get right out so we don't create a traffic problem with the other teams coming in behind you.'

When the boat hit the shore and the ramp went down everybody did supposedly what they had to do. The riflemen were fanning out but the casualty rate was very bad. We couldn't determine where the firing was coming from because there was something like 100 yards of open beach ahead of us and all we could see were the houses along the shoreline. I can remember dropping into the sand and taking up my rifle and firing it at one of the houses. Sergeant Wilkes said to me, 'What are you firing at?' I said, 'I don't know. I don't know what I'm firing at.'

Most of the men in the boat team were either wounded or dead. I didn't see anybody except Gil Murdoch, who was lying next to me. The tide was coming in rapidly and I said to him, 'Gil, how do you feel?' He said, 'I can't see – I've lost my glasses.' And I said, 'Well, can you swim?' He said, 'No, I can't swim too well.' I said, 'Well, look, we can't stay here – there's nobody around here that seems to have any idea of what to do. Let's get back into the water and come in with the tide.'

At that point I had lost all my equipment. So I took Gil and we got back into the water. I was holding on to him, I think he had been wounded. I got him to a position where there was a knocked-out tank, or a DUKW or something like that, and I got situated on that in the water and stayed with him for a while. I realized I couldn't stay there indefinitely, but Gil was in no position at that time to move. I felt that I did all I could for him and I said, 'Look, there's a patrol boat that's supposedly in the area to pick up survivors. Can you stay here and will you be OK?' He seemed to indicate that he would.

I started to swim in towards the shore and almost made it when I was picked up by a boat that had been hit and was kind of floundering near the sea wall. One of the officers in the boat pulled me on board and I promptly fell asleep.[18]

Corporal Gilbert G. Murdoch, A Company, 116th Infantry:

As the coxswain of the assault craft thought he had reached the beach, he stopped engines and had the ramp lowered. The lieutenant ran off down the middle of the ramp and was immediately killed by machine-gun fire. Rodríguez, who was a private, ran off at the right side and was immediately cut in half by the machine guns. I jumped off from the left side and found myself in about nine feet of water. As I came back up I punched my CO_2 tubes for buoyancy and turned round and faced out to sea.

The coxswain of the landing craft had reversed out to sea again, sixty or eighty feet, and was now coming forward at me, full speed with the ramp down, to try and get over the sandbar. The ramp hit me and knocked me under the water and I came up on the port side of the craft, facing towards the beach. I grabbed the one-inch hawser line which it used as a bumper and the landing craft hit the beach with me still hanging on to it.

As soon as I could get myself oriented and get the strength to get up, I realized I could hardly see because I was wearing glasses and my glasses were coated with salt. Eventually I saw our mortar team about twenty yards onto the beach, with the men lying down next to the mortar, not firing. I called to ask them what was happening and they said they were hit and they just couldn't fire the mortar, even though it was set up for firing.

The sergeant in charge asked me to fire it. I fired two or three rounds and they flew out, but did not explode. The sergeant yelled, 'Murdoch, you dumb bastard, you're not pulling the firing pins.' I had never fired mortar rounds before, so for the remainder of the rounds I pulled the firing pins, so we knew we got some mortar fire on the beach, but with the smoke and my fogged glasses I couldn't tell what we hit.

Then I started to move forward, creeping and crawling, and I realized that my rifle wouldn't fire because the sand had cemented the operating rod. I smashed it with my bayonet handle, but it still wouldn't work.

As I moved inland on the beach with a weapon that wouldn't fire, I came across one of our riflemen, wounded, a man named McSkimming from Washington DC. He was wounded in the arm and he asked me to give him a shot of morphine, which I did. We wished each other luck and I moved on.

I kept crawling up the beach and in another couple of minutes a tank came out of the water, dropped its flotation gear and came rumbling towards me. I don't know whether it could see me or not, or whether it cared, but it kept coming right at me, no matter how fast I went. It was only about twelve or fourteen feet behind me when it got hit and blew up.

I finally came to one of the underwater obstacles which, since we landed at high tide, was out of the water. There were two people there. I spoke to them for a few moments and then I saw George Roach, who had been in the flame-thrower tank. He said all the officers were dead, all the noncoms were dead and that as far as he could see he and I, as Pfcs, were the senior men on the beach. There were thirteen of us alive out of 205.

Tracer fire was coming in over our heads, presumably aimed at the mine on top of the obstacle. I mentioned the mine to the other soldiers and the man on the right, whose name I don't remember, said he was thinking of getting out of there. At that minute I saw that his left legging was bloody and I said, 'You're hit.' He said, 'You damn fool, so are you.' I looked down and saw that two machine-gun bullets which had gone through his leg had spent themselves in my right ankle.

I suggested that we move to the left where there was a mound on the beach covered by grass which was on fire. George Roach said yes, the other two said no. So George and I got up and ran as all kinds of small arms fire came at us, but we made it. We stayed there a while, but almost choked to death from the smoke, so we both agreed we would have to get off the beach.

George said, 'Look, I'm a good swimmer and you're not badly hurt, let me swim you out to that knocked-out tank in the water out there.' We both took off most of our clothes. I had a picture of my fiancée in my helmet lining and I was looking at it when George grabbed the helmet liner and the helmet out of my hand, threw it up the beach and said, 'Let's get going.'

We got out to the tank, which was in about three or four feet of water, in about fifteen minutes, mainly due to his efforts, and hung on to the port side. At the rear there were three heads bobbing in the water. They were three men from the tank crew with their faces all powder burned. The tank commander, a buck sergeant, was sitting behind the turret with his left leg off at the knee and the bone and the artery floating in the water. He said that his men were of no value to him, they wouldn't do what he said and he was very upset with them.

He asked us to get him a shot of morphine. Although my ankle was numb, I felt so happy to be on a firm surface that I crawled inside the turret, grabbed the first-aid pack and gave him a shot.

After about ten or fifteen minutes, the sergeant said he wanted to get to the beach as he thought it would be safer. George and I said, 'No, the beach is not safer,' but he wanted to go and he finally coaxed his three men to come from the rear of the tank and help him into the water. They were all wearing orange navy-type Mae West jackets so we could see them going towards the beach, but as they got closer a long shore current moved them to the left and the last I saw they were still kicking and trying to make the beach without success.

George and I were now the only two on the tank and we started to draw fire. As the tide was coming in, we were forced to stand first behind the turret and then on top of it. George, who was still in pretty good shape, said he would swim out to get one of the small craft out there. I shook his hand and wished him well and he took off. I was thankful that he had got me where he did, but I figured I was dead anyway. The last I saw of him was his arms pumping as he swam away.

Tracer fire was coming in at me and I got so damned angry that I stood on the turret and fired the fifty-caliber machine gun until there were no rounds left. Whether I hit anything I don't know. I could hardly see the beach, my glasses were so fogged over with salt spray and I had nothing to clean and dry them with.

Now the tide was coming up so that about every third wave knocked me off the turret. I thought this can't go on, so I took an empty jerry can from inside the tank, made sure it was watertight and jumped off the tank, figuring I would try and make the beach myself. But I also got swept up by the current and carried off a mile or two towards the left, to where there was an LST with its nose on the beach and its stern on fire. The Germans were pouring round after round of heavy-caliber artillery into it, trying to blow it up.

As I was drawn closer and closer I felt the shells were almost blowing me out of the water. Every time I heard one coming I put the jerry can under my stomach to try and absorb some of the impact.

I finally did make it past the LST and saw a small control craft come by. It stopped right next to me and a crew man threw out a life preserver which hit me on the head and almost knocked me out. Then the Germans started to fire again and the small boat took off in a roar. I was very unhappy and cursing my bad luck, telling God what I thought of Him, but after a few moments the boat came back. Two men in the stern tried to pull me in, but couldn't do it. Finally they got me along the side of the craft and rolled me in.

They took me back to the APA boat that I had come across the Channel in and I was taken down to the sick bay and offered some medicinal brandy. Being a non-drinker, I was not for that. The chief pharmacist's mate said, 'Are you sure you don't want it?' I said, 'No, I don't.' So he picked up the small bottle, it would just fit into your hand, and disposed of it with a happy grin.[19]

Pfc Robert Koch, C Company, 116th Regiment:

The water was very rough. There wasn't any question about it, it was rough. A lot of the boys got themselves caught up in the nets coming down off the side of the ship and we had quite a time getting them loose. Their legs got caught and they dropped their rifles and dropped their ammunition and the smaller ship was bouncing up and down against the side of the other ship.

When we started our run in for the beach we were receiving shells from the enemy. Naturally they were hitting quite close and we were just hoping and praying that our ship would make it in. In my particular ship a sergeant who was at the front raised his head to see how far we had to go to reach land and he was struck right in the forehead by a bullet. He fell back, dead. He was the first dead man I had ever seen in my life. This made me pray even more.

We were about 300 feet off the beach when our LST got hit slightly and so we had to swim in. As soon as the front opened, machine guns opened up and a lot of men were killed. This meant you had to crawl over the bodies of your dead comrades, buddies that a few minutes ago you'd been talking to.

But your only concern at that time was to reach your goal of the beach and the only way to do it was to get rid of the equipment. We had brought flamethrowers and machine guns on the LST which were vital to our attack but we had to let them go because the weight of them would have taken us under and we couldn't have possibly gotten in. We were in about twelve feet of water and there were mines all around, small mines that were scattered in the water and blowing some of the men up.

When I arrived on the beach, believe it or not, the only thing I had was myself. I had dropped my rifle in the water and when I hit the beach I laid there and thought to myself, 'What am I going to do here? Am I going to wrassell, or fist fight, or what?' But other boys had come along and some of them, my buddies, had been shot and were laying near me and I took their rifles and belts.

Our mission was to go up a valley and hold the top ground, but very unfortunately we had landed 1,500 hundred yards south of our goal in front of cliffs going straight up. The Germans were up there with machine guns and we laid on the beach and crawled to find as much cover as possible. A lot of boys would try to make a dash for the bottom of the cliff and when they did they were shot down.

In my particular case, along the beach I had a buddy who was struck through the throat by a bullet and I was trying to press the veins to stop the bleeding, trying to hold it in. I just couldn't stop it. I tried and was doing the best I could but he died in about two or three minutes. We pulled a lot of the other boys who'd been hit into safety behind rocks or what not.

You knew you couldn't stay on the beach, you knew you were exposing yourself to enemy fire. You could do one of two things. You could either make up your mind to go right then or you could wait and watch the enemy and wait until they were firing at another angle before you made your move. A lot of men were killed, in my opinion, because fright caused them to move when they shouldn't have, when the enemy was zeroed in on them and as soon they moved they were gone. Some of them froze and you had to hit them on the shoulder and say, 'Come on, John, let's go.'

When we made our run for cover we were being machine-gunned and it was the miraculous thing about life in such a situation when men on the right of you would drop and men on the left would drop, but you seemed to keep coming. You weren't getting hit at all.

We finally made it to the bottom of the cliffs where we had more safety because the Germans could not fire their machine guns straight down on our position and they also couldn't fire their rifles because they had to expose themselves over the cliff which would give us an opportunity to get them. We remained in that position, well, I would say it was a lifetime, but it was probably about four or five hours.

Let me say that in our original company of 213 men, eight hours after we landed only thirty-eight were still in action.[20]

Captain Charles Cawthon, Headquarters Company, 2nd Battalion, 116th Infantry:

The first assault wave already on the beach did not resemble a battle line so much as it did heaps of refuse deposited there to burn and smoulder unattended. The water was waist-deep and we were moving faster. I would judge the time to be about 07.30 and the first shots directed at us keened above the sound of the wind and surf. To my left a high cry in hurt surprise announced, 'I'm hit!' I looked round. The white face, staring eyes, and open mouth of the first soldier I saw struck in battle remains with me. My first words in battle were not an exhortation to the troops but a useless shout to attend the wounded man. I think he was gone before the medics reached him.

With the burst of fire we all submerged neck-deep in the surf. I lay flat out supporting my head above water by my hands on the shifting sands and gave my attention to the fact that a few more surges of the surf would eject me onto the beach where there were many dead things, both men and machines. All around was incredible chaos: bodies, weapons, boxes of demolitions, flamethrowers, reels of telephone wire, and personal equipment from socks to toilet articles. Discarded life belts writhed and twisted in the surf like brown sea slugs. The waves broke around the wrecked tanks, 'dozers and landing craft, thick here in front of the heavily defended exit road.

From my prone position the beach rose like a steep, barren hillside. There was a stretch of sand, being narrowed by the minute by the tide, then a sharply rising shingle bank of small, smooth stones that ended at the sea wall. Against the shingle bank and the wall were the men of the first wave. Some were scooping out holes; a number were stretched out in the loose attitude of the wounded; others lay in ultimate stillness. I still could not make out the exit road, but we had come in not far off our appointed place.

While I was straining to see above the debris and still stay in the dubious protection of the water, one of the explosions that were rippling up and down the beach erupted close by. There was a hard jar to the side of my face, and blood started streaming off my chin. I don't recall any particular emotion on being hit for the first time, but I did realize that this was no place to linger; those along the embankment seemed much safer. My boat team had completely disappeared in the debris. Having decided that survival, never mind valour, lay forward, I tried to rise but seemed to be hoisting the English Channel with me. The assault jacket's pockets, the gas-mask case, boots, leggings and uniform all held gallons of salt water. I had long preached the maxim that a good soldier never abandons his equipment, but I now jettisoned the assault jacket and lumbered up the beach, streaming with water.

Gasping for air and retching salt water, I reached the embankment. All around were familiar faces from F, G, H and Headquarter companies. Those who had arrived with me were in about my condition, others were more recovered. Gradually my lungs and stomach stopped heaving. I took my .45 service automatic from its plastic bag and found it sticky with salt and gritty with sand. When I pulled the slide back to load a round into the chamber, it stuck halfway. The embankment was strewn with rifles, Browning automatics and light machine guns, all similarly fouled.

About this time the battalion commander came over the embankment with some half-dozen soldiers in tow. He had been trying to get up the bluff at this point but was baulked by weapons that wouldn't function. His first words, 'This is a débâcle,' remain with me. He told me to sort out the boat teams and round up some firepower, and then he left on the run down the embankment to find a way up the bluff.

I left some of the able-bodied trying to clean weapons and ran down to the waterline, taking cover behind a blown-out tank 'dozer. From here the face of the bluffs and the exit road were visible and I expected to see flashes and smoke from German guns. The only smoke visible on the enemy side, however, was from brush fires started by the naval cannonade. Under their smoke a few brave souls were climbing the bluff.

I splashed down the waterline through the debris in the direction the battalion commander had taken and acquired a second bloodying. This time I didn't hear the shell, but there was another jar to the side of my face – opposite to the first one – and again I started leaking blood. My injuries, though much less serious than most, were spectacular by being so visible. Two soldiers advised me I'd been hit and guided me to a busy aid station. A medic looked over the wounds on both sides of my face and announced with professional authority that here was a rare case of a shot having gone cleanly through one cheek and out through the other without damage to teeth or tongue.[21]

Captain Albert H. Smith Jr, aged 25, executive officer, 1st Battalion, 16th Infantry Regiment, 1st Infantry Division:

When we were about 500 yards offshore I began to realize we were in trouble. Because of the numerous beach obstacles, we now had five LCVPs going in abreast and very close together. The intervals between the craft could be measured in inches rather than in the tens of yards our amphibious doctrine called for.

As its bottom scraped a sand bar, our LCVP shuddered to a stop. Almost simultaneously German machine-gun fire hit the steel ramp. I yelled to the seaman not to drop the ramp and, for once, the navy obeyed the army. Then, as the German machine gunners swept down the line of landing craft, I called for the ramp to be dropped. All but two of us raced safely into waist-deep water; the last two men were hit before they could leave the craft.

The beach bottom was firm under our feet, but the going was tough because of the surf and the heavy loads we were carrying. Our wet woollen clothing didn't help our mobility, either.

The closer we got to the beach the more certain I became that the landing was a disaster. Dead and wounded from the first waves were everywhere. There was little or no firing from our troops. On the other hand, German machine guns, mortars and artillery pieces were laying down some of the heaviest fire I had ever experienced.

Unknown to us, regiments of the 352nd Infantry Division (part of Rommel's reserve) were conducting anti-invasion manoeuvres in the Omaha beach area on 5–6 June. Their presence more than doubled the number of defenders our amphibious assault had to overcome.

Somehow, Captain Hank Hangsterfer, the headquarters company commander, and I were able to get our half of the battalion headquarters across the soft sand and into the defilade afforded by the shingle embankment. I don't recall any casualties. Then, seeing some movement off the beach to our east, we began to move in that direction.

En route we ran into Brigadier General Willard Wyman, our assistant division commander, who had landed minutes earlier and was trying to organize the scattered forces. We had been taught at infantry school that a combination of fire and movement was the best way to advance against a dug-in enemy. But in this situation and at this hour – it was about 08.00 – when General Wyman asked whether we were advancing by fire and movement, I answered, 'Yes, sir. They're firing and we're moving.'[22]

Carter Barber, combat correspondent on board Coast Guard Rescue Cutter 16:

The cutter had just made a round trip to discharge some ninety casualties picked up earlier in the morning, when she saw a stricken LCT which was slowly capsizing as it sank. On the decks, over thirty men were trapped, including a wounded man with nearly severed legs, dangling only by pieces of flesh. We threw heaving lines to men in the water. Two or three of them were screaming, 'Oh, save me . . . I'm hurt bad . . . please, please, please!' and I yelled back, 'Hang on, Mac, we're coming,' and looked astern at the guys on our boat hauling other wounded men aboard, and wondered at the inadequacy of everything. We needed ten pairs of hands more.

Arthur Burhard Jr, a member of the cutter's crew, jumped over the side to help the man with the injured legs. He secured a line around him, completely disregarding the smoke that was beginning to pour from the LCT's hatches. We had a hell of a time getting him aboard because his clothing was waterlogged and he was weighted down with helmet, rifle, pack, ammunition, et al. The man screamed as we helped him aboard, but we had to be a little callous so that we could get the man on the deck and move to another group of survivors.

I watched one man from the bow. He shouted, 'I can't stay up, I can't stay up.' And he didn't. I couldn't reach him with a heaving line and when we came towards him his head was in the water. We didn't stop and went on to seven or eight more men who were just about ready to sink too. When we got them aboard, the first lad had completely disappeared, apparently slipping out of his life jacket.

Although it seemed like hours, we quickly got all the men aboard, including one old man who was so soaked in water that he was almost drowned. His face was almost awash and his head was laid open almost to the brain. His eyes fluttered and his jaw moved, however, so we knew he was alive. It took five of us on the boat's fantail to hoist this man aboard, by placing boat hooks under his armpits. We got him on deck, got the water out of his chest and covered him with a tarpaulin. No more than two minutes after we had picked up the rest of them, the burning ship completely turned turtle and disappeared from sight. We took them to a ship which was leaving immediately for England.

Only one died on board the cutter, apparently from shock. Rigor mortis had already set in and we couldn't close his eyes. When we searched his pockets for identification, I thought it was the first and last time anyone ever rolled this guy right under his eyes. He had a wallet tightly secured in a condom with hundreds of pound notes and an American silver dollar round his neck. Been in the navy five months, thirty-nine years old.

We stripped his clothes from him to his underwear, tied him to a rusty piece of steel and prepared to bury him. I tried to cross his arms over his chest but they were too stiff. His flesh was green.

McPhail, the skipper, reappeared on deck with his Bible, intoned the words, and we stopped the cutter's engines. I took off my helmet and the rest of the boys followed suit. We slid the body into the sea.[23]

Sergeant Alan Anderson, aged 27, B Battery, 1st Platoon, 116th Combat Team, 467th AAA Battalion:

Shortly after the first initial wave was on shore the counter fire began in earnest. I could see machine guns ripping into the ramps of some of the larger vessels unloading men further out into the Channel and the men were tumbling, falling dead into the water, just like corn cobs off a conveyor belt.

At about 08.00 hours we were due to land and the navy or coast guards units in charge of putting us on shore started to maneuver into position. As we came in toward the shore we came under intensive machine-gun and artillery fire. We milled around a bit, because it was obvious that there were no vehicles surviving on the beach. Some amphibious tanks had landed and had been promptly destroyed and the few DUKWs and other craft that were on the beach were burning and disabled.

As we were watching the slaughter around us, we thought we perhaps could help neutralize some of the German fire, so we turned the gun turret on a half-track around to get some fire onto the gun emplacements on the shore. As we did so, an 88 shell came through the side of the boat and exploded directly underneath the half-track. One of the men had already climbed into the turret. His name was Everett C. Martin, and he took the full blast of the exploding shell, which blew him off the half-track onto the deck of the LCV.

He was badly wounded. We picked him up and put him on a blanket. A hospital rescue craft was nearby and we lifted him over the side and the men from the navy got hold of him and managed to transfer him to the rescue vessel. The blanket was soaked in blood and I thought he had practically no chance of survival, but I heard afterwards that he did live, although he had 206 pieces of shrapnel removed from his body.

The naval officer in charge of the landing was up on the bridge at this time, with a flag alongside his head, and about that time a barrage of machine-gun fire cut that flag off. He had that kind of bewildered look that sometimes comes on men's faces when they're first under fire and realize how close they had come to being killed.

When we got in pretty close to the shore we saw a black man in the water. He was part of the crew removing underwater obstacles and was badly wounded, raising his hand for someone to help him.

We were trying to find a rope or a buoy or something to throw to him, but then the naval officer received orders to put back to sea because they were afraid of losing all the vehicles.

I remember with horror this poor man, as he lay in the water waving his hand and then sliding back under the water, which was tinted red with the blood that was obviously flowing from his wounds.[24]

Captain C.N. Hall, assistant battalion surgeon, 2nd Battalion, 16th Infantry:

We touched beach on Easy Red gently and yelled, 'Ramp down!' It crashed and every man grabbed stuff to get off. I and Sergeant Lambert began pushing them off, but they were glad to get off. Several 88mm shells landed near and rocked us. I was at the back of the boat and behind the crowd. There was a lot of machine-gun fire and tracers were going over the boat; some hit the boat. Men in the water were yelling, 'Get out of the way,' etcetera. Finally we all got off in three or four minutes. Some equipment was left behind, but we could not take it all. We were the biggest boat on the beach so we were a target. Several machine guns were hitting near and machine guns were splattering. I thought I saw tracers.

There were a lot of men in the water, wading waist deep in order to land. A lot of men in the water were wounded. I saw a man in a 'fugue' state, screaming and yelling, waving his arms. He had thrown all his equipment away. Saw 88s land to right and wound one man, who yelled for aid and wept. He had had his hand blown off. Boats were sinking, half a dozen LCTs were landing within 100 yards left and right.

MG fire and 88s got heavier. As we got knee-deep, 88s hit twenty-five feet to right and front, in the surf. A fragment hit me in the leg; it felt like a push, but didn't hurt. Some shell hit the sergeant. We floundered in.

All our men took cover behind tetrahedral obstacles at the edge of the water and fell on the sand when they heard bullets clanging on the rails of the obstacles. I hid behind my helmet, but peeped out and saw all the men in the remnants of the first and second waves hunched behind shingle. There was fire from pillboxes off to left and right, also small-arms fire, 88s landing in the water.

The men went in a few at a time. Some got in unhurt, some did not and there were yells from the wounded, but it was not our job to help them. I tried to run, but had to hobble with the wound in my thigh, so went up the shingle on all fours. Firing shifted to the left. We got behind the shingle but could not dig in because if we dug a hole the pebbles would roll back in. Lambert was wounded but not too badly.

We lay on cold pebbles, shaking with fear and cold. It caused me to notice my leg was hurting. Two hours later I had to give myself one dose of morphine. I looked round and saw men who were still coming up the beach and having a lot of trouble from the machine-gun fire. Many were hit in the water, and the wounded were drowned by the rising tide. I yelled to some and urged them to crawl in and some of them did. Many did not seem to be functioning at all, mentally; they were just sitting or sprawling around. They could move their limbs, but would not answer or do anything. Several officers started to go and get them but higher officers yelled at them to come back and they did. Some men were clinging to an LCVP, the highest end of which was grounded. I saw that if something was not done the rising tide would get them. They toppled off one by one and drowned. I saw one with a chest wound and the water eventually covered his face and he drowned.

One boy came across from the tetrahedral obstacles strolling casually up the sand. Someone yelled to him to get down as a burst of machine-gun fire made a circle of sand bursts all around him, but he came in safely. There was an old major who just made it to us. He was worn out, so I gave him a dose of morphine. I saw one boy pick up rifle after rifle and try to shoot it but they were all filled with sand and no good. Finally he got a pistol and fired it at the pillboxes, but he was told to stop as he was only drawing fire.

In all this fire, when you could hardly get across the beach and expect to live, Corporal Jones, a puny kid who was the last one to expect anything spectacular of, went out six times and brought men in. He checked one man over and could not move him. He came back to me, described the wound and asked me what he should do. He went back and did what he could. The man was shot through the chest. Jones could not drag him up, but he dragged in four men and survived. He should have got the DSC. Jones put on the best show that I saw on that beach.[25]

Lieutenant William H. Jones, 7th Battalion, 467th Anti-Aircraft Artillery:

I will never forget the navy lieutenant that was running the ship that brought us to the beach on Omaha. I gave him two dollars, a lot of money at that time, to take pictures of me going off the LCT and landing on the beach. I wanted to mail the pictures back to my wife's address and he wrote it down and put it in his pocket. It wasn't but just a very short time, a few minutes, until he was picked off by enemy fire and killed. I often wondered if they sent his personal things to his wife and what in the hell she thought about this address of this woman from Seneca, South Carolina, that he had in his pocket.

We had half-tracks mounted with quadruple 50-caliber machine guns and dual 37mm automatic rifles. I felt it was my Christian duty to go in on the first half-track. The navy guy that was taking soundings must have got a false sounding because I went off on the first half-track and that darn thing went down for twelve feet into the ocean. The fellow that was driving it, I kept pulling at him, I could feel the muscles on his back as he was under water. The exhaust pipe was completely under water and I could feel him flinching as he mashed on the starter. Finally I jerked him up out of there and he was spitting water out of his mouth as he said, 'You told me this damn thing would run under water.' I said, 'No, I never said it would run with the exhaust pipe under water.'

We inflated our Mae West jackets and swam on in shore. I have never seen as many dead people before in my life. It was absolutely unbelievable. There was nothing on the beach but dead bodies and the sand was red with blood.

I remember they gave us a little vial of morphine to break and stick yourself in the arm with in case you got hit and was dying, it made dying easier. I don't think I had that morphine over one minute after I got on the beach. I gave it to another fellow. All these screaming things, mortars and artillery shells and all, you'd hear them whistling and you'd hit the dirt, well, when you hit the dirt every time you hit it on top of another dead GI. There wasn't any such thing as digging a foxhole in that sand.

The only thing I wanted was a cigarette and I asked this medic that was running across, 'You got a dry cigarette?' And he handed me a cigarette and he was hit with something, I don't know what it was, but his entire body, his insides and everything, was flown all over me. It must have been a mortar that hit him, I don't know.[26]

Corporal Robert L. Miller, aged 20, B Company, 149th Combat Engineer Battalion, 6th Engineer Special Brigade:

We reached to within what I suppose to be nearly 100 yards from the beach when our LCT stopped and the ramp was lowered. The skipper said this was it – we were to disembark there and then as we had grounded on an underwater sand bar. Our platoon commander objected in no uncertain terms, reminding the skipper his orders were to run us on to the beach, but the skipper refused to budge.

The jeep was first off and immersed completely under water but made it to shore as it had been waterproofed and the exhaust pipe extended well above the jeep itself. The trucks were next and they also made their way to the shore, thanks to the waterproofing system.

The men started to unload at that point and, as we jumped off the ramp, we sunk completely under with the weight of all our gear. I will never forget the feeling of panic I experienced at that moment. Thankfully, we had been taught in training how to strap on our packs and equipment in such a way as to get rid of it in a hurry should such a predicament present itself. I was able to eject all my equipment, with the exception of gas mask and steel helmet, and leap upward from the ocean floor, finally getting my head above water.

I started swimming for the beach. It was a very tough swim and frightening, to say the least. The weight of the soaked clothes, boots, gas mask and steel helmet made it near-impossible but I did finally reach water hip-deep and was able to stand up. I was near exhaustion by this time and felt as though my body weighed at least 300 pounds.

As I started wading toward the beach I remember hearing some guys from other boats screaming as they were drowning in their attempt to reach the shore. As I continued wading I saw ahead of me GIs huddled behind a shale ridge for protection just beyond the water line.

At last I reached shore and was about fifteen feet up the beach when a big white flash of nothingness enveloped me. I had been hit. And the next thing I knew I was flat on my back looking up at the sky. I tried to get up but could not and reasoned, my God, my legs had been blown off, since I had no sensation of movement in them and could not see them for the gas mask on my chest blocking my view. I wrestled around and finally got the gas mask off to one side. I saw my feet sticking up and reached my upper legs with my hands and so felt relieved that they were still whole, but could not understand my immobility or lack of sensation in them.

One of the fellows from our group soon crawled beside me, crouching for protection behind a mine-detector case he had found floating in the water. I told him I had been hit and needed the medics as I couldn't move. Within a few minutes, which seemed more like an eternity, they reached me behind the shelter of a half-track and gave me a shot of morphine. Shock from the injury overcame me at that point and I passed out.

When I regained consciousness I hazily recall being in a first-aid station on the beach with medics going over me and cutting off my clothes to determine my injury. I soon passed out again and when I next awoke I was on an LST with a navy medical aide asking what he could do to make me comfortable. It must have been early afternoon or late morning on D-Day, as I heard the clatter of guns being fired on deck.

I was to learn later that a round of sniper fire had passed through my body, severing my spinal cord. I would never be able to use my legs again.[27]

Rifleman Hal Baumgarten, aged 19, B Company, 116th Infantry:

At about 7.00 a.m. I saw the beach with its huge sea wall at the foot of a massive 150-foot bluff. An 88mm shell landed right in the middle of the LCA to the side of us and splinters of the boat, equipment and bodies were thrown into the air. Lieutenant Donaldson cautioned us to get down. Bullets were passing through the thin wooden sides of our vessel. The ramp was lowered and the inner door was opened.

In a British LCA only one man could get out at a time. Clarius Riggs was hit in front of me as he exited the boat and went under. I got a bullet through the top of my helmet and then, as I waded through the deep water, carrying an M1 rifle at port arms, a bullet hit the receiver plate. I was able to fire the gun one time, then the stock broke in half. I threw the thing away. Private Nicholas Kafkalas picked it up, handing it back to me, thinking I had given up. Bullets ripped through my field jacket and one glanced off my helmet. I left my assault jacket on the LCA. As we worked our way to the sand, I noticed three amphibious tanks and two of them were knocked out. Many Company A soldiers were hanging on to the tanks, one of which was firing its 75mm gun into the pillbox to the right flank of Dog Green. The bunker just kept firing back.

About eight or ten feet to my right, a little in front of me, Private Robert Dittmar was hit in the chest. I heard him yell, 'I'm hit, I'm hit!' and watched him as he continued to go forward about ten more yards. He tripped over a tank obstacle and as he fell his body made a complete turn and he lay sprawled on the damp sand with his head facing the Germans and his face looking skyward. He seemed to be suffering from shock and was yelling, 'Mother, mother . . .' as he rolled around on the sand.

Sergeant Barnes got shot down right in front of me and Lieutenant Donaldson. Sergeant 'Pilgrim' Robertson had a gaping wound in the upper right corner of his forehead. He was walking crazily in the water, without his helmet. Then I saw him get down on his knees and start praying with his rosary beads. At this moment, the Germans cut him in half with their deadly crossfire which was coming from pillboxes and what I thought was a reinforced building overlooking the beach.

Shells were continually landing all about me and fragments from an 88mm which exploded about twenty yards in front of me hit me in my left cheek. It felt like being hit with a baseball bat, only the results were much much worse. My upper jaw was shattered, my left cheek blown open. My upper lip was cut in half, the roof of my mouth was cut up and teeth and gums were lying on my tongue.

I washed my face in the cold Channel water and managed somehow not to pass out. I got rid of most of my equipment. Here, I was happy I did not wear the invasion jacket. I wore a regular army zippered field jacket with a Star of David drawn on the back and 'The Bronx, New York' written on it. I crawled forward, trying to take cover behind bodies and water obstacles made of steel.

Finally I came to dry sand and there was only another hundred yards, maybe less, to go. I started across the sand, crawling very fast, with Germans in the pillbox on the right flank shooting the sand all about me.

When I reached the sea wall, blood was gushing from my left cheek. I met Pfc Dominic Surro, who was then unhurt. He was a rather large kid from Georgia. He and I were the same age, nineteen. He tried to help, but we were under intense fire from the pillbox.

I picked up another M1 rifle and followed Surro, who was moving left toward the Vierville Draw. We were seeking safety from the pillbox. I then found my best buddy, Pfc Robert Garbett, lying face down and dead.

My adrenalin was pumping and I got up to cross the road above the wall when Gilbert Pittenger from New Jersey tackled me and probably saved my life, because just as I started a hail of bullets came my way, barely missing me. I helped Sergeant Frazier, who was wounded and paralysed, to get behind the sea wall. That was the last I saw of him.

A mortar shell exploded and three pieces of shrapnel got me in the left side of the head. My helmet had three holes, but probably saved me from much worse. More mortar shells began falling nearby so we dived back behind the wall. One of the medics, Cecil Breeden, leaned over me, shells and bullets flying, and applied a pressure bandage and sprinkled sulfa powder to my face wound. I tried to pull him down to safety, but he hit my hand away and said, 'You're hurt now. When I get it, you can take care of me.'[28]

Sergeant Cecil Breeden, medical aid man, A Company, 116th Infantry:

Every man was a hero, never saw a coward. When I found Baumgarten, he had his cheek about over his ear. I patched him up and went on my way. I glanced now and then at the boys trying to take that damned pillbox. As I remember, it took six or more to do it. As far as I know, none of them lived. I couldn't tell you who any of them were. I was just too busy to know what was going on around me.

I remember patching up Butch, the A Company mail clerk, and Lieutenant Rany Nance. Then 'Big Bill' Presley [M/Sergeant, B Company] came by and I asked him what he was doing. He said, 'Looking for a damn rifle that will work.' Pointing up the hill, he said he saw some men up there. Then he told me to get down or I was going to get hit. I said, 'What the hell are you talking about, you're a damn sight bigger target than me.' He just grinned and went on up the beach. Soon he came back with a rifle, just waved and went on.[29]

Sergeant Debs H. Peters, 121st Combat Engineers:

There was a tank on fire in the middle of the sand, between us and the sea wall. We reached the tank and crouched down behind it, but as we did so a shell hit the tank. Shell fragments hit him [Captain Bainbridge] in the face and cut his face up. It looked real bad, a lot of blood. One piece hit me in the chest and cut it open. I asked him how bad he was hurt and he said it was a scratch, but it looked bad to me. I didn't see him again.

I made my way over to the sea wall and found Captain John McAllister, who was from my unit, and Major Robert Stewart, who was our exec. We agreed we should get out of there if we wanted to live and Major Stewart told me to go ahead. I knew where the mines were buried, since I had studied the terrain carefully from aerial photos and intelligence. So I said, 'Let's go,' and we jumped up on the road and went across on the other side, fell down into the ditch, up again, through a briar patch, then up against the hill, which was fairly steep, but it was good because we were out of the line of fire from some of the machine guns.

We continued to the top of the crest and, in spite of being in perfect physical shape, we were all out of breath. The artillery and mortars had set fire to the foliage and there was a terrible lot of smoke. We had to put on our gas masks it was so bad. At that time, the major instructed me to go forward and make a reconnaissance to see what was ahead. In spite of the fact that the machine-gun fire was intense, I reluctantly did so. Fortunately the grass was high and there was a good bit of brush. I stayed very close to the ground and had got about 100 yards when I was caught by machine-gun fire, which tore my pack up and put a hole in my helmet.

I tried to get into a small depression about a foot deep and finally I got my weapon turned around and put a grenade in it. I fired this grenade in the direction the fire was coming from. It quit and I got out of there real fast and found a deeper hole.[30]

Staff Sergeant William H. Lewis, aged 22, Anti-Tank Platoon, 1st Battalion, 116th Infantry Regiment:

On the beach I ran over to the sea wall, cold and scared. Larry Rote piled in on top of us and said, 'Is that you shaking, Sarge?' I said, 'Yeah, damn right!' He said, 'My God! I thought it was me.' I could see him and he was shaking all right. Both of us were.

We huddled there just trying to stay alive. There was nothing we could do except keep our butts down. There was no place to go and the automatic fire became heavier. As others landed they, like us, took cover behind the wall.

There were dead guys washing back and forth in the surf with their shirts stained with blood. I remember a tractor of a bulldozer hitting a land mine and it blew into nothing. Two pieces of track was all that was left where that baby hit. Even the camouflage nets were blown to pieces.

There was a 1st Division sergeant, who had seen combat in North Africa, and he said, 'See that bunker next to the exit, get some fire on that baby.' A fire-control sailor got on the radio and tried to direct fire on the pillbox but the shells were ineffective. The sergeant with the Big Red One on his jacket then ordered, 'Everyone start firing on that embrasure! Keep them away from that hole!' He sure knew what he was doing. We got up there and started firing on that embrasure. The sarge took some men with a bangalore torpedo and placed it under that baby. He stopped that thing from murdering us with its 88s. The bunker was in the face of the cliff and they were using it as a command post. It was a killer and the man with the Big Red One on his shoulder helped us to blow it up.

We were disorganized because everyone was in the wrong place and three out of four of the company commanders were killed. Many officers and noncoms were casualties so we became disorganized and didn't move off the beach as we would have liked. We were caught between a tank that had gotten ashore and some fortified houses that were shooting at us. There was a huge naval dud from one of the battleships laying next to me. I was afraid the thing would explode.

From the top of the hill the view of the fleet out in the Channel was awesome. Looking down on the slaughter of the men and the destruction of equipment was hard to fathom. I never heard one man say, 'Hell, this is not what it is supposed to be like! Let's go back!' There was so much going on that all you could think about was to keep your ass alive.[31]

Stanley Stypulowski, aged 21, Anti-tank Company, 16th Infantry Regiment:

We got the beach OK. I drove the track about 300 yards down the beach and I was stopped by our engineers, who were still trying to remove land mines to make it passable. We were directed to take cover. At this point my squad became separated. I took cover near a burned-out Sherman tank, my logic being the Germans wouldn't expend any further ammo on a disabled tank.

As I took cover behind the tank, I found myself sitting on the ground beside a soldier with a severe leg wound asking for help. I called to a couple of medics nearby and then tried to help him and found I was unable to move my arms. At this point my mind didn't quite function as it should have, I guess, and I thought to myself, 'What the dickens is happening to me that I can't help this poor fellow?' I just sat there, kind of numb.

The medics came over and one medic worked on the wounded soldier and the second asked me how badly I was hit. I told him I didn't know I was hit. The medic removed my gas mask, which was worn chest-high for buoyancy, and showed me a hole through it and then he showed me a hole in my shirt. He cut away my shirt and I saw a hole in my chest the size of a silver dollar, no bleeding. The medic told me I wasn't bleeding because I had been hit by a large piece of shrapnel that was still red hot and had sealed the blood vessels as it entered my body.

Being raised as a Roman Catholic, as a child we were taught in the event of serious illness or an injury which may result in death, to repeat the following: 'Jesus, Mary and Joseph have mercy on my soul,' which I did.

The medic, in the meantime, doused my wound with sulfa powder and bandaged it. He helped me up and started walking back through the surf to an LCT discharging troops. The medic told me to try and make it to the boat on my own and left me to go back to the beach. After taking a few shaky steps in the surf, the salt water got in the wound and I apparently passed out. When I came to I was lying on my back on an inflated raft, looking up at two sailors who had apparently pulled me out of the surf. I remember the sun was in my eyes.

An LCT took me back to the USS *Dorothy Dix* and I was put in a body basket and hoisted aboard. While I was being pulled over the rail, one of the sailors called out, 'Hello, Ski, remember me from St Casimir's?' It was the church I attended in my home town, but at that point I was pretty well out of it and couldn't recognize anyone. That night, the ship brought us back to England.[32]

Captain Edward Wozenski, E Company, 2nd Battalion, 16th Infantry:

Just before the landing all of our web gear, standard web gear, issue gear, fine battle-proven gear, was taken away from us because some theorist figured that it would be far easier and much more practical to wear a hunting-type jacket. So at the last minute we were issued with these canvas jackets with fantastic pockets all over the place and we transferred all our gear into these pockets.

When we hit the bottom we had approximately four hundred yards to struggle through the water to the beach. There was small arms fire all around so you were up and down, ducking down, as terrified as anyone could be. Every time I got up I thought it was pure terror that was making my knees buckle until I finally hit the beach and realized I had about one hundred pounds of sand in the pockets of my jacket, sand that had accumulated on top of the fifty or sixty-pound load we were all carrying in.

When I finally got up the shale I had my first sergeant with me and I asked him, 'For God's sake get a packet of cigarettes out,' and he had to dig out handfuls of sand before he could get a pack out for me . . .

I was praying for smoke, any kind of smoke, so that we could get up through the wire. Heroics have nothing to do with it – their automatic weapons were trained on us and people cannot advance in daylight against automatic small arms. There were tanks burning, some landing craft had caught fire and the general smoke and haze of a battlefield began to develop and then, through all this, off on a flank, I saw a yellow smoke flare.

I knew this was one of our basic signals. All platoon leaders and platoon sergeants had yellow smoke flares and I had said the first son of a gun that gets up on top of that bluff will set off a smoke flare. I thought I would try and assemble as many people as I could and move down to the point where I thought the smoke flare went off and make a move up there because I knew I couldn't get up where I was.

I remember distinctly taking my trench knife and pressing it into people's backs to see if they were alive. If they were alive I would kick them or roll them over and say, 'Let's go!' I picked up half a dozen people this way, but I didn't realize that terror could be so great in a man that he would not turn round to see who was sticking a knife into him. Later on it dawned on me that two or three of them were alive but just wouldn't turn round because of absolute terror.

We assembled maybe a dozen people and about opposite the point where I saw the yellow smoke flare I started working my way up a path. Half-way up I'm climbing the bluff and I see one of my platoon sergeants coming down the other way with a big grin on his face. Right in front of my nose, as he steps down he puts his foot on a teller mine. I said, 'My God, how stupid can you be?' and he said, 'Oh, don't let it worry you, it didn't go off when I stepped on it going up.'

When we got up to the top of the cliff I had a head count. I landed 180 men and eight officers. I counted thirteen men and one other officer beside myself.[33]

Sergeant Hyman Haas, commanding a section of anti-tank guns mounted on half-tracks:

Omaha beach was my first combat. Like everyone else, I guess I was shocked and amazed at my first sight of the beach and like every other guy I found it was impossible to carry out the assignment I'd been given. I was supposed to drive my half-track straight across the beach away up one of the valleys to the village of St Laurent-sur-Mer. Then I had to set up my guns on top of the bluffs. I found the valley OK, but I found something else, too. That shingle bank no guy who was there will ever forget. This side of it was littered with wrecked tanks, dead men and hundreds of guys crouched down taking cover. Nobody could get past it. Before I even stopped the half-track, an officer ran towards me. He pointed out a pillbox 300 yards away that was giving the guys seven kinds of hell. I brought the half-track stern-on to the pillbox, trained the gun and laid it on the target. Then I fired ten rounds. As far as I could see they all exploded in the pillbox. After that the German gun was silent.[34]

Eldon Wiehe, HQ Battery, Division Artillery, 1st Infantry Division:

We were going in, we were landing an hour after the first troops went in. We got close to the beach and the ship ahead of us caught an 88 right in the middle. Flak was flying everywhere. Our skipper, I suppose he had gotten scared, turned around and took us back out to sea, out of gun range. No other ship that I saw turned around. We stayed there a couple of hours and he decided to go in again, so we went in one more time. We came under very heavy gunfire again and again the skipper turned around and went back out to sea. We didn't blame him, we were all scared. We stayed out there until about noon, when a speedboat came by and someone in command, a high authority, took a bullhorn and yelled, 'The skipper of that ship, you've been in twice. Take it in and this time do not come back until it is unloaded.'

Our lieutenant informed us to undo our backpacks and take everything off. He said we probably wouldn't get in all the way, so just grab a rifle and whatever ammunition you have. Sure enough, we were pulling in and we came under heavy fire again. The skipper lowered the ramp. Our lieutenant yelled that we weren't in far enough and couldn't get our vehicles off, but the skipper insisted that we get off. We drove the first truck off and it sank. Again our lieutenant yelled at the skipper to take us in further, but again the skipper refused, insisting that we unload. We drove all the trucks off, as we were ordered to do by the ship's commander. All seven sank.

We had to swim in. We had quite a ways to swim, and being under fire, it seemed like thirty minutes. When we got to where our feet could hit the sand we got up and started walking. When we hit the shore we heard a shell coming in and we all immediately hit the dirt. There happened to be a shellhole near where I was and I jumped into it without looking. When that shell burst I guess I panicked. I started crying. There was a ship to our right that had dry-docked and my buddies got me behind that ship, where I cried for what seemed like hours. I cried until tears would no longer come. Suddenly I felt something, I can't explain it, but a warm feeling went through my body and I stopped crying and came to my senses.

We stayed there for a while. We were without vehicles, at least four hours late, had no idea how to get off the beach or where we were. We were sheltered by the ship from four pillboxes and soon we saw two bulldozers head for them with their blades up. They put their blades down and closed the holes the guns were shooting out of and stopped the machine guns firing. On the return trip one of them took a direct hit and the man on it seemed to fly into pieces.

We knew we had to get off the beach and the lieutenant went off to see if he could find a way out. He soon returned and told us the bulldozers had made a road through the mines. We talked it over and everyone agreed we had to get off the beach as soon as possible. So we picked up our carbines and ammunition and ran.[35]

Sergeant Victor H. Fast, aged 21, 5th Ranger Battalion:

When I crawled up the beach to the sea wall I had an M1 rifle, two bandoliers of ammo and several grenades. No helmet, no gas mask, no pack, because I had peeled them all off so I could swim. I crawled around to find a helmet from a dead buddy only to find it half full of head – I quickly found another.

We were lying behind the sea wall re-grouping when General Cota walked up and said to Colonel Schneider, 'I'm expecting the Rangers to lead the way.' We started inland through a smoke haze and a field of bouncing Betsies and captured some Germans. I was Colonel Schneider's interpreter and he told me to interrogate them. He didn't tell me who or what to ask, he just said get whatever information you can.

Now I used my head and country breeding and picked the youngest, most timid-looking, lowest-ranking Kraut I could find. I took him away from the other prisoners and told him straight – you are going to tell me what I want to know. First, I told him the war was over for him and to relax. I asked him if he had observed all the American and British bombers overhead earlier that morning. He said, 'Yes.' That was good – I wanted to get him in a 'yes' mood.

Then I told him I'd give him three choices. One, if he told me nothing, nothing at all, just kept his mouth shut, I would send him over to the Russians. (Of course, I couldn't do anything of the sort.) Second, if he gave me information about minefields and number of troops in the immediate vicinity but left me in any doubt that he was telling the truth, I would turn him over to my Jewish buddy, Herb Epstein, who was standing next to me. Herb had not shaved that day, was big and burly. With a .45 on his hip, a Ranger knife in his boot and a Thomson sub-machine gun, he looked mean enough to scare the living daylights out of anybody. Thirdly, I said that if he told me what I wanted to know and convinced me he was telling the truth, I would send him to America where he would have a good life until the war was over and he could go home.

He told me about the little mines, the 'bouncing Betsies' and about the fortifications on Pointe du Hoc. He told me there were no troops as such in Vierville, but inland there were numerous elite Panzer divisions. He added that the beach area was covered with criss-cross fire from 88s and machine guns. I said yes, I knew, because we had come through a barrage on the way up the slope.

We proceeded up the Vierville draw and drew fire from both sides and sniper fire from the church steeple. Colonel Schneider called for a naval bombardment of the church and it was promptly demolished. A girl sniper was found in the rubble.

Another thing I remember about that day was that one of our HQ Rangers boasted that he was going to have sex with a French woman within eight hours of hitting the beach. Sure as hell, Herb Epstein cracked a door when we were clearing Vierville and saw the knucklehead in the act.[36]

Robert E. Adams, US Coast Guard, aged 25, coxswain on LCVP No.22 from US Samuel Chase, APA 26:

I don't know how close we were to the beach when we saw the haze and smoke and you could smell cordite. It was like going into a new world. A few of our soldiers were seasick and I suspect they were anxious to get out of the boat. I don't recall any German 88 shells, and we knew that noise only too well, but we could hear the chatter of – it had to be machine guns.

We were getting ready to hit the beach. There is almost always a sandbar out from any beach and our routine was to cut the motor for a second and let our backwash carry us over, and I must have unconsciously done this, because I was able to get my boat right up to the edge of the beach.

At this time all was confusion and it seemed like all hell was breaking loose. We had to maneuver between the obstacles to get to the beach and I recall the army had an amphibious vehicle that we called ducks. I think they were spelled 'dukks' or something like that. And they were a disaster. Already I could see bodies of soldiers and their rumps sticking out of the water, because for their life belt they just had a belt round their waist and not their chest and obviously they couldn't keep their head up when they hit deep water, and so they drowned, and all the belt did was keep their ass up out of the water. I suspect that the waves engulfed all of these army vehicles very easily, as they did not appear to be all that seaworthy.

Our ramp opened and our brave group from the Big One bounded out and I recall looking to my left and two soldiers were holding up another one between them and they were yelling something, words of encouragement. He looked half-drowned. I suspect he had escaped from one of those sunken army DUKWs. In my memory I remember seeing something lying up ahead. We saw several fall. You saw guys fall right in front of you. We knew they were expected to be eight miles inland and this was not happening and right away you knew automatically that something was wrong. Soldiers seemed to be all huddled in groups.

About the maneuvering of an LCVP boat. When you hit the beach, you keep your boat in forward gear at low speed because you must keep enough steerage on so that your boat will be at right angles to the beach, particularly in Normandy where the high waves were washing in behind you. If your boat got just a wee bit broadside, you would be broached, in other words washed up sideways on to the beach. Keeping too much forward motion was touchy because the tide, in my opinion, was outgoing and if you didn't broach you could end up high and dry on the beach.

Backing the LCVP away from the beach could be just as perilous. You had to back it out, keeping your boat as straight as possible. If you went just a little bit sideways, you stood an excellent chance of being washed up on the beach. Fortunately for me and my crew, I was lucky enough to back out without mishap. Backing out I saw something I will remember all my life: my boat grazed a telegraph post placed by the Germans as a hazard and on top of it, so close I could almost reach out and touch it, was a Teller mine. It could have blown us all to bits.

So our first landing was successful. Our orders then were to seek out any support boat and take whatever directions they gave us. We approached a support boat and picked up a one-star general and about four or five people on his staff, officers and a couple of sergeants. I recall he said to me, 'Son, how is it on the beach?' And I guess at this time we were a couple of hundred yards off the beach and I responded, 'Pretty hot, sir.' He said, 'Well, take us in as close as you can.'

I remember as a kid reading cowboy and indian stories as to how the enemy, whichever side, liked to kill the leader, the man in control, usually obvious by his insignia, or whatever. I kept thinking, here I've got the man with the helmet on and as I recall, the one star was white or silver. Anyway, it was extremely visible. I just kept thinking, why don't I have the guts to ask him to turn around? I'm gonna get killed just because I know he's a general and they'll try to blow this boat out of the water.

Well, neither happened. I didn't ask and we didn't get hit. I put him so close he and his group hardly got their ankles wet.

Even at this time everything was stagnant on the beach and we saw those poor bastards topple over, some of them. Not the ones that we let out, but we could see it.

As we were on the beach, we were summoned by an army provost marshal to take three men on a stretcher back to our ship and two or three others, I can't remember exactly how many, who were standing evidently shell-shocked, because they were like mummies. They were like dead guys – they were walking but they didn't say anything. The order to go back to the ship was received by us in the crew as 'Boy, how lucky can you get.'

The sea was still rough, but we made it back to our ship. It was a different world. The gun crews were all relaxed, some drinking coffee. Not a shot had been fired. We had not seen one single *Luftwaffe* plane on the beach and neither had the ship's crew.

Our boat was lifted aboard. Someone took care of the men who were wounded. As I recall, I think one or two had died en route back to the ship.

Alongside our ship was an LCI that had received several direct hits but had somehow made it back to the safety zone and the people on our ship were in a rescue operation. Looking down on this LCT was a terrible scene. You could see bodies, dead and wounded, all over the deck.

So, anyway, we were aboard and I thought we had a reprieve from the beach. How lucky to be able to return from all the smoke and gunfire.

Thirty minutes later, over the public address system came an announcement: 'All available boats return to Red Two beach.' Now, Red Two, that's in my memory. I see where it was called Easy Red, but in my memory it was Red Two beach.

Earlier that morning we had a great deal of confidence heading for the Normandy beaches. Now, it seemed like this was a death sentence. How could we go back and fool around that beach without getting shot, or blown up by a mine, or simply broached on the beach and then shot?

The crew and I made our way back to what we now knew as an inferno, and the next two hours are fuzzy. We took another general with some soldiers to the beach again from a larger boat. By this time, our troops had been able to break out some. The stalemate, I think, had been broken, but we continued to have shells dropping around us spasmodically.

Finally we lucked out and were given some wounded soldiers to take back to the ship. Getting on deck, I saw a sight that I will never forget. On the port side aft, dead soldiers were stacked up like cardboard. Helmets were in a big pile. Most of these dead boys still had their boots on. It was a sight you simply had to turn away from.[37]

CHAPTER THIRTEEN

SWORD

On Sword beach, the eastern flank of the invasion, British infantry came ashore supported by floating tanks and armour to face up to a German panzer division known to be in the area. Within an hour, advance units had got off the beach and were penetrating inland . . .

Telegraphist Clifford Palliser, aged 19, on board HMS Largs:

As dawn broke the coastline of Normandy came into view. We were about six miles out and already the warships had commenced their bombardment of the shore defences. I was having a quick smoke on the upper deck and could see the lighthouse at the entrance to Ouistreham harbour, the church steeple at Hermanville, a gas-holder behind the villas and houses along the seafront and empty beaches. It was approximately 6.00 a.m., one-and-a-half hours before the first landing on Queen sector of Sword beach.

It was at that time, waiting for the first landing to go in, that the Germans reacted. I assume that the smokescreen laid on our left flank had attracted the attention of the German navy at Le Havre. Several E-Boats came out of that harbour to investigate. Coming through the smoke and seeing the mass of shipping, they fired ten or twelve torpedoes towards the fleet before turning back for Le Havre. One or two torpedoes hit the Norwegian destroyer, *Svenner*, which sank immediately. I saw her go down in the shape of a letter 'V'. I did not see the two torpedoes that tracked towards our ship, but the bridge saw them and went full astern. One torpedo passed feet in front of the bow and the second one a similar distance astern.

With all the noise and excitement around, the adrenalin was pumping through my veins. I was all hyped up and, not wishing to miss those first few minutes of the actual landings, my fellow operator and I took it in turns to step out of the cabin to see what was happening. The small assault craft were slowly making their way ashore, bobbing and weaving.

Just before the actual landing the officer came to us and said, 'Go and watch a piece of history in the making.' This we did. I watched the inspiring sight of a rocket landing craft slowly position itself, turning sideways to the beach and releasing more than a thousand rockets. The craft vanished in its own smoke and a few seconds later an oblong section of the beach simply erupted. The craft then withdrew to reload. I could just see the engineers among the beach obstacles at half tide destroying the various explosive devices in the water.

My last sight before I returned to the cabin was to see the DD tanks swim ashore and stop on the waterline to blow away the canvas sides that had allowed them to float. I remember being stunned, thinking that one after another the tanks were being knocked out before they saw any action. It was a real surprise when, through a break in the smoke, I saw the tanks lumbering on up the beach.[1]

Marine Edwin Webb, aged 18, landing craft bowman:

As soon as it was daylight we had to get to the boats. We were about eight miles off France; you could just see it in the distance. While we were loading up the boats there was a God almighty bang and we saw a Norwegian destroyer, the *Svenner*, blow up. The stern went up and met the bows and she went down in about two minutes. We couldn't do a thing for the crew; she was about half a mile away and there were lots of other ships around. It was our first taste of war and it sort of hit you in the gut.

We lowered away at about five-thirty or six in the morning. There was a hell of a swell on. We had thirty-six fully equipped troops on board and some of 'em, poor devils, could hardly stand up for the amount of stuff they had on their backs. I thought to myself then, God, if we go under, three parts of 'em will never make it.

We circled round for about a quarter of an hour, maybe longer, until everybody was lowered away and cleared off the parent ship and then away we went. As we were going in we saw a squadron of aircraft come over and strafe the beach. They had white stripes on the wings and round the fuselage to denote they were Allied aircraft. We also passed pretty near to one of the rocket ships. It was the first time I'd ever seen one. Basically it was a tank landing craft with several hundred rockets on it. When they pressed the button the rockets went off with such force that if the boat was going full steam ahead it would start going full steam astern. They had to wait half an hour for the decks to cool down before anyone could step on them. I can still feel what it was like when those rockets fired by my right ear.

We were due to go in on the extreme left of Sword beach and we got through the obstacles all right and got our chaps off. They hardly got their feet wet. There was sniping and bits and pieces going on, but we had too much to think about to worry about it. After I pulled up the ramp the corporal put her in full astern to get out. As we swung round we caught an obstacle and it ripped through the bottom of the craft. It went down like a stone and we had to swim for it. When we got on the beach there was nothing we could do but lie low, because we'd lost our weapons in the water when the craft went down.

Eventually we teamed up with some other Marines who'd lost their craft as well, then one of our officers turned up and said he was going to see the beachmaster to see if we could join up with the commandos. I thought, bloody hell! He was a nutter this bloke, a real madhat. When we was on exercises up in Cromarty he used to get us up out of our bunks and have us dashing around half an hour before reveille. That was his nature. Anyway, this nutter went off and we didn't see no more of him.

There were little footpaths through the dunes and the odd German were coming through with their hands up. They all wore felt caps – I didn't see one with a tin hat. One had his face all done up in bandages and I heard some medical orderly say, take him up behind the tent, so whether they took him up there and shot him because he was too far gone I don't know.

All the bigger landing craft coming in were flying barrage balloons and there was so much stuff flying around them that whenever one came in right in line with us we moved. I'd say to my colleague, 'Frank, we've got to move, mate.' One time we went to sit with a sergeant in the army who had a little truck and trailer. We were chatting with him in it, taking in all what was going on, and another landing craft started coming in opposite us. I said, 'Sarge, we've got to move in a minute. That one's coming in here and I don't fancy staying when he's here.' He said, 'Sorry, mate, I've got my orders and I've got to stay here.' Lo and behold, we moved on and there was a big bang and I looked behind me and he was no longer there. I turned to my mate and said, 'That poor devil's gone.'

We was ducking and diving, keeping out of the way of anything going on. The beachmaster, who was walking up and down with his walking stick as if he was in Hyde Park, told us to keep out of the way until he could get us off the beach. About eleven o'clock, or half past, this LCI came in and we were told to get on it. We scrambled on board with Jerry having a pot shot at us and a naval chappie in the bows blasting away in the direction the fire was coming from.

Once we got out, the navy brought us a mug of hot coffee laced with rum. Daft as it may seem, I went below and went to sleep.[2]

Marine Derek Pratt, aged 19, bowman on an assault landing craft from the SS Empire Broadsword:

We were all assembled with the troops on our various landing craft still hanging from davits on the side of the *Broadsword*. They hung in tiers, one row above the other. The chaplain said a few words and blessed us after which the first tier started to lower away. So far so good.

The sea was mighty rough and the waves must have been twenty feet high. We hit the crest of a wave and I started to take off the forward hook. I managed to release it, but unfortunately my stern sheetsman, Marine Joe Beardsley, couldn't release his because by that time we had dropped into a trough and the cable had gone taut.

Consequently we were hanging by the stern hook and all the troops on our landing craft fell forward all on top of one another. I dashed to the stern and when the next wave brought us up level we managed to release the stern hook, at which time we dropped with an almighty splash in the drink.

The troops sorted themselves out and we started to circle clockwise away from the carrier to allow the rest of the landing craft to be lowered and then we all formed up and proceeded to make our way seven miles to the beach.

The sea was so rough that when a landing craft hit the trough of a wave it vanished from view until it rose on the next crest. The coxswain found it very difficult to keep on station. Previous to being lowered away we had all been issued with a hay box of stew to give the troops a hot meal. After we had been travelling for about two or three miles I decided to see if the troops would like anything to eat and I opened the hay box. What an unholy mess! The grease from the stew had all come to the top and as soon as the troops smelled it and saw it the majority were sick on the spot and I spent the next hour swabbing the decks of vomit, by which time I was beginning to feel most unwell myself.

We eventually saw the coastline and with me reading off the yards to go – 1,000, 500 and so on – we prepared to hit the beach. We had to thread our way through the beach obstacles and one of my jobs was to hold the poles with the Teller mines on them out of the way, quite an experience for a nineteen-year-old who had only seen the sea on cinema before he joined up.

We eventually managed to get all the troops off without any casualties and proceeded to back off the beach with the same difficulty we had had going in. With a great sigh of relief we started back to the *Broadsword*. Suddenly a voice from the stern said, 'Look what I've found.' It was our stoker, Blanco Taylor, and he was holding a grenade in his hand.

'Bloody hell, Blanco,' I said, 'throw it over the side. We've got this far. Let's make sure we all get back.' With that, he threw it over the side. Half-way back to the *Broadsword* we passed the second wave coming in on our starboard side and gave them the thumbs up. Out of the nine landing craft in the first wave, all got back safely. But in the second wave only two made it back.[3]

Dr J.H. Patterson, RAMC, medical officer No.4 Commando:

I was in S4, the last boat on the starboard side. We stepped gingerly over the gap with our heavy loads and began to pack in. As always, the last man couldn't sit down. Soon 'Lower away' sent the LCAs down into the water, to bump and wrench on their davits as the swell took them; but quickly the shackles were cast off and we rode free – very free – in that sea. The LCA flotilla, like tiny corks afloat, were lifted into view and then sank between the waves of the huge swell. The various assault craft were forming up, the first wave already on its way towards the shore.

We were rolling heavily in a big south-west swell, which broke continually over us, drenching us to the skin. My hands grew numb and dead and my teeth were chattering with cold and fright. I had a look at my batman, sitting on the thwart. He was looking awful, but gave me a grin through his green. It was zero hour and the first infantry were going in. We passed round the rum and those who were not sea-sick took a good swig. The sea was dotted with 'bags, vomit'.

The chaps in the other boats were passing round the rum and I could hear snatches of song through the hellish din. Hutchie Burt's boat went in singing 'Jerusalem'. We didn't sing in our boat. My mouth was bone dry and I was shaking all over; I doubt if I could have produced a note.

The shore was obscured by smoke, but I made out the fountains of shellbursts and the rattle of small-arms fire cut through the roar of the heavy shells. Something was hit on our starboard bow and a huge cloud of black smoke went up, with orange flame licking against the murk of battle. Bullets rattled against the craft and splinters went whining overhead. We cowered down.

We touched, bumped and slewed round. Then the order, 'Ramps down'. The boat began to empty and, being at the stern, the medics were the last to leave. I seized a stretcher. No one seemed ready to take the other one, so I picked it up too, staggered to the bows and flopped into the water. It was thigh deep, as the craft had grounded on some softish object, probably a body.

The next stretch of time is muddled in my memory. I have no idea how long it took from the boat until I reached the enemy wire. There was thick smoke over the beach and the tide was low but flooding. There were many bodies in the water; one was hanging round one of the tripod obstacles. The shoals were churned with bursting shells. I saw wounded men among the dead, pinned down by the weight of their equipment.

The first I came to was little Sapper Mullen. He was submerged to his chin and quite helpless. Somehow I got my scissors out and with my numb hands, which felt quite weak and useless, I began to cut away his rucksack and equipment. Private Hindmarch appeared beside me and got working on the other side. He was a bit rattled, but steadied when I spoke to him and told him what to do. As I was bending over I felt a smack across my bottom, as if someone had hit me with a big stick. It was a shell splinter, but it hit nothing important and I swore and went on. We dragged Mullen to the water's edge at last.

The commandos were up at the wire and clearly having trouble getting through. Hindmarch and I went back to the wounded in the water. I noticed how fast the tide was rising and wounded men began to shout and scream as they saw they must soon drown. We worked desperately; I don't know how many we pulled clear, though it wasn't more than two or three.

Then I saw Donald Glass at the water's edge, badly hit in the back, and we went to him and started to cut away his equipment. Doing so I became conscious of a machine gun enfilading us from the left front. In a minute I was knocked over by a smack in the right knee and fell on Donald, who protested violently. I cautiously tried my leg and found that it still worked, though not very well. Donald was too bad to walk, so I got Hindmarch to open a stretcher. I looked for help but the only standing figure anywhere was my batman, who was working on his own with the drowning wounded in the water. He smiled and I left him to get on with it. I tried my leg again and took one end of the stretcher.

Hindmarch is a big strong fellow and between us we began to carry Donald up towards the wire. I had to have one rest and at the finish I was beat to the wide and just lay there and gasped for some minutes. We took the stretcher from Donald and left him in a bit of a hollow in the sand, where he had a certain amount of cover. The troops had got through the wire, and I stumbled after them across a minefield to the demolished buildings, which the air photographs had shown so clearly and which were our assembly area. I am a little vague about the minefield, but I remember thinking that it might be wise to walk in footprints.

I found the unit assembling among the buildings. Someone gave me a swig of rum, which did me good, and Lance Corporal Cunningham put a dressing on my leg. It turned out to be a lucky wound, through the muscles and tendons behind the knee-joint, which had missed the popliteal artery very narrowly. The shrapnel in my buttock made me stiff but was not worth worrying about.[4]

Captain Robert Neave, aged 26, second in command, B Squadron, 13th/18th Royal Hussars:

We were originally going to launch our DD [swimming] tanks at 5,000 yards, but the launching officer told me he had been given instructions to go in to 4,000 yards because of the weather. The decision did not directly concern me – my concern was to lead the column ashore, something of a hazardous task in view of the weather, and as far as we were concerned the shorter the better. There was no question at all that we shouldn't go, none at all. I remember saying, well, we're off boys, good luck to you. Get into your tanks and follow.

We were given the signal to launch and I was the first off our LCT. Once in the water, to our surprise, all went well despite the rough sea. The morning was dark and black, rough, but not cold. Standing up on the turret I could see the light coming up over the Le Havre peninsula, the lights of the French coast and I noticed the bows of a sunken ship away to the left. I don't know why I saw this, but I did. You saw the other LCTs ranged behind you and it was a very remarkable indication of enormous support that you were going to get. I hung about rather close to the LCT while the others were getting off. I remember waiting for them to get in line behind and away we went. There was no activity at all, except occasional shells bursting on the shore line.

The coast in front of us looked dark and forbidding – a few straggling houses behind dunes. Our destination was the extreme left-hand end of Sword beach and our guide point was the Ouistreham lighthouse at the mouth of the Orne. There was meant to be a midget submarine also acting as a guide post and while I am sure it was there I don't remember seeing it.

It took about half an hour, three-quarters of an hour, something of that sort, to get into the beach. The trip was relatively uneventful except for shots falling short from behind or misdirected shots from in front that splashed into the sea around us from time to time. At that stage most of us were more frightened of being swamped by the sea than we were of the Germans. When the tank was under way you could see nothing except right in front of you, nothing behind you. The bow was much higher out of the water than the two sides, which were only about a foot above the water. The extraordinary thing was I remember feeling entirely secure, although the weather was rough, because for some reason or another, the response of the tank to the rough weather was such that we shipped extremely little water, or at least, *we* did. The weather was coming up the Channel and was therefore behind us. That was one of the reasons, I am sure.

When we touched down at about H minus six or seven the tide was absolutely rock bottom low and I discovered we had landed among a variety of flimsy poles on top of which were balanced a series of large 7.5 shells, each with an instantaneous fuse sticking out like a pimple. When we hit the shallow water, I had collapsed the screens because I wanted to see what I was about and I wanted to have my tank in a fighting position. You could press a button and the air came out of the thing and released the steel knee joints and the whole thing then collapsed under its own weight. You left it behind you, like an old lady stepping out of her skirts.

I remember directing the driver, telling him for goodness' sake to keep in the middle of these posts otherwise you'll knock one of these things over. If we had, then it would have meant a hole in the tank or blown up a track. There were whole rows of these things but only two in front of me and I went in between them, delighted to discover that there was about two inches to spare on each side of the tank once the canvas screen had been deflated. There were a few tracer bullets going across but one of the feelings I had, as I landed (and you had a great many feelings as you landed) was of how empty it was – no attacking army, no figures to receive me, how remarkable that the place was so empty.

Having pulled out of the water we fired at all before us, partly to revive our confidence, partly to scare the other side. I remember seeing a pillbox in front of me, a big concrete pillbox. I can remember seeing unpainted houses on the dunes, an absolutely empty shoreline and beach. The pillbox wasn't firing at me because I think somebody had dealt with it, but I thought I'd give it a bang and fired at it and quite suddenly I saw four or five little chaps in enormous helmets coming off the beach, running towards me with their hands up. I paid no attention to them at all, I don't remember seeing what happened to them, because they didn't get near enough.

The beach was half a mile wide, or seemed so to me, and I made my way, followed by my four tanks, straight up the beach, trying to discover somewhere to get off. We had one or two stonks coming from the other side, which made me feel we ought to hurry up and get on with it. Having ascended a line of dunes, which weren't very big, I remember thinking to myself, now, where do we find the most likely route through to the first lateral? I got out of the tank to tell the other people behind me what I was doing and as I was getting back into my tank I remember feeling the wind of a bullet going under my nose and then going between my two fingers. It just broke the skin; it really was remarkable, feeling the wind and the sting of the bullet.[5]

Captain Albert Cooke, aged 28, 101st Amphibious Company, RASC:

I was to be in the recce party and my job was to mark the beach exits so that the DUKWs coming ashore later would land at the right place. This meant I would be among the first to land. I had some aerial photographs, known as 'obliques', and they were extremely good, because as we were approaching the shore, I could recognize various features right in front of me, so I knew where we were. There was a great deal of activity going on around, ships and so on, and a lot of noise, but it was difficult to know where it was coming from.

The LCT went right into the shore and I was able to recognize that we were coming into the right place. The lieutenant RN who was in charge of the craft told me that our party had to take a barrage balloon ashore. I was the only one who could really take it. I'd never been near a barrage balloon before, but he showed me how the quick-release mechanism worked and so I strapped on this kind of harness and got over the side onto a ledge, probably about a foot wide. This was when the craft had actually landed in very very shallow water. He'd got right up, this chap, and down went the ramp. As the tanks were leaving I started wrestling with the quick-release mechanism of the barrage balloon, but it worked much more quickly than I expected and suddenly took me up in the air on a nice breeze, which gently floated me onto the sand. I landed without getting my feet wet.

You were supposed to attach the barrage balloon to whatever you could find. I saw a wrecked truck and thought that would do, but as soon as it was attached it was shot down and it went way off along the beach, its cables flapping onto tanks and other vehicles.

The four of us in the recce party were supposed to crawl along the beach so we didn't make too conspicuous a target and we were doing this when we came to a main beach exit where there was a military policeman standing directing the traffic, which was as busy as Piccadilly Circus. When I saw him, I stood up and started walking with the others following behind. There were bullets shooting into the sand quite near, so there were obviously snipers about and as I was going past this MP, he said, 'Get down, sir, it's dangerous.' So I got down again and he continued to stand there, directing the traffic.[6]

Major Patrick Porteous VC, aged 26, No.4 Commando:

There was a hell of a chop in the sea and as my landing craft was lowered she hit a very big wave and we took in a lot of water. There was a hand pump to pump out the bilges, but it wasn't working very well so we all started bailing like mad. We managed to keep the water down, but every time a wave came along we took a bit more water and we were constantly bailing all the way in. It was very cold, very miserable, and I was frightened that the thing was going to go down when we were still miles off the beach.

Anyway, we got within sight of the beach and there was a hell of a lot of smoke and muck and stuff flying about and when we were still, I suppose, about sixty yards out, our poor landing craft finally gave up the ghost and sank in about three feet of water. We waded ashore, about waist deep. It wasn't too bad, but there was a lot of stuff flying about from some big German pillboxes just to our left. I saw the troop commander in the landing craft next to mine shot dead on the spot – he just dashed out and keeled over.

At the edge of the water we found a hell of a lot of chaps from the previous unit to have landed, I think it was the East Yorks. They were all dead or wounded, just swilling about in the water.

We started crossing the beach. A flail tank just to my right, with its flail going looking for mines, got a direct hit by an anti-tank shell and blew up. I ordered all my chaps to throw their smoke grenades which created a big belt of smoke down our left-hand side and protected us from the pillbox. A little while later a subaltern from my unit managed to creep up to it and put a grenade into the firing slit; he won an MC.

Anyway, we got across the beach and into some sand dunes, where we organized a bit, although a lot of my chaps had been wounded. At that point I think I had lost about a quarter of my troop, either killed or wounded. Our job was to make our way to a coastal battery on the outskirts of Ouistreham, about a mile-and-a-half away, and destroy the guns with special charges made of plastic explosive. We moved straight away and found a château with a sort of walled garden, where we cleaned our weapons and dumped our rucksacks, and then set off towards the battery.

We had to cross a big anti-tank ditch and when we got there we found someone had left a plank across it, which was just as well because one of the blokes who was carrying a specially made collapsible bridge had been killed on the beach and the bridge had been smashed to pieces.

On the way we passed a small house and a frantic Frenchman came running out and said that his wife had been wounded and asked if we had a doctor. At that very moment I heard a mortar bomb approaching and threw myself flat on the ground. The Frenchman was a little slow on the uptake, presumably he had never been mortared before, because there was an explosion and as I looked up I saw his head rolling down the road. It was very sad, kind of off-putting.

When we got to the battery, we found that the guns were dummies, just telegraph poles lashed onto wagons, and we learned afterwards from a Frenchman that the battery had been withdrawn some three or four days previously and had been re-sited a couple of miles back. In the centre of the position was a huge concrete observation tower, an enormous thing with walls about ten feet and some Germans who were at the top of it started firing at us. My signaller, who was just beside me, was shot and killed, and one of my subalterns, who had got up close to the tower, was killed when they dropped a grenade on him. He was a great friend of mine; I'd been best man at his wedding only two months before. He was trying to see if we could smoke them out, but the only access was up a single staircase in the middle and so the men inside were as safe as houses.

They obviously also had communication with the new gun position because we started getting shelled. I realized there was no point in staying there, but several more of my chaps were killed by shell fire as we were withdrawing.[7]

Archibald Doon Campbell, Reuters war correspondent:

We hit the beach, the ramps went down and the commandos, many of them with collapsible bicycles and their faces smeared black, went down the ramp. When it was my turn I fell off, up to my chest in the

Channel, and with the pack on my back I would never have made it, but for a lunge forward accelerated by a push from a huge commando behind me. I staggered up the beach, dripping wet, crossed a mined road into a field and stumbled into a ditch some 200 yards from the beach. The commandos were racing on ahead through a lot of mortar fire and small-arms fire.

In the ditch the wounded were being treated and one literally clawed at the earth to try and get deeper because of the withering fire coming from woods some two or three hundred yards ahead of us and into which the commandos had disappeared. I got the pack off my back and undid it, took out my portable typewriter and put some paper in. I had landed at six minutes past nine on the morning of D-Day and I have been told since that it was the most incongruous spectacle in that sector of the beach, Campbell of Reuters trying to beat out a message on his portable typewriter with all hell breaking loose around him.

Anyway, it was no good. A mortar hit the lip of the ditch in which we were lying and threw earth all over the typewriter, clogging the keys. So I put it away and on a notebook with a dateline 'In a ditch, 200 yards away from the beach' described in 200 or 300 words just what was happening: that we had landed, that we were 200 yards inland, we had seen the first prisoners being taken and more tanks, guns and men were landing. Having written it, I put it in an envelope addressed to Reuters, London, and then, in one of the occasional pauses in heavy fire, sort of wriggled and crawled and stumbled back to the beach, where one could see little boats coming in, dropping supplies and men then beating back to the UK. I gave the envelope to one of these men, with £5 and said, 'Try and get it to Reuters.' That was the first dispatch from Sword beach.[8]

Commander L.R. Curtiss R N VR, captain LCI No.519:

Our job was to touch down on the middle of Queen Red beach – a strip of sand some 800 yards wide – in a five-mile stretch of smoke-covered coastline between Ouistreham and Lion-sur-Mer.

In the last three miles we saw landing craft closing the beaches with their loads of armoured vehicles and troops and others coming away. We could see nothing of the beaches, which were obscured by smoke and haze until we were quite close in. When, at last, we were able to discern the silhouettes of the houses, our lookout picked up the château-like building at the eastern end of Queen Red. By the Grace of God, it seemed to me, we were spot on.

I recall how, in those moments of touch down, the smallest detail seemed to assume microscopic clarity. My mind concentrated on finding a path through the underwater obstructions. Fortunately, at that state of the tide, the tops of many of them were still visible, sprouting above the surface of the sea. I felt I could discern a clear path through the menacing stakes and we emerged unscathed. I called for more power from the engine room and thrust our bows hard onto the beach to ensure as dry a landing as possible.

At that moment we were hit by armour-piercing shells, which zipped through the port Oerlikon gunshield, but fortunately missed both gunners. I gave the order for the troops to land, the ramps were manhandled over the bows and the commandos began to land in about three feet of water as calmly as though on exercise. We bade goodbye to Lord Lovat and wished him good luck and I carry in my mind a mental picture of him wading ashore with his men. As the commandos crossed the fire-swept sands, the skirl of Bill Millin's pipes gave heart and encouragement to all.[9]

Trooper M.G. Gale, 44th Battalion, Royal Tank Regiment:

Being the last tank to be loaded, ours was of course the first to disembark. On our way over we were given a pep talk by our CO and a tot of rum and we were reminded that we would land in six foot of water. Ease her off lads, we were told, you have all done this many times before, and of course we had, twice in action and many times in practice.

We knew when we were told to man our tanks and start the engines that the time was close. The ship slowed to a halt, the bows opened and the ramp went down and there, in the morning light, was the beach. Fighting was going on, we could hear gunfire, other tanks were landing to our right and we could see them moving up the beach.

Sitting in the driver's seat, I began to move our Sherman very slowly down the ramp. I began to ease her off the end, waiting for the drop into what we expected to be six feet of water. We were all battened down and well waterproofed, which was just as well as it turned out, because instead of six feet, we fell into twelve feet of water. Unknown to the ship's captain, we had stopped right in front of a shell hole and our tank had fallen into it.

Before I could decide what to do, voices came over the radio telling us not to try and move. The water was almost at the top of our air intake and if we had tried to pull out of the hole the tank would have gone down and we might all have drowned.

Instead I was told to cut the engine and wait for instructions as the ship pulled out to come in again and unload. We sat there under the water for almost two hours, waiting for the tide to go out. We were able to follow what was going on on the radio, but we could see nothing except water through our periscope. When at last the water went down and we could see, we were able to rejoin our regiment. By then they were well off the beaches and they had, I am sorry to say, sustained a number of casualties. Two tanks in my own troop had been hit. We had not enjoyed our enforced stay underwater, but it perhaps saved our lives.[10]

Lance Corporal Pat Hennessy, aged 19, 13th/18th Royal Hussars:

The first tank off was Sergeant Charlie Rattle's of 4th Troop. We followed and as we righted in the water we could see other DD tanks launching on both sides of us. There was much noise and smoke and it was quite a struggle to keep the tank on course.

Apart from our driver, Trooper Harry Bone, we were all on deck and I remember vividly witnessing the tragedy which befell Captain Noel Denny's tank, which was overtaken and run down by its own LCT.

It took us well over an hour to get close to the beach. The sea was rough and the noise increasing. As we felt the tracks grind on the shelving bottom, we dropped our float screen and opened fire on the line of houses which were our targets.

We had a quick discussion as to whether we should move up on the beach and chance the mines which had not yet been cleared, but suddenly the problem was solved for us. We had landed on an incoming tide and the water was getting deeper. Then one large wave swamped the engine compartment and that was that! We couldn't move, even if we wanted to.

For a while we continued firing, but the tank was flooding, so, grabbing the .303 Brownings and as much ammunition as we could, we launched the rubber dinghy and began paddling for shore. But within a minute machine-gun fire hit our little boat, and co-driver Joe Gallagher, in the ankle.

We were tumbled into the water, losing the guns and ammunition, but somehow we managed to get Gallagher and ourselves to the beach. I remember hanging on to a post sticking out of the water for a breather and glancing up I saw a large black mine attached to it.

We finally dragged ourselves ashore, soaking wet and shivering. Then from somewhere there appeared a tin of self-heating soup. As we lay there gasping, and gulping down the soup, an irate captain in the REs came up to me and said, 'Get up, Corporal! That's no way to win the Second Front.'[11]

Lieutenant Alexander Badenock, Armoured Support Group, Royal Marines:

We came off the craft all right, just as the infantry were landing, and slid into the water. The Germans had put rows of long iron posts in a triangular shape all along the beach and we could see the mines on top of them. It was tricky getting my tank through but we didn't touch them. We stayed just out of the water and fired everything we could up the beach. The infantry had quite a long way to go up the beach and the Germans were fighting back hard and doing a lot of damage.

I saw two craft on my left go up in flames and on my right there were several craft bumping up and down on the beach with holes in their waterline. The dust and smoke made the whole thing seem unreal. I could only see as far as the top of the beach but there was a large house there, which we discovered later was used by the Germans as an HQ, which we fired on.

The tide was running in fast and before we knew where we were it was round the top of our tracks, so we went on up the beach to the sand dunes at the top. My tank was the first to lead up the beach and knowing the German love for mines these moments were very nerve-racking. We didn't hit one, though, just one of the bits of luck one has.

Out of the German dug-outs in the sand dunes a white handkerchief appeared, waving frantically. It was followed by a German who tried to give himself up to our tank. Whether he wanted a ride in it I don't know, but I couldn't do anything about him, so pointed to some infantry nearby and he went off to give himself up, breathing great sighs of relief.

Another German, an officer this time, got up out of his dug-out right in front of the gun barrel. I saw a lot of infantry going past now, a very good sign, although at this stage I didn't know how things were going. Fire seemed to be coming from all around and Germans were holding out in the bottom floor of some houses near us and sniping us badly. They had to be shot out ruthlessly and didn't seem to give a thought for their own lives. There were a few of them who were still firing from the same lot of houses the whole day.

We captured a German sergeant major whom we led all round the position we were in and through their dug-outs just to see whether there were any booby traps left anywhere. He told us, through the help of a French commando, that they hadn't had time to lay any, that they had all been taken completely by surprise and had never thought that we would try to invade in that sort of weather. A Frenchman I spoke to had exactly the same idea. He said that when May passed the French were settling down to another year of occupation, saying we wouldn't be coming this year at all. A party of them came down to help with the wounded. One of them had all his papers signed ready to be dispatched to Germany on the very evening of D-Day. He was simply bubbling with joy.[12]

Sapper A.J. Lane, aged 23, Field Squadron, Royal Engineers:

I remember my first moments of dragging myself out of the sea holding on to my Bren gun, magazine boxes and other kit. I looked around to see instant death and destruction all around me. But I was conscious that, even so, the beach was perhaps no worse than staying on the boat where I felt I would have died of sea sickness anyway.

I sought cover behind an AVRE which had just been hit but I moved quickly away when I realized that it was blazing away and could blow up at any second. I succeeded in making the bank of dunes at the high-tide mark and hoped that somehow I could get my Bren gun into a position to fire over and beyond the dunes in the enemy direction, wherever that might be.

I remember as well as anything else what happened just then – damned silly, considering the circumstances – and that was my annoyance and irritation at the sea lice, or beach bugs, or whatever they were, that were crawling all over me.

Getting into an attacking position was not easy because of the mortars, shells and bullets that were hammering down onto a relatively small and concentrated area. On at least two occasions I was an eyewitness to shells or mortars making direct hits on soldiers moving close to me and seeing them literally disappear in a flash.

Until that time I had never seen a live or dead German soldier in my life. Here suddenly there were two of them almost jumping over me as I crouched low behind the sand bank. One of the Germans appeared to throw a hand grenade as he came over the top, although it was difficult to know one explosion from all the others happening at the same time. Another British soldier must also have thought a grenade was thrown because he managed to kick the German in the behind to send him sprawling and then, by blasting away with his sten gun, I figured that whether a grenade was thrown or not was hardly a matter for a board of inquiry in the circumstances.

I moved to a position to be able to view the ground over and beyond the sand bank. The area all around seemed to be covered by a barrage of shell fire, raging and rolling over the ground as if threatening to overwhelm us all.

In the circumstances I decided to do something about helping some of the badly wounded soldiers – many of my own comrades among them – who were lying around in exposed positions on the beach. The best I could do was to drag a few of them to a low position in the sand dunes, where things were almost just as bad. I caught up with someone who had a stretcher and the two of us worked as we had never worked before. Truly in every way – emotionally, mentally, physically – the most awful job in the world. It was, I suppose, made worse for me because there were no medics around, obviously no hospital and no sanctuary other than a dip in the ground where we dumped those we carried. It is also true to say that quite a few of those who were placed there were hit a second time; some were killed. I saw many mutilated bodies and grey-green-yellow faces on that morning, some became silent and still for ever. I was a stretcher bearer until I was physically exhausted, depressed and sick, when I could do no more. I handed over the stretcher to someone else, firmly resolved in my own mind that a stretcher bearer's job would never, never again be one for me. Before moving away from the beach my final effort was directed towards trying to plug, unsuccessfully, a fist-sized hole in the back of a poor fellow who had himself been hit when tending to another wounded man.[13]

Sergeant Major H.E. Harrison, Royal Engineers:

We were all well provided for in the way of creature comforts, having been thoughtfully issued with a tin each of self-heating cocoa and soup. None of my companions appeared enamoured at the idea of hot soup just then, but I thought we would need them when we got ashore so I collected up as many of the tins as I could find and stuffed them in the pockets of my combat jacket.

I began to wonder when the ramp went down and we were in deep water if I would sink, dragged down by the tins of cocoa and soup, and come to a particularly inglorious end. But my fears were unfounded – the water was not so deep as it looked and I made it.

Then there were other things to think about. The soup may not have been hot but our reception was. The sight of so many of my comrades falling around me was one I shall never forget.

Then came my own turn – I felt a severe blow in the abdomen. I did not feel any pain but this figured: we had been told there was often no pain when actually struck and at any rate I was still upright. But it was serious, that I knew, because I was covered in blood.

In shock or fright, I don't know which, I managed to stagger to a casualty station without, miraculously, being hit again. There I discovered, to my embarrassment, that I was not covered in blood, but in tomato soup.[14]

CHAPTER FOURTEEN

JUNO

Juno beach was assigned primarily to the 3rd Canadian Division. Delayed by half an hour because of the weather, the Canadians swarmed ashore and quickly fought their way inland undeterred by stiff opposition . . .

BBC correspondent Colin Wills:

Hello BBC! This is Colin Wills recording on board an infantry landing craft on June 6th 1944. The day has broken now, the day has become clear and the sky is blue but there is still a good deal of cloud about but the sun is streaming through. The whole sea is a glittering expanse of green with white crests everywhere, and everywhere, too, there are ships, every kind of ship one imagines that would be needed in an invasion. There are all our landing craft for tanks, for infantry for every type of supplies. There are great troopships in great number, there are battleships, smaller warships, destroyers, patrol craft, escort ships and in the sky overhead there are aircraft of about half a dozen different kinds that I can see at this moment.

One could not imagine a more stupendous scene: all of these ships all taking their various part in the invasion. The whole sea itself seems restless and excited with the tension of the moment . . . and in this dramatic, natural setting we are moving towards the shore, the battleships and other bombardment ships over on the flank are pouring in their fire and now other warships, moving up front in our path, are laying a smoke screen and now there is a signal from the flagship: 'All hands to beaching stations.' That's a signal for our sailors on board this craft to get ready for the landing and, of course, for the soldiers down in the hold to get ready with all their kit on the deck. We have started our run-in to shore – we are still some distance out but I may be able to report a little bit more of the landing.

This is the day and this is the hour! The sky is lightening, lightening over the coast of Europe, as we go in. The sky is lighter and the sea is brighter but along the shore there is a dense smoke screen as the battleships and the smaller warships sweep along there, firing all the time against the shore. The sun is blazing down brightly now, it is almost like an omen the way it has suddenly come out just as we were going in. The sky is bright, the sea is a glittering mass of silver with all these craft of every kind moving across it and the great battleships in the background, blazing away at the shore.

There go the other landing craft past us. Some are left behind, the slower ones, each taking their part and going in at the right time for their right job. I can hear the sound of anti-aircraft fire. I can't see yet whether it is our people who are being attacked. There is an enormous cloud of smoke along the shore, not only from the smoke screen but from the terrific bombardment. All the ships are blazing away now. All around this great grey-green circle of water there are ships, ships moving in, ships on patrol, ships circling, ships standing to and firing. We are passing close by a cruiser, a cruiser that has been taking part in the bombardment but is now, I imagine, on some sort of general patrol.

You cannot imagine anything like this march of ships, like soldiers marching in line. I have never seen anything so expressive of intent. It is a purpose shared among ships and among many hundreds of thousands of men, who are going in now to the coast of Europe to do the biggest job they have ever had to do. I can't record any more now because the time has come for me to get my kit on my back and step off on that shore and it's a great day . . .[1]

Captain Dan Flunder, adjutant, 48 Commando:

As adjutant, I was OC Troops and spent the night with them in a cramped little mess-deck; almost everyone was sick. I had the men up on the superstructure early because I thought the fresh air would restore them and because men are always happier when they can see what is going on.

Soon we were running into the beach and I walked up and down the bows keeping an eye on the Navy people responsible for lowering the ramps. The sea was covered with craft as far as the eye could see. The shore was under bombardment, craft were sinking, and from where I stood it certainly didn't look as if the Canadians had secured the beach – things didn't look good at all.

I didn't realize we were under fire until I saw two men collapse and fall over the starboard side. By then it was too late to beat a retreat and I later found three bullet holes in my map case – they must have passed between my arm and my body during that period. The tide was high and we had craft hitting the beach obstacles. The CO had our two-inch mortars firing smoke from the bows, so at least we were not getting aimed fire. When we grounded we got the starboard ramp down, which wasn't easy with the waves thrashing the stern about. I was half-way down when a big wave lifted the bow and somersaulted the ramp and myself into the sea. I saw the great bows coming over me and the next thing I remember is walking up the beach, soaking wet, with some of my equipment torn off, including my pistol, but still clutching my stout ash walking stick. When I got to the top of the beach, I was violently sick.

The beach was covered with casualties, some Canadian, some ours. The surf was incredible, with beached and half-sunken craft wallowing about in it. Offshore, other craft came steadily on. Some tanks struggled ashore and some bogged in the shingle. Those that were advancing had their turret lids shut and were heading for a large group of wounded. I was sickened to see one run over two of our wounded and it was heading for our good padre, John Armstrong, who had been badly wounded in the thigh. I had spoken to him on the way up the beach; typically, he had been vehement that I should not stop by him, exposed to enemy fire. I ran back down the beach and hammered on the turret, to get someone to put his head out. When this failed I stuck a Hawkins anti-tank grenade in the sprocket and blew the track off – that stopped it.[2]

Sergeant Harold Fielder, aged 27, 26 Field Company, Assault Engineers:

I was a tank commander on a Churchill fitted with fascines. We were called 'the Funnies', that was our name. Our job was to fill in anti-tank ditches, or whatever, to make the gap for the main assault to come through.

It was about six o'clock in the morning when we first saw the coast. You could see fire going every way. Our people were still shelling and there was still bombing going on. As we were going in we were fired at from a pillbox, but then one of the gun tanks on another craft fired at it and hit the aperture and they weren't able to fire again, so we were lucky there.

It was about seven o'clock when we landed. We were slightly late. The Canadian infantry had gone in before us and were laying all over the beach and in the water. We thought at first they were Germans, but they weren't and we ran over some of them because we didn't realize who they were. It was only later we found out they were Canadians. We felt terrible, absolutely terrible, because we didn't even know if they were already dead or not.

We were supposed to go up over the dunes to where they thought, from aerial photographs, that there was a ditch. But as luck would have it, when we got up there there was no ditch. Then we started getting fired on by some Jerries in a dugout. We fired back at them with our Browning and they came out, about five of them, with their hands up. They were only youngsters. We sent them back to the beach, where there was a pen for prisoners. We shed our fascines and went on a little, but then I decided myself that we could do more by going back to the beach. So we went back and started clearing the beach of tetrahedrons, connecting them onto a couple of tow ropes and pulling them clear. In a matter of hours we'd cleared the beach completely. We were still under fire, but more and more troops were coming in, thick and fast.[3]

Sergeant Leo Gariepy, aged 31, B Squadron, 6 Armoured Regiment, Canadian Armoured Corps:

At dawn, approximately 04.30 hours, the fuzzy coast of France could be seen in the distance. The sea was raging, LCTs were being tossed all over the place. In the distance could be heard and seen the detonation of bombs on the coastal area and immediately on my left the shape of a large destroyer was visible.

After a short while the mine-sweeper leading us in slowed down and began making a semi-circle. Signals were exchanged: the mine-sweepers had completed their task and were wishing us God speed on our mission. The flotilla of LCTs began manoeuvring for launching our DD tanks. This meant it was necessary for them to head into the wind, showing a broadside to the enemy supposedly alert on the coast.

The men were grim, expecting at any moment retaliation from the coast. It seemed incredible that we had not been seen. Our LCT was having great difficulty trying to maintain its position for launching. Orders to start tank motors had been given, all gear stowed on board, wirelesses tuned to a pre-determined frequency. Silent prayers could be observed on every grim face, the well-oiled mechanism of the gun breeches could be heard being worked and some of the men were doing innocent little things, watched intensely by the others.

Finally the launching officer called us together and said that High Command had vetoed launching in such a rough sea. This had the effect of a firecracker among the troops. They were fighting mad, but no amount of cursing or pleading would make him change his mind.

The LCT began manoeuvring again to bring us right into the beaches. We were then approximately 9,000 yards out, and the spirit had gone out of everyone. We were discouraged and disheartened to realize that all our training had been in vain and we would now be dropped on the beaches like 'gravel crushers' (infantry) at the mercy of the navy.

Suddenly, at 7,000 yards, our squadron commander, Major Duncan, asked us if we would prefer to risk it. Cheers went up, we were all for it, and the CO, knowing very well what we were facing, agreed and we prepared to launch. The LCT once again took its launching position in the wind, the ramp was lowered and we each, in turn, rolled off. The manoeuvre was difficult owing to the wind and waves. DD tanks had been conceived for a Force 4 wind and we were operating in about a Force 7.

All our five tanks were successfully launched and we ploughed into the water, trying to adopt a pre-determined attack formation. (We couldn't fire our guns in the water, because they were hidden behind the huge canvas screen which kept us afloat.) Standing on the command deck at the back of my turret, trying to steer and navigate, that 7,000 yards to the beach was the longest journey of my life.

Enemy fire was discernible now. Machine-gun bullets were ripping the water all around me and an occasional mortar shell fell among us. I looked behind to see how the others were faring and noticed that many of the tanks had sunk and the crews were desperately trying to board bright-yellow salvage dinghies.

A midget submarine appeared just a few yards in front of me. His duty was to lead me to my primary target on the beach – a blockhouse sheltering a naval gun. High wind was forcing me to drift and the man in the submarine was trying to wave me back into line. It was impossible, the wind was too strong. The struts which kept the rubberized skirt around the tank were groaning and I had visions of them giving out at any moment.

I called on my crew to bring up fire extinguishers and tools to try and brace the struts. I could hear the pinging of enemy bullets ripping through the canvas and hitting the hull of my tank.

We were due to land at 07.30 and when we were a few hundred yards from the beach the destroyer started firing salvo after salvo with a deafening roar. As the water became shallower, the submarine stopped, its occupant stood up and wished me luck with his hands clasped over his head.

Of the nineteen tanks we should have launched I could now only see nine. I was a few yards off my target, but not too bad, and at exactly 07.45 I touched the sand and drove out of the water. On the beach I gave orders to deflate the canvas skirt and what happened next will always remain vivid in my memory. The German machine gunners in the dunes were absolutely stupefied to see a tank emerging from the sea. Some of them ran away, some just stood up in their nests and stared, unable to believe their eyes. We mowed them down like they were corn on the cobs. The element of surprise was a total success.

Making my way up the long expanse of sand, destroying obstacles as we moved on, I approached the blockhouse which was my target. It was camouflaged with a superstructure to make it look like a beach house, but seeing that the roof had been demolished I assumed it was out of commission and stopped as close to the walls as possible.

I ordered the crew to open cans of self-heating oxtail soup. We needed it very badly, because we were still suffering from the effects of sea-sickness. While we were drinking our soup I looked around to try and get a general picture of the situation. Several tanks were still wallowing in the water, although many had foundered. Heavy shelling from at sea was still going on, landing craft and infantry assault boats were coming in. It was like a scene out of Dante's Inferno.

While I was observing all this, our tank was suddenly lifted off the ground by a tremendous blast. I was sure we had copped one, but looking out I saw a huge gun recoiling into the blockhouse by which we were sheltering. It was far from out of action. I realized we were too close for him to get a bead on us and that we were safe for the moment. We withdrew a few yards obliquely from his line of sight and from that position, at almost point-blank range, I ordered several rounds of armour-piercing shells to be fired into the embrasure. Then I went round behind the blockhouse and pumped eight or ten high explosive rounds through the steel doors of the entrance.

We then started to head into the town of Courseulles. Fearing a mine pattern on the unused street leading away from the beach, I ploughed through the back gardens of the houses. My rendezvous was at the town graveyard, on the Rue Emile Heroult.

A frantic Frenchman appeared in front of my tank, gesticulating wildly. I stuck my head out of the turret and asked him what he wanted and he shouted 'Boche, Boche' in an excited voice and pointed up the street. When he tried to explain in extremely bad English, I cut him short in French and asked him what was the matter. He was flabbergasted that I could speak French but I finally cooled him long enough for him to tell me that there was a group of enemy hidden inside a large park behind an eight-foot-high wall. A naval shell had made a large hole in the wall and every time the infantry tried to advance past the hole the enemy sprayed them with machine-gun fire.

An officer in the Regina Rifles asked me if I would block the hole with my tank so his platoon could get by, but not being too fond of being a 'stopper', I suggested that I should go inside the park with my tank and try and dislodge the machine gunners.

I took a position directly in front of the wall, butted through it with my tank and fired a smoke shell into a large enclosure, following it up with machine-gun fire. Then we fired two HE shells into a sentry box in the far corner of the area. This had the desired effect and some thirty-two German prisoners gave themselves up. I believe this was the first large group of the enemy taken on the beach area. It was then about 08.30.[4]

Captain L.N. (Nobby) Clark, No.1 Movement Control Unit, 3rd Canadian Division:

At about 08.00 our craft formed line and we were going in. Most of the fellows were all ready, their Mae Wests giving them all an outlandish shape. I was very interested in the expressions on their faces. Some looked like 'wounded spaniels', some were quite nonchalant, others made a feeble show of gaiety. What amused me most was a fat boy trying to whistle, but the best he could do was blow air with a squeak now and then. Just between ourselves, I was pretty scared myself about that time.

Those last few moments were pretty awful. We were coming under intense small-arms fire and everyone was down as much as possible. I manoeuvred into a position to be as near as possible to the front. I wanted to be one of the first to land, not because of any heroics but because waiting your turn on the exposed ramp was much worse than going in.

A sergeant and a corporal started down. I was third. The sergeant couldn't touch bottom but pushed away and swam in towards shore. The corporal started to follow and I plunged in after him but the weight of my 'light assault jacket', filled with enough canned goods to start a grocery store, pulled me under in spite of my Mae West. While I was floundering in the water the corporal got into trouble: there was a terrific backwash and only quick action by a brave merchant navy lad saved him from drowning. I got back onto the ramp and the skipper of the LCI very sensibly decided to pull off and try to come in a bit better.

The next run at the shore put us in about five feet six inches of water. A naval fellow in a lifebelt went in with a rope and I followed. I must have been a ridiculous sight, holding onto my pistol in one hand and a bag of valuables (mostly cigs) in the other as well as trying to hold onto the rope. Some of the men had great difficulty getting ashore, particularly the short ones. One poor chap was crushed to death when the ramp broke away in the heavy seas and slammed him between it and the side of the ship. Many of the lads on our LCI never got ashore: a Spandau opened up just when the water was full of men struggling to get ashore.

The beach was littered with those who had been a jump ahead of us and a captured blockhouse being used as a dressing station was literally surrounded by piles of bodies.

I didn't lose much time getting to the back of the beach where there was a bit of protection and wriggled out of my assault jacket which I swore then and there never to wear again.[5]

Revd R.M. Hickey, chaplain, North Shore Regiment, won MC on D-Day:

Joel Murray from Cross Point and I landed together in the water but we could reach bottom and made shore. A young lad next to me fell, a bullet got him. I dragged him ashore, and there in that awful turmoil I knelt for a second that seemed an eternity and anointed him – the first of the long, long list I anointed in action.

There was a long fifty yards of wide, open beach between the water's edge and the cement wall; if you could make the wall you were safe, for a time at least, from the enemy fire; but, ah, so many of our fine young men didn't make it. There on the open beach they lay, dead or dying. It was our duty to get to them, so, with our stretcher bearers and first aid men, Doctor Patterson and I crawled back again across that fifty yards of hell.

The beach was sprayed from all angles by the enemy machine guns and now their mortars and heavy guns began hitting us. Crawling along the sand, I just reached a group of three badly wounded men when a shell landed among us killing the others outright. That is why the report got around that I had been killed in action. Someone saw the shell hit and figured I had got it too.

The noise was deafening; you couldn't even hear our huge tanks that had already landed and were crunching their way through the sand; some men, unable to hear them, were run over and crushed to death. A blast shook the air like an earthquake, it was the engineers blowing the wall. All the while enemy shells came screaming in faster and faster; as we crawled along, we could hear bullets and shrapnel cutting into the sand around us; when a shell came screaming over, you dug into the sand and held your breath, waited for the blast and the shower of stones and debris that followed; then when it cleared a little, right next to you, perhaps someone you had been talking to half an hour before, lay dead.

Others dying, might open their eyes as you reached them. By the little disc around their neck I knew their religion. If Catholic, I gave them Extreme Unction with one unction on the forehead, but whether Catholic or Protestant, I would tell the man he was dying and to be sorry for his sins, and often I was rewarded by the dying man opening his eyes and nodding to me knowingly.

It was a hard job to get the wounded on the stretchers and carry them to the shelter of the wall. I will never forget the courage of the stretcher bearers and first aid men that morning. If some men are living today, next to Almighty God they can thank men like Lieutenant Hisslip of Vancouver and his stretcher bearers, and I will always remember the bravery of these first aid men from our own regiment, Edward Hachey, Buddy Daley and Bob Adair. They stayed with us on the open beach until we carried all the wounded we could to safety behind the wall and gave them what help we could.

Major Ralph Daughney crept along the wall to where I was.

'Father,' he said, 'there's some of our men badly wounded up among the houses.' I followed him. A ramp had been placed against the wall by now. Over it we went to what could have been sudden death, for the houses facing us about fifty yards away were still held by German snipers. I often wonder why we both weren't picked off as we came over the wall. I like to think a German sniper spared me; I like to think that a German sniper had me in his telescopic sight but when he saw by my collar and red cross arm band that I was a chaplain, he stayed his finger – well, I like to think it.

Ralph and I never reached those men. Two stretcher bearers ahead of us stepped on a mine just as they reached them and a terrific explosion killed the stretcher bearers and all the wounded. The awful concussion drove Ralph and me back; half dazed, we jumped down again behind the wall.

Like a hospital patient, you lose all idea of time in action. Time meant nothing. We were told after that we had been on the beach for two hours.[6]

Captain Jack Fawcett, aged 27, 1st Battalion, Canadian Scottish Regiment:

It was rough going in. I had been in small boats off the coast of British Columbia many times and never been sea-sick; this was the first and only time in my life when I was sick. Before we were too close to the shore I got my bag, vomit, did my bit and threw it over the stern.

The sailors manning the landing craft did a magnificent job. As we went in, we had to change from single file to line abreast and as we did so a navigating patrol boat moved across our front to protect us from being bothered by the enemy. A signaller was standing on the side of the craft, making a semaphore message. I had learned signalling in the boy scouts and the message was, 'Good luck, Canada.' I read it out to the fellows in our landing craft and it bucked us all up.

The other thing that impressed me about the navy – I'm a bit of a romantic in some ways, I guess – was that as we made our final approach, the marine corporal at the stern rigged up a little mast and broke out the White Ensign. I looked out and saw all five landing craft in our line were also flying White Ensigns.

It was very strange. I felt the tension draining away and I had the feeling that this was going to be a successful affair, that no matter what happened it was going to go right. Looking at the men in our craft, the way they were, I think they felt the same. We were so intent on getting to the beach that if the engines had stopped or broken down, sheer willpower alone would have driven the craft ashore.

We came under fire as we went in – this was H + 5 – with rifle bullets ricocheting off the bow doors. There was a little apprehension as we went out the door. The sergeant carrying the wireless set was due to be the first one in our group to go out and he wasn't too happy about it. The drill was that if he got hit I could pick up the set and operate it. He said, 'Why do I have to go first?' I said, 'Well, somebody has to be first – it's the wireless set that is the important thing here.'[7]

Captain Vassar Hall, aged 35, Regina Rifles:

We hit the beach about 7.30 a.m. or thereabouts, by which time there were quite a number of wounded Regina Rifles on the beach. There was little we could do for them. I remember seeing one poor chap who had always been first up at the entertainments we had in England. If there was a dance or something, he would always be on the floor, swinging around and having a great old time and I can remember my last image was of him sitting there, holding his stomach, bent over. I said to him, 'What's the trouble?' and he said he had a bullet in his stomach and was just waiting for the medics to get him out.

Machine-gun fire continued for a little while after that and there was a large number of casualties. One of the boxers of the regiment, I found him afterwards dead at the edge of the water, he'd been killed in the water, and our signals officer, he was lying right beside him. We were lucky. Charlie, Able and Baker companies got through the obstacles on the beach all right and landed with all their company intact, but Dog company, five or ten minutes behind us, lost two of their craft coming in.

I was beach quartermaster for the Regina Rifles, so I just hung around the beach. There was lots to see, people to help. We started to collect casualties. German prisoners of war started to come on the beach in fair numbers. They were very docile at that time because they were under guard and didn't have their weapons. Later in the day, when the tide went out, we saw a lot of the casualties that had been drowned and were still out in the water, so I got a party of

German prisoners to go and start to pick up bodies, including the body of the company commander who had followed me in but didn't make it.

We brought them in and part of my job was also gathering the effects of those killed in action, turning money over to the paymaster and anything else belonging to them over to the padre. I still have my little notebook that I kept for checking off the casualties on the beach and I even made notations in my notebook on how they were killed – shell wound, drowning and so on.[8]

Private Roland Johnston, aged 24, gunner/driver 3rd Anti-tank Regiment:

I was driving an M10 tank destroyer with waterproofed periscope sights and we could see gunfire as we approached the shore and, as we came in up closer, you could see bodies all over the beaches. When we got to the beach we drove straight off and we had to run right over a lot of casualties to get up the beach. It was a big worry but you had to put it out of your mind, just forget about it. There was only one way up and you gotta realize that your tracks cut down so much in the sand that I wondered at one point if we were going to make it.

Our orders were to go straight up the beach, to go as far as you could. The machine-gun fire was wild, it was unreal. A lot of the infantry was still in the water, they were pinned down and they couldn't get in. Every tank that went in, the infantry took cover behind.

I forget at what point we blew off our waterproofing, but we came into a corner, maybe 100 yards, and we met the British commandos. We were about the first troops that they had run into and one of their officers said, in his British accent, 'You have to turn left heah!' I looked and saw there were bodies lying on the road and I said, 'Oh my God, not for a minute.' I said, 'We're gonna have to move some of those bodies because I am not going to run over any more of my own bodies today.' The bodies were still warm, I know because we moved them. There were lots, I guess they got caught by a machine-gun nest or something.

We went round the corner – you have to realize I was only looking through a periscope sight and you can only see so far down – and came across a slit trench behind a pillbox. We dropped the muzzle of our 50-calibre into the trench, gave it a couple of blasts and a couple of grenades and we heard 'Komrad' and they was coming out. I don't know how many we killed but we took twenty-one men and an officer out of there as prisoners.

The prisoners were shaken up pretty good. The order of the day was 'no quarter', that meant no prisoners to my way of thinking. So one of my buddies wanted to shoot them, which was the proper thing to do under those orders, but our officer, as I still say, was a good guy and he said, 'No.' So we took 'em back and by this time the engineers were trying to build this compound and we brought these prisoners in there. Now these prisoners we took you've got to realize these were the first prisoners we took. One of our guys, Joe Bryson, the gunner on our vehicle, had a Bren gun and every time these guys would slow down he'd let off the Bren over their heads and got their jackboot heels going like you wouldn't believe.[9]

BBC correspondent Howard Marshall:

I have just come back from the beaches and as I have been in the sea twice I'm sitting in my soaked-through clothes with no notes at all; all my notes are sodden and they are at the bottom of the sea, so as it is literally a matter of minutes since I stepped off a craft, I'm just going to try to tell you, very briefly, the story of what our boys had to do on the beaches today as I saw it myself.

I won't go into the build-up, which has taken place, as you know, over a very long time, but I will start with first light this morning, when the great invasion fleet had arrived off the coast of northern France and we were having breakfast. We were having breakfast just before first light, at four o'clock, as a matter of fact, in the particular landing craft for barges, in which I was, with certain regiments. We had breakfast early and we were at first light assembling into our landing craft.

Still, the landing crafts were lowered and as the light broke and we really could see around us, we began to become aware of the formidable character of this invasion fleet of which we were a part. All over the blue-green water, water which was extremely choppy and wind-flecked, we saw various types of craft which go to make up an invasion fleet and before very long we were among them. I was in a barge which was due to pick up the brigadier of an assault group and we were going in with the first assault wave. So we circled round with the various types of vessels, opening fire on the beach, which we could see quite plainly in the dim morning light, at the appointed time. First of all, the cruisers started with a rather loud bang and soon the air grew heavy with the smell of cordite and loud with the sound of explosions and, looking along the beach, we could see the explosions of our artillery creating a great cloud and fog of smoke.

Well, my particular craft picked up our brigadier, not easily because, as I say, the sea was very rough, and we headed straight for our appointed portion of the beach. We could see as we went in that that particular portion of the beach wasn't altogether healthy and as we drove towards it with our planes overhead, giving us the sort of cover we had been hoping for and which we had been expecting, as we drove in, we could see shell bursts in the water along the beach and just behind the beach and we could see craft in a certain amount of difficulty because the wind was driving the sea in with long rollers and the enemy had prepared anti-invasion, anti-barge, obstacles sticking out from the water, formidable prongs, many of them tipped with mines, so that as your landing barge swung and swayed in the rollers, and they are not particularly manageable craft, it would come into contact with one of these mines and be sunk.

Well, that was the prospect that faced us on this very lowering and difficult morning as we drove into the beach. I tell you this, as I say, because it was the experience of so many other men at just this same time. We drove into the beach, swinging rather broadside on in the wind and waves, seeing the jets of smoke from bursting shells near us in the water, and slightly further away on the beach itself, and suddenly as we tried to get between two of these tri-part defence systems of the Germans, our craft swung, we touched a mine, there was a very loud explosion, a shudder in the whole craft and water began pouring in. Well, we were some way out from the beach at that point. The ramp was lowered at once and out of the barge drove the Bren-gun carrier into about five feet of water, with the barge settling heavily in the meanwhile.

Well, the Bren-gun carrier somehow managed to get through it and we followed, wading ashore. That was one quite typical instance of how people got ashore. When they got ashore they seemed to be in perfectly good order because the troops out of that barge immediately assembled and went to their appointed places and there was no semblance of any kind of confusion. But the scene on the beach, until one had sorted it out, was at first rather depressing because a great many barges were in difficulties because of these anti-tank screens and we noticed that a number of them had struck mines, as ours had struck a mine. But then we began to see that in fact the proportion which got through was very much greater and that the troops were moving all along the road, that tanks were out already and going up the hills and that in fact we were dominating the situation and that our main enemy was the weather and that we were beating the weather, that we had our troops and our tanks ashore and that the Germans weren't really putting up a great deal of resistance.

Well, after spending some time on the beach, talking to troops, finding them in tremendous fettle, very, very delighted they were having this crack at the Germans, the next problem became to get away and to come back and do this news bulletin. Well, very quickly, I'll tell you what happened. It was again a question of wading out, picking up a barge which was leaving the beach, finding it had been holed by the enemy, the port engine had been shot up and the bows were sinking and therefore transferring to another craft, getting onto a headquarters ship and finally getting into an ML and getting back just in time to tell you that all is going well, and that there is reason – if one may judge – from the individual spirits from the men on the beaches, not from the military picture alone, which obviously I haven't been able to see, there is every reason for the highest confidence.[10]

CHAPTER FIFTEEN

GOLD

British troops assaulting Gold beach, in the centre of the invasion front, had little difficulty piercing the defences and fighting their way inland; by midday they had established a bridgehead three miles wide and two-and-a-half miles deep . . .

Major R.J.L. Jackson, 6th Battalion, The Green Howards:

As beachmaster, my job was like that of a traffic controller except that my traffic was on foot. I had to see that everyone was directed to their correct positions as soon as they arrived.

The beach was completely deserted as we approached and I remember being puzzled by the comparative silence. Of course, the Allied bombardment was landing far ahead and we could see some of the big shells passing over us, but the absence of any fire directed at us was strange. Our biggest fear concerned the first few seconds when the landing-craft doors were opened and we presented a tight, congested target for any machine-gunners. Because of this we lost a sergeant, who jumped too soon into the sea when we hit a false bottom. The water there was some eight feet deep, but he thought we had struck the beach. He was carrying so much equipment that he sank straight away and was drowned.

Ironically his fears were without foundation. When we landed the doors opened, we jumped out, but there were no bullets. The beach was apparently still deserted. The water was only about a foot deep and I quickly advanced up the beach, flanked by a radio operator and a regimental policeman carrying a sten gun. At every step we expected to be fired at, but were not. The lack of opposition became eerie.

Then, after about 200 yards, we must have reached a German fixed line. Suddenly they threw everything at us. The mortars took us first and I was hit badly in the leg. My radio operator and policeman were both killed outright by the same explosion. Fortunately, although I could not move, the radio was intact and I was able to keep in touch and help troop movements for a while. The first wave of infantry passed me by, and the next, and after a time the field of fire receded.

I was conscious that my particular D-Day was over and then I realized that the tide was coming in. It was the worst moment of the war for me. I could not move and no one was there to drag me beyond the high-tide mark. The water came swirling in until it covered my dead companions. Then it lapped my legs and reached my chest. It was a clear sunny day but the sea was icy cold. I knew I was badly wounded, but not mortally, and it seemed absurd to die like that in inches of water. But then the sergeant of regimental police, from my home town, came along the beach, saw me in time and carried me to a sand dune, where I lay all day.[1]

Private Dennis Bowen, aged 18, 5th Battalion, East Yorkshire Regiment:

Reveille was about three-thirty, four o'clock. I washed and shaved and had breakfast and as we came out of the dining saloon we were given two twenty-four-hour ration packs containing the usual thing, oatmeal biscuits, tea, sugar and powdered milk.

A high percentage of people, not everybody, was sea-sick. Yes, I was sick. Every day, as soon as I'd had me breakfast, I'd go straight and throw it up in the scuppers. Some of the Royal Navy personnel had said to me whatever you do, don't do without food; if you're going to be sick, let your stomach have something to be sick on. People were saying, 'I'll be bloody glad to get off this boat,' even though it meant landing on the beach.

It was even worse when we got in the assault landing craft. We had a certain amount of trouble getting on the assault craft because the sea was extremely rough. We got down the netting down the side of the ship. The ship was rolling and the landing craft were bouncing right up in the air and back down again, probably twenty feet . . .

30. An American driver who intends to enter France freshly shaved.

31. Colonel Nathaniel R. Hoskot, *left*, the day before D-Day.

32. Major Peter Martin.

33. Sergeant John R. Slaughter

34. Oberleutnant Helmut Liebeskind.

35. Obergefreite Heinrich Severloh.

36. Two Consolidated Liberators of the USAF returning home from a bombing mission in the early hours of D-Day overfly the Allied Armada.

37. Part of the Armada, protected by barrage balloons.

38. Landing craft forming up.

39. HMS *Warspite* firing on German coastal batteries.

40. HMS *Rodney* pounds enemy positions.
41. British sailors man an anti-aircraft gun.

42 & 43. Two of the famous Robert Capa photographs of the first landings by US troops at dawn on Omaha beach. Capa's film was damaged during development.

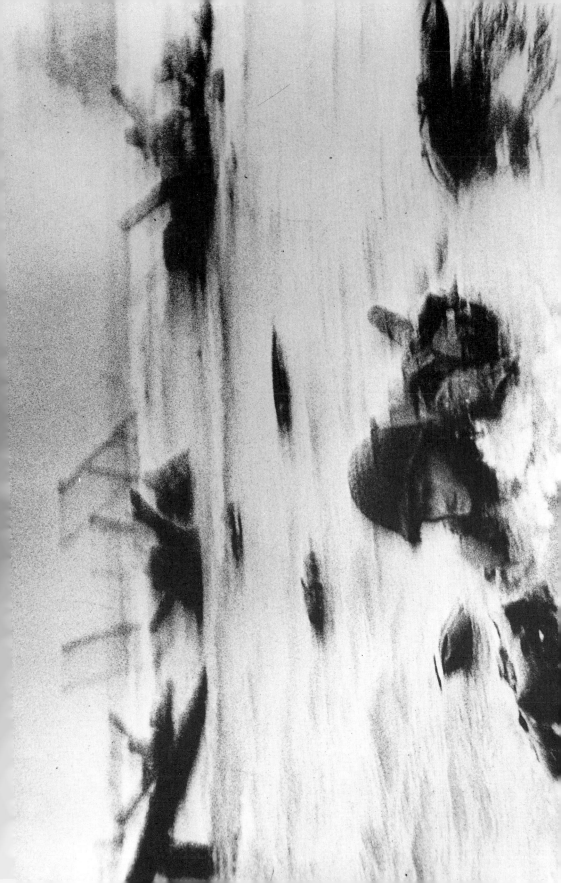

44. Scottish troops landing in France.

45. US troops under fire crouch behind tanks and obstacles.

46. Men of the Regiment de la Chaudière coming ashore.

47. Lieutenant George Honour on an X Craft used to guide landing craft into the beaches.

48. Royal Marine Commandos.

49. Survivors of a capsized craft wade ashore.

50. Survivors of a capsized US landing craft giving artificial respiration to a fellow infantryman.

51. British troops taking cover.

52. British troops moving forward on Sword beach.

53. The face of battle: a GI is tended to by a US medic.
54. The Sixth Airborne Division's landing zone near Ranville.

55. A British tank and glider near Ranville.

56. British airborne troops digging in, with their glider in the background.

57. No turning back: the scene on Omaha beach.

58. Canadian wounded wait for transfer next to a captured German bunker.

59. Read all about it: the first news of the invasion comes out in England.

perhaps that's an exaggeration, but certainly six to twelve feet . . . and you had to time it so that you could step from the netting on to the landing craft when it came up on a wave. I was fortunate, the thing came up and I sort of stepped off and then went down with it. There were quite a few men who got hurt, mistimed the jump and fell quite heavily and never got to the shore at all. They were taken straight back onto the ship with broken limbs or dislocated shoulders.

It took about twenty minutes to half an hour to fill the LCA, then they circled round and waited. They had RN speed boats with loud-hailers and you could hear all the orders coming over, you know, '4986! Follow me!' Everybody was bellowing and shouting, actually shouting orders to get into position.

Then we started heading in. Of course, I didn't see anything then because you are down in the boat and it's got high sides. You could have climbed up the sides to look, but nobody did. The naval barrage had started by then, it seemed to me as if every ship in the Channel was firing onto the beach.

The landing craft was flat-bottomed and it was lifting up in the air and banging down. Everybody was spewing over everybody else. I was keen to get off the damn thing, although I knew I was going into action. I didn't see it as me, an individual, fighting. I merely felt that I was a little tiny person in the middle of a whacking great event that was going to happen. In my mind, all that was happening was that I was on this boat, I was sick, so were all the other people, the front of the ship was going to go down, I was going to get off and I was going to run up that beach. I didn't think anything about firing my weapon or that the enemy would be firing at me. The front of the ship was going to go down and I was going to get off and say 'Thank God.'

The run-in took about three quarters of an hour or an hour.

As we got close to the beach, the ramp went down. I was near the front and I ran off down the ramp, which becomes like a little gang-plank, and started to scoot up the beach. I looked back to see if everybody else was coming with me and saw that the LCA was going backwards. The water had only come up my ankles when I landed, but when I looked back I could see the men getting off were dropping into water up to their waists. I thought, my God, it's going backwards, they're never all going to get off, I'm going to be left here with just the few people who had got off with me! But they started up the engines again and forced it back up the beach.

On the little piece of beach where I landed there was a road built on top of the sea wall and we all ran up and got close up underneath the edge of that. There were lots of explosions on the beach and quite a few casualties, though it was difficult to say how many men were dead, how many were wounded and how many were just there because they thought the best thing to do was to just get down on the sand. There was a tank burning, which exploded. I seem to remember just a continual roar of sound; there was no individual sound of bang-bang-bang, it was a roar. Whether it was us firing at Jerry or Jerry firing at us, I don't know.

Remember, there was lots of smoke and dust and it was hot, even though the sun hadn't come up properly, because we had loads and loads of equipment, so much equipment I can't imagine why we had it all. Everything was sort of stuffed in your pockets in addition to what we'd got in our battle order and anybody who could have grabbed extra rations had done so. So everybody was covered in sweat and of course steel helmets always make you sweat.

Of the thirty men in our little group, our platoon, I should think twenty-five got up and under this wall. There were lots of people laid out on the beach but I feel sure they weren't from our group, although I couldn't look round and think, 'Ah, so-and-so is missing, he must have been . . .' I never even thought about it. I just knew there were some people wounded, some people dead. I don't think I was frightened. I was exhausted, hot, tired, worried, eager for it all to be over, but I don't think I was frightened. Your heart is pounding like mad, of course, and you're hoping and hoping that you won't get hurt, but I wasn't frightened.

The tide started to come in so it was imperative that we got off the beach and some laddie, a private soldier, I really don't know who he was, jumped up on top of the wall with his sten gun and said, 'Look, come on you lot, get over this wall, get over it!' So we got up onto the road and ran like mad across this marsh, wetland, on the other side. As I ran across I heard rounds flying off the tarmacadam, so I presume Jerry had a fixed line on it. I could hear ricochets coming off the road and whining across the beach. It wasn't our stuff coming in from behind us, it was stuff that was coming in from Jerry, it was their small-arms fire I could hear and a lot of men were going down.

I could hear Sergeant Mayhew shouting, 'Keep going! Keep going!' We got right across the marsh into some houses on the other side and got ourselves into position there and dug in in the gardens.

There were civilians in the houses, French. We saw them but didn't speak to them. Some of the blokes attempted to, but they only spoke French and we only spoke English.[2]

Sergeant Major Jack Vilander Brown, aged 29, 147th Essex Yeomanry:

We started firing just after six, when we were probably about two or three thousand yards offshore. Everybody opened up, the noise was horrific, it was ear-shattering. It was bad enough our people firing, but there were rocket things on either side, there were capital ships, destroyers dashing backwards and forwards ... it was, well, we'd never experienced anything like it.

That running shoot, you know, those guns got so hot the blokes could hardly handle them. Grease was running out of the breech blocks and the cartridge cases were being thrown over the side. We fired 150, 200 rounds – as soon as one's gone, you put another one in – and the noise, well! We didn't have time to be afraid, you don't get time to think. But from where I was, as we got nearer, I could see it was very rough. Some assault landing craft had overturned, some had hit the mines on the poles. One thing I will never forget is seeing these poor chaps struggling in the sea, these infantry blokes being kept afloat by their life belts. We had to get to the beach and there was no way we could avoid them; we just went through them, just passed them by. I don't know what happened. You couldn't help the poor souls.

We were getting closer and closer and we had just finished firing, we couldn't have been more than 500 yards off the beach, when we were hit. Lieutenant Gregson, our GPO [gun position officer], had gone forward with the navy to supervise the ramp going down when there was a violent explosion and the LCT shuddered. A shell had hit the ramp and wounded him and at least three of the navy people; one may have been killed. Everybody then struggled to try and get the ramp down, but it was jammed. We couldn't get it down, so we couldn't go in, so we hove to and started to drift with the tide, while they tried to fix the ramp.

They brought Lieutenant Gregson back down right next to where I was and I could see he was badly hurt. We did what we could for him. Then another shell hit the little bridge just behind me but it was a dud. I didn't know it at the time – there was so much noise you didn't know what was coming this way and what was going that way, honestly you didn't. Right next to us was this rocket ship – it was an LCT with all these rockets on. When they went off, you never heard anything like it. I heard them going off and glanced over and I thought, you lucky so and sos, that's your lot, now you're going to swing round and hop it. Just as I said it two or three shells hit them and they disappeared in smoke and flames.

Anyway, they managed to get the ramp partly down and the first SP went off and was hit the moment it got to the beach. The bloke who was wounded was a great friend of mine, poor old boy. Then we all got off. As we went down the ramp I realized we were completely on our own and that we had landed in the wrong place – there was an enormous sea wall in front of us that had certainly not been mentioned at the briefing.

The first thing we had to do was detach our ammunition sledges to prevent them getting tangled in our tracks. In order to carry as much ammunition as possible we had these sledges underneath our SPs, attached by wires, and as they moved off they dragged them along. They were getting thrown about in the breakers, so I had to get some blokes, very brave blokes too, to go into the water, get underneath and un-hook them.

I don't remember seeing our LCT get off the beach, but I know some commandos landed just after us. Their boats had been completely tipped up and so they swam ashore. They had lost most of their small arms, so we gave them some of ours, ammunition and what not. Their CO was a brave bloke; I remember seeing him standing on the top of the sea wall, waving his stick to direct the blokes where to go.

By this time I was beginning to think a bit more clearly and I walked round a sort of promontory – there was a hell of a shambles on the beach of blokes and vehicles – but I couldn't see the rest of the regiment. I couldn't even see Le Hamel, which was where we should have landed. I thought, Oh, God! I realized we had to get off the beach, the quicker the better, particularly as the tide was coming in. There were a lot of REs with bulldozers and all sorts of things and I arranged with them to breach the sea wall with TNT so we could get off. Then of course we started firing and then I suddenly saw '*Achtung Minen!*' and realized there was a big minefield in front of us. But it was very well marked, including where we could go through! The first Germans we saw were some prisoners who had been told to go back to the beach. One was a colossal bloke and he said to me, in pretty good English, something like: 'You so-and-so English will soon be driven back into the sea. Adolf Hitler told us it will be so.' I was so taken aback I didn't say anything to him and off he went back to the beach. I'll never forget it.[3]

Company Sergeant Major H.W. Bowers, 1st Battalion, The Hampshire Regiment:

My main concern when we landed was to get a nice pair of German boots, because my own were killing me. The assault craft landed and we made a dash up the beach. Terrific fire was coming from our right, from a pillbox which we didn't know was there. We decided to attack this pillbox. At this moment, a wireless message came through to the company commander to return and take over the remnants of the battalion. He went off with a runner, leaving me and the wireless operator there, who at that moment got killed, leaving me alone and not feeling too happy.

I decided it was impossible for me to attack the pillbox on my own and I tried to return to my original position. On the way I found the commanding officer badly wounded. He said, 'Hello, Bowers, you still living?' I said, 'Yes, just about!' and explained the position to him. He said, 'OK, you carry on.' I thought, Christ, he must think I can take on the whole German army! However, I edged back a bit to get through the wire and I picked up a couple of naval commandos, who in their humorous way asked if they could come along for a bit of fun. We crawled through the minefields, across a couple of fields, eliminating the Germans that were in the slit trenches there and eventually reached the sanatorium building, the end of which was the pillbox. I put them into a firing position and crawled into the sanatorium and so down onto the top of the pillbox. The Germans immediately put out a white flag. I thought, to hell with you, after all this trouble, and I slipped in a 36 Mills grenade. After the explosion a few seconds passed and out they come running, with their hands up, shouting, 'Russkis! Russkis!' I was not interested in their nationality. All I was interested in was those nice, soft boots they were wearing and it was my intention, without any shadow of doubt, that a size-eight pair of them would belong to me in the very near future.[4]

Lance Corporal N. Travett, 2nd Devons:

We were on Jig section. As we were going in, we could see the shore
and we could see the shells going over and we could see burning
assault craft that had been hit. You could see that other assault craft
were being hit by looking over the top. You kept your head down
below the side of the boat, which was steel all the way round, but
then you would occasionally pop your head over the top to see what
you could see. All I could see was the beach with smoke rising from
the bombing which was going on. The aircraft, of course, were
bombing and the battleships were firing shells overhead and that was
causing quite a kerfuffle.

We weren't hit; we were very fortunate. When we beached we had
to jump into the water and it came up roughly waist high. While I
was wading ashore, I lost a couple of friends – the beach having been
bombed beforehand, had left bomb craters in the water which you
could not see. Some people actually walked into these craters and
were drowned because of the weight of their packs. There were dead
bodies in the water, quite a number, dozens probably. Not necessarily
from my own regiment because we went in as a second flight. I think
the Dorsets were in front of us, then it was the Devons, but prior to
that the Engineers had been in to demolish these mines on poles, to
make room for the tanks to come ashore.

We managed to get to the shore and we had to run up the beach. I
think there was a wall at the top of the beach. It seemed to take a
long, long time just to get from the boat to the wall. You could see
bullets splashing into the water beside you and you could see bullets
landing in the sand. We got what cover we could underneath the wall
because there was still considerable enemy firepower from pillboxes.
It was a low wall and I think it formed part of a road that ran along
the top of the beach. There were lots of soldiers with me, everyone
was trying to get as much cover as they could. We'd all landed not
necessarily in exactly the same spot, but there were a lot of us,
anyway, taking cover under that wall. There were officers and senior
NCOs but I was only a lance corporal then, so I was well down the
list of seniority. I knew the people in charge, some of them were
fearless, the only way I can put it. There was the average chap who
took as much cover as he could, and then there was the other chap
who'd say, 'Come on, come on. We can get from that wall to this
wall, it's all right.' Though you thought twice about it, sometimes.

People were being killed because the shelling was still coming from inland onto the beach. In no way could you possibly advance until these pillboxes had been destroyed. So we lay there in our wet trousers, water oozing out of our boots, for what seemed ages and eventually the most troublesome pillbox – it was on our right, I remember – was silenced. That was where I saw my first dead Germans. Gruesome. I thought, really, those chaps had probably been called up for service like myself and had no wish to be where they were, but they didn't stand a chance, not there. They just . . . well, what could they do?[5]

Private Francis Williams MM, aged 22, 6th Battalion, Green Howards:

When we climbed into the LCA from a Landing Ship Infantry called the *Empire Lance* and were lowered into the English Channel, then formed up with the other LCAs, the craft were rolling and pitching. As we headed for the beach about six miles away I stood up all the way as I knew I would be sea-sick if I sat down. Quite a few of the lads were sick, spewing into special paper bags that had been given to us.

I stood and watched the beach getting closer and the planes going in to bomb and the fighters roaming around. Then the navy opened fire with their big guns and the rocket ships opened up. Whoever survived that day will never forget it. I know I won't.

As we came in close to the beach some landing craft were hit, some of the occupants being killed, drowned, others being good swimmers were picked up or managed to struggle ashore, not many managing this. Everyone had their belts unfastened so that if the craft was hit you could throw off your gear, which consisted of Bren pouches, small pack on the back and lots of extra ammunition, grenades galore, water bottle on the side. In the pack were the essentials an infantryman needs, number one being shaving gear. Then two twenty-four-hour food packs consisting of sugar, milk and tea cubes, oatmeal blocks, a few sweets and cigarettes, a chemical block to heat your water for tea or porridge. I can't remember what else was in them.

The doors of the craft opened, the ramp went down, belts were fastened and this was it. Sergeant William Allen Hill (nicknamed Rufty) and my best mate was first to go, followed by two privates whose names I can't recall. That was the last I saw of them. The landing craft had not run aground and they were sucked under, the three of them drowning.

I didn't know my mate was dead when I left the craft and when I was wading ashore the water was nearly up to my chest. I had to carry my Bren above my head. There was a small sandy ridge just off the beach. I got behind that, asking different lads if they had seen my mate Rufty Hill. One lad told me he was dead in the water, along with a few others. I couldn't believe it. He had got out of Dunkirk a few years earlier, had been through all the battles in the Western desert and Sicily, now he was dead without even getting ashore.

On our left a flail tank went forward and blew up, whether from a shell or a mine I don't know. One of its wheels rolled right along the beach and just missed one of our sergeants, who was lying on the sand with a wound in his leg and half his jaw blown away.

Just fifty or sixty yards in front of me was a Spandau firing to our right. One of our platoons was moving up the road which was to have been our left boundary, but we had landed well to the left of it. I jumped up and ran at the machine-gun post, firing short bursts from the hip. I was on them before they knew what was happening. I shot two of the occupants and shouting '*Hande hoch!*' the other six gave themselves up. I ran them towards the track with their hands on their heads and when we reached it, there in the ditch was about six or so of 18 Platoon, all of whom had been hit in the legs. I ran the six Germans down to the beach and left them as there was a lot of people ashore now. Before I left them I noticed one of them had a sort of band around the bottom of his sleeve and on it were the words Afrika Korps. I had a few words with him. As far as I can remember I said to him, 'You Rommel's man?' He said, '*Ja.*' Pointing to my Africa Star I said, 'Me 8th Army.' It was a bit like Tarzan and Jane. I shook his hand and went back to what was left of 17 Platoon.[6]

Private Joe Minogue, 7th Armoured Division:

Our first sight of the coast was just a kind of low black line on a rather grey morning. Everything was very quiet and we were told that we were so well ahead of schedule that the invasion fleet had kind of pulled up for a ten-minute rest. I suppose this would have been about half past six, about an hour before we were due to land.

There was a bit of lurking about, as it were, then the softening-up barrage began.

The amazing thing to us was these rocket ships they had got. They were tank landing craft with a vast number of down spouts – you could call them nothing else but that – sticking out of the side. They turned lazily to one side and fired a vast number of rockets at the beach, then manoeuvred to fire the other side. This seemed to be some kind of signal for us to move and the six landing craft that we were with suddenly began to pull away from the rest of the fleet. We saw at that stage that the infantry were debarking from their bigger ships into these smaller landing craft which were to follow us in. And we thought, hello, well, you know . . . this is it.

We unshackled the chains that were holding the tanks onto the deck and climbed aboard. Once we were aboard, that was it, because you could see nothing. We had been offered a drop of rum beforehand if we wanted it, but I think most of us settled for those self-heating cans of cocoa. I think some of us were brought up on stories about the First World War when they used to give liquor to the troops to persuade them to go over the top and we were determined that nothing like that was going to happen to us.

You can imagine the position with five of us in the tank crew, each man with his own thoughts, each dependent on the other. We were fairly confident we would be able to perform the jobs we were going to be asked to do. We had just one job really, that was to get off the landing craft and once we had reached the high water mark on the beach we had to begin flailing – beating mines with the chains at the front of the tank – and keep going until we reached the road. Then we were to turn right and rendezvous in the village of Le Hamel in twenty minutes' time.

H-Hour, as they called it, was at 7.30, but I remember the driver looking at his watch and saying, 'Christ, we're five minutes early – I hope this isn't a bad sign.' We saw the first couple of tanks go off, then the third one. We were the fourth tank off the landing craft and we were very, very apprehensive, as I've said, about this business of being in the water. I think the driver of the tank was a bit more apprehensive than the rest of us because he blew part of the waterproofing a little bit before he should have done and we all thought, 'Oh, this is it. We've been hit, this is the end of it.'

Anyway, we plugged on and to our great relief we finally found the water was well away from us. I was the gunner and I only had a forward view but I could see that the three tanks in front of us were not doing too well. The first tank had stopped because its commander had been killed, the second tank had been a bit too close to him and had slewed to the right and hit a clay patch on the beach and the tank behind him had had a hit in the side, which had set it on fire. I saw the crew busily scrambling out. This didn't do a great deal for our confidence.

Fortunately, at that moment the tank commander hit me on the head with his microphone, which was his famous signal to do a 360-degree traverse in the gun turret to break the waterproofing round the turret ring. This gave me an absolutely fantastic view of the whole thing. There was absolutely nothing one could see on the beach in the way of opposition; I mean there weren't thousands of people waiting to fight us off, which is the kind of thing we vaguely expected.

As I began a traverse to the left I saw an odd pillbox here and there, but I wasn't quite sure whether anything was coming from it or not. Then as the turret came back towards the sea I could see the infantry just beginning to come ashore. It was all a bit like a cartoon, a bit unreal. I suppose there must have been a couple of machine guns raking across the beach. You could see infantrymen getting into the water from the small landing craft, some chest-deep, some waist-deep, and they would begin to run across the beach and suddenly you'd see the odd figure fall here and there.

It wasn't a matter of a whole line of men going down; it seemed as though just one in five, or a small group, might go down. A chap would be lying doubled up on the beach and some people would run past him and then a couple of his mates might get hold of the epaulettes on his battledress and drag him forward to the shelter of the sand dunes.

By this time we had reached the high-water mark and we began to flail and I remember hitting the first mine on the first rise of the sand dunes. How many mines we actually flailed I've no idea but when we reached the road the tank commander told us that the tank behind was doing well and was following us along. We turned right when we reached the road and when we reached the first corner there was a dead German there. It was like something from a film. He was young, huddled up and hatless, or rather his helmet had fallen off and he was very, very blond. It seemed so stupid, in a way, that there should be a blond dead German on the very first corner.

Further along the road we were trying to negotiate a bomb crater right in the centre of the road and suddenly the tank began to slide into the crater. We obviously couldn't move and so we got out and by this time the infantry – I think it was the Hampshires, and the Dorset Regiment – had got off the beach and were breaking through onto the road. Their officers were most impatient about the fact that we were holding up their advance and they cursed and swore in those fancy voices that ordinary soldiers learned to imitate so well, things like, 'I say, old chaps, can't you move that damn thing out of the way?'

Eventually another tank came along and gave us a tow out of this hole and the infantry moved on. Of course they'd been glad of the short rest, because they all got their fags out and had a bit of a breather. Then nobody really knew what to do with us and the rest of the day we were never more than half a mile from the beach and we kept being moved on by military policemen who would come up and say, 'Get this damn thing out of the way.' We finally finished up in the garden of a Frenchman who smoked about forty of our fags in about three hours.[7]

Signaller I.G. Holley, aged 20, 1st Battalion, The Royal Hampshire Regiment:

I had already been in action in the Middle East and I felt like an old soldier, answering questions about what it is like. 'Brakey', one of our reinforcements was not yet nineteen and very apprehensive about going on his first operation. I tried to reassure him.

On our LCA there was a small keg of rum and a couple of bottles of whisky, put there by some unknown person, I never found out who, probably with the intention, good or bad, that we might need a little Dutch courage. One drink was enough for me, in the hope that it would settle a queasy stomach caused by the flat-bottomed boat tossing about in the swell. On board we had a naval sub lieutenant who, either from the magnitude of the event or from *esprit de corps* obtained from the rum, felt impelled to stand up and give forth a little speech on the great thing we assault troops were about to do.

Overhead there was the continuous whizz of naval shells homing in on their targets to soften them up for us. We were soon in range of mortars, a weapon we had grown to respect, and we could hear the sharp crackle of machine-gun fire. We had the word to get ready and tension was at its peak when the ramp went out. I was with the second in command of the company, a captain. He went out with me close behind. We were in the sea to the tops of our thighs, floundering ashore with other assault platoons to the left and right of us. Mortar bombs and shells were erupting in the sand and I could hear the burp-burp of Spandau light machine guns through the din. There were no shouts, only the occasional cry as men were hit and went down.

To my right I spotted my friend, Laffy, another signaller, crawling on his hands and knees, with the radio floating in the water behind him, attached to him by the long lead from the microphones still on his head. I thought he had been hit and only learned later that he had a relapse of malaria (a legacy quite a few of us had from the Middle East) and had no idea what he was doing.

The beach was filled with half-bent running figures and we knew from experience that the safest place was to get as near to Jerry as we could. A near one blasted sand over me and my set went dead. (I discovered later that it was riddled with shrapnel.) A sweet rancid smell, never forgotten, was everywhere; it was the smell of burned explosives, torn flesh and ruptured earth.

High up on the beach a flail tank was knocked out. I saw B Company's HQ group take cover behind it as a shell scored a direct hit on them. They were gone in a blast of smoke out of which came cartwheeling through the air a torn shrieking body of a stretcher bearer with the red cross on his arm clearly discernible.

We got to the sea wall, where Spandau from a pillbox to our left flattened us until it was silenced a few minutes later. We got on the road, running as fast as our equipment would allow. A Sherman tank had collapsed in a great hole, its commander sticking his head out of the turret going mad with rage. Past this we turned off the road through a wire fence with signs on it saying '*Achtung Minen*'. A long white tape ran straight across the minefield, a corridor repeated twice again before we reached a cluster of trees where we were able to take stock of ourselves. There were six of us left.[8]

Sergeant W.E. Wills, 2nd Battalion, The Devonshire Regiment:

Few of us slept well that night and at about 3.30 a.m. we were roused for breakfast, which consisted of almost-cold liver and onions and a lukewarm mug of tea. Then we assembled in our pre-determined positions to load into our landing craft.

My LCM, being first off, had to cruise round and round the 'mother ship' until all the LCPs were lowered from the davits and the officers and men had used the scrambling nets to get from the decks and into their allotted landing craft. On board my LCM was the CO and part of battalion HQ, the MO, some stretcher bearers, a few supporting-arms personnel as well as the CO's jeep and the RAP jeep.

The choppy sea caused a little sea-sickness, helped I suppose by fear, and sitting in front of me was a stretcher bearer called Wally Hodkin who was using a bucket because he had diarrhoea and he was at the same time being sick into a bucket in front of him. The smell was frightful and combined with the action of the very choppy sea several others became sea-sick – me too, eventually.

Once all our assault craft were loaded and assembled in flight order we set off for the shore, which could now be seen a few miles away. Most of the sea-sickness seemed to terminate then for there was so much of interest going on around us. There seemed to be, within sight, hundreds of small, medium and large assault craft and behind us dozens of large mother ships, some still lowering assault craft, and countless naval ships.

A sneaky little thought crept into my mind, which was 'How's this for a wedding anniversary?' June 6 1944 was the sixth anniversary of my marriage and I felt I had more fireworks for its celebration than any other living person. Rocket ships, assault ships, battleships, cruisers, frigates and destroyers were all thumping away at the shore and fighter and fighter/bomber aircraft were passing overhead.

As we got closer to the shore we could hear the swish of bullets overhead and splashes and bangs as shells hit the water around us, but I didn't see any craft hit, although an occasional 'clang' told me that a bullet or a piece of shrapnel had struck our metal sides.

When about 1,000 yards from the beach, I could see assault troops running from their landing craft and a few Bren-gun carriers leaving their LCMs and moving along what was to be our landing beach. Then I noticed the tripod-type obstacles still partly covered by the sea and I saw one LCA thrown over by a large wave, or maybe a bursting shell, and it drifted upside down in the choppy sea.

When about 300 yards from the shore, our LCM stopped and the front ramp was lowered for us to disembark. Both our jeeps were able to drive off together and into the sea we went – the CO and the rest followed. Unfortunately the sea was deeper than anticipated and after only a few yards both jeeps drowned as water poured into the extended exhaust pipes and also shorted out all our electrics.

Grabbing the Bren gun, but leaving all my personal belongings, I started to leave the jeep, as did the driver, but the water was too deep at that point for walking, so I ditched the Bren gun and started swimming for the shore. All around me men were swimming and I saw our MO helping his batman, Private Stone, who couldn't swim and almost sank like a stone from the weight of his battle order.

After about twenty-five yards I could walk safely and was able to see more of what was going on. The CO, a fairly tall man, was on the beach and shouting for his signaller. The MO had set Private Stone safely on his feet and as he waded ashore he kept stopping to examine floating bodies, but as all were obviously beyond help he let them float away.

There were already one or two amphibious tanks moving up the beach from the sea and towards the sand dunes about thirty yards from the water. The LCTs were off-loading more tanks and shells and mortar bombs were falling, but not in any concentrated manner, fortunately.

As I walked along the beach, trying to locate the track up which it had been intended the vehicles should drive to the de-waterproofing area, I heard a voice say, 'Hello, Wills. Get me a blanket if you can.' There was a bedraggled figure half sitting, half lying, against the sand dunes. He had a Devon Regiment shoulder badge and a major's crown. I looked hard at his badly smashed face and was eventually able to recognize Major Howard, who commanded C Company of our battalion.

Looking around the beach the only blankets to be seen were draped, regimentally, around the haversacks on the backs of the military policemen who were sign-posting the various beach areas. As I walked by one he dropped suddenly and lay very still, except for twitching in his hands. A bullet, maybe from a sniper, because I could not hear automatic fire, had gone straight through his tin hat from front to back and taken some of his brains with it. There was nothing I could do for him, so I removed his neatly folded blanket and took it back to Major Howard. It was then that I learned he had been in the LCA which had capsized and that several of his company had been drowned.

At this stage I felt no fear, only discomfort and disgust at losing my kit, my gun, and the jeep. Making my way along the beach I saw

many dead men and quite a number of stretcher bearers carrying
wounded off the beach and I could see order was coming into the
activities of all on the beach, but one incident upset me more than a
little. An amphibious tank came from the sea, paused a little and then
made its way along the beach with its canvas screen still up. A sapper
went to move across its path but fell about ten yards in front of it, hit
by a bullet. The tank driver obviously could not see him and drove
on. One track passed over the pelvis and buttocks of the fallen man,
killing him, of course.[9]

Major R.B. Gosling, 147th (Essex Yeomanry) Field Regiment, RA:

As we neared the coast of France, our naval hosts gave us hot tea and
a double rum ration. This, added to the choppy seas, the oil fumes
and the general nervous excitement, made some of us violently sick
and thankful to see the coast of Normandy more clearly. We climbed
down a rope ladder into an LCA en route for landing sector Jig
Green West. Regardless of our carefully synchronized watches and
the fact that we were not due to land for another ten minutes, the
colonel urged our LCA on towards the beach through the obstacles
and stakes. Soon our 'driver' reckoned he was close enough; pleading
that he had to return for another load of passengers, he let down the
ramp and we plunged into the sea to an uncomfortable height. We
were holding hands in case of unexpected deep holes and sure
enough, almost at once, I found only a hand behind me protruding
from the water and Sergeant Cecil Hall was temporarily submerged.

When the assault companies went in, our own run-in shoot and the
rockets had finished and the naval bombardment had lifted, so the
beaches suddenly appeared relatively quiet and empty. As we moved
into shallow water, however, a swarm of angry bees buzzed just
above our heads; our Hampshire comrades, war-experienced,
recognized German heavy machine-gun fire and ran forward. In front
of us the sand furrowed and spurted from Spandaus firing down the
beaches in enfilade on fixed lines from Le Hamel. The colonel
shouted to us to lie down, but the wet sand was unattractive, so we
sprinted for the cover of the dunes fifty yards ahead.

Some mortar bombs and 88mm shells were falling and one of the
former landed just behind Lieutenant Colonel Nelson-Smith and me,
smashing one of his arms and filling my left leg with small fragments.

We managed to make it to the dunes and flung ourselves in a depression in the sand. Intermittent bombs and shells continued to fall and the bees swarmed through the reeds above our heads. We laid very flat and still.

With my First World War entrenching tool, providentially issued just before sailing, I dug my head and shoulders into the sand. After a few minutes German fire seemed to have switched down to the beach again and I crawled up the dune to peer over the other side. Horrified to see a German uniform some twenty yards away, I fired my revolver in his general direction and hastily slid back. A Hampshire corporal lying near me, already wounded, knelt up to look over the dune and was at once shot through the chest by a sniper.

The first member of the regiment I saw was Major Vere Broke, standing up in his half-track, which had landed at H + 60 with C Troop's guns, and moving west down the beach towards Le Hamel. At that moment a Spandau again opened fire and I shouted to him to keep his head down. He waved to me and, typically, continued on imperturbably, merely tipping his tin hat over his eyes.

Thereafter, the full activity of D-Day continued all around while I and other wounded lay ignominiously in the dunes. Good news kept filtering back and, later medical orderlies got us into a German sleeping-bunker being used as a first-aid post. The remains of the Germans' stand-to breakfast still lay on a table with wine from the night before; also a note from a French girl to 'Hans chéri' that she would meet him behind the bunker at 8 p.m. on Tuesday June 6. She never turned up.[10]

Major C.J. Sidgwick, 147th (Essex Yeomanry) Field Regiment RA:

As the tide began to ebb, horrible spikes and obstacles appeared, Teller mines and the like. Within ten minutes we hit one of the obstacles and holed our stern. The skipper did his best, but the sea rushed in and he dumped us all into the sea, luckily only thigh-high, so we waded ashore minus wireless sets, amidst some of the horrible sights of men at war, dead, drowning, and splintered wood from craft destroyed.

We plodded on over the beach, past the casualty stations, on to the little hills inland. Came across Cecil Gosling and his party at 09.00, eating a haversack ration. 'Just like Monte Carlo,' I said. 'Glad you think so,' he replied. 'What's happening?' I inquired. 'Don't quite know, but the regiment are firing somewhere,' was his answer.[11]

Trooper Charles Wilson, regimental survey party, 147th (Essex Yeomanry) Field Regiment, RA:

I was one of the 'roly-poly team', whose job it was to drag out to the shore a huge roll of matting and wire mesh, which was intended to prevent following vehicles getting bogged down in the sand. The 'roly-poly' was about eight feet in diameter, with an axle to which ropes were attached. Most of us stripped down to vest, pants and gym shoes.

We hit two mines going in, but they didn't stop us, although our ramp was damaged and an officer standing on it was killed. We grounded on a sand bank. The first man off was a commando sergeant in full kit who disappeared like a stone in six feet of water. We grasped the ropes of the 'roly-poly' and plunged down the ramp into the icy water. The 'roly-poly' was quite unmanageable in the rough water and dragged us away, towards some mines. We let go the ropes and swam and scrambled ashore. All I had on was my PT shorts as I had lost my shoes and vest in the struggle. Someone offered cigarettes all round, but they were soaking wet.

George Chapman in the Bren carrier was the first vehicle off the LCT. It floated a moment, drifted on to a mine and sank. George dived overboard and swam ashore. The battery CP half-track got off along the beach, with me running behind. The beach was strewn with wreckage, a blazing tank, bundles of blankets and kit, bodies and bits of bodies. One bloke near me was blown in half by a shell and his lower part collapsed in a bloody heap in the sand. The half-track stopped and I managed to struggle into my clothes. Several shells burst overhead and shrapnel spattered the beach. Machine-gun bullets were kicking up the sand.

Our survey jeep came off the LCT and went down like a stone, being so overloaded. Our MO's jeep followed and met a similar fate and the driver was just pulled out in time, half-drowned. The rising tide helped the LCT lift off the sand bank and it moved inshore, squashing the two jeeps flat.

Eventually a way was cleared off the beach and the battery half-track moved inland. I walked along behind it with the rest of the command post staff, as it crawled along a narrow lane which the engineers were sweeping for mines. Then we came to fields and hedges, two poor stone cottages and our first Frenchmen, two grey-stubbled old men who kissed us on both cheeks and jabbered away in the Normandy dialect. The road was crowded with vehicles and infantry moving inland.[12]

Lieutenant Stuart Hills, commander of a DD tank, C Squadron, Sherwood Rangers:

When dawn first broke we found ourselves, rather disconcertingly, in the lead and apart from the other landing craft bearing the rest of the squadron there was not another ship in sight. However, as it became lighter we could see, over the very rough and very grey sea, hundreds of ships of every description and as the French coast came into view one sensed for the first time that the battle was on. Every now and then there were terrific explosions from shore which was soon a large haze of smoke and small fires, and I distinctly remember I experienced the same 'stomach sensation' which I always used to suffer from before going in to bat.

As the ramp was lowered about 700 yards from the shore I could see two flail tanks brewing up just to my front and I could not help wondering what caused them to be knocked out and catch fire and whether our tanks would meet the same fate when we reached the shore. For those who do not know, a DD tank is an ordinary Sherman tank with certain technical modifications which enable the tank to be launched from a landing craft and then to swim off under its own steam to the shore, navigated by the commander. The launching operation is comparatively simple as long as the sea is calm, but in rough weather the whole affair becomes rather danger-ous, as the tank is inclined to become waterlogged and sink.

We were just going down the ramp when I noticed the hawsers weren't quite tight and this took several minutes to rectify. During this time I had to sit on top of the ramp, a huge white target for any German gunner who liked to take a pot shot. Sure enough, the shots soon came, one on the side of the ramp, the other on our starboard beam, wounding Sergeant Sidaway. Without more ado, I gave my driver the order to go and down the ramp we went.

As soon as we hit the water I knew something was very wrong. The screen was very flimsy in the rough sea and water poured in everywhere. I gave a few technical orders to try and save the day, but when I saw that things were hopeless I gave the order to bail out. I can only imagine that the first shell was our undoing and that it must have holed one of the bottom plates. Corporal Footitt pressed the button on our rubber dinghy which inflated automatically and Trooper Kirman, the only non-swimmer, put it over the side. I scrambled inside the turret to get my mapcase out, but we were going down so fast that I had no time to retrieve it and in my haste to get out I tore the headphones out of the set altogether.

I followed Troopers Reddish and Storey over the side and a few seconds later our tank, 'Bardin Collos', disappeared into the murky depths. Even during these hectic and exciting moments I could not help wondering what Old Father Neptune would think about the sudden appearance of a tank on the sea bottom. My next feeling, as is often the case when no one has been hurt, was one of annoyance at losing my kit, but it soon became evident to all of us that our position was not over-entrancing. We were now about 500 yards out, and by this time the German gunners seemed to have woken up a bit and there was a certain amount of stuff flying about. Moreover, there was a strong current running from west to east which we were unable to combat, our hands being the only means of propulsion. Our chances of reaching the shore therefore were about nil. The rubber dinghy was extremely small; we were wet and cramped. The only hope was that we would be picked up.

I looked back on our own landing craft and saw that things had developed rather badly there too. SSM Robson was sinking fast, likewise Sergeant Sidaway. I could see nothing of Captain Bill Enderby or Sergeant Saunders.

Soon after, we managed to hail an LCG which came over to pick us up, and we were bracketed by high-explosive as we climbed on board. The navy, as always, treated us magnificently and we breakfasted on whisky and Mars bars – an admirable combination. I also heard the announcement of the invasion over the British radio.[13]

Wireless Operator A. Baker, 4th/7th Dragoon Guards:

The first sight of the French coast gave me a queer feeling. Everybody stared at it without saying very much as we slowly drew towards it, passing the big troopships which lay at anchor, having sent their infantry towards the beach in small assault boats.

There were several cruisers lying out there too, firing broadside after broadside inland. We passed within a couple of hundred yards of one, which I seem to remember was the *Belfast* – the noise of her guns was ear-splitting. There was a battleship firing in the distance – the *Rodney*, so the skipper announced over the loud-hailer on the bridge.

Two squadrons of rocket-firing Typhoons roared over, after the 88 which we knew was on the beach. They didn't get it. The 88 knocked out two Churchills before we arrived and was itself knocked out by a flail tank. We saw a terrific explosion on shore, which was presumably one of the Churchills going up.

There were destroyers right in close to the beach, firing like mad. They must have been almost aground. Rocket ships – LCTs carrying batteries of rocket guns – and SP guns firing from LCTs added to the general din. Smoke hung over everything and we could see the flashes of exploding shells on land. We couldn't tell which way they were arriving. About half a mile from the beach a navy motor boat drifted past with a dead sailor lying across the foredeck. I'd never seen anybody dead before.

We were still two or three hundred yards offshore when a big spout of water shot up near our starboard side, followed by another in almost the same place. 'We are now being shelled,' the skipper said dramatically. It was very novel and unpleasant.

By now the beach was black with men and machines and scores of LCTS were discharging their cargoes. The sea was still rough and obviously making things very difficult. I saw several lorries overturn in the breakers.

Our LCT went in and the bows touched bottom. Handling it must have been tricky, as the beach was lined with metal spikes, some with Teller mines fixed to them. Before the ramp could be lowered the current swung the craft round and the skipper had to back her out again among the infantry, who were wading ashore up to their necks in water.

We went in a second time and weren't so lucky. There was a terrific crash and the LCT jerked back. It had hit one of the mines. I was sitting in my seat at the time, with my head sticking out of the hatch – the operator's seat on an ARV being next to the driver's. I was thrown forward and hit my mouth on the rim of the hatch, breaking a tooth and making me feel a bit dizzy. I lowered the seat quickly, shut the hatch and watched things through the periscope.

The number one, who had been standing in the bows, had been blown into the air. I think he broke a couple of ribs, but he got up and carried on directing the lowering of the ramp, which was damaged but went down OK.

Captain Collins' scout car was first down the ramp and it was immediately knocked out by a shell. Collins was unhurt but Steeles, his driver, was wounded. All the rest of the vehicles, our ARV included, got safely ashore.

My memories of the beach are very confused. I remember noticing a number of DD tanks still there, but I couldn't see whose they were. Dabby, our commander, seemed to know where he was going fairly well, and in quite a short time we were off the beach altogether and going up a track with a procession of other vehicles. There were grassy banks on either side, and notices bearing skulls and crossbones and the words 'Achtung Minen'. In one place a big hole had been blown in the middle of the track and filled in with fascines.

Before long we were in Ver-sur-Mer itself. The village was quite a mess and about half the houses had been flattened by the naval bombardment, but the people still came out to cheer and throw flowers. No firing seemed to be going on and Benny, the driver, and I both had our heads stuck out of the hatches.

We went straight through the village and out the other end and, quite suddenly, I realized that all the other vehicles had disappeared and we were alone. We were charging up a quiet country lane all by ourselves. I knew this was wrong because I had seen the orchard where we were to rendezvous on the map and I knew that it was on the very edge of the village. I told Dabby this and we had a bit of an argument – the first of many that I had with various commanders over similar things – before I managed to convince him. We turned round in a field, about a mile up the lane, and went back towards the village.

On the way back we met Muddy Waters (late C Squadron SQMS) with the leading troop of B Squadron, advancing up the road with their infantry. They had no idea anybody had gone ahead of them. The infantry had collected several Jerry prisoners from the fields and ditches. When we got back to Ver we found Captain Collins standing in the middle of the road waving us into an orchard on the right. This was just opposite the original one, which had turned out to be mined. Everybody seemed to have got there safely.[14]

Letter, written 4 July 1944, from Lieutenant Hugh Bone, 2nd East Yorks Regiment:

As our flotilla swung into line behind its leader we raised our flag, a black silk square with the white rose of Yorkshire in the centre. The navy had sewn their red anchor into the top left corner and the brass marine badge was soldered to the blade of the spear on which the flag was suspended. It blew taut in the wind and spray. As we left the ship our bugler blew the general salute and then again as we passed the HQ ship, the senior officer returning our CO's salute.

It was some distance to the beaches and it was a wet trip. All of us had a spare gas cape to keep us dry and we chewed our gum stolidly (mine was still in my mouth twelve or fourteen hours later; usually I hate the stuff and never touch it). Promptly at H-Hour I began listening on my wireless set for the first news and crystal clear came messages from the assaulting companies: 'Heavy opposition, pushing on.' We could hear the tach-a-tach-a-tach of machine guns and the explosions of enemy mortars on the beach.

It was a very dull morning and the land was obscured by mist and smoke, so that, except for the flotilla leader and the CO, no one actually saw the land until the metal doors opened in front and the ramp was down. The doors opened as we grounded and the colonel was out. The sea was choppy and the boat swung a good bit as one by one we followed him. Several fell in and got soaked through. I was lucky. I stopped for a few seconds to help my men with their heavy wireless sets and to ensure they kept them dry. As we staggered ashore we dispersed and lay down above the water's edge. Stuff was falling pretty close to us and, although I did not see it happen, quite a number of people from my own boat were hit. Instinctively, where we lay we hacked holes with our shovels.

The colonel moved forward. I tried to collect my party of sets and operators, but could only see a few of them. I began to recognize wounded men of the assault companies. Some were dead, others struggling to crawl out of the water because the tide was rising very rapidly. We could not help them since our job was to push on, but I saw one of my signal corporals with a wound in his leg and I took his codes with me, promising to send a man back for his set before he was evacuated.

Getting just off the beach among some ruined buildings, we began to collect the HQ. The other boat party was mostly missing, also three-quarters of my sets. The colonel was getting a grip on the battle and I was sent back to the beach to collect the rest of us. I did not feel afraid, but rather elated and full of beans. There were some horrible sights there and not a few men calling for help. I wanted to pull a body out of the waves, but he looked to be dead and I had no time or duty there; the beach medical people would gradually get round to them all. Under the side of a tank that had been hit I saw a bunch of my people and I bawled to them to get up and get moving since they were doing no good there and could quite safely get along to HQ. I felt a little callous when I found that nearly all of them had been hit and some were dead. But sorting them out I made up half of a wireless team and then went in search of some more. By persuading a couple of blokes with shrapnel in their legs and feet that they were good for a few hours yet, I got my wireless lifted and back to HQ, which was just moving inland.[15]

Sergeant John Bosworth, 25 Beach Recovery Company, REME:

The ramp came down with a clatter and the LCL started to shudder. I thought for a moment we had been hit, but what was happening was that we were beaching. Looking through my visor on the D8 armoured bulldozer I saw a large house, then smoke blanked out everything.

A sailor waved me forward and revving up I was under way towards the ramp. The sea was just covering the bottom of the ramp and I moved steadily forward and down into the sea. I should think about 200 yards to go, and about four foot of water gradually receding as the beach came up, the D8 was getting a firmer grip with the tracks, so I drove straight between the white tapes and just as I was about twenty yards from the sea wall I felt a sharp pain in my left hand. I thought I had banged my hand against the armour plate, as there wasn't a lot of room when steering.

The beach guide pointed to the sea wall where I eventually stopped. To my left was a Sherman tank which was half-way up the wall and firing its gun. Between the tank and me was a sand-bagged emplacement with corrugated sheeting on top and some soldiers looking out from a hole between the bags.

I switched off my engine and climbed out of the D8 to unreeve the winch rope and carry out de-waterproofing when an explosion went off near the sea wall, which blew sand all over the place. 'Come in here, you silly bugger,' someone shouted from the emplacement. 'Jerries are dropping grenades from up top.'

It didn't take me long to get under cover and I found about six soldiers from the Royal Pioneer Corps who had been ashore about an hour. As they couldn't find the RE section they were attached to, they had built the shelter. They had found three bottles of rum and several packs of compo and a corporal said they were waiting until something happened. I thought it had!

The infantry were not coming ashore and a lot of firing was going on behind. Rocket-firing Typhoon aircraft were flying up and down the beach engaging targets we couldn't see. Several other landing craft had now beached and I could see other D8s that were part of my section ashore so I thought that it was time I showed myself. But a naval officer beachmaster for King Red said that we should stay where we were and clear the entry points, and as soon as the wall was breached we were to drag all casualties to a point out of the way, subject to the Germans allowing it.

He then gave us a large tot of rum from a stone jar, and taking off my left-hand glove I noticed there was blood and something stuck in the palm of my hand. 'You had better get that fixed up,' said the officer. 'The FAP is over there. Take my dog with you. The walk will do her good and I can't leave here yet.'

I put on my steel helmet, got hold of the dog's lead and went to the FAP where the MO was up to his neck in wounded troops. He looked like a butcher, with blood stains all over his white gown. 'Take that bloody dog out of here,' he said. 'Whose is it?' I told him that it belonged to the beachmaster and it wanted a walk. The MO then asked me what I wanted. I showed him my hand. 'That's an easy one,' he said. 'Sergeant, take out this shrapnel and sew him up. Don't forget the injection. Next.'

The sergeant removed a lump of metal from my hand, put some stitches in, gave me an injection and said, 'Come back in three days' time.' I got hold of the dog and went back to the beachmaster. He was now questioning some German prisoners. 'Bloody Russians,' he said. 'Thanks for walking my dog and take it easy. Have another rum.'[16]

CHAPTER SIXTEEN

UTAH

The first American assault troops heading for Utah, most westerly of the D-Day beaches, were swept off course and landed, by chance, in an area where the enemy defences were much weaker; by the time the Germans had moved up to try and repel the invaders, the landing on Utah was unstoppable . . .

Pfc Joseph S. Blaylock Sr, aged 24, B Battery, 20th Field Artillery, 4th Motorized Division:

We climbed down the rope ladder, down the side of the boat, and got onto the LCT. It was kind of rough at that particular time, which I remember because I had a hard time with the waves getting onto the boat. With everybody taking a position, we started circling. I don't know how long we circled, but we made a big circle and kept on going around and around. After a while, all the boats had gathered and we started in towards Utah beach. All of us were pretty quiet at that particular time. There was not much going on and I think everybody was thinking about what their reaction was going to be on the beach and what was ahead of us. If there was anything said at that particular time, it was said in a nice, quiet voice.

As we were going in, a plane returning from the paratroop drop got shot down right in front of us, about three or four hundred yards, and we all voted to see whether or not we should pick up the crew. The coxswain got outvoted and we decided to pick up three men on a rubber raft and carry them in with us. We figured it would only throw us off maybe six or eight minutes. You're talking about a happy group of pilots; they were real happy that we stopped and picked them up and then we proceeded on in. Everybody again was quiet. Every now and then we'd take a peep over the front or over the side, to see what we could see.

During that time, I went back to the back part of the ship and ran into a can of coffee which I put into my pack, because coffee was precious at that particular time.

We'd got to I'd say about three or four hundred yards from the beach when the ramp went down and Lieutenant Fitzpatrick asked me to get off to see if I could feel any mines. I had learned to tread water in Black and Red Creek in Mississippi, so I got off and treaded water and told them no, there wasn't anything, no mines or anything, so to come on off.

So twenty-five assault troops from the 101st Airborne Division came off, then next came the jeeps. The first one that went off went right down to the bottom, then the other two came off and proceeded on in towards shore.

In the meantime I had lost my carbine and I wondered what I was going to do for a gun when I got in. Anyway, I hung on to the back of the jeeps, kind of pedalling and pushing the jeeps on in towards the shore. There were some 88s and some ack-ack and some mortar shells coming in, and as we got into the shore, the jeep proceeded on ahead towards the causeway. Bieganski and I ran up against a sand dune while we caught our breath a little bit.

After a while we moved on down to the causeway, which was about 100 yards from us, then turned right and went about fifty yards. We were getting ready to have a meeting with General Teddy Roosevelt and as he started talking a German fighter plane came over and started strafing. I dove into a foxhole and just as I went down I started praying. About that time somebody dove on top of me and knocked the breath out of me. He asked me did I mind and I said, 'No, the more the merrier.'

So after that was over with, we got together with General Roosevelt and he said, 'Men, you've landed about 2,000 yards south of where you were supposed to have landed. We will start the war from here.'[1]

Bruce Bradley, aged 24, radio operator, B Battery, 29th Field Artillery Battalion:

I was attached to an infantry regiment that was to go in the first assault wave. We would be the first people to wade ashore on Utah beach. I was to be the radio operator for Lieutenant Blanchard, who I had trained with and liked as an officer and person. We were told we were expendable in the first wave. I remember nobody responded to those chilling words. We were also cautioned to loosen our helmet straps as if we lost our grip on the rope ladders going down the side of the ship, we could plunge down with force enough to break our necks when the water hit the helmet rim. So I made sure I had a good grip. Better some battered knuckles than drowning.

The sea was rough and it was dark. The navy guys had remarked that they were glad they were navy at this point. I'm sure they were. We got V for Victory signs from them as they helped us over the side. Victory didn't seem possible at the time, to me. Survival, maybe.

Making the run into shore the sky was intermittently lit by explosions, some of them of tremendous force. Bombs, shells from the battleships standing out to sea, rockets whooshing overhead, ack-ack from German positions and tracers were coming and going. An awesome display.

As we drew closer to the beach we could see the shape of the land. Also geysers of sea water were coming from shell fire, aimed at us. We had to keep our heads down. I remember I had been so tired from all the tension, lack of sleep, fear, etcetera, but all of a sudden I was not tired any more. I was very alert.

The noise of the shelling and counterfire was much louder, then there was a deafening blast and we were thrown down or knocked sideways. We had been hit by a shell. The coxswain was gone, the ramp was down, the boat was sinking. Sideways. I was thinking about how I would inflate my Mae West somehow. I did this automatically. Most guys in that boat drowned.

My citation reads that I waded ashore, but the water was very deep and rough, so I dog-paddled toward the shore until my feet found sand. There were obstacles, triangular steel shapes, sticking up, but no barbed wire in my path. I waded onto the beach and hit the ground. I had lost my carbine, but still had the radio.

I saw what looked like a low wall ahead and I crawled for it.

Gaining some cover gave me a chance to pull myself together and assess my surroundings. To my right was a dead GI about ten feet away, to my left, about thirty to forty yards away, were some GIs in the process of regrouping. As I watched they went over the wall, so I decided to flip over it also. When I looked ahead, no more sand. It was a swamp of shallow water, but I was on my way, so I started sloshing forward. A shellburst to my left threw me down, but I was OK. I thought maybe I am better off alone. The guys on my left were drawing fire. I made it across the swampy area and joined some other infantry guys.

We headed for Ste Mère-Eglise, a little town. It was only then that I realized I had a nose bleed and my right ear pained, must have been from the explosion on the landing craft. From then on until I found Lieutenant Blanchard, who I figured came in on the second wave, things happened in a sort of haphazard way, no pattern to it. Some dazed Germans had been hiding in a basement of a church and were my first encounter with the enemy. Dead paratroopers were hanging in the trees still in their harnesses. This jolted me more than the bodies lying here and there in the swamp. I don't know why.

Taking cover behind a low hedgerow I found myself next to another GI and offered him a cigarette. While I was looking for my Zippo lighter I heard a snap and when I looked up at him he was dead, hit in the head. He was sitting higher than me.

I crawled away and heard a BAR and other firing and went toward it. The sniper was on the ground. He had been up in a tree and shot down from it. I had yet to fire a shot. I had thrown two grenades but had no way of knowing whether they did any good.

I then found the artillery was ashore and went in search of Lieutenant Blanchard. I first found the sergeant for communications; he was happy to see I had a radio. He directed me to Lieutenant Blanchard and we took off to find an OP where he could direct fire on targets of opportunity. We found a high point, a sort of ridge, and in a short time spotted a bunch of artillery coming toward the area on a country road that intersected another road. The lieutenant got a fix and I relayed his commands and little did we know that a battleship would get in on the act, because in addition to 105s, 16-inch shells came over, bracketing the road and destroying the artillery. The whole battery went up in the air – men, guns, equipment and all.[2]

Captain George Mayberry, aged 24, unit TK:

The landing craft drove onto the shore at 6.30 in the morning, within a minute of the time of H-Hour. I jumped off into four feet of water. Never before in my life had I wanted so badly to run, but I could only wade slowly forward. It was approximately 100 yards to the edge of the shore and it took me two minutes to reach the shallow water. Those two minutes were extremely long. Even on the beach I couldn't run as my uniform was sodden and heavy and my legs were numb and cramped.

Heavy shells commenced exploding on the beach, as well as sporadic mortar fire from a short distance inland. A soldier just ahead of me was blown to pieces by a direct hit. The instant it happened, something small hit me in the stomach – it was the man's thumb. About then, General Theodore Roosevelt Junior came striding along the beach. He was waving his cane and bellowing at everybody to get moving across the dunes. We kept moving as fast as possible. Some enemy rifleman began firing at me, so I picked myself up and began to run forward over the top of the dunes. Facing me were five of the enemy. I shot the one with his hand raised to hurl a grenade, the rest threw down their rifles and put up their hands. I handed them over to a wounded corporal and went forward again.

A couple of hours later I came to Exit One, the most southerly causeway across the flooded area. While the three soldiers I had collected and I were shooting and crawling towards the bridge, we heard shooting from the direction of Pouppeville. There couldn't be any Americans there unless they were paratroopers. I hoisted my small identification flag. The paratroopers stared at me as though I were the first American they had ever seen – because I had come to Normandy by sea. I looked at my watch. The first meeting between American airborne and seaborne forces had been effected at 11.05 a.m.[3]

Private George 'Mac' McIntyre, aged 33, B Company, 4th Engineers:

We headed up the Channel for half an hour, then turned sharply for the shore. Spray splashed over the sides of the LCT and we were soon soaked to the skin. I began to check the shells in my rifle and cartridge belt. Why, I don't know, for I had checked them a dozen times since we left the assembly area. Maybe I was just plain nervous and wanted something to do. One by one, I took them out, polished them, and put them back. Mike Keane watched me for a few moments and then remarked, 'This isn't Trenton, is it, Mac?' I didn't know exactly what to say, so I blurted out, 'Or Brooklyn either, Mike.' Mike was from Manhattan, but he didn't correct me. He handed me a cigarette and we dropped down beneath the squad truck and lit up. This very act was what we needed and we chatted amicably about nothing in particular.

Ten minutes later we approached the shore and looking over the side we could see that we had already taken prisoners. A group of them, under guard, were at work carrying ammunition from a landing craft to the shore. The water around us was cluttered with debris – crates, life belts, discarded clothing, an orange, a haversack, a book, several K Rations – and several bodies. They were floating face downwards and were American.

With a jar, the LCT struck bottom. I climbed up on the hood of the squad truck and peered over the tailgate of the LCT. We were still about 100 yards from shore. In between was the fouled up shoreline waters of the Channel. Landing craft, trucks, jeeps, auxiliary craft, artillery pieces, launches and just plain junk littered the waters. Since it was impossible to go ashore here, we pulled back and made another try a little farther down. We hit with a jar again, still too far out for an effective landing. We made a third try and a salvo of 88s all but blew us out of the water. This convinced the navy officer in charge of the LCT that we would have to wait for high tide to land.

By this time we were so anxious to set our feet on land that we fought a desire to swim ashore, pack and all. We floated around for about half an hour, then something happened to change the officer's mind. Two Jerry planes broke out of the clouds and dropped a couple of bombs just a little too close for comfort – so close that pieces of shrapnel hit the LCT and a huge wave almost swamped us. In no time at all, we were headed back for the shore. This time we managed to get a little closer and the ramp was lowered. All of our vehicles had been waterproofed, so Captain Smith ordered the driver of the first jeep to take off.

The jeep made the short run down the ramp and hit the water. Down it went until the driver was forced to stand on the seat to keep his head above water. If he could have kept his foot on the accelerator and his hands on the wheel, he could have driven to shallower water and thence to shore. As it was a rope had to be tossed to him and he was dragged back into the boat. The bulldozer, with its higher seat, also became stranded.

The LCT pulled back and made a new run for shore, getting about twenty feet closer. Captain Smith ordered his men to try for the shore. Not knowing how deep the water was at that point, we were a little apprehensive. 'Go ahead, McIntyre, you're first,' he said. I said, 'Yes, sir-r-r-r,' and made a running jump from the end of the boat. Just as I was about to sink from sight, my feet struck bottom. For a moment I couldn't gain traction and floundered around. Finally, my toes dug into the shifting sand and I started for dry land, with just my head and rifle above the water.

I never knew what cold water was until that moment. Looking back, I could see the others had plunged into the swirling surf. It was a long, cold walk to the shore and each of my legs weighed a ton by the time I reached it. I was supposed to dash up the beach, like they do in the movies, but I was so tired that all I could do was stagger up.

Who is the first person I meet when I finally make it? A military policeman, yellow banded helmet and all. As a joke, I started to head back to the Channel, but I didn't go far as Mike was just behind me and together we went back up the beach.

'How did you get here so soon?' I asked the MP.

He laughed and answered: 'I'm a leftover from the last war, mac.'[4]

Pfc William E. Jones, aged 25, 1 Company, 8th Infantry Regiment, 4th Division:

As soon as we hit the beach there was a sign sticking up all along the beach '*Achtung Minen*!' That meant it was a minefield we were fixing to go through. But we were the spearhead outfit, we were first, so we pushed through the engineers on the beach. We hit a single column across that minefield and went over and didn't bother with it. I don't really know if it was a minefield or not. It probably was. We didn't have time to check it out.

The Germans had flooded a big area in behind the beaches. There were big canals, or drainage ditches, filled with water. We were trying to get across that thing. They had one little old road that led across to a little old village and one of our Sherman tanks had come up and was trying to cross that thing. It hit a mine and caught on fire and blew up and killed everybody on the thing. One of the crew was hanging outside the hatch, dead.

We passed him up and went on. Whoever could get on that road did and the rest of us swam across those ditches. We got to this little old village, maybe a dozen houses. French people, of course, lived there. Us being there was as big a surprise as anything in the world to those people. They didn't really know how to take us, I guess. One man started to run and we hollered for him to halt. He didn't halt and one of our men shot him and left him there.

We were going to search those houses. I remember one house a couple of us went in and hollered, trying to tell them to come out. We didn't know any French. Nobody came out. We took a rifle butt and knocked the door in. I threw a grenade in the door, stepped back and waited until it exploded. Then we went on in.

There was a man, three or four women and two or three kids in that room. The only damage done was that the old man had a cut on his cheek. It was just a piece of luck that they didn't all get killed.

We left that village and were trying to get to higher ground. As we started up our first hill, I decided that the big satchel charge packed with ten pounds of RDX explosive was killing me, so I set that thing down in a hedgerow and left it there. I always wondered if some Frenchman ever stuck a plow into that thing – he would be in orbit. That stuff packed a wallop you would not believe.[5]

Tom Treanor, war correspondent, Los Angeles Times:

I hit the beach myself early during D-Day. The coastguard cutter on which I was stationed went close inshore to pull aboard some men who had capsized in a DUKW. They came aboard shivering and shaking with cold and as soon as they got below, proceeded to get sea-sick all over the place. I ceased interviewing them then and asked my skipper, Lieutenant Raymond Rosenbloom of Baltimore, if he would hail a passing landing craft inward bound to the beach and put me aboard. The transfer was made and my new skipper, Lieutenant Edward Raymond, said, 'I don't think we can get in. It is all these obstacles that are messing the thing up before we even get to the beach.' I couldn't see any obstacles. 'That's the trouble,' he said, 'neither can we. The tide is running high and they're covered. Those are heavy posts, driven into the sand with boobytraps attached. At low tide, we can avoid them. At high tide, you see,' he pointed at various landing craft up and down the beach which had been stove in and now swung idly back and forth with the surf. 'They got it,' he said.

We piled up the coast a mile, looking for an opening, and then heard a loud-hailer behind us. A sleek looking patrol craft slid by and the skipper shouted, 'Hold off! Don't put your craft ashore until you get further orders!' 'Now what?' I asked Raymond. 'We'll see if we can get you on something smaller,' he said. He got out his loud-hailer and called a landing-craft personnel, which was heading in to the beach. Motor machinist mate John Kramer of Albany, New York and Seaman First Class Jack Whitney of Columbus, Ohio, took me aboard. 'OK,' said Kramer and Whitney, 'let's go keep an eye out for the trap.' We came sliding and slewing in on some light breakers and grounded.

I stepped ashore on France, walking up a beach where men were moving casually about carrying equipment inshore. Up the coast a few hundred yards, German shells were pounding in regularly but in our area, it was peacefully busy. 'How did you make out?' I asked one of the men. 'It was reasonably soft,' he said. 'The Germans had some machine-gun posts and some high velocity guns on the pallisades which made it a little hot at first. They waited until the landing craft dropped their ramps and then they opened up on them while the men were still inside. In a few cases we took heavy casualties, but then the navy went to work on the German guns and it wasn't long before they were quiet.'

The general lack of fortifications at this point was astonishing. The barbed wire consisted of four single strands, such as we use at home to fence in cattle. A man could get through by pushing down on one wire and lifting up on another, providing they weren't booby-trapped. The engineers and beach battalions had blown gaps in the wire through which we could drive vehicles. A few dead lay about and some wounded were here and there on stretchers, awaiting transfer to ships at sea.

All the way up and down the broad beach as far as I could see, men, jeeps, bulldozers and other equipment were moving about like ants. A few columns of black, greasy smoke marked equipment which had been hit by shell fire and set afire. The German shelling continued steadily at various points up and down the beach but had so far not reached the area in which I was walking. It would work over an area and then move on to another. It was accurate, landing for the most part close to the water's edge, and I saw one small landing craft catch fire after taking a hit. Men came spilling out of it into water waist-deep. From time to time there were huge concussions as the engineers set off demolitions. The ground would shake and the troops would throw themselves violently on the ground. I climbed a rock embankment and came to a piece of flat land where hundreds of men were digging slit trenches. When they got down about a foot and a half, they struck water. Some of them were lying in the water and I asked if there was much shelling. 'There is when there is,' one man said. 'Now there isn't. But when it comes, it sure comes.' I asked him what German fortifications he could point out. He showed me some tunnels at the top of the pallisade which rises above the beach along this stretch of coast. There were five or six positions I could make out, nothing particularly formidable.[6]

Michael Jennings, aged 18, seaman/wireman, Royal Navy, on LCT 795:

When our turn came to go in it felt like all the practice runs we had been through. My job was to brake the drum on the kedge anchor cable and it all seemed routine.

As we approached I looked above the armour protection to see what was going on. Craft were landing and discharging transports and men amidst occasional splashes in the sea. In my ignorance I thought these were underwater obstacles being blown up by the engineers. They were, in fact, shells from a German battery which was getting its range from our anti-aircraft balloons.

We should have unloaded and backed off the beach, but due to the flatness the tide ran out, leaving us high and dry. With all the troops ashore the skipper opened up the rum and I had a large neat tot along with the others, even though I was under-age.

This seemed to make the day much more pleasant until there was a loud bang close by and something whizzed past our heads. Some shrapnel holes had been made in the winch housing forward and suddenly the effect of the rum wore off.

We decided it would be safer ashore, so we left the craft and ran, dropping whenever a shell burst. We jumped into a trench with an American soldier chewing gum, who asked us if we were commandos. Our reply was that we were sailors waiting to get out as fast as we could.

The soldier shared a choc bar with us from his K rations and when more shells landed nearby, my shipmate 'Lofty' stood up and shouted that he was going to write to Congress about it, which got a laugh from the Americans. Some of the lads went off and found a dead German near a bunker and brought back his Very pistol and helmet with holes in it. I wondered who he was, and thought of his family.

When the tide began to come in we got back on board, started the engines and pulled off the beach.[7]

Major John L. Ahearn, aged 30, commander C Company, 70th Tank Battalion:

When we got inside the sea wall, we proceeded laterally between the sea wall and the road, where we saw a number of infantrymen from the 2nd Battalion of the 8th Division, who were going northward. As we looked down towards the south, we saw another German strongpoint and, although we saw no activity there, I had our tanks fire some shells into it.

With this, a number of Germans came out with their hands in the air and began running towards us. So I dismounted from my tank to take them prisoner and as I did so a most unusual thing happened. (I shouldn't really say most unusual, because a similar thing happened to me in Sicily.) As I got out of the tank and began to approach them, they began yelling at me and gesturing me to stay still, yelling '*Achtung Minen!*' I gestured to them to move toward the road and the tanks moved toward the road and I delivered these thirty-odd prisoners to the infantry.

Along with a couple of other tanks I continued to proceed down this rather narrow road, across the dunes and hedgerows, to see if there were any further strongpoints that we might assault. Shortly after this my tank hit a land mine and the front left bogie was blown, immobilizing it. I radioed this information to Lieutenant Tighe, one of my junior officers, and then proceeded on foot to see if there was anything we might take a look at.

At this time I heard cries for help and looking towards the beach I saw three figures who I surmised were injured paratroopers. I immediately returned to the tank and got the first aid kit and tried to cross the hedgerows to get as close to them as I could. I was going through a break in the hedgerow when a personnel mine went off under me.

The explosion threw me into the hedgerow and I was unconscious for a while. Subsequently I wakened and heard two of my crew yelling for me. It was hard to find me, because I had rolled up against the embankment, but when they did I cautioned them not to come over because of the presence of mines. (I later learned there were some 15,000 mines in that vicinity, so the odds were not very good that I was not going to be harmed.)

Anyway, they went back to the tank and got a long rope and threw the rope to me and then dragged me out from the hedgerow. Subsequent to that time my memory is a little bit fuzzy as to how I got back to the field hospital, but I do know that I was on stretchers and on jeeps and that I was transferred from one group to another before I finally arrived at the hospital.

During that night, it was decided I would need surgery. I had heavy paratroop boots on and both feet, I guess, were terribly mangled and they decided they would have to operate on me. Before this I had been given about six bottles of plasma and had been visited by the chaplain.

Then, in the early evening, in this makeshift tent with white sheets covering the walls, I was operated on. A decision was made that they would just amputate the one foot because they felt I would not be able to withstand both operations. So during the night the one foot was amputated and I was prepared for transport back to England.[8]

CHAPTER SEVENTEEN

THEY'RE HERE!

For the French people in Normandy, the day of liberation was also a day of terror as the massive naval bombardment battered the coast, then swarms of Allied bombers launched mass attacks on the major towns in the path of the planned Allied advance . . .

Madame d'Anselm, Asnelles:

We had dug a little trench in the garden, just big enough to shelter the eight of us and a couple of others. It was not very well protected, or covered. When the bombing attacks started we were in the house, but it was so bad that we had to go into the garden and take refuge in the trench, which was fortunate because the windows and parts of the house were soon smashed. Then, somewhere between three and four o'clock, two of the children took advantage of a pause to go back to the house to fetch something. One of them seized the opportunity to climb onto the garden wall to see what was happening. There was a German gun just the other side of the garden wall. Suddenly he shouted excitedly. 'Mummy! Mummy! Look, the sea – it's black with boats!'[1]

Jean Deslandes, aged 14, son of the baker at Lion-sur-Mer:

It was impossible to sleep, everyone kept their clothes on and was outdoors or at the windows. The planes buzzed round in circles, ceaselessly. The sky was being swept by anti-aircraft fire. Everyone was asking each other what was going on. No one knew, naturally, about the release of parachutists on Ranville and its surroundings.

Come the dawn, the news poured out: countless ships on the sea. I climbed into the loft and I saw clearly this armada of ships. A state of nerves and of fear. Shoppers arrived to buy as much bread as they could and hurried to get back home. Everything went very quickly. The fishermen who were watching the ships from a distance saw them line up and turn towards the coast. 'Hurry up, hurry up and get in your shelters, it's the big one and it is coming our way.' A neighbour of ours, a veteran of Verdun, had dug a trench for his family and ours and that was where we huddled together, thirteen of us, two of whom were the wounded of 14/18.

Through the morning and midday hours we crouched in the dug-out, which was little more than a tube sealed at either end with a piece of cloth. From time to time, during respites in the bombing, M. Legal and M. Lecoutillet, the two ex-servicemen who guarded the two ends of the ditch, would stick their heads up and report on the damage. 'Madame Deslandes, your building has taken a hit. No roof on those buildings at the bottom.' M. Lecoutillet said, 'Yes, my place as well. The chimney has gone and taken a piece of the roof with it.'

Later, much later, when we were all tightly pressed together waiting for death, a complete silence fell. The two veterans understood its meaning: the infantry was about to arrive.

We climbed out of the ditch just as the first commandos arrived, wearing not helmets but green berets on their heads, their faces blacked up. Seeing us, they stopped. With emphatic gestures, we warned them that the Germans were not far away. 'They're waiting for you down there,' we told them and we showed them the château, which was about forty metres away.

The Germans had seen us and a violent fusillade followed. The commandos melted away and we threw ourselves into the trench. A few more minutes and we heard the report of a rifle and a bullet shot into the trench. 'They want to kill us!' screamed M. Legal. Another shot, another bullet. 'I'm going outside,' said M. Legal and as he did so, the German who had fired was standing less than five metres away. He pulled a grenade from the turn-up of his boot. 'Civilians, women and children,' shouted our friend.

'Everybody out,' came the order and soon we were surrounded, pistols pointed at our chests, rifles in our backs. 'You traitors, you spies! Give us the information,' said one of the officers, adding some incomprehensible words.

'We saw you! You, go and stand by that post.' Fortunately for us, it was only the *Wehrmacht* and the sight of two wounded ex-servicemen and a baby calmed the officer in charge who was chasing us with a resounding '*Raus.*' We left at a run.

A few metres further on, I saw the first dead soldier. It was a commando who was killed scaling a slope. In one hand he still carried a rifle, in the other, the branch of a tree.[2]

Pierre Cardron, aged 40, baker, Ste Marie-du-Mont:

I had to bake 100 loaves every night for the village, all over a wood fire, and it was very difficult to work with the grey flour, which was all we could get in those days.

A German had been billeted in our house but he left forty-eight hours before the invasion. He used to listen to the BBC with me every night. One day he told me that he and some other soldiers had been up in the steeple of the church looking at a map with all the batteries marked on it when the wind had suddenly blown it away. They saw it float down into the village square but by the time they got there it had gone. He said it was a bad day for the Third Reich and of course I commiserated with him. I did not tell him I knew all about the map and that it had immediately been passed on to the Resistance.

On the night of June 5 I heard planes and I thought at first it must be Germans flying from Carpiquet. I opened the window to hear better and saw paratroopers coming down. I ran upstairs to wake my wife.

At around five-thirty we heard a lot of shooting. We didn't dare go out. I went upstairs to see my son, who was in bed because he had had his tonsils taken out the day before. I looked out of the first-floor window, still wearing my white baker's hat, and saw an American parachutist pointing a gun at me. I think he must have thought I was a medic from my hat.

At seven o'clock M. Le Caplin walked in. He was a guard at the railway station at Carentan and had just come off night duty. He kissed me and said, 'They're here! They're here! They've landed, and if you don't believe me, here's an American cigarette.'

He said he had cycled four times across German and American

lines and so we did not know who was in control. At 7.30 my wife saw four Americans being marched down the road as POWs and we thought, 'Damn! The Germans are back.' But then a German jeep came down the road with two men in it and a paratrooper in the steeple of the church opened fire and killed them both.

At ten o'clock the Americans arrived in the village centre. I threw my arms around them and cried. Then I helped them look for the remaining Germans. I opened a slab leading down into the cellar of the church and they dropped hand grenades in there. Then somebody noticed a movement of the red curtains across the confession box. Underneath they saw two pairs of boots. A paratrooper yanked the curtain aside and there were two seventeen-year-old Germans, white as sheets and trembling.[3]

Jean-Pierre Fauvel, aged 18, resident of Vernière-sur-Mer:

I lived in my parents' house about 200 metres from the sea. It was in a *zone inderdit*, a forbidden area, only open to people who lived there. Heavy artillery fire began about six o'clock and lasted for about an hour and the few Germans who were in the village left very rapidly on motor bikes. Then, at about 7.30, we heard one of our neighbours shouting, 'It's the English! It's the English!' Sure enough, there were soldiers running up along the entire length of the wall of the house. They were either English or Canadian. They said absolutely nothing at all to us, I think they were rather surprised to find civilians in the area. They laid down or crouched behind the wall; some were poking into the ground with their bayonets, looking for mines.

Our first reaction was to go down to the beach to see what was happening and we set off down a path, but were stopped by some English soldiers who said we could not go any further. I remember they took photographs of us.

At about nine o'clock armoured tanks appeared in a field close by. I invited one of the English officers to come into our house to get a view of what was going on from the upstairs window. He was very suspicious, took out his pistol and made me walk in front of him as we went up the stairs. After looking round for several minutes, we came back downstairs again.

The soldiers were very well informed with detailed maps marked with the exact positions they were to occupy at the moment of invasion. They came ashore fully equipped and even brought their own drinking water because they were afraid the wells would be poisoned. We lit a fire to boil some water and the English officer offered us tea and biscuits.

By eleven o'clock most of the houses in the village, ours included, had been damaged by shelling and almost all the animals in the fields had been killed. There was a thick smell of gunpowder in the air and there was a continual dreadful noise of guns firing, tanks and lorries going by and all the time more and more soldiers. The field opposite our house was turned into a prisoner-of-war camp and the entire length of the main road through Vernière was choked with tanks and trucks, one behind the other. The sea was black with ships trailing barrage balloons. It was a beautiful sight.[4]

Raymond Paris, aged 20, assistant to the notary, Ste Mère-Eglise:

At dawn, or perhaps half-an-hour before dawn, we saw an aeroplane coming from the east, flying extremely low and apparently damaged by flak. We could hear no motor, simply the sound of the wind passing the wings. About four or five hours later, a woman who was in the courtyard and who was a baker announced that she was going to start baking for the day. She walked down the corridor to the front door and within minutes she was back, saying that the streets and the square were full of soldiers and they weren't Germans.

Rather suspicious, we did not go straight out into the street, but went upstairs to the bedrooms, opened the windows and looked out and saw that, indeed, the streets and the square were filled with a large number of soldiers. Two things struck us immediately. We had not heard them marching – we were used to the sound of marching from the presence of the German soldiers – and the other thing was the smell of blond tobacco, of which, as you can imagine, we had been deprived. It was most agreeable.

As the soldiers appeared to be making friendly signs, this encouraged us to go downstairs and outside onto the street. Very quickly we established that the soldiers were Americans, which we could see from the flags sewn onto their upper sleeves. Everyone was very moved by this, especially when we considered that every one of those boys had come all the way across the Atlantic and the Channel just to land in Ste Mère.

We wanted to speak to them, naturally, but I left school at twelve and most of my comrades were like me and we had none of us learned any foreign languages. While this was going on we saw a car driving up the road towards us. Now none of us had seen a car for ages, because of fuel rationing, and no one had seen anything like this one and no wonder, because it was a jeep, the first ever. We naturally were surprised to see it and more than curious how it had got there. We later learned it had arrived by glider.

It is the custom here to brew Calvados so my father and our neighbour, M. Leclair, brought the Calvados out into the street to toast the Americans, who were keen to drink but, because they were not entirely trusting, insisted that my father or M. Leclair drank first. This was not to continue for long, because the first dozen or so soldiers enjoyed it so much that they told their friends to come and try it and soon a queue formed.

I crossed the road to see if I could find the body of the parachutist we had found the previous night. I went to the spot where we had left him under the canopy, but there was no body to be seen. Not far from where I stood were three abandoned German lorries, fuelled by gazogene, which the Germans had clearly not been able to start up quickly and had simply left. Sitting on the running board of one of them there was a parachutist, relaxing. He called to me and I was very surprised that he spoke perfect French. He saw my surprise and explained that he was from Louisiana. Needless to say, I had no idea why anybody in Louisiana should speak French.

He asked me what I was looking for and I explained how we had found the body of one of his comrades the previous evening and that it had disappeared. He laughed and told me that it was him. What had happened was that he had received a bullet in the shoulder and he realized that if he moved even slightly, the German would shoot him in the head to make sure he was dead, so he played dead. When he heard me and my father approaching that night, he had no idea if we were French or German, so he continued to pretend to be dead.

We talked for a while and then I went off to look at the site where the house had been burning the previous night. The two dead parachutists were still suspended from the trees. When I got back to the square, my friend had gone and I never saw him again; I never knew what became of him.

At this time all was calm and everybody got their flags out and draped their houses – Ste Mère was *en fête*. Some people said that everywhere from Cherbourg to Bayeux was liberated and everyone was feeling very optimistic and joyful. This calm lasted until about

8.15 a.m. when the Americans made it clear to us that they were expecting a counter-attack by the Germans.

In the two minutes that followed, the first shells began to fall and explode. My parents gathered together what little food there was, covers, a little money and a few precious objects and we went to hide out in the trench which I had dug at the bottom of the garden. In order to reach it, we had to cross the courtyard, our own garden and a neighbour's garden. When we reached the trench, our neighbours had already arrived and dug in. I had, at the time, a sister of fourteen years and a small brother, Gérard, who was only sixteen months old.

Within a few minutes the bombardment had become so intense that I swear there were fifty shells exploding a minute; I do not exaggerate. It was absolutely terrible, they were coming from all sides, all concentrating on Ste Mère. We were in the trench for about half an hour when my mother suddenly said she hadn't brought any milk for the baby and I said, 'Right, I'll go back to the house and find some milk.'

There were periods of lesser bombardment. You see, we had the impression that the Germans were systematically bombarding and destroying the town, section by section and as they finished shelling one section, they moved on to the one next door. In those in-between periods the shells seemed to explode rather less intensively around us and it was in one of those periods that I ran into the house to look for some milk for my brother. I was standing by the table trying to pour the milk into a bottle when suddenly there was a terrific explosion in the street outside. You understand there were lots of explosions going on all the time, but none of them was very close. This was right in front of the house and all the roof tiles fell down into the house.

In the wake of the explosion, I heard women wailing. I went to the door to investigate and realized the sound was coming from the house opposite ours. However, remembering what my father had told me about shells during the war of 1914–18, that another could follow swiftly, I turned and made for the trench at the back of the garden to rejoin the family.

At this moment, however, the Germans had decided to start saturating our sector of the town with shells and in the time it took me to cross the courtyard to the trench, some ten or fifteen shells exploded in my immediate vicinity. At this point I had learned to recognize when and where shells would explode by the sound they made. If the whistling noise was thin and shrill, they would explode some distance away; if the sound was muffled and low, they would explode close by. So, when I started to cross the garden, I heard a shell coming close by and threw myself to the ground, still holding onto the bottle of milk. I was lying on the central path, close to a framework of climbing peas and it exploded in a pear tree about fifteen metres away from me, ripping it out of the ground. I continued running to the trench and I had hardly gone ten metres when a second shell exploded behind my back. I threw myself to the ground and when I looked back, I saw the pea frame had completely disintegrated. The shell had exploded more or less on the spot where I had been lying.

When I got into the trench I was overcome by a fit of violent trembling, retrospective fear, I suppose, such that I wrapped my arms around myself to try to stop it. The trembling ceased minutes later when our neighbour ran into the courtyard screaming that her husband was dead. I left the trench, accompanied her to her house, and discovered that her husband had been killed in his shop by the explosion out in the street. His chest had been crushed and his right arm was missing, but worst of all his cranium had split open and his brain was lying two or three metres away from his body. I was dreadfully upset and frightened. I could hardly bear it, as one who cannot stand the sight even of an injection. I had to do something for the family. I dragged his body over onto a small couch, but I knew I had to do something about the brain which was just lying there. I took a salad bowl which happened to be handy and with some shards of glass picked up the brain, put it in the salad bowl and pushed it under the divan.

Back in the trench, branches of trees had fallen on to us as a result of the many different explosions. We sent up many prayers for deliverance and told our beads with great energy.[5]

André Lebreton, aged 22, member of La Resistance de l'Orne:

On the night of the invasion I was working making illicit alcohol, Calvados, in a still in the barn of a friend. At about 5.30 in the morning the ground began to tremble and we realized that there was a massive bombardment going on in the direction of Caen. I went into the house and all the glasses and crockery were rattling. We didn't know what was going on, but it was obviously something more than just a bombing raid.

The farmer turned on the radio, hoping for news, but there was none for a long time. Then at 8.30 we tuned in to the BBC and learned that the invasion had begun. There were no other details and I was very disappointed; so great was my faith in the Allies that I expected to hear talk of victory in the first minutes of the broadcast.

I decided to stop work and make contact with my Resistance chief. I felt it was absolutely crucial to get orders, to do something to help. I got on my bicycle and set out for Flers, but about two kilometres from the farm, I spotted a Mercedes with four Germans in it, hidden under the foliage in a copse of trees. The driver was sitting at the wheel; the other three must have been staff officers and were in vehement debate, all smoking furiously. I was able to distinguish an olive-green trouser leg with a red stripe. It was clearly someone of superior rank and his head was bandaged. The others were wearing the tall caps of Nazi officers.

I took in all these details and decided it was the moment for action. I had no orders, no precise instructions, but I felt I had to do something. I had a slight case of the jitters, but my mind was made up. I knew there was a cache of weapons back at the farm. I returned on my bicycle, found the weapon store, took a rifle and loaded it. I set out once again, hoping to find a place where I could conceal myself and shoot the Nazis.

All kinds of ideas were churning in my head, but when I reached the brow of the hill I realized I was too late – the car had disappeared. I was disappointed, yes, but also in some perhaps cowardly way I was also relieved. I realized that it was not all that easy, and rightly so, to be a killer.[6]

Leaflet dropped by Allied aircraft:

Urgent message from the Supreme Allied Commander of the Expeditionary Force to the inhabitants of this town. If the common enemy is to be vanquished, the Allied Air Force must attack all centres of transport as well as all the enemy's vital ways and means of communication. Orders to this effect have been issued.

Read this leaflet. You are located either in or near a centre which is essential to the enemy to achieve the movement of its forces and supplies. The target area near which you are situated will be intensively bombarded.

It is vital that you and your family distance yourselves without delay in the next few days and move out of the danger zone in which you live.

Do not encumber the roads. Disperse into the countryside as swiftly as possible.

Leave for the countryside. You do not have a moment to lose.[7]

Madame Helene Hurel, resident of Caen:

Towards midnight I woke up, like everyone else, because of the dull sounds from the direction of the coast. Nobody was ever really surprised by this because we had suffered bombing raids nearly every day for several months. Meanwhile, the noise was growing hour by hour, the windows were rattling and you could see the Allied fighters by the jagged light in the sky. All along the ridge, which overlooked us, you could see blackish smoke clouds rising into the sky. The white heads of small balloons passed over the surrounding heights. The vibrations of the raid grew stronger and stronger.

All over the neighbourhood, windows flew open, the shutters clattered and opinions were aired. There was no question of it: the landing had obviously occurred.

At 4 a.m. we all got up and bundled down to the cellar. Despite four years of waiting, nothing was ready – well, virtually nothing. Cupboards and chests were emptied in no time at all as bursting suitcases were piled up. The bathtub was filled with water as well as all available bottles. Activity was at its height.

The radio, listened to at 5.30, 6.30 and 7.30 a.m., gave out not one detail. Only opinions flowed, the principal one being that 'a new phase of the airborne offensive' had just started. 'Please evacuate towns and villages within thirty-five kilometres of the coastline and as far as possible you will be warned of any raids.'

Eventually, at 8.30 a.m., the announcer stated that 'the Grand Quartier general informs you that Allied troops have begun operations to land in the North of France.' Now the North of France for us was Pas de Calais, so surely not our region. The streets of Caen were full of people, each with a bit of a smile despite their anxiety. The noise was deafening. Electricity, water, gas, telephone – everything was cut off. Cars were driving at a most unfamiliar speed, no one showed up at work or few did. It seemed that life as we knew it was brusquely suspended.

Despite the bombing raids and the restrictions on going out, lots of people came to the town in order to find bread. Nobody had thought to lay in stocks as a consequence of the obligatory closing times of Sundays and Mondays.

It was about four in the afternoon and a few folks were gathered at our entrance gate, where there was lots of talk and discussions. Our neighbour, Madame Legrain, was determined to go out and look for bread, despite the reservations of her daughter, Antoinette. As for us, we decided to go around to another neighbour, Madame Vancoppenolle. We had hardly crossed her threshold when there was a horrendous drumming of heavy motors. Madame Gournay with her son and her mother dashed for the shelter under the stairs. The earth shook and through the window by the light of an explosion we saw the aeroplanes and their bombs falling to the ground, causing an apalling impact. Mother and I joined the others at the back of the room. Monsieur Gournay and Monsieur Vancoppenolle threw themselves to the floor. The whole company trembled as they prayed. Then came a second wave of bombers, more explosions and then silence.

Those of us who had relatives in town went to look for them in a state of great anxiety, seeking news of them. Mostly they found each other but Antoinette arrived at the house and threw herself into my arms. 'I've lost my mother,' she cried. 'I'll never see her again.' I did not come to that conclusion necessarily, but a little while later a covered handcart arrived with the body of poor Madame Legrain. There were no more coffins to be had, so M. Legrain made a coffin from wood he found around his place. The coffin was carried to the bottom of the garden and put into the ditch dug that very morning at the request of Madame Legrain.[8]

André Heintz, aged 24, student, member of the Resistance in Caen:

My sister was a nurse in the improvised hospital – a former lunatic asylum where Beau Brummel had once been confined – and as she helped the surgeons who were already hard at work, operating on British soldiers as well as civilians, several bombs fell on one of the wards near her, killing some patients, and she realized that something had to be done to warn the Allies that the building was being used as a hospital. By then two other hospitals had been hit, all the firemen in the city had been killed and their equipment lost, and the only place where coffins could be made had been destroyed.

We wanted to do something quickly. Painting red crosses on the building would have taken too long and finding the paint itself was a problem. We decided to look for the red carpets that were usually laid out in church for weddings but could not find the key or anyone who could help us. So my sister decided to take four of the big sheets that had been used in the operating theatre and were already smeared with blood. We dipped them into pails of blood that stood there and went to spread them in the hospital garden.

As we were spreading the fourth sheet to make the fourth arm of the cross, a small plane came down. We thought it was going to strafe us and we were tempted to abandon the job and run into hiding, but we decided to risk finishing our cross. Then we noticed that it was a spotter plane and that it was waggling its wings to let us know it had seen the red cross.[9]

Madame Pernelle, resident of Hérouville-St-Clair, near Caen:

It was 13.20 hours and a squadron of planes was approaching overhead. Bombs whistled and exploded quite close to us. I pressed myself up against a nearby wall. Things were falling all around us, everything was upside down. There was a second's lull and then the explosions shook the facades of the buildings and there was a wild rush of the population to the ditches.

People were carrying more or less what had fallen into their hands – suitcases, coats, blankets. Men and women carried small, crying children in their arms. A young neighbour of ours shouted in horror, 'They're going to wreck my house!' A clamour arose, 'Get to the shelters, get to the shelters.'

The residents of the bombed areas milled around. There were twenty of us in our trench, including a tiny baby with curly hair, carried by its parents. One couple were with their elderly mother, of whom they took absolutely no notice. The poor old thing cried out and groaned at each noise. A young woman whose husband was a prisoner in Germany called out 'Mother' and shouted furiously at each bomb as it fell.

One sensed that she was at the edge of a crisis. My husband, Robert, said briskly to her, 'That's enough shrieking now. If you don't stop immediately, I'll slap you.' She was instantly silent. It was plain that such brutality was quite appropriate to prevent panic breaking out.

Later that day I moved to a shelter in Caen which was being bombarded without a pause by ships anchored off Ouistreham. By then, the explosions were very close indeed. I felt a violent shockwave and the walls of the trench began to cave in behind my back and I was hit by a torrent of blinding, suffocating dirt. I shouted out, 'That's it,' and freed my head from the morass. There were cries close to us. I disentangled myself from the grasp of the old lady who was shouting, 'Pull me out of here,' and Robert and I went to the help of others. There were three people laid out, covered by dirt and slabs of cement. These were enormous and very heavy . . .

Another shell exploded and in the light I saw the face of one of my neighbours, quite close and obviously dead. I quickly put my blanket over her body, to avoid the horror that would ensue. Later that day, Robert looked at me anxiously and asked if I was wounded. My dress, from the shoulder to the hem, was covered with a thick streak of earth which had stuck to something glutinous – it was blood. Then I realized what had happened. The woman had been killed by a huge piece of cement falling on her chest and the blood had jetted from her mouth and covered me from head to foot.[10]

Madame Pierre Quaire, a resident of Caen:

We had just sat down at the table to eat when the explosions began. Through the window, we could see the town in flames. Thick smoke extended everywhere and in the distance we could hear a growing noise. All our appetites had gone, so we abandoned the meal. M. Battu of the Civil Defence came to our house, asking us if we had any water. It was important, he said.

Later the refugees began to appear, fleeing towards the heights of the town. There were people in slippers and dressing-gowns, carrying suitcases and bundles of clothes. We tried to help them, but I was fearfully tired and the baby I was expecting was kicking me with some violence. I had to stretch out on my bed for a while and I had hardly done so when I heard the sound of a wave of aeroplanes, getting closer and closer, a vast and menacing sound. 'Quick, quick, everyone downstairs,' shouted Pierre. We dragged Mamie, who could barely walk, and there we were, tightly pressed against each other under the stairs, listening to the bombs falling closer and closer. The house rattled, the children cried. Then there was another bomb, even closer, and everything went black. For a second or two, we thought we were dead, stupefied by the noise, the fear, the dark and the dust. Then we began to breathe again. We were all alive but I had started to haemorrhage. I knew we had to leave. We crept out and saw an armchair suspended in the telegraph wires, along with curtains and bits of paper. 'That's it,' I said. 'It's the end. We've got to get out of here.'[11]

CHAPTER EIGHTEEN

IS IT THE LANDING?

While German soldiers manning defences along the Normandy coast fought bravely to repel the invasion, they fought alone; the High Command refused to commit reserve divisions to the battle for fear that the operation was a feint and that the real invasion was still to come . . .

Obergefreite Heinrich Severloh, aged 20, 1st Battery, 352 Infantry Division:

We had stages of alarm. The highest was 'imminent danger' and that was given at midnight. This was definitely it. When you got the highest alert, you knew there was no possibility of it being false. We got our stuff together and drove off to the shoreline; it took about half-an-hour. We just stood around in the trenches, it was still night and we weren't expecting any light until about four o'clock. There were about eighteen of us on that stretch of one kilometre.

I know that I was the first to see the ships. They were mine-sweepers, I saw the silhouettes and they were about ten kilometres out to sea. We didn't realize it then that the Allies had created artificial fog, but in one spot, the fog had lifted and you could see ships. I called to the Oberleutnant and said, 'Sir, there are ships out there.' But when he came to where I was, the hole had already closed and the fog had thickened again. But he had caught a glimpse of them although it was still very, very dark.

When the fog finally disappeared in the early morning there was what looked like a city out there, ship upon ship upon ship. You could not see the water between them. It defied description; there were no words for it. Bombers flew overhead and started dropping bombs near us and the naval artillery opened up. I cannot describe how it was. You couldn't tell what was exploding because you couldn't hear anything any more.

Then the first landing craft arrived and the soldiers got off and it was only when we saw that they were not wearing flat English helmets that we realized they were Americans. Then we saw the white strip on the front of their helmets and recognized the 1st Division.

Diagonally opposite to where I stood was not a landing craft as such but some kind of ship I had never seen before. It was a largish ship, and on either side were steps down to the water wide enough for men to come down them side by side. They seemed to be heading exactly in my direction at a distance of about 250 to 300 metres.

We had to hold our ground. We had two mortars and a number of grenade launchers and machine guns and so we started firing. Very few survivors came off that first Allied ship because at that stage all our weapons were functioning properly. Shortly afterwards, other craft landed but they were smaller. The time seemed to go very quickly, I can only remember looking at my watch once. Then ammunition began to run out. At the depot in Houteville, there was nothing left. We had about fifty rounds left in the barrel of the machine gun and I believe Oberleutnant Freagin also had about fifty rounds.

We retreated up onto the cliffside, it was bushy and on fire. It was all uphill and in doing that climb we found ourselves directly in the firing line of the American infantry. We were crouching in foxholes and the impact of the firing was so violent that the ground shook. I was not exactly afraid, I just didn't feel very well. In those days we could all still pray and that is what I did.

As I was running from that position I was wounded, one shot in the hip, the second in the face. Although I was in a great deal of pain, I was still mobile after a fashion. I had caught the bullet on the hip bone and it had entered through the pocket where I kept my pay book and letters. It was absolutely forbidden to carry your papers and paybook into battle, but if I hadn't had them on me, I don't think I would have survived.

At the battery commander's post, I received injections or some kind of pills because I no longer felt any pain. I must have been lying there for an hour or so, when the commander, a major, asked me if I was fit enough to guard three American prisoners that had been taken. I had thrown my machine gun away, so I took a carbine from one of the prisoners and sat in front of the bunker guarding them. A fourth prisoner was brought and I remember he came from Texas because he had TEX written on his battledress jacket. He had been shot in the chest and the bullet had pierced his lungs. I still had four cigarettes which I shared with the prisoners and even he smoked one.

One of the prisoners could speak German and said, 'When are you going to shoot us?' I told him that I wasn't even allowed to touch him and if I did worse I would be punished instantly. I asked him where he came from and how come he spoke German. He said he came from Uelzen, not far from my home. His father had had a farm and he wanted to marry a particular woman but his parents objected because she was a servant, so the two eloped to Hamburg and sailed to America.[1]

Gefreite Joseph Haeger, aged 19, 4th Company, 1st Battalion, 736th Infantry Regiment, 716th Division:

I was in a foxhole in a field north of Colleville. Ahead of me was a minefield and behind me a concrete bunker capable of holding twelve men. But for several days we had not been allowed to sleep in the bunker at nights in case it got a direct hit when the invasion came. So we had to sleep in our foxholes.

I was a Catholic; my grandfather used to write to me regularly to say that he was praying for me and that God would protect me. I didn't believe in the war. My father had told me, back in 1939, that Germany could not possibly win and it would be like it was in the 1914–18 war, when the whole world was against us.

I was even more convinced that our position was hopeless when we arrived in Colleville. There were no defences worth talking about and although there was a great lot of work going on, planting obstacles and so forth on the beaches, everyone in the company knew that a good bombing would destroy everything.

On the night of 5 June we sat around as usual talking about how badly prepared we were and when the invasion would come. At midnight, the bombing started.

Although I felt the situation was hopeless, when the invasion actually started I knew that it was a battle for survival, that it was either the enemy or me. So when the Canadian troops started pouring across the beaches I opened fire with my machine gun and kept firing for several hours at everything that moved in front of me. I think I fired about 2,000 rounds; I don't know how many men I killed or wounded.

At about eleven o'clock we were forced to withdraw and with Lance Corporal Huf, who carried the ammunition, I helped cover the retreat through Colleville. At one point I was firing away and I suddenly ran out of ammunition. I shouted to Huf, who was lying beside me shoulder to shoulder, 'Where's the ammunition? Where's the ammunition?' I turned round and, as I did so, Huf toppled over. He had been shot through the head; a trickle of blood was coming out of a small hole in his forehead.

My first instinct was to run, because I was sure the next one would be for me. All around me, men were leaving their foxholes and starting to move back. I was very scared and the noise was terrible. I clipped on a new magazine and began to pull back, firing as I went. When I got back to the barbed wire, the hole was blocked by the body of a sergeant. I knew him; I remembered he could play the violin very well. I had to climb over his body, which I hated, but somehow I got through and started running back along the road towards Colleville.

I heard mortars coming over and threw myself into a ditch at the side of the road. I saw a cow killed in a field nearby and about ten other cows gathered round the body and as they did so another mortar shell exploded in their midst and killed them all. I was horrified.

I got up again and continued running until I got into Colleville where I found the remainder of my company. There were less than twenty men from the 120 who had been in our area. I hoped that some of them were still cut off and would join up with us later, but they never did. We lost 100 dead in the first two hours of the invasion. Luckily Ferdie, Lance Corporal Ferdinand Klug, who was one of my best friends, was among the survivors, although his face was streaming with blood. He was firing his machine gun from a bunker when a shell burst on the outside and sprayed the inside with fragments of concrete. Ferdie had more than forty splinters embedded in his face.

More mortar shells began to burst around us and one hit the post box where we had posted all the letters we had written on the previous day. I said to Ferdie, 'They'll never get them now.'

Shooting was coming from all sides now, including from the French, who were firing from the windows of their houses. The noise was so terrible and firing so intense that I felt absolutely numb and unable to think. It took us nearly an hour to cover the 200 yards to a big bunker, where the battalion headquarters was located. We got into the communication trenches surrounding the bunker and started firing back.

We held our position in the trenches for more than an hour. It was the most terrible time of my life. We were continually shelled and under fire from snipers. One of our bazookas hit a Canadian tank. We saw the flap opening and a soldier was half-way out when there was another explosion and it burst into flames with the soldier still hanging from the turret. I said to Ferdie, 'I hope we have a better death than that. I'd rather have a bullet.'

After about an hour we were ordered into a bunker, which was a command post almost entirely underground with a small observation hatch on the top. It was already full of wounded men. There were about thirty of them lying on straw blankets, absolutely terrified and crying out all the time. There was hardly any air inside and a man in the observation hole shouted that the Canadians were starting to pile earth up against the ventilators. It started to get very hot and difficult to breathe.

The company commander told us to breathe together: 'Breathe in when I say IN and out when I say OUT.' The battalion commander was firing a machine gun through a small aperture by the door. I will never forget the smell and the heat and noise inside that bunker, the cries of the wounded, the stink of exploding bullets and gases from the machine gun and the company commander yelling, 'IN, OUT, IN, OUT . . .'

Finally the company commander said to the battalion commander: 'Sir, we can't carry on. The wounded are suffocating.' The battalion commander said it was out of the question. 'We'll fight our way out of here if we have to. Count the weapons and the men preparatory to getting out.'

At that point there was almost a mutiny and some men started pulling the bolts out of their rifles in defiance. They knew that the door out of the bunker lead to a trench and that on the other side of the trench the Canadians would be waiting for them.

Ferdie said to me: 'You're the only one beside the battalion commander who's got a machine gun. You'll be the first out of here, believe me.' I said: 'No, I'm not going to do it,' and I pulled out the locking pin that held the machine together. Just then the man in the observation post shouted: 'My God, they're bringing up a flamethrower!'

We heard the 'woof' of the flame-thrower, but the flames couldn't get through the staggered sections of the ventilation shaft, although it turned red hot before our eyes. Now there was near panic. One German could speak two words of English and he kept shouting, 'Hello boys, hello boys, hello boys . . .'; the wounded were shouting their heads off and a radio operator in the corner was shouting to try and establish contact with headquarters. The battalion commander seemed oblivious to what was going on and kept firing his machine gun out of the aperture without once looking round.

People were shouting, 'We've got to do something, we've got to do something,' and eventually we took one of the dirty white sheets from one of the wounded and with the help of a broomstick pushed it out through the observation hatch. A voice from outside shouted, 'All right then, come on out.'

We dropped our weapons and made for the door, more scared of what the battalion commander would do than of the Canadians outside. Suddenly he turned round and asked the radio operator if he'd made contact. The operator shook his head. The battalion commander went very white, stepped back and then dropped his machine gun.

One of the soldiers opened the door and went out carrying the broomstick with the white sheet. Through the opening, we could see Canadian troops standing on either side of the trench. They started to shout, 'Oucha come, oucha come.'

We were made to lay down on the grass at the end of the trench, take off our equipment, boots and tunics. I said to Ferdie, 'Well, it's all over for us now.'[2]

Obergefreite Werner Kortenhaus, aged 19, 4th Company, 22nd Panzer Regiment:

At midnight on the night of June 5/6th, I was on a patrol consisting of an NCO and five men which had to walk to the next village under cover of darkness. The purpose of these patrols was to examine the countryside in between the villages. Soldiers were always trying to get out of this duty and so a system of passwords was devised to show that everyone who should have been there was there.

It was about six to eight kilometres to the next village, not so bad
a distance, and so we could pretty well take our time. We passed
another patrol in the dark and exchanged a few words with them.
The NCO was limping noticeably and he told us he had been
stepped on by a horse. He had gone into a field to stroke a horse and
the beast had stepped on him.

We had gone about a third of the way when suddenly we heard the
noise of a very low-flying aircraft. Naturally, at night, we always
heard lots of aeroplane noises but they flew very high on their way to
bomb railways and things and they never really disturbed us. There
were a lot of clouds, which the moonlight penetrated from time to
time. And we heard from the aircraft noise that it was climbing
steadily, but we couldn't see it and it was beginning to irritate us.
What was it, we wanted to know. It was something quite unfamiliar,
so we started looking into the country on either side of the road,
because at first we thought maybe some agents had been dropped.

We couldn't clarify the situation, so we turned round and headed
back to make a report. As we reached the edge of Epinay we were
surprised to see, by the light of the moon, the silhouettes of the
crews working away on the tanks. As we got to the first tank, we
asked what was up, were we doing a night exercise? No, came the
answer, it's full alert! We reported to the company office in the
middle of the village and found it in a state of some excitement. The
orders were to get the tanks ready to move.

The village women would do your laundry for a small payment
and I had given my laundry in that day, so in order to get ready to
march I had to retrieve my things, which of course were sopping
wet, and pay the woman. Nevertheless, we got all our stuff together
and ran to our tanks which were still dug in. So we stowed our
things, got the tanks ready and by 02.00 we were ready to move from
our position thirty kilometres south of Caen, waiting for the order to
march. But nobody gave it.

We stood around our tank and simply waited. The driver switched
on the motor to warm up the engine, thinking we would be driving
off at any moment, then he switched it off. After an hour, he
switched it on again and then off again. We kept asking ourselves,
why doesn't the order come through? We didn't really know what
was happening, all we knew was that we were on standby and ready
to fight.

It wasn't until nearly 08.00, after we had been standing around for six hours, that we finally got the order to march. The route was the road between Falaise and Caen, which we reached by the back roads. We were ordered to drive the tanks at a distance of fifty metres apart, because of air attacks. And so we did this and each of us tried to camouflage ourselves by standing under the trees.

And so, from eight in the morning until five in the afternoon we progressed slowly, advancing a little way, stopping and waiting, and then advancing some more, and so it went on. Why did we keep stopping? Well, by then there was quite a lot going on. The first of the leaflets were dropped on us which told us, 'We have breached the Atlantic Wall extensively and until now we have only encountered old men and babies.' By 'babies' they meant the HJ (Hitlerjugend), which was rubbish because they didn't arrive on the scene until the following day.

If we had been able to move off at three in the morning, we could have been in the area around Caen by six in the morning. As it turned out, by 14.00 it was impossible to go through Caen since wreckage from the air raids made the streets impassable.

During the march we were pretty convinced that by that evening we would be back in our quarters, that's how naive we were. We thought we would just do what we had to do and then be back by night time. On the road to Caen there are long stretches when the road gradually rises and you cannot actually see Caen, so when we finally reached the top of the rise we saw huge black clouds in the distance over the city. In that moment I had the feeling we were now actually in the war, a picture with which I was not familiar. It was then I realized that there was no chance of us being back in our quarters that night, it looked too serious to me. I just had the feeling that I could not tell how things were going to develop, but there was still a sense of optimism and we did want to know what was going to happen.[3]

Generalleutnant Edgar Feuchtinger, commander, 21 Panzer Division:

I first knew that the invasion had begun with a report that parachutists had been dropped near Troarn a little after midnight on 6 June. Since I had been told that I was to make no move until I heard from Rommel's headquarters, I could do nothing immediately but warn my men to be ready. I waited patiently all that night for some instructions. But not a single order from a higher formation was received by me. Realizing that my armoured division was closest to the scene of operations, I finally decided, at 6.30 in the morning, that I had to take some action. I ordered my tanks to attack the English 6th Airborne Division which had entrenched itself in a bridgehead over the Orne. To me this constituted the most immediate threat to the German position.

Hardly had I made this decision when, at seven o'clock, I received my first intimation that a higher command did still exist. I was told by Army Group B that I was now under command of 7th Army. But I received no further orders as to my role. At nine o'clock I was informed that I would receive any further orders from 84th Infantry Corps and finally at ten o'clock I was given my first operational instructions. I was ordered to stop the move of my tanks against the Allied airborne troops and to turn west and aid the forces protecting Caen.

Once over the Orne river, I drove north towards the coast. By this time the enemy, consisting of three British and three Canadian Infantry Divisions, had made astonishing progress and had already occupied a strip of high ground about ten kilometres from the sea. From here the excellent anti-tank gunfire of the Allies knocked out eleven of my tanks before I had barely started. However, one battle group did manage to by-pass these guns and actually reached the coast at Lion-sur-Mer, at about seven o'clock in the evening. I now expected that some reinforcements would be forthcoming to help me hold my position, but nothing came. Another Allied parachute landing on both sides of the Orne, together with a sharp attack by English tanks, forced me to give up my hold on the coast. I retired to take up a line just north of Caen. By the end of that first day my division had lost almost 25 per cent of its tanks.[4]

Oberleutnant Herr, aged 25, 22 Panzer Regiment:

I was the commanding officer of one of those unfortunate tank units which was expecting the invasion in the environs of Blocqueville, near Falaise. I was stationed in the château at Couliboeuf.

I was catapulted out of bed by the alarm at about two or three o'clock in the morning. Because I had been advised by naval experts that the invasion would only come at high tide, I did not think it was particularly serious at that point. I believed that it was simply a

regimental exercise and therefore issued my first instructions from
my bed, still groggy with sleep.

A sonorous droning could be heard coming from aeroplanes flying
over the château where I was quartered. I thought I was hearing the
sounds of manoeuvres and assumed that the CO of our regiment was
using these circumstances to instigate an exercise for us.

But then, suddenly, it was serious. I was presented with a leaflet
that was found in the courtyard of the castle. The message actually
read: 'Leave this building in which the enemy is quartered. It will be
attacked without delay. Get out into the open for your own safety.' I
was asked what I thought about it and I said I thought that these
orders to attack probably referred to cities like Falaise, rather than to
the château. I suggested that instead of heading for open country
they should get themselves into the deepest cellars of the castle in the
event, as was being threatened, of the castle being attacked.

I withdrew from the location at about 6.30 a.m., without receiving
orders, since the high command was unable to make any decisions.
They simply did not know if the invasion would occur east or west
of the Orne at that point. So we marched without orders from higher
echelons. It was also understood that the order to deploy the tanks
would come directly from the high command or from Hitler himself.
The next difficulty then was, would the regiment have to be split in
order to go east or west of the Orne? I myself was west of the Orne,
having pushed so close to the coastline that I could see, like an
appalling swarm of grasshoppers, the flotilla of ships lying off the
coast and also, much to my dismay, low-flying aircraft, whose
whistling I could hear passing over my tanks. It later transpired that
these were freight-carrying gliders, flying low over us, away into the
hinterland, east of the Orne, unfortunately out of range of our
weapons. The most I could do was to observe the gliders through
my field glasses, see how they landed, how flaps at the back opened
and jeeps and heavy equipment emerged. I heard that possibly even
light tanks were delivered in this way. I remember this incident with
the aeroplanes very clearly, and how we staggered onwards.

The platoon leader of No. 2 platoon, Lieutenant Doell, had made
an advance on foot with his infantry and had retrieved about thirty
English soldiers from a bomb crater. In a pause in the fighting, I was
able to speak to the POWs and explained to them that I was ordered
to carry their wounded to the nearest field hospital, but could not
prevent myself adding sarcastically, 'I'm not sure if all of them will

arrive safely, since enemy aircraft don't seem to acknowledge the Red Cross.' One officer stepped forward and asked politely if he might ask a question. Certainly, I said, go ahead. He then asked if the aircraft shelling the Red Cross were American or English. I could tell from his question that it was a matter of restoring his honour and I was able to tell him that it was Americans and that they literally fired on anything that moved, whether it was because they were trigger happy or because they did it on orders from above. Everybody who found themselves in this murderous territory and who had to go down those long, straight roads from Caen to Falaise knew that they were the streets of hell.

Going through Caen presented some problems. There was a bridge, the last one intact, over the Orne, which was being ceaselessly bombed by fighter bombers. I got out my watch and timed the intervals at which the bombers flew over and then, as coldly as if I had been timing athletics, sent my tanks over the bridge. On your marks, ready, go, and in this way I was able to get all my tanks over the bridge without a single loss. I can't remember the exact interval of seconds but basically, once each machine had dropped its bomb load, it pulled up in order to allow the next to make a run and that gave us the time. Amazingly, the bombs fell right and left into the river, but none hit the bridge. I was proud to get my company across. Caen was intact as we went through, I suppose the murderous airborne raids must have come later. Anyway, once we had crossed the bridge, the subsequent progress was much more like a peace march.

I can't remember how long the advance to the coast from Caen actually took, but I certainly recall a stop, a sort of briefing pause, where we stationed ourselves in some woods to stay out of sight of fighter aircraft, waited for orders and took the opportunity to discuss progress and plans. It was as we left the woods that we ran into confrontation with the enemy tanks.

It was afternoon by now and we came upon a stationary column of Sherman tanks, at about 500 or 600 metres' distance. It was really spooky, they just stood there and nothing moved. I gave the order to attack, to drive round these tanks in order to attain better positions for shooting at them, as the range of my Panzer IV was not great enough from that distance. The decision was, however, taken out of my hands as the other side opened fire.

The 'skirts' over the tracks of the tank, that were to protect us from hazards and mines etcetera, just swirled up and literally flew through the air round us. I personally had always been frightened of being burned to death in the cockpit of my tank, so I lengthened the lead of my neck microphone so that I could sit behind the turret. It was not sensible of me, but I had had such appalling experiences earlier, when I had to extract the bodies of comrades from tanks that had been burned out, and put them in coffins that were as little as three-quarters of a metre long. The consequence of this was that when my tank received a hit the shrapnel struck me and the result was that I fell to the ground and had to feel around my knees with my hands to check that I still had legs. Blood was pouring out of me.

Lieutenant von Oppel Bronikowski, in despair, asked me what to do, to which I replied, if you don't know, then how on earth should I know?

I managed in any case to get myself with my unit and the remaining tanks into a sort of secure rearguard position. By this, I mean a position which allows us to see the terrain, with the tank itself protected but the barrel up for us to be able to look along it.

We were only able to resume radio communication once we had made contact with the enemy, which made things somewhat difficult. Along the whole stretch of the crossing of the Orne radio silence had been imposed and so we knew nothing about what was going on. We drove by vision only and that held true for the followers as well. I am absolutely certain that one of my own panzers was fired on from behind, not by the enemy, but by one of our own that had got us confused.

I am not able to describe exactly how things proceeded, but after we had disengaged ourselves from the enemy and re-grouped in a rearguard position of safety I wanted to re-position the tank of Lieutenant Lehman with which I was in radio contant and which was about fifteen metres distant from my tank. I wanted him to move backwards a little further when I got the strict command, 'No tank moves even a centimetre.' Barely ten minutes later, his tank received a direct hit; in fact, while I was in the middle of a radio conversation with him. The Panzer IV has a 7cm-thick glass observation window in the turret which gives one a vision of 360 degrees. The shell must have directly hit this spot. The black forage cap that Lehman always wore was hurled out and landed on my tank in the shock waves of the explosion. I looked over and saw that the whole dome had been blown away – it was an appalling situation. I was so furious that I jumped out of my tank and ran to my commander and reported that, 'I have just sacrificed another tank on direct orders.' It was a dreadful situation.

However, what puzzled us was that the enemy did not follow through and come after us. If not now, then when would it be? We had no infantry, we were completely alone. We were desperate, the situation was desperate.

As far as I know, we had penetrated the furthest forward. Everybody tried to do their best, what else was there to do? Stop firing, run away and attempt to save myself? The thought never crossed my mind, and I never heard of anyone doing such a thing as deserting the flag. The other side clearly expected something else, the question the English officer asked about shooting on the Red Cross clearly illustrates that. I was asked another question. Why are you fighting so doggedly, when we will have to fight Russia together? We never had this universal view of things that maybe should have been expected from us subsequently.

Each side had a picture of the enemy so firmly embedded that the 'alternatives' were never a possibility. We had stepped up to do the very best for our country and that was to throw the enemy back into the sea.[5]

Hauptmann Wilhelm von Gottberg, aged 29, group commander, 22nd Panzer Regiment:

By 2.30 a.m. all our tanks had their engines running and we were ready to go. We were burning to fight. We had done so many exercises that we knew every nook and cranny of Normandy and could have proceeded to any point, even in the darkness. But no orders came. We couldn't understand it. I was furious. I kept imagining that while we were waiting the Allies would be busy occupying all the strategic hills.

At last, at 7.15 we got orders to move and to assemble in Chicheboville wood. I ordered my group of seventy-three tanks to get under way. Then came another order – it still makes me mad when I think about it – to detach one of my companies to join another outfit fighting on the right of the Orne at Cagny.

We got to Chicheboville wood and by noon, along with Feuchtinger's division, we had passed Caen. North of Caen we were ordered to attack the Periers heights, but, just as I feared, the Allies had occupied all the strategic positions. Ten of my tanks were knocked out by the British even before their tanks were within our firing range. We had to give up. We dug in around a farmhouse at Lebisey.

I am still convinced that, if we had been given orders to attack during the early hours of the invasion, we would have succeeded in throwing the enemy back into the sea. But there was nothing I could do except curse the short-sightedness of my own high command.[6]

Oberleutnant Hans Hoeller, commander anti-tank platoon, 2nd Battalion, 21st Panzer Division:

I was quartered in a private house in Cairon, a village about eight miles north-west of Caen and about the same distance from the coast. The family of the house conducted themselves with great politeness and friendliness and when the alarm was sounded at 2.00 a.m. on 6 June, they brought me all their available provisions, food and drink, and bade me farewell with tears in their eyes.

We were equipped with French transport, armoured Renault half-tracks fitted with mortars. Our vehicles were loaded in the shortest possible time with munitions and were soon ready to go. Before we left Cairon we dropped off our private belongings in the local château, thinking we would pick them up again later. We never saw them again, for the Tommies took Cairon a few hours later without a struggle.

Under cover of early-morning darkness, and with enemy aircraft roaring overhead, we reached our point of engagement, Bénouville, without any trouble. Our command was initially rather indecisive and whether or not the order to attack came from the regiment or the battalion I cannot say.

We were able to storm Bénouville and occupy half the town, but we were not able to take the exit road to the coast and this remained out of our hands for the whole day. The mass of enemy paratroopers fought doggedly and received continuous reinforcements from the coastal area. We had to watch, with great bitterness, the endlessly growing numbers against us, knowing we would receive no support. The most we could do was hold the position and try to interrupt the advance.

At about midday or very early afternoon, a very old man, who appeared to have difficulty in walking, turned up at our defences having apparently come from the enemy's territory. He came to a halt at our trenches, then turned round and started off in the direction of the enemy again. We discussed among ourselves whether or not he should be allowed to do this, but minutes later two enemy tanks appeared and their very first shot scored a direct hit on our defences. Soon, however, our left-hand gun knocked out one of the tanks and the other one disappeared down a side street.

From a copse of thickly planted trees and bushes at the outermost perimeter of our position I had a good view of Pegasus bridge, about 600 metres away, which the Tommies had overcome during the night and were still holding. We could see an enemy tank stopped outside a house; the tank officer was talking to the inhabitants. Our right-hand gunner was unable to crank down the barrel of his anti-tank gun low enough to fire and we could not risk starting the engines because of the noise. We decided to push the vehicle over the edge of the incline so that it could get a shot and after several dramatic moments we managed to do so without being noticed. Lance Corporal Wleck targeted his objective and fired. The enemy tank exploded and the house alongside it collapsed. The English could not grasp where the shot had come from and began firing in all directions, but not in our immediate vicinity and we were able to retreat in the confusion and noise of battle.[7]

Feldwebel Rainer Hartmetz, aged 19, No.2 Company, Schell Battalion, 77 Division:

I was standing in the door of our tiny blockhouse on the coast road talking with the lieutenant who was outside when a motor cyclist stopped and I heard the lieutenant say, 'What? They've landed?' An hour later we got the order to leave and go to Le Vivier, where the company was to assemble.

We reached Le Vivier at about dawn. It was a grey, rainy morning. We had our cars parked under the trees, waiting for the other squads and platoons to arrive. The captain appeared and it looked for a moment as if he wanted to say something to us, but he only gave us the sign to mount the cars and drive on.

The convoy was very strung out, with a long distance between the cars. Each squad had a small truck with a machine gun for air defence. When we got near to Avranches, fighter bombers were over the town. Twenty or thirty Thunderbolts curved out of the sky diving down on the roads. We heard the dry rattle of their weapons and got our cars under the trees beside the road and waited until the sky was clear. Then we pushed on at high speed through the town.

Avranches was not yet seriously damaged but we saw people leaving their homes and the town. At the entrance to Granville we had to stop for a short time. The town was heavily bombed and a lot of civilians were leaving in big columns, burdened by their property, necessary and unnecessary things. Some were crying, the eyes of others were full of hate when they saw us.

In the crowd of refugees a Mercedes with a paymaster came slowly nearer till it came to a stop beside our cars. We had time to look at the guy, who was going in the wrong direction. He had cut a hole in the roof of the car to look for fighter bombers. He looked out of that hole as if he was imitating a tank commander. His face was red with anger and he was shouting at the refugees to make way.

First we were amused by that fat guy, but when we saw that his car was packed full of baggage and carpets and luxury stuff we got bitter and we got mad when he started to shout at us to give him way. What did this son of a bitch know about combat?

The lieutenant jumped out of the car ahead of us and went over to the Mercedes with three or four soldiers. He didn't shout, but he was pale like death. He said calmly to the fat guy, 'Get out of that car!' The soldiers dragged him out, didn't listen to him when he protested, pushed him and his driver between the French people, where they disappeared. They took all the petrol cans out of his car and pushed it into the ditch beside the road. We hated to fight for people like that and we knew there were a lot of them.

It seemed to be a long way, a dreadfully long way. Every few kilometres we had to stop and hide under the trees because of the fighter bombers, but we had good fortune and none of our cars was damaged. There was a rumour that airborne forces had dropped somewhere, but nobody knew exactly where. We had no information. I wondered only that the boys still fooled and joked around like always. They said things like how they always wanted to cross the Mississippi and they wouldn't mind doing it as POWs. It was just fooling.[8]

Obergefreite Anton Wuensch, aged 23, 2nd Company, 2nd Battalion, 6th Parachute Regiment:

At four o'clock we got word to get out and assemble on a road nearby, where we met the company commander, Lieutenant Schulz. We all stood in a little group around him as he said, 'Well, it's started. Now we are going to see who are men.' Then he read out the official orders from the battalion commander: 'Strong enemy forces, both airborne and infantry, have begun to land. Others are approaching from the sea all along the coast. The task of 6th Parachute Regiment is to destroy these units and throw the enemy back into the sea.'

I thought to myself, this is bad, we really will have to make a go of it because if we don't there are no reserves behind us. It seemed that our regiment was the only thing between the enemy and the whole of France.

We marched off at double time and reached the outskirts of Le Mesnil, some time between five and six. We could hear shooting to our left and right. To the north of Le Mesnil we found a Volkswagen completely burned out, with oil and blood on the road. Nearby were three American parachutes, which we tore into strips to make scarves for ourselves.

We carried on marching silently through one village after another until suddenly the machine gunner up ahead threw himself on the ground and started firing his Spandau at some US paratroopers who were about 400 yards away. I ran up to the machine gunner and told him he was wasting his ammunition because they were out of range. I tried to pick off one of the Americans with my rifle but he was too far away.

By seven o'clock we had reached the outskirts of Carentan and just as we did so we saw twelve medium bombers flying over the town. As we watched, I saw the bomb doors opening. We all threw ourselves into the ditch at the side of the road as the bombs started to fall. It seemed they were directly over us and I was sure we were going to be hit. I wrapped my head in my arms and waited for the explosions. When I looked up I saw the bombs had destroyed some big gasoline storage tanks just ahead of us and the whole area was in flames. I was horrified and frightened that the bombers would return for another sweep, but they didn't.

Then we heard a horrible, horrible screaming and we saw a

hysterical young woman of about twenty-five or twenty-six running towards us. Her face was black, her hair was hanging down everywhere and her dress was streaked with white. She pushed a baby carriage with two children in it and another child held onto the handle. She was screaming and all the children were crying. Her house was close to the gasoline tanks and had been completely demolished. I was chilled by the sight of them and I remember thinking, 'God, if this is going to be war, let it be man-to-man, not like this.'

The woman seemed to be almost blind, either with terror or from the explosion. We tried to stop her, to tell her that she could stay where she was, but she just ran on. It seemed as if she couldn't see us or hear us.

As we approached a bridge on the other side of Carentan we heard the 'express train' sound of heavy naval gunfire. Once again we dived into the ditches as the heavy shells began wobbling through the air towards us. They landed in the swamps ahead of us, close to an anti-aircraft battery. A small spotter plane flew overhead, so low that I could see the pilot's face. This made me very angry and I shouted to the crew of the anti-battery to shoot the bastard down. Someone yelled back, 'Go lick your arse. We've got no ammunition.' So we just lay there, sweating our guts out.

When the bombardment lifted we went across the bridge and saw some other parachutists from our battalion in the yard of a farmhouse. They were standing around drinking. We went over and found the French farmer, with a cigarette drooping from his mouth, doling out cider for cash. I thought to myself that times were changing for the Germans but nothing changes for Norman peasants.

Just then we saw a captured American paratrooper being marched along the road towards us. He was enormous, a big husky giant of a man with red hair. I said to my mate, 'Jesus, if they're all as big as that they'll beat the hell out of us,' but I cheered up a bit when I saw that he was being marched along by a very small German with a sub-machine gun. I yelled at the prisoner: 'Good luck! I hope you enjoy chopping wood in Germany.'

By three o'clock in the afternoon, walking across fields and narrow country lanes, we came to the village of Vierville. As we approached, a sergeant came running towards us to say that there were American paratroopers in a barn to our right. They had been firing at a small château where we had a command post and had killed several of our soldiers.

Lieutenant Schulz ordered me to take my mortar team and attack the barn, to set it on fire with phosphorous shells. We approached along a sunken road, set up the mortars and got ready to fire. The first three shells missed, but the fourth scored a direct hit and went straight through the roof. We saw a burst of white smoke and the top floor of the barn began blazing furiously. There was no more fire from the Americans. It was the first time we'd been in action and we felt good about it, about having struck back at the invaders.

After this we moved on and we were marching along a sunken road when bullets started whistling around us. We flattened ourselves in a ditch and it did not take long to work out that there was a sniper somewhere ahead. We looked around carefully and one of my men suddenly said, 'Look, there's an American up that tree.' I took up my binoculars and as I did so a man on the other side of the road was hit. I looked at the clump of trees very carefully and finally saw the sniper.

I put down my glasses, spat on my hands and lifted my rifle. Taking careful aim, I fired. I don't know whether I hit the American, but at least I forced him to change his tactics because I saw him start to climb down from the tree. I aimed at a spot on the tree trunk that was clear of foliage and waited. As he came into the clear area I said, 'All right, my boy, now I'm going to get you.' I fired. Then I fired twice more and I saw the sniper throw up his arms and fall backwards out of the tree. I thought I would feel some reaction, but I felt nothing.

As the sniper fell from the tree, my men cheered and we all ran forward. The American was dark-haired, handsome, of medium height and very young. His eyes were open and blood was trickling from his mouth. He'd been shot several times through the back, one bullet had passed out through his left breast. As I stood looking at him I felt some kind of pity, but it was more like the sickening sight of looking at a dog which had been run over.

We went through his pockets and found his K rations in a small water-proofed box. There was a small pack of Lucky Strike, some biscuits, a can of cheese, a little package of Nescafé and some chewing gum. In his pockets we found a wallet with two photographs and a letter. One of the photos was of the soldier sitting with a girl, who we thought was perhaps his wife. The other was of the couple on a verandah with a family, the soldier's family, I suppose. One of my men started to put the photos and the letter in his pocket but I stopped him. I told him that if we got captured and the Americans found the stuff on him he'd be in trouble. We had been told that American paratroopers would show no mercy if they captured us.

We continued to move north towards where the real battle area was and not far from where I had shot the sniper we saw a blue parachute hanging from a tree with a container under it. There was a lot of rifle fire and machine-gun fire ahead of us, but we decided we would try and get the container. We thought there might be weapons and ammunition in it.

Getting to that clump of trees was not easy, because there was quite a lot of fire about and Thunderbolts were strafing the ground in front of us. We moved along a ditch towards the trees, then I told my men to wait while I crawled forward on my stomach to the tree. I took off the scarf I'd made from the parachute silk earlier that day and tied it round the trunk of the tree, then I hung two grenades in the scarf, pulled the pins and ran back to where my men were waiting. The grenades went off and the tree toppled. We cut the parachute lines from the container and dragged it to a patch of hollow ground where we had some shelter.

Instead of ammunition or guns, to our amazement the container was packed with an enormous quantity of food. It was food the like of which we hadn't seen for years. There were cans of milk, sugar, cigarettes, chocolate, pineapple juice, orange juice, butter and candy. Right there, in the middle of a lot of fighting that was going on all around, we started to gorge ourselves, eating as much as we could. When someone asked if we shouldn't be moving on, I told them not to worry, that the war was certainly going to last long enough for us to catch up with it. Friedolin poured packets of Nescafé into his mouth and washed the powder down with cans of condensed milk, saying over and over again, 'Oh, this is just wonderful.' For a full half hour we stuffed ourselves and when we could eat no more, we filled our pockets with as much as we could. The biggest disappointment was that we had to leave so much behind.

Better fed than we had been for months, we pressed on. By nine o'clock the fighting was much heavier. Now the firing was no longer sporadic. About one hundred yards outside the little village of St Côme-du-Mont, we suddenly saw our machine gunner fall forward on his gun. He'd been shot through the head. It was the first time we'd seen someone shot so quickly and so close to us. The number two in the crew grabbed the gun, ran around a hedge and opened up on the US troops along the ridge. He had hardly fired before he, too, was shot. A third man, apparently infuriated by the death of his comrades, grabbed a Schmeisser sub-machine gun, ran out into the open and began blasting away at the US positions. He suddenly threw up his arms and with a frightful scream fell back dead.

We saw all this from our position only a few yards away. I kept my men busy firing the mortar to help them keep their courage up. All of us had been shaken by these three sudden deaths. Two more men of the machine-gun company were hit and so we moved back about 100 yards. The fighting continued for some time, then we saw a small group of German infantry moving up on the left-hand side of the ridge.

We started to move up again to support them and I had nearly reached the road when I was hit by a burst of machine-gun fire in the upper part of my legs. It felt like I had been hit by a red hot iron. I fell flat on my face and lay on the ground in terrible pain, although I could feel nothing in the lower part of my legs, nor could I move them. I turned over on my back and to my amazement saw more bullets hitting the ground around me.

Friedolin crawled over and dragged me back into a ditch. He propped me up against a tree, took out a knife and cut my pants down on both sides and as he did so all the food I had stuffed in my pockets spilled. I can remember seeing it lying all around me in all the blood. I got the feeling I was burning from my own blood, as if it was molten lava. Then I saw that both my feet were completely twisted around as if my legs had reversed.

Later on, some stretcher bearers appeared and started to carry me at a run away from the area, but then artillery or mortar fire started landing all around and they dropped me and ran for cover. I screamed with pain and yelled at them, 'You bloody idiots.' I don't know how long I lay there under the shelling; I was in too much pain to care. I was certain I was going to die.

The next thing I can remember was Friedolin coming back with a Volkswagen. I was taken to a French house that had been turned very hurriedly into a casualty clearing station and I was put on the floor beside a lot of other wounded men. In the centre of the room was a table where a doctor was hard at work. All around him were wounded men in various degrees of pain, some were crying, some were mumbling, some were silent. A French woman was walking around looking at the wounded men, shaking her head in disbelief.

When I was put on the table I was given morphine and I asked the doctor if I was really going to die. He slapped my face and said there was nothing wrong with me. Then he turned to an assistant standing at the end of the table and said, 'Hold him.' This man grabbed my shoulders and pressed me firmly to the table, then the doctor said, 'This is going to hurt a bit,' and pulled my leg and twisted it back into position.

I can remember hearing the crunching noise as the bones twisted inside my leg and I can remember screaming long and hard. Then the same thing happened to my other leg. When I came to I was in splints, back on the ground.

One thing that stands out in my mind on that day was that, as I was being driven in the Volkswagen to the clearing station, I can remember hearing terrific artillery barrages and thinking that this time we weren't going to win.[9]

Gefreite Walter Hermes, aged 19, motor-cycle messenger, 1st Battalion, 192nd Regiment, 21st Panzer Division:

I was stationed at Carpiquet airfield just outside Caen. Around nine o'clock the company commander came in and told us the invasion had begun. 'The British have landed,' he said. 'The time has come to stand by our Führer in defence of the nation. Each one of us must do our duty as soldiers.' I suddenly felt very happy. I'd been waiting for this for a long time and I thought there would be a certain glory about going into battle.

But even after this news there were still no orders for us, so I just hung around the duty room with my friend Schard to see what would develop. I said to Schard: 'I'm going to take a nap. Why don't you write a letter and when you're through, wake me. We may not get a chance later on.' I slept for three hours and then I sat down and wrote a letter to my parents: 'My dear parents: The British have landed! I am taking this opportunity to write you a line before going into action. I'm well and healthy. Don't worry about me, I'm sure I'll see you soon. This is a small thing. We'll soon throw those British back into the sea.'[10]

Gefreite Heinz Herbst, aged 23, H Company, 613 Long-Range Reconnaissance Unit:

At about four or five o'clock, the news came through that there had been an invasion. It was still dark when the phone call came with the news and at first we thought it might be diversionary tactics to draw the troops away from Calais (towards Normandy) and then actually land around Calais. That the invasion should occur with such massive numbers was never imagined, nor had we been able to pick up on that from listening in to broadcasts.

At the time of the invasion, I was working at the HQ along with the company commander and the adjutant. They lived in one house and we wireless people lived in another and our teleprinter was in the company HQ. From there we sent the news to Fontainebleau or OB West. Now, our men were picking up the Allied advance on their sets – they were landing here, there and everywhere. On the wall, we had a large map on which we marked the progress of the enemy with tiny flags and coloured thread.

It was like a thriller, following the movements of the various English regiments. You would locate them on the map and then hear from the transmissions that they had been transferred down there, another one went somewhere else. The individual units were very well known to us, so were the divisions and battalions; we knew each and everyone of them and, wherever they moved, we were on to them; it was like a puzzle. You pushed around the bits of information and thought, well, there must be some purpose to this. Sometimes there were movements that were intended to deceive us. You would notice that a regiment was ordered to a particular place and then suddenly it would appear somewhere else entirely and then you realized what had happened. Then they would change the call sign, but from the style of transmission of the individual operator, you would recognize the unit again and so you would monitor it very closely and eventually discover that it was indeed the unit you suspected.

I was very busy during the day. Previously, things had been dead and now it was starting again. We had had no sleep the night before and now we had to start tracking movements again. Also, as we did not know what was going to happen, we had to be ready for action, machine guns at the ready in case paratroopers landed. We snatched a couple of hours' sleep whenever we could.

I didn't burn to encounter the enemy, I have to say. I wanted to do my job and get home as quickly as possible. When the invasion began on 6 June, we realized that there was nothing left for us to gain with this war. We had suffered Stalingrad in Russia; the Russians were advancing; the Allies were in Italy and Africa; the Italians had capitulated. We just said to ourselves, let's get out of this as unscathed as we possibly can.[11]

General Warlimont, deputy chief, Armed Forces Operations Staff:

About midday the usual assemblage collected for the briefing conference, but on this particular day there was a Hungarian state visit in honour of which the conference took place in Klessheim castle, at least an hour by road from the offices of those involved. As usual when visitors were involved, it was a showpiece, but in view of events in the west a preliminary conference took place in a room next to the entrance hall. I and many of the others were keyed up as a result of the portentous events which were taking place and, as we stood about in front of the maps and charts, we awaited with some excitement Hitler's arrival and the decisions he would take. Any great expectations were destined to be bitterly disappointed. As so often happened, Hitler decided to put on an act. As he came up to the maps he chuckled in a carefree manner and behaved as if this was the opportunity he had been waiting for for so long to settle accounts with his enemy. In an unusually broad Austrian, he merely said, 'So, we're off.'[12]

Telephone journal, 7th Army:

16.55 hours. Chief of Staff Western Command [von Rundstedt's HQ] emphasizes the desire of the Supreme Command [Hitler] to have the enemy in the bridgehead annihilated by the evening of 6 June, since there exists a danger of additional sea and airborne landings for support. In accordance with an order by General Jodl, all units will be diverted to the point of penetration in Calvados. The beachhead there must be cleaned up by not later than tonight. The Chief of Staff declares that such would be impossible. The commander of Army Group B [Rommel] states that 21 Panzer Division must attack immediately regardless of whether reinforcements arrive or not. The Supreme Command has ordered that the bad weather conditions of the night of 6–7 June be utilized for the bringing up of reserves.[13]

CHAPTER NINETEEN

AFTERNOON

By the afternoon of D-Day, order had been created out of chaos on four of the five invasion beaches and reinforcements and supplies were steadily pouring in. On Omaha thousands of troops were still pinned down. Inland, fighting continued . . .

Vincent J. DelGiudice, aged 22, pharmacist's mate assigned to USS Bayfield:

While we were having chow – lunch was called at 12.00 – a call came through saying that a number of LCTs would be coming on board with casualties from Omaha beach. We were told that Utah beach was secure and that the 7th Corps under General Collins was well on its way to Cherbourg, but that the 1st Army was pinned down under the cliffs on Omaha.

About two o'clock, three LCTs came aboard with at least 100 stretcher cases on each of them. It seemed like an overwhelming number of wounded people and I felt the situation would be very difficult to manage. As the men were brought aboard, the chief medical officer was running around giving orders. He assigned me all the head casualties and told me to take them down to the army officers' quarters. Some of the non-medical members of the crew acted as stretcher bearers.

The most dramatic case I recall was a robust young Ranger with blood dripping from under his helmet. When I took his helmet off, I discovered a piece of shrapnel had cracked open the cranium and as the helmet came off, his brain oozed out of the laceration that was created. I grabbed an 8 × 8 sterile gauze, put it over his head and in my naïveté tried to push the brain back into his skull, with very little success. I secured a bandage round his head, washed his face and neck, gave him some morphine and plasma and called the medical officer over. Dr Walsh said there was nothing more that I could do for him and he would probably die very shortly. He did, within the hour.

The next person I attended to had his ear blown off. He complained of a considerable amount of pain. He was given some morphine. I put some sulfa powder over his wounded ear and the wounds on the side of his head and gave him a bottle of plasma.

The wounded kept coming aboard. Those casualties that did not require immediate treatment were placed to one side, those that required immediate surgery were brought down to the sick bay and given some sort of surgical treatment, and those who were going to die were given some plasma and some morphine and left alone to whatever fate would befall them. I can only say at this point there was a considerable amount of confusion. There was more work than twenty men could take care of. We just kept working. Every person involved kept as busy as he could and did the best he could under the circumstances.

Later we had the main operating room going, the dispensary operating room going and we were called upon to use part of the mess hall as another operating room. I was in charge of getting the equipment and the portable operating table in position. I have to admit that some members of the crew didn't like it. Those that could eat, ate, but those that couldn't stomach it didn't bother.

We also got maybe fifteen or twenty German casualties and the one I most vividly recall was a tall, thin corporal, a rather handsome chap with blond hair. He had been wounded in his right hand and all five fingers were dangling. I had to amputate all his fingers with my bandage scissors. After I had bandaged his hand, for my effort I got a smile and a '*Danke schoen*', which I believe means thank you.

I don't remember the details of all the other men I took care of that day. It certainly isn't a very pleasant memory. I do recall that three men died and my good friend George Norman from Massachusetts and I got some canvas bags, put the bodies into the bags and stored them in the ship's refrigerator until they could be taken back for burial.[1]

Lance Corporal Peter Masters, No.6 Commando:

We were cycling inland to link up with the airborne when someone in front was shot by a machine gun. Captain Robinson, our troop commander, told me to go down into the village to see what was happening. It was rather obvious what was happening: they were shooting at us. I asked him how many men I should take with me and he said none. That was fine by me, we'd been trained in just this kind of work. I told him I'd go round the left flank, reconnoitre the village and come back from the right flank, which is what we'd been taught to do. 'No, no,' said Robinson. 'I just want you to walk down that road and see what's going on.'

It was now quite clear to me that what he wanted was for me to be shot at by the machine gun so he could see where it was positioned. It was a bad moment for me and I began to think feverishly. I knew he had to know, but that didn't help me. We'd been trained to try and figure an angle to improve the odds. I remembered an old Cary Grant film, set in the Khyber Pass or somewhere. He had walked straight into a rebel stronghold and said, 'You're all under arrest,' which I'd always thought a very funny line indeed. So I decided to do the same. I walked down the centre of the road, where everyone in the village could see me, and began shouting in German: 'All right, everybody out with your hands on heads. It's no use fighting, you're totally surrounded. For you the war is over. Come on, give yourselves up.'

No one came out, of course. On the other hand no one shot me, either. Below me was a parapet wall. On the left was a ten-foot hedge, quite impenetrable. There was no ditch but a grass border a few feet wide, no place to hide at all. I guess they didn't shoot because they were curious to see what else would show. They knew they could always shoot me when they wanted to, and this is eventually what they decided to do. A man popped up from behind the parapet and shot at me with a Schmeisser. He missed because he fired too quickly, and perhaps he was a bad shot anyway. I didn't see where the bullets went but assumed they went right high, because that's how a Schmeisser fires. Then he ducked back and as he ducked I went down on one knee and fired. My Tommy gun fired one round then jammed.

I couldn't look because my eyes were glued to where the man had been. I cleared the gun quickly, but when he popped up again and missed me again, it jammed without firing. By this time I was lying down in the grass by the verge, and I forced myself to look and see what had gone wrong and saw that two rounds were crumpled in the breech. I cleared them and thought that this time I had to get him otherwise he was bound to get me. But then I heard a noise behind me and saw the rest of the troop charging down the road with fixed bayonets. One of them was firing a Bren from the shoulder – most unusual – and it was he who shot the machine gunners, who had retreated a little way down the Ouistreham road. Then some of our tanks turned up and put some shells into the village and we were able to move across the bridge.[2]

Brigadier the Lord Lovat DSO MC, commander 1st Commando Brigade:

At a crossing [in the village of St Aubin] a knot of civilians gesticulated outside a low-roofed edifice damaged in the morning's blitz. The occupants – old people – had been badly injured; the family begged for a doctor and bandages. As I turned to point out the medical team bringing up the rear, a sniper's bullet smacked the wall beside my head with a crack like a whip. A near miss, that showered the relatives with chips and rubble. 'He's over there, top storey,' shouted Bobby Holmes, charging across the street to a house at the corner. Someone tossed a grenade through the window as Bobby kicked the door down and cut loose with his Tommy gun. He looked out at us with shocked surprise. 'This one was dressed in civvies, but he had a Jerry rifle and there's a parachute silk under the bed.' The commentary ended with, 'My God, I'm coming down. More Huns are advancing over fields to the south.'

Our fire would certainly halt the approaching enemy – who, leaving their horse-drawn vehicles at the side of the road, were now closing in on the village in open order across green patches of standing corn. The enemy – a platoon about thirty strong – looked a soft touch: the sun was in their eyes and we were unobserved. I made a quick decision to ambush them.

It was a relief to get the rucksack off – the straps were already burning my shoulders – then tee up behind its bulk and go into action with a light, short-barrelled US army carbine. Joe Lawrence and Salbury's brother, a despatch rider, sneaked one of the quick-firing K guns up on to a shed. The Germans were 500 yards away. We had not been seen. They were in the bag.

The fire order whispered down the ambushing party is not to be found in training manuals – 'Pick the officers and NCOs and let them come right in.' The ragged volley caused a surprise: dust flew off the back of the fair-haired platoon commander as he spun round and fell; half a dozen others, who had bunched in the centre, went down in a heap. The rest took cover in the corn. The fight was over before a tank from the 13th/18th Hussars arrived; either the rumble coming closer or the long swinging gun had an electrifying effect on the survivors, who leapt to their feet, throwing their weapons away. All shouted their surrender in an unknown language. With shaven heads and smelling to high heaven, they turned out to be Russians press-ganged into service, commanded by a German officer and NCOs. They appeared delighted to be led into captivity.[3]

Dr J.H. Patterson, RAMC, medical officer No.4 Commando:

We moved off to the main east–west road, which leads straight into Ouistreham. The road was under heavy mortar fire and I came on six of our men lying dead along the way. I was very lame, but Marine Boyce carried my rucksack and gave me an arm.

Farther on we passed two more of our chaps, one dead, and the other almost gone, with his head smashed. I pushed his beret over his face and went on. Then we found Lance Corporal Farnese, quite dead. The same mortar bomb had killed another man, an old French-man who had come out to welcome us, and severely wounded another commando in the shoulder. A bad case: his shoulder was practically severed, with blood gushing from it. With some trouble we got the bleeding under control with finger pressure in the neck, and, holding on to this point, we put him on a stretcher and carried him the rest of the way to the point where the assaulting troops left their rucksacks, 300 yards further on.

Here I set up my RAP, on a patch of grass under some pine trees. The attack on the battery and the coast defences was well under way, but I was pre-occupied with my badly wounded man, and packed the wound as best I could before giving him a pint of plasma, which brought back his pulse. Now casualties were pouring in.

A lot of officers were hit. The CO had a split temple and some fragments in his leg, but refused to be evacuated. The Germans persistently mortared the road junction beside us: the bombs were clearly visible as they sailed overhead, skimming the roofs of the adjacent houses. Later we put as many of the wounded as possible inside, under cover. Casualties kept coming in all the time, but luckily some jeeps turned up and I began to get the severely wounded back to the beach-head, which cleared the congestion.

I talked French with the locals as I drove around the town collecting more wounded in a jeep, getting cautious as it became clear that the only troops left in the town were probably Germans. I drank *à bas les Boches* with the white-bearded local doctor in the little hospital, across the bodies of civilians and soldiers. I had a cup of hot sweetened milk and a wash at the cottage across the road. I flattened to the ground as we were straddled by a stick of small armour-piercing bombs and practically disappeared when a rocket-firing Focke-Wolf strafed the streets.

More than once I looked out at my wounded on the beach. Nothing was being done for them: there was no plasma or blood, and they lay there being bombed and machine-gunned all night long. Very few were taken off that day.[4]

Letter, written 4 July 1944, from Lieutenant Hugh Bone, 2nd East Yorks Regiment:

The move inland was not much fun, since Jerry was mortaring us pretty badly. We had to cross a marsh and in places we were up to our armpits in muddy water and slime. The mortars had our range and as I helped my wireless people through the deep parts they were bursting only fifty yards behind us. In spite of all my efforts, the wireless set that weighed so much and was of such importance, would not work – a vital part had been lost dodging the mortars.

The next battle I saw only from the back, but its aftermath gave me my first real taste of fear. We had moved forward into one already-taken enemy position in order to mount an attack on a stronger one beyond it. This was rash since Jerry had his mortars laid on the last position. It was a small thick wood by the side of a road and he fairly laced into us. I cannot tell you how many were wounded and killed there, but I lost some more signallers and a whole crowd round me got hit. We could not get away, neither could we dig. The ground was hard and tangled with roots and the bombs were bursting literally everywhere all the time.

I laid on my face for a few moments, then, seeing the provost sergeant hit five yards away, I pushed over to him and shoved my field dressing on the back of his neck. He had a piece of shrapnel through his shoulder, but it was not serious and we got him out of it. (Curious how everyone turns yellow when hit.) We all had to get out of it and we did. The attack went in from the rear instead and was successful, lots of Jerry prisoners being captured, but Dicky was killed and Hurch wounded, as well as a good many others. After this, having reached our objectives, all but one, we began to collect ourselves.[5]

Private Francis Williams MM, aged 22, 6th Battalion, Green Howards:

We moved forward all day, losing men to snipers and booby traps. By then we had lost most of our NCOs and our three platoon commanders had all been killed or wounded. I would say that, owing to the loss of officers and NCOs, there were several of our lads that should have received decorations but didn't. One in particular was Private Bernard Charles Elmer, who was known as 'Before Christ' because of his initials. Charlie and I were both No.1 Bren-gunners and we were on our own going along a track with a thick hedge on one side and open ground on the other. We heard an artillery piece being fired and also the rattle of a couple of Spandaus. We looked through the hedge and fifty to sixty yards away was a field gun and two machine guns firing on our lads down the way a bit. Charlie and I were undecided what to do, when up the track came a Sherman tank. We asked the tank commander to fire a couple of shots at the field gun, but the tank commander spoke into his intercom and the tank buggered off, leaving Charlie and me on our own again. BC, being a good bit older than me, worked out a plan of action. Not far behind the enemy position was the beginning of a wood. BC would work his way behind them and, as soon as I saw him come into the open ground behind the position I was to open up and fire as fast as I could through the hedge. Charlie moved off and after a few minutes I saw him appear out of the wood. I fired three magazines into the position. Charlie ran at them firing from the hip and they gave up very quickly. I scrambled through the hedge and joined up with Charlie. There were five or six dead, some wounded and eight prisoners, who we made run back down the track towards the beach with their hands on their heads.

Charlie and I sat down at the corner of the track and the wood, opened up one of our twenty-four hour packs and brewed up a pot of char with the water out of our bottle and ate our oatmeal blocks and a few sweets. Then some of our lads came up the track and we moved on. We were passing through a village when my number two on the Bren saw a shutter move on the window of a house. While I covered him with the Bren, he lobbed a 69 grenade, a plastic type of flash grenade, up at the window. As he did so, a gust of wind blew the shutter closed, the grenade hit the shutter and bounced back and exploded near Private Sedgewick, another Middlesbrough lad. He had bits of plastic in his hands, face and a few other places. He asked me to dig them out with his jacknife. I got some out but some were in too deep and I told him to go back and get medical attention, which he did. I never saw him again from that day to this.

I had no idea of the time, but it would have been early evening, still light enough to see easily, and we were coming out of open ground into a road running through a village which, if my memory serves me right, was called Villiers or Villers-le-Sec. Just as we were nearly onto the road a barrage of mortars or shells landed nearby. I was hit in the upper arm. A two-inch piece of shrapnel went into my arm horizontally, breaking the bone and hanging out the back of my upper arm. We dived into a ditch at the side of the road and old faithful BC cut off my battledress sleeve and my shirt sleeve and put a field dressing on my wound. We had lost four killed and another four or five wounded beside myself.[6]

Captain L.N. (Nobby) Clark, No.1 Movement Control Unit, 3rd Canadian Division:

The afternoon and evening was devoted to 'de-lousing' the houses behind the beach of snipers and quite a job it was. We were a bit clumsy at first and lost quite a few because of it, but it soon became more or less a drill. I had a small group of two sergeants and six sappers with plenty of guts. Some of the houses just refused to be de-loused and so we burned them down. We set one on fire which had caused us a lot of grief and when it really started to brew a young Jerry made an effort to escape through a window. He got partly out when a gunner on an LCT saw him and hit him with a streak of about 50 Œrlikon rounds.

By dark most of the houses in our vicinity were clean. My loot up to that point was a swastika flag which I had torn from the wall of a sort of headquarters.[7]

Private John Chalk, aged 23, medical section, D Company, 1st Battalion, The Hampshire Regiment:

I was beginning to wonder what was going to happen to the wounded when one of the battalion signallers told me the wounded were collecting in the church at Asnelles-sur-Mer. I took some of the walking wounded to the church, where I found that a friend of mine from B Company, Lance Corporal Roy Butt, had set up an aid post. The place was full of wounded and he was being assisted by some French nuns and some other women from the village. We had no idea where the medical officer was, so we just did our best.

I remember bringing in a tank officer with a gunshot wound in the face, some of his jaw and a lot of his tongue shot away. He walked with me to the church, but there was not a lot we could do and he just sat on the pews waiting patiently, and losing blood.

It was about this time that I realized we were out of practically everything – dressings, morphine, etcetera – so I decided to look for the RAP (Regimental Aid Post). I went back down to the beach, but never found it. Then someone told me there were medical supplies in one of the pillboxes and to help myself, which I did.

Whilst on the beach this time I was amazed at how far the tide had come in since we had landed. It appeared chaotic to me, with smashed landing craft and quite a few bodies moving in and out with the waves. Engineers were still blowing up mines and some German prisoners were helping to clear things up. However, I couldn't hang around, so I made my way back inland as fast as I could, up a lane to the east of Asnelles, because I knew D Company had to go inland around the back of Le Hamel to attack a gun position on high ground.

I was destined to be delayed again because going up this lane I heard two heavy explosions up ahead. Turning a corner I knew I had more work to do. The lane was littered with dead and wounded from a section of the Devons, about eight men, and one of our officers, who had been caught by what I reckon was heavy mortars. The corporal of the section was laying in the road with both legs blown off as close to the body as it was possible to get. As I stood wondering where to start, he asked if I had a fag. Although I was a non-smoker, I always carried cigarettes for this very purpose. One of the first things most wounded ask for is a fag. I put one in his mouth and lit it for him, and he was talking to me as if this was an everyday happening.

I did what I could for the wounded – those who were not dead were all wounded – and while kneeling among those poor fellows a section of battalion HQ picked their way through, headed by the adjutant, Captain Walters, who asked me if I knew where battalion HQ was. I couldn't help him and he couldn't tell me where the RAP was.

After they moved through I looked up to see a young girl with a bicycle, just standing there crying and sobbing. I realized she was afraid to move through what must have looked like hell to her, so I picked up her bicycle, took her by the hand and led her through. Goodness knows where she had come from or where she was heading for.

I knew I couldn't leave those poor fellows there without more help, so I decided to go back to the beach again. This time I was luckier, because just coming up from the beach was the medical officer of the Devons, who had just landed with his RAP. I told him about his men and he said I should leave it to him.

Once again, I set off inland, taking a short cut to where I thought the company should be. By this time the weather had improved no end and the sun was shining when I came across a couple of battalion signallers who had set up their radio in front of a cottage and one of them asked if I would like a drop of char, as they had just brewed up. While enjoying this welcome drink I noticed the roses growing on the walls of the cottage and for some reason thought of the song, 'The Roses of Picardy'.

I was then informed that someone thought there were some wounded in the cornfield which ran from the back of the cottage to a ridge of high ground. I found one dead sergeant at the top of the field and then made my way through the cornfield, searching. Suddenly I was fired on by a machine gun from the high ground. Fortunately they missed, and I went to ground with the bullets cracking through the corn. I then crawled to the edge of the field and, under cover of a hedge, made my way to the bottom end where I found a group of wounded from my own company who had been caught by the machine gun while making their way across the field.

Among this group was the company's second in command, whose upper arm was shattered. Also in the group was a young chap wounded in the head, the bullet entering his mouth and lodging in the skull somewhere at the back of his eyes. His face was swelling badly and I really didn't have a lot of hope for him. (Months later I met him again in England and he was all right, apart from losing one eye.)

After doing what I could for this group, I had to get a message back to battalion HQ about them because, although fighting was going on all around, it was quiet in that corner of the field and it would be some time before they were found. So I trekked back to the cottage to get a message sent, then went back to the wounded to assure them that help was on its way. Then I continued on my way to catch up with the rest of the company.[8]

Captain John Madden, C Company, 1st Canadian Parachute Battalion:

We drove down into the small village of Bénouville, where a group of soldiers sat at the sidewalk tables of a small café, while not ten yards away a 20mm gun mounted on a jeep poured shot after shot into the spire of the church where hid a sniper. Even as I tried to adjust to this madness, up came an officer I had known in England. He wore a sturdy pair of German jackboots. Before I thought to ask him of my brigade, my unit, we fell into discussing the difference between their boots and ours.[9]

General Omar N. Bradley, commander US First Army:

The whole of D-Day was for me a time of grave personal anxiety and frustration. I was stuck on the *Augusta*. Our communications with the forces assaulting Omaha Beach were thin to non-existent. From the few radio messages that we overheard and the first-hand reports of observers in small craft reconnoitring close to shore, I gained the impression that our forces had suffered an irreversible catastrophe, that there was little hope we could force the beach. Privately, I considered evacuating the beach-head and directing the follow-up troops to Utah Beach or the British beaches. Chet Hansen recorded later that I remarked to Monty: 'Someday I'll tell General Eisenhower just how close it was those first few hours.' I agonized over the withdrawal decision, praying that our men could hang on.

They did – barely. Then, at 1.30 p.m., I received a heartening message from Gerow: 'Troops formerly pinned down on beaches . . . advancing up heights behind beaches.' I sent my chief of staff, Bill Kean, and Chet Hansen to the beach for a first-hand look. Their report was more optimistic than I dared hope for. The situation everywhere on the beach was still grave, but our troops had forced one or two of the draws and were inching inland. Based on their report, I gave up any thought of abandoning Omaha Beach.

By nightfall, the situation had swung in our favor. Personal heroism and the US Navy had carried the day. We had by then landed close to 35,000 men and held a sliver of corpse-littered beach five miles long and about one and a half miles deep. To wrest that sliver from the enemy had cost us possibly 25,000 casualties. (No exact accounting has ever been arrived at.) There was now no thought of giving it back.[10]

Lieutenant Colonel Donald V. Bennett, 62nd Armored Artillery:

About noon, we were able to take the first hill, about 100 yards inshore. This was about five hours after we landed [on Omaha]. In our landing area we had a company of tanks, Shermans with a shroud on them so they could swim in. Out of the total, we had *one* able to reach our beach. It was just short of high water when it hit a mine and knocked off one of its tracks. The crew was still in there. We had some fires burning around there and you couldn't see very well. There was an entrance to a dug-out right there; the crew couldn't see it from their tank, but I could see it from where I was lying down on the beach. I got their attention and directed fire at 100 yards with the 75mm on the tank. We got some hits in the enclosure and knocked it out.

Sergeant O'Brien, one of the men with me, and I were moving up the beach and it was hard going. At one time we came across one of these great big black rubber boats that the engineers had used coming in. It was lying up on the beach and we flopped down behind it. I've never felt so safe in my life. No one could see us. We hid behind this big black thing. Then we got our wind back and our senses and it dawned on us what we were hiding behind. Air! So we decided to move and we went about fifty feet down the beach and karoom! A mortar shell hit that black boat and just blew it to hell.

About this time I found my A Battery; they had landed a little to the right. They were in a position below high water, mixed up with a company of the 116th and some of the 16th. Sergeant Patrick, one of the chiefs of section, saw me and said, 'Hey Colonel, do you want some coffee?' Now this was about three o'clock in the afternoon and

I hadn't had anything since two o'clock the previous night. I said, 'Sure.' So he ticked off two people to go out and make some coffee. And they pumped up the Coleman stove, put some water in a can, put the can on the stove and got down on their hunkers and started watching this thing boil.

Literally the stuff was flying all around there and every once in a while you'd hear something hit on the side of the track. But these two men were just down there watching and stirring the water. A platoon sergeant from the 116th had been in a hole; he had all his platoon around him. Now, he got up and looked over there and he saw these two lads down on their hunkers, stirring this coffee. 'Hey, Jim,' he called, and a corporal stuck his head out of another hole. 'Look at that son-of-a-bitch over there, look at that son-of-a-bitch making coffee.'

Pretty soon the sergeant said, 'All right, gang,' and got what was left of his outfit moving. As far as I was concerned, the nonchalant manner in which these two lads were going about making coffee for the colonel had told the sergeant that perhaps they could live. So one platoon, or what was left of it, marched off to go to war.[11]

Notes scrawled on two pages of memorandum book and three envelopes by Major Stanley Bach, liaison officer, HQ 1st Army, attached to advanced headquarters of 29th Infantry Division on Omaha:

12.00 – BEACH HIGH TIDE, BODIES FLOATING ... MANY DEAD AMERICANS ON BEACH AT HWM [High water mark].

12.15 – HEAVY MORTAR AND 88 FIRE STARTED ON BEACH FROM E. END TO W. END – SERIES OF FIVE SHELLS IN SPOTS – DIRECT HIT ON SHERMAN TANK, MEN OUT LIKE RATS – THOSE ALIVE.

12.30 – LCT HIT TWO MINES CAME ON IN – HIT THIRD DISINTEGRATED AND REAR END SUNK – AT BURST OF SHELL TWO NAVY MEN WENT FLYING THROUGH THE AIR INTO WATER – NEVER CAME UP.

12.50 – SAW A CAPTAIN, INF, PULL FIVE MEN TO SHORE OUT OF WATER.

13.00 – TIDE GOING OUT – NOW RHINO FERRY IN BUT BURSTING SHELLS FORCED IT TO GO BACK OUT TO SEA AFTER UNLOADING TWO VEHICLES.

13.20 – SAW DIRECT HIT ON BEACHED LCM, FLAMES

everywhere, men burning alive. beach can now be seen by aid of glasses entire distance about two miles east and two miles west — with tide slowly going out — long runnels appear in beach, also obstacles with deadly teller mines on top of beach.

14.00 – Fire on beach increasing – aid man go to help man that was M.G. [machine-gunned] but hit by bullet himself, another aid man pulled him back to foxhole.

14.30 – Just heard from above that Capt T. Ernest of 115th Inf is above us in field hit by bullet – four aid men go get him – he comes back smiling despite shoulder wounds. says get two jerries for him.

14.40 – More mortar fire and more men hit – LCVP unload five loads of men, they lie down on beach, mortar fire kills five of them – rest up and run for foxholes we left couple of hours ago.

15.00 – Snipers in large brick house on beach only 50 yards from HWM keep men in holes.

15.20 – Direct hit on $2\frac{1}{2}$ ton truck gasoline load – canvas flames – another catches fire – then entire load goes up. area 100 yards square – men's clothes on fire – attempt to roll in sand to put out flames – some successful – others die in flames.

15.40 – Infantry moving by us up path over crest and moving forward – we endeavor to move on – M.G. holds us for a few minutes, then lifts, we get to open field – follow path – see one man that had stepped on mine, no body from waist down – just entrails and chest organs.

16.00 – We reach wood through field 500 yards from top of cliff we just came up. see man on knees. we think he is praying or scared, roll him over and he is dead, died on knees praying.

16.30 – Barbed wire, mines, mortars, M.G. rifle and 88 fire everywhere it seems – prayed several times – 'why do these things have to be forced upon men?'

16.50 – Reach town of st laurent $\frac{3}{4}$ mile from beach, snipers holding up our advance – established CP and saw first time the 1st Div friends who were quiet, fighting mad – gave me heart, too.[12]

Sergeant Thomas Valance, aged 23, A Company, 116th Infantry Regiment:

I remember floundering in the water with my hand up in the air, I guess trying to get my balance, when I was first shot through the palm of my left hand. I remember feeling nothing but a little sting at the time, although I was aware I was shot. Next to me in the water a fellow called Hank Witt was rolling towards me and I remember very clearly him saying, 'Sergeant, they're leaving us here to die like rats. Just to die like rats.'

I made my way forward as best I could, but I was hit several other times, once in the left thigh, which broke a hip bone, although I didn't know it at the time. I remember being hit in the back a couple of times and feeling a tug as the chin strap of my helmet was severed by a bullet. I worked my way up onto the beach and staggered up against a wall and sort of collapsed there.

I spent the whole day in the same position. Eventually the bodies of the other guys washed ashore and I was the only live one among so many of my friends, all of whom were dead and in many cases severely blown to pieces. It was not a very pleasant way to spend a day.

The day wore on and I worried somewhat about my left hand, which had swollen considerably and was changing colour. I knew that I had a sore left hip and the blood there was matted to my uniform.

Some time that afternoon there was a caterpillar tractor going down the beach, parallel to the waterline, and the driver stopped when he saw me alive. He came running up to me and handed me three comic books, which I guess he thought was the right thing to do, the humanitarian thing to do. Needless to say, I was not in the mood for reading comic books or anything else. Sometime after he went on his way, another fellow came up and bandaged my hand and later on still another fellow came up and gave me a can of soup.

I guess about dusk, a couple of litter bearers came down and moved me.[13]

Sergeant Jerry W. Eades, aged 25, commanding No.4 Gun Section,
B Battery, 62nd Armored Field Artillery Battalion:

About 3.00, or in that vicinity, the ramp went down. Our motors
were revved up and I was looking at the lieutenant standing behind
the half-tracks and close to the jeep, and he had his arm up and when
he dropped his arm forward I kicked the driver on the back of the
head, on the helmet, and that meant for him to let the sticks go and
let her roll, and off we went.

I vaguely remember seeing the 3rd Section gun fall off the front of
the boat and into the water and then I heard a kind of glubb-glubb-
glubbing sound. The water was deeper than our air intake and of
course it immediately flooded.

The thing I was thinking about then was all the stuff we had lost.
The navy boys had given us fifty pounds of sugar, twenty-five or
thirty pounds of coffee and forty or fifty cartons of cigarettes and we
had lost it all. There was also a picture of Dorine Villiers, I remember
that. She was a girl who used to sing songs on the BBC. She sang a
request sent in by me and two other guys and dedicated it to Joe,
Jerry, Lee and the boys of Battery B. We sent her a V-Mail letter
asking for a picture and she sent us an 8 × 10 picture of herself, from
the waist up, which we taped to the inside of the gun carriage where
all the guys could see it. Anyway, we lost the picture of Dorine
Villiers and all our coffee and all our cigarettes.

I didn't even have time to see where the guys were at when we
went down. I had my cartridge belt on but I didn't have it buckled
up and I had a carbine, I think it might have been on my shoulder, I
don't know, but anyway my thought was that with all that weight I
might drown. I knew the water was more than twelve feet deep or
our shroud would have stuck out, so I threw off the rifle and
cartridge belt. All I could see was just a blur in front of me and I
could see guys trying to swim one way so I went that way too and
the next thing I knew I was touching down on bottom. I was
standing maybe armpit deep in water and trying to move forward
and little waves were coming in and just shoving me back as I
walked in.

Then I saw what chaos was going on up on the beach and I could
hear the mortar rounds, possibly artillery rounds, hitting up there. I
could hear rifle and machine-gun fire. They had some big steel
crosses sticking out of the water and I remember going up to one

and trying to stay behind the steel. There were so many guys around there I felt kind of guilty trying to stick behind something. I could see across the beach, maybe thirty-five to forty yards, there were cliffs and guys beginning to gather up there and I knew if I could get up under that cliff I'd at least be safe from small-arms fire and possibly from the mortars.

So I finally inched my way up out of the water and all of a sudden I realized how cold I was. I was shaking quite a speed. I didn't realize how scared I was and how cold I was, I guess. Anyway I jumped up and started running and as I ran along I picked up a rifle from a guy lying on the beach who looked like he was dead. He could have been in shock, I don't know. I didn't stop and kept running and when I fell down beside the cliff the first guy I saw was a fellow named Clarence E. Figgins, from Fort Scott, Kansas, who was in my gun crew. I think I remember asking him, 'Where's the rest of our crew?' and he just gave me a kind of blank stare. He just didn't know, or couldn't say anything.

We could still hear machine-gun chatter here and there and I could still hear the swoosh of the mortar rounds when they were hitting, but they were going further out to sea from me. I just sat there, kind of numb, trying to realize what was going on and asking myself just what in the hell I was doing in that place.

As we were sitting there too scared to get up, there was a colonel, I think he was a lieutenant colonel, coming down the beach. He nonchalantly walked up to where we were and said, 'Who's the non-commissioned officer around here?' I didn't say a word. I didn't see any other non-commissioned officers making any move to get up, either. Then this fellow in my gun crew – and if I ever wanted to strangle anybody it was him, right then – said, 'He's my sergeant.' The lieutenant colonel turned to me and said, 'Are you an NCO?' I said, 'Yes, I'm a sergeant in the artillery.' He said, 'Well, since you are the only one here that is a sergeant, gather up as many of these men as you can and report to Lieutenant so-and-so . . .' He pointed to a place down the beach. I said, 'I'm not an infantryman, I'm an artilleryman.' He said, 'I don't care what you are, you're in the infantry now.'

Everybody that we could gather up there we formed into a kind of provisional platoon and went inland to a little town called Colleville-sur-Mer, I think, or something like that. We made it in that night. And although I had lost my gun and had gone through a very confusing day, I was still alive and I hadn't been wounded. I considered myself very lucky.[14]

Colonel David Bruce, London chief of OSS, with General 'Wild Bill' Donovan, head of OSS:

When we finally got ashore in Normandy I had maladroitly, in taking evasive action when fired upon by enemy aircraft, fallen on the general and gashed him badly in the throat with my steel helmet. It must have cut close to the jugular vein, for he bled profusely. At this time he wore, and it was the only occasion when I knew him to do so, the ribbon of the Medal of Honor, in those days everywhere recognizable.

We sauntered inland to an American anti-aircraft battery, the furthermost position occupied by our people in that sector. Beyond was a huge open field, enclosed at the far end by a tight hedge. In the field, three presumably French peasants appeared to be digging up roots or vegetables. Donovan approached the battery and said he was going forward to question his three French agents, who were expecting him. The captain, looking at his bloody throat and the Congressional medal, warned him this was dangerous, but let him proceed.

As we progressed, our alleged agents disappeared; Donovan and I came to a halt in the lee of a hedgerow that was being subjected to intermittent German machine-gun fire. Flattened out, the general turned to me and said: 'David, we mustn't be captured, we know too much.' 'Yes, sir,' I answered mechanically. 'Have you your pill?' he demanded. I confessed I was not carrying the instantaneous death pellet concocted by our scientific adviser. 'Never mind,' replied the resourceful general, 'I have two of them.' Thereupon, still lying prone, he disgorged the contents of all his pockets. There were a number of old hotel keys, a passport, currency of several nationalities, photographs of grandchildren, travel orders, newspaper clippings, and heaven knows what else, but no pills. 'Never mind,' said Donovan, 'we can do without them, but if we get out of here you must send a message to Gibbs, the hall porter at Claridges in London, telling him on no account to allow the servants in the hotel to touch some dangerous medicines in my bathroom.

This humanitarian disposition having been made, Donovan whispered to me: 'I must shoot first.' 'Yes, sir,' I responded, 'but can we do much against machine guns with our pistols?' 'Oh, you don't understand,' he said. 'I mean, if we are about to be captured, I'll shoot you first. After all, I am your commanding officer.'[15]

Pfc Carl Weast, aged 22, 5th Ranger Battalion:

We went through Vierville-sur-Mer and proceeded on the coastal highway towards Pointe du Hoc. Now we had just gotten out of town, I suppose maybe 4–500 yards, when our point men came under machine-gun fire. Fortunately these machine gunners weren't very good; they didn't hit anybody. Our guys merely hit the ground and crawled back to the cover of the hedgerow.

A messenger came back from our company commander and he instructed our platoon officer to go down the hedgerow perpendicular to the road, get behind that machine gun and get rid of it. OK, now this lieutenant we had, I'm not going to mention his name, he had come in as a replacement for an officer who was injured in training, and he was a real goof-off. So we started going down the hedgerow and instead of flanking, or getting that gunner from the rear, this lieutenant apparently went off his rocker, because we just kept going inland until we came to a gravel road, where we halted in an orchard.

Shortly after we halted, a hell of a barrage of artillery hit the orchard and my good friend Elmer Banning was killed and the first section leader, Sergeant McElwain was hit in the right arm pretty bad. When the smoke cleared and we got ourselves together again, we checked Elmer, determined he was dead, and the medic we had fixed up Mac's arm as well as he could and gave him a shot of morphine.

About this time, approximately twenty yards to our left, where another hedgerow took off, comes out some US officers, I think it was a captain and a couple of lieutenants, and they asked us who we were and what our unit was. We told them we were a platoon from the 5th Rangers. They were the headquarters staff of the 116th Regimental Combat Team. They had apparently managed quite nicely to get up to their planned CP, a château on the other side of the orchard, but they found it was full of Germans. Since they only had a couple of enlisted men, we were impressed as the CP guard, so we more or less stayed in that area, which had fairly good cover even though within spitting distance, practically, was a château full of Germans.

While they were trying to make up their mind what they wanted to do, a German riding a bicycle comes along the road from the direction of the château. He was obviously a dispatch rider, with a case slung over his shoulder, and he was unarmed except for a pistol. At first I don't think he realized that we were enemy troops because he got, oh hell, I suppose within twenty yards of us when he suddenly realized, hell, everybody had their rifles trained on him.

When he realized we were enemy he stopped his bicycle and I think he might have been going to get rid of that dispatch case but some of the guys thought he was going for his pistol and he must have been hit with about, I would say, nine or ten rounds real quick. Naturally he dropped, but unfortunately he wasn't dead. He laid face down near the edge of the road, bleeding profusely. The blood gathered under his face and he was breathing into it, making a bubbling sound, and it was as nerve-racking as hell. One of the fellows, I don't know who the hell it was, committed an act of mercy, went over to this guy and put a bullet right through the back of his head.

We had set out what you might call outpost positions and one of them was at a junction of the gravel road with a paved road from the direction of Vierville. I was on that outpost position with a friend of mine, Blacky Morgan, and lo and behold these Germans came out of the château, formed up in a column of twos, put their wounded on an old two-wheel horse buggy, two guys pulling and two guys shoving, and started down towards this crossroads.

Apparently they didn't know we were there either, because they had their rifles over their shoulders. So we waited until they were real close, I'm saying maybe ten yards, and we step out into the road with our weapons pointed at them and of course they surrendered immediately, all of them. There must have been thirty-five, maybe forty, in the whole bunch, including the wounded. We put them in an orchard and put one man guarding them and tried to interrogate them. Hell, there was no Germans there! They were all Hungarians, Romanians, Russians, anything but Germans. I think there was one German cadreman, a noncom, and he had been on the Eastern front. He was middle-aged and looked like he wanted to do anything but fight a war, believe me. This guy was as happy as hell to be a prisoner, although he was concerned about a German counter-attack, although not nearly as concerned as we were.

We started sending out light patrols, I'm talking two or three men, to our flanks and even back towards Vierville. There were a few little exchanges of gunfire, but at no time did anybody ever see any friendly troops and it was getting late into the evening. As the evening gave way to darkness we had these prisoners and had to decide what in hell we were going to do with them. We laid them down to sleep, real close to each other, and put a man with a BAR at the end and we made it plain to them that when it got dark we wouldn't be able to observe them but we could hear them and if anybody made any motion we were going to machine-gun the whole bunch of them. They got the message loud and clear and they lay there and, believe me, those were some damn quiet enemy, didn't hear a tick all night long from them.

Normandy – hey, if we'd have been confronted with first-class German troops they'd have just tore our ass up. Fortunately, we were up against some of the lousiest troops in the German army. These guys didn't want to fight, none of them did, and we were fortunate in that. Otherwise . . .

We talk about leadership. Where was the leadership back on those beaches? I think the men would have moved if somebody would have led them. In our outfit, we were fortunate, we had leaders. Captain Whittington was one of the first ones over that goddamn sea wall. The officers went first. Later on I heard our adjutant criticizing Captain Whittington for unnecessarily exposing himself and I remember he [Whittington] says, 'You saw it happen back on that goddamn beach. Now when you know how the hell you lead men from behind, you tell me. It just doesn't work.'

Believe me, on Omaha beach there was precious little leadership anywhere. It was simple fear that stopped those guys at the sea wall and they lay there and got butchered by rocket fire and by artillery fire for no damn reason other than the fact that there was nobody to lead them off that goddamn beach. We were fortunate, we had some of the best officers in the army. Those guys did it, they led us. And like I say, I'm no goddamn patriot. I did my job, but somebody had to lead me, man.[16]

Joe Palladino, aged 19, DUKW driver, 462nd Amphibious Truck Company, 1st Engineer Special Brigade:

We were told to stay down with our DUKWs in the hole and my friend Marty Mirtel, from Cleveland, Ohio – we used to call him Mert – we were sitting there all day smoking and talking and trying not to think what was going on. We said to each other we were going to watch out for one another. We'd stick together. I'd follow him or he'd follow me. You know, stay together, give ourselves a little confidence. We couldn't see what was going on, being we were down below deck. All we could do was hear the navy guns booming and shelling the beach.

Finally, about 1.00 in the afternoon, they opened the hatch and daylight rushed in like a spotlight. I remember that. They lowered the ramp and one by one our DUKWs went off into the Channel and kept circling until everyone was out. Then we started off towards the beach, about fifty yards apart. I remember the sergeant yelling: 'Keep fifty yards apart.'

I never saw so many ships in my life. There were hundreds and hundreds of ships and aeroplanes, all kinds of planes going over. But outside of the navy guns peppering the beach there wasn't much other action going on and it was a nice sunny day.

Half-way into the beach, this Focke-Wulf 109 came swooping down out of nowhere and started strafing everybody. All you could do was duck your head to the wheel and shrug your shoulders. Luckily no one got hit. As he pulled out of his dive, a British Spitfire came out of nowhere and got right on his tail and chased him off.

That was our first taste of any kind of action, but that all changed as soon as we got close to the beach, because the Nazis had a pillbox up on the end of the beach that had the beach zeroed in and they kept shelling that beach, I believe it was with an 88.

Once we hit the beach there were MPs more or less in charge of keeping everything moving. They were screaming 'Get going! Get going!' and pointing to a road cut right through the sea wall. This went through to swamps, all swamps, and you had to go through that road and they just kept waving you through. 'Get going! Get going! Keep moving!'

In the meantime all the shelling was going on while we were going through that swamp and all of a sudden two 109s came swooping down and started strafing again. The sergeant was yelling 'Hit the ditch! Hit the ditch!' I stopped, jumped out of the DUKW and jumped into a ditch. As I hit the ditch I looked down and I remember there was a handkerchief full of blood lying there. I had jumped right next to a dead German soldier. I didn't know what to do, I just wanted to get away from him. I remember getting out of that ditch and running across to the other side of the road and jumping into the ditch over there.

That was my first sight of a dead German soldier, but from then on along that road there were quite a few more. They were all over the place, laying in the fields. It was terrible. I just wanted to get where I had to go, which was a field being used as an ammunition dump. Finally the MPs directed me to it. They unloaded me right away, stacked up the ammo and then I was on my way back to the beach again.

When I hit the beach, a sergeant yelled out a ship number and I went back into the Channel again, looking for that number on a ship, to bring back another cargo.

It was still daylight. It wasn't too bad because you could see where you were going. There were a lot of sunken ships and stacks sticking out of the water, but at least you could see where you were going. You would hook up to the ship and the ship was bobbing and you were bobbing and they sent a net over the side loaded with all kinds of shells.

At night it was worse because you couldn't see where you were going. There were no lights, you couldn't have any lights on. All you had to guide you were little reflectors stuck on the beach on little pieces of wood that reflected the night light. You had a compass on the dashboard of the DUKW which you had to use to make sure you were going in the right direction, back to the beach. The Channel had very strong currents, so that you would think you were going straight but it would carry you down to the next beach. You would be way out of your way and you would have to come up along the beach to get to where you were going. It was no picnic.[17]

Don Malarkey, aged 22, E Company, 2nd Battalion, 506th Parachute Infantry Regiment:

As the battalion proceeded towards the causeway that we were to take, we had not gone more than five or six hundred yards when machine-gun fire started breaking out and the column halted. Colonel Bob Strayer, the battalion commander, ordered E Company to make an attack on the position. I believe there were twelve of us, led by Lieutenant Dick Winters from Pennsylvania, the platoon leader, and Lieutenant Buck Compton from Los Angeles, the assistant platoon leader.

We went through an orchard area to approach the position and when we were very close by, Lieutenant Winters stopped us all and had us line up along the hedgerow looking into the position, which incorporated an emplacement of four German 88s. We all lined up and placed withering fire into the position with all our weapons, prior to making an assault.

Buck Compton went first and as he dropped into the entrenchment he saw a German standing about fifteen feet from him. He drew his Tommy gun and fired, but the gun jammed. In the meantime, the German ran away down the trench. Compton turned and waved us all across and we proceeded towards the first gun. Robert 'Popeye' Wynn, from Virginia, was with me and got hit half-way across.

As I neared the gun I could see the crew of a German 88 firing straight down the field. They couldn't traverse on us, but they were firing at whatever enemy forces they might hit in that vicinity. I pulled a grenade and threw it, but the two gunmen were already hit either by Buck Compton or by Lieutenant Winters. Both of them, I think, fired simultaneously.

When I got there one of the crew was lying dead under the gun and the other had run out into the field about fifty yards before he went down. I could see that he had a case on his hip, which I thought was a German Luger. I thought, well, I'd better go and get that gun, so I ran out on the field and as I knelt down Lieutenant Winters saw me and started yelling at me, that I was stupid and should get the hell out of there as the place was crawling with Germans.

Across the main hedgerow, towards the family farm of Brecort, the whole road was lined with German infantry with machine guns. They apparently thought I was a medic because they didn't fire at me when I was going out to where the German lay. But when Winters yelled and I jumped up and started running back, four or five machine guns started firing at me and the bullets were kicking up the ground all round me.

I dove under the gun, which was dug in below the surface of the ground about eighteen inches. I lay there, face up, as they kept firing into the gun and fragments of bullets dropped into my face. I finally turned over to keep that from happening and they kept firing intermittently.

I was stuck until Bill Guarnere, my sergeant, got along the hedgerow to about five or six feet away from me. He said, 'We'll time their bursts.' So he started timing the bursts of the machine-gun fire that came in and he said, OK, as soon as you hear the next burst, jump up and run to me.' I did that, and I got out of there without being hit.

From then on, we fought there through a good part of the day and eventually captured three of the guns.[18]

Lieutenant Eugene D. Brierre, aged 20, C Company, 501st Parachute Infantry Regiment:

We did not have any trouble taking the little village of Boutteville. In the village, I went into a house where a German was lying on the floor. His gun was near him. I almost shot him when I realized he was seriously wounded. He signalled me to hand him something. I saw that he was pointing towards a rosary. I grabbed his gun, unloaded it and put it on the other side of the room. I then picked up the rosary and handed it to him. He had a look of deep appreciation in his eyes and began to pray, passing the beads through his fingers. I learned later that he died shortly afterwards.

After capturing Boutteville, General Taylor ordered me to take a patrol and go and make contact with the soldiers coming from the beach. Some Germans had been reported on the road heading towards the beach. I took eight men and went along a hedgerow about fifty yards to the east of the road. We got to a place where there was no more cover and started to head back to the road, which seemed to be clear. At that time we were fired on from the beach. I shot an orange flare up into the air to show that we were friends. The firing stopped and we could see troops starting to come up the road. When they got to the bridge, about six Germans came out with their hands up and surrendered.

I made three patrols for General Taylor. We never did run into any live enemy. We did find many dead Germans. We cut off their insignia and brought it back to General Taylor. On my first patrol I noticed a wedding band on a dead German. I never gave it another thought, but on the second patrol I passed the same location and saw that the ring finger of the dead German had been cut off. This shocked and angered me. I thought that out of respect for the dead soldier's family, that ring should have been returned to his family.[19]

Ross Munro, correspondent The Canadian Press:

The shelling had stopped on the beach and we walked into Bernières with the reserve brigade infantry which had just come off the craft. The French civilians, who had fled to the fields for shelter during the bombardment, were returning to their shell-raked village now. Old men and women, young girls and children, stood on the sidewalks of the littered main street, clapped their hands, waved the troops on their way and tossed roses in their path.

This first spontaneous reaction of these Norman people was an almost unbelievable thing to see. Our shells and rockets had blown down their homes; they had lost everything they owned; their town was a shambles, with even the fine church on the square scarred by battle; they had been terrified by the bombardment and some of the people of Bernières had been killed. But there they stood in little groups on this dusty street amid the havoc of their village and smiled and laughed and cheered our men along the road that wound up the slope through the wheat fields to battle.

A girl handed me a crimson rose and there were tears of despair and joy in her eyes as she said: 'There is my home, over there. It is gone. It is ruined by the bombardment, but the Allies are here! The Canadians are in our village now and the Boche has gone.'

She smiled, and seemed to forget about her personal tragedy as she picked another armful of flowers and tossed them to the tank crews as the Shermans thundered by.[20]

Revd R.M. Hickey, chaplain, North Shore Regiment:

The first French people I saw that day were some men, women and children crouching in a little cave near the beach. Up in the village the people had run to whatever protection they could find in cellars and out in the fields; some, unable to get away, were killed, others badly wounded. A man ran across the street, he wanted help; we followed him into his house and there on the floor lay his young wife badly wounded. Doc stopped the bleeding with a first aid dressing, and she tried to bless herself when I told her I was a priest and would give her absolution and extreme unction.

Their children, three little girls of about four, six and eight, looked on terrified, maybe as much because of us as of their mother. I spoke to them, but only seemed to terrify them all the more. Then I remembered I had three chocolate bars in my pocket, part of my day's rations. I gave them to the little girls. Oh, the power of a chocolate bar! The terror vanished from six brown eyes and even there as terror reigned, three little girls attempted a smile as I patted their curly heads.

'I think she'll live,' said Doc. I told the husband what the Doctor had said. 'Thank God. Thank God and you,' he answered.[21]

Sergeant Harold Fielder, aged 27, 26 Field Company, Assault Engineers:

Later that afternoon we were sent up to an orchard, about a mile-and-a-half from the beach, where we dug a dug-out and pulled our tank over it. There was a farm nearby with a rabbit in a hutch so we decided we would have it for dinner. We pulled up some spuds from the field, skinned the rabbit and boiled them on a little stove we had. It was good, too.

The French farmer was very cross. He came over and said, '*Les anglais sont pas bon*,' and went storming off. He wasn't at all happy that we'd eaten his rabbit.[22]

Second Lieutenant David Holbrook, aged 21, East Yorkshire Yeomanry:

Once we got off the beach we pulled into a field behind a wall to blow all the waterproofing off. You pressed a button and it exploded strings of cortex all around the tank which busted the waterproofing. Then you had to get out and pull it all away before it got in the tracks. You couldn't move your turret until you had done that.

While we were doing all this there was a colossal hail of fire coming over the top of the wall. The Germans had these fast-firing machine guns called Spandaus and they were literally ripping an orchard to pieces. You've never heard anything like it. You suddenly find yourself enveloped in a sort of hail of tracer, wondering what the hell was happening. That was our first experience of being under fire, although it wasn't actually direct at us. It was horrible seeing this very pretty landscape being ripped to pieces and the noise was absolutely incredible. It was more than just a noise: it was an assault on your skin and ears. The blast just sort of slams into you with all these bits of tree and wall flying about.

The army's term for it was shit. Day and night there was some kind of shit flying at you. If it wasn't these machine guns it was tank guns, if it wasn't tank guns it was artillery, if it wasn't artillery it was some bugger in an aeroplane dropping bombs on you.

There wasn't any kind of confrontation you could call a confrontation. You'd just move along in your tank and then suddenly a great wave of shit would start flying at you and you'd blast off in that direction and then it all stops and there's a lot of dust and smoke and you back behind a wall. Then you come out the other side and start driving along and nothing happens and you think that's all right and then suddenly a bloody great branch flies off a tree and you see that somebody else is shooting at you and then you dodge behind a house.

On exercises they had tried to indicate to us what shell fire would be like, but the reality of war is that everything goes horribly wrong and people get killed. It's not like it is in the books. You find a nice place behind a hill to shelter from fire and then you suddenly get a barrage from the other direction, which you least expect, and you get this terrible feeling that it's all going wrong. Your nice experience of army organization is all buggered up all at once and you have to start relying on your own resources, keeping your little patch OK, hoping you will survive.

I think what war teaches you is how fantastic human hate can be. Because it's clearly insane, really, this spectacle of men and machines trying to destroy one another. It's really quite hideously insane. And one wonders whether there is any future for an animal that can do this.[23]

CHAPTER TWENTY

HOME FRONT

Back in Britain, there was little to do but wait for news and pray that the landings had been a success; little to do, that is, until the wounded started coming home . . .

Tom Hiett, aged 14, telegram boy, Southampton:

I knew D-Day was getting close because I used to deliver telegrams to a lot of the military units and headquarters in Southampton and I was one of the few people allowed free access to the embarkation area. I'd seen the battleships *Revenge* and *Resolution* at New Docks. They told me they were 'stokers' training ships'; a weak story – I knew they were there to support the invasion even though it was the best kept secret ever.

On 4 June I had had to deliver a telegram to the temporary naval barracks and I couldn't find anyone there. I finally found a matelot and said: 'Where have they all gone?' He said they had embarked. When I got home I told my parents to listen to the news next morning, but of course there was nothing. I didn't know they were still laying out in the Solent because of the postponement.

I was on a district round on the morning of 6 June. Southampton was absolutely deserted, but you could hear the distant rumble of guns and I saw a squadron of B17s fly over, very high up. At 11.00 I had the first death telegram to deliver. The lady came to the door and was horrified to see me standing there. I gave her the telegram, muttered, 'No answer,' and fled.

It seemed I could hear crying all down the road and I thought, 'Good God, how many more?'[1]

Sergeant James Rider, aged 21, US Army Medical Corps, Rhodes General Hospital, Utia, New York:

The bulk of our patients were members of various units stationed in England who had come back after being injured in training exercises: paratroopers, injured combat soldiers, truck accidents, tank accidents. I was assigned to a ward of orthopaedic injuries: broken arms, legs, all sorts of broken bones in accidents. You didn't get sent back to the States unless you needed a long period of either continued surgery or recovery. The troops called it being 'ZI'ed', which meant being sent to the Zone of Interior, that is, the United States.

June 6 was like any other morning. I was doing a twelve-hour shift, from 7.00 a.m. to 7.00 p.m. and as usual I went to work on the ward at 7.00. I recall having breakfast but I didn't listen to the radio.

Going to the ward, I sensed some excitement along the corridors, but you couldn't put your finger on it. As I entered the ward, the lights were bright and blazing, which you just didn't get at 7.00 in the morning, most people wanted to steal a last minute of sleep if they could. But this morning every patient was sitting straight up in bed or in a wheelchair listening to the radio.

Many, many of them were crying. Most of them knew their outfits were in the invasion. They could see their buddies on the landing craft and see them being killed as the news came back that there was a great deal of resistance and that casualties were expected to be high.

I guess that was the thing that got me most, the men crying. Nobody seemed ashamed of this. I guess they felt a sense of guilt that they weren't there. Their outfit was there, their buddies were there and they felt they should have been there.[2]

Mrs Nellie Nowlan, Basildon, Essex:

I remember D-Day, 6 June. I was working in Plessey's underground tunnel at Redbridge, Wanstead, making Spitfire vacuum pumps. I was walking to the top of the road towards East Ham High Street to get my 101 bus from Woolwich when I heard such a noise and thundering. I reached the High Street and thousands of lorries and tanks loaded with soldiers were making their way to Woolwich.

They were laughing and waving their hands and Mrs Larkin from Larkins sweetshop was throwing them packets of cigarettes and chocolates and peanuts. They were catching them and saying, 'Thank you, darling.' The older people were standing by the kerb crying and saying, 'Good luck, boys, God bless you!' When I walked across the road to get my bus, they all gave me the wolf whistle. I smiled and waved my hand . . . needless to say, I was crying, too.[3]

Statement to the House of Commons by the Prime Minister:

I have to announce to the House that during the night and the early hours of this morning the first of the series of landings in force upon the European continent has taken place. In this case the liberating assault fell upon the coast of France. An immense armada of upward of 4,000 ships, together with several thousand smaller craft, crossed the Channel. Massed airborne landings have been successfully effected behind the enemy lines, and landings on the beaches are proceeding at various points at the present time. The fire of the shore batteries has been largely quelled. The obstacles that were constructed in the sea have not proved so difficult as was apprehended. The Anglo-American Allies are sustained by about 11,000 first-line aircraft, which can be drawn upon as may be needed for the purposes of the battle. I cannot of course commit myself to any particular details. Reports are coming in in rapid succession. So far the commanders who are engaged report that everything is proceeding according to plan. And what a plan! This vast operation is undoubtedly the most complicated and difficult that has ever taken place. It involves tides, wind, waves, visibility, both from the air and the sea standpoint, and the combined employment of land, air and sea forces in the highest degree of intimacy and in contact with conditions which could not and cannot be fully foreseen.

There are already hopes that actual tactical surprise has been attained, and we hope to furnish the enemy with a succession of surprises during the course of the fighting. The battle that has now begun will grow constantly in scale and in intensity for many weeks to come, and I shall not attempt to speculate upon its course. This I may say, however. Complete unity prevails throughout the Allied armies. There is brotherhood in arms between us and our friends of the United States. There is complete confidence in the Supreme Commander, General Eisenhower, and his lieutenants and also in the commander of the expeditionary force, General Montgomery. The ardour and the spirit of the troops, as I saw myself, embarking in these last few days, was splendid to witness. Nothing that equipment, science, or forethought could do has been neglected, and the whole process of opening this great new front will be pursued with the utmost resolution both by the commanders and by the United States and British governments whom they serve.[4]

Wren J.E. Laughton, cypher trainee at Lee airfield:

At breakfast rumours sped around but it was not until I arrived at the office that I heard the definite news. The wireless was on and, with everybody gathered round, we heard the first communiqué from the Supreme Headquarters of the Allied Expeditionary Force that landings had been made in northern France. Later we heard the voice of the Supreme Commander, General Eisenhower, and afterwards Mr Churchill's statement to the House of Commons.

What a thrilling day it was! In the morning I spent an hour on the aerodrome, no longer the orderly field of routine activity but a scene of incredible movement with a tense operational hum about it. Everywhere there were lorries, vans and crash tenders speeding back and forth. Mechanics and fitters crawled around and over the planes, and pilots climbed in and out of the cockpits. Mustangs were taking off two at a time, sweeping along the runways and up over our heads, while two more swung into position and followed in their wake. The whole flight was up and away in ten minutes. Beyond this nearest runway, Spitfires were landing after their fifth sortie of the day.

Round at the tennis club in the evening, a few pilots came in for a quick drink. They looked tired and strained, but told us their experiences. One had bailed out into the sea, another said he had beaten up a gun post and had knocked out the crew by machine gunning them in the pants. Another had limped home on one engine. And then the rumours began about those who had been our friends and who were now missing . . .[5]

Letter from a Wren at Heathfield, Sussex:

My darling Mummy & Daddy,
As you can gather by the heading we are on watch and on this night of nights I'm free enough to write a letter – let's hope it's as quiet as this all night. The less work the better the crossing . . .

It is now Tuesday evening and what a day. I still can't believe we have actually landed in France, that what we've all been waiting and waiting for for such ages should at last have happened and so far apparently successfully. Captain Sinker (our S.S.O.) told each office individually last evening about 9.00 that 'we were off'. You can imagine even though we could split the watch last night there wasn't much sleep for anyone! The security seems to have been magnificent and I believe it really must have been a bit of a surprise – gosh, I wouldn't be anywhere else today . . .

Well my darlings, all possible love – God bless you and all the invasion forces.

Veronica x x x[6]

Air Marshal Sir Arthur Tedder:

We in London eagerly awaited each scrap of information. The first reports from the Army Headquarters and from Coningham were favourable. The airborne operations, however, were not a complete success as only one-sixth of the force landed on their correct drop zones, but casualties were less than anticipated. I believed that we had achieved tactical surprise, in part because the enemy had not been expecting us in such conditions. That we had not been expected, and that our ships had been able to cross to Normandy without loss from air attack, indicated how great a degree of advantage was conferred upon the power with air supremacy. During the day, both the King and the Prime Minister arrived to see our War Room. Both were satisfied with the early promise of the assault.[7]

Naina Beaven, aged 16, Red Cross nurse, Portsmouth:

It was about two o'clock when Miss Hobbs, my nursing commandant, came into the office where I was working and said I was needed up at QA, which was Queen Alexandra's Hospital, that there were so many wounded coming back from the beaches that they desperately needed help. I ran home to tell my mother, got my uniform and then rushed up the hill to the hospital.

Another girl who I saw once a week at lectures checked in shortly after I did and we reported to Matron together. She checked our names and told us to go to this particular ward. It took us some time to get there because all the corridors were laid end to end with stretchers. Lorries were coming up from the dockyard so quickly that there wasn't room for all the wounded. The army stretcher bearers knew who was badly wounded and those who were less seriously wounded were put on the floor.

When we got to the ward we were told to start cleaning people up, giving them drinks and things. Many of them were filthy – well, they were quite young and when you're frightened you know what happens, you're all messy and dirty – so the main thing was to clean them and bed-bath them. We didn't have to treat their wounds or anything, if you took somebody's filthy battledress off and found something bad, then you would call a sister.

Mostly they were conscious but not talking much; they were mostly really, really tired and later on in the day we were told that these were the first exhaustion cases. A lot of them were so completely exhausted they didn't care one jot what happened to them. They had been on standby since the day before.

Some of them could speak, but when you are completely exhausted, not just very tired, when you are too tired to care about anything, you just want to be cleaned up and have something to drink. They weren't hungry.

As I worked with these poor exhausted soldiers, I was thinking, 'How long will it go on? If I come tomorrow and the next day, will I still be doing this?'

While I was washing and cleaning up filthy and dreadful and horrible messes and giving out water and cold milk to people who were allowed such things, two sisters came round and asked if I would be willing to work in the German prisoners' ward. They needed the same kind of help, but some nurses refused to go into their ward.

I had to go and see Matron first. I went with my friend, Win. Matron said, 'You know we have a lot of German prisoners – they were picked up very early from the beaches.' I said I didn't know, but had just been told. She said, 'Well, a lot of people won't work with them, they are either walking out or refusing to work with them. Will you do what you're doing, for them?'

Well, I was a bit meek and mild and I didn't say anything and Win looked at me and Matron said, 'Hurry up and make up your minds, because if you are not going to do it, I'll try somebody else.' Win looked at me and said, 'Oh, come on, Naina. My Eddie is out there and if somebody said they wouldn't clean him up, Mum would feel terrible.' So with that, I felt that if Win was going to do it, I'll do it. We would do it together and protect each other! I also couldn't bear the thought of my commandant saying to me, 'One of my girls wouldn't even give a prisoner a cup of water?'

Once we got to the Nissen hut where the Germans were being kept, we found there were four armed guards, two on the outer doors who had rifles and two on the inner doors with pistols. The guards checked who we were, checked the papers Matron had given us, then the sister checked us and said, 'You know what you are here for, don't you? Get on with it.'

These people were just lying on top of their beds in an assortment of dirty clothes. None of them was particularly badly wounded, but they were filthy dirty, absolutely stinking dirty, very white, unhealthy, unwholesome looking people. They had the dirty pallor of tramps, a horrible, yellowy-grey unhealthy look. And nobody said anything. None spoke English to my knowledge, they just pointed.

I sat somebody up – in those days you had feeding cups – and the smell was awful but by then it was too late to say you didn't like it. The main thing I remember was them staring, a sort of a glazed staring. They hardly talked to each other at all, I hardly heard a word, just the odd grunt or the odd word; nobody had any brightness or any life. Everybody was lying down, nobody sat up unless we propped them up. It was very silent. I remember Win saying wasn't it strange how quiet it was.

I don't really think I felt sorry for them and I didn't hate them or anything like that. I know that when I gave them a drink or a wash or cleaned them up a little bit, there was a feeling of gratefulness that you could sense. They were pleased to be helped. They, too, were terribly tired and I think they had a feeling of humiliation. Some of them were only kids, they weren't really much older than me.

One of the rules of the Red Cross is that you are there to help everybody. I'm glad I didn't refuse to help those men.[8]

Mary Verrier, Hants 12th Detachment, VAD, Portsmouth:

When the chaps started coming back I went down to the South Parade Pier with a charabanc converted into a stretcher carrier. I was waiting beside my charabanc while the chaps were being loaded on and Dr Roberts, the medical officer, came along and looked at me and said, 'Are you going with this charabanc?' I said, 'Yes, Dr

Roberts.' He looked sort of doubtful so I said, 'My commandant said I should come here and I am more than capable of doing this job.' I wasn't much more than a girl myself, barely nineteen. I stepped on that vehicle a bright-eyed bushy-tailed young girl and stepped off a woman.

We took the chaps straight up to Queen Alexandra's Hospital where the whole front was laid out with stretchers.

The sister there was a young girl from London and she looked at us and said, 'Now look here, my girls, I want none of this nonsense with your hats.' Our commandant, Miss Wheldon, always made us wear our hats right down on our heads with not a vestige of hair showing. She said, 'When my boys come in I don't want them looking at you as freaks of nature – you girls might be the last thing these boys see on earth, so get out in the bathroom and put your hats back.'

We went and pulled our hair out from under our hats and put on a bit of powder and lipstick and went back to the sister. I remember her saying, 'I don't want you to be laughing all the time like hyenas, but I want a gentle smile, and I don't want it to drop under any circumstances, and when you bend over my boys have a nice look in your eyes and don't let your eyes reflect what you see.'

It was a privilege to serve those lads. They never moaned or asked people to hurry up when they were laid on their stretchers waiting to come in. They laid there with patience, a joke and a smile. One chap who was very badly burned said to me, 'I'm quite good-looking really, you know, Nurse.' I said, 'Your eyes are not bad now, they're quite saucy.' So he said, 'You wouldn't like to give us a kiss, would you nurse?' We weren't allowed, but I looked around and I bent down and kissed him on his horribly burned lips with the awful smell coming off his burns.'

CHAPTER TWENTY-ONE

THE END OF THE DAY

By the evening of 6 June 1944 the Allies had established a firm toehold on the continent of Europe, with miraculously fewer casualties than anticipated by many of the planners. Eisenhower's great gamble on the weather had paid off, as had the gamble of the operation itself. If the invasion had failed, history might have been written differently, for no one could predict how long it would take to assemble sufficient men and material for another attempt. Although there was disappointment about the extent to which the invaders had been able to penetrate inland, the fact was that they had come to stay. The segments of the great artificial harbours were already being towed across the Channel; more men and equipment would pour into Normandy during the ensuing weeks to prepare for the inexorable advance into Germany. D-Day marked the beginning of the end of the Second World War . . .

War Diary, 7th Army High Command:

18.30. Channel Coast Navy Command reports on the Normandy situation:

1. Strong enemy ship concentrations at mouth of Seine. Shore batteries are having a duel with enemy naval artillery south of Le Havre.
2. On both sides of the Orne canal north of Blainville, strong enemy pressure has pinched off some bridges and our own forces are slowly withdrawing.
3. Arromanches has been surrounded and the guns have been destroyed.

4. Northwest of the Vire estuary, enemy landings are continually in progress.

5. The Marcouf battery is under strong fire from 380mm naval guns. Two guns have been knocked out by direct hits and one is continuing the battle. We are also receiving effective rocket fire from enemy ships. Enemy airborne units are between this battery and Ravenoville.

6. In front of the Grandscamp-Barfleur line, 6 battleships and heavy cruisers, 20 destroyers and between 30 and 40 transports have been observed.[1]

Oberleutnant Helmut Liebeskind, aged 22, adjutant 125 Panzer Grenadier Regiment, 21 Panzer Division:

One thing we did not expect was the might of the armada of ships, that was a real shock. Wherever we went, or positioned ourselves, five minutes later, as if at the touch of a button, there was a massive barrage. As you know, marine gunners are trained to shoot at a moving target from a moving ship and here they were in calm waters off Caen firing on us – we were served up to them as on a platter and they only needed to line us up, press the button and draw the curtains, the automatic fire did the rest; it was inhuman. We simply had not imagined it would be like that, despite our experience.

That night we sat down in the company of the commanding officer and sundry others and started to analyse the events of the day. Things looked rather sad as we saw no possibility of throwing them out. We were also hoping that finally some reinforcements might arrive. The Waffen SS Division and the Panzer Lehr Division were within two days' travel, but they didn't come. We heard next day that they had been held up so badly by enemy air activity that no movement was possible.

The feeling of not being able to drive out the Allies, that everything was in vain, had already seeped into our thoughts on that very first night. In war there is nothing more demoralizing than when one acknowledges that one has the forces and yet, whatever they do, it is futile. It has a way of blighting the spirit. I remember well how this feeling overcame us. 'What will become of it?' we asked one another.

Above all, we were bitterly disappointed by the total non-participation of the German air force. We had always worked so well together with the air force and that it had dropped out of sight so completely we found incomprehensible. If we had had the support of the air force, things would have been different.

Going to bed properly was out of the question. We were in the command bus, where there were two desks and a bunk, and we took it in turns to stretch out there, or on an air mattress on the floor.

The day ended with a very funny incident. During the morning, in a lull in the firing, my orderly had brought me a wash bowl full of strawberries and whipped cream because he knew I was passionately fond of them. At the command post we had a bus and I told him to put the bowl underneath the bus, which he duly did. That night, at about 11 p.m. when it was pitch black and there was a pause in the fighting, I suddenly remembered the strawberries. Right, I said, go and get me those strawberries now. He dived under the bus and withdrew the bowl. Not a strawberry, not a smear of whipped cream was left. The others, messengers or whatever, had gobbled the lot. It was such a disappointment.[2]

Unteroffizier Rudi Escher, aged 23, 1058 Infantry Regiment, 91st Airlanding Division:

In the evening the freight gliders started arriving and one landed very close to where we were, having been fired on from the ground. The pilot was dead, but the co-pilot was only wounded in the legs and we tried to get him out to take him to the field hospital, but as we did so we were fired on by American soldiers. I suppose they wanted to save their own people in the glider, I don't know. We tried repeatedly to get back to the glider as we had noticed there were useful supplies inside and eventually succeeded. The wounded man was taken away and then we opened a side door in the glider and two Americans were sitting there, absolutely still, their weapons at the ready. They must have been absolutely petrified, they probably shat their pants, because they remained rooted to the spot. We hauled them out, took them prisoner and told them to open the rear door so we could roll out the transport. They just shook their heads, perhaps they were so scared they simply couldn't understand what was going on. So, shortly afterwards, we destroyed the plane with fire bombs and hand grenades.[3]

Gefreite Walter Hermes, aged 19, motor-cycle messenger, 1st Battalion, 192nd Regiment, 21st Panzer Division:

It was about 11.30 at night and we were retreating towards Caen. As we were assembling in a little village, I can't remember the name, we were suddenly ambushed. I remember the company commander shouting, 'Fix bayonets, close combat, we're surrounded!' Suddenly there was an explosion and the motor cyclist standing next to me was hit in the stomach and died instantly. I was knocked off my feet but I wasn't hurt. I had never seen anyone die before and I was suddenly very scared, really for the first time that day. Bullets were kicking up dust all round us and everyone seemed to be running in different directions to escape. So I ran too and hid in a doorway, praying that I would live.

Finally I crossed the road and jumped over a wall and made my way to the outskirts of the village with another man. A German jeep came along and we waved it down and jumped on it, literally jumped on it as it was going along. Ahead we saw a group of armoured cars and I felt very relieved. I said to the man with me, 'It's the company.' But then there was a fire which lit the night and by the light I could see that the troops standing around the armoured cars wore flat British-type helmets. We stopped about twenty-five yards away. It was very dark. Then the machine-gunner on our jeep began firing. The British fired back and we jumped out and threw ourselves into a ditch. One of us, I think it was the driver, didn't make it. I heard him grunt and give a deep sigh as he got to the ditch and I tried to pull him in but I couldn't get hold of him. As I reached forward to get a better grip, to my horror my hand went straight into his wound. I could feel his blood and his body still quivering; it was like grabbing death itself. I was sick and petrified.

We took off our equipment, but held onto our weapons, so we could move faster, and on the count of three we jumped up out of the ditch and raced across the field. There was no fire. We had almost reached the hedge on the other side of the field when a British voice said, 'Halt! Hands up!' A British captain and five soldiers came out with their guns aimed at us. We dropped our weapons and threw up our hands. I said to one of the men with me, 'Thank God we are not going to die.'

We were led away and put under guard in the corner of a nearby field. While we were sitting there I began to think about my family, my mother and father and my sisters and I remembered the letter I had written that morning. I didn't feel too bad about being captured and I was thankful to be alive.[4]

Hauptman Helmut Lang, aged 36, adjutant to Feldmarschall Rommel:

We arrived at La Roche Guyon at about 9.15 in the evening. On the journey, the Field Marshal was tense and worried; he kept urging the driver to go faster. I remember him punching one gloved fist into another as he said, 'You see, Lang, I was right all the time. I should have had the Panzer Lehr and the 12th SS under my command near the beaches.'

He didn't talk much on the way, but he kept repeating that he was right about wanting those divisions under his command. At another point he said, 'If I was commander of the Allied forces right now I could finish the war off in fourteen days.' And later, 'If Montgomery only knew the mess we are in, he'd have no worries tonight.'

The moment the car pulled up outside the headquarters, I jumped out and ran ahead of the Field Marshal up the steps into the hall. As I did so, I was conscious of loud music coming out of General Speidel's office. It sounded like the strains of a Wagnerian opera. Speidel came out and was walking forward to meet Rommel. I said to him, in a sort of surprised way, 'General, the invasion, it's begun, and you're able to listen to Wagner.' He just said, 'My dear Lang, do you honestly believe that my listening to Wagner will make any difference whatsoever to the course of the invasion?'

Speidel greeted Rommel and the two men went into his office. I was very depressed by what was happening because everyone knew by then that the landings had been a success.

I remember almost the first thing I said to him that night was, 'Sir, do you think we'll be able to manage it, hold them back?' He replied, 'Lang, I hope we can. I have always succeeded up to now.'[5]

Generalleutnant Josef Reichert, aged 53, commander 711th Division:

In the afternoon I went with Generals von Salmuth and Hofmann, commander and chief of staff of the 15th Army, to a battery at a place called Mont Canisoy from where, through binoculars, we were able to see the whole invasion fleet, the movement of the landing barges back and forth, indeed the whole panorama of the invasion as men were landed on the beaches west of the Orne.

Nevertheless, I still did not believe that this was the main invasion. I thought it was a Dieppe-type raid, aimed at creating a situation where various German units would be sucked into a vortex and that this would follow with a major invasion elsewhere. I did not think this operation would succeed because I knew that there were two Panzer divisions in reserve – the 12th SS and the Panzer Lehr – and I expected them to attack at any moment.

I spent most of the day waiting for these divisions to attack because I was convinced that when they did they would throw the invaders back into the sea. That night when I went to bed, I was still convinced that this was no more than a diversionary attack and that the real *Schwerpunkt*, or spearhead of the attack, could be expected elsewhere.[6]

Foreign Armies West Headquarters. Appendix to situation report No. 1288, 6.6.44:

While the Anglo-Saxon enemy landing on the coast of Normandy represents a large-scale operation, the forces employed comprise only a relatively small portion of the troops available.

Of the 60 large formations held in southern Britain, only ten to twelve divisions, including airborne troops, appear to be participating so far.

The execution of the operation followed the established technique for large-scale landing operations. It included bomber raids at night on coastal fortifications, parachute and glider landings making use of the moonlight, and most remarkable of all, landings on the beaches without consideration of the state of the tide. The weather must have caused the operation some difficulties. In particular, it is bound to have interfered with the operations of the enemy air force.

The progress of the landing so far can hardly have lived up to the expectations of the enemy command as it included numerous setbacks and many abortive attempts to reach land. All the same, the success should not be underestimated. The enemy has gained a bridgehead which is 30 kilometres wide and in places up to 8 kilometres deep. The weakness of this bridgehead must be seen in its shallow depth in some places and the lack of an efficient port . . .

According to a believable Abwehr report of June 2, the forces in southern England are divided into two army groups, the 21st British Army Group and the 1st US Army Group . . . Not a single unit of the 1st US Army group, which comprises around 25 large formations north and south of the Thames, has so far been committed. The same is true of the ten to twelve combat formations stationed in central England and Scotland.

This suggests that the enemy is planning a further large-scale operation in the Channel area, which one would expect to be aimed at the coastal sector in the Pas de Calais area . . .[7]

Nun at Bon Saveur convent, Caen:

As refugees and wounded began to pour into our convent, we made hurried preparations to convert the wings of the vacant mental homes into temporary hospitals. Just after vespers, three vast buildings of our mental home were hit, with nuns and patients buried beneath the debris. The wounded became panic-stricken; they would not remain in bed, but struggled down to the basements. And to add to the poignancy of the scene, the poor mothers from the maternity home appeared, clinging to each other for support, their babies clasped in their arms, crying pitifully. We heard the screams of terror and the roar of gunfire and above it all a voice raised in prayer to God for protection. We could see fire bombs drop and huge buildings blazing; we could see the planes swoop down, then rise up, having done their deadly work; hear bombs and the sound of machine guns.

At midnight, 400 nuns of the Order of Our Lady of Charity, and as many girls, sought shelter with us. Their convent and home had been burned, 16 nuns had perished in the flames. Almost every convent in Caen had been hit.[8]

Madame Aude Verne, resident of St Lô:

At about eight o'clock in the evening I fled into the countryside to try and escape the bombing. The prominent factor was the apocalyptic illumination caused by the explosions. It made the forest virtually transparent and when I looked at the leaves, I could see all their veins.

It was the end of the world, a flood of fire, of iron, of earth, of tree branches. I was thrown into the air by the shock of a bomb which landed close by. I was in total darkness and felt that I was almost part of the elements. I fell to the ground on a heap of earth and broken branches. I had the sensation of my skin covering being too small for my body, because it seemed to be pulling at me all the time. I did not know at that time that I had been burned all over my body. I started to howl like everyone else and to flee to save my life. I remember bursting through a thorn hedge, catching my plaits on it. I followed the sound of other people's voices to guide my path. Someone called out – she had found another path and the survivors fell on it in a rush and so I found myself with them, carried along by the scrimmage. Those who had been on the path had been crushed to pulp. One heard the most dreadful death rattles. The town resembled a furnace worthy of the devil. A single idea dominated – to flee, to flee this hell.[9]

Wing Commander Desmond Scott, 123 Wing, RAF:

It was not until the evening that I was able to head for the Normandy beaches, and was just in time to join a sky train – a stream of tugs and gliders that reached out southwards from Selsey Bill as far as the eye could see. Hundreds of four-engined bombers were strung in a narrow stream, each pulling a large Hamilcar glider, all bound for the Normandy bridgehead. It was the largest glider-borne force yet to fly into battle. Most of the 6th Air Landing Brigade, including artillery and light tanks, were on their way to Normandy.

During the time I overhauled the leaders of this massive aerial armada as they passed to the west of Le Havre, and kept with them as they crossed the enemy coast near the mouth of the River Orne, not a single enemy aircraft put in an appearance. The only enemy reception was light flak in spasmodic and scattered bursts, and this was swiftly dealt with by swarms of low-attack aircraft. They were like angry bees as they worked below us, eloquent proof of our command of the air.

When the tugs began releasing their gliders I became so fascinated by the performance of these powerless wood and canvas monsters I could not take my eyes off them and almost flew straight into a squadron of Spitfires that crossed my path on their way to Bayeux.

One glider was shot down by flak, but the rest ploughed on into the fields alongside the Orne like a flock of exhausted black swans. Some skimmed along the ground and finished up in a cloud of yellow dust. Others hit the ground at too steep an angle and burst open like paper bags.

As the numbers mounted and the fields on the landing zone became congested, some gliders seemed to have no place to go. But they just dropped down into the smallest of spaces and elbowed their way in among the dust, splinters and torn fabric. I was surprised how quickly the tanks left their winged carriers. No sooner had one touched down than out crawled a tank like a crustacean hurriedly vacating its shell.

The German gunners were quick to size up the situation and began shelling the gliders from across the nearby Carentan Canal. Several burst into flames. I went into a steep dive towards Colombelles, hoping to catch sight of some of these German batteries, but I could see other aircraft busily engaged in strafing attacks and flew on to the south-east of Caen.

Two motor cycles and what appeared to be a staff car were racing along a road near Cagny, and I swept down and raked them with cannon fire. All three came to a sudden and dusty stop, but I did not see what became of them. A loose flight of Mustangs suddenly turned towards me and for a brief moment I mistook them for enemy fighters. But by the time I had realized my mistake I was ringed by several streams of light flak and quickly moved myself back and out to the coast near Ouistreham.

All along the fringe of the bay, as far as visibility would permit, I could see smoke, fire and explosions. Inland some areas were completely smudged out by evil clouds of smoke. Underneath it great flashes of fire would erupt and burst like bolts of orange lightning. Normandy was like a huge, fire-brimmed boiling cauldron. To seaward ships of all shapes and sizes lay patiently at anchor. Between them and the beaches an extraordinary regatta was taking place as hundreds of smaller craft dashed hither and thither.

I turned and flew westwards towards Bayeux and had gone as far as St Aubin-sur-Mer when I was fired on by the Royal Navy. I removed myself from above the D-Day shipping and to give the trigger-happy navy gunners a wider berth I set off home by way of the enemy port of Le Havre. Further to the east the landscape was already beginning to fade into twilight. Streams of coloured tracer climbed slowly but brightly into the darkening sky away to the north of me, probably from Cap d'Antifer or Fécamp.

Like homing seabirds, many aircraft accompanied me back across the Channel. At various distances were lone Spitfires, and here and there a lumbering four-engined bomber, ragged packs of Typhoons,

Mustangs and Thunderbolts, all heading for the peace and security of their home bases on the south coast of England. For us it was the end of D-Day.[10]

20.00 hours. Lieutenant Arthur Newmyer, USNR, speaking over the public address system of Rear Admiral Hall's flagship, the Ancon, off Omaha beach:

This has been a long, and tough, day. On the whole, our naval bombardment this morning was accurate and powerful. Generally, our first waves reached their designated beach areas within five minutes of their scheduled time. But, as you know, we were faced with strong winds and choppy seas. And on the way in, in certain instances, our small landing craft capsized and there we lost valuable equipment and precious lives.

On some beaches the landing was successful from the start. On others the going was very hard. One of the principal objectives of Admiral Hall's force was a powerful battery on Pointe du Hoc, at the westernmost end of our initial target area. At and near this point the Nazis had placed six 105mm guns. Even though we were 20,000 yards offshore, our transports and the *Ancon* were within range of those guns. Those guns were mounted in concrete and were firmly embanked on top of a rugged cliff which rose sharply, almost at the water's edge, to a height of 200 feet. The American Rangers really went after that Pointe du Hoc battery. They captured it amazingly quickly.

As must be expected, however, on a beachhead as large as the one assigned Force O, in other areas, particularly towards the eastern end of our beach, it was not so easy. At first it wasn't the larger guns that bothered the invading troops – it was the steady stream of machine-gun fire that pinned down our boys as they attempted to go ashore. Added to the steady stream of machine-gun fire were the difficulties we had with certain beach obstacles in those areas.

The choppy seas hampered our demolition units. They were unable to clear entrance channels as fast as they, and we, had hoped. So in some of those areas our landing craft tangled with these obstacles, many of which contained mines, and we had other losses of men, supplies and landing craft here.

When word of this condition reached our fire-support ships they moved in, and moved in fast. Destroyers, cruisers and battleships supported those boys on the beaches. Our bombing aircraft poured in, fast and effectively. By noon, some of those troops that had been trapped were moving inland at a satisfactory pace. By early afternoon the APAs had unloaded nearly all their troops. They already have left us to start back to England. Their first mission has been accomplished.

A few hours ago, Force B of the Western Task Force arrived. Force B is the support force, commanded by Commodore Campbell D. Edgar, USN. Commodore Edgar's force, containing a large number of LSTs and LCI(L)s, already is unloading.

Generally, we feel we surprised Hitler and his cohorts this time. But the Germans were quick to announce that we had landed, and undoubtedly large Nazi reinforcements are on the way. Certain guns, we suspect, already have been moved up, and the going, at the moment, is again hard.

Our aircraft, which for weeks have been pounding vital bridges and other transportation arteries, will continue to disrupt these German attempts to reinforce. But to be really in position to face the German counter attack, our boys on the beaches have got to get more supplies, more equipment and more men.

That job is up to the navy.[11]

Sergeant Alan Anderson, aged 27, B Battery, 1st Platoon, 116th Combat Team, 467th AAA Battalion:

The navy started firing against the pillboxes in our area. These big 12 and 16-inch shells were landing not more than thirty or forty yards or less in front of us. It created such a vacuum that those shells practically pulled you right out of the hole. I remember being lifted up as the shells went over and then being kind of slammed back down when they exploded. It was an awful experience and the concussion was beyond belief. We were showered with debris, sand and smoke and this continued for a considerable time. I was deaf for three days afterwards.

How we survived there I will never know. At around 9.30 at night the firing let up enough for us to pick ourselves up. There were about eighteen or nineteen of us in the area and we had, I recall, two guns. I managed to get hold of an M1 rifle and clean it up a bit and then we went up the hill off Omaha beach towards Vierville-sur-Mer, which was the village just above us.

I remember as I walked around the corner there was a pillbox being used as an aid station and some man, an American soldier, came running up holding his intestines in his hands. He had been hit by shrapnel and was hollering, 'Help me! Help me!' and his intestines were kind of hanging and running out through his fingers. He fell, probably dead, I don't know, within maybe five or ten feet of the aid station.

It was now beginning to get dark and there was a ditch just to the left-hand side and I went over and saw four or five soldiers, Rangers, there. I said to one of them, 'Where is the front line?' and he said, 'This *is* the front line. There are Germans over there and they've got machine guns. There's a lot of fire, so stay down.'

So we joined them in the ditch. About this time I was absolutely overtaken by fatigue. You have to remember I had not slept for two nights and all of that day. Well, not really sleeping. My clothes were still wet and that chemical-impregnated material used against the possibility of being gassed smelled to high heaven. It was hardly bearable.

I remember I had a chocolate bar from my C-rations and I had picked up a canteen, so I had a little water. My lips were parched and I could hardly close my mouth because it was full of sand and other debris from the artillery pounding on the beach.

One of the Rangers said, 'Well, Sergeant, why don't you catch a little nap here. I'll stay awake for a couple of hours and then I'll wake you and maybe I can get a little sleep.'

So I laid down and I remember where I laid there was a burst of machine-gun fire and it was coming at a kind of angle that was pretty close to my head, so I just moved over a little bit and thought, 'Well, he can't get me here,' and I fell sound asleep.[12]

Pfc Walter P. Shawd, aged 22, L Company, 2nd Battalion, 116th Regiment:

We got up on top of a hill and there was ten of us got up there: Lieutenant Skrek, Sergeant Armstrong and eight enlisted men. We came upon a house. There was a hedgerow and we saw three Germans run around the house and Lieutenant Skrek says, 'Don't fire.' Why he said that I'll never know. But we didn't fire and we hit the ground. Then three rounds of mortar came in, killing the lieutenant and wounding Sergeant Armstrong. That left us with no one except eight enlisted men.

We kept crawling across fields, trying to meet up with larger groups. Finally we came to a road and most of our outfit was there so we joined up with them. The navy was shelling us as we tried to signal them that we were Americans, but they kept sending back, 'Surrender to the Americans.' Finally we got them to stop.

I thought I was hungry. We had K rations and I took a little cheese out of the tin and took a bite, but I wasn't hungry. I threw it away.

And so we started up this field and there were some machine guns and Germans up there and they had a line of fire on us and were just picking us off. We couldn't get up there, so we swung around the road and started towards St Laurent. There was a farmhouse and farm buildings and we were getting fire from that. We set up the bazooka and fired it into the building, but to no avail.

It was beginning to get dark, so they told us to dig in. But I was so tired I just laid on top of the ground. I heard some tanks coming up the road. Thank God they were ours.

That night, or that day, we probably made a thousand yards off the beach and that was it. There were two fellows in our company that weren't wounded or killed. I was one of them, and Goodman Paisley Dallas from South Carolina was the other one. That night, we felt like veterans.[13]

Captain James L. Ballard, 29th Divison HQ:

I was the G3 liaison officer with the 29th Division Headquarters and at about 8 p.m. I was in the division command post, in a stone quarry on the road from the beach up a slight hill towards Vierville-sur-Mer. Our communication with 1st Division on our left, which was supposed to have its headquarters at St Laurent-sur-Mer, was out. Our whole headquarters was more or less confined to the quarry and things were in rather bad shape.

General Gerhardt turned to me, a little after 8 p.m. I think it was, and asked me if I could try and make contact with elements of the 1st Division. I asked for an enlisted volunteer to accompany me and Staff Sergeant Ted Josephs from Brooklyn, New York, stepped up immediately. After receiving a few hasty instructions from the Chief of Staff, Sergeant Josephs and I started out. He, as I remember it, was armed with a rifle and I had a carbine and a pistol. I carried a map of our positions inside my field jacket.

The night was very dark. However, Vierville-sur-Mer was lit up, for the most part, by fires which were still burning. We sneaked up the road to Vierville and at the little intersection which comprised the heart of the town we turned left on the road running to St Laurent. My plan was to walk on the road until we got out of town and then slip off to either side, if possible, using the road only as a guide. I was on the left side of the road, Sergeant Josephs was on the right, about five yards behind.

When we had gone about 400 yards beyond the outskirts of Vierville, a dog at a farmhouse off to the right started barking. We hit the ground and lay perfectly motionless for what seemed like ages. After the dog had stopped barking I whispered loudly to Sergeant Josephs and we started off again, sneaking along half in and half out the ditch at the side of the road.

After we had gone about 400 yards, I guess, I was suddenly startled when a man jumped up in front of me, so close I could have touched him, and darted off to the right. Immediately I heard a sharp whistle and a volley of shots rang out in our direction, generally passing over my head. Almost at once three men came towards my position, which was prone at the edge of the road. I could see them silhouetted against the sky. When I hit the road I dropped my carbine, so I pulled my pistol and fired at almost point-blank range several times. Two men fell with shouts. I don't know what happened to the third, it all happened so fast. I dashed some distance to the right rear, jumped a hedge and took cover in a field to gather my thoughts. I had lost Sergeant Josephs and thought he was either killed or captured.

I reasoned that I had encountered either a patrol or a strong-point and that it was more important that I report the presence of enemy between us and the 1st Division rather than continue to attempt to reach the 1st Division. Also, if Sergeant Josephs had been captured he may have disclosed information of our own situation, despite his best intentions. So I worked my way back to division headquarters as quickly as I could and there found that contact had been established with the 1st Division via the beachhead. It also turned out that I was supposed to go to the 1st Division via the beach as it was believed there were enemy along the highway, but I had not been so instructed.

At dawn next day I set out in a commandeered tank to try and find Sergeant Josephs and we had only gone about a mile or so when he jumped out of a ditch and hailed us. I was never so glad to see anyone in my life. He said he had lain deathly still all night right beside a group of Germans whom he could hear talking; fortunately, they had pulled out just before dawn.[14]

Private Dennis Bowen, aged 18, 5th Battalion, East Yorkshire Regiment:

Every time we stopped for more than a few minutes, we would dig in or make some kind of a shelter. I had really no idea of where we were. I knew I was in France and I could see these peculiar French road signs and things and thought how weird it all was. We kept moving until we got to the outskirts of a town which I know now is Bayeux. I should think we did about twelve miles that first day. I can remember looking at the tower on the cathedral and some old timer saying, 'That'll get blown away because it's obviously an OP.'

We'd no shortage of ammunition. We had loads and loads of canvas bandoliers and everybody carried a couple of Bren magazines as well. Every time we stopped you'd got a few more empty magazines and somebody would say, 'Fill 'em up, fill 'em up!'

If a German soldier appeared, everybody fired at him. It was no bother, we didn't think of them as human beings. When I say we were brainwashed that sounds a bit over the top, but you literally didn't even think about it. You are there, there is noise, everybody is shouting and screaming and suddenly you see this figure. In the excitement you fire at him. Oh, yes, I hit people. I personally saw people that I was firing at fall, on more than one occasion. I can say that without any hesitation. Without bragging about being a good shot, a man only 100 or 150 yards away is an awful big target. And if it's an enemy soldier you don't just fire one shot, you fire a round, re-load and fire another, as quick as you can, another and another. Even when he has fallen you still keep firing.

Some Germans were trying to surrender but in the excitement we fired on them before they had any chance to put their hands up. You see, a lot of them were in prepared bunkers and they could only come out of the bunker in single file and they would come out quite slowly, but as soon as they appeared, everybody would start firing. The first couple or three coming out of the bunker would buy it, then the remainder would come out hands way up in the air. Some people still kept on firing but I don't think our lads were saying, well, I don't care if that man wants to surrender or doesn't want to surrender, I'm going to shoot him anyway. I don't think that was in anyone's mind. I think it was the excitement of constantly stuffing fresh ammunition into magazines and blazing away. A lot of men were just firing from the hip as we walked forward, not taking their rifles up to the shoulder and taking individual aim, but just firing away from the hip. There was a lot of small-arms fire, much more than you would think or expect. You would think a lot of enemy casualties were caused by artillery shelling, but there must have been a lot caused in the later stages of any attack, in the last 100 yards or so, by small-arms fire.

It was all very exciting, but bewildering, because, although we'd done manoeuvres, we'd never done a manoeuvre with the urgency of what was happening at that time and, of course, I'd never seen wounded or dead men. When some fellow shouts out, 'I'm hit! I'm hit!' and you look round and you see blood, well . . . We'd quite a lot of casualties. I should think there was anything up to a half the platoon became casualties on the first day.

I never got hit and I thought it was because I was such a good soldier and could always find a bullet-proof piece of cover. It was probably just dead luck, but at the time I was thinking, well, these may be battle-hardened warriors, but I have done two years' training and I know how to leopard-crawl, how to keep me backside down and that kind of thing.

We started digging in for the night at about nine o'clock, just as it was coming dusk. We were absolutely knackered. There was a farmhouse close by and Corporal Stephenson went down to the farmhouse and spent the night in there with one of the girls, on that very night. He crawled round all the trenches and when we were stood down, he came round and said, 'If anybody wants me, I shall be in there,' nodding at the farmhouse. I, as a young boy, thought he's going to go in there because it is a building rather than spend the night in a trench. Then a couple of the old timers said, 'You know why he's in there? 'Cos there's a French girl in there.'

I never stopped to eat all day; I hadn't even taken the cork out of my water bottle. I had grabbed water from water butts and out of streams. I obviously wasn't hungry, hunger is the last thing you worry about. Some of the older soldiers were already brewing up on the beach. I thought, my God, what are they doing? We were sheltering under the wall and they were brewing up, not a bit worried by the battle. It became a point later on, you always had your mug, one pint, enamel, on the outside of your pack, not inside, because if ever you got anywhere where someone was brewing, that was your ticket.

I never closed my eyes all night, I was far, far, far too excited. I did get a sense of relief that I'd got through the day. When we first got into the landing craft and all hell let loose around us with every possible type of weapon firing and making this awful din, I felt if I was going to get killed, that would be the place it would happen. But once I'd got through that, then I was OK. Once I started going forward with the rest of the platoon, and men around me were being hurt, but not me, I was OK. But we were awful thin on the ground: ten of us set off that morning but only four or five of us were still there that night when we finally dug in.

By and large, it didn't enter my head that it was a war; it was just something that was happening, something that was just going on. If somebody had put their hand down and picked me out of it and said, 'Right, now this is a battle, what is happening?' I couldn't have told them, all I could have said was we're going forward.[15]

Cleaves A. Jones, HQ 29th Infantry Division:

At 19.00 we were a mile off Omaha beach. At the water's edge was a confused huddle of craft and vehicles and beach obstacles. Behind us, the warships still fired rapidly. DUKWs, patrol craft, LCVPs and small vessels continuously kept moving in and out of the larger craft. At 20.00 we hailed two LCVPs, who refused to heed us until our craft intercepted them and practically by show of arms forced them to come alongside and take us off.

The trip to the beach took seventy minutes. The sea was heavy and running rapidly eastwards. The craft tossed viciously, shipping much water and causing additional sea-sickness. The sickest man of all was Staff Sergeant George Joseph of the G3 section. He made utterly inhuman noises getting up what disturbed him. We were 2–300 yards offshore, but could get only occasional glimpses as the craft tossed and rolled. It took most of my strength to remain upright in harness, pack, gas mask, weapon and hold my briefcase out of the water.

We touched down and landed almost dryfoot on a pebbly beach. I almost stepped on a half-submerged body as I left the craft. I saw some dozen bodies washing at the water's edge and others on the patch of ground between the road and the sea. We were about a quarter of a mile from the exit to Vierville and immediately proceeded there. At this time came a lull in the firing on the beach.

Toward the cliff-line was level ground, swampy, with high grass for 100 yards, then the rise of the cliff. Facing seawards, on the land side of the road, was a low stone wall. Behind this wall were dead, wounded and soldiers sheltering from fire.

Possibly a dozen small houses had stood between road and cliff, but were utterly wrecked. Bits of metal and shreds of the houses crunched underfoot. Wire was in coils in the swampy ground. The beach and the road was littered. I saw several broken bits of rifle. There was clothing, K Ration particles, gas masks or part of them, pieces of flesh, letters and paper in shreds, covers of first-aid packets, belts, ammunition expended and whole, pieces of boxes, cans, parts of walkie-talkies, dented helmets. Everything dusty, dirty and stained.

Dead lay in the most grotesque of postures. What seemed to have been two bodies slithered across the road in tank tracks. One thing, which seemed to have been killed by a mine, lay at the road's edge completely stripped of uniform and shoes by the blast, no head, legs reversed and blown into jelly-like lumps under the shoulder blades, the scrotum torn away and the testicles laid bare.

At the point where the beach road turned inland to Vierville, engineers were burning out a pillbox which gave forth a dense, almost solidified gush of oily black smoke. Several houses at that point had been shattered and blocked the road. A dozer was working, and we picked our way through the rubble. A first-aid station had been set up in the lee of a shattered house.

Fifty feet inland from the turn were the remnants of a road block, with small pillboxes on the hills right and left. At this road block it appeared a soldier had sheltered and further lightened his pack, because strewn in a yard-square area were toothpaste, soap, toothbrush and other toilet articles.[16]

BBC correspondent, Alan Melville:

This is Alan Melville, Despatch 13, 21.00, 6 June, from the beach west of Ouistreham. Hello, everyone, this is Alan Melville speaking from the beach just west of the little village of Ouistreham. The paratroops are landing, they are landing all round me as I speak.

They have come in from the sea and they are fluttering down, red, white and blue parachutes, fluttering down, and they are just about the best thing we have seen for a good many hours. They are showering in, there is no other word for it, pouring in, in threes and fours. They are fluttering down in perfect formation, just the way we've seen it on the newsreels, the way we've seen it done in exercises, and here they are doing it, the real thing, and believe me, they haven't come any too late.

They'll be a very unpleasant surprise to the enemy, whose fighting I can still see, the signs of a typical panzer battle. You can hear the aircraft roaring over me, I expect, as I speak. I can still see the signs of a typical panzer battle being waged on the slightly high ground just about three or four miles ahead of me. And these paratroops are coming down between where I am speaking, which is just above the sand dunes. Down they come ... they're being attacked pretty harshly, as you can hear, but they are landing in great force, between the sand dunes, between the beach area and the battle and they may have a very decisive effect on that battle.

Jerry is putting up to try and stave this surprise eventuality off, but he isn't able to cope. The aircraft are sweeping inland, letting go their valuable cargo, sweeping round as if nothing mattered and turning again out to sea. They are still coming in. I am just turning round to look out to sea and I can see, way out to the very horizon, they are coming in in flood after flood.[17]

Brigadier General James M. Gavin, Commander Task Force A, 82nd Airborne Division:

As darkness descended, I moved up to see what the situation looked like. The 1st Battalion of the 505th had taken heavy casualties. It was well organized and had the situation in hand, but the German defenses on the causeway seemed quite strong and there was no way to force a crossing of the causeway that night. From the causeway a road went directly back to the east, to our rear, to the town of Ste Mère-Eglise, about five miles away. I went back to where the road crossed the railroad and decided that I would establish my Command Post there. In that way I could control the situation at the causeway and stay in touch with the 507th at Chef-du-Pont. I established contact with division headquarters.

General Ridgway was back near Ste Mère-Eglise and knew where we were and what we were doing. There was still a great deal to be done in sorting things out. I had one officer who spoke German, Captain Miller, and one jeep that I had obtained from division headquarters. It helped me keep in touch with the various fragments of my command. We established radio communication with Lieutenant Colonel Thomas J.B. Shanley's battalion of the 508th, which was across the Merderet River and about three miles from the La Fière bridge, well behind the German lines. They were under fire but intact.

I decided to get some rest. June nights in Normandy can be very cold. I looked around for something to cover me; all I could find was a dead paratrooper with his parachute over him. He must have been killed in descent and some trooper had covered him with his own parachute. Although I was shivering with cold, I did not have the heart to take it away from him. I finally found, of all things, a camouflage net that had arrived in the battle area. I chose a place against a hedgerow, so as to be protected from artillery fire, which was coming in spasmodically during the night, and I rolled up in the camouflage net. It was surprisingly warm.

I had hardly fallen asleep when someone shook me and told me General Ridgway wanted to see me. This was unlike General Ridgway; he always went forward to see his officers in combat rather than take them away from their tactical commands. I checked again; there was no question about the accuracy of the message. I had not been back that way, but his Command Post should have been near the road to Ste Mère-Eglise. I took Captain Olsen with me, and we started along the road. It was as light as day in the full moonlight, and we walked in the shadows, one each side of the road. We did not realize it at the time, but during the night a German infantry battalion had passed between my Command Post and that of General Ridgway, so it was just as well that we moved along the road with care. I felt bone weary, having been up for two nights and a day. In addition to the physical exhaustion, combat itself, with its tension and excitement, takes a great deal out of you.

After several miles of walking, I came on the Command Post off to the left of the road. I went to the Operations Center, which was in a tent, and asked for General Ridgway. They pointed out that he was asleep in a small ditch off to the side. I went over and shook his shoulder and woke him up. He didn't seem too happy about it and said he had nothing for me and didn't need me. No doubt a zealous staff officer, thinking it might be a good idea to get a first-hand report on the situation along the Merderet River, had sent a message in the name of General Ridgway, and by the time I arrived, the message had been forgotten or the staff officer who sent it was fast asleep.[18]

Noel Monks, war correspondent:

Just before dark we went back to Hermanville for the night and were in time to witness one of the most thrilling sights I have ever seen. As we entered the town, we heard the drone of what seemed to be many hundreds of aeroplane engines, and we wondered if the Luftwaffe was coming in force to wipe out the bridgehead, still little more than a toehold. But no, it was hundreds of our own aircraft, towing gliders. They came over us so low we felt our cheers would have been heard in the noiseless gliders as they slipped their tows.

In the gliders were welcome reinforcements of men, artillery and light tanks for General Gale's courageous 6th Airborne Division. It was still an hour to darkness – nearly 9 p.m. – but the gliders, nearly 300 of them, blacked things out as, like giant bats, they settled beyond the Orne river. We could hear the din of battle break out as the Germans reacted to this daring operation, and we went to sleep on the floor of a deserted, empty house with a silent prayer for the welfare of the gallant men who had just flown in.[19]

Captain John Tillett, aged 25, 52nd Air Landing Battalion, Oxfordshire & Buckinghamshire Light Infantry:

As soon as we landed, we leapt out of the glider, as trained. I suppose I must have been one of the first to leap out, as the leader of the party, and to my astonishment there in front of me, in a trench, was a real, live German. We had been training for three years to fight real, live Germans, but we weren't really prepared with our weapons so I think I said to my sergeant major something like, 'Er, sergeant major, what about that German?'

We decided we ought to shoot him, but looking at him I could see he was absolutely terrified and there was no question of him shooting at us. He was about fifteen yards away and seemed to be all on his own in a slit trench and I remember he wasn't wearing a helmet and didn't seem to have a weapon; I suppose he must have thrown it away. I happen to speak a little German, so I said to him, '*Haende hoch! Sie sind Gefangener.*' [Hands up! You are a prisoner.]

So we took him prisoner, but we didn't know where the hell we were or which direction to go in. But there was a ridge with a hedge along the top behind the glider and I thought if we went up to the ridge we'd be able to see where we were. So we set off in formation, as it were, up towards this ridge and just as we got to it we could hear tank noises and two tanks came up the other side of the hedge, and to my horror I saw the leading tank had a swastika on the side.

We turned tail and disappeared over this cornfield at what seemed like Jesse Owen-speed, looking for some sort of hole to get into, while the tank swung its turret towards us.

So within two minutes of landing we had (a) taken a prisoner (b) advanced boldly and (c) were put to full flight!

Actually we lost our prisoner when we were running for our lives and then we found out that the tanks were British and they'd chalked swastikas on the sides of their bloody turrets to indicate that they had knocked out German tanks.[20]

Captain John Madden, C Company, 1st Canadian Parachute Battalion:

Commandos held Amfreville, so we took up a position on their right flank and dug in for the night. I established myself in the kitchen of the farmhouse we defended. Foremost in my mind is the food they gave us; even now I recall with pleasure the big plate of stew, the two eggs and the good brown bread they set before me. It disappeared in short order.

As I mopped up the final morsel with my last crust of bread, I couldn't help but think of the picture I presented. Here was I, an officer in Canada's finest regiment, with a loose airborne smock flopping about my frame. My boots were caked with cow dung and mud. My face was still black where sweat had not washed away the camouflage cream. My badges of rank and unit flashes were hidden beneath layers of dust. My clothes sagged and slouched as I did. We were very, very tired.

By the end of the meal, darkness had fallen. The old man lit a stubby candle and with a knowing smile disappeared into the musty loft. He reappeared wearing a battered old helmet and carrying a bottle of Calvados. Pouring a goodly tot, he motioned me to drink.

Liquid flame seared my mouth. With much gesturing I convinced him that I was unequal to the task. Not at all disturbed but somewhat disgusted, he reached up and pulled a jug of cider from the low rafters.

Distasteful it was, but none the less effective. In a warm haze I groped my way through inadequate French to learn the story of the German occupation from the old farmer, his daughter and his son. Then I left the kitchen. Outside I rolled up in my gas cape and went to sleep. My first day in France was finished.[21]

Rifleman Alex Kuppers, aged 22, Anti-Tank Platoon, Winnipeg Rifles:

We didn't have any contact with the Germans during the day, not until the evening or during the night. I guess a lot of them had taken cover in woods or barns or something, but a group of them – I don't know how many there were – tried to march through our lines. We were supposed, maybe, to think it was our own people, or something, but somebody challenged and put a flare up and they scattered and some of them just hit the ground. One fellow threw a grenade and I guess it must have exploded right beside this German officer's head, because he didn't have a head next morning.

Somebody accused our guys of cutting his head off. It wasn't. It was blown off. And I remember someone went through his pockets and I felt kinda bad because he had a wife and two little children in Germany. Course, they would have blown our heads off if they'd had first chance.

It wasn't any big action, that night, not where I was. My sergeant put two of us in the middle of what seemed an awful big field for two men. That's where we dug our trenches and spent the night, near Creuilly. We didn't get any sleep at all that night.[22]

Sapper A.J. Lane, aged 23, Field Squadron, Royal Engineers:

I found a German foxhole on the far river [Orne] bank alongside the bridge abutment and road approach. Steel duckboards lay scattered around and some of these I used as a parapet for protection against bullets and shrapnel.

I settled into my lonely foxhole position. I felt isolated and pretty vulnerable, since opposite me were menacing fields and trees. It was getting to be late evening with light fading fast and I cannot say that at that moment I was looking forward to passing my first night on foreign and hostile soil. I was not particularly cheered by the immediate company of corpses close to me. I could almost reach out and touch the most gruesome of the three, a German who had had his brains blown out through a jagged hole in his steel helmet.

I was in truth cold, frightened, confused, terribly tired and hungry, not a very brave young soldier who had been cast into a nightmarish world of awful reality.[23]

RQMS Ed Meekison, 5th Black Watch:

We were directed up to a causeway leading to a small town which we could see by the light of the AA [anti-aircraft fire]. There was a deep ditch alongside the road which we found very useful because we twice had to leave the vehicle and take cover from air attacks. We reached the main street of the village and contacted an MP who was directing traffic. He put us on a road leading inland, no doubt anxious to get rid of us from a fireprone area: several of the houses were blazing. Our maps showed no relationship to this particular area, so for the time being we were lost. Shortly we were joined by other vehicles from our unit and formed a convoy under a young officer who was equally unaware of our exact location and just as confused as we were. Seeing what I thought was a row of sleeping soldiers just off the road, I halted and made my way over to them to ask them where the Highland Division was operating, only to find these lads were beyond answering any questions. They were covered by gas capes.

Some distance up the road we pulled into a tree-lined field and were told to camouflage our vehicles and try and get some rest. Leaving my vehicle I wandered across to a hedgerow to relieve my bladder and proceeded to spray the nearest bush. To my complete amazement, an apparition arose from the opposite side of the bush, clad in a camouflaged jacket and a steel helmet not quite like any I had seen before. He was absolutely terrified. Somewhat anxious myself, I demanded who he was and received a reply in an unintelligible language. Backing up to the three-tonner, and keeping my eye on him all the time, I grabbed my Lee Enfield rifle, pushed a round into the breech and demanded my acquaintance put his hands up pronto. During this time, of course, he could have disposed of me quite easily as I was otherwise unarmed, but with a despairing wail he shouted, 'French Canadien!'[24]

Captain Robert Neave, aged 26, second in command, B Squadron, 13th/18th Royal Hussars:

At the end of the day I can recall extreme tiredness! And sleeplessness. I remember going to sleep that night, unrolling my bedding roll, which you kept on the back of your tank. I had a very splendid wireless operator called Danny Mason. He was an absolutely splendid little man who was more than a friend, he was a real companion and always concerned with one's welfare. Mason would always see that your bedding roll was taken off the tank, unrolled and he found a decent spot for you. You would sleep near the tank. It wasn't a good idea to sleep under it as there were occasions when it slowly sank into the ground and you would get squashed.

I had the feeling that we had had a very successful day. I had a feeling that perhaps we ought to have got further inland; I felt that the position was slightly tenuous on the basis that we had progressed only the first couple of miles inshore, but I personally felt very pleased at what had happened. We'd lost nothing – that is, Squadron HQ had lost nothing – but I knew the troops had had a rough time. Certainly I felt that we were luckier than we might have expected to have been.[25]

Major Peter Martin, aged 24, 2nd Battalion, The Cheshire Regiment:

At nine o'clock we had our compo stew, followed by treacle pudding. Somebody milked a cow and we had a super brew of hot chocolate. Everyone was in tremendous form. My sister had insisted that I take along her portable gramophone, one of those wind-up affairs, so we got it out and played some Vera Lynn songs and a favourite with the soldiers called 'Paper Doll'. Then, much to my amazement, a dispatch rider arrived with mail. I had a letter from my mother in which she said she had a very strong feeling the invasion was imminent. I just burst out laughing.[26]

Pfc Harry Parley, aged 24, E Company, 116th Infantry:

The last hours of 6 June are quite vivid in my memory. As darkness came, we found ourselves in a field enclosed by hedgerows. Dirty, hungry, dog-tired, and with no idea as to where we were, we decided to dig in for the night. We could hear the far-off sound of artillery and even see the path of tracer fire arching in the distance. We knew someone was catching hell. As we spread around the field, I found myself paired off with a sergeant; however, the foxhole we started was never completed. The ground was rock hard and we were both totally exhausted by the time the hole was about three inches deep. Finally, standing there in the dark and aware that it was useless to continue, the sergeant said, 'Fuck it, Parley. Let's just get down and get some rest.'

I had had nothing to eat all day except for a few bites of a rock hard D-ration chocolate bar that I carried in my back pocket. I had also had no urge whatsoever for a bowel movement during the day. I think I had experienced first-hand what being 'scared shitless' really meant.[27]

Lieutenant Colonel N.P.H. Tapp, commanding 7 Field Regiment RA, 3 British Division:

As it got dark we settled down for a little rest. Sleeping was difficult owing to the presence of a few German aircraft and a never-ending stream of AA of all sorts from the Royal Navy. Although I was very tired at the time I can remember reflecting as I lay on my blanket on the hay in a barn that it was nice to be back again about four years and five days after I had left from Dunkirk, and although we had not advanced as far as we had hoped on the first day, there was no doubt in our minds that we were securely ashore and no one would get us off again.[28]

Private Zane Schlemmer, aged 19, HQ Cpy 2nd Battalion 508 Paratroop Infantry Regiment:

We dug in at the forward observation post. I was beastly tired by that time. We were issued with Benzedrine pills and I used mine that night. I was on watch from midnight to four, but the thing that amazed me was that I had these hallucinations. The cows out in the field were white and black and brown and very dark, and with the spots on these cows and with the hallucinations I'm having from this Benzedrine, I'd swear there were people coming in. It was scary. In order to stay awake, I pulled the pin from a hand grenade and held it in my hand all through my watch. I wouldn't want to go through that night again, even though we experienced no German probes. It was the hallucinations . . .[29]

Lieutenant Donald Holman, aged 23, commanding amphibious platoon RASC:

About midnight I went down to the beach alone. I wanted to have a look, to see what was going on and to see what we had to do to get ready for next morning. I commanded a platoon of DUKWs amphibious vehicles which would be helping to unload ships on the following day. It was fairly quiet by then, a few things coming in but not many. There was still gunfire going on, but it was mostly in the distance.

It was actually a beautiful night and as I walked along the beach I thought I was stepping on soft seaweed, but when I looked down I saw it was the bodies of our men washed up on the tide. I was actually walking on the bodies of British soldiers. I didn't go any further; it was a bit shattering.[30]

Private Joe Minogue, 7th Armoured Division:

During the period when we were waiting for someone to tell us what to do we had a bit of time to think about what had happened. I would hate anybody to think there was any kind of heroism about it. Each of us had been building up secret little fears that we might not survive. We were aware that we had been very lucky indeed and that our fears, fortunately, had not materialized. I don't think any of us were patriotic men in the sense that we would stand rigidly to attention and wave flags, but we were rather proud that this army, which had done so many daft things, in which we had been bellowed at and shouted at and generally mucked around and spent thousands of hours on exercises standing about in the rain and the mud and the snow, had finally managed to bring off what, when you look at it in a fairly cold light, was a pretty big adventure.[31]

Midnight. Wireless messages between Oberst Krug, commander 736 Grenadier Regiment, and HQ 716 Infantry Division:

'The enemy are on top of my bunker. I have no means of resisting them and no communications with my men. What shall I do?'

   '*I can give you no more orders. You must make your own decision now. Goodbye.*'[32]

NOTES

Chapter 1: Night Raiding

1. Author's interview
2. Ibid.

Chapter 2: The Invasion of the Yanks

1. Keegan, John: *Six Armies in Normandy*, pp.11–14
2. Eisenhower Center, University of New Orleans
3. Second World War letters of Robert W. McCormick, typescript, US Army Military History Institute
4. *As Mac Saw It*, typescript, US Military History Institute
5. Author's interview
6. Eisenhower Center
7. Author's interview
8. Eisenhower Center
9. *Army Talks*, Vol.11, No.11, March 1944
10. *A Yank In Britain*, typescript, Hoover Institution
11. Eisenhower Center
12. Letter, archives D-Day Museum, Portsmouth

Chapter 3: Dry Runs and Wet Runs

1. Author's interview
2. Eisenhower Center
3. Ibid.
4. Balkoski, Joseph: *Beyond the Beachhead*, p.55
5. *Wartime Memories of John R. Slaughter*, unpublished manuscript loaned to author
6. Eisenhower Center
7. Author's interview
8. Ibid.
9. Manuscript, D-Day Museum
10. Letter to author

11. Letter loaned to author
12. Handwritten account supplied to author
13. Author's interview
14. Edwards, Jimmy: *Six of the Best*, pp.149–50
15. Archives, D-Day Museum
16. Letter to author
17. Unpublished manuscript, US Army Military History Institute
18. Eisenhower Center
19. Ibid.
20. Ibid.

Chapter 4: Spies and Lies

1. Cave-Brown, Anthony: *Bodyguard of Lies*, p.464
2. Eisenhower Papers, SHAEF SGS 000.7
3. Miller, Francis P.: *Man From The Valley*, p.110
4. Francis P. Miller Collection, George C. Marshall Research Library
5. Eisenhower Center
6. Royal Engineers Journal, no date
7. *Army*, Vol.30, June 1980, pp.18–25
8. Public Record Office (PRO), Air 20/8932
9. Unpublished typescript loaned to author
10. PRO, WO 219/88
11. Author's interview

Chapter 5: Behind the Atlantic Wall

1. Liddell-Hart, Basil: *The Other Side of the Hill*, p.133
2. Author's interview
3. Unpublished manuscript, National Archives, Washington DC
4. Author's interview
5. Ibid.
6. Warlimont interview, National Archives
7. Unpublished manuscript loaned to author
8. Author's interview
9. Ibid.
10. Cornelius Ryan Archives, Vernon R. Alden Library, Ohio University
11. Author's interview
12. Ibid.
13. Wilmot, Chester: *The Struggle For Europe*, p.218

Chapter 6: Sealed!

1. Letter, D-Day Museum
2. Author's interview
3. Unpublished manuscript, D-Day Museum
4. Manuscript loaned to author

5. Imperial War Museum (IWM) Sound Archives, 9577
6. Unpublished manuscript, D-Day Museum
7. IWM Sound Archives, 8761
8. Unpublished manuscript, IWM
9. Manuscript supplied to author
10. Author's interview
11. Unpublished manuscript, Centre for Military Studies, King's College, London
12. Eisenhower Center
13. *Wartime Memories of John R. Slaughter*, op. cit.
14. Eisenhower Center
15. Thames Television, *World at War* series

Chapter 7: On the Move at Last

1. BBC Sound Archives, SR 1604/H/C
2. Letter, D-Day Museum
3. Typescript, US Army Military History Institute
4. Brereton, L.H.: *The Brereton Diaries*, p.270
5. Eisenhower Center
6. Willis, Leonard: *None Had Lances*, p.131
7. Eisenhower Center
8. *The Silver Bugle*, Autumn 1984
9. Eisenhower Center
10. Typescript, D-Day Museum
11. *The News*, Portsmouth, Overlord Supplement, June 1984
12. Letter, D-Day Museum
13. BBC Sound Archives, SR 1602/H/A
14. Monks, Noel: *Eye Witness*, pp.223–4
15. Author's interview
16. Typescript loaned to author
17. Author's interview
18. Typescript, Royal Marines Museum, Eastney, Hampshire
19. MG30 E269, Public Archives, Canada
20. Typescript, US Army Military History Institute
21. Brown, Lt John Mason: *Many A Watchful Night*, pp.6–7
22. Manuscript loaned to author
23. Eisenhower Center
24. Archives, HQ Company, 116th Infantry Regiment

Chapter 8: Sunday 4 June 1944

1. Smith, General Walter Bedell: *Eisenhower's Six Great Decisions*, pp.41–2
2. Thames Television, *World at War* series
3. Army Medical Services Magazine, Vol.38, October 1984
4. Eisenhower Center

5. *The Covenanter*, July 1945
6. Edwards, op. cit., pp.165–6
7. Karig, Walter: *Battle Report*, pp.309–11
8. Author's interview
9. Thames Television, *World at War* series

Chapter 9: Monday 5 June 1944

1. Eisenhower Papers, No.1735, Dwight D. Eisenhower Library, Abilene, Kansas
2. Eisenhower Papers, No.1734
3. Hollister, Paul, et al: *D-Day Through to Victory in Europe*, p.75
4. *The Silver Bugle*, Vol.46. No.3
5. Saunders, Hilary St George: *The Green Beret*, p.267
6. Typescript, D-Day Museum
7. Eisenhower Center
8. Munro, Ross: *Gauntlet to Overlord*, pp.51–3
9. Willis, op. cit., p.133
10. Eisenhower Center
11. Unpublished typescript loaned to author
12. Eisenhower Center
13. Lovat, Lord: *March Past*, p.305
14. *Army*, Vol.30, June 1980
15. Typescript, D-Day Museum
16. Typescript, RAF Museum, Hendon
17. Chauvet, Maurice: *D Day ler DFM*, p.15
18. Thames Television, *World at War* series
19. Typescript, Hoover Institution
20. Author's interview
21. Unpublished manuscript, Centre for Military Archives
22. Lovat, op. cit., pp.369–70
23. BBC Sound Archives, SR 1653/2
24. Delmer, Sefton: *The Counterfeit Spy*, p.193
25. *World War Two Resistance Stories*, no date
26. Delmer, op. cit., p.194
27. Ibid.
28. Warlimont interview, National Archives
29. Wilmot, op. cit., p.229

Chapter 10: Chocks Away

1. McCormick archive, op. cit.
2. Ridgway, Matthew B.: *Soldier: The Memoirs of Matthew B. Ridgway*, pp.2–3
3. Gale, Lt Gen. Sir Richard: *With the 6th Airborne Division in Normandy*, p.72
4. Rapport, Leonard et al: *Rendezvous With Destiny*, p.82
5. Letter loaned to author

6. Typescript loaned to author
7. Author's interview
8. Thames Television, *World at War* series
9. Unpublished manuscript, RAF Museum
10. Keegan, op. cit., pp. 84–5
11. Eisenhower Center
12. Unpublished manuscript loaned to author
13. Letter, D-Day Museum
14. Eisenhower Center
15. Author's interview
16. Ibid.
17. Eisenhower Center
18. Ibid.
19. Tape loaned by Manchester & District Normandy Landing Association
20. Author's interview
21. McCormick archive, op. cit.
22. Typescript loaned to author
23. Ibid.
24. Author's interview
25. Ibid.
26. Ibid.
27. Letter loaned to author
28. Ibid.
29. Jefferson, Alan: *Assault on the Guns of Merville*, pp.117–18
30. Letter loaned to author
31. Ex Coelis, *Canadian Army Journal*, January 1957
32. Neville, Lt Gen. Sir J.E.H. (ed.), *Oxs & Bucks Light Infantry Chronicle*, pp.61–2

Chapter 11: They're Coming!

1. Ministry of Information: *By Air to Battle*, pp.5–7
2. Typescript, D-Day Museum
3. Author's interview
4. Reynaud, Alexandre: *Ste Mère-Eglise*, pp.42–4
5. Author's interview
6. National Archives, Washington DC
7. Telephone log, 7th Army, National Archives, Washington
8. Cornelius Ryan archives
9. RAC Journal, Vol.IV
10. Ryan archives
11. Ibid.
12. Author's interview
13. Ibid.
14. Ibid.
15. Ibid.

16. Ibid.
17. Ryan archives
18. Ibid.
19. Author's interview
20. Ryan archives

Chapter 12: Omaha

1. Karig, op. cit., pp.320–1
2. Ewing, Joseph: *29, Let's Go!*, pp.36–8
3. Second World War eyewitness, no date
4. Ibid.
5. National Archives, Washington DC
6. Eisenhower Center
7. Slaughter memoirs
8. Eisenhower Center
9. Ibid.
10. National Archives
11. Eisenhower Center
12. Ibid.
13. Slaughter memoirs
14. IWM Sound Archives, 2702/03
15–19. Eisenhower Center
20. Thames Television, *World at War* series
21. Second World War eyewitness, no date
22. *Infantry*, May–June 1985
23. Typescript, D-Day Museum
24. Eisenhower Center
25. National Archives
26. Eisenhower Center
27. Ibid.
28. Slaughter memoirs
29. Ibid.
30. Eisenhower Center
31. Slaughter memoirs
32. Eisenhower Center
33. Thames Television, *World at War* series
34. BBC Sound Archives, SR 1653/2
35–37. Eisenhower Center

Chapter 13: Sword

1. Typescript, D-Day Museum
2. Author's interview
3. Letter to author
4. Lovat, op. cit., pp.371–2

5. Author's interview
6. Ibid.
7. Ibid.
8. IWM Sound Archives, 9577
9. London Flotilla Bulletin, Nos 2 & 3
10. Typescript, D-Day Museum
11. *Soldier* supplement, June 1984
12. Typescript, Royal Marines Museum
13. Manuscript, IWM
14. *Portsmouth News*, June 1984

Chapter 14: *Juno*

1. BBC Sound Archives, SR 1623/G/F
2. Neillands, Robin: *By Sea and Land: The Story of the Royal Marine Commandos*, pp.150–1
3. Author's interview
4. Typescript, National Archives, Canada
5. Typescript, D-Day Museum
6. Hickey, Revd R.M.: *The Scarlet Dawn*, pp.195–6
7. Author's interview
8. Ibid.
9. Ibid.
10. BBC Sound Archives, SR 1625/E/A

Chapter 15: *Gold*

1. *Green Howards Gazette*, June 1974
2. Author's interview
3. Ibid.
4. BBC Sound Archives, SR 1653/2
5. Author's interview
6. Letter to author
7. Thames Television, *World at War* series
8. Letter, D-Day Museum
9. Letter to author
10. *Essex Yeomanry Journal*, 1969
11. Ibid.
12. Ibid.
13. Lindsay, T.M.: *Sherwood Rangers*, pp.102–3
14. Typescript, D-Day Museum
15. Typescript, IWM
16. *Soldier* supplement, June 1984

Chapter 16: Utah

1. Eisenhower Center
2. Ibid.
3. BBC Sound Archives, SR 1653/2
4. *As Mac Saw It*, op. cit.
5. Eisenhower Center
6. BBC Sound Archives, SR 1630/H/A
7. Letter, D-Day Museum
8. Eisenhower Center

Chapter 17: They're Here!

1. Tute, Warren, et al: *D-Day*, p.199
2. *Ouest-France*, June 1984
3. Ryan archives
4. Author's interview
5. Ibid.
6. Ibid.
7. Document loaned to author
8. *Ouest-France*, op. cit.
9. Typescript loaned to author
10. *Ouest-France*, op. cit.
11. Ibid.

Chapter 18: Is It the Landing?

1. Author's interview
2. Ryan archives
3. Author's interview
4. Shulman, Milton: *Defeat in the West*, pp.102–3
5. Typescript loaned to author
6. Ryan archives
7. Author's interview
8. Manuscript loaned to author
9. Ryan archives
10. Ibid.
11. Author's interview
12. Warlimont, Walter: *Inside Hitler's Headquarters*
13. Telephone Journal, 7th Army (1st Canadian Army Intelligence Summaries, August–October 1944)

Chapter 19: Afternoon

1. Eisenhower Center
2. Dear, Ian: *Ten Commando*, pp.131–2
3. Lovat, op. cit., pp.319–20
4. Ibid., pp.374–5
5. Typescript, IWM
6. Letter to author
7. Typescript, D-Day Museum
8. Letter to author
9. Ex Coelis, op. cit.
10. Bradley, Gen. Omar: *A Soldier's Story*, pp.251–2
11. Typescript, US Army Military History Institute
12. National Archives, Washington
13. Eisenhower Center
14. Ibid.
15. Smith, R. Harris: *OSS: The Secret History of America's First Central Intelligence Agency*, pp.184–5
16–19. Eisenhower Center
20. Munro, op. cit., pp.67–8
21. Hickey, op. cit., pp.196–7
22. Author's interview
23. Ibid.

Chapter 20: Home Front

1. Letter, D-Day Museum
2. Eisenhower Center
3. Tute, op. cit., p.111
4. *Hansard*, 6 June 1944
5. Typescript, IWM
6. Letter, D-Day Museum
7. Tedder, Lord: *Without Prejudice*, pp.548–9
8. Author's interview
9. Typescript, D-Day Museum

Chapter 21: The End of the Day

1. 7th Army War Diary, National Archives, Washington
2. Author's interview
3. Ibid.
4. Ryan archives
5. Ibid.
6. Ibid.
7. Appendix, sit. – rep. West No.1288

8. McKee, Alexander: *Caen: Anvil of Victory*, p.66
9. *Ouest-France*, op. cit.
10. Scott, Desmond: *Typhoon Pilot*, pp.109–11
11. Karig, op. cit., pp.321–3
12. Eisenhower Center
13. Ibid.
14. Typescript loaned to author
15. Author's interview
16. Typescript, National Archives
17. BBC Sound Archives, SR 1626/E/B
18. Gavin, Lt Gen. James M.: *Airborne Warfare*, pp.110–11
19. Monks, op. cit., pp.228–9
20. Author's interview
21. Ex Coelis, op. cit.
22. Author's interview
23. Memoirs of A.J. Lane, IWM
24. Typescript loaned to author
25. Author's interview
26. Ibid.
27. Eisenhower Center
28. Typescript loaned to author
29. Author's interview
30. Ibid.
31. Thames Television, *World at War* series
32. McKee, op. cit., p.68

SELECT BIBLIOGRAPHY

BALKOSKI, Joseph: *Beyond The Beachhead* (Stackpole Books, Harrisburg, Pennsylvania, 1989)

BRADLEY, General Omar N.: *A Soldier's Story* (Eyre & Spottiswoode, London, 1952)

BRERETON, L.H.: *The Brereton Diaries* (William Morrow, New York, 1946)

BROWN, Lt John Mason USNR: *Many A Watchful Night* (Hamish Hamilton, London, 1944)

CAVE-BROWN, Anthony: *Bodyguard of Lies* (Harper & Row, New York, 1975)

DEAR, Ian: *Ten Commando* (Leo Cooper, London, 1987)

DELMER, Sefton: *The Counterfeit Spy* (Harper & Row, New York, 1971)

EDWARDS, Jimmy: *Six of the Best* (Robson Books, London, 1984)

EWING, Joseph: *29, Let's Go!* (Infantry Journal Press, Washington DC, 1948)

GALE, Lt Gen. Sir Richard: *With the 6th Airborne Division in Normandy* (Sampson Low, Marston, London, 1948)

GAVIN, Lt Gen. James M: *Airborne Warfare* (Infantry Journal Press, Washington DC, 1947)

HICKEY, Revd R.M.: *The Scarlet Dawn* (Tribune, Campbelltown, New Brunswick, 1949)

HOLLISTER, Paul and STRUNSKY, Robert (eds): *D-Day Through to Victory in Europe* (CBS, New York, 1945)

ISMAY, Lord: *Memoirs* (Heinemann, London, 1960)

JEFFERSON, Alan: *Assault on the Guns of Merville* (John Murray, London, 1987)

KARIG, Commander Walter USNR: *Battle Report* (Farrar & Rinehart, New York, 1946)

KEEGAN, John: *Six Armies in Normandy* (Cape, London, 1982)

LIDDELL-HART, Basil: *The Other Side of the Hill* (Cassell, London, 1951)

LINDSAY, T.N.: *Sherwood Rangers* (Burrup, Mathieson, London, 1952)

LOVAT, Lord: *March Past* (Weidenfeld & Nicolson, London, 1978)

McKEE, Alexander: *Caen: Anvil of Victory* (Souvenir Press, London, 1966)

MILLER, Francis P.: *Man From The Valley* (University of North Carolina, Chapel Hill, 1971)

MONKS, Noel: *Eye Witness* (Frederick Muller, London, 1955)

MUNRO, Ross: *Gauntlet to Overlord* (Macmillan, Toronto, 1945)

NEILLANDS, Robin: *By Sea and Land: The Story of the Royal Marine Commandos* (Weidenfeld & Nicolson, London, 1987)

NEVILLE, Lt Gen. Sir J.E.H. (ed.): *The Oxfordshire and Buckinghamshire Light Infantry Chronicle* (Gale & Polden, Aldershot, 1954)

RAPPORT, Leonard and NORTHWOOD, Arthur Jnr: *Rendezvous With Destiny* (Infantry Journal Press, Washington DC, 1948)

REYNAUD, Alexandre: *Ste Mère-Eglise* (Julliard, Paris, 1984)

RIDGWAY, Matthew B.: *Soldier: The Memoirs of Matthew B. Ridgway* (Harper, New York, 1956)

SAUNDERS, Hilary St George: *The Green Beret* (Michael Joseph, London, 1949)

SCOTT, Desmond: *Typhoon Pilot* (Leo Cooper, London, 1982)

SHULMAN, Milton: *Defeat in the West* (Secker & Warburg, London, 1947)

SMITH, R. Harris: *OSS: The Secret History of America's First Central Intelligence Agency* (Dell Publishing, New York, 1972)

SMITH, Gen. Walter Bedell: *Eisenhower's Six Great Decisions* (Longmans Green, New York, 1956)

TEDDER, Lord: *Without Prejudice* (London, Cassell, 1966)

TUTE, Warren and COSTELLO, John: *D-Day* (Sidgwick & Jackson, London, 1964)

WARLIMONT, Walter: *Inside Hitler's Headquarters* (Praeger, New York, 1966)

WILLIS, Leonard: *None Had Lances* (24th Lancers Old Comrades Association, 1986)

WILMOT, Chester: *The Struggle for Europe* (Collins, London, 1950)

INDEX

Adair, Bob, 328
Adams, Robert E., 297–300
Adsett, Pte, 215
Ahearn, Major John, 371–2
Aitken, Capt. Douglas, 125, 163
Albemarle aircraft, 187–9
Aldbourne, 30–2
Alex, Pfc (Private first class) George, 182–3
Alford, Lieut Parker A., 181
Algonquin, Canadian ship, 162
Alliance Resistance network, Bayeux, 175
Alvalio, Pfc Joseph, 40
Ambrose, Dr Stephen, xv
Amfreville, 468
Ancon, USS, 132, 246–7, 456–7
Anderson, Sgt Alan, 282–3, 457–8
Anderson, Lieut, 260
Andrews, Celia, 32–3
Anselm, Mme d', 373
Apanasewics, Capt., 262
APAs, 246, 275, 297
Arkansas, USS, 247
Armstrong, John, padre, 322
Armstrong, Sgt, 458
Army Vehicle Inspectorate, 45
Arromanches, 64, 83, 97, 161, 447

Asnelles, 97, 373, 419
Atlantic Wall, xiii, 79, 92, 93, 224, 240, 394
Augeri, Pte Sal, 253
Augusta, USS, 137–8, 166, 247, 268, 421
Avranches, 402
AVRE (Armoured Vehicle Royal Engineers), 317
'Axis Sally', 115–16

Bach, Major Stanley, 423–4
Baddeck, HMS, corvette, 135
Badenock, Lieut Alexander, 316–17
Bailey, Lance Cpl John 'Bill', 42–3
Bainbridge, Capt., 261, 290
Baker, A., 161, 355–7
Baker, Major, 161
Baldwin, Hanson, W., 64–6, 166
Ballard, Capt. James L., 459–61
Banning, Elmar, 429
BAR (Browning Automatic Rifle), 431
Barber, Carter, 280–1
Barker, Brig. Richard, 58
Barnes, Pfc John, 37–8, 255–7
Barnes, Sgt, 288
Baumgarten, Rifleman Hal, 287–9
Bayer, George, 18

Bayeux, 69, 70, 175, 378, 454, 455
Bayfield, USS, 411–12
BBC, 69–70, 80, 85, 121–2, 130–1, 320–1, 332–4, 426, 464–5; French Service, 175, 381
Beardsley, Marine Joe, 304
Beaulieu, 105, 111–12, 119
Beavan, Naina, 22–3, 443–5
Beavers, Jim, 201
Becker, Frederick, 116
Bedell-Smith, Gen. Walter, 143–4, 145
Beibst, Gefreite Werner, 79–83, 242–3
Belfast, HMS, 356
Bennett, Lieut Col Donald V., 54–5
Bénouville, 400, 421
Bernard, Professor, 2
Berry Pomeroy, 20–2
Bieganski, Pfc, 362
Bingley, Violet, 130
Bixler, Sgt John, 250
Black Prince, HMS, 166
Blanchard, Lieut, 363, 364
Blandford, 117
Blaylock, Pfc Joseph S., Sr, 163, 361–2
Block, Major, 244
Bluff, Sgt, 73
Boccafogli, Edward C., 149–50

Bond family of Torquay, 15
Bone, Trooper Harry, 315
Bone, Lieut Hugh, 358–9,
    416–17
Bon Saveur convent, 453
Booth, Constable Sidney, 128
Bortzfield, Charles, 190–2
Bosworth, Sgt John, 359–60
Bournemouth, 43, 47
Bowdidge, Cpl Bill, 34–5
Bowen, Pte Dennis, 101–4,
    132–4, 336–9, 61–3
Bowers, Coy Sgt Major H.W.,
    341
Box, Mrs Marjorie, 122
Boycott, Charles, 139
Bradley, Bruce, 125, 364
Bradley, Gen. Omar, 247,
    421–2
Brancaster beach, 1
Brandon, 43
Branham, Felix, 35–7
Breeden, Sgt Cecil, 289
Brereton, Lieut Gen. Lewis,
    124
Brevands, 240
Brewer, Gunner Ernest, 100–
    1
Brierly, Flight Lieut Denys
    S.C., 189–90
Brierre, Lieut Eugene D., 435
Bristow, Flight Lieut P.M.,
    183–5
BRITISH ARMY UNITS:
21st Army Group, 64, 247,
    453
Second Army, 247
'4th Army', phantom, 58
Royal Army Medical Corps,
    173, 305–7; 21 Field
    Dressing Station, 148–9
Royal Army Service Corps:
    101st Amphibious Coy,
    310–11; amphibious
    platoon, 473; Tipper Coy, 45
Royal Engineers, 1–4, 318–19,
    342; 246 Field Coy, 138–49;
    Field Squadron, 109–10,
    317–18, 469–70; 3rd
    Parachute Squadron, 110–
    11, 205–11
Royal Pioneer Corps, 360

2nd Airborne Div., 231
3rd Div., 131, 162, 472
6th Airborne Div., 110, 169,
    178–9, 219, 395, 467
7th Armoured Div., 344–7
50th Northumbrian Div., 102
1st Commando Brig., 165,
    414–15
1st Special Service Brig., 196
3rd Parachute Brig., 110
6th Airlanding Brig., 111, 454
8th Infantry Brig., 160
5th Black Watch, 470
Cheshire Regt, 2nd Battn, 471
Devonshire Regt, 14, 348–51;
    2nd Battn, 105, 342–3
Dorset Regt, 342, 347
4th/7th Dragoon Guards,
    161, 255–7
Durham Light Infantry, 6th
    Battn, 126–7
East Yorkshire Yeomenry,
    311, 437; 2nd Battn, 358–9,
    416–17; 5th Battn, 101–4,
    132–4, 336–9, 461–3
147th Essex Yeomenry, 43–4,
    111–13, 229–41, 351–2,
    352–4
7th Field Regt, RA, 472
Glider Pilot Regt, 49; A
    Squadron, 192–4
Green Howards, 6th Battn,
    335–6, 343–4, 417–18
24th Lancers, 125, 163
52nd Oxfordshire and
    Buckinghamshire Light
    Infantry, 42–3, 48, 467–8
Parachute Regt, 45–6, 179–80,
    197–8, 211–18
5 RHA, G Battery, 100
Royal Hampshire Regt, 347,
    351, 352; 1st Battn, 52–3,
    341, 347–8, 429–21
13th/18th Royal Hussars, 44–
    5, 315–16, 415; B Squadron,
    172–3, 308–10, 471
Royal Tank Regt, 44th
    Battery, 314–15
Royal Ulster Rifles, 1st Battn,
    104–5, 111
Royal Warwickshire Regt, 2nd
    Battn, 34–5

Sherwood Rangers'
    Yeomenry, 43–4;
    C Squadron, 354–5
7th Parachute Battn, 150
8th Parachute Battn, 207
9th Parachute Battn, 211–18;
    A Coy, 45–6, 179–80, 213–
    17
13th Parachute Battn, 197–8
52nd Air Landing Battn, 48,
    467–8
4 Commando, 161, 173–4,
    305–7, 311–12, 415–16;
    French Troop, 168–9
6 Commando, 413–14;
    3 Troop, 113–14, 173
10 Commando, X Troop, 72–8
22nd Independent Parachute
    Coy, 47, 187–9
25 Beach Recovery Coy,
    REME, 359–60
101st Amphibious Coy, 310–
    11
Brize Norton, RAF, 49–50
Bronikowski, Lieut von
    Oppel, 398
Brown, Sgt Major Jack
    Vilander, 43–4, 111–13,
    339–41
Brown, Lieut John Mason,
    137–8
Brown, Sgt Owen L., 24–5
Browning, Lieut Gen.
    F.A.M., 66
Bruce, Col David, 428–9
Bruce, Robert, 248
Brumbaugh, Cpl J. Frank,
    186–7, 196–7
Bryant, Col, 163
Bude, 42
Buff, Sgt Thomas, B., 179
Bulford, 45–6, 110
Bull, General, 145, 147–8, 158
Bures, 207
Burford, Signett Hill, 32–3
Burhard, Arthur, Jr, 281
Burns, Robbie, 184
Butt, Lance Cpl Roy, 419

C-47 aircraft, 190–1, 201, 204
Cabourg, 189, 231
Caen, 84, 87, 90, 143, 153, 161,

175, 207, 229, 230, 237, 382–3, 384, 385–6, 393, 394, 395, 397, 399, 400, 448, 450, 453, 455; Résistance in, 67–70, 223–4, 383–4

Cairon, 400

Calais, 87, 95, 408

Caldwell, Ginger, 173

Campbell, Archibald Doon, 105–6, 131, 312–13

Campbell, Sir Malcolm, 2

Camrose, HMS, 135–6

Canada/Canadians, xiii, 162, 207, 214, 219–20, 320–34, 390, 391, 392, 395, 435–7, 468–9

CANADIAN ARMY UNITS:

Armoured Corps, 323–6

3rd Div., 326–7, 418

3rd Anti-Tank Regt, 331–2

6th Armoured Regt, B Squadron, 323–6

Assault Engineers, 26 Field Coy, 322–3, 437

Canadian Scottish Regt, 1st Battn, 329–30

North Shore Regt, 327–9, 436–7

Regina Rifles, 326, 330–1

Winnipeg Rifles, Anti-Tank Platoon, 469

1st Parachute Battn, 214, 219–20, 421, 468–9

48 Commando, 321–2

No. 1 Movement Control Unit, 326–7, 418

The Canadian Press, 435–6

Canhan, Col Charles 'Stoneface', 141–2

Canning Town, 101–3

Canyon, Harold 194–6

Capa, Robert, xiv–xv

Cardron, Pierre, 375–6

Carentan, 227, 229, 232, 240, 375, 403, 404, 455

Carpiquet airfield, 230, 375, 408

Cartledge, Pfc Carl, 115–17

Cass, Brig. E.E.E., 160–1

Castognola, Pilot Officer 'Caz', 168

Cawthon, Capt. Charles, 248–50, 277–9

Cayeux-sur-Mer, 74

CBS News, New York, 160

Chalk, Pte John, 52–3, 419–21

Chapman, George, 353

Charlton, Thurman, 165

Chauvet, Cpl Maurice, 168–9

Chef-du-Pont, 465

Cherbourg, 8, 83, 89, 119, 160, 229, 230, 378, 411

Cheshire, Wing Commander, 168

Chouvaloff, Capt., 227

Churchill, Sir Winston, 2, 58–9, 93, 171, 441–2

Clark, Capt. L.N. 'Nobby', 326–7, 418

Clements, Lieut John, 38

Clift, Captain Maurice, 38–9

Clogstoun-Willmott, Lieut Cmdr Nigel, 4–6, 7, 8, 9–10

Coast Guard Rescue Cutter 16: 280–1

Cockburn, Dr, 167

Colleville, 389–90

Colleville-sur-Mer, 427

Collins, Capt., 357

Collins, General, 411

Combined Operations Pilotage Party (COPP), 5

Compton, Lieut Buck, 433, 434

Coningham, Air Vice-Marshal Sir Arthur, 443

Cooke Capt., Albert, 310–11

Corbett, Cpl, 187, 188

Courseulles, 326

Cota, Gen., 296

Cotentin peninsula, 83, 89, 229, 230

Couliboeuf, 395

Courbet, French ship, 135, 136

Crawford, Major J.A., 140

Creasey, Admiral, 145, 156

Crown Hill barracks, Plymouth, 35–7

Cunningham, Lance Cpl, 307

Curtis, Rupert, 165, 166

Curtiss, Commander, L.R., 313–14

Daily Mail war correspondent, 131–2

Dakota aircraft, 48, 49–50, 151, 183–5

Daley, Buddy, 328

Dallas, Goodman Paisley, 459

Dallas, Major Thomas S., 260

Damski, Gefreite Aloysius, 96–7

Daniell, Ray, 64

Dartmouth, 123

Daughney, Major Ralph, 328–9

Daum, Johnny, 149–50

Davis Submarine Escape Apparatus, 44

deception and cover plans, *see* Fortitude, Operation

DelGiudice, Vincent J., 411–12

Denny, Capt. Neel, 315

Deslandes, Jean, 373–5

Devlin, Rifleman Patrick, 104 5

Dittmar, Pte, Robert, 288

Doell, Lieut, 396

Donaldson, Lieut, 287, 288

Donovan, Gen. 'Wild Bill', 428–9

Dorothy Dix, USS, 292

Dover, 87, 95

Downs, Mrs, of Warsash, 24–5

Drake, Sgt Len, 47, 187–9

DUKWs (Duplex-Drive amphibious trucks), 56, 121, 257–8, 272, 282, 297, 310, 368, 431–3, 463, 473

Du Maurier, Daphne, 66

Duncan, Major, 324

Dunfee, Sgt William T., 177, 201–2

During, Hauptmann Ernst, 240–2

Dyson, Bill, 184

Eades, Sgt Jerry W., 426–8

Eagle, Exercise, 116

E-Boats, German, 55, 56, 301

Eden, Sir Anthony, 126

Edgar, Commodore Campbell, 457

Edwards, Flying Officer
Jimmy, 48–50, 151–2
Eisenhower, Gen. Dwight D.,
vii, 28, 57, 58–9, 107, 115,
136, 143, 144, 145, 146,
147–8, 156, 157, 158, 159,
160, 161, 181, 421, 441, 442,
447
Elmer, Pte Bernard Charles,
417–18
Elsey, Lieut George, 132
Empire Broadsword, SS, 304,
305
Empire Javelin, HMS, 163–4,
257
Empire Lance, HMS, 343
Empire Windrush, HMS,
260
Enderby, Capt. Bill, 355
England, Sgt, 271
Epstein, Herb, 296, 297
Ernest, Capt T., 424
Escher, Unteroffizier Rudi,
228–9, 449
ETO campaign ribbon, 20
Etreham, 243
Evreux, 99
Exeter, 14
Expert Infantryman's Badge,
39

Fairford airfield, 150
Falaise, 237, 394, 395, 396,
397
Falkingham aerodrome, 149
Farnese, Lance Cpl, 415
Fast, Sgt Victor H., 296–7
Fauvel, Jean-Pierre, 376–7
Fawcett, Capt. Jack, 329–30
Fawley, 53
Ferrari, Gino, 37
Feuchtinger, Generalleutnant
Edgar, 394–5, 399
Fielder, Sgt Harold, 322–3,
437
Figgins, Clarence E., 427
Fitzpatrick, Lieut. 362
flamethrowers, 44, 53, 271,
273, 392
Flunder, Capt. Dan, 321–2
Focke-Wulf aircraft, 432
Footitt, Cpl, 355

Foreign Armies West HQ,
appendix to situation report
1288: 452–3
Fortitude, Operation, 58–78
Fowey, 65; Menabilly House,
65–6
Fox, Captain Freddy, 111
Frazier, Sgt, 289
Free French, 36, 135, 168–9,
257; *see also* Résistance
Freeland, Lieut Stephen, 152–
3
Frénouville, 90–1
Friedolin, German soldier,
232–3, 406, 407
Fromm, Hauptmann Curt,
92–4, 237–8
Fuerst, Leutnant Heinrich, 98
Furlong, Sgt Dan, 193–4

Gale, Trooper, M.G., 314–15
Gale, Gen. Richard N.
'Windy', 145, 178–9, 467
Gallagher, Joe, 315, 316
Garbett, Pfc Robert, 289
Gariepy, Sgt Leo, 323–6
Gaulle, General Charles de, 70
Gavin, Brigadier Gen. James
M., 465–7
Gearing, Lieut, 256
Georges Leygues, French ship,
166
Gerhardt, Gen., 459
German Armed Forces
Operations Staff, 89–90,
176, 410
GERMAN ARMY UNITS
(*Wehrmacht*): 79–99, 228–45,
387–410, 447–52
Army Group B, 229, 395, 410
Panzergruppe West, 88, 238
7th Army, 229, 230, 395, 410,
447–8
15th Army, 79–83, 229, 242–3
16th Army, 230–1
81st Army, 231
84th Army Corps, 229, 233
84th Infantry Corps, 395
. 12 SS Panzer Div.
(Hitlerjugend), 99, 238, 451,
452
21 Panzer Div., 87–8, 230,

235–6, 394–5, 400–1, 408,
410, 448–9, 450–1
22 Panzer Div., 92–4, 237
77th Div., 90–2, 401–2
91st Airborne Div., 229
91st Airlanding Div., 228–9,
449
352nd Infantry Div., 83–4,
240–2, 243–5, 280, 387–9
706/8 Festungsdivision, 98
711th Infantry Div., 230–1,
236, 238, 451–2
716th Infantry Div., 175, 223,
229, 236, 389–92, 474
Panzer Lehr Div., 60, 448,
451, 452
Waffen SS Div., 448
100 Panzer Brigade, 92–4, 237
6th Parachute Regt, 232–3,
403–8
22nd Panzer Regt, 84–6, 392–
4, 395–400
125th Panzer Grenadier Regt,
87–8, 235–6, 448–9
192nd Regt, 230, 408, 450–1
352nd Artillery Regt, 243–5
357th Regt, 96–7
736th Grenadier Regt, 474
736th Infantry Regt, 389–92
914th Regt, 240–2
1058 Infantry Regt, 228–9,
449
Flak Assault Regt, No. 1,
233–4
Schell Battn, 90–2, 401–2
613 Long-Range
Reconnaissance Unit, 94–6,
408–9
German Navy Signals Corps,
234–5
Gerow, Gen. L.T., 171, 421
Gestapo, 7, 60, 70, 78
Gillard, Frank, 121–2
Gillen, Leading Signalman
I.J., 135–6
Gillingham, Pte, 269
Glasgow, HMS, 166
Glass, Donald, 307
gliders, 48–50, 151, 182, 192–
4, 204–5, 396, 467;
Hamilcar, 454; Horsa, 49–
50, 151, 215; Overlord

Administration Instructions for Pilots, 50–2
Glover Family of Paignton, 23–4
Goathland, HMS, 160–1
Goebbels, Dr Paul Josef, 29
Gold Beach, 335–60
Gondrée, Georges, 221–3
Gonneville-sur-Merville, 214
Good, Col Paul R. 'Pop Good', 124
Goodwin, Dick, 139
Gordon, Lieut R.G., 138
Gosling, Cecil, 352–3
Gosling, Major R.B., 351–2
Gottberg, Hauptmann Wilhelm von, 399–400
Gournay, M. et Mme, 383
Grandscamp, 233, 448
Granville, 402
Gregson, Lieut, 339
Grimes, O.T., 269
Growler, tug, 135
Guarnere, Sgt Bill, 434
Guderian, Gen. Heinz, 88
Guerin, Jean 'Alain Chartier', 69–70
Guingand, Major Gen. Sir Francis de, 145, 156

Haas, Sgt Hyman, 127–8, 294
Hachey, Edward, 328
Haeger, Gefreite Joseph, 389–92
Hahn, Capt., 261–2
Hall, Sgt Cecil, 351
Hall, Capt. C.N., 283–4
Hall, Rear Admiral, 246, 456
Hall, Capt. Vassar, 330–1
Halton, Matt, 131
Hamlett, Lee, 270
Hamlett, Pfc Warner 'Buster', 268–71
Hampstead Marshall, 115–16
Hangsterfer, Capt. Hank, 280
Hansen, Chet, 421–2
Harries, Sgt Jack, 45–6, 179–80
Harrison, Sgt Major H.E., 318–19
Hartmetz, Feldwebel Rainer, 90–2

Hawkes, Bill, 269
Hayling Island, 53
Heine, Heinrich, 96
Heintz, André, 67–70, 223–4, 383–4
Hemingway, Ernest, 132
Henderson, Sgt Joe, 210
Hennessy, Lance Cpl Pat, 315–16
Herbst, Gefreite Heinz, 94–6, 408–9
Hermanville, 301, 467
Hermes, Gefreite Walter, 230, 408, 450–1
Hérouville-St-Clair, 384–5
Hérouvillette, 207
Herr, Oberleutnant, 395–9
Herrig, Gefreite Klaus, 234–5
Hickey, Revd R.M., 327–9, 436–7
Hiett, Tom, 439–40
Hilary, HMS, 162–3
Hill, Brig., 45–6
Hill, Sgt W.A. 'Rufty', 343, 344
Hills, Lieut Stuart, 354–5
Hillshure, Lieut, 269
Hilton-Jones, Bryan, 73
Hindmarch, Pte, 306, 307
Hisslip, Lieut, 328
Hitler, Adolf, 1, 7, 12, 76, 79, 84, 89, 90, 99, 171, 176, 247, 341, 410
Hobart, Gen. Sir Percy, 44, 119
Hoeller, Oberleutnant Hans, 400–1
Hofmann, Gen., 451
Holbrook, Second Lieut David, 437–8
Holbury, 122
Holley, Signaller I.G., 347–8
Holman, Lieut Donald, 473
Holmes, Bobby, 414
Holodnak, George, 20
Honiton, 118; RAF, 16
Honour, Lieut George, 153–4
Hoskot, Lieut Col Nathaniel R., 24, 198–201
Howard, Major, 350
Hudson, Capt. Hal, 212–13, 218

Huf, Lance Cpl, 390
Huffstickler, Pte, 118–19
Hurel, Mme Hélène, 382–3
Hythe, 53

Ingram, Jack, 250
Irving, Lance Sgt, 209–11
Isigny, 164, 240
Isle of Wight, 160, 161, 165, 172
Ivybridge, 37, 39, 41

Jacks, Pte, 57
Jackson, Major R.J.L., 335–6
Jefferson, Lieut Alan, 217–18
Jennings, Michael, 370–1
Jodl, Gen. Alfred, 176, 242, 410
Johnson, Colonel 181
Johnston, Pte Roland, 331
Jones, Cleaves A., 463–4
Jones, Cpl, 284
Jones, Lieut William H., 285–6
Jones, Pfc William E., 118–19, 165, 367–8
Jordan, Sapper Benny, 110–11, 205–6
Joseph, Staff Sgt George, 463
Josephs, Staff Sgt Ted, 459–61
Jungclas, Raymond, 182
Juno beach, 320–34

Kafkalas, Pte Nicholas, 287
Kean, Bill, 421–2
Keane, Mike, 366
Keegan, John, 11–13
Kilpatrick, Sgt, 135
King, Cpl, 73
Kingston, Herefordshire, 17–20
Kirman, Trooper, 355
Kistowski, Oberst Werner von, 233–4
Klopp, Sgt, 232–3
Klug, Lance Cpl Ferdie, 390–2
Knilans, Lieut H. 'Nick', 167–8
Koch, Pfc Robert, 170, 276–7
Koenig, General, 70

Kortenhaus, Obergefreite Werner, 84–6, 392–4
Kramer, John, 369
Krause, Lt Col 'Cannonball', 201
Krug, Oberst, 474
Kuppers, Rifleman Alex, 469

La Cambe, 233
Lambersart, near Lille, 94
Lambert, Sgt, 283, 284
Lancaster aircraft, 168, 214
Lane, Sapper A.J., 109–10, 317–18, 469–70
Lane, Lieut George (Lanyi Gyorgy), 72–8
Lang, Hauptman Helmut, 451
Largs, HMS, 132, 301–2
La Rivière, 161
Larkhill, 47
Lassen, Major E.H., 148–9
Laughton, Wren J.E., 442
Lawrence, Joe, 414
LCAs (Landing Craft Assault), 40, 174, 250, 256, 287, 288, 305–6, 337, 343, 347, 350, 351
LCC No. 70: 152–3
LCIs (Landing Craft Infantry), 36, 65, 169, 261–2, 299, 304, 327, 457; No. 519: 313–14
LCMs (Landing Craft Mechanical), 152, 349, 423–4
LCTs (Landing Craft Tank), 1, 36, 43, 54–5, 152, 162, 172, 247, 254, 257, 280–1, 283, 285, 286, 292, 308, 310, 323–4, 339, 340, 353, 356, 361, 367–7, 411; No. 795: 370–1; rocket ships, 257, 302, 303, 340, 345, 356
LCVPs (Landing Craft Vehicles and Personnel), 36, 40, 41, 246, 247, 279, 284, 463; No. 22: 297–300
Lebreton, André, 380–1
Le Caplin, M., 375
Le Chevalier, M. et Mme, 241
Leclair, M., 378
Lecoutillet, M., 374
Lee, Tiger, 197

Lee, Major Gen. William, 179
Lee airfield, 442
Legal, M., 374
Legrain, Mme, 383
Le Hamel, 340, 351, 352, 419
Le Havre, 89, 160, 234–5, 301, 308, 447, 454, 455
Lehman, Lieut, 398
Leigh-Mallory, Air Chief Marshal Sir Trafford, 145, 147, 148, 156, 157, 178
Le Mesnil, 403
Lennox-Boyd, Major, 187
Le Rousset d'Acon, 239
Les Moulins, 243, 254
Levenson, Staff Sgt Leonard, 62–3, 181–2
Le Vivier, 401
Lewis, Staff Sgt William H., 257–8, 290–1
Liebeskind, Oberleutnant Helmut, 87–8, 235–6, 448–9
Lion-sur-Mer, 313, 373–5, 395
Liverpool, 13, 23, 36
Longues, 69, 84
'Lord Haw Haw', 115
Los Angeles Times, 368–70
Lovat, Brig. the Lord, 106, 165–6, 314, 414–15
LSTs (Landing Ship Tank), 41, 56–7, 275, 276, 287, 457; No. 47: 136–7; No. 983: 140–1
Luc-sur-Mer, 3; lighthouse, 2, 3
Lundgren, 2nd Lieut Kent, 261–2
Lunenberg, HMS, 135
Lunsford, Sgt Ewell B., 55–6

McAllister, Capt. John, 290
McCanless, Pte Ernest, 252, 253
McCormick, Pfc W., 17–20
MacDuff, Cpl, 206
McElwain, Sgt, 429
McIntyre, Mrs Betty, 21
McIntyre, Pte George 'Mac', 20–2, 123–4, 136–7, 365–7
MacLeod, Col Rory, 58
MacMillan, Wee Johnny, 110

McNabb, Lieut Ed R., 253–4
McSkimming, Rifleman, 273
Madden, Capt. John, 421, 468–9
Malarkey, Don, 433–5
Marshall, Howard, 332–4
Martin, Everett C., 282
Martin, Major Peter, 471
Mason, Danny, wireless op., 471
Masters, Lance Cpl Peter, 413–14
Matze, Mervin L., 269
Maude, Major R.M.S., 138–40
Maurice, M., 224
Mawson, Trooper, M.E., 44–5
Mayberry, Capt. George, 365
Mayhew, Sgt, 104, 338
Mead, Margaret, 25–8
Meekison, RQMS Ed, 470
Melville, Alan, 464–5
Mercader, Guillaume, 175
Merifield, Cpl William, 45
Merville, 214
Mescki, Cpl John, 197–8
Messerschmitt 210 aircraft, 192
Meyer, Generalstabsoffizier Hubert, 99, 238–40
Meyer, Irmgard, 238–40
Meyer, Kurt, 239
midget submarines, 1, 5–6, 7–10, 308, 324–5; X23: 153–4
Miller, Col Francis P., 59–60
Miller, Glenn, 22
Miller, Capt. Robert M., 124
Miller, Staff Sgt Victor 'Baseplate', 260
Millin, Bill, 314
Mills-Roberts, Derek, 165
mines/minefields, German, 67, 74–5, 82, 84, 97, 216, 296, 340, 348, 353, 356, 357, 362, 367, 371, 423; 'bouncing Betsies', 296; Teller, 73, 258, 263, 352
Minogue, Pte Joe, 119–20, 344–7, 473
Mirtel, Marty, 431–2
ML (Motor Launch), 334
Monks, Noel, 131–2
Monson, Ronald, 131

Montcalm, French ship, 166
Mont Canisoy, 451
Montebourg, 229
Montgomery, Field Marshal
  Sir Bernard Law, 43, 60, 77,
  110, 131, 142, 145, 148, 157,
  161, 168, 247, 421, 442
Morgan, Blacky, 430
Morgan, General, 145
Morris, Lance Bombardier C.,
  113–14, 173
Mosley, Leonard, 131
Mosquito aircraft, 60, 192
Mountbatten, Admiral Lord
  Louis, 73
Moyer, Jack, 124
MTBs (Motor Torpedo
  Boats), 2, 4, 10, 72
Mulberries (artificial
  harbours), xiv, 63–4, 136
Mulberry B., 136; Port
  Construction Force, 63–
  4
Mullen, Sapper, 306
Mumford, Lieut Col, 127
Munro, Ross, 162–3, 435–6
Murdoch, Cpl Gilbert G.,
  247–8, 272–5
Murray, Sgt Frank, 161–2
Murray, Joel, 327
Mustang aircraft, 442, 455,
  456
Myers, Bernie, 20

NAAFI, 47, 108, 109, 113,
  119
Nance, Lieut Rany, 289
Neave, Capt. Robert, 172–3,
  308–10, 471
Nelson-Smith, Lieut Col, 351
Neptune, Operation, 124, 136
New Forest, 53, 105
Newmyer, Lieut Arthur, 246,
  456–7
New York Times, 166; London
  Bureau, 64–5
Nivens, Gen., 145
Norfleet, Sgt, 251, 252, 253
Norman, George, 412
Norton, Ursula, 128–30
Norway, Norwegians, 58, 85,
  170

Nottingham, Players' cricket
  pavilion, 24
Nowlan, Mrs Nellie, 440–1

Obenshain, Sgt, 40
O'Brien, Sgt, 422
Ogden-Smith, Sgt Bruce, 2–4,
  7–9
O'Leary, Sapper, 209
Olsen, Capt., 466
Omaha beach, 7, 8–9, 117,
  164, 243, 246–300, 411,
  421–2, 423, 431, 456, 457,
  463
Orne, river, 153, 231, 237,
  308, 395, 396, 398, 447, 452,
  454, 467, 469
OSS (Office of Strategic
  Services), 59, 428–9
Otlowski, Sgt William B.,
  258–9
Otway, Lieut Col Terence,
  211–12, 218
Ouistreham, 168, 301, 308,
  312, 313, 385, 414, 455,
  464–5
Overlord, Operation, 1, 50–2,
  59, 66, 70, 72, 124, 144

Padley, radio op., 256
Paignton, 23
Palladino, Joe, 56–7, 431–3
Palliser, Telegraphist Clifford,
  132, 301–2
Paris, Raymond, 224–6, 377–
  80
Parley, Pfc Harry, 266–8,
  471–2
Parry, Major Allen J.M., 213–
  18
Pas de Calais, 1, 93, 235, 236,
  242, 382, 453
Patrick, Sgt, 422–3
Patterson, Dr J.H., 173–4,
  305–7, 328, 415–16
Paul, Vernon L., 140–1
Peachey, Sam, 211
Pegasus Bridge, 221, 401
Peill, Second Lieut Hans,
  92
Pemsel, Chief of Staff, 7th
  Army, 230

Pernelle, Mme et Robert,
  384–5
Peters, Sgt Debs H., 261, 290
Petite Roche-Guyon, La, 75–6
Pilck, Sgt Joe, 265–6
Pittenger, Gilbert, 289
Pluskat, Major Werner, 243–5
Plymouth, 35, 39, 56, 118,
  132, 166
Pointe du Hoc, 296, 429, 456
Poitevin, Arthur, 69
Pont-l'Abbé, 229
Pont-l'Evêque, 229
Port-en-Bessin, 5–6, 243
Porteous, Major Patrick, 311–
  12
Portland naval base, 171
Portsmouth, 22, 106, 197, 128,
  160, 172, 174, 443–6;
  SHAEF HQ, Southwick
  House, 144–8, 155
Pratt, Marine Derek, 304–5
Presley, M/Sgt 'Big Bill', 289
Prince family of Totnes, 21–2

Quaire, Mme Pierre, 385–6
Queen Alexandra's Hospital,
  443–5, 446

Radio Calais, 234
RAF (Royal Air Force), 19,
  26, 30, 73, 144, 182;
  Bomber Command, 189–90;
  123 Wing, 454–6; 161
  Squadron, 167; 271
  Squadron, 48–50, 151; 570
  Squadron, 189–90; 575
  Squadron, C Flight, 183–5;
  617 Squadron, 167–8
Ramsay, Admiral Sir Bertram,
  145, 146, 148, 157
Ranville, 187, 210, 374
rationing, 21–2, 25, 31, 35
Rattle, Sgt Charlie, 315
Raymond, Lieut Edward,
  368–9
Reach, George, 248
Red Cross, 17, 25, 186, 297,
  399, 443–5
Reddish, Trooper, 355
Reichert, Gen. Josef, 451–2
Renaud, Alexandre, 226–7

Résistance, French, 7, 66–72,
  89–90, 93, 176, 223–6;
  Bayeux, 175; Caen, 67–70,
  223–4, 383–4; deliveries by
  air to, 66–7; l'Orne, 224–6;
  plans for interference with
  communications, 71–2;
  sabotage, 70–1; Ste Mère-
  Eglise, 224–6
Resolution, HMS, 439
Reuters war correspondent,
  105–6, 131, 312–13
Revenge, HMS, 439
Rhodes General Hospital,
  New York, 440
Richter, General, 175
Rider, Sgt James, 440
Ridgway, Gen. Matthew B.,
  177–8, 465–7
Riggs, Clarius, 287
Riley, Geoffrey, 139
Riva Bella, 237, 238
Roach, Pfc George, 271–2,
  273, 274–5
Robb, Air Vice Marshal, 145
Roberts, Capt. James Milnor,
  171
Robertson, Sgt Pilgrim, 288
Robinson, Capt., 413
Robson, SSM, 355
Roche Guyon, La, 451
rocket ships (LCTs), 257, 302,
  303, 340, 345, 356
Rodney, HMS, 356
Rodriguez, Pte, 272
Romano, Phil, 179
Rome, Allied occupation of,
  87, 166
Rommel, Feldmarschall
  Erwin, 1, 76–8, 81, 82, 88,
  90, 93, 176, 230, 247, 280,
  344, 394, 410, 451
'Rommel's Asparagus', 67,
  81–2, 93
Roosevelt, President Franklin
  D., 171
Roosevelt, Gen. Teddy, 362,
  365
Rosenbloom, Lieut Raymond,
  368
Rosevere, Major 'Rosie', 207–
  8, 209, 210–11

Rote, Sgt Larry, 290–1
Rothesay, 43
Royal Marines, 132, 134, 135;
  Armoured Support Group,
  316–17
Royal Navy, 13, 29–30, 43,
  107–9, 132, 135–6, 162, 336,
  370, 455, 472; 11th
  Submarine Flotilla, 153–4
Royal Victoria Docks, 130
Rundstedt, Feldmarschall
  Gerd von, 79, 90, 99, 176,
  410
Russia, 1, 81, 91, 92, 96, 240

sabotage, xiv, 70–1, 75, 77
St Alban's Head, 174
St Aubin, 414, 455
St Côme-du-Mont, 406
St Landeuil, 83
St Laurent, 424, 459, 460
St Lô, 453–4
Ste Marie-du-Mont, 229, 375–
  6
Ste Mère-Eglise, 200, 201,
  202, 205, 224–7, 228, 236,
  241, 364, 377–80, 465, 466
St Pierre-du-Mont, 84
Sales, Sgt Bob, 262–4
Salisbury Plain, 47
Salmuth, Gen. von, 451
Sammon, Lieut Charles E.,
  202–5
Samsonsia, tug, 135
Samuel Chase, USS, 297
Saunders, Sgt, 355
Schilling, Capt., 40, 164
Schlemmer, Pte Zane, 472–
  3
Schneider, Col, 296, 297
Schulz, Lieut, 403, 405
Schweppenburg, General
  Geyr von, 88
Scotland, 41–2, 43, 58, 161
Scott, Wing Cmdr Desmond,
  454–6
Scott-Bowden, Major Logan,
  1–4, 7–9
Sedgewick, Pte, 418
Seine, Bay of the, 136, 166,
  246
Selsey, 64

Severloh, Obergefreite
  Heinrich, 387–9
SHAEF (Supreme HQ Allied
  Expeditionary Force), 7, 58,
  66, 442; Chief Met. Officer,
  144–8; Southwick House,
  Portsmouth, HQ of, 144–8,
  155; Scottish Command, 58;
  SFQ monthly progress
  report to, 70–2
Shanley, Col Thomas J.B.,
  466
Sharp, Dougie, 197
Shawd, Pfc Walter P., 458–9
Sidaway, Sgt, 354, 355
Sidgwick, Major C.J., 352–3
Skrek, Lieut, 458
Slade, Lieut Dennis, 217
Slapton Sands, 39–40, 54, 57
Slaughter, Sgt John R., 39–41,
  117, 163–4, 250–3, 264–5
Small, Sgt, 191
Smith, Capt., A.D.C., 161
Smith, Capt. Albert H., Jr,
  279–80
Smith, Bill, 179
Smith, Capt., 123, 136, 366,
  367
Smith, Major David, 139
Smith, Mack, 263
Smith, Major Thor M., 28–30
Smith, William C., 41–2
Southampton, 53, 108, 113–
  14, 439
South Brent, 23
Southsea, 128–30
Speidel, Gen. Hans, 230, 451
Spitfire aircraft, 162, 432, 442,
  454, 455
Stagg, Group Capt. James,
  144–8, 155–8
Stalin, Josef, 87
Steele-Baume, Major E.H.,
  150
Steeles, driver, 357
Stevenson, Cpl, 104, 462
Stewart, Lieut, 191
Stewart, Major Robert, 290
Stirling aircraft, 167
Stone, Pte, 350
Storey, Trooper, 355
Strayer, Col Bob, 433

Struke, Doug, 185
Studland Bay, 43, 53
Stypulowski, Stanley, 291–2
Surplice, Group Capt., 178
Surro, Pfc Dominic, 288–9
Sussex, Operation, 59–62
Svenner, Norwegian destroyer, 301, 302
Swindon, 30, 31
Sword beach, xiv, 174, 230, 301–19

tanks, 43–5, 53, 119–20, 247, 265–6, 301, 314–15, 316, 371; Churchill, 322–3, 356; DD (Duplex-Drive amphibious Sherman), 43–4, 53, 302, 308, 309, 315, 323–6, 354–5, 357; flail, 44, 53; flame-throwing, 53; Panzer IV, 395, 397–9; Sherman, 44, 291–2, 348, 359, 367, 397, 422, 423, 436
Tapp, Lieut Col N.P.H., 472
Tarbrush, Operation, 73
Tart, Pfc Vernon W., 13–17
Tavistock, 36
Taylor, Blanco, 305
Taylor, Gen., 179
Tedder, Air Chief Marshal Sir Arthur, 115, 116, 144, 145, 147, 148, 156, 157, 443
Tempsford, 167
Texas, USS, 166, 247, 248, 250, 257
Thunderbolt aircraft, 402, 456
Tiger, Exercise, 57
Tighe, Lieut, 371
Tillett, Capt. John, 48, 467–8
Tillières-sur-Avre, 238, 239
Tomasi, Doctor, 255
Torquay, 14–16, 125
Totnes, 20, 21
Traux, Sgt Louis E., 185–6
Travett, Lance Cpl N., 342–3
Treanor, Tom, 368–70
Troarn, 111, 207, 210, 211, 236, 394
Tway, Pfc, 270
Typhoon aircraft, 356, 360, 455

USAF, 167; Ninth Air Force, 124; 441st Troop Carrier Group, 100 Squadron, 190–2
US Army Medical Corps, 440
US ARMY UNITS:
1st Army Group, 453
1st Army, 247, 411, 421–2, 423–4
7th Army, High Command War Diary, 447–8
V Corps, 171
VII Corps, 411
1st Infantry Div., 246–300, 459, 460
4th Div., 118, 165, 367–8
4th Motorized Div., 163, 361–2
7th Armoured Div., 119–20, 473
8th Div., 371
12th Div., 55–6
29th Infantry Div., 35–7, 117, 124, 423–4, 459–61, 463–4
82nd Airborne Div., 177–8, 182–3, 465–7; Divisional HQ, 62–3, 181–2
101st Airborne Div., 24, 30, 179, 198–201, 362
1st Engineer Special Brig., 56, 431–3
6th Engineer Special Brig., 13–17, 23–4, 286–7
4th Engineers, B Coy, 20–2, 123–4, 136–7, 365–6
8th Infantry Regiment, 118–19, 165, 367–8
16th Regt, 270; 1st Battn, 279–80; 2nd Battn, 283–4, 293–4; Anti-Tank Coy, 291–2; Cannon Coy, 258–9; E Coy, 293–4; G Coy, 265–6
18th Infantry Regt, HQ Coy, 161–2
20th Field Artillery Regt, B Battery, 163, 361–2
62nd Armored Artillery, 54–5, 422–3
83rd Field Artillery Regt, 57
115th Infantry Regt, 38, 424; F Coy, 41–2

116th Infantry Regt, 41, 141, 170, 247–59, 260, 422, 425; A Coy, 1st Battn, 37–8, 247–8, 251, 255–7, 271–5, 289; B Coy, 262–4, 287–9; C Coy, 170, 276–7; D Coy, 1st Battn, 39–41, 117, 163–4, 250–3, 264–5; E Coy, 266–8, 471–2; F Coy, 268–71; H Coy, 233–5; HQ Coy, 2nd Battn, 248–50, 277–9; L Coy, 2nd Battn, 458–9; T Coy, 35–7, 38; Anti-Tank Platoon 1st Battn, 257–8, 290–1
121st Combat Engineers, 261, 290
171st Infantry, 124
467th AAA, 285–6
501st Parachute Infantry Regt, 3rd Battn, 181; C Coy, 435; Intelligence and Reconnaissance Sectn, 115–16
505th Parachute Infantry Regt, 465; 2nd Battn, 202–5; 1 Coy, 3rd Battn, 177, 201–2
506th Parachute Infantry Regt, 1st Battn, 185–6; E Coy, 2nd Battn, 433–5; F Coy, 30–2
507th Parachute Infantry Regt, 24, 198–201, 465
508th Parachute Infantry Regt, 193–4, 466; B Coy, 3rd Platoon, 149–50; HQ Coy, 2nd Battn, 194–6, 472–3; 1 Coy, 186–7, 196–7
618th Ordnance Regt, 13–17
1st Medical Battn, A Coy, 261–2
2nd Ranger Battn, HQ Coy, 24–5
4th Medical Battn, 55–6
5th Ranger Battn, 260, 294–5, 429–31
29th Field Artillery Battn, B Battery, 125, 363–4
62nd Armored Field Artillery Battn, 426–8

US Army Units – *contd*
70th Tank Battn, C Coy, 371–
    2
149th Engineer Combat Battn,
    23–4; B Coy, 286–7
174th Ordnance Battn, 13–17
467th AAA Battn, A Battery,
    127–8; B Battery, 282–3,
    457–8
696th Armored Field Artillery
    Battn, Medical Detachment,
    17–20
116th Regimental Combat
    Team, 429; 1st Platoon,
    282–3, 457–8
462nd Amphibious Truck
    Coy, 56–7, 431–3
US Marines, 134–5
US Navy, 13, 132, 137, 140,
    422
USNR, 137–8, 152–3, 246–7,
    456–7
Utah beach, 143, 361–72, 411,
    421

V1 and V2 rockets, 88
VAD, Hants 12th
    Detachment, 106–7, 445–
    6
Valance, Sgt Thomas, 425
Vancopenolle, M. et Mme,
    383
Vandenberg, Lieut Gen. Hoyt
    S., 145
Van der Voort, Sgt Charles,
    260
Van de Voort, Lieut Leo, 257
Van Fleet, Col, 118
Varaville, 207, 214, 219
Vere Broke, Major, 352
Verne, Mme Aude, 453–4
Vernière-sur-Mer, 376–7
Verrier, Mary, 106–7, 445–6

Ver-sur-Mer, 161, 357
Victory, HMS, 160
Vierville-sur-Mer, 5, 9, 117,
    164, 256, 289, 296, 297, 404,
    429, 430, 457, 459–60, 464
Villemont, 236
Villiers, Dorine, 426

Wallace, Percy, 174–5
Walsh, Dr, 412
Walter, Brig. A.E.M., 63–4
Walters, Capt., 420
war correspondents, xiv–xv,
    105–6, 131–2, 162, 163, 166,
    280–1, 312–13, 320–1, 332–
    4, 368–70, 435–6, 464–5,
    467
Ware, Capt. Robert, 263
Warlimont, Gen. Walter, 89–
    90, 176, 242, 410
Warsash, 24–5
Waters, SQMS 'Muddy', 357
Weast, Pfc Carl, 429–31
Webb, Marine Edwin, 302–4
Webster, Pfc, David Kenyon,
    30–2
Wenn, J.T., 134
Western Task Force, 137;
    Force A, 465; Force B, 457;
    Force O, 456
Weymouth, 135, 153, 161
Wheatley, Wing Commander
    Dennis, 178
White, Jim, 153
Whitney, Seaman First Class
    Jack, 369
Whittington, Capt., 431
Wiehe, Eldon, 294–5
Wilkes, Sgt, 272
Wilkins, Staff Sgt, R.A., 23–4
Williams, Pte Francis, 343–4,
    417–18
Wills, Colin, 130–1, 320–1

Wills, Sgt W.E., 105, 348–51
Wilmot, Chester, 131
Wilson, Trooper Charles,
    353–4
Wilson, Sgt John, 192–4
Winstanley, Alan, 107–9
Winters, Lieut Dick, 433,
    434
Wise, Lieut Ernest, 270
Witt, Frau, 239, 240
Witt, Hank, 425
Witt, Major Gen., 238, 240
Wleck, Lance Cpl, 401
Wood, Major George L.,
    126–7
Woodbridge, Roy, 73–4, 75,
    78
Woodward, Flying Officer
    Colin, 167
World, Lieut, 190, 191
Wozenski, Capt. Edward,
    293–4
Wrigglesworth, Air Vice
    Marshal, 145
Wright, Staff Sgt Dick, 262,
    263
Wright, Technical Sgt Richard
    T., 134–5
Wuensch, Obergefreite
    Anton, 232–3, 403–8
Wuensch, Frau, 239, 240
Wuensche, Max, 239
Wyman, Brig. Gen. Willard,
    280
Wynn, Robert 'Popeye', 434

Yarmouth, 44
Young, Peter, 165
Yvetot, 92–3

Zappacosta, Capt., 262, 263
Ziegelmann, Oberstleutnant,
    83–4